Sarah Crowe

Studies in Medieval and Ren

5

EUROPEAN MUSIC,

Studies in Medieval and Renaissance Music

ISSN 1479-9294

This series aims to provide a forum for the best scholarship in early music; deliberately broad in scope, it welcomes proposals on any aspect of music, musical life, and composers during the period up to 1600, and particularly encourages work that places music in an historical and social context. Both new research and major reassessments of central topics are encouraged.

Proposals or enquiries may be sent directly to the editors or the publisher at the addresses given below; all submissions will receive careful, informed consideration.

Professor Tess Knighton, Institucio Mila i Fontanals/CSIC, c/ Egipciaques 15, Barcelona 08001, Spain

Dr Helen Deeming, Department of Music, Royal Holloway, University of London, Egham, Surrey TW20 0EX

Boydell & Brewer, PO Box 9, Woodbridge, Suffolk IP12 3DF

Previously published titles in the series are listed at the back of this volume

European Music
1520–1640

edited by
James Haar

THE BOYDELL PRESS

First published 2006
The Boydell Press, Woodbridge
Paperback edition 2014

ISBN 978 1 84383 200 3 hardback
ISBN 978 1 84383 894 4 paperback

The Boydell Press is an imprint of Boydell & Brewer Ltd
PO Box 9, Woodbridge, Suffolk IP12 3DF, UK
and of Boydell & Brewer Inc.
668 Mt Hope Avenue, Rochester, NY 14620–2731, USA
website: www.boydellandbrewer.com

A CIP catalogue record for this title is available
from the British Library

This publication is printed on acid-free paper

Designed and typeset in Adobe Garamond Premier with Tory initials by
The Stingray Office, Manchester

CONTENTS

PREFACE

THE authors who have loyally stuck with this volume over a period longer than any of us care to remember will recall that the original core of these essays was intended to form one of a series of books on the history of Western music. Owing in part to the dilatory behavior of some contributors, in part to the editor's procrastination, the project got behind schedule, and the original publisher, losing confidence in it and indeed tiring of the whole series, agreed with me that it might be as well to drop it.

I did so with regret, not just for letting down the colleagues who wrote for the book but because the essays contain a lot of good stuff, very little affected by the passage of a few years. Here enters the *deus ex machina* of this tale: Bruce Phillips, who got me started on the original project, not only agreed that it was too good to let go but managed to interest another publisher in taking it up. The old publishers gave me free rein; new commissions were sent out to replace the incorrigible no-shows; the long-suffering contributors were coaxed into revising and updating their essays. A new volume—what is before the reader here—was the result.

The publishing house of Boydell and Brewer is the heaven-sent means through which this was accomplished, and I know that the authors of these essays join me in expressing our gratitude to them. I hope that they and the readers of this book will agree that the project was indeed worth saving. Special thanks are owed to Jeffrey Dean for his expert copy-editing and his refined choice of elements of typographical design.

The original plan for the volume, which has survived essentially intact, was to combine a group of essays on topics relevant to the musical culture of Europe in the sixteenth and early seventeenth centuries with a series of chapters outlining the chronological development of this culture. The dates chosen, 1520–1640, were not and are not arbitrary: 1520 marks the establishment of the *ars perfecta* represented (for Glareanus) by the completed work of Josquin; 1640 is an appropriate if approximate terminus for a late-Renaissance/early-Baroque period including the career of Claudio Monteverdi. The essays were to be concerned with genres (mass, motet, madrigal, chanson, etc.); contemporary events and phenomena with important consequences for music (the Reformation, Protestant and Catholic; printing, humanistic currents) and musical thought characteristic of the period (theory) as well as terminology used to characterize the period ("Renaissance" and "Baroque," now much criticized but surely no worse than the lame and linguistically clumsy "early modern"). These essays were to be followed by the second part of the book—in no way second in importance—comprising accounts of the music of the Italian peninsula, France, the Netherlands, Germany and Central Europe, England, and Spain, each divided (not very precisely) into chronological segments. In the book's present state the two sections have been mixed, themes alternating with chronologies so that their complementary nature may stand in better relief. The chapters may be read as they come or in any order the reader prefers; but, kind reader, if you do skip about, keep going back to the table of contents so that you don't miss anything.

Not wishing to limit the authors' independence any more than was absolutely necessary, I imposed very few guidelines on them. This was just as well, since few of them paid much attention to what I did tell them. They are—the scholars represented here—an independent-minded bunch. For me this individuality of approach and style adds interest and life to the volume. Since it is no longer one of a series of all-but-textbooks, uniformity is of no particular value here. Some effort has been applied to keep single contributions internally consistent, but that is all. What is important is that every one of the contributors is either an established authority in his/her field or, in a few instances, an up-and-coming scholar from whom much may be expected in coming years. They have given of their best, and I am proud of each and every one of them.

James Haar

Chapel Hill, North Carolina
April 2005

ABBREVIATIONS

Books

Brown	Howard Mayer Brown, *Instrumental Music Printed before 1600*
CEKM	Corpus of Early Keyboard Music (American Institute of Musicology)
CMM	Corpus Mensurabilis Musicae (AIM)
DDT	Denkmäler deutscher Tonkunst
DTB	Denkmäler der Tonkunst in Bayern
DTÖ	Denkmäler der Tonkunst in Österreich
EDM	Das Erbe deutscher Musik
MSD	Musicological Studies and Documents (AIM)
RISM A/I	Répertoire international des sources musicales, *Einzeldrucke vor 1800*
RISM B/I/1	Répertoire international des sources musicales, *Recueils imprimés, XVIe–XVIIe siècles: Liste chronologique*
RISM B/VIII	Répertoire international des sources musicales, *Das deutsche Kirchenlied*

Libraries

B: Belgium	*Br*	Brussels, Bibliothèque Royale Albert Ier
CH: Switzerland	*Bu*	Basel, Universität Basel, Öffentliche Bibliothek, Musikabteilung
	N	Neuchâtel, Bibliothèque publique et universitaire
	SGs	St. Gallen, Stiftsbibliothek
	Zz	Zurich, Zentralbibliothek
D: Germany	*Bs*	Berlin, Stadtbibliothek preussischer Kulturbesitz, Musikbibliothek
	Mbs	Munich, Bayerische Staatsbibliothek
E: Spain	*Bbc*	Barcelona, Biblioteca de Catalunya
	Mn	Madrid, Biblioteca Nacional
	OL	Olot, Biblioteca Popular
	PA	Palma de Mallorca, Biblioteca Fundación Bartolomé March Severa
	SIM	Simancas, Archivo General
	TZ	Tarazona, Catedral, Archivo Capitular
F: France	*Pc*	Paris, Bibliothèque du Conservatoire (in *Pn*)
	Pn	Paris, Bibliothèque national de France
GB: Great Britain	*Cfm*	Cambridge, Fitzwilliam Museum

GB (cont.)	*Lbl*	London, British Library
	Ob	Oxford, Bodleian Library
	WRec	Windsor, Eton College Library
I: Italy	*Fn*	Florence, Biblioteca Nazionale Centrale
	Fr	Florence, Biblioteca Riccardiana
	Ma	Milan, Biblioteca Ambrosiana
	MOe	Modena, Biblioteca Estense e Universitaria
	Nn	Naples, Biblioteca Nazionale Vittorio Emanuele III
	Rc	Rome, Biblioteca Casanatense
	Rv	Rome, Biblioteca Vallicelliana
	Rvat	Rome, Biblioteca Apostolica Vaticana
	Tn	Turin, Biblioteca Nazionale Universitaria
P: Portugal	*La*	Lisbon, Biblioteca de Ajuda
PL: Poland	*Kp*	Cracow, Biblioteka Polskiej Akademii Nauk

1

RENAISSANCE HUMANISM AND MUSIC

Gary Tomlinson

FOR students of the Renaissance, "humanism" is a term that sends up warning flares. Its use is entrenched, its usefulness unquestionable, but it remains unsettled in meaning and hence worrisome, begging apology and qualification even from writers who have done much to define it. Thus Paul Oskar Kristeller opened his watershed Oberlin lectures half a century ago by noting that, although "the term 'Humanism' has been associated with the Renaissance and its classical studies for more than a hundred years, . . . in recent times it has become the source of much philosophical and historical confusion"; his became, then, a mission of delimitation and definition. More recently Donald R. Kelley began in a similar tone his admirable survey of the subject: "'Renaissance humanism' joins two debatable abstractions, one that suggests a cultural revival and the other a secular philosophy, perhaps divested of higher religious concerns." Such ambivalence is found also among musicologists. James Haar ventured so far as to entitle a chapter in his *Essays on Italian Poetry and Music* "The Early Madrigal: Humanistic Theory in Practical Guise"; but he only came around to addressing humanism, near the end of the chapter, in order to complain that "The term is overworked in general in scholarly and popular writing on the Renaissance and so often misused in discussions of music that I considered not using it at all."[1]

This caution includes a good measure of valor, and it certainly has the virtue of forthrightness. Too often, instead, discussions of humanism evade the term's historiographical difficulties. Anyone versed in modern writings on the Renaissance, musicological or otherwise, knows the frustration aroused by sidelong references to an undefined humanism, to unspecified humanists, or to a vague humanist "orientation," "inclination," or "spirit." Renaissance humanism has provided

[1] Haar has since helped set straight some of this misuse, contributing the admirable overview "Humanism" to *The New Grove Dictionary* (where however the subject entry had to await the edn of 2000 for its first appearance). See Paul Oskar Kristeller, *Renaissance Thought: The Classic, Scholastic and Humanist Strains* (New York, 1961), 8; Donald R. Kelley, *Renaissance Humanism* (Boston, 1991), 1; and James Haar, *Essays on Italian Poetry and Music in the Renaissance, 1350–1600* (Berkeley, 1986), 74.

a historiographical terrain more congenial than many to the persistent growth of an undisciplined *Geistesgeschichte*—a particular fertility that lives on from the earliest uses of the term, in which it was connected to such broad and, for the Renaissance, questionable notions as individualism and secularism. The caution of students of humanism such as Kristeller reacts against this ongoing nomenclature-creep.

On the positive side, both the caution and the carelessness gauge the richness of the concept of humanism, the multiplicity of meanings that have accrued to it in the century-and-a-half of its usage to describe aspects of Renaissance culture. This multiplicity and its connections to music history will emerge more clearly in what follows. I should say at the outset, however, that they will emerge under the auspices of my conviction that the usefulness of humanism as a concept increases as its implications are understood to be more and more diffused through Renaissance culture, to seep across permeable boundaries into sometimes unexpected spaces in the manner of all complex cultural phenomena. "No neat definition of humanism will be meaningful," Brian Copenhaver and Charles Schmitt have written,[2] and any helpful measure of its significance will need to embrace conceptual profusion while skirting intellectual anarchy. This careful control within multiplicity is, finally, the historiographical task at hand. The remedy for the sprawling proliferation of Renaissance humanisms is not to constrain artificially and *a priori* the term's range of implication but instead to plot ever more carefully the many situations in which appear cultural tendencies we might usefully term humanist.

OVER the last century-and-a-half a number of paradigmatic interpretations of humanism have been advanced by general historians and taken up by music historians. In these we may trace, side by side, the general and musical historiographies of humanism. No doubt the earliest of these paradigms to take hold was what I will call WHIG HUMANISM. In this view humanism was seen as a prominent force—even the guiding force—in the assumed emergence during the Renaissance of modern forms of subjectivity and worldliness. Humanism here takes the form of an emergent individualism, the Renaissance moment in a putative progress of humankind toward a modern sense of autonomous selfhood and of the Enlightened liberalism and egalitarianism that were its political reflections. The Whig interpretation arose from nineteenth-century conceptions of the Renaissance that were themselves closely in touch with Enlightenment progressivism and anticlericalism, above all Jules Michelet's famous notion of the Renaissance "discovery of the world and of man" (from his *Histoire de France* of 1855), borrowed by Jacob Burckhardt as a central theme of his *Die Kultur der Renaissance in Italien* (1860). From such sources the Whig view constructed teleologies guided by individualist,

[2] Brian P. Copenhaver and Charles B. Schmitt, *Renaissance Philosophy* (Oxford, 1992), 24–25.

humanitarian principles and leading, it would imply, to ever freer forms of society and expression.[3]

Among music historians the chief exponent of Whig humanism has no doubt been Edward E. Lowinsky. Lowinsky came honestly by his stance, inheriting it in a direct line from Burckhardt via German musicologists, especially his teacher Heinrich Besseler. Lowinsky saw the musical Renaissance as an "emancipation" from the supposedly rigid strictures and structures of medieval music-making, a liberation that allowed the forging of newly flexible musical styles capable of expressing—as he put it, echoing Michelet and Burckhardt—"the outer world of nature and the inner reality of man." In the course of this liberation a novel conception of musical creativity was discovered, one that adumbrated later notions of innate, unteachable genius. Most importantly, humanist musicians turned their attention more and more to the meaning and affect of the poetry they set and away from its formal outlines; for Lowinsky this indubitable tendency of certain sixteenth-century styles and genres was part and parcel of the more general emancipation. In this these composers set in motion nothing less than a sweeping "humanization" of music that pointed the way to the glories of Bach, Mozart, Beethoven, and Schubert. The individualism of Burckhardt's Renaissance man, we cannot but conclude, found its consummation in the Hegelian culture-hero. Meanwhile the humanist liberation of the musical spirit did not proceed unopposed. Lowinsky's famous hypothesis of a "secret chromatic art" in the Netherlands motet, formulated long before he had said much about humanism, posits a musical subversion of illegitimate religious authority that is in hindsight entirely in keeping with the liberal goals of his Renaissance humanism.[4]

The difficulties of the Whig view are obvious enough, perhaps, even in this brief sketch. However much it might touch on basic shifts in European society from the thirteenth to the seventeenth centuries—above all the burgeoning of certain societal forms associated with the resurgence of cities and towns—and despite its helpful highlighting of the sense on the part of Renaissance writers themselves of cultural progress and enlightenment, it troubles in its progressivism, in its limited vision of medieval society and culture as a crimped foil for Renaissance developments,[5] and in the confidence with which it maps modern modes of subjectivity

[3] See Burckhardt's *The Civilization of the Renaissance in Italy*, trans. S. G. C. Middlemore, ed. Irene Gordon (New York, 1960); for individualism, Part 2; for his dependence on Michelet, Part 4 and specifically 225 n.

[4] Lowinsky developed these views in essays that sometimes do not speak specifically of humanism, especially "Music in the Culture of the Renaissance" (1954) and "Musical Genius: Evolution and Origins of a Concept" (1964); he connected his views explicitly with historians' conceptions of humanism in "Humanism in the Music of the Renaissance" (1982, with a long genesis reaching back to the 1950s). All these essays are republished in Edward E. Lowinsky, *Music in the Culture of the Renaissance and Other Essays*, 2 vols., ed. Bonnie J. Blackburn (Chicago, 1989); see esp. 38–39, 50, 56–57, and 218. See also Lowinsky, *Secret Chromatic Art in the Netherlands Motet* (New York, 1946), esp. chs. 8 and 9. For Besseler's views, see his "Das Renaissanceproblem in der Musik," *Archiv für Musikwissenschaft*, 22 (1966), 1–10.

[5] This inability to take account of the societal and expressive vitality of the Middle Ages is surely the most fundamental weakness of Whig humanism; in the Lowinskian view it should

onto a pre- or early-modern world. Moreover, because of its sweeping conclusions and resonant political progressivism it has a special attraction for authors of generalizing accounts. This has given it an unfortunate staying power and a propensity to turn up, unexamined and unelaborated, in elementary music-history texts and similar locales.

The Whig paradigm of humanism is not the only one rooted in Burckhardt's *Kultur der Renaissance.* For him an important force in the emergence of a new Renaissance individualism was the revival of ancient letters and thought, which brought with it a new corpus of themes, topics, and modes of self-expression. Looking over his shoulder at German educators of the generations preceding his, he termed this emphasis on ancient Greek and Latin writings *Humanismus.* Since Burckhardt's time this revival has exerted a guiding influence on Renaissance studies, so powerfully indeed that there is scarcely a conception of humanism formed over the past century that has not reserved an important place for it.[6]

In strict application this second paradigm might be called PHILOLOGICAL HUMANISM. Here humanism is equated with scholarship on ancient texts *tout court.* Like the Whig interpretation, this view tends to be suggested especially in surveys that make only synoptic reference to humanism, for the simple reason that any more careful scrutiny of Renaissance study of ancient texts inevitably opens deep and wide questions of its aims, ideals, and strategies. Kristeller himself pointed out that in its narrowest formulations the philological view is insufficient to characterize the novelty of humanist agendas; in particular it "fails to explain the ideal of eloquence persistently set forth in the writings of the humanists,"[7] a positive valuation of rhetorical suasion we will examine below. Neither does this strict view explain, from the other side, the fact that the philological emphases and expertise the humanists pioneered in their efforts to exhume and interpret certain ancient texts were quickly exploited by many scholars of very different temperament (reading very different texts). We need, in order to construct a rich panorama of Renaissance scholarly culture, to reserve a place for anti-humanist scholarship on ancient texts. Philological expertise should not retain the name "humanism" when stripped of other humanist emphases.

Perhaps the most famous Renaissance advocate of a philology brimming with broader agendas, and a scholar who sits near the heart of most recent interpretations of humanism, is Lorenzo Valla (1405–1457). It is useful to introduce him here not so much because his studies brought him, by virtue of his redating of the Donation of Constantine, to the center of Roman ecclesiastical politics. More to

probably be understood as the reflection of political dichotomies Lowinsky witnessed in his own lifetime. Lewis Lockwood sums it up well as a failure "to allow for the possibility that the Renaissance can be distinguished from the Middle Ages by other means than as a period of alleged 'freedom' in contradistinction to—the contrast is inevitable—'tyranny.'" See Lockwood, "Renaissance," *The New Grove Dictionary of Music and Musicians* (2nd edn., 2001), XXI: 184.

[6] See Burckhardt, *The Civilization,* Part 3. For the coining of the term *Humanismus* in the early 19th century, see Kristeller, *Renaissance Thought,* 8–9.

[7] *Renaissance Thought,* 98.

the point is the fact that his approach to philology raised large issues that will help us define humanist views through the later Renaissance.

Valla's readings of ancient Latin texts, outstripping those of his predecessors (and most of his followers) in precision, constructed a history for the Latin language more elaborate than had ever before been achieved. In the process he made clear the great changes that had occurred in the evolution of Latin from Cicero's time to his own. He suggested that languages in general were inextricable from particular societal and cultural circumstances, and by doing so he distanced ancient Latin from modern concerns—paradoxically, in the light of the Burckhardtian model of humanist classicism—and portrayed it as a historical, now-dead vernacular, equivalent in its ancient usage to modern vernaculars. This tendency to understand past utterance in its own setting advanced a kind of humanist historicism rooted in the study of linguistic usage and situated self-representation. In some later Renaissance voices, especially after the mid-sixteenth-century revival of ancient skepticism, this view could approach an almost relativistic sense of historical and cultural difference (Montaigne's is the most notable such voice); Kelley justifiably points to its connection to the post-Renaissance poetic historicism of Giambattista Vico.[8] Finally, in his philosophical writings Valla justified his emphasis on philology by proposing that human reason itself was not abstractable from everyday language use but rather shaped by it. We will return below to the radical implications of Valla's philology.[9]

Most musicological writings on humanism adopt in some fashion the philological interpretation. But they usually do so in a moderated form that, if it does not examine the deepest values embedded in humanist scholarship, at least does not strip away the particular and specific agendas individual scholars pursued *through* philology. Two music historians who worked most productively along these lines are Claude V. Palisca and D. P. Walker. Neither hesitated to explore the motives—personal, polemical, institutional—behind Renaissance classical scholarship. Walker set out, in his pathbreaking essays on "Musical Humanism in the 16th and Early 17th Centuries," now more than half a century old, to lay to rest the notion that imitation of ancient musical practice had no impact on late-Renaissance music-making. He sketched the outlines of such impact by describing scholarship and debate on four topics of special interest to ancient writers on music: the

[8] It is no accident that one of Montaigne's most striking essays in this mode, "Of Cannibals," concerns non-European peoples, for humanist tendencies toward historical relativism found ample support in growing European awareness of non-Europeans through the late Renaissance. For Vico, see Kelley, *Renaissance Humanism*, 101, 103, 109–10, and 128.

[9] The secondary literature on Valla has burgeoned in recent decades. See *inter alia* Paul Oskar Kristeller, *Eight Philosophers of the Italian Renaissance* (Stanford, 1964); Cesare Vasoli, *La dialettica a la retorica dell'Umanesimo* (Milan, 1968); Jerrold E. Seigel, *Rhetoric and Philosophy in Renaissance Humanism: The Union of Eloquence and Wisdom, Petrarch to Valla* (Princeton, 1968); Salvatore Camporeale, *Lorenzo Valla: Umanesimo e teologia* (Florence, 1972); Anthony Grafton and Lisa Jardine, *From Humanism to the Humanities* (Cambridge, Mass., 1986); and Richard Waswo, *Language and Meaning in the Renaissance* (Princeton, 1987). For good surveys of Valla's significance, see Kelley, *Renaissance Humanism*, and Copenhaver and Schmitt, *Renaissance Philosophy*.

melodic genera; intonation systems; modes and their varying ethos; and music's reflection or expression of the words it sets. Palisca examined the Renaissance exhumation of ancient musical thought in a series of essays extending from the 1950s, through his publication (in 1960) of the correspondence between Girolamo Mei and Vincenzo Galilei, to his book of 1985, *Humanism in Italian Renaissance Musical Thought.* Across this body of work, Palisca remained sensitive to the variety of uses to which revived ancient knowledge was put.[10]

Both Walker and Palisca highlighted the new emphasis in the sixteenth century on the emotional and ethical powers of music, as Lowinsky had; but instead of viewing this as a march toward spiritual emancipation they linked it to the rhetorical aims of much humanist thought and activity—to the humanist "ideal of eloquence," as Kristeller put it. This brings us to a third paradigm of humanism, one that begins to ground and explain the new place in Renaissance culture of suasive oratory: RHETORICAL HUMANISM. This interpretation starts from curricular rearrangements in schools and universities of the fourteenth and fifteenth centuries. Although it is already signaled, again, by Burckhardt, it is owed above all to Kristeller, especially to a series of foundational essays he produced in the 1940s and '50s.

Kristeller argued that humanism spread as a set of curricular emphases in liberal arts education apparent in Italian universities and schools by the fifteenth century. They arose especially in reaction to the importation of scholastic methods and priorities from France during the fourteenth century; later they were taken up in northern universities as well. In the trivium of verbal arts passed down from late antiquity, including grammar, rhetoric, and logic, scholastic thought had given pride of place to logic as a means of understanding natural philosophy and theology. The humanists laid more emphasis on grammar and especially rhetoric in their teaching; to these they added the study of poetry, history, and ethics. By the late fifteenth century these five subjects could be referred to collectively as the *studia humanitatis* or "humanities," and a teacher of them could be called a *humanista.* The humanist emphases of grammar and rhetoric answered to the communal needs of Italian urban culture of the late Middle Ages and were manifested in the writing and speechmaking techniques of the *dictatores,* the notaries and public scribes of the period. From this heritage humanists took their tendency to see education in the verbal arts as serving pragmatic ends, preparing young men for civic, governmental, or religious service. The humanists differed from their medieval pre-

[10] Walker's "Musical Humanism in the 16th and Early 17th Centuries," orginally published in *The Music Review*, 2 (1941), 1–13, 111–21, 220–27, 288–308; 3 (1942), 55–71, has been reprinted several times; see D. P. Walker, *Music, Spirit, and Language in the Renaissance*, ed. Penelope Gouk (London, 1985). For Palisca, see *Girolamo Mei: Letters on Ancient and Modern Music to Vincenzo Galilei and Giovanni Bardi* (American Institute of Musicology, 1960), *Humanism in Italian Renaissance Musical Thought* (New Haven, 1985), and, for a collection of essays published across three decades, *Studies in the History of Italian Music and Music Theory* (Oxford, 1994); for a summary of his views see his "Humanism and Music," in *Renaissance Humanism: Foundations, Forms and Legacy*, 3 vols., ed. Albert Rabil, Jr (Philadelphia, 1988), III: 450–85.

decessors, however, in the strength of their insistence that elegant and persuasive speaking and writing needed to be patterned after classical models.[11]

Kristeller's curricular paradigm offered a number of advantages not found in earlier interpretations. First, it suggested how the rhetorical emphases of the humanists arose in response to particular conditions of late medieval Italy, more fully and quickly urbanized and commercialized than northern Europe. Second, by elaborating the agendas of humanist scholarship it proposed that classical studies in themselves were not a sufficient determination of humanist orientation. Instead the specific priorities of humanist classicism—especially the humanists' exaggerated reverence for Cicero and, later, Quintilian—were a means to achieve a new, more forceful and persuasive eloquence. Third, it countered the unsubstantiated but widespread assumption that humanism was a systematic philosophy that displaced an earlier scholasticism. In place of this view it offered the more nuanced picture of academic turf wars, so to speak, between the rhetorical culture of Italy and the fashions of scholastic logic and argumentation introduced there from France at the end of the Middle Ages. Finally, it portrayed this opposition as a lasting one, thus bringing the confrontation of humanist and scholastic orientations to the fore as an issue for late-Renaissance historiography. As Kristeller concluded, "The humanism and the scholasticism of the Renaissance arose in medieval Italy about the same time, that is, about the end of the thirteenth century, and . . . they coexisted and developed all the way through and beyond the Renaissance period as different branches of learning."[12]

For music historians Kristeller's curricular view has had, in its specific arguments, less impact than it might. Musicologists still have far to go in understanding the relations between music as it was presented in humanist schools, music as included in university curricula, music as taught to the choirboys from whose ranks polyphonic composers most often matured, music as it was mastered by courtly purveyors of semi-improvisatory solo song, and so forth.[13] In a more general sense, however, the emphasis on eloquence in rhetorical humanism has been so richly suggestive that few recent studies of late-Renaissance musical expression do not

[11] In Kristeller's large output, see especially two essays in *Renaissance Thought*, "The Humanist Movement" (3–23) and "Humanism and Scholasticism in the Italian Renaissance" (92–119), and his more recent summary of his views, "Humanism," in *The Cambridge History of Renaissance Philosophy*, ed. Charles B. Schmitt, Quentin Skinner, Eckhard Kessler, and Jill Kraye (Cambridge, 1988), 113–37. See also Hanna H. Gray, "Renaissance Humanism: The Pursuit of Eloquence," in *Renaissance Essays*, ed. Paul Oskar Kristeller and Philip P. Wiener (New York, 1968), 199–216; and, for a refinement of Kristeller's connection of humanists and *dictatores*, Ronald Witt, "Medieval 'Ars Dictaminis' and the Beginnings of Humanism: A New Construction of the Problem," *Renaissance Quarterly*, 35 (1982), 1–35. For Burckhardt's emphasis of humanist rhetoric, see *The Civilization*, Part 3, passim; for universities and schools, 166–69.

[12] "Humanism and Scholasticism," 116. For details of the confrontation of these contrasting curricular agendas in the later Renaissance, see Erika Rummel, *The Humanist–Scholastic Debate in the Renaissance & Reformation* (Cambridge, Mass., 1995).

[13] Kristeller's own contribution along these lines, "Music and Learning in the Early Italian Renaissance," in *Renaissance Thought II: Papers on Humanism and the Arts* (New York, 1965), 142–62, points up the scantiness of evidence concerning musical education in the period but offers tantalizing suggestions as to humanist musical priorities and education.

embody it in some form. It anchors our understanding of the conditions that fostered one of the most important tendencies of the Renaissance: the pervasive and finally selfconscious rhetoricization of musical technique and expression. It underscores how music was perceived during the Renaissance to be suspended between two categories of knowledge: the mathematical arts of the quadrivium, in which music had found its intellectual niche since late antiquity and to which it still looked for its theoretical and rational foundation, and the speaking arts of poetry and rhetoric. Of course this ambivalence of music had long been palpable, captured already in Platonic juxtapositions of musical mathematics with musical ethics, codified later in divisions like Boethius's *musica mundana*, *humana*, and *instrumentalis*, and in any case ever implied in the Western division of musical thought from musical practice. But both humanist rhetoric and humanist attention to ancient accounts that allied music with verbal arts and emphasized music's ethical and affective powers exacerbated the ambivalence and helped broach music's performative dimensions in ways that countered the abstractions of Boethian theory. They fostered the musical polemics characteristic of the late Renaissance, polemics that often turned on questions of the relative weight given to performative eloquence on the one hand and mathematical demonstration on the other in the creation and judgment of musical styles.[14]

Indeed, in Italy such debates took their place in a larger polemical literary culture also engendered in some degree by humanism. The strengthening of music's alliance with verbal arts prepared the way for writers on music to pose a counterpart to the late-sixteenth-century floodtide of treatises on poetic theory. If music-theory treatises of the fifteenth and early sixteenth centuries usually remained far afield from the humanist verbal arts, it is clear that from the middle of the sixteenth century on they often engaged the kinds of questions then being debated by the literary theorists: questions of genre and generic decorum, of definition of style, of imitation of earlier styles, and of stylistic evolution.[15] The confluence of these two bodies of theory, musical and literary-rhetorical, is captured emblematically in the title of the most important music treatise of the century, Zarlino's *Istitutioni harmoniche*, framed to recall Quintilian's *Institutio oratoria*. The distance music theory had traversed in the century preceding Zarlino is measured in his scorn for the mensural concerns that still preoccupied a writer like Tinctoris (whatever the other tendencies—such as an interest in ancient accounts of music's powers and

[14] Many of these topics are taken up by Ann E. Moyer in her study of the changing affiliations of musical thought in late-Renaissance structures of knowledge, *Musica Scientia: Musical Scholarship in the Italian Renaissance* (Ithaca, NY, 1992).

[15] The issue of imitation of earlier styles has proved especially fertile in musicological discussions. For essays particularly concerned with parallels between musical and rhetorical imitation, see Warren Kirkendale, "Ciceronians versus Aristotelians on the Ricercar as Exordium, from Bembo to Bach," *Journal of the American Musicological Society*, 32 (1979), 1–44, and Howard Mayer Brown, "Emulation, Competition, and Homage: Imitation and Theories of Imitation in the Renaissance," *Journal of the American Musicological Society*, 35 (1982), 1–48; for cautions regarding such parallels, see Honey Meconi, "Does *Imitatio* Exist?", *Journal of Musicology*, 12 (1994), 152–78.

a progressive sense of historical change—that made Tinctoris a harbinger of musical humanism).[16]

In northern Europe, meanwhile, rhetorical humanism influenced musical thought along a somewhat different route. There a university culture emphasizing Ciceronian rhetoric, led by scholars such as Philipp Melanchthon and Johann Sturm, suggested musical analogues. Nicolaus Listenius, Gallus Dressler, and other writers on music picked up on the suggestion, elaborating a new theoretical category, *musica poetica* (roughly, composition), and comparing the organization of musical works to that of formal oratory. By the 1590s Joachim Burmeister, trained in both rhetoric and music, transferred rhetorical terms and techniques to the parsing of musical works, inventing a practice he termed—after the Greek *analyein*, to unloose, dissolve—analysis.[17]

Thus curricular and rhetorical humanism has deep and broad implications for the music historian. Nevertheless it shares a limitation with philological humanism: like that view, it tends to describe the symptoms of humanist culture rather than diagnosing its internal condition. Just as studies couched in the philological paradigm sometimes trace the patterns of scholarly activities while barely questioning what ends were served by renewed interest in the revival and emulation of classical authors, so the curricular view often only hints at the cultural and ideological sources of its rhetorical priorities. The question of the deep roots of the humanists' ideal of eloquence remains unanswered.

Another paradigm of humanism, CIVIC HUMANISM, has built upon Kristeller's rhetorical view in an attempt to answer this question. It took its impetus from the insight that humanism's roots reach back to medieval Italy and its burgeoning town and city society. In this view, the exigencies and pressures of civic life and governance fostered the new emphasis on effective and persuasive communication. The humanist revaluation of rhetoric sprang from the particular social requirements of the *polis*. This interpretation was adumbrated already in the 1940s by Eugenio Garin and came into sharp focus in Hans Baron's *The Crisis of the Early Italian Renaissance* (1955). Baron argued that rhetorical humanism matured in the heat of political crisis, specifically in 1400–1402 in a Florence threatened with invasion by the armies of Giangaleazzo Visconti of Milan. In this crucible the armament of humanist rhetoric was fired and tempered. The wavering of earlier humanists such as Petrarch between a life of solitary study and a life of political commitment was settled firmly in favor of the latter. The special significance of Cicero for the humanists was discovered in his own political struggles, parallel to those of modern Florentines, and was defined by his use of rhetoric in defense of republicanism and political pluralism. This involved a view of ancient Rome not as some unattainable golden age but rather as a society parallel to modern Florence

[16] See Tinctoris, Dedication of *Proportionale musices* (1473–74), and Zarlino, *Istitutioni harmoniche* (1558), Book 3, ch. 71; both are translated in *Strunk's Source Readings in Music History*, III: *The Renaissance*, ed. Gary Tomlinson (New York, 1995), 123–29 and 158–84.

[17] See Palisca, "Humanism and Music," 474; for an analysis of a Lasso motet from Burmeister's *Musica poetica* (1606), see *Strunk's Source Readings*, III: *The Renaissance*, ed. Tomlinson, 189–93.

from which real-life political lessons might be learned. In turn, this novel historical perspective accorded a greater dignity to modern society and in particular to vernacular Italian writing. The effects of this whole congeries of views, finally, lived on in later ideas of freedom, political self-determination, and individual dignity.[18]

Both in its particulars and in its broadest sweep Baron's argument has been challenged. Nevertheless the general notion has endured that the rhetorical emphases of humanism were related to the politics of city life, were rooted in the revival and proliferation of cities in late-medieval Italy, and were sustained across the Renaissance by the ideological, political, and military struggles of Italian city-states. The legacy of Baron's work has lived on in a series of self-conscious attempts to understand the links between humanist rhetorical culture and individual urban political contexts, especially republican ones.[19]

Musicology, until recent years loath to knock about overmuch in political concerns, has been slow to exploit this understanding of humanism, even in the 1980s, when Renaissance regional and city studies burgeoned. One recent study clearly enough indebted to the civic-humanist paradigm is Martha Feldman's *City Culture and the Madrigal at Venice* (1995). Although Feldman does not take up Baron's thesis or address explicitly the topic of humanism, she examines the development of the mid-sixteenth-century Venetian madrigal from the broad context of the city's expressive culture and the rhetorical ideals it gave rise to and embodied. She traces across various strains of Venetian society connections musicologists have long suspected between the Ciceronian poetics of Pietro Bembo and the *Musica nova* style of Willaert and its offshoots. She demonstrates the illumination of musical styles (even styles as opaque as the *Musica nova*'s) to be gained from close reading of local urban cultures. Along the way she deepens our understanding of the dispersion and implications of humanist rhetoric.[20]

A fifth paradigm of humanism stems from the opposition Kristeller and others had discerned of humanism to scholasticism—an opposition not, remember, of a Renaissance philosophy to an earlier, medieval one but of strains of culture emerging simultaneously in Italy and intertwined throughout the Renaissance. This view, which we might call ANTISCHOLASTIC HUMANISM, interprets the later Renaissance in the light of broad divergences that divided against itself the elite culture of the time. It emphasizes a continuing tension, through the period

[18] See Hans Baron, *The Crisis of the Early Italian Renaissance*, 2 vols. (Princeton, 1955; rev. edn 1966); also Eugenio Garin, *Italian Humanism: Philosophy and Civic Life in the Renaissance*, trans. Peter Munz (New York, 1965), esp. ch. 2.

[19] The arguments against Baron are marshaled in Jerrold Seigel, "'Civic Humanism' or Ciceronian Rhetoric? The Culture of Petrarch and Bruni," *Past and Present*, 34 (1966), 3–48. A more recent assessment is James Hankins, "The 'Baron Thesis' after Forty Years, and Some Recent Studies of Leonardo Bruni," *Journal of the History of Ideas*, 56 (1995), 309–38. For an overview of Baron's civic humanism thesis and its reception and for summaries of humanism in five Italian cities, see *Renaissance Humanism*, ed. Rabil, vol. 1, chs. 7–12. The case for the afterlife of civic humanism in 16th-century Florence and in 17th- and 18th-century England and America is made by J. G. A. Pocock, *The Machiavellian Moment: Florentine Political Thought and the Atlantic Republican Tradition* (Princeton, 1975).

[20] Martha Feldman, *City Culture and the Madrigal at Venice* (Berkeley, 1995).

and beyond, between opposed visions of history, authority, humankind, and the world: visions of change, mundane instability, and partial truth on the humanist side, of stability, transcendent constancy, full knowledge, and appeal to authority on the scholastic. This interpretation understands humanist rhetoric as a means of channeling and controlling unpredictable human passions in an early-modern world haunted by novel anxieties—a world destabilized by geographical, technological, and anthropological discoveries, by a burgeoning of printed matter on a wealth of subjects, and by cataclysmic disease and warfare. It attempts to explain the humanist ideal of eloquence, in other words, as a pragmatic recourse to persuasion in a world considered mutable and capricious.

The antischolastic interpretation was elaborated, in a way that showed its indebtedness to Baron's civic-humanist model, by William Bouwsma in *Venice and the Defense of Republican Liberty* (1968). Bouwsma analysed the events leading up to the Venetian interdict of 1606 so as to lay bare the deeper oppositions embedded in them. He conceived these oppositions in terms of large medieval and Renaissance "visions" that were not successive cultural stages but coexisted in late Renaissance culture and were closely tied to scholasticism and humanism respectively. The medieval vision embodied in his view an optimistic estimation of human potential for attaining truth and understanding the order of things, while the Renaissance vision reflected the pessimistic view that the human intellect could at most aspire only to a dim, partial comprehension. In its on-the-ground operation the medieval vision encouraged a constant and even rigid response to worldly vagaries, a response based on the confidence that a stable and whole truth was perceivable behind them; Bouwsma allied it with political authoritarianism. The Renaissance view instead fostered a flexible adjustment to changing circumstances whose causes could not be fully known, an approach that depended on a fluid, persuasive interaction in language with others; it found its political metier in republicanism.[21]

This antischolastic view of humanism has remained an important one, because it recognizes and accommodates the persistence through the Renaissance of scholastic modes of thought, and above all because it aims to characterize the chasmal divides that, by any account, cut through late Renaissance culture. But the particular ideological and political spin that Bouwsma put on his opposed visions has certainly been challenged. Anthony Grafton and Lisa Jardine, in *From Humanism*

[21] William J. Bouwsma, *Venice and the Defense of Republican Liberty: Renaissance Values in the Age of the Counter Reformation* (Berkeley, 1968); see esp. ch. 1, where Bouwsma details his medieval and Renaissance visions and their connections to scholasticism and humanism. For Bouwsma's views on humanism, see also "The Culture of Renaissance Humanism," American Historical Association, pamphlet no. 401, 1973, and his essays collected in *A Usable Past: Essays in European Cultural History* (Berkeley, 1990), esp. essays 1, 2, and 9. His last book, *The Waning of the Renaissance, 1550–1640* (New Haven, 2000), attempts from a cultural-historical vantage to celebrate the liberatory aspects of Renaissance thought and describe their decline amid the growing anxiety and malaise of the period about 1600; behind this analysis stand, still, the cultural divisions Bouwsma had perceived in his study of the Venetian interdict. For the northern, especially academic dimensions of this cultural divide, see Rummel, *The Humanist–Scholastic Debate.*

to the Humanities (1986), have even turned on their head the kind of political and intellectual affiliations Bouwsma perceived. They depict the later humanism of the sixteenth century as a force that was above all one of intellectual and social orthodoxy, serving European rulers by reinforcing the superiority of hereditary elites and forging a docile bureaucracy of educated functionaries. For them humanism led to the orthodoxy codified in the educational pragmatism of Petrus Ramus, divorced by now from the ethics that had once formed a part of humanist schooling. The political usefulness of humanism to those in power insured its "victory." Humanist, not scholastic, education encouraged meek acceptance of authority, and "Scholasticism bred too independent an attitude to survive."[22]

The difference between these two interpretations is certainly consequential—but not as much so as the recognition both share of the fundamental ideological divisions that ran through sixteenth-century society and culture. Humanism played a major role in the making and expression of these divisions; given the variety of definitions we have already surveyed, however, it should not surprise that there is no consensus as to the nature of this role. The position of humanism in the at times contentious emergence of the new science provides an example. In one view, typified by the work of Lynn Thorndike and John H. Randall, Jr, a bookish, poetizing humanism was antithetical to experimental method and empirical observation of the world, which instead arose directly from the continuing development of Aristotelian scholasticism. A more recent, revisionist argument voiced eloquently by Eric Cochrane describes instead a worldly and venturesome humanism, one encouraging anti-authoritarian observation and hypothesis, a productive but un-Aristotelian merger of mathematics with technology, and the persuasive vernacular argumentation deployed most famously by Galileo.[23]

The emphasis of the divisions of Renaissance culture, and in particular the divide between humanism and scholasticism, has proved suggestive in musicological work aiming to discern the underpinnings of stylistic changes and contrasts. My own *Monteverdi and the End of the Renaissance* (1987) brings the views of Bouwsma, Cochrane, and others to bear on late-Renaissance poetic ideologies, aligning Monteverdi's shifting allegiances to Petrarchan and Marinist styles with the broader flux of humanist and scholastic values about 1600. A more general antischolastic interpretation, parallel to Bouwsma's if not influenced by it, was advanced by Nino Pirrotta. His essay of 1966, "Music and Cultural Tendencies in 15th-Century Italy," contrasted the musical predilections of two types of educated

22 Anthony Grafton and Lisa Jardine, *From Humanism to the Humanities* (Cambridge, Mass., 1986): see p. xiv. For a nuanced response to Grafton and Jardine's views from the perspective of English humanist pedagogy, see Rebecca Bushnell, *The Subject of Humanism: Rereading Early Modern Pedagogy* (Ithaca, 1995), esp. ch. 1.

23 For the negative assessment, see for example Lynn Thorndike, *Science and Thought in the Fifteenth Century* (New York, 1929), and John H. Randall, Jr, *The School of Padua and the Emergence of Modern Science* (Padua, 1961); for the positive one, Eric Cochrane, "Science and Humanism in the Italian Renaissance," *The American Historical Review*, 81 (1976), 1039–57; for a recent survey leaning toward Cochrane's position, Pamela O. Long, "Humanism and Science," in *Renaissance Humanism*, ed. Rabil, III: 486–512.

men, scholastic and humanist. Scholastic clerics, Pirrotta argued, preferred elaborate polyphony while humanists, who gained increasing power and prominence in the mid-fifteenth century, sponsored a more overtly rhetorical art: the (generally unwritten) accompanied solo song of *improvvisatori* like Serafino Aquilano. In the shifting prominence of these differing types, with their different musical tastes, Pirrotta sought some explanation for what he and others have seen as the submergence of elaborate polyphony in early- to mid-fifteenth-century Italy.[24]

It is clear enough that Pirrotta's dichotomy has sometimes been overstated by his supporters and even by Pirrotta himself.[25] Recent work by Lewis Lockwood and Allan W. Atlas on particular musical centers in fifteenth-century Italy has suggested no general humanist distaste for written polyphony, and indeed Margaret Bent has discerned humanist sponsorship of such music in Padua in the early decades of the century. These studies do not attempt to dismiss unwritten or little-written musical traditions of the Renaissance or to make them disappear by assimilating them to written polyphonic traditions (as Reinhard Strohm has recently done); Lockwood, for example, pays special attention to the famous singer-lutenist Pietrobono of Ferrara. Attempts such as Strohm's fly in the face of too much musical and anecdotal evidence to be convincing. The stylistic, repertorial, and performative distinctions we have tended to gather under the written/unwritten dichotomy were recognized facts of elite Renaissance music-making. Whatever the degree of overlap between various traditions of unwritten song and written polyphony, we need a clearer explanation of the distinct cultural niches they occupied, either along Pirrotta's or other, yet-to-be-suggested lines.[26]

[24] See Nino Pirrotta, "Music and Cultural Tendencies in Fifteenth-Century Italy" (1966) and "Novelty and Renewal in Italy: 1300–1600" (1973), both reprinted in Nino Pirrotta, *Music and Culture in Italy from the Middle Ages to the Baroque* (Cambridge, MA, 1984), 80–112 and 159–74; also Gary Tomlinson, *Monteverdi and the End of the Renaissance* (Berkeley, 1987).

[25] In "Novelty and Renewal," 167, for instance, Pirrotta wrote: "With the spreading of humanistic thoughts and attitudes, the new breed of literati came to despise polyphony as a contrived, unnatural form of musical expression, and to see its procedures and theory as typical examples of medieval lore."

[26] For area studies, see Allan W. Atlas, *Music at the Aragonese Court of Naples* (Cambridge, 1985); Lewis Lockwood, *Music in Renaissance Ferrara, 1400–1505* (Cambridge, MA, 1984): and Margaret Bent, "Humanists and Music, Music and Humanities," in *Tendenze e metodi nella ricerca musicologica*, Atti del convegno internazionale (Latino 27–29 sett. 1990), *Historiae musicae cultores* Biblioteca, 71, ed. Raffaele Pozzi (Florence, 1993), 29–38. For Strohm's view of unwritten songs as "reduced or simplified" renderings of written repertory see Reinhard Strohm, *The Rise of European Music, 1380–1500* (Cambridge, 1993), part 4, ch. 4, passim and especially 565–66. Strohm's whole account, which doubts "whether Italy's unwritten music-making was in itself so typically Italian" (542), seems tendentious in its merger of a congeries of song traditions in Italy—some written, some unwritten, some partially written—under the single banner of written polyphonic art-song. Such a merger carries to excess Strohm's more moderate view (585) that across Europe "polyphonic song around 1500 was developing along parallel lines," a view that can still accommodate, within limits, the interaction of practices differing in regional and social affiliation, style, and performance means. For evidence from these years of stylistic and performative distinctions that intersect with questions of written and unwritten transmission see the passages from Paolo Cortesi's *De cardinalatu*, Vincenzo Calmeta's *Life* of Serafino Aquilano, and Castiglione's *Courtier* translated in *Strunk's Source Readings*,

The persisting opposition of humanism and scholasticism throughout the later Renaissance inevitably raises the question of the affiliations of both to the large religious divisions of the time. Such questions have formed another humanist paradigm: CHRISTIAN HUMANISM. In this interpretation the triumphant ratiocination of late-medieval theology—manifested above all in the synthesis of faith and philosophy in Aquinas's *Summae*—answered to the centralized, hierarchic, authoritarian structure of the church of that period, and would see a strong resurgence, in the later sixteenth century, as both Roman and Reformed clerics moved to consolidate and strengthen their own authority. In the intervening centuries, however, various evangelical movements undermined clerical power and institutions and sought a simpler lay piety that might facilitate direct and individual relations between Christian believers and Gospel. Such movements came to be allied with humanist rhetoric.

This alliance could arise because both humanist eloquence and lay piety espoused a novel view of the human organism that questioned the primacy scholastic thought granted to the intellect over the will and its associated passions. Petrarch reflected this anti-scholastic voluntarism when he wrote: "The object of the will, as it pleases the wise, is to be good: that of the intellect is truth. It is better to will the good than to know the truth." Such a view tended to reorder the relations to faith of knowledge on the one hand and rhetorical persuasion on the other. Valla's rhetorical studies and ideals were rooted in this Petrarchan belief that persuasion was a more forceful means of inculcating faith than logical demonstration. Erasmus linked the stylistic propriety to be gained from the study of ancient classics to the rhetorical force of Christian homiletics: "Religious matters," he wrote, "can be made to shine more brightly with the aid of the classics, provided that only purity of style is sought." Both writers saw a direct relation of believer to Scripture as crucial, and both brought their philological expertise to bear on the New Testament, Valla in a collation of the Latin and Greek texts and Erasmus in a monumental new edition and translation of the Greek.[27]

III: *The Renaissance*, ed. Tomlinson, 38–51. Such evidence is found even in Strohm's book: on p. 543, where the distinction of French, Venetian, and Sicilian songs at a Venetian banquet of 1448 bespeaks a clarity of regional styles Strohm at times blurs; or in music example 85, whose part-writing—especially the prevalent parallel 6ths between cantus and tenor—is not so indistinguishable from northern styles as Strohm suggests (574). Recent research has also emphasized unwritten, improvisatory practices in church polyphony; see below, n. 33. For a survey with much to say about the interaction of written and unwritten practices in the 16th century, see Haar, *Essays on Italian Poetry and Music* (cited n. 1 above).

[27] A chief exponent of Christian humanism is Charles Trinkaus; see esp. his *In Our Image and Likeness: Humanity and Divinity in Italian Humanist Thought*, 2 vols. (Chicago, 1970), and, for summary statements and extension of the argument there, two essays in his *The Scope of Renaissance Humanism* (Ann Arbor, 1983): "The Religious Thought of the Italian Humanists: Anticipation of the Reformers or Autonomy?" (237–62), and "Themes for a Renaissance Anthropology" (364–403). For Northern Europe, see William Bouwsma, "Renaissance and Reformation: An Essay on Their Affinities and Connections" (1974), reprinted in *A Usable Past*, 225–46; for the quotation from Petrarch's *On His Own Ignorance and That of Many Others*, see *The Renaissance Philosophy of Man*, ed. Ernst Cassirer, Paul Oskar Kristeller, and John Her-

Singing too could be seen as an effective evangelizing force in movements of lay piety. Indeed some such movements—for example the much-studied *laudesi* companies of Florence, active from the thirteenth century to the sixteenth—are so clearly associated with centers otherwise implicated in humanist currents that it behooves us to consider their devotional song as a manifestation of new rhetorical ideals in a Christian context.[28] More generally, the many sixteenth-century voices advocating the reform of sacred and liturgical music, from whatever doctrinal orientation, may be seen to participate in this Christian humanism. From Erasmus to Calvin, from Luther to Bernardino Cirillo, most who spoke on the topic argued that excessive complexity and overtly secular features needed to be pruned from sacred song in order to allow the words it conveyed more effectively to enter and inspire the soul. Through such reform, they aimed to achieve a propriety of musical style that might better shape the will—thus functioning like Valla's persuasive rhetoric—and that would be the musical equivalent of Erasmus's classicizing stylistic "purity." Their critique, in other words, reflects both the humanist ideal of eloquence and the general rhetoricization of musical practices described above. Such musical thought was not concerned exclusively (or even, in some cases, primarily) with polyphony. Instead the reformers aimed to create new repertories of sacred monophony or purge the improprieties of old ones even as they spelled out new, usually restricted roles for polyphonic song. Nevertheless the impact of such thinking was felt by many polyphonists and may be witnessed in works as different as the modest homophonic psalm-settings of the Huguenot Claude Goudimel and Josquin's vast psalm-motet *Miserere mei Deus*.[29]

All these paradigms—even in some measure the Whig interpretation, with suitable qualification to avoid egregious imposing of anachronistic views of subjectivity on the fifteenth and sixteenth centuries—offer important insights into the musical thought and practice of the Renaissance. They have not tended simply to disappear when newer interpretations have emerged, but instead have been absorbed into those interpretations, or rather overlaid on one another, as our views have become more complex and nuanced and have been redirected by changing present-day historiographical agendas. Just as the paradigm of civic humanism sprang from, incorporated, and aimed to explain that of rhetorical humanism, so it also endorses a novel worldliness in Italian urban culture not unrelated to the Whig view and at times smacks of a Whiggish progression toward Enlightened

man Randall (Chicago, 1971), 105; Erasmus is quoted by Eugene F. Rice, Jr, "Erasmus and the Religious Tradition, 1495–99," in *Renaissance Essays*, 162–86; see 180.

[28] For a survey of the Florentine companies, see Blake Wilson, *Music and Merchants: The Laudesi Companies of Republican Florence* (Oxford, 1992).

[29] For a sampling of the reformers' views, see *Strunk's Source Readings*, III: *The Renaissance*, ed. Tomlinson, section 3 ("Music and Religious Reform"); for the probable influence of Savonarola in Josquin's motet, Patrick Macey, "Savonarola and the Sixteenth-Century Motet," *Journal of the American Musicological Society*, 36 (1983), 422–52.

autonomy and freedom. The paradigm of antischolastic humanism incorporates both the rhetorical and the civic paradigms in an interpretation of the ongoing evolution of Italian city-states, and also at times smacks of progressivism. The paradigm of Christian humanism points up the religious goals of humanist redefinition of rhetoric and incorporates humanist/scholastic divisions as they played themselves out in the later Renaissance. And, finally, all these interpretations involve a continuing re-evaluation of the Renaissance classicism featured in the philological paradigm.

In the meantime it has become clear that these various views, taken together, barely touch on some of the most basic epistemological issues that might be seen to set humanist thought apart from other strains in the Renaissance and that might have their own large impact on music. These issues are revealed above all in humanists' attempts to annex the one verbal art near the center of scholastic agendas: logic. At least from Valla on, certain humanists defined logic along Ciceronian, topical lines. This logic of *topoi*, or place-logic, was originally an Aristotelian discipline of probable argumentation, an alternative to his formal demonstration by means of syllogism, and had long occupied a marginal place in scholastic logical curricula. It differed from syllogistic in that it did not proceed according to abstract, language-transcending formulas. Instead it developed in linguistic usage itself, unfolding in rhetorical acts of dialogue and argumentation that traced a less easily codified but none the less logical path from topic to topic. In this discursive dimension topical logic accorded well with the humanists' rhetorical and pragmatic concerns; to emphasize it humanists preferred the term "dialectic" to "logic."

Dialectic became, then, an expression of the humanists' shift of emphasis from the scholastics' formally valid demonstration to compelling, discursive persuasion; in advancing it they tended to reverse the scholastic hierarchy of *ratio* over *oratio* and to subsume wisdom in eloquence. Humanist dialectic approached a kind of early-modern "ordinary language" philosophy rooted in views like Valla's, which tended to place all reasoning under the aegis of language use. (The Schoolmen's logic of the late Middle Ages had, instead, distanced reason from the deployment of language.) After Valla dialectic was developed and disseminated by writers like Rudolph Agricola, whose *De inventione dialectica* of ca.1480 was enthusiastically embraced as a textbook fifty years later, and Juan Luis Vives, who described pious, Christian grounds for relinquishing the certain knowledge sought through scholastic method.[30]

[30] Two early and important analyses of this shift in dialectic are Walter J. Ong, *Ramus: Method and the Decay of Dialogue* (Cambridge, MA, 1958), which describes Agricola's topical logic as backdrop for a history of Petrus Ramus' educational reforms, and Cesare Vasoli, *La dialettica* (1968, cited in n. 9 above), which gathers essays published from 1952 on concerning figures from Valla to Ramus. By now topical dialectic and its implications are well entrenched in the secondary literature, occupying an important niche even in general surveys of Renaissance thought and thoroughly identified with humanist rhetorical interests and strategies. For secondary works on Valla, see n. 9 above; for Vives, see Copenhaver and Schmitt, *Renaissance Philosophy* (cited in n. 2), esp. 200–6; and for Agricola and his influence, see, in addition to

Richard Waswo's *Language and Meaning in the Renaissance* (1987) is a suggestive study dealing with such issues. Waswo sees in humanist positions on language and dialectic a "Renaissance semantic shift" analogous to—indeed, in some respects anticipating—the linguistic turn of the twentieth century: a shift from essentialist views of thought that see language as referential, as a "cosmetic" overlay on our conceptions and perceptions, to a contextual view that sees language as actively "constitutive" of our thoughts through its use in particular social contexts and discursive situations. For Waswo this constructivist idea of language is implicit in humanist emphases of rhetoric and dialogue, in the echoes of Valla's rhetorical dialectics through the later Renaissance, in the reformed readings of Scripture that asserted its historical situatedness and thus suggested the temporality of its meanings, and in the manufacturing of authorial subjectivity through text that is marked in a writer like Montaigne. In these and other instances we witness an awareness of "the intoxicating and terrifying possibility of *making* meaning" through language that forms, in Waswo's view, "one of the principal defining energies of the entire Renaissance."[31]

This latest paradigm of humanism—call it ORDINARY-LANGUAGE HUMANISM—may have profound implications for musical culture, though it has not yet been taken up by musicologists in any direct or detailed way. In this humanism, with its emphasis on the pragmatics of discourse, we may deepen our understanding of the constitutive, social dimensions of written and unwritten musical traditions alike throughout the Renaissance. We may reconceive the pervasion of later Renaissance musical culture with what Pirrotta once called the *maniera* of polyphonic techniques—a manner that may come to seem, at the broadest level, a musical analogue to the emphatically social-linguistic presentation of humanist dialogue.[32] We may also find a framework in which better to comprehend improvisatory polyphonic practices like Tinctoris's shadowy *cantare super librum*, which musicologists have recently located in complex interrelation to fully written polyphony about 1500.

Ong, Lisa Jardine, "Inventing Rudolph Agricola: Cultural Transmission, Renaissance Dialectic, and the Emerging Humanities," in *The Transmission of Culture in Early Modern Europe*, ed. Anthony Grafton and Ann Blair (Philadelphia, 1990), 39–86. Humanist logic still tends to receive scant attention from historians of logic and philosophy "proper," probably since philosophers' perspectives have tended to be shaped by later outgrowths of formal, syllogistic logic. For a juxtaposition of divergent approaches to the history of scholastic and humanist logics that is instructive in this regard, see the chapters "Traditional Logic" and "Humanist Logic" in the *Cambridge History of Reniassance Philosophy* (Cambridge, 1988), respectively by E. J. Ashworth and Lisa Jardine.

[31] Richard Waswo, *Language and Meaning in the Renaissance* (Princeton, 1987); quotation from 132.

[32] Here I take up James Haar's suggestion in *Essays on Italian Poetry and Music* (cited in n. 1 above; see 57) that polyphonic song (and specifically the madrigal) enabled "not just a straightforward declamation of a text but a ruminative, multi-layered reading of it"; such multi-layered interpretation, it seems to me, has affinities with the multiple perspectives of humanist dialogue and dialectic. For Pirrotta's *aperçu* on the 16th century's polyphonic *maniera*, see "Novelty and Renewal in Italy" (cited in n. 24 above), 173.

Moreover, ordinary-language humanism, with its view that reason is immanent in discourse and only inappropriately reduced to abstract formulas, provides an ideological context for musical practices and polemics that resisted to some measure the quadrivial demand for mathematical formalization and abstraction: Monteverdi's practices criticized by Artusi, for example, or Vincenzo Galilei's recommendation, ridiculed by Zarlino, that musicians observe the intonation and gestures of play-actors in order to learn to express the words they set. Here this view of humanism may capture a deep cultural rationale (deeper than is offered by the rhetorical paradigm) for the nudging of musical thought away from the transcendental numericalism of the quadrivium toward the speech-act pragmatics of the trivium.[33]

More broadly still, ordinary-language humanism casts a new light on the whole late-Renaissance exaltation of music's affective powers. We have already had occasion to mention this aspect of Renaissance musical culture. By the end of the period it was dispersed across the whole of Europe, displayed in a myriad of forms ranging from the late, expressionist madrigals of Marenzio, Luzzaschi, or Gesualdo to Dowland's melancholic songs; from the civic ethics of Baïf and Mauduit's *musiques mesurées*—a civic humanism gauged in precise musical technique—to the dark religiosity of Lasso's late Lamentations of Jeremiah; from Caccini's ornamental expression of text and affect to Peri's declamatory one; from discussions of modal ethos and polyphonic modality to Burmeister's rhetorical analyses of polyphony; from the themes of courtly musical festivities at Paris in 1581 to the themes of those at Florence in 1589. All these instances of Renaissance musical culture, and the overarching concern for music's expressive powers they manifest, are clearly if generally related to the rhetorical emphases of earlier humanist historiography. But the ordinary-language view of humanism may well uncover deeper roots for them. It suggests the intriguing possibility that the abiding interest through this era in music's powers may be allied with a widespread and novel language constructivism, that it may reveal a conception of musical discourse as itself formative of affect or ethos and not merely the conveyance for pre-formed states of the soul.

This hypothesis is encouraged by the paradoxical affinity of ordinary-language humanism to ostensibly very different Renaissance cultural strains: the varieties of Neoplatonic and magical thought revitalized in the late fifteenth century and subsequently spread through large areas of European culture. Late-Renaissance psychology and magic located the source of music's power in its own kind of constructivism—Platonic-numerical rather than rhetorical—in which speech-acts (or, better, song-acts) built sounding structures that acted to reshape psychological or spiritual formations within the human organism. Many magicians, philoso-

[33] For suggestive analyses of Tinctoris's improvised polyphony in relation to fully written polyphony, see Margaret Bent, "*Resfacta* and *Cantare super librum*," *Journal of the American Musicological Society* 36 (1983), 371–91, and Rob C. Wegman, "From Maker to Composer: Improvisation and Musical Authorship in the Low Countries," *Journal of the American Musicological Society* 49 (1996), 409–79; for relevant texts in the Zarlino–Galilei and Monteverdi–Artusi polemics, see *Strunk's Source Readings*, III: *The Renaissance*, ed. Tomlinson, 184–89, and IV: *The Baroque Era*, ed. Margaret Murata, 18–36.

phers, and musicians shared the notion that musical affect occurred when music's physical motions altered the innate motions of listeners' souls. The belief in this physico-psychological power of music is not new in the Renaissance, of course—Renaissance thinkers were sensitive to its antecedents stretching back to ancient thought—but it is perhaps more acutely and pervasively felt from the late fifteenth century through the sixteenth than ever before in the West. It seems likely that this development was encouraged by the spread of constructivist notions of language and its relations to the world and the psyche—notions, once again, that are increasingly clearly associated with humanism.[34]

The musical issues I have preliminarily linked to this humanist position did not disappear at the end of the Renaissance. They were left to evolve further in changed cultural circumstances: in the categorical Cartesian approach to affect of the later seventeenth century and the ruminations on it of the Enlightenment, reflected in their own music styles and debates; in the resurgence of linguistic constructivism and Platonic transcendentalism, with music at its heart, that preoccupied Romantic thought; and in the linguistic turn, still fundamentally concerned with the problematic status of musical language, whose structuralist and poststructuralist implications we live with today—a turn already seen in hindsight as a most characteristic gesture of the twentieth-century human sciences. The ghosts of Renaissance humanism, though they assume for us different forms than they took on for Burckhardt, still rise up before us.

[34] For the workings of magical language and song in this period, see Gary Tomlinson, *Music in Renaissance Magic: Toward a Historiography of Others* (Chicago, 1993), esp. chs. 2, 4, and 5.

2

THE CONCEPT OF THE RENAISSANCE

James Haar

ONCE the proudest of words identifying periods of Western history, the term "Renaissance" has in recent years had a bit of a hard time. There are several reasons for this. First, some scholars argue that there have been many periods of political, social, and artistic renewal, many renaissances rather than one to be set apart with an assertive capital letter. This is a useful idea, and we will presently turn to it.

Next, proponents of continuity in cultural history have pointed out the multiple aspects of medieval life and thought that continued, changing in various ways and at different times, into the period (late fourteenth century to early seventeenth century) most generally if admittedly roughly defined as the Renaissance.[1] If on the other hand what we have been used to calling the Renaissance marks the beginning of modern life more than the continuation of medieval culture, and more than the simple revival of ancient thought and art, "early modern" might be a better term for the period, and it has been employed by music historians as well as by scholars in other fields. Supposing a trifold division, ancient–medieval–modern, of Western culture, as was already done in the late seventeenth century, this might do.[2] But "modern" is a tricky word, increasingly so in our contemporary world as scholars and critics have turned to calling their own culture "post-modern." There are even more "modern" periods in cultural history than there are "renaissances."[3]

[1] The scholar most frequently cited for this view is Johann Huizinga, in whose *The Waning of the Middle Ages* (1919; Eng. trans. 1924) 15th-century culture, particularly that of the court of Burgundy, is seen as essentially medieval. Some use of overtly medieval themes may be seen in 15th-century Italy as well; an example is the selfconscious revival of the themes of medieval epic in the chivalric romances so popular in Ferrara and elsewhere.

[2] Christoph Cellarius, *Historia universalis . . . in antiquam et medii aevi ac novam divisa* (1696).

[3] For an assemblage and discussion of "modern" movements in music, from the 14th to the 20th century, see the papers of Kurt von Fischer and H. H. Eggebrecht, "The Concept of the 'New' in Music from the Ars Nova to the Present Day," *International Musicological Society: Papers of the Eighth Congress, New York 1961*, ed. Jan LaRue, 2 vols. (Kassel, 1961–62), I: 184–202, II: 112–17.

"Modern" and "reborn" strike me in any event as nearly antithetical terms. And in the history of music the break between ancient and modern—between the end of the late hellenistic tradition and the documentable rise of Western music—could be seen as deeper than anything in our subsequent history, even though recognizing it as such does away entirely with the Middle Ages.

More fundamental objections to use of the word "Renaissance" come from scholars who object to an often strongly Italian focus joined with elitist presuppositions and who are tired of Hegelian dialectic, seeing on both counts little that is salvageable in nineteenth-century historical writing of even partially Hegelian cast; in particular they are opposed to the work of Jacob Burckhardt, whose *Civilization of the Renaissance in Italy* put the term on the historiographical map.[4] This is not the place to debate the merits and demerits of Burckhardt's work; but if his optimism and his emphasis on novelty and on the individual creativity of the period need qualification, and his omissions, particularly those of philosophical, economic, and sociological topics now seen as of central importance, need filling in, his book remains I think a vitally important work on the subject (the reader will detect that I have decided that the Renaissance *is* a subject).[5]

Burckhardt, interested as he was in the arts, did not write about them, and certainly not about music, in his great book.[6] Many musicologists have however studied the Renaissance in Burckhardtian vein; among them may be mentioned three of special prominence in the twentieth century, Leo Schrade, Alfred Einstein, and Edward Lowinsky.[7] A turn away from Burckhardt was inevitable; in other fields it began early in the century, and in music new directions, some of them evident in this volume, in the approach of music historians to the period are now to be seen, but no single one would seem as yet dominant. It seems premature to try to

[4] The first scholar to make prominent use of the term was Jules Michelet (d. 1874), who gave the title "Renaissance" to a volume of his *Histoire de France*, introducing it as "l'aimable mot de Renaissance" and declaring that "le xvie siècle est un héros" (ix: 5, 14 in the edn of 1870). Burckhardt's *Die Cultur der Renaissance* appeared in 1860; the first English translation was published in 1878. Its early reception is outlined by Wallace Ferguson, *The Renaissance in Historical Thought* (Cambridge, MA, 1948), ch. 8.

[5] For a sympathetic recent view of Burckhardt's work, along with an attempt to see elements of the Burckhardtian Renaissance as lasting until the time of Descartes, see William Kerrigan and Gordon Braden, *The Idea of the Renaissance* (Baltimore, 1989).

[6] *Die Cultur der Renaissance* was preceded by Burckhardt's *Der Cicerone* (1855), a guide to Italian painting. He also wrote on architecture (*Geschichte der Renaissance in Italien*, 1868). There are a few pages on music in his book of 1860; Burckhardt knew little of the subject (the pioneering work of A. W. Ambros was yet to appear), but he did make some interesting remarks on the prevalence of amateur cultivation of music in the early 16th century.

[7] Leo Schrade, "Renaissance: The Historical Conception of an Epoch," *Report of the International Society for Musical Research, Fifth Congress, Utrecht 1952* (Amsterdam, 1953), 19–32; Alfred Einstein, *The Italian Madrigal*, trans. A. H. Krappe, R. H. Sessions, and O. Strunk, 3 vols. (Princeton, 1949); Edward E. Lowinsky, "The Concept of Physical and Musical Space in the Renaissance" (1941); "Music in the Culture of the Renaissance" (1954); "Music of the Renaissance as Viewed by Renaissance Musicians" (1966); "Humanism in the Music of the Renaissance" (1982). These and other essays of relevance may all be found reprinted in Lowinsky, *Music in the Culture of the Renaissance and other Essays*, ed. Bonnie J. Blackburn, 2 vols. (Chicago, 1989), to which citations below refer.

summarize current post- or anti-Burckhardtian theories, and useless to argue with those who would do away with the notion of the Renaissance altogether. In this essay I shall in any event continue to use, because I think them still useful, some Burckhardtian concepts.

It is not so difficult to describe changes—in genres and styles of composition, in performance and reception, in patronage and cultural milieu—affecting the music of the period, the second part of which is addressed in this book. Doing all this and then simply saying, here is the Renaissance in music—at least in its later phases—is of course possible, but it does not get us far. And rather than discussing the music of the period 1520–1640, then concluding that this is "what happened" during the Renaissance,[8] we might try to isolate aspects of European life that have been agreed upon, by Burckhardt and others, as defining the term and that can apply to the musical culture of the period. Not everything that Burckhardt and his successors saw as Renaissance-defining phenomena applies to music; and, more important here, not everything in the musical culture of the period can or need be thought of as possessing "Renaissance" character.

Before postulating Renaissance categories for music, we must face some geographical and chronological questions. The Renaissance is an era to which I have given a broad temporal span, without geographical limitation; but as a period of intellectual and artistic "rebirth" readable in the work of scholars and writers and visible in architecture, sculpture, and painting it has, from the time of Burckhardt, been commonly thought of as beginning in Italy in the late fourteenth century and only gradually spreading north of the Alps; and in the land of its birth the period has often been considered to be over by the middle of the sixteenth century if not a generation before (the Sack of Rome in 1527 and the end of the Florentine republic a few years later are convenient exterior events for this view, the death of Raphael in 1520 or that of Ariosto in 1533 appropriate signposts of cultural change).[9] How can we justify using "Renaissance" as an epithet for a period of pan-European music history beginning in 1520? And what about the still current view that the Renaissance in music, unlike the other arts, traveled from North to South?

An answer to these questions has already been suggested at the beginning of this essay, namely that there have been many "renaissances" in European culture. As for geography, the importance of Franco-Flemish musicians in the fifteenth century is unquestioned, even if Quattrocento Italy is no longer seen as the musical desert described by earlier scholars. But whether anything is gained by giving their art the

[8] This is essentially the approach of Gustave Reese, *Music in the Renaissance* (New York, 1954), still a remarkably complete and acute survey of the music of the 15th and 16th centuries. The same period is covered in Leeman L. Perkins, *Music in the Age of the Renaissance* (New York, 1999), a work that opens with a defense of the traditional view of the Renaissance. For a brilliant if slightly idiosyncratic view of 15th-century musical culture, see Reinhard Strohm, *The Rise of European Music, 1380–1500* (Cambridge, 1993). Strohm has little use for the Renaissance as term or concept.

[9] Burckhardt's book has no set chronological boundaries, but he has little to say about later-16th-century culture.

epithet "Renaissance" is to me very doubtful.[10] With regard to chronology, I have already said that the term "Renaissance" is best used as characterizing certain distinct aspects of life, not as a cover-all; and not all of these developed at the same time, making chronological precision difficult. The revival—as opposed to mere recovery—of ancient musical thought is, for example, more marked in the period after 1520 than in earlier generations. Conceptualizing music as a rhetorical art imitative of the natural world and, more importantly, of human passions is far more characteristic of sixteenth- and early-seventeenth-century Europe than it is of the fifteenth century. The sixteenth-century Reformations, Protestant and Catholic, spurred musical activity that was certainly thought of at the time as renewal and rebirth. The notion of the composer and the performer as artists, not mere craftsmen, aspiring to and achieving fame through individual *virtù*, was perhaps never as fully realized (before the nineteenth century) in music as it was in the other arts; still, it is more markedly evident in our period than in the early Renaissance. To say that the High Renaissance in music ended with the death of Josquin des Prez (1521) once seemed very *au courant*; it now seems no more meaningful than the citation of dates given above for the political and artistic spheres of life in Italy. Perhaps one might consider these "endings" to be beginnings as well, part of the inevitable overlap in accounts of human history, with political catastrophe in Italy leading to new developments of the Renaissance concept of state (sixteenth-century monarchy), artistic achievements constantly giving rise to new art (Michelangelo coming out of Raphael, Willaert out of Josquin). For the end of the period 1520–1640 such a phenomenon as the rise of opera can surely be seen as another overlap, partaking of both Renaissance and Baroque aspirations.

There is, then, plenty of reason to consider as "a" Renaissance a set of cultural directions applicable while not limited to sixteenth- and early-seventeenth-century music. As to what aspects of the musical life of this period might best be said to partake of Renaissance values, some caution is indicated. I have already listed a few things that I think do qualify: the revival of ancient musical theory; the importance of rhetoric and hence of text–music relationships; religious renewal; the achievement of personal fame, of at least temporary immortality, if the oxymoron may be excused, through artistic excellence. Each of these topics is related to the others, and each is broad enough to subsume a number of related phenomena, to be discussed below. I am not inclined to add to the list.

Other scholars have been more generous; Edward Lowinsky in particular has postulated a much longer list.[11] I do not wish to argue here the validity of Lowinsky's points; but I would repeat that not everything that happened in the period—

[10] Musicologists as early as R. G. Kiesewetter (d. 1850) emphasized the priority of Northern musicians in many musical developments. Some late-19th-century French scholars, notably Louis Courajod, maintained that the Renaissance began with the Valois dynasty in 14th-century France. See Ferguson, *The Renaissance in Historical Thought*, 316–18.

[11] See in particular the concluding pages of his "Music in the Culture of the Renaissance," 38–39. Lewis Lockwood, "Renaissance," *The New Grove Dictionary of Music and Musicians*, 2d edn, ed. Stanley Sadie, 29 vols. (London, 2001), XXI: 179–86, esp. p. 184, gently but firmly rejects some of Lowinsky's views, seeing some of the latter's categories as inappropriate and

including some of its most striking advances—gains in meaning from having the "Renaissance" tag applied. For example, the commercial success and wide circulation of printed music from *c.*1530, with the broadening of musical culture and the vast increase in musical literacy that resulted, is really an early-modern, not a Renaissance phenomenon. Abandonment of fixed poetic forms in musical settings, apart from the exaggerated importance given it by some scholars, is a change of taste that may be a break with tradition but is in itself hardly a renewal of lost artistic values. Changes in musical language, in particular the mid-sixteenth-century tonal revolution that Einstein referred to as the "clearing up" of the harmonic palette,[12] may have some tangential relationship to Renaissance-inspired thought (see below) but are I think better viewed as part of the stylistic course of sixteenth-century polyphony, as nearly as can be independent of ideological trends outside music. Thus "music in the Renaissance" is merely a conventional abbreviation for a chronological period; "Renaissance music," the subject of this essay, may have real meaning but is far from an inclusive term.

The Revival of Ancient Musical Thought

THE intensity and pervasiveness of interest in classical antiquity is what above all else has given meaning to the Renaissance.[13] For music this interest has been looked on as less important than it was for the other arts, since no Roman music and only a few scraps of ancient Greek music survived, fragments chiefly of late hellenistic origin and hard to interpret even after the notation has been deciphered, as it was in the sixteenth century. But the situation is not terribly different for painting, for which surviving classical prototypes known in the Renaissance were largely in the nature of decorative ornament. The absence of a written record of ancient music may have been a kind of blessing in disguise, since it forced on even the most classically inclined of sixteenth-century musicians both greater adherence to the living Western musical tradition and greater originality of interpretation of what the ancients said about music.

What did survive from the classical past was a body of theoretical literature and a wealth of anecdotal lore about the origins and affective powers of music. The transmission of the theory treatises through the Middle Ages has been carefully

his general view of the Renaissance as a movement of emancipation of medieval fetters as misguided.

[12] *Italian Madrigal*, 606. Einstein is here referring to the end of the century; but elsewhere he sees this kind of change of language as taking place a generation earlier, in the late work of Cipriano de Rore and in the music of Orlando di Lasso.

[13] The work of Paul Oskar Kristeller has eloquently reiterated this view. See for example his "Humanist Learning in the Italian Renaissance," *Renaissance Thought II: Papers in Humanism and the Arts* (New York, 1965), 1–19. Of course there have been other periods of intense interest in antique culture, such as the Carolingian revival at the end of the 8th century, a poetic and philosophic renaissance in the 12th century, and the Winckelmannian neo-classicism of the late 18th and early 19th centuries.

delineated by Thomas Mathiesen;[14] the fifteenth-century recovery of the treatises and of the principal sources for classical anecdote about music has been admirably described by Claude Palisca.[15] By 1520 the earlier stages of this process—collection of manuscripts, translation of a number of treatises into Latin, even the printing of some treatises (notably the *De institutione musica* of Boethius, which had been known in the Middle Ages but was now studied with new intensity)—was virtually complete. Sixteenth-century theorists began to deal with this material in earnest, and composers to act upon it in various ways. Individual topics of importance in this activity include scale and mode; tuning; the relationship of word and tone; the priority of solo song (or lack of polyphony) in ancient music; music as imitation, of the physical world and of human action and emotion; and, dependent on this last, the fabled powers of music to move human hearts and minds.

From Boethius, and indeed from Plato's *Timaeus*, known in excerpts for centuries, theorists had already learned something of Greek scales, modes, keys, and genera. Now they had much more to read on the subject. By a natural if mistaken process they, like their medieval predecessors, identified Greek octave-species and keys with the modes of ecclesiastical chant; not until late in the sixteenth century was it conclusively demonstrated that this connection was false, and then only to a select few.[16] Whether the extension of modal thought and practice from chant to sacred and secular polyphony that took place in the sixteenth century was the direct result of study of ancient theory may be argued, but the prestige of classical sources surely played an important role in the process.[17] And if changes in sixteenth-century harmonic language, leading to increased use of root-position chords in tonally coherent patterns (not necessarily the patterns to be codified in the late seventeenth century), were chiefly the result of such purely musical—

[14] Thomas J. Mathiesen, "Hermes or Clio? The Transmission of Ancient Greek Music Theory," *Musical Humanism and its Legacy: Essays in Honor of Claude V. Palisca*, ed. Norma K. Baker and Barbara R. Hanning (Stuyvesant, NY, 1992), 3–35. See also the later section of Mathiesen's *Apollo's Lyre: Greek Music and Music Theory in Antiquity and the Early Middle Ages* (Lincoln, NE, 2001).

[15] Claude V. Palisca, *Humanism in Italian Renaissance Musical Thought* (New Haven, 1985). This book is a culmination of Palisca's years of work on the subject of Renaissance humanism in music. Other valuable contributions of his include *Girolamo Mei: Letters on Ancient and Modern Music to Vincenzo Galilei and Giovanni Bardi: A Study with Annotated Text* (Rome, 1960), *The Florentine Camerata: Documentary Studies and Translations* (New Haven, 1989), and numerous articles.

[16] See Palisca, *Humanism*, ch. 11; D. P. Walker, "Musical Humanism in the Sixteenth and Early Seventeenth Centuries," *The Music Review*, 2 (1941), 1–13, 111–21, 220–27, 288–308; 3 (1942), 55–71.

[17] Harold S. Powers/Frans Wiering, "Mode," *New Grove*^{2}, XVI: 775–823, esp. pp. 797–823; cf. Jeffrey Dean, "Okeghem's Attitude towards Modality: Three-Mode and Eight-Mode Typologies," *Modality in the Music of the Fourteenth and Fifteenth Centuries*, ed. Ursula Günther, Ludwig Finscher, and Jeffrey Dean, MSD 49 (Neuhausen-Stuttgart, 1996), 203–46. Theorists most often cite classical authority for their views on mode when they espouse what Bernhard Meier has called the "pseudo-classical" system (of mixed ancient and medieval origin) equating modes and octave species. See Meier, *The Modes of Classical Polyphony*, trans. Ellen S. Beebe (New York, 1988), ch. 2, esp. pp. 43 ff. It should be noted that by "classical" Meier means the music of the middle and late 16th century.

hence non-Renaissance—phenomena as the popularity of dance-song and of instrumentally accompanied song, the organization of the music into tonal/modal patterns—a process not equally clear in every piece—was at least a partial cause, with the classically sanctioned prestige of mode a contributing factor.

Odder, but demonstrably classicizing in nature, is the preoccupation of some sixteenth-century musicans with the Greek genera, the diatonic, chromatic, and enharmonic scale segments explained in a number of classical sources. Western music used, apparently, only the diatonic genus; but in the hope that some of the secrets of ancient music's fabled power lay in the chromatic, with its use of successive semitones, and the enharmonic, with its employment of quarter-tones, a few musician-theorists advocated use of these genera and even composed in them. Not the earliest to do so, but certainly the most flamboyant, was Nicola Vicentino, whose *L'antica musica ridotta alla moderna prattica* of 1555 defends and advocates the use of these genera as a way of renewal and rebirth for music.[18] Sixteenth-century expansion of the tonal palette through the use of many sharps and flats is, by the way, only loosely connected with interest in the chromatic genus; it is much more an outgrowth of medieval hexachordal thought, hence by our definition a non-Renaissance feature of musical life.

Systems of tuning or intonation for medieval musicians and especially for their successors were matters in part theoretical, in part practical, and resolution between theory and practice was not easy.[19] On the authority of Boethius, writers in the fifteenth and early sixteenth centuries championed Pythagorean intonation as the theoretical basis for all music even as they admitted that in practice it was difficult to use.[20] The earliest theorist to challenge Pythagorean hegemony, Ramos de Pareia, seems to have proceeded along practical rather than humanistic lines.[21] But rediscovery of or renewal of interest in ancient sources, chiefly Euclid's *Elements* and Ptolemy's *Harmonics*, gave both new investigative method and classical precedent for an alternate theory of intonation. Such a theory, utilizing the *diatonic syntonon* of Ptolemy, was elaborated by Ludovico Fogliano (*Musica theorica*, 1529). This system (what we have come to know as just intonation), with its pure thirds and large diatonic semitone, was espoused by later theorists, notably Gioseffo Zarlino, whose *Istitutioni harmoniche* of 1558 established it as the new theoretical

[18] See Maria Rika Maniates' Eng. trans. of Vicentino's volume, *Ancient Music Adapted to Modern Practice* (New Haven, 1996). See also Henry W. Kaufmann, *The Life and Works of Nicola Vicentino, 1511–c.1576* (American Institute of Musicology, 1966). Serious interest in the genera on the part of Ramos de Pareia in the late 15th century and of his student Giovanni Spataro, a Bolognese theorist and composer active a generation before Vicentino, is evident in the latter's correspondence. See *A Correspondence of Renaissance Musicians*, ed. Bonnie J. Blackburn, Edward E. Lowinsky, and Clement A. Miller (Oxford, 1991), 66–70.

[19] See the relevant articles of Mark Lindley in *New Grove*^{2}: "Just intonation", XIII: 290–95; "Pythagorean intonation", XX: 643–45; "Temperaments", XXV: 245–68; cf. Palisca, *Humanism*, chs. 9–10.

[20] Theorists as late as Gafori (d. 1522) and Spataro (d. 1541) upheld the Boethian tradition. By the mid 16th century Pythagorean tuning was all but abandoned by most theorists, but it persisted here and there into the 18th century.

[21] Palisca, *Humanism*, 232–34.

basis for Western tuning. Its victory may be seen both as renewal—or better adaptation—of ancient musical thought and as triumph of "tonal" principles.

A new relationship of word and tone, in part a formal adjustment of melodic and rhythmic values to quasi-declamatory speech patterns and in part the forging of a musical vocabulary imbued with rhetorically persuasive and affectively powerful qualities, is generally regarded as one of the most important of Renaissance achievements in music.[22] Indeed it is so, to such an extent that it deserves treatment as a separate topic. At this point I will simply stress its perceived precedent in ancient musical thought. Both Plato, for his insistence on the priority of words in song (*Republic* III, 398), and Aristotle, for his theories of art as imitation of human life and feeling (*Poetics*), could be and of course were cited. Not far behind were Cicero (*De oratore* and other works) and Quintilian (*Institutio oratoria*). With such authorities to hand, it was easy for sixteenth-century writers to move to "the ancients say" every time the subject came up. And it came up often, in the writings of humanistically inclined theorists (Glarean and Vincenzo Galilei, among others) and also in the work of practical musicians, resulting in such oddities as quantitatively exact musical settings of classical and humanistic verse (Latin and vernacular), as well as in declamatory Protestant chorales and Catholic preoccupation with the reformation of "barbarous" medieval chant in its perceived indifference to textual values.[23]

An aspect of ancient music related to, sometimes thought of as essential to, effective and affective declamation of text is its fundamentally solo nature. The Greeks may have accompanied their songs in some way and they may have sung homophonic choruses, but they never mention counterpoint and presumably never thought of it. For some theorists (and presumably most composers before the end of the sixteenth century) this did the ancients no credit; in the eyes of Tinctoris, Gafori, Heyden, Spataro, Zarlino, and Zacconi modern music could boast of glories the Greeks had never achieved.[24] For others, such as Glarean, in whom humanistic interests were uppermost except when he was speaking of his favorite polyphonists, ancient monody was admirable in the abstract and worthy of being reborn in the work of modern musicians.

Unaccompanied solo song had of course never disappeared from Western music.

22 It is one of the main concerns of Edward Lowinsky. See for example his "A Treatise on Text Underlay by a German Disciple of Francisco de Salinas (1961)," *Music in the Culture of the Renaissance*, 868–83.

23 On humanistic settings in quantitatively exact style, see Lowinsky, "Humanism in the Music of the Renaissance," and the bibliography there cited. On chant reform at the end of the 16th century see Bernhard Meier, "Choralreform und Chorallehre im 16. Jahrhundert," *Geschichte der katholischen Kirchenmusik*, ed. Karl Gustav Fellerer, 2 vols. (Kassel, 1972–76), II: 45–53; Robert Hayburn, *Papal Legislation on Sacred Music, 95 A.D. to 1977 A.D.* (Collegeville, MN, 1979), chs. 3–4; James Haar, "Monophony and the Unwritten Tradition," *Performance Practice: Music before 1600*, ed. Howard Mayer Brown and Stanley Sadie (London, 1989), 240–47.

24 For example, Zarlino despite his proudly displayed humanistic erudition criticizes the "imperfections" of ancient music, among them the fact that "their songs were not composed of many voices as is our practice today" (*Istitutioni harmoniche* [Venice, 1558], book ii, ch. 4).

But after the fourteenth century little secular monody was preserved in writing, being replaced by polyphonic settings doubtless considered more artful. So much the norm did this become that the frottola, in essence accompanied solo song, was circulated in prints and manuscripts in "correct," that is four-part, polyphonic dress.[25] Yet solo performance of this repertory and contemporary French song was not only common, it was much admired—was indeed for Castiglione the most distinguished kind of music-making—partly because, as Burckhardt would have it, it emphasized individual achievement, and partly because it corresponded to an ancient practice.[26] *Improvvisatori* of varied skill and different social levels sang solo settings of epic and lyric poetry to unwritten melodies known popularly or of their own devising, accompanying themselves or using a *tenorista* playing a bowed or plucked string instrument. Some were known for the high quality of their singing; but on the whole their music perished with them unless imitators could catch something of their style, sometimes called *aria*.

From the second half of the sixteenth century there are in Italy manuscripts and even a few prints containing *arie*, solo melodies with one or two accompanying parts.[27] These are, like the *modi di cantar versi* scattered through Petrucci's song prints, quite simple, mainly syllabic, and affectively neutral; they came to life only in expert performance. And throughout the century there are chordally declamatory choruses, usually written for celebratory occasions.[28] To what extent, apart from overtly humanistic pieces, this tradition of solo song and declamatory choral writing is indebted to imagined classical prototypes is not easy to determine. What is important is that when Vincenzo Galilei, Giovanni Bardi, and others began to champion solo song as a vehicle for recapturing ancient musical ethos, there was an active tradition to draw on. The affective ornament and rhythmic *sprezzatura* of Caccini's *Nuove musiche* and that of his contemporary monodists masks an essentially simple style related to the sixteenth-century *aria* and so not particularly

[25] The repertory could of course be performed in four parts, but this arrangement does appear to have been a matter of convention. In a letter of 1535 to the Venetian theorist Giovanni del Lago, the composer Bartolomeo Tromboncino speaks of a frottola that he had written "to be sung to the lute," that is, without an alto part; he is willing to revise the piece for four voices at Lago's behest. See *A Correspondence of Renaissance Musicians*, 869–70.

[26] *Il cortegiano*, 2.13. See James Haar, "The Courtier as Musician: Castiglione's View of the Science and Art of Music," in *Castiglione: The Ideal and the Real in Renaissance Culture*, ed. Robert W. Hanning and David Rosand (New Haven, 1983), 165–89, esp. pp. 173–76.

[27] Many of the *arie* appear singly in madrigal prints, or can be found imbedded in polyphonic pieces. One collection that does survive is the 1577 reprint of *Aere racolti . . . dove si cantano Sonetti, Stanze & Terze Rime*, collected and in part composed by the Neapolitan musician Rocco Rodio. See Howard Mayer Brown, "The Geography of Florentine Monody: Caccini at Home and Abroad," *Early Music*, 9 (1981), 147–68; idem, "Petrarch in Naples: Notes on the Formation of Giaches de Wert's Style," *Essays on Italian Music in the Cinquecento*, ed. Richard Charteris (Sydney, 1990), 16–50.

[28] The *ne plus ultra* of the declamatory chorus may be Andrea Gabrieli's music for *Edipo tiranno* (Sophocles' play in Italian translation), written for the opening of the Teatro Olimpico in Vicenza. See Leo Schrade, *La Représentation d'Edipo tiranno au Teatro Olimpico (Vicence 1585)* (Paris, 1960).

"classical."[29] But the whole impulse toward solo song, culminating in the mix of dramatic speech-song and *aria* in Peri's *Euridice* of 1600 and, more colorfully, Monteverdi's *Orfeo* of 1607, owes a great debt to the power of suggestion of ancient writing about music; it is thus a Renaissance phenomenon even though it is informed by evolving Baroque sensibilities.

The last two topics I listed as part of the revival of ancient musical thought, imitation and the fabulous powers of music, might be better described as part of the newly intense preoccupation with music as rhetoric.

The New Connection of Music and Rhetoric

Ancient music, particularly the instrumental art of cithara and aulos, may have been descriptively imitative in concept and intent.[30] The conventions of style or gesture that made such imitation effective to listeners are lost to us and were certainly unknown in the sixteenth century. There was a tradition in Western music, presumably independent of antique precedent, of onomatopoetic gesture and of melodic and rhythmic convention—fast–slow, up–down—representing sounds of nature and physical activity. This battery of imitative devices was enormously expanded in the sixteenth century, resulting in widespread use of what have become known familiarly if not altogether accurately as "madrigalisms."[31] In itself this is not a revival of ancient musical ideas; it takes on meaning for our purposes only as part of a larger phenomenon, the rhetoricizing of music. By this term I mean both the shaping of melody and rhythm to fit text in "naturalistic" declamation and also a quite steady increase of effort at making music more expressive of the text it set. By heightening the rhetorical level at which verbal texts depicted human passions, composers hoped to move the "affections" of singers and listeners through successful imitation of these passions.

Medieval music is of course not without rhetorical qualities. Examples abound, including such striking ones as the soloistic decoration superimposed on plainchant in Notre-Dame organa; the matching of music to verbal artifice in the work of the greatest of medieval *rhétoriqueurs*, Guillaume de Machaut; the troubadour

[29] Giulio Caccini, *Le nuove musiche*, ed. H. W. Hitchcock (Madison, WI, 1970). Caccini's elaborate use of vocal ornament and his recommended use of rhythmic freedom (*sprezzatura*) in performance make the music seem more innovative than it basically is. Only occasionally, as in the *aria* "Occh' immortali", does Caccini show, almost unadorned, the roots of his song style. *Arie* were customarily embellished in performance throughout the 16th century; see Brown, "Petrarch in Naples", 25, citing a Neapolitan amateur writing in 1562.

[30] Aristotle included all major forms of poetry (and by inference their musical settings) as imitative in concept; he even included instrumental music. See *Poetics* 1.2.1447^{a}; cf. Palisca, *Humanism*, 397.

[31] These imitative devices deserve to be taken more seriously than many modern scholars have done. They were certainly admired in their day; and early-17th-century writers, particularly in Germany, went to some trouble to catalogue them. The most elaborate of such efforts may be the chapter on texts in Wolfgang Schonsleder's *Architectonice musices universalis* (Ingolstadt, 1631). See George J. Buelow, "Schonsleder", *New Grove*^{2}, XXII: 613–14.

turned polyphonist in the Trecento madrigal repertory. Little of this rhetoric is perceptible, at least to us, as imitative of speech-defined emotion; and polyphony was not, as its late sixteenth-century detractors never tired of saying, a natural vehicle for rhetorical naturalism in music. It took several generations, beginning about 1500, for composers to achieve declamatory precision in setting texts, and even at its best this quality was evident more to singers than to listeners, who could not help but be distracted by the contrapuntal overlapping of voices. As late as the 1530s serious musicians cared only intermittently for perfect "rightness" of declamation.[32]

A real change took place after 1530, led by Adrian Willaert in the motets and madrigals later to be collected and published as *Musica nova* (1559). In this music the prime factor was respect for the text; its physical sound, its verbal accents, its syntactic structure determined the course of the polyphonic fabric.[33] I think there is reason to doubt the extent to which humanistic interest in the antique blend of music and rhetoric determined earlier movement toward declamatory settings; the influence of popular song may have been equally important for composers at the turn of the century. But for Willaert and his circle the theories of Pietro Bembo, advocating classical purity in both Latin and Italian, and recommending close attention to the sound of language, were of determining influence. Willaert was described as the "new Pythagoras" by his pupil Zarlino; he could as well have been called the "new Plato." And in the work of Willaert's contemporary Cipriano de Rore a vividness of musical declamation, blended with contrapuntal fluidity in his earlier work and later on tending to emphasize strongly colored chordal passages, gave music a newly perceived strength of rhetorical persuasiveness and of imitative affect. Not without reason was Rore proclaimed at the end of the century as the father of the *seconda pratica*.

For its admirers this music recaptured the power attributed to the art by the ancients; thus the work of Orlando di Lasso, in the words of the humanist Samuel Quickelberg, portrayed its verbal subjects more vividly than any painting could.[34] Late sixteenth-century polyphony in the hands of master musicians like Lasso, Wert, and Marenzio achieved ever more persuasive rhetorical qualities, constantly expanding the number and kind of conventions that enabled listeners to hear music imitating the content of words—sometimes iconically, through direct word–tone equivalence, sometimes in broader or subtler strokes.

Yet not everyone was convinced. To impassioned neo-classicists such as Vin-

[32] It is not a subject for serious treatment by theorists before mid-century. Many musicians of his time may have shared the view of Spataro that text and its disposition in music was of secondary importance. See *A Correspondence of Renaissance Musicians*, 106–7. For a survey of text–music relationships, see Don Harrán, *Word–Tone Relations in Musical Thought from Antiquity to the Seventeenth Century* (American Institute of Musicology, 1986).

[33] See Martha Feldman, *City Culture and the Madrigal at Venice* (Berkeley, 1995).

[34] Quickelberg's statement is in a commentary on Lasso's Penitential Psalms, a volume accompanying the illuminated manuscript dedicated to these works. See Lowinsky, *Music in the Culture of the Renaissance*, 206. A generation earlier the printer Johann Ott said something rather similar about the music of Josquin; see Lowinsky, ibid., 26.

cenzo Galilei and, later, G. B. Doni, as well as to sober musical humanists like Girolamo Mei, the decorum imposed by polyphonic structure impeded musicians from achieving perfect rhetorical coherence, perfect imitative identification, complete affective strength. Only by breaking through this convention could the goal of recapturing the powers of ancient music be reached. In the work of the monodists and in the first musical dramas the goal was attained—at least in its own terms; in the madrigals of Claudio Monteverdi it was adapted with striking success to polyphony. There is no question here of "progress" toward "better" music; but there is achievement in musical terms of the chief aim of the Renaissance, the creative renewal of ancient art. By one of the ironies that historians create for themselves, this culmination of Renaissance musical thought coincides with the growth of Baroque sensibilities that were to lead music in quite different directions after the first few decades of the century.

Religious Renewal

To this point everything that I have identified as being a part of Renaissance music has had a a more or less close bond with strivings to renew the art of classical antiquity. This might seem not to be true of the religious ferment that gripped sixteenth-century society; after all, it was not ancient Greek religion that reformers turned to for inspiration. Some early students of the Renaissance stressed its pagan character (Burckhardt is not guilty of this).[35] But despite the ubiquity of reference to classical deities and the half-playful pagan vocabulary of some humanist scholars, there was no serious interest in, indeed little knowledge of ancient religions.[36] Nonetheless there is a connection; both Protestant and Catholic reformers wanted a return to a supposed purer form of Christianity, represented historically by the period of the Church Fathers (or in extreme cases by the apostolic beginnings of Christian belief). However little interested people, even many scholars, were in the chronology of ancient culture, they did know that Christianity developed in the midst of late-classical society. If the Christianizing of ancient philosophy is an essentially medieval activity, a religious syncretism, chiefly Neoplatonic in nature, is characteristic of the fifteenth and to some extent of the sixteenth century.[37] To put it simply, one might say that religious reformers wanted a revival not of ancient religion but of the Christianity of antiquity.

How this was reflected in music is the subject of other essays in this volume. Here I shall simply review a few of the topics I have touched on earlier, looking

[35] The work of John Addington Symonds, *The Renaissance in Italy*, 7 vols. (London, 1875–86), views the Renaissance as essentially pagan in character.

[36] See Jean Seznec, *The Survival of the Pagan Gods: The Mythological Tradition and its Place in Renaissance Humanism and Art* (1940; Eng. trans. by Barbara F. Sessions, New York, 1953). Seznec deals with the ambivalent feeling of churchmen about the pervasive love of antiquity (see esp. pp. 263–69); he does not suggest that ancient religion, as opposed to ancient mythology, was an important factor in Renaissance culture.

[37] See Kerrigan and Braden, *The Idea of the Renaissance*, chs. 5–7.

at them in a (I hope not dim) religious light. First of all, the verbal text of music for worship was in the minds of reformers a matter of prime importance. Calvinists used unaccompanied psalmody, a throwback to what they saw as the earliest Church music. Lutherans, following their music-loving leader, used chorale melodies in part new, in part derived from older music (including plainchant). Chordal settings and some polyphonic elaboration were allowed, but the settings were syllabic and carefully adjusted to agree with text accents.

Catholic reformers in the period after the close of the Council of Trent (1563) also stressed intelligibility of text. Sacred polyphony was probably never seriously threatened, despite the later mythical claim that Palestrina "saved" it with his Marcellus Mass.[38] Still, Carlo Borromeo and other prelates concerned with musical reform directly influenced composers such as Vincenzo Ruffo to write works stressing simultaneous or at least easily followable text delivery.[39] Polyphonic laude, chordal or modestly contrapuntal, appeared in abundance as the institution of the oratorio developed. In all this music, Catholic or Protestant, classicizing features such as choice of mode played a role.

That polyphony could, paradoxically, serve to heighten sacred as well as secular texts was something easily grasped by Catholic, Anglican, Lutheran, and even some Huguenot reformers. Sacred contrafacta of madrigals, chansons, and lieder appeared in abundance, sometimes closely related to the spirit of the original text, sometimes wildly at odds with it.[40] "Spiritual" chansons and madrigals were newly composed, employing the same rhetorical devices used in secular music. At the turn of the century sacred monodies followed suit; the Italy of Bernini's ecstatic sculptures saw the creation of Baroque monodies and solo cantatas, similar in aesthetic intent and in exceptional cases, such as Monteverdi's sacred music, equal in artistic realization. Here again Renaissance strivings and Baroque attitudes are blended, the fabled powers of ancient music brought back to serve militantly Christian purposes.

[38] This story appears to have started with Agostino Agazzari, a musician and writer active in Rome in the decade after Palestrina's death. See Lewis Lockwood, ed., *G. P. da Palestrina: Pope Marcellus Mass*, Norton Critical Scores (New York, 1975).

[39] Lewis Lockwood, *The Counter-Reformation and the Masses of Vincenzo Ruffo* (Vienna, 1970).

[40] See, for example, Richard Freedman, *The Chansons of Orlando di Lasso and their Protestant Listeners* (Rochester, NY, 2000).

The Quest for Personal Fame

Burckhardt begins the pages devoted to Renaissance striving for immortal personal glory with Dante, referring to a celebrated passage in the Divine Comedy:

> Ben non sare' io stato sì cortese
>   mentre ch'io vissi, per lo gran disio
> dell'eccellenza, ove mio core intese.
>
> (I should not have acted the courtier
> while I lived had I not been moved in my heart
> by such a great desire for excellence.) *Purg.* xi, 85–87

The speaker[41] did win fame; but all fame is fleeting:

> Non è il mondan romore altro che un fiato
>   di vento, che or vien quinci ed or vien quindi,
> e muta nome, perché muti lato.
>
> (Earthly fame is nothing but a puff
> of wind, blowing now here, now there;
> it changes name as it changes direction.) *Purg.* xi, 100–102

After Dante's time people took the first of these passages more seriously than the second. In emulation of ancient Greeks and Romans celebrated for military, political, and cultural excellence, Burckhardt's Italians of the fourteenth through sixteenth centuries strove mightily for personal distinction, coveting literally or figuratively the laurel that conferred immortal fame; and they were imitated by Northerners to a greater extent than Burckhardt tells us.

In music the first notable seeker of posthumous fame was not an Italian but a Frenchman, Guillaume de Machaut, who during his lifetime supervised the orderly copying of his complete literary and musical works.[42] Individual musicians did not follow Machaut's precedent (which was probably unknown to them) for a long time, indeed not until the age of printed music. Others occasionally acted for them; thus the copying of the Squarcialupi Codex (*c.*1415) was surely meant as memorial to the Trecento composers, each represented by a portrait as well as by name, contained in it. The Chigi Codex, copied at the very end of the fifteenth century, is in part a tribute to the fame of Ockeghem, nearly all of whose masses

[41] The 13th-century painter Oderisi of Gubbio.

[42] Machaut's activity in this regard is not without precedent or without the influence of patrons, but in scope it far exceeds what anyone else had done. It was perhaps fear of imminent death (from the plague) that led him in mid-career to start collecting his work. See Lawrence Earp, "Machaut's Role in the Production of Manuscripts of his Works," *Journal of the American Musicological Society*, 42 (1989), 461–503. The Florentine organist-composer Francesco Landini (d. 1397) is said to have been crowned with laurel in Venice; see Filippo Villani (d. 1405), *De origine civitatis florentine et de eiusdem famosis civibus*, ed. Giuliano Tanturli (Padua, 1997), 152.

are contained in it. There are sixteenth-century examples as well, among them a magnificently illuminated manuscript devoted to the motets of Rore.[43]

Most of these are presentation manuscripts, done at the behest of or as a gift for an exalted recipient; the composers may not even have been directly involved in their compilation. With printed music things are different. In an age when writers such as Pietro Aretino and Ludovico Ariosto took care over the publishing of their work, composers including Arcadelt (possibly), Layolle and Corteccia (certainly) saw to the printing of their collected madrigals, Carpentras of his sacred music. We know that Adrian Willaert revised his *Musica nova* for the opulent print, sponsored by a music-loving Ferrarese prince, which the composer must have regarded as his artistic testament. In the later sixteenth century Orlando di Lasso would seem to have been as much concerned about the publication of his music as any nineteenth-century composer; and after his death his sons published his collected motets with the title, obviously of monumental intent, *Magnum opus musicum*.[44] Monteverdi took great pains over the printing of his madrigals and sacred music; only his operas remained mostly unpublished, a fate that was to befall opera for centuries to come.

It thus seems clear that composers were as interested as any other artists in acquiring personal glory; for Glarean sixteenth-century composers had an "immoderate thirst" for fame. Were they in fact famous outside a narrow circle of fellow musicians? Fifteenth-century composers such as Du Fay, Ockeghem, and Busnoys were well known during their lives and commemorated after their deaths by musicians and a few poets, and were admired, not always for their musical skills alone, by their patrons and employers. The first composer to enjoy a wide and suprisingly lasting reputation among cultured amateurs as well as fellow professionals was Josquin des Prez. By the time of his death in 1521 Josquin was famous all over Europe. His name was proof of excellence to Castiglione, to Folengo, to Rabelais, to Pope Leo X, to Martin Luther.[45] Many of his works, including nearly all the masses (these in collected form), were published during his lifetime, and the printing and reprinting of his music (along with pieces attributed to him for the value of his name) went on into the second half of the century. To the theorist Glarean, writing some fifteen years after the composer's death, Josquin's music represented

43 On the Squarcialupi Codex, see the volume of studies published with a sumptuous facsimile, especially F. Alberto Gallo's Introduction and John Nádas, "The Squarcialupi Codex: An Edition of Trecento Songs, 1410–1415," in *Il Codice Squarcialupi: Ms. Mediceo Palatino 87, Biblioteca Medicea Laurenziana di Firenze*, ed. F. Alberto Gallo (Florence, 1992), 9–17, 19–36. For the Chigi Codex (*I-Rvat* Chigi C VIII 234), see Herbert Kellman's introduction to the facsimile (New York, 1987). The Munich manuscript (*D-Mbs* Mus. ms. B) is the subject of Jessie Ann Owens, "An Illuminated Manuscript of Motets by Cipriano de Rore" (PhD diss., Princeton University, 1978).

44 See James Haar, "Orlando di Lasso, Composer and Print Entrepreneur," in *Music and the Cultures of Print*, ed. Kate van Orden (New York, 2000), 135–62.

45 See Helmuth Osthoff, *Josquin des Prez*, 2 vols. (Tutzing, 1962–65), 1: 79–80; Jessie Ann Owens, "How Josquin became Josquin: Reflections on Historiography and Reception," in *Music in Renaissance Cities and Courts: Studies in Honor of Lewis Lockwood*, ed. Jessie Ann Owens and Anthony M. Cummings (Warren, MI, 1997), 271–80.

an *ars perfecta*; and until the end of the sixteenth century Josquin's name was held in honor even as his music disappeared from currency.

The Florentine academician Cosimo Bartoli, writing about mid-century, compared Josquin to Michelangelo as a "prodigy of nature."[46] High praise; and valuable as evidence that the work of individual composers was at least occasionally being considered as great art, a real change from earlier times when music received praise in general but individual works were rarely singled out.

Michelangelo's fame endured; Josquin's eventually faded, not to be revived until the birth of modern musical historiography at the end of the eighteenth century. Composers in the sixteenth century suffered the fate of painters described in another part of Dante's speech on fame:

> Credette Cimabue nella pittura
> tener lo campo, ed ora ha Giotto il grido,
> sì che la fama di colui è oscura.
>
> (Cimabue was thought to lead the pack
> in painting, and now Giotto is all the rage,
> so much so that the glory of the former is faded.) *Purg.* xi, 94–96

This was put succinctly for music by the German theorist Othmar Luscinius:

> And how strange that we find in matters of music a situation entirely different from that of the general state of the arts and letters: in the latter whatever comes closest to venerable antiquity receives most praise; in music, he who does not excel the past becomes the laughing stock of all.[47]

As the century progressed, writers successively placed Willaert, Rore, and Lasso at the pinnacle of earthly fame.[48] At the century's end Palestrina, put on a pedestal by his Roman students, began his centuries-long reign as the quintessential Renaissance composer, a phenomenon that lies outside the boundaries of this book. Still, Josquin occupied a place of special honor; the composer-theorist Adrian Petit Coclico (1552) set him at the head of a group of composers who transcended the work of early *musici mathematici* by employing their art for truly expressive goals and thus preparing the way for the modern *musici poetici*, masters of the new rhetorical art of music.[49] Thus composers were seen to combine the traditional quadrivial science of music with rhetorical values associated with verbal art, a view that, however

[46] "Un monstro della natura, sì come è stato nella Architettura Pittura & Scultura il nostro Michielagnolo Buonarroti." See James Haar, "Cosimo Bartoli on Music," *Early Music History*, 8 (1988), 37–79, esp. p. 54.

[47] *Musurgia seu praxis musicae* (1536), cited by Jessie Ann Owens, "Music Historiography and the Definition of 'Renaissance,'" *Notes* 47 (1990), 305–30; p. 307. Owens's article is a valuable summary of 16th- and early-17th-century remarks about the fame of past and present musicians.

[48] Owens, "Music Historiography," 312–13.

[49] *Compendium musices* (1552; facs. ed. Kassel, 1954). See Marcus van Crevel, *Adrianus Petit Coclico* (The Hague, 1940), 51–53. The term *musica poetica* was used by German theorists, beginning with Nikolaus Listenius (1537), to refer to the art of composition.

exaggerated (and based on very incomplete knowledge), retains some validity and is closely related to the notion that individual composers and their works could achieve real artistic fame.

Performers, then as now, acquired fame more easily than composers, and were readily compared to ancient virtuosos. Lists of distinguished singers and instrumentalists are not uncommon in the sixteenth century. Occasionally one finds descriptions and anecdotes telling us something about them; Cosimo Bartoli provides not only praise but interesting information about performers, chiefly Florentine, of his acquaintance.[50] Individual performers, singers or masters of one or more instruments, reached levels of reputation high enough for them to become subjects of admiring poetry or prose. Among such musicians we might mention the Ferrarese lutenist-singer Pietrobono (d. 1497), compared—to his advantage—by a local humanist to Amphion, Arion, Orpheus, and Apollo.[51] Pre-eminent among *improvvisatori*, singers of their own verse and that of others, including Petrarch and his growing flock of imitators, was Serafino Aquilano (d. 1500), active at various Italian courts but especially Naples and Milan; the "divino Serafino" was extravagantly praised as both poet and musician.[52] A mid-sixteenth-century example of a performer achieving extraordinary personal fame is Francesco da Milano, lutenist and composer of exceptional virtuosity, another musician crowned with the epithet *divino* and called the "prince of lutenists."[53] From the late sixteenth century there are many famous names; the most celebrated (or perhaps the best at self-promotion) was Giulio Caccini, active in Florence, Rome, and Paris as singer and composer of monody; his daughter Francesca, also famed as both singer and composer, carried the reputation of the family to the end of our period.[54]

There were of course performers of distinction in earlier periods; but we know much less about them. There was an undoubted growth of virtuosity in the period from 1450 to 1650. More important for our purposes is the desire, new to this period, and achievement of personal reputation, glory attained through possession of the *virtù* once possessed by ancient artists and now regained.

[50] Haar, "Cosimo Bartoli on Music."

[51] See F. Alberto Gallo, *Musica nel castello* (Bologna 1992), ch. 3: "Orpheus christianus," p. 113. Gallo gives examples of other testimony of this kind for 15th-century performers. For a full account of Pietrobono's extraordinary career and reputation, extending over most of the second half of the century, see Lewis Lockwood, *Music in Renaissance Ferrara, 1400–1505* (Cambridge, MA, 1984), 95–108.

[52] See Antonio Rossi, *Serafino Aquilano e la poesia cortigiana* (Brescia, 1980); Giuseppina La Face Bianconi and Antonio Rossi, *Le rime di Serafino Aquilano in musica* (Florence, 1999).

[53] H. Colin Slim, "Francesco da Milano (1497–1543/44): A Bio-bibliographical Study," *Musica Disciplina*, 17 (1964), 63–84, 19 (1965), 109–28. Another famous Italian lutenist of the time was Albert de Rippe, active at the French court; see Victor Coelho, "Alberto da Ripa," *New Grove*^{2}, XXI: 434–35, XVI: 49.

[54] For details of the careers of Giulio Caccini and his daughters Francesca and Settimia, see Warren Kirkendale, *The Court Musicians in Florence during the Principate of the Medici* (Florence, 1993), nos. 36, 82, 87.

EVERYTHING that I have said here about the music of the sixteenth and early seventeenth centuries has pointed toward connections in the minds of its creators, performers, critics, and amateurs with the musical culture of antiquity. Thus I have tried to depict the Renaissance in music in the way in which it has traditionally been approached in other fields. These pages represent far less than a sketch of the history of music in the period; they are meant instead to suggest aspects of musical culture that may be legitimately considered as partaking of Renaissance values. Many other forces were at work in shaping the efforts of musicians and the attitudes of performers and listeners, forces that would gain little in our understanding if the label "Renaissance" were to be stuck on them. Printing; the rise of broadly based musical literacy; the development of families of musical instruments; changes in ecclesiastic and secular patronage: these are a few of the features of the musical world from the death of Josquin to that of Monteverdi that are unconnected with the desire for a renewal of ancient culture. Above all the steady development of the musical language itself, the shaping of patterns of sound by composers emulating one another or grappling alone with the notes, this remains central to the art; shaped in part by exterior forces such as Renaissance strivings but possessing a life—what the Germans call *Eigendynamik*—of its own.

3

THE CONCEPT OF THE BAROQUE

Tim Carter

WHEN Jean-Jacques Rousseau claimed (in his *Dictionnaire de musique*, 1768) that "a baroque music is that in which the harmony is confused, charged with modulations and dissonances, the melody is harsh and little natural, the intonation difficult, and the movement constrained," he was writing from the rather smug viewpoint of the French Enlightenment. Here "baroque" is used in an early sense of extravagant, bizarre, even "gothic." The broader notion of the Baroque as a distinct style-period from the mid or late sixteenth century to the early or mid eighteenth century gained ground instead in the nineteenth century, particularly in art history by way of Jacob Burckhardt, Heinrich Wölfflin, and Willibald Gurlitt. Wölfflin later expanded his argument to embrace a range of stylistic alternatives distinguishing the Baroque from the Renaissance (painterly rather than linear styles, open rather than closed forms, etc.) and also reflecting broad pendular motions within the Western tradition. Various attempts to apply these categories to music have been brave but controversial—comparisons between music and painting always founder on the rock of metaphor—but the force of (and clearly visible evidence for) notions of the Baroque in art history established terms that (as Wölfflin himself suggested) literary and music historians could scarcely ignore, even if the detail might be different in their own fields.[1]

The search for common factors underpinning the arts of a given period tends to focus either on ill-defined but seductive notions of a "spirit of the times" or on a more precise articulation of contextual perspectives. Robert Haas's *Die Musik des Barocks* (1928), the relevant chapters of Paul Henry Lang's *Music in Western Civilization* (1941), and Friedrich Blume's entries on "Renaissance" and "Barock"

[1] This all-too-brief survey, and much of what follows, owes an obvious debt to Claude V. Palisca, "Baroque," in *The New Grove Dictionary of Music and Musicians*, 2d edn, ed. Stanley Sadie (London, 2001), II: 749–56. In general terms, I have also found both Arnold Hauser, *The Social History of Art*, II: *Renaissance, Mannerism, Baroque* (London, 1962), and Peter N. Skrine, *The Baroque: Literature and Culture in Seventeenth-Century Europe* (London, 1978), useful introductions to the period.

for *Die Musik in Geschichte und Gegenwart* variously followed the trend for music.[2] A more autonomous stance was adopted by Manfred Bukofzer in *Music in the Baroque Era: From Monteverdi to Bach* (1947)—focussing on the music's inner stylistic unity—Suzanne Clercx's *Le Baroque et la musique* (1948), and Claude Palisca's *Baroque Music* (1968): here "Baroque" runs the danger of being treated more as just a label of convenience. However, the past three decades have tended to favor the contextual approach, often influenced by "soft"-Marxist modes of historical enquiry, as in Lorenzo Bianconi's *Il Seicento* (1982).[3] It is significant, as a result, that Bianconi avoids the period-label. But such an approach is predicated upon the notion that music has always fulfilled, and not just reflected, specific cultural, social, and political—however broadly defined—requirements, which have influenced to a significant degree the styles, techniques, and genres available to the composer.

It is always difficult to locate precise dates for any period and its subdivisions. Such attempts depend on notions of congruence between and within the arts, on the features chosen to define a given style-period, and indeed on the social, political, and geographical terrain under discussion. Wölfflin's claims for early, high, and late phases in Baroque art (from around 1570, 1680, and 1700 respectively) may or may not square with Bukofzer's division of Baroque music into early, middle, and late periods (1580–1630, 1630–80, and 1680–1730). Similarly, any attempt to identify a starting date for the musical Baroque is hampered by a problem not yet fully acknowledged within music-historical enquiry: the Renaissance as a broad cultural phenomenon seems to some to have ended, in effect, by the 1530s, at least in Italy (convention extends the concept in England to the early seventeenth century, but the Elizabethan Renaissance is a very different case). For most art and literary historians, Italian culture of the mid-to-late sixteenth century breathes a different air, which some have identified with Mannerism—a preoccupation with form over content—and with self-conscious virtuosic display, often for none-too-expressive ends.[4] Mannerism has also become aligned, perhaps wrongly, with Marinism, an allegiance to the artful, conceit-ridden verse of the prominent early-seventeenth-century poet Giambattista Marino, whose *concettismo* and search for "meraviglia" was thought by some critics to have brought the entire literary century into disrepute.[5] Whether one views Mannerism as a *fin de siècle* tendency of the Renaissance or as a period in its own right, the term is slippery—like the art it seeks to categorize—because of both its limited location within the rarefied atmosphere

[2] Blume's entries are translated in his *Renaissance and Baroque Music* (London, 1968).

[3] *Music in the Seventeenth Century*, trans. David Bryant (Cambridge, 1987).

[4] The classic text is Craig Hugh Smyth, *Mannerism and "Maniera"* (Locust Valley, NY, 1963).

[5] James V. Mirollo, *The Poet of the Marvelous: Giambattista Marino* (New York, 1963); idem, *Mannerism and Renaissance Poetry: Concept, Mode, Inner Design* (New Haven and London, 1984). Vestiges of the pejorative view of Marino, which has precedents in the Arcadian movement towards the end of the seventeenth century and was also taken up with some passion by later critics such as Benedetto Croce and Francesco de Sanctis, remain in musical readings such as those presented in Gary Tomlinson, *Monteverdi and the End of the Renaissance* (Oxford, 1987).

of the north Italian courts (extending to Rome, but Venice, for example, is usually excluded) and its pejorative overtones. Indeed, some are happy to project such overtones onto the arts themselves, whether dismissing Mannerist art outright or interpreting it as a result of the various socio-economic crises perceived as affecting Europe in the sixteenth and early seventeenth centuries. But with only a few exceptions (for example, in the case of the madrigals of Gesualdo), the category of Mannerism has been slow to gain acceptance in musicological circles.[6] Here, instead, the Renaissance is often extended at least through to the death of Giovanni Pierluigi da Palestrina in 1594, if not beyond. This is, of course, a particular problem for contextualists—how can music be said to lag behind the other arts (a common enough idea) if all the arts exist in the same contexts?

Any historical survey crossing over conventional period boundaries, as does the present book, can often create enough continuities and coherences to warrant treating such boundaries with more than a grain of salt. Yet there is also enough contemporary comment to suggest that not a few musicians, particularly in Italy, did indeed perceive some kind of change in the air in the decades around 1600: witness the polemics surrounding early opera, or the Artusi–Monteverdi controversy and the consequent notion of a *prima* and a *seconda pratica.* Similarly, Giovan Battista Doni—a prominent theorist of the 1630s—called the Renaissance masters "an abomination from past time."[7] This suggests that as the musical Renaissance reached its end along with the sixteenth century, something different was emerging, with concepts previously viewed as embodying important truths now (dis)regarded as inadequate, irrelevant, or, at best, peripheral.

A Contextual Approach

The two poles defining the spheres of activity (and most often, the fields of employment) of the late-sixteenth- and early-seventeenth-century musician—as with his or her forebears—were the church and the court.[8] Churches needed choir-masters, organists, and singers in order to celebrate the liturgy; courts needed musicians for the necessary public pomp and circumstance and for private entertainment. The place of music in Renaissance sacred and ceremonial life—not to mention its value as a social pastime—had already guaranteed a new

[6] The most fervent advocate is Maria Rika Maniates, *Mannerism in Italian Music and Culture, 1530–1630* (Manchester, 1979). A more measured stance is adopted in James Haar, "Classicism and Mannerism in 16th-Century Music," *International Review of Music Aesthetics and Sociology*, 1 (1970), 55–67; see also idem, "Self-Consciousness about Style, Form and Genre in 16th-Century Music," *Studi musicali*, 3 (1974), 219–32, and the other articles in this issue of that journal.

[7] Blume, *Renaissance and Baroque Music*, 28.

[8] The following discussion is drastically condensed from material in my *Music in Late Renaissance and Early Baroque Italy* (London, 1992), where full footnotes and a bibliography can be found. *Man & Music*, III: *The Early Baroque Era: From the Late 16th Century to the 1660s*, ed. Curtis A. Price (London, 1993), also has much of relevance to the period under discussion here.

status for the composer and skilled performer (a situation that also finds parallels in the other arts). But this status was further enhanced as religious and political institutions went through various constitutional crises, using the arts to articulate a response to the problems that beset a difficult period in European history.

There was optimism in the air as the Catholic Church emerged from the rather gloomy self-reflection dominating the period of the Council of Trent (1545–63) and the overwhelming, and almost entirely unprecedented, challenge of the Protestant Reformation. In Counter-Reformation Rome, the Jesuit Church of the Gesù, begun in 1568, was finished in 1584, and the Chiesa Nuova (replacing Santa Maria in Vallicella) was built in 1575–7. Pope Sixtus v (reigned 1585–90) revitalized the city and its institutions, with a radical building program—including the completion of the dome of St Peter's—and bureaucratic reforms (which also involved reorganizing the papal choir). These initiatives continued during the reigns of Clement VIII (1592–1605) and Paul V (1605–21). The architectural projects emphasizing the glories of the Church Triumphant were matched by ambitious endeavours in the visual arts, and also in music. The large-scale polychoral works for various groupings of voices and instruments favoured in Rome (they were by no means a predominantly Venetian phenomenon) offered a powerful reflection of the so-called "colossal Baroque."[9] The Church was also quick to exploit the rhetorical and emotional powers of the "new music" for its own ends, whether in the motet or in the dramatic context of sacred dialogues, sacred operas, and oratorios.[10] And were an adherence to orthodoxy required, the Church could always take advantage of the music of Palestrina, whose classically balanced polyphony was soon canonized as the "official" style for church music, counteracting the centrifugal tendencies of the period and representing a golden mean as a powerful expression of the new-found permanence of the Church and the glory of God.

Church and state could be powerfully intertwined—as the civic liturgies of Venice revealed—and even within the north Italian courts, notions of grandeur, persuasion, and orthodoxy (in this case, the orthodoxy of absolutism) were no less useful as guiding forces for the arts. The Medici in Florence had long exploited the politics of spectacle in the context of courtly celebration: the comedies with flamboyant *intermedi* and related theatrical genres (including, if briefly, opera) regularly staged during Medici wedding festivities provide clear examples of the arts being used for political ends.[11] Court dances (whether or not exploiting some kind of dramatic framework) and tournaments also fostered the social cohesion and distinction of an élite class, not to mention the acquisition of princely skills useful

[9] See Graham Dixon, "The Origins of the Roman 'Colossal Baroque,'" *Proceedings of the Royal Musical Association*, 106 (1979–80), 115–28; Noel O'Regan, *Sacred Polychoral Music in Rome, 1575–1621* (DPhil diss., University of Oxford, 1988).

[10] Howard E. Smither, *A History of the Oratorio*, I: *The Oratorio in the Baroque Era: Italy, Vienna, Paris* (Chapel Hill, NC, 1977); John Walter Hill, "Oratory Music in Florence, I: *Recitar cantando*, 1583–1655," *Acta musicologica*, 51 (1979), 108–36.

[11] Aloys M. Nagler, *Theatre Festivals of the Medici, 1539–1637* (New Haven and London, 1964; repr. New York, 1976); Cesare Molinari, *Le nozze degli dèi: Un saggio sul grande spettacolo italiano nel Seicento* (Rome, 1968).

in other contexts (for example, on the battlefield). The power of the arts to impress both one's subjects and foreign visitors, not least with lavish displays of wealth signalling the political and economic health of the state, also found its counterpart on the more intimate scale of private performance. In the 1580s, the renowned *concerto di donne* of Ferrara supported by Duke Alfonso II d'Este—a virtuoso performing group focussing (but not exclusively) on female voices—was a subject of both admiration and emulation even as the duke attempted to keep its performances and repertory a private *musica segreta*.[12] Many north Italian princes—not least the Gonzaga at Mantua—similarly prided themselves on their virtuoso singers, instrumentalists, and composers.

But for all the importance of church and court for contemporary musicians, music-making could also take place in less formal environments. The mercantile proto-capitalist strategies of the great Renaissance states fostered an economic environment that granted the nobility and even the rising bourgeoisie relatively high levels of disposable income that could be devoted to conspicuous private consumption in the arts.[13] Similarly, developing urban environments created a need to project civic identity. Indeed, the market for which composers potentially catered broadened considerably in the sixteenth and early seventeenth centuries, a broadening that was encouraged, to say the least, by music printing. The need for music for domestic use (the cultured individual singing to the lute, the convivial gathering around the dinner table, moments of family celebration or commemoration), or for the meeting-places of various social groups such as confraternities and academies, remained strong, despite the acknowledged threat of excluding such groups from music-making posed by the increasing professionalization of modern musical endeavour. As in the Renaissance, the academy, whether as a formal institution or more loosely organized as a salon, played an important part in cultural life. For example, early opera in both Florence and Mantua had its roots in this environment, and the remarkable flowering of opera in Venice from the opening of the Teatro S. Cassiano as a "public" opera house in 1637 stems from much the same academic context.[14]

These apparent continuities reinforce one theme of this chapter—the difficulty of enforcing period boundaries—but they also counteract a prevalent trend in historical treatments of the period. The seventeenth century has often been labelled

[12] Anthony Newcomb, *The Madrigal at Ferrara, 1579–1597* (Princeton, 1980). Useful material can also be found in Iain Fenlon, *Music and Patronage in Sixteenth-Century Mantua*, I (Cambridge, 1980).

[13] Richard A. Goldthwaite, *Wealth and the Demand for Art in Italy, 1300–1600* (Baltimore and London, 1993).

[14] For early opera, see most recently Tim Carter, *Monteverdi's Musical Theatre* (New Haven and London, 2002), 17–46, 110–18. However, reference should still be made to Nino Pirrotta's seminal "Temperaments and Tendencies in the Florentine Camerata," *Musical Quarterly*, 40 (1954), 169–89, repr. in idem, *Music and Culture in Italy from the Middle Ages to the Baroque: A Collection of Essays* (Cambridge, MA, 1984), 217–34. The academic context of Venetian opera is clearly described in Ellen Rosand, *Opera in Seventeenth-Century Venice: The Creation of a Genre* (Berkeley and Los Angeles, 1991), 37–40.

one of "crisis,"[15] embracing political upheaval (the English Civil War), religious turmoil (the Thirty Years' War from 1618 to 1648, which cut swathes through much of northern and central Europe), fundamental shifts of scientific paradigms (Galileo, Descartes, Newton), plague (for example, in Italy from 1630 to 1632), economic disasters (beginning around 1620), and even drastic climate change. One can speculate on whether such natural and man-made disasters and their undoubtedly catastrophic consequences, or these scientific and philosophical paradigm shifts, had any greater effect in this period than those of previous centuries. But it is probably more useful to consider why viewing the seventeenth century in this particular light has proven so attractive in the literature. The century has tended to receive a bad press from historians and critics, and not always on reasonable grounds. The predominantly Protestant ethic of recent historical discourse (at least in Anglo-American circles)—with its aversion to Catholic triumphalism—finds its counterpart in a dialectic of Whig versus Tory readings of history (the labels emerge in the 1680s) that, from the Whig perspective, favour an anti-monarchic and anti-absolutist rhetoric. Both the church and the court, then, become symbolic of outmoded regimes to be crushed in the inexorable drive towards the political and intellectual liberties reaching fruition in the eighteenth-century Enlightenment and then the Age of Revolutions. The "crisis" of the seventeenth century therefore inserts itself within a teleology as old world-orders pass to new, and as "early modern" society relentlessly pursues its path towards modernity.

These issues probably have had even more impact on the historiography of Baroque music than they did on its history. For example, the tendency to locate the emergence of new "Baroque" styles chiefly in secular spheres (opera, solo song) ignores the fact that the bulk of musical activity in the early seventeenth century remained focussed on the sacred and the spiritual.[16] Still more pernicious is the notion that opera only found its "real" home in the ostensibly public opera houses of an ostensibly republican city (Venice), where it could develop untrammelled by the whims of princely patronage, and, instead, insert itself within a "free" market. To be sure, musicians could not always escape the professional and personal consequences of the various crises of the seventeenth century. Yet for many, business carried on as usual.

[15] Recent historical studies of the "crisis" of the seventeenth century rise from *Crisis in Europe, 1550–1650: Essays from "Past and Present,"* ed. Trevor Aston (London, 1965). The issues have been further explored, and in part reconsidered, in *The General Crisis of the Seventeenth Century*, ed. Geoffrey Parker and Lesley M. Smith (London, 1978), while revisions of the "crisis" scenario appear both in Theodore K. Rabb, *The Struggle for Stability in Early Modern Europe* (New York, 1975), where the emphasis is more on the reconfiguration of European institutions, and in the Marxist interpretations advanced in V. G. Kiernan, *State and Society in Europe, 1550–1650* (Oxford, 1980). Important for an economic historian's view of the seventeenth century is Jan de Vries, *The Economy of Europe in an Age of Crisis, 1600–1750* (Cambridge, 1976), but cf. the revisionist reading in Richard Tilden Rapp, *Industry and Economic Decline in Seventeenth-Century Venice* (Cambridge, MA, 1976).

[16] See the remarks in Tim Carter, "Music Publishing in Italy, c.1580–c.1625: Some Preliminary Observations," *Royal Musical Association Research Chronicle*, 20 (1986–7), 19–37.

Some Geographical Problems

The emphasis on Italy in the discussion thus far is one often encountered in the literature. It also raises a broader question: To what extent is the Baroque just an Italian phenomenon, rather than a pan-European one? To be sure, most of the above remarks on music in ecclesiastical, courtly, civic, and domestic contexts could be applied, *mutatis mutandis*, to France, Germany, Spain, the Low Countries, and England, and even to music in the far-flung reaches of Eastern Europe or the New World. The musical establishment of the dukes of Bavaria in Munich (particularly under Albrecht V, with his passionate if uneven support for Orlande de Lassus) rivalled and indeed surpassed many performing groups in Italy. The French, Spanish, Habsburg, and English courts exploited entertainments on a scale no less extravagant than their Italian counterparts. And the burghers of Antwerp, Paris, Leipzig, London, or even Mexico City were surely no less interested in civic and domestic music as a sign of urbane accomplishment.

Italian music permeated Europe and beyond, whether by way of music prints, of musicians themselves crossing national boundaries (in various directions), or of broader religious/cultural networks. Italian music prints reached northern Europe through the standard trade routes (not least by way of the Frankfurt Book Fair), and northern printers such as the Phalèse press in Antwerp, Adam Berg in Munich, and Paul Kauffmann in Nuremberg willingly reprinted popular Italian repertories. They made their selection with a keen eye on the local market—music of the *avant garde* clearly was not a commercially viable proposition—and thus appear fairly conservative: the lighter madrigals, canzonettas, and ballatas of composers such as Luca Marenzio, Orazio Vecchi, and Giovan Giacomo Gastoldi found striking favour. Italian music also found its way to the nascent music-printing trade in London, as in the anthologies of madrigals with translated texts such as Nicholas Yonge's *Musica transalpina* (1588; a second book appeared in 1597) or Thomas Watson's *The First Sett, of Italian Madrigalls Englished* (1590). Thomas Morley may have complained in his *A Plaine and Easie Introduction to Practicall Musicke* (1597) of "the new-fangled opinions of our countrymen who will highly esteem whatsoever cometh from beyond the seas (and specially from Italy) be it never so simple, condemning that which is done at home though it be never so excellent,"[17] but he himself did much to import Italian styles to England by way of his canzonets, balletts, and madrigals.

Morley never visited Italy, although his colleague, the lutenist and song-composer John Dowland did, journeying to Venice and Florence in the mid 1590s (he also hoped to meet Marenzio in Rome): the experience presumably made itself felt in Dowland's declamatory lute songs. The Dresden composer Heinrich Schütz paid two extended visits to Venice, the first in 1609–12—his studies with Giovanni Gabrieli had a profound effect on his own polychoral settings published in the *Psalmen Davids* (1619) and to the end of his life—and the second in 1628–9,

[17] Thomas Morley, *A Plain and Easy Introduction to Practical Music*, ed. R. Alec Harman (London, 1952; repr. 1966), 293.

when he met and worked with Claudio Monteverdi. The later English madrigalist Walter Porter also claimed to have studied in Italy with Monteverdi. There were close connections between Italy and the Danish court of King Christian IV in Copenhagen, where composers such as Mogens Pedersøn and Hans Nielsen produced Italianate madrigals (like Schütz, both studied in Venice with Giovanni Gabrieli). Spanish control of Naples and Milan made for easy commerce between Spain and Italy, and Tomás Luis de Victoria was neither the first nor the last Spanish composer to study and work in Rome before returning home, taking back Italian styles of sacred music to establish firm roots in Spain and also the New World. Musicians from Italy also headed northward: Giovanni Gabrieli to Munich in the mid 1570s, Luca Marenzio to Poland in 1596–8 (the Roman Giovan Francesco Anerio was also there in the late 1620s), Giulio Caccini and his family to France in 1604–5 (a visit to England was also planned), and Angelo Notari to London in 1610, where he entered court service until the establishment of the Commonwealth and published in 1613 an important collection of Italianate solo songs that clearly influenced other English composers attempting to emulate Italian styles (such as Henry and William Lawes).

Much of this movement of musicians across Europe traced routes established by commerce or by lines of political or religious affiliation. The foreigners who came to Italy for training often followed well-developed patterns for broader education, not least through the seminaries and colleges of Rome. And the Jesuits, with their emphasis on education, established elaborate institutional and individual networks stretching across Europe and into the New World:[18] wherever they extended their influence, they exploited the visual, musical, and dramatic arts in the ways they knew best, disseminating Roman confessional, ceremonial, and artistic orthodoxies throughout the Catholic communion with only minor concessions to local practice.

This suggests some limits that one might choose to place upon notions of a European Baroque, focussing less on its geographical origins than on its religious affiliations. Catholicism was spread widely through Europe, even into Protestant enclaves. In England, for example, an interest in things Italian was prominent in recusant circles—even if it was not quite the marker for recusancy that it has been assumed to be[19]—and although Dowland and other English Catholic musicians

[18] Thomas D. Culley, *Jesuits and Music*, I: *A Study of the Musicians Connected with the German College in Rome During the 17th Century and of Their Activities in Northern Europe* (Rome and St Louis, 1970); idem, "Musical Activity in Some Sixteenth-Century Jesuit Colleges, with Special Reference to the Venerable English College in Rome from 1579 to 1589," *Analecta musicologica*, 19 (1979), 1–29; T. Frank Kennedy, "Jesuits and Music: Reconsidering the Early Years," *Studi musicali*, 17 (1988), 71–100. For missions to the Americas and Asia, and the place of music therein, see *The Jesuits: Cultures, Sciences, and the Arts 1540–1773*, ed. John W. O'Malley *et alia* (Toronto, 1999).

[19] Compare the myth surrounding Francis Tregian the younger, traditionally associated with the Fitzwilliam Virginal Book (Cambridge, Fitzwilliam Museum, Music MS 168) and with various manuscript collections of Italian music, including London, British Library, Egerton 3665 and New York, Public Library for the Performing Arts at Lincoln Center, MS Drexel 4302, all reputedly copied while Tregian was imprisoned for recusancy in the Fleet from 1609

(John Bull, Peter Philips) found temporary or permanent employment in safer religious and political environments in northern Europe, Dowland returned to England, and other practicing Catholics stayed there (Byrd is the obvious example). Many Protestants, especially those of a more puritan bent, may have been deeply suspicious of Italian culture: the English pedagogue Roger Ascham (in his *The Scholemaster* of 1570) warned of "the inchantementes of Circes, brought out of Italie, to marre mens maners,"[20] and he was not alone in fearing corruption from an Italian lasciviousness and effeminacy (a common parlance of the time) too redolent of popery. But it would be a mistake to emphasize unduly the differences between Catholic and (at least some) Protestant environments: musicians of either faith could often—with discretion—live and work in either context. Similarly, Protestant and Catholic styles could interact (witness the music of Schütz), even if the mixture of ecstatic vision and a dogmatic adherence to authority typical of the Baroque in its deepest sense was alien to many Protestant world-views. It is true that although the Baroque may not have been an exclusively Italian phenomenon, in its early stages it was essentially a Catholic one, and when Protestant cultures latched on to the stylistic tropes, they sometimes went in different directions. Yet often all it took was to give a "popish" work a different text (i.e., to produce a contrafactum), or just to treat it as an abstract instrumental piece, to sanitize it for general consumption.

Style and Transmission

In many music histories, the rise of opera and solo song in Florence in the 1590s—and the emergence of new styles of music for virtuoso voice(s) and basso continuo—are deemed a watershed not just distinguishing the Baroque period from the Renaissance, but also marking the birth of what could be recognized, in however primitive a form, as "modern" music. Closely associated with these new styles, so the historiography would have it, are supposedly new modes of musical thinking, emphasizing vertical harmony (witness the basso continuo and its "figured bass") at the expense of linear counterpoint (which becomes an archaic, and archaizing, device), and a shift from so-called modality to so-called tonality. More recently, the trend has been to locate these "new" styles in a more traditional context, not least by way of improvisatory and other performing practices common in the Renaissance. Similarly, it is impossible to distinguish so clearly between vertical

to 1619. This has in effect been demolished in Ruby Reid Thompson, "Francis Tregian the Younger as Music Copyist: A Legend and an Alternative View," *Music & Letters*, 82 (2001), 1–31. For the broader phenomenon of English collectors of Italian music, see Lydia Rigmor Hamessley, *The Reception of the Italian Madrigal in England: A Repertorial Study of Manuscript Anthologies, ca.1580–1620* (PhD diss., University of Minnesota, 1989).

20 Tim Carter, "Secular Vocal Music," in *The Blackwell History of Music in Britain*, II: *The Sixteenth Century*, ed. Roger Bray (Oxford, 1995), 147–209, at 181–82. See also Steven J. Masello, "Thomas Hoby: A Protestant Traveler to Circe's Court," *Cahiers Élisabethains*, 27 (1985), 67–81.

and linear processes within a given compositional praxis: Renaissance polyphony pays clear attention to vertical sonorities, and the figures used to indicate the inner parts above the continuo bass are often strongly indicative of linear voice-leading. As for modality and tonality, they are difficult enough concepts in musical terms, quite apart from the problem of identifying any transition (smooth or otherwise) between the two.[21] Certainly matters of style and structure did change from the Renaissance to the Baroque periods, but not as dramatically as we may have led ourselves to believe.

What is perhaps most striking about music of the early Baroque period is its stylistic variety, ranging from *stile antico* polyphony for four or more voices to the most up-to-date recitative for solo voice and continuo: this variety can be found even in the work of single composers (for Italy, Claudio Monteverdi is the prime example). Such a range of styles doubtless reflects the various contexts in which music was produced, and also a heightened self-consciousness concerning the place of music in changing social and artistic worlds. However, one should be wary of imputing to the Renaissance a single musical style that somehow becomes fragmented towards the end of the sixteenth century, however convenient such a notion might be for ideas of change as Renaissance certainties were replaced by Baroque doubts. Renaissance music clearly had its own languages and dialects—from the studied polyphony of Franco-Flemish masses and motets to the homophonic simplicity of the Parisian chanson or the Italian *canzone villanesca alla napolitana* and its derivatives—and especially if one takes into account improvisatory vocal and instrumental practices (including a Humanist-inspired "recitative" style) for which scant evidence has survived.[22] Nor should the simple presentation of much Renaissance music—dictated largely by the commercial and technical requirements of the music-printing industry—mislead us into thinking that this is how the music was actually heard. Imagining a performance of, say, a Palestrina motet with vocal embellishments and instrumental participation—not a necessary scenario but certainly a plausible one in some contexts—may give a better sense of the sounds that perhaps most frequently struck late Renaissance ears.[23] Indeed, what changes

[21] Carl Dahlhaus, *Untersuchungen über die Entstehung der harmonischen Tonalität* (Kassel, 1968), trans. Robert O. Gjerdingen as *Studies on the Origin of Harmonic Tonality* (Princeton, 1990); Bernhard Meier, *Die Tonarten der klassischen Vokalpolyphonie* (Utrecht, 1974), trans. Ellen S. Beebe as *The Modes of Classical Vocal Polyphony* (New York, 1988); Harold S. Powers, "Tonal Types and Modal Categories in Renaissance Polyphony," *Journal of the American Musicological Society*, 34 (1981), 428–70; Eric T. Chafe, *Monteverdi's Tonal Language* (New York, 1992).

[22] These improvisatory styles and their ramifications for our understanding of a "Renaissance" music in Italy have been most extensively discussed by Nino Pirrotta in his "Music and Cultural Tendencies in Fifteenth-Century Italy" and "Novelty and Renewal in Italy, 1300–1600," repr. in Pirrotta, *Music and Culture in Italy from the Middle Ages to the Baroque*, 159–74, 175–97. Pirrotta's *Li due Orfei: Da Poliziano a Monteverdi* (2nd edn, Turin, 1975), trans. Karen Eales as *Music and Theatre from Poliziano to Monteverdi* (Cambridge, 1982) is also important.

[23] The techniques are covered in Howard Mayer Brown, *Sixteenth-Century Instrumentation: The Music for the Florentine Intermedii*, MSD 30 (American Institute of Musicology, 1973); idem, *Embellishing Sixteenth-Century Music* (London, 1976).

as we move from the Renaissance to the Baroque may be not so much musical or performing styles themselves as the fact that these styles are recorded through notation in different ways.

The effects of printing on music of this period (and the associated notion of a "print culture") are covered elsewhere in this volume (see especially Chapter 15). But some issues now seem particularly to have come to the fore. For example, although printing could establish a definitive text relatively immune from the corruption of manuscript transmission—Giulio Caccini said as much in the preface to his *Le nuove musiche* of 1602[24]—it created a distance between composer and performer that was only partly bridged by composers' attempts to offer more precise instructions for the performance of their music, whether verbally or through notation. As several composers had already realized, there were dangers in releasing to a broad public their prized musical possessions, which might thereby be plagiarized and/or otherwise devalued. And the increasing incorporation of virtuoso performing elements as essential, rather than incidental, to the compositional fabric posed technical problems that could not always be solved by the single-impression method of music printing: engraving was a better but more expensive solution.[25]

The new use of score formats for some repertories at the turn of the century—opera, solo song, instrumental music—reflects not just the emergence of new genres but also the changing technical demands of performance contingent upon changing musical styles (for example, the need for continuo players to have a clear view of the music they had to co-ordinate). It also affirmed the tendency noticeable in most of the arts through the sixteenth century to reify the art-work as a "text" to be valued and appreciated in abstract and not just functional terms. Regardless of the role of the score in the compositional process (a matter of some debate), music in score could be studied and imitated in ways not possible with partbooks, where some manner of performance is the only way of coming to know the piece;[26] it could also be admired by connoisseurs and collectors as a record of

[24] *Giulio Caccini: Le nuove musiche*, ed. H. Wiley Hitchcock, Recent Researches in the Music of the Baroque Era, 9 (Madison, 1970), 43: "It seemed to me that these pieces of mine had been honoured enough—indeed, much more than they merited—by being constantly performed by the most famous singers of Italy, male and female, and by other noble persons who are lovers of the profession. But now I see many of them circulating tattered and torn . . . . Thus I have been forced (and also urged by friends) to have these pieces of mine published." For the broader issues, see Tim Carter, "Printing the 'New Music,'" in *Music and the Cultures of Print*, ed. Kate van Orden (New York and London, 2000), 3–37.

[25] See the editions of Luzzasco Luzzaschi, *Madrigali a uno, doi e tre soprani* (Rome, 1601), and Girolamo Frescobaldi, *Toccate e partite d'intavolatura di cimbalo* (Rome, 1615). For the printing of the latter, see Arnaldo Morelli, "Nuovi documenti Frescobaldiani: I contratti per l'edizione del primo libro di *Toccate*," *Studi musicali*, 17 (1988), 255–65.

[26] Early examples of scores for study or commemorative purposes are *Tutti i madrigali di Cipriano de Rore a quattro voci* (Venice, 1577) and Carlo Gesualdo, *Partitura delli sei libri di madrigali a cinque voci* (Genoa, 1613). See also Edward E. Lowinsky, "On the Use of Scores by Sixteenth-Century Musicians," *Journal of the American Musicological Society*, 1 (1948), 17–23; Jessie Ann Owens, *Composers at Work: The Craft of Musical Composition, 1450–1600* (Oxford and New York, 1997).

a performance (the score of Monteverdi's *Orfeo* of 1607 published in 1609 seems to be a good example) even if they had no intention of performing it themselves. Indeed, the elaborate detail with which some composers loaded their scores sometimes seems to have been designed more to inhibit than to encourage future performance, thereby claiming the advantages of print (prestige, reward) while mitigating its perceived disadvantages (too ready accessibility to something that must, for the composer's sake, appear rare and unique). But whether in partbook or in score, the new complexities of much music of the early seventeenth century tended to exclude one mainstay of the market for printed music in the sixteenth century: the amateur musician of fairly limited abilities and resources. Just as the fixity of print threatened to divorce the art-work from the artist, so did it tend to alienate the artist from his or her public. After the first golden age of printing in the sixteenth century, there was a significant reversion to manuscript as the chief means of preserving and transmitting (or not, as the case may be) musical works of art.

Function and Content

Musical debate in the period focussed on the significant functions of music, and also on its non-functional significance. Gioseffo Zarlino's conservative definition of music as "sounding number" (1558) invoked an external world of order and proportion that was duly reflected in the sounds and silences of day-to-day musical life. The harmony of the spheres—the sounds of a cosmos regulated by the fixed and constant motions of the planets—was audible to God but not, since the Fall, to man. However, so the Boethian trope goes, this divine harmony (*musica mundana*) found its reflection in the harmony of the well-regulated soul (or the well-regulated state) as *musica humana* and was imitated by the balanced harmonies and proportions of *musica instrumentalis* (incorporating both vocal and instrumental music), which in turn became a potent metaphor for the harmony both of the soul and of heaven. The whole world was conceived as an interlocking chain of resemblances from the heavenly to the earthly spheres, with each element on one level finding its precise analogy on others, all a product of, and working for, the ineffable dominion of a Divine Creator lauded by choirs of angels and choirs of men. For all its status as a commonplace, this powerful vision of a world literally in harmony with itself is both mystical and magical, imposing a fervent wish for order to mitigate the fear of chaos.[27]

Chaos was an ever-present threat, as the political and social turmoil of the period constantly revealed. Not for nothing did invocations of harmony take on an incantatory tone, whether in political terms—court entertainments across Europe in the period make the point clear—or within contemporary theoretical speculation on music. Zarlino's emphasis on the perfect numbers and proportions

[27] For these invocations of harmony and their consequences, see Gary Tomlinson, *Music in Renaissance Magic: Toward a Historiography of Others* (Chicago and London, 1993).

expressed within musical harmony—not least through the *senario*, the number six construed to contain all the rational consonances (the octave, fifth, fourth, third, and sixth)—was more than just a theoretical conceit: it also invoked powerful ideological resonances. And any threat to so ordered a scheme had ramifications far beyond the mathematical note-crunching often typical of *musica speculativa*. When Vincenzo Galilei dismissed the relevance of the *senario* to any practical musical endeavour—given the impurity of the intervals used in contemporary systems of tuning and temperament—Zarlino and his supporters did have one defence: man is *de facto* imperfect and so cannot rise to so ideal a vision of divine perfection. But it was a rear-guard action.

The pages devoted to the matter in contemporary treatises make for dull reading, but there was a crucial issue at stake: the stability of the Renaissance worldview. Galilei, however, had different concerns. His debunking of the *senario* takes second place to the exploration of a new function for music drawing on his own experience (and those of his mentors, including the noted Florentine philologist Girolamo Mei) of sources on music from classical antiquity.[28] The renowned musicians of classical myth, and classical writers on music, offered an alternative message, namely that music exerted powerful ethical and emotional effects upon its listeners. The question now was whether such effects should be both censured and controlled (as Plato argued in his vision of the ideal Republic) or be put to good political and aesthetic use by the virtues of emotional catharsis (an Aristotelian view). As in the Hellenic and Hellenistic periods when these matters were first debated, the one stance encouraged a conservative retention of the old order, while the other offered a radical defence of the new. The debate between Artusi and Monteverdi over the novel dissonance treatment and text-expressive strategies of the so-called *seconda pratica* had been prepared some 2000 years before.[29]

For all the temporal distance between the early seventeenth century and the great thinkers of classical antiquity, the conceptual distance had been lessened by the Humanist endeavours of the Renaissance (a period that claimed a special relationship with classical Greece and Rome) and by the recovery of sources that retained an immediate and considerable presence. But although the Humanist impulse was intrinsic to the Renaissance, it was also separate from it, and thus it could continue as one driving force through the seventeenth century and indeed into the Enlightenment, anchoring contemporary endeavour in much the same ways as beliefs in a *musica mundana* had done for an earlier period. However, the new

[28] The important texts are all by Claude V. Palisca: "Vincenzo Galilei and Some Links between 'Pseudo-Monody' and Monody," *Musical Quarterly*, 46 (1960), 344–60, repr. in idem, *Studies in the History of Italian Music and Music Theory* (Oxford, 1994), 346–63; *Girolamo Mei (1519–1594): Letters on Ancient and Modern Music to Vincenzo Galilei and Giovanni Bardi; A Study with Annotated Texts*, MSD 3 (2nd edn, American Institute of Musicology, 1977); *Humanism in Italian Renaissance Musical Thought* (New Haven and London, 1985); *The Florentine Camerata: Documentary Studies and Translations* (New Haven and London, 1989).

[29] Martha Maas, "Timotheus at Sparta: The Nature of the Crime," in *Musical Humanism and its Legacy: Essays in Honor of Claude V. Palisca*, ed. Nancy Kovaleff Baker and Barbara Russano Hanning (Stuyvesant, NY, 1992), 37–52.

historicism of the sixteenth and early seventeenth centuries prompted a slightly different view of classical texts from the rather uncritical (some might say) admiration motivating early Renaissance thought. The notion of Plato and Aristotle conveying truths of universal import (at least, once mediated by Christian syncretism) was mitigated by the sense that they were, after all, men like any other men: the ground shifted from universal "truths" to "matters for debate," important but with outcomes predicated on their contemporary relevance. Monteverdi, for example, felt it necessary to invoke Plato in his discussion of the *seconda pratica* and the search for a "natural path to imitation," but Plato, he said, offered only a dim light that was more suggestive than instructive: the composer was left essentially on his own.[30]

A new sense of history also affected notions of an *ars perfecta*. Zarlino claimed that the greatness of music in classical antiquity had been lost in the corrupt Middle Ages (the "dark" ages) but recovered in the Renaissance, not least by his "new Pythagoras", Adriano Willaert. Monteverdi, on the other hand, was well aware that Willaert existed in a particular historical space, and that his achievement—for all its significance—was essentially transient. The processes of history, once discovered and articulated, could not be stopped by one great musician, whatever the attempts of theorists—and sometimes institutions (witness the Palestrina "myth")—to establish a paragon of unsurpassable perfection. For Monteverdi, Willaert certainly marked the peak of the *prima pratica*, but Cipriano de Rore, Willaert's pupil and successor at St Mark's, Venice, had initiated a new practice and new ways of conceiving the relationship between music and word that lay at the heart of a modern text-expressive style.[31]

Such lessons of history were rendered concrete by the powerful preserving force of print that expanded the chronological frame of musical knowledge to a significant degree: Monteverdi wrote a parody mass—the *Missa "In illo tempore"* (1610)—on a motet by Nicolas Gombert first published in 1538, and in 1627 he oversaw a new edition of Arcadelt's *Il primo libro de madrigali a quattro voci* written almost a century before. Composers could be classified as *antichi*, *vecchi*, and *moderni*—as became common in contemporary treatises[32]—and the *moderni*

[30] Monteverdi refers to Plato both in his controversy with Artusi (see the documents in Oliver Strunk, *Source Readings in Music History*, rev. edn, IV: *The Baroque Era*, ed. Margaret Murata [New York and London, 1998], 18–36) and in a letter to Giovan Battista Doni of 22 Oct. 1633, given in Denis Stevens (trans.), *The Letters of Claudio Monteverdi* (rev. edn, Oxford, 1995), 420–22. For the latter, see also the discussion in Gary Tomlinson, "Madrigal, Monody, and Monteverdi's 'Via naturale alla immitatione,'" *Journal of the American Musicological Society*, 34 (1981), 60–108.

[31] Claude V. Palisca, "The Artusi–Monteverdi Controversy," in *The New Monteverdi Companion*, ed. Denis Arnold and Nigel Fortune (London, 1985), 127–58, repr. in Palisca, *Studies in the History of Italian Music and Music Theory*, 54–84; Tim Carter, "Artusi, Monteverdi, and the Poetics of Modern Music," in *Musical Humanism and its Legacy*, ed. Baker and Hanning, 171–94.

[32] Jessie Ann Owens, "Music Historiography and the Definition of 'Renaissance,'" *MLA Notes*, 67 (1990), 305–30; eadem, "How Josquin Became Josquin: Reflections on Historiography and Reception," in *Music in Renaissance Cities and Courts: Studies in Honor of Lewis*

could see themselves within, and therefore potentially outside, the context of one or more musical traditions. Reifying the art-work on the printed page also prompted a shift on the part of contemporary theory away from arcane mathematics in favour of a more humane criticism, catering for the musically sophisticated audiences that printing itself had done so much to create.[33] A shift from the whats and hows of musical creation to the whys and wherefores of musical perception exposed the need for a poetics of music, of the art and craft of modern musical expression, and thus for a critical language to explore notions of value in contemporary musical art. Given the essential lack of such critical thought in previous music theory, it is not surprising that modes of argument, and even terms themselves, were taken over from the other arts, not least poetry: the Artusi–Monteverdi controversy owed much to contemporary debates over Battista Guarini's famously controversial pastoral play, *Il pastor fido*.[34] There was more at stake than just providing the critical tools for evaluating musical art-works: contemporaries sought a definition of music that hinged more on the interaction of content and function to an immediate end (moving the listener) than on some vague appeal to universals or to divine authority. And the search for an effective and affective musical presentation of the text naturally drew those who sought a poetics of modern music to the field wherein classical sources placed considerable emphasis on music's power, the art of rhetoric.

In his *Musica poetica* (1606)—even the title is significant—the German theorist Joachim Burmeister established a theory of music predicated directly upon rhetoric and its associated system of tropes and figures: the lesson is emphasized by a "rhetorical" analysis of a motet by Lassus, *In me transierunt*.[35] This seems to have been particularly a north-European concern, for reasons that merit exploration. But rhetoric had more influence than just by way of a series of figures matched to emotional states on principles that later (German) musicologists would identify as the *Affektenlehre* (the Doctrine of the Affections). Rhetoric categorized the processes involved in bringing an oration to fruition and defined the structures by which it might be organized (in one scheme: *exordium, narratio, propositio, confirmatio, confutatio, peroratio*): these structures would *de facto* appear in music set to texts constructed along appropriate rhetorical lines, and could even be transferred to wordless music, i.e., for instruments, which in turn began to gain a rhetorical power of its own. Rhetoric also defined the styles (plain, middle, grand) appropriate to specific types of oration, and thereby generated intersecting taxonomies that

Lockwood, ed. Jessie Ann Owens and Anthony M. Cummings, Detroit Studies in Musicology, 18 (Warren, MI, 1997), 271–80.

33 James Haar, "A Sixteenth-Century Attempt at Music Criticism," *Journal of the American Musicological Society*, 36 (1983), 191–209. I also discuss the issue in "Artusi, Monteverdi, and the Poetics of Modern Music."

34 Tomlinson, *Monteverdi and the End of the Renaissance*, 17–21.

35 Discussed in Claude V. Palisca, "*Ut oratoria musica*: The Rhetorical Basis of Musical Mannerism," in *The Meaning of Mannerism*, ed. Franklin W. Robinson and Stephen G. Nichols, Jr (Hanover, NH, 1972), 37–65, repr. in Palisca, *Studies in the History of Italian Music and Music Theory*, 282–311.

linked genre, style, and function. Finally, rhetoric also recognized the utility of its apparent rigidities: once rules were fixed, they could be broken for special effect. The lessons for music theory were obvious.

The Bolognese theorist Adriano Banchieri made an early attempt to establish new criteria for assessing musical achievement in his *Conclusioni nel suono dell'organo* (1609). Here he reconciles the extreme positions adopted by Artusi and Monteverdi in their controversy over the *prima* and *seconda pratica*. Banchieri distinguishes between the *osservanza* and *inosservanza* of the traditional rules of counterpoint, claiming that observance is appropriate in works without words (instrumental toccatas, ricercars) and in pieces where the text does not require "unobservance," whereas to "express" a madrigal, motet, sonnet, or other kind of poetry, the musician must be free to exploit unobservance so that he can "proceed imitating the affections with the harmony." These incipient notions of genre- and function-specific styles are taken further in the preface to Monteverdi's Eighth Book of madrigals, the *Madrigali guerrieri, et amorosi* (1638), which elaborates taxonomies defining two- and threefold categories based on genre and function (*musica da camera*, *da teatro*, and *da ballo*), genre and style (*canti senza gesto* and *opuscoli in genere rappresentativo*; *madrigali guerrieri* and *amorosi*) and style and expression (the three *generi*—*concitato*, *temperato*, and *molle*—which in turn match the ranges of the voice and the "passions or affections of the soul").[36] The overlapping and interaction of these categories map out (not entirely clearly) the domains of modern secular music. Such systems owed a clear debt to the urge for classification in the "new science" of the early seventeenth century. They also offered—by revealing gaps within the current state of knowledge—the potential for new invention: according to Monteverdi's preface, "In all the works of the former composers I have indeed found examples of the 'soft' [*molle*] and the 'moderate' [*temperato*], but never of the 'agitated' [*concitato*], a genus nevertheless described by Plato . . . ."[37] He then proceeds to describe his discovery of the *concitato genere* and its present popularity in music for church and chamber.

The most complete taxonomy of modern musical endeavour was offered by the Italian composer and theorist Marco Scacchi, *maestro di cappella* at the Polish court from 1628 to 1649.[38] Scacchi distinguishes between three classes of music: church (*ecclesiasticus*), chamber (*cubicularis*), and scenic or theatrical (*scenicus seu theatralis*). The church style further divides into masses, motets, etc. without organ for four to eight voices, motets with organ or for several choirs, and vocal music *in concerto* (with instruments and in the modern style). The chamber style is made up of (unaccompanied) madrigals sung round a table (*da tavolino*), vocal pieces with continuo, and vocal pieces with instruments. The theatrical style consists

[36] Barbara Russano Hanning, "Monteverdi's Three *Genera*: A Study in Terminology," in *Musical Humanism and its Legacy*, ed. Baker and Hanning, 145–70.

[37] Strunk, *Source Readings in Music History*, IV, ed. Murata, 157–9.

[38] Claude V. Palisca, "Marco Scacchi's Defense of Modern Music (1649)," in *Words and Music—the Scholar's View: A Medley of Problems and Solutions Compiled in Honor of A. Tillman Merritt by Sundry Hands*, ed. Laurence Berman (Cambridge, MA, 1972), 189–235, repr. in Palisca, *Studies in the History of Italian Music and Music Theory*, 88–145.

of "speech perfected by song, or song by speech." Scacchi's divisions established important precedents for later theorists such as Christoph Bernhard and Angelo Berardi. They also supported his powerful plea (in the *Breve discorso sopra la musica* of 1649) for tolerance in accepting the multiplicity of styles available to the modern composer. Like Monteverdi and Banchieri, Scacchi had learnt perhaps the most important lesson of the early seventeenth century: that different groups of composers, regardless of their orientation, could coexist in relative equanimity within a pluralist musical context.

Signifier and Signified

Another theorist taking a critical eye to contemporary genres and styles was the Florentine Giovan Battista Doni, resident in Rome and active within the artistic circles of the Barberini family. In his various treatises, the *Compendio del trattato de' generi e de' modi della musica* (1635), the *Annotazioni sopra il Compendio de' generi e de' modi della musica* (1640), and *De praestantia musicae veteris* (1647)—others were published much later in the collection *Lyra Barberina amphichordos: accedunt eiusdem opera* (1747)—Doni treads the well-worn Humanist path of comparing the music of classical antiquity with modern musical endeavour. But given the Barberini interest in opera—and doubtless Doni's pride in his native city—he devotes considerable attention to that Florentine invention, the *stile recitativo* (or *stile monodico*), and to its use in the theatre as the *stile rappresentativo* ("representative style"), which is classified in various ways.

According to the theorists of early opera and monody, music gained its power by being a heightened, yet still verisimilar, representation of oratorical delivery: early recitative was a form of musical speech (*recitar cantando*). This music did not simply tickle the ear's fancy, nor did it confuse the listener by its mixture of sounds high and low, or fast and slow, as Vincenzo Galilei claimed of contemporary polyphony. By virtue of its speech-like nature, it also aroused the emotions by way of reason rather than just through the senses, using the word (or in sacred music, the Word) rather than mere sounding number to make its effect. True, this was special pleading, reinforced by the subject-matter of the first operas—the great poet-musicians of classical myth (Apollo and Orpheus)—or, for that matter, by the most popular sources of texts for sacred music in the new style, the first-person "songs" of David (the Psalms) and of Solomon (the Song of Songs). But in contrast to polyphony, one voice could represent one speaker, using all musical/rhetorical means to teach, move, and delight the listener.

The term *stile rappresentativo* had a distinguished history in the early seventeenth century. According to Pietro de' Bardi (1634), "il canto in istile rappresentativo" was developed by Vincenzo Galilei in Giovanni de' Bardi's Camerata;[39] the

[39] Pietro de' Bardi's letter to Giovan Battista Doni detailing events in his father's Camerata and early opera in Florence is translated in Strunk, *Source Readings in Music History*, IV, ed. Murata, 15–17.

term also first appeared in print on the title-page of a work associated with the Camerata, Giulio Caccini's *Euridice* (1600: "composta in stile rappresentativo"). Other composers linking it with the theatre include Girolamo Giacobbi (his *Aurora ingannata* [1608] includes "canti rappresentativi") and Monteverdi in his *Madrigali guerrieri, et amorosi* (1638). But like the term *stile recitativo* it was not restricted to stage music. "Stile rappresentativo," "musica rappresentativa," "genere rappresentativo," etc. are used for solo songs or dialogues (in the preface to Caccini's *Le nuove musiche* [1602], the "lettera amorosa" and "partenza amorosa" in Monteverdi's Seventh Book of madrigals [1619], and Francesco Rasi's *Dialoghi rappresentativi* of 1620), for sacred *concerti* (Bernardino Borlasca in 1609), and even, somewhat paradoxically, for polyphonic *seconda pratica* madrigals (Aquilino Coppini describing Monteverdi's Fifth Book in 1608). Thus it denotes music for the theatre, music in a recitative style, or music that (re)presents a text in a particularly dramatic or emotional way.

It remains unclear exactly what is "represented" in the *stile rappresentativo*, whether a text, the emotions behind (or aroused by) that text, or something else (the act of representation itself?). But the notion of representation signals a significant epistemological shift not just in music but also in language and in the history of ideas as the Baroque broke away from Renaissance paradigms.[40] It also focuses critical attention (both contemporary and modern) on the relationship between signifier and signified, a relationship hitherto unquestioned due to the elaborate chains of resemblance dominating the Renaissance world-view but now placed in doubt by new modes of scientific endeavour and of philosophical thought. In a cosmos saturated by webs of analogy and metaphor, the place of any element was fixed within a hierarchy from macrocosm to microcosm by virtue of its resemblance to elements both higher and lower on the scale. Identities were thus forged by similarities (whether revealed or hidden) that allowed the Renaissance to make sense of its world. Music's relationship to the harmony of the spheres was one of resemblance articulated as metaphor; texts set to music were to be "imitated" by musical analogues through word-painting (whether aural or visual, as in *Augenmusik*). And although such word-painting was roundly condemned by the proponents of the Florentine "new music," this music, too, sought validation on the grounds of resemblance, in this case to oratorical speech.

Of course, the perceptual and conceptual identity of signifier and signified predicated upon resemblance—and the related emphasis on verisimilitude (the "imitation of nature") in art—remained a powerful force for notions of representation: Baroque music has its literal word- or mood-painting (Monteverdi's *concitato genere* is only an extreme example) in ways little different from Renaissance models.

[40] This discussion owes some debt to Michel Foucault, *Les Mots et les choses* (Paris, 1966), trans. as *The Order of Things: An Archeology of the Human Sciences* (London, 1991); see also Tomlinson, *Music in Renaissance Magic*, passim; Tim Carter, "Resemblance and Representation: Towards a New Aesthetic in the Music of Monteverdi," in *"Con che soavità": Essays in Italian Baroque Opera, Song and Dance, 1580–1740*, ed. Iain Fenlon and Tim Carter (Oxford, 1995), 118–34. No doubt, one should also heed the warnings presented by Karol Berger in his review-essay on Tomlinson's book in *Journal of Musicology*, 13 (1995), 404–23.

But the idea that the relationship of signifier to signified is instead one of difference, for all its possible grounding in similarity and identity, prompts a more analytical mode of critical enquiry (we have already seen some of the results), and also a restructuring of the links between a sign and its meaning. These links are now cemented less by resemblance—although that may still be an issue—than by representative conventions fostered by tradition or created by invention, establishing a code to be learned by and shared between producer and receiver. The sign also takes on a life of its own, permitting an exploration of its intrinsic nature and effects. For music, a comparison of two laments by Monteverdi makes the point clear. The recitative setting of the *Lamento d'Arianna* (the only surviving part of Monteverdi's opera *Arianna* of 1608, to a libretto by Ottavio Rinuccini) presents the impassioned speech of a woman (Ariadne) abandoned by her lover (Theseus): so powerful was its effect that it moved the audience to tears and spawned numerous imitations.[41] But the *Lamento della ninfa* "in stile rappresentativo" published in Monteverdi's *Madrigali guerrieri, et amorosi* (1638) is very different.[42] A nymph deplores her desertion by a lover, wandeing distractedly through the fields under the gaze of three shepherds. The text (again by Rinuccini) is a strophic canzonetta, and the central lament is in a suave triple time, with a sinuous melody projected over a descending tetrachord ground bass (an "emblem of lament")[43] repeating obsessively throughout the setting. This is, in effect, an aria not just in the technical (early-seventeenth-century) sense of a setting of strophic poetry but also in terms of nascent musical styles. In most real worlds, of course, lamenting lovers rarely sing triple-time arias—Monteverdi's signifier bears scant resemblance to its signified—but while this intense music may not be verisimilar, it is a powerful statement of impassioned despair. It also establishes crucial precedents for the later Baroque period, not just in vocal repertories but also in instrumental music, where the sign would be divorced from any textual content and yet could still convey its meaning, and thus grant affective power to seemingly "abstract" styles and genres.

Whatever the power of the naturalistic setting of the *Lamento d'Arianna*—so it has been lauded by modern scholarship—Monteverdi's first published version of the lament was an arrangement for five voices (in the Sixth Book of madrigals of 1614), pursuing an intensely musical expression even at the expense of realistic declamation. As with the *Lamento della ninfa*, Monteverdi seems to have realized above all that in setting a text, to quote Mozart, "music must always remain music." Recovering the ground for music as music rather than as some spurious form of

[41] William V. Porter, "*Lamenti recitativi da camera*," in *"Con che soavità,"* ed. Fenlon and Carter, 73–110.

[42] The *Lamento della ninfa* ("Non havea Febo ancora") has gained iconic status in recent scholarship; see the discussions in Tomlinson, *Monteverdi and the End of the Renaissance*, 213–14; Susan McClary, "Excess and Frame: The Musical Representation of Madwomen," in eadem, *Feminine Endings: Music, Gender, and Sexuality* (Minnesota and London, 1991), 80–111; Tim Carter, "*Possente spirto*: On Taming the Power of Music," *Early Music*, 21 (1993), 517–23; Tomlinson, *Music in Renaissance Magic*, 229–46.

[43] Ellen Rosand, "The Descending Tetrachord: An Emblem of Lament," *The Musical Quarterly*, 55 (1979), 346–59. But note the caveat in Carter, "Resemblance and Representation," 129.

speech was a significant endeavour for the early seventeenth century—for all the importance of the *stile recitativo* and the Florentine "new music"—and one reflecting the fullest realization of the representational powers of the *stile rappresentativo*. It also marked the arrival of a truly Baroque style in contemporary musical endeavour.

4

ITALY, *i*: 1520–1560

Giulio M. Ongaro

THE period from 1520 to 1560 was one of profound change in the Italian peninsula. An informed observer in the year 1520 could have hardly foreseen some of the political developments that were to take place by 1560. Certainly it would have been difficult to guess in 1520 that a bothersome, but somewhat limited, reform movement in Germany would lead by 1560 to a divided Europe and to one of the great internal efforts at reform by the Catholic Church, arguably the greatest to occur between the Renaissance and the twentieth century; or that Rome would sacked by the Imperial forces in such a savage manner that emotions were aroused almost everywhere in Europe—even the Emperor Charles v had to distance himself from the behavior of his troops. Perhaps our observer, living in war-torn Italy, would have thought it even less likely that a lasting peace—sanctioned by the 1559 treaty of Câteau-Cambrésis—could put an end to several decades of fighting between the Emperor and the king of France and therefore to the almost constant clash of foreign armies on Italian soil. In 1520, when the French controlled the duchy of Milan, it might have also been difficult to foresee that the peace of 1559 would sanction an almost total Imperial and Spanish dominance in Italian affairs for some time to come, a turn of events that has culturally influenced Italy (especially its Southern regions) up to the present day.

The political events of these four decades had profound repercussions on the arts in general, and on music in particular. As the balance of power shifted, courts were created and destroyed, political influence and wealth were absorbed by the struggle for survival (or for expansion), and the cultivated and tolerant ideals of Castiglione's *Cortegiano* were sacrificed to the harsh realities of political and religious strife, becoming increasingly detached from reality. The later boundaries of our period also mark the true beginning of the Catholic Reformation, a time when the edicts of the Council of Trent had to be put into practice, and the role of polyphonic music within the Catholic liturgy was debated and clarified.

In short, the middle of the century represents in many ways the end of the true Renaissance, artistically as well as politically, hastened perhaps by the sack of Rome and by the less destructive but still traumatic siege of Florence. In the visual arts, the break was recognized by contemporaries: already in 1557 Lodovico Dolce defined and defended *manierismo*, the artistic trend that was fast becoming dominant in Italy. Only in Venice did the influence of Titian keep *manierismo* at bay a little longer. In music, a sophisticated commentator of the early seventeenth century, Claudio Monteverdi, could look back at the madrigals of the Flemish composer Cipriano de Rore (d. 1565) as the beginning of a new manner of composition, a *seconda pratica* ("second practice"), thus recognizing a break with past attitudes.[1]

The balance of power of musical patronage was greatly affected by political events. Two of the major musical centers of the fifteenth century, Milan and Naples, played a reduced role in the central years of the sixteenth century, partly because of changed political conditions. The end of the Sforza dynasty in Milan occurred when Francesco II died without heirs in 1535, thus returning the duchy to the Imperial fold. Although not entirely devoid of musical activity—particularly in the case of lute music, where Milanese performers and composers set a standard—Milan never returned to her glory days of the fifteenth century, when famous composers and theorists such as Gaspar van Weerbeke, Johannes Martini, Loyset Compère, and Franchino Gaffurio populated her musical life.[2] In Naples, which lost its independence to the Spanish crown in 1504, music did not regain the position it held during the Aragonese years; nevertheless Naples gave to the rest of Italy one of the most popular (and popularesque) genres of the sixteenth century, the *canzone villanesca alla napolitana* (also known as *villanella*, *villanesca*, and *napolitana*), whose first appearance in print occurs in 1537. The works of Neapolitan composers such as Giovanni Domenico del Giovane da Nola and Tommaso Cimello, who published collections of *napolitane* in the 1540s, were instrumental in the diffusion of the genre outside Naples.[3] A typical example of this repertory is Giovanni Domenico da Nola's "O dolce vita mia" (Example 4.1). The voices move mostly together, setting the text in a rather syllabic manner with much repetition of pitches, in a declamatory style. The choice of words in the text shows an intent to imitate popular expression, particularly that of the Neapolitan area ("haggio" for "ho," "toi" for "tue," etc.). The three parts often outline simple triads in root position, with a tendency to thin the texture by having a pitch doubled at the octave. The musical phrases are short and regular, and the bass provides an unambiguous harmonic foundation, by leaping to the roots of the chords. The sense of regularity is enhanced by having two out of three subdivisions of the piece repeat without any

[1] A translation of the manifesto of the *seconda pratica,* officially written by Giulio Cesare Monteverdi as a "Dichiaratione" appended to Claudio's *Scherzi musicali* of 1607 (though surely representing the latter's thought), can be found in Piero Weiss and Richard Taruskin, *Music in the Western World* (New York, 1984), 172–73.

[2] For the Sforza period, see Paul A. Merkley and Lora L. M. Merkley, *Music and Patronage in the Sforza Court* (Turnhout, 1999); Robert Kendrick's interesting *The Sounds of Milan, 1585–1650* (Oxford and New York, 2002) covers a slightly later period.

[3] The standard work on *napolitane* is Donna G. Cardamone, *The Canzone Villanesca alla Napolitana and Related Forms, 1537–1570* (Ann Arbor, MI, 1981).

Ex. 4.1 Giovanni Domenico da Nola, "O dolce vita mia" (*Villanelle, libro 2*, 1545). Adapted from *Nine villanelle*, ed. B. Thomas (London, 1984).

modifications. The simplicity of these pieces, far from being a hindrance, is in fact the basis of their appeal to musical amateurs, similar to that of the frottola.

Private patronage of music by the nobility in Naples did continue in the sixteenth century, subject however to the vagaries of the rule of the Spanish viceroy, and famous musicians were still active in the city. One of the most prestigious was the theorist and composer Diego Ortiz—the author of one the first manuals for

O dolce vita mia, che t'haggio fatto
Che me menaz'ogn'hor con toi parole
Et io mi struggio come nev'al sole.

bowed string instruments, the *Tratado de glosas* (1553)—who was maestro at the royal chapel in Naples from 1555 to 1570. More interesting is the phenomenon of serious involvement of members of the Neapolitan aristocracy in music making. Noblemen like Luigi Dentice—who published his *Due dialoghi della musica* in 1552—Giulio Cesare Brancaccio, and later Carlo Gesualdo, Prince of Venosa, are examples of this trend, which is, at least in part, due to the near total loss of power by the Neapolitan nobility in the political affairs of the province. Music and, until their ban in 1547, the *accademie* and their theatrical productions—where noblemen acted, sang, and played—were surely considered safer outlets for the energies of the aristocracy than political activity.

Two other major centers suffered greatly because of political events, but managed to retain their varied musical life. In 1520, at the beginning of our period, Rome was under the influence of Pope Leo X (Giovanni de' Medici), perhaps the most musical pope of the Renaissance, and a true heir to the Medici tradition in his patronage of the arts. Protector of artists and intellectuals such as Raphael, Pietro Bembo, Erasmus, and Aldo Manuzio, Leo did not refrain from interceding personally in order to secure the services of a favorite artist or musician, as he did in 1520, when he wrote to the doge of Venice asking for the temporary loan of the cornettist Zuan Maria dal Cornetto, one of the great virtuosos of the early sixteenth century.[4] Leo was succeeded (after the brief interlude of Adrian VI) by another Medici, Giulio, whose policies as Clement VII were in part responsible for the disastrous Sack of 1527. Rome was financially and artistically affected by the Sack, but the decline was only temporary, and soon the Eternal City was once again attracting fine musicians from all over Europe, although the geographical expansion of Protestantism limited somewhat the area from which they were recruited.[5]

Florence made a brief and unsuccessful attempt at re-establishing a republican government, but she could not withstand a siege by the Imperial army, in spite of the presence of Michelangelo as military engineer on her side. The capitulation of the city following the defeat of her army at Gavinana (3 August 1530) spared Florence the horrors of a sack similar to that of Rome, and resulted in the return of the Medici, who were installed by the Emperor as *de jure* as well as *de facto* rulers. With typical Medici flair, after succeeding the murdered Duke Alessandro, Duke Cosimo I, the patron of Giorgio Vasari, soon found ways to celebrate dynastic events with elaborate pageantry involving a great deal of music. At his 1539 wedding to Eleanora of Toledo, the festivities included *intermedi* set to music by Francesco Corteccia.[6] These types of courtly entertainments punctuate the whole century in Florence, and the musically rich *intermedi* formed one of the bases for the development of opera in the waning years of the century.

At Ferrara and Mantua, in the meantime, the strong musical traditions developed in the fifteenth century by the Este and Gonzaga families were continued by their sixteenth-century descendants. Ercole II d'Este (ruled 1534–59) attracted to his Ferrarese court the likes of Maistre Jhan, Alfonso dalla Viola, and most importantly Cipriano de Rore. Ercole's 1528 wedding to Renée of France, who often

[4] The response of the Venetian government, which mentions a letter coming directly from the Pope, is in Archivio di Stato di Venezia, Collegio, Notatorio 18, fol. 149^r.

[5] A good introduction to musical life in Rome in this period is Christopher Reynolds, "Rome: A City of Rich Contrast," in *Man & Music*, II: *The Renaissance: From the 1470s to the End of the 16th Century*, ed. Iain Fenlon (Basingstoke and Englewood Cliffs, NJ, 1989), 63–101.

[6] The music of these entertainments can be found in *A Renaissance Entertainment: Festivities for the Marriage of Cosimo I, Duke of Florence, in 1539*, ed. with comm. by Andrew C. Minor and Bonner Mitchell (Columbia, MO, 1968).

embarrassed the Este family with her Protestant leanings, established a strong link to France, and Ferrara remained for a while one of the most important channels of diffusion of French music into Italy. In addition, under the patronage of Ercole Ferrara established a musical press that, while not comparable to that of Venice, nevertheless made important contributions to the printed repertoire. It is fitting that towards the end of the period under examination, the successor to Ercole II and the patron of the last great flowering of music in Ferrara, Alfonso II, would be the dedicatee of one of the most celebrated music prints of the sixteenth century, Adriano Willaert's *Musica nova*. The brother of Ercole, Cardinal Ippolito II, was also an enthusiastic patron of music: the theorist Nicola Vicentino completed his influential treatise *L'antica musica ridotta alla moderna pratica* (1555) when under his patronage.

In Mantua, where the first permanent *cappella* was of recent coinage, having been established by Francesco II Gonzaga in 1510, the situation was, if less splendid, somewhat similar. The musical life of the city was dominated by the French composer Jacquet of Mantua, who served from 1526 until his death in 1559, rising to the post of *maestro di cappella* of the Mantuan cathedral. The real change on the Mantuan musical scene occurs with the accession to the dukedom of Guglielmo Gonzaga (ruled 1550–87), a fervent music lover and amateur composer—a letter by Palestrina to the Duke criticizes in very diplomatic terms a ducal composition that had been sent to the composer for evaluation. Guglielmo supervised the construction of the ducal church of Santa Barbara in 1562–65, hiring as *maestro di cappella* one of the last famous Flemish composers to serve in Italy in the sixteenth century, Giaches de Wert.[7]

Other musical centers, although definitely of secondary importance, made noteworthy contributions to sixteenth-century music. For example, Bologna, though hampered by the lack of an independent court, was an important center for instrumental music, and at least two first-rate groups of instrumentalists—the Concerto Palatino and the instrumentalists of the church of San Petronio—were active there. Similarly, Bergamo was the home of the Italian composer Gasparo de Albertis (d. 1560), one of the first Italians to break the monopoly of the *oltremontani* on sacred music. The music of De Albertis, influenced by humanistic and Italian taste in its clear texture and attention to text declamation, includes also *cori spezzati* pieces that are contemporary—and can be compared—with those of Willaert.[8]

It is, however, in the city of Venice, the *Serenissima*, that the most dramatic changes occur between 1520 and 1560.[9] Although deeply affected by the early

[7] See Iain Fenlon, *Music and Patronage in Sixteenth-Century Mantua*, 2 vols. (Cambridge, 1980–82); an archival study of sacred music in Mantua can be found in Pierre Tagmann, *Archivalische Studien zur Musikpflege am Dom von Mantua, 1500–1627* (Bern, 1967).

[8] See Gary Towne, "Gaspar de Albertis and Music at Santa Maria Maggiore in Bergamo in the Sixteenth Century," (PhD diss., University of California, Santa Barbara, 1985).

[9] There is a growing literature on music in Venice in this period. For the social milieu that fostered secular music, see Martha Feldman, *City Culture and the Madrigal at Venice* (Berkeley, 1995); the rich pageantry of the confraternities is illustrated in Jonathan Glixon, *Honoring God*

stages of the War of the League of Cambrai, and particularly by the disastrous defeat suffered at Agnadello (Ghiara d'Adda) in 1509, by 1520 Venice had somewhat recovered and could take pride in its stability in an unstable Italy, and in the fact that the city had not been violated by foreign armies. Musically Venice had been the site of the first music printing press, that of Ottaviano Petrucci, and there is evidence that she had a varied and flourishing musical life in her churches, confraternities, and private homes well before 1520. On the other hand the Venetian Republic failed to attract a composer of the first rank until Adrian Willaert accepted the post of *maestro di cappella* at the ducal church of St Mark's in 1527. By the time of his death in 1562, Venice had become a musical capital, where musicians came to study with "il divino Adriano," whose music-publishing firms—most notably those of Gardano and Scotto—produced an enormous quantity of volumes, and where a characteristic Venetian sacred style, which found its most distinctive expression in the works of the Gabrielis, was being shaped. These changes were not solely due to Willaert's arrival: in fact they were also the result of an astute cultural policy pursued by the Venetian government, particularly by the Doge Andrea Gritti, who was bent on exploiting the political misfortunes of other Italian cities to create a "second Rome" in Venice. Another feature of Venetian musical life also makes Venice unique among the major Italian musical centers of the sixteenth century. It can be said that living in Venice enabled Titian to establish a new working relationship between patron and artist in which the artist attained a new dignity and status *vis-à-vis* the patron, or that the relative freedom of the Serenissima allowed Pietro Aretino to invent a practically new literary role for himself. Similarly we can perceive that, owing to the particular circumstances surrounding the church of St Mark's, and the government of the Republic, the status of Willaert and of the other musicians of the basilica and their relationship to those in power was different from that of almost any other court musician elsewhere in Italy. The Venetian penchant for a legalistic approach to labor relations, the absence of a ruler with absolute power, together with the collegial elements of the Venetian governmental system and with the mercantile roots of her ruling class, the stress on continuity, all contributed to create a situation where duties and rights of musicians were clearly defined, where musicians (particularly the most successful) seem to have been treated with a new degree of respect, where something of a personality cult was established for the *maestri di cappella* of St Mark's. Venetian documents are full of signs of this new condition, which becomes evident around the time of Willaert's hiring in 1527. As late as the seventeenth century, in a famous letter to his unreliable former patron in Mantua, Monteverdi outlined the condition of the maestro at St Mark's and the many advantages, both social and financial, of his position there.[10]

In general, the decades between 1520 and 1560 represent a further step towards the establishment of an Italian musical language, shaped by Italian composers.

and the City: Music at the Venetian Confraternities, 1260–1807 (Oxford, 2003), which devotes large sections to the 16th century.

[10] See *The Letters of Claudio Monteverdi*, trans. and introd. by Denis Stevens (London, 1980), 187–93.

There is definitely in this period an important and noticeable dichotomy between secular and sacred music in Italy that is perhaps the sign of a transitory phase. The fifteenth and early sixteenth centuries encompass the period when French-speaking or Flemish composers came to Italy and composed almost exclusively music in the Northern tradition—although sometimes influenced by Italian traits—for their Italian employers, who accepted gladly this cultural hegemony from beyond the Alps. Even the appearance of the frottola in the later part of the fifteenth century, though undeniably important, did not threaten the status of French secular music as the most sophisticated and desirable genre of the period. The French hold on the musical life of the peninsula begins to loosen in the late 1520s, with the arrival of the madrigal on the musical scene. As a cultural and musical phenomenon, the rapid rise in popularity and longevity of the madrigal and its sub-genres, its diffusion and influence abroad—most notably in late sixteenth-century England—and its cultivation by masters and amateurs alike, is one of the most intriguing and fascinating musical events of the sixteenth century. The birth of this genre in the cultural circles of Rome and Florence owes much to the musical contributions of two foreign composers, the northerners Philippe Verdelot (d. *c.*1530(?); before 1552) and Jacques Arcadelt (d. 1568), whose madrigals were so popular that they were still being reprinted a century after their composition. Franco-Flemish composers, faced with the task of setting to music a through-composed text in a way that would reflect the sophistication of humanistic courts, probably relied on their experience setting French chansons and Latin motets and employed a texture made up of four or five independent vocal lines. In terms of texts, poetic forms, and musical settings, the madrigal constituted a break from most of the frottola repertory and opened up expressive possibilities that composers continued to explore throughout the century.[11] Foreign composers were not alone in creating the madrigal, however: as we might expect, native composers also made a vigorous contribution to the budding genre. The compositions of Costanzo Festa (d. 1545) in Rome and the madrigals composed by the Florentine Francesco Corteccia (d. 1571), *maestro di cappella* for the Medici dukes, more than hold their own against those of the *oltremontani*. It is true also that the foreign musicians active as madrigalists, most notably Willaert and Rore, became often so culturally assimilated that the sensitivity shown in their musical response to Petrarchan (and Petrarchist) texts suggests that they possessed an understanding of the text and of literary aesthetics that went well below the surface. Example 4.2 shows a passage from the madrigal "Giunto m'ha Amor," written by Adrian Willaert and published in his *Musica nova* in 1559. Compared to earlier madrigals, this presents a more sophisticated setting of the text. Willaert takes advantage of the five-voice medium by writing in a flexible texture, where voices are sometimes paired in varying combinations, and where the text appears in an overlapping fashion among voices, with a fair amount of repetition (leading to an emphasis on selected ideas of the text). Although the

[11] An old but still valuable survey of the genre is Alfred Einstein, *The Italian Madrigal*, 3 vols., trans. Alexander H. Krappe, Roger H. Sessions, and Oliver Strunk (Princeton, 1949); see also the shorter volume by Jerome Roche, *The Madrigal* (2nd edn, Oxford, 1990).

Ex. 4.2 Adrian Willaert, "Giunto m'ha Amor" (*Musica nova*, 1559), mm. 9–24. *Adriani Willaert Opera omnia*, ed. H. Zenck et al. (American Institute of Musicology, 1950–), XIII.

entrances of the voices can be staggered, this does not imply imitation, as each part tends to have a distinctive line. See, for example, the way in which the first cited phrase is presented by each voice in turn: there are similarities among the voices,

but also a clear effort to avoid literal repetition. The first phrase of the text ("Che m'ancidono a torto," "which kill me wrongly") overlaps with the second ("e s'io mi doglio," "and if I complain") in measures 15–16, and the two textual ideas ("e s'io mi doglio" and "doppia il martir," "my suffering redoubles") also overlap at first, although by measure 20 the voices join in near homophony. Willaert further emphasizes the text by introducing an E-flat in measure 19 and turning towards a C-minor chord. This works both on the harmonic level and on the melodic level, by outlining the movement from D to E-flat and back to D, a type of melodic motion often employed in the sixteenth century at particularly poignant moments.

One important landmark was achieved in the mid sixteenth century: the first collection of music composed by a woman to appear in print, a book of madrigals by Maddalena Casulana, was published in Venice in 1566. The names of women performers do appear with increasing frequency in musical accounts of this period, and music at convents in several cities also begins to be better documented.[12] It is fair to say that the period from 1520 to 1560 prepares the way for the professionalization of women musicians and the expansion of their role in music that we notice towards the end of the Renaissance.

12 See, among recent studies, Craig Monson, *Disembodied Voices: Music and Culture in an Early Modern Italian Convent* (Berkeley, 1995); Robert Kendrick, *Celestial Sirens: Nuns and Their Music in Early Modern Milan* (Oxford, 1996); and, for a slightly later period, Colleen Reardon, *Holy Concord Within Sacred Walls: Nuns and Music in Siena, 1575–1700* (Oxford, 2002).

The careers of Festa and Corteccia, both of whom held important appointments in church chapels, illustrate also the gradual shift away from the hegemony of foreign composers in the field of sacred music. If from 1520 to 1560 the composition of sacred music in Italy remained largely dominated by the *oltremontani*, we can also see that a generation of native composers begins to assert itself, and glimpses of Italian practices can be caught at times in the music of the foreign composers. While the prevalent style of motets is still that introduced and perfected by Franco-Flemish composers of the period, other styles also begin to appear in printed collections. For instance, Willaert and Jachet demonstrate in their *cori spezzati* psalm settings the willingness to adapt their music to an Italian style, more declamatory and chordal, already explored by native composers such as the Paduan Francesco Santa Croce—one of the earliest composers in this style—and, as we have seen earlier, Gasparo de Albertis. An example of a sacred piece in simple chordal style is a setting by Alberti of selected passages from the Passion narrative, an excerpt of which is presented in Example 4.3. This short passage, taken from Matthew 26: 1 and 26: 5, presents the words of Christ, sung by a four-part choir, and a short answer by the *turba* ("crowd"), setting words spoken in the Gospel by the priests. In some churches, when a polyphonic Passion was sung the choir was divided so that the words of Christ were sung with one singer to a part, while the "turba" text was sung by all the remaining singers, thus placing the words in Christ in dramatic relief. The four voices proceed mostly in note-against-note style throughout the entire piece, as they do in this excerpt. Settings like this were sung during Holy Week, often as part of a procession touching the Stations of the Cross within a church: the simple musical setting not only made the text clearly audible by the congregation but might also have been easier to sing while the singers took part in the procession (this is one of the few occasions when we know the music was sung from memory in some places).

De Albertis is also important in the development of the polyphonic mass among native composers. His book of masses of 1548 is the first such printed collection dedicated solely to the works of an Italian composer, paving the way for Palestrina's first book of masses of 1554. Works by Italian composers appear only very rarely in anthologies of masses in this period: even accounting for the fact that such anthologies were published much less frequently than motet collections, it is striking that the only names to appear between 1520 and 1560 are those of Vincenzo Ruffo, who published his *Missa "Alma redemptoris mater"* in a 1542 collection printed by Scotto in Venice (sufficiently popular to be reprinted two years later by Gardano); and of Ippolito Ciera, active in the Veneto region, whose appearance in a 1555 Scotto print may be due at least in part to his ties to Venice. The relative absence of Italians from the printed collections does not reflect their total output in this genre, as many Masses by Italians are preserved only in manuscripts, but it does reflect the taste of the public (and also perhaps a certain degree of snobbery) in their preference for foreign composers. It is noteworthy that this taste extended also to the field of secular music, where, for example, the French chansons of Janequin seem to have been much in demand by the Italian public. At any rate, sacred compositions by Italian composers significantly increase in number after 1560, and

Ex. 4.3 Gasparo Alberti, *Passio D. N. Jesu Christi secundum Mattheum*, mm. 1–23. Adapted from *Italia sacra musica*, ed. K. Jeppesen (Copenhagen, 1962), III: 75–76.

(*cont.*)

this is an indication of the changed conditions in the peninsula: where before 1560 a majority of *maestri di cappella* at important churches had been foreigners, after that date Italians, trained in many cases by those foreigners, took over the most prestigious posts at Italian churches.

It is also in this period that polyphonic masses turned increasingly to newer compositional techniques meant to unify the various movements of a mass while displaying the inventiveness and resourcefulness of their composer. The fifteenth-century mass had been unified primarily by the use of the cantus-firmus technique, in which a pre-existing melody was used as a foundation for the polyphony, or by

Ex. 4.3 (*cont.*)

[Christus:] Scitis quia post biduum pascha fiet, et Filius hominis tradetur et crucifigatur. [Turba:] Non in die festo, ne forte tumultus fieret in populo.

the paraphrase of chant models. The mass in the sixteenth century was often based on a pre-existing polyphonic model, utilizing all voices of that model in an organic manner. Thus, a composer would first select a motet, a madrigal, or a chanson, then rework the existing material, sometimes adding voices, rewriting the imitative entrances, adapting the model to the needs of the text of the mass. By 1588 the theorist Pietro Pontio in his *Ragionamento di musica* discusses the composition of the mass in terms that clearly show that this procedure was the one to be usually followed. In the twentieth century these masses have been often called "parody masses," although it might be better to label them with the contemporary label of "imitation masses," that is masses that imitate a pre-existing model. One measure of the popularity of this technique is that about half of the surviving masses by Palestrina employ it.[13]

The decades between 1520 and 1560 mark also the beginning of a momentous change in music printing. The beautifully crafted pioneering volumes of Ottaviano Petrucci, which were expensive and technically difficult to produce, gave way to the cheaper and easier (though less elegant) system developed by Attaingnant in Paris in the late 1520s and soon afterwards introduced to Italy. The number of editions published with the new system increased dramatically, led by the output of the two giants of sixteenth-century Italian music printing, Girolamo Scotto and Antonio Gardano in Venice.[14] Their output included, together with the works of the acknowledged masters, also the compositions of lesser musicians, and a fair number of volumes that can only be described as "vanity" prints, whose appeal to the general buying public must have been minimal. It is impossible to overestimate the impact of this new method of diffusion compared with the old, slow manuscript copying. Printed music books circulated widely in Europe, and the democratization of taste generated by this new medium influenced in turn composers and publishers. For the first time it is possible to gauge the popularity of a composer not just by the praises written by a few aristocrats and theorists, or by the inclusion of his works in a manuscript that often reflects primarily the idiosyncratic taste of a court or of a ruler, but simply by the frequency with which his compositions were reprinted throughout Europe—in short, by his commercial success.

Instrumental music benefited from this new medium, and as a result this is the first period from which a large amount of instrumental music survives, together with much information on instrumental practices and techniques. The manuals of Silvestro Ganassi, musician of the Venetian Republic, are examples of the type of information on fingering, tuning, articulation, and ornamentation that were made available for the first time to a much broader section of the public. His manual for the recorder, the *Opera intitulata Fontegara* of 1535, breaks new ground in the level of detail and sophistication of the instruction provided, and the two volumes of his *Regola rubertina* of 1542–3 for the viola da gamba are similarly organized. Printed lute tablatures, containing both instrumental forms—many of which were established in this period—and intabulations of vocal models, began to flood the market in the mid 1540s, spurred by the popularity and versatility of the lute. These publications surely helped swell the ranks of the cultivated amateur; they made much music easily available to large segments of the bourgeoisie, and in doing so also increased the demand for other similar publications. The ramifications of this development are multifaceted. For example, during these decades we see evidence of an almost modern organization of the instrument-making business in some centers: perhaps the demand for instruments increased with the diffusion of

[13] For more detailed discussion of the mass see below, Ch. 7.

[14] For the output of these two printers, see the definitive works by Mary S. Lewis, *Antonio Gardano, Venetian Music Printer, 1538–1569: A Descriptive Bibliography and Historical Study*, 2 vols. (New York, 1988–97); and Jane A. Bernstein, *Music Printing in Renaissance Venice: The Scotto Press (1539–1572)* (New York and Oxford, 1998).

musical literacy, and the greatest beneficiary of this increase was surely the lute, for which a large amount of music was composed and arranged. Lute makers—among them a number of recent immigrants from German-speaking lands—produced large quantities of affordable instruments, together with a few elaborate ones.In some centers, such as Venice, for instance, the production of the leading lute-making workshops seems to have been too large to be absorbed by the city, and we know that the export trade in lutes to other European countries was brisk.

An important mark is reached in the year 1546, when Italian lutenists published more than a dozen books of lute tablature, thus surpassing the total number of Italian collections for the instrument that had appeared over the previous thirty years. The composers or arrangers of these collections were from the region of Milan (Francesco da Milano, Joan Maria da Crema) or from the Venetian area (Giulio Abondante, Domenico Bianchini, Melchiorre de Barberiis, Francesco Vindella) and were primarily known as virtuoso performers on their instruments. One famous description of a court performance by Francesco da Milano (1497–1543), the first Italian Renaissance instrumentalist to gain international recognition, contains perhaps a fair amount of exaggeration, but is indicative of the effect that some aristocratic audiences of the time, imbued with humanistic ideals, expected from such virtuosi:

> He had barely disturbed the air with three strummed chords when he interrupted the conversation that had started among the guests. Having constrained them to face him, he continued with such ravishing skill that little by little, making the strings languish under his fingers in his sublime way, he transported all those who were listening into so pleasurable a melancholy that . . . they remained deprived of all senses save that of hearing . . . and I believe that we would be there still, had he not himself —I know not how—changing his style of playing with a gentle force, returned the spirit and the senses to the place from which he had stolen them, not without leaving as much astonishment in each of us as if we had been elevated by an ecstatic transport of some divine frenzy.[15]

Keyboard music also made impressive strides in this period. Indeed, some of the first wholly instrumental collections printed in Italy—the *Frottole intabulate da sonare organi* (1517) of Andrea Antico and the *Recerchari, motetti, canzoni* (1523) by the organist and singer Marc'Antonio Cavazzoni—were dedicated to keyboard music. Although the emphasis is on keyboard arrangements of vocal pieces, we can see in the works of Cavazzoni, especially in his *ricercari*, an instrumental language in the process of gradually moving away from its vocal models. The *ricercare* as an instrumental genre is itself central to the development of a new instrumental language in Italy in the decades up to 1560. The first *ricercari*, beginning with those of Spinacino's *Intabolatura de lauto, libro primo* of 1507 (the first recorded use of the term) were essentially pieces in an improvisatory style, often short and sometimes

[15] Quoted in Arthur J. Ness, *The Lute Music of Francesco Canova da Milano (1497–1543)* (Cambridge, MA, 1970), 2.

intended as actual preludes to other pieces. Cavazzoni already used imitative passages in his compositions in this genre. A more consistently imitative style can be seen in the works of Marc'Antonio's son Girolamo Cavazzoni, and the *ricercare* of the sixteenth century moves towards a more severe contrapuntal style, primarily in the hands of organists such as the Flemish Jacques Buus and the Italians Annibale Padovano, Claudio Merulo, and later Andrea Gabrieli. Four-part *ricercari* by these and other composers, usually published in collections that bore the indication "da cantare et sonare" (to be played and sung), probably in order to appeal to the widest possible audience, are among the first manifestations of the trend that would lead to the flowering of instrumental-ensemble music later in the sixteenth century. Other terms of great importance for the history of instrumental music, such as toccata, fantasia, and sonata, also made their first appearance in instrumental collections of this period, a symptom of an interest in instrumental music that increased gradually throughout the sixteenth century.

In spite of the important role of manuscripts and prints in the circulation of music in mid-sixteenth-century Italy, we should not forget that paper or parchment were not necessary for the performance of much music of the period. Although the peak of the popularity of the *improvvisatori* (the performers who improvised music, poetry, or both) was perhaps in the past, nevertheless their craft did not entirely disappear from the musical scene. Well into the century there were still *cantimbanchi* plying their trade on the squares of Italian cities, singing popular tunes to their audiences, but also providing a varied entertainment by dancing, acting, and juggling. On the other end of the scale, the courtly improvisers performed their versions of epic or erotic poetry, using their skills in varying a number of basic formulae. Echoes of the popular tradition seeped into the art music produced during this period. For example, certain musical features found in the sub-genres of the madrigal were surely imitating (or even quoting) popular music, and this type of imitation, triggering in the listener the pleasure of recognition, must have been at least partly responsible for their popularity.

Finally, the long and vital tradition of Italian music theory of the fourteenth and fifteenth centuries was continued in this period by several important figures. The works of Pietro Aaron and Giovanni Spataro, whose lively correspondence, in addition to more formal treatises, gives rare insights into the theory of the time, are typical of Italian theory at the beginning of the century. In the years 1520–60 Italian theorists, though, became increasingly influenced by humanistic concerns while expanding the theoretical discourse on music.[16] The theoretical works of the second half of the century attempt to deal with the heritage of antiquity in ways that would have been impossible before the study of Greek expanded beyond an extremely small circle to become a staple of humanistic education. An example of this approach is the treatise *L'antica musica ridotta alla moderna pratica* by Nicola Vicentino, in which the author tried to reconcile Greek theory with sixteenth-century practice. The fact that this treatise was controversial from its publication

[16] For an overview, see Ann E. Moyer, *Musica Scientia: Musical Scholarship in the Italian Renaissance* (Ithaca, NY, 1992).

(and that Vicentino's understanding of the principles of ancient Greek music was somewhat flawed) did not prevent Vicentino from being a clear influence on later composers, by providing a set of theoretical justifications for the experimentations that culminated in Monteverdi's *seconda pratica*. The landmark of mid-sixteenth-century Italian theory, however, is undoubtedly the *Istitutioni harmoniche* of 1558 by Gioseffo Zarlino: his erudite exposition of theoretical ideas in this and subsequent works (*Dimostrationi harmoniche*, 1571 and *Sopplimenti musicali*, 1588) make Zarlino a giant of later-sixteenth-century theory, while his post as *maestro di cappella* at St Mark's in Venice from 1565 to his death in 1590 put him in the position to influence directly the development of music at one of the most important musical centers of the Renaissance, supervising the work of, among others, Claudio Merulo, Andrea and Giovanni Gabrieli, and Baldissera Donato.

In view of what we have seen so far, it is obvious that the overall appraisal of this period in Italy must be seen as positive. This is, after all, the period when a major musical genre, the madrigal, is introduced and becomes successful, when Italian composers begin to take control of many of the most important positions in musical establishments, even as foreign musicians continue to be attracted to Italy in large numbers, when Italian music theory contributes significantly to the field, and when Italian music printing dominates the industry in quantity and quality. Many of the seeds of future developments in Italian music were sown in this period. By the early seventeenth century these would bear fruit in a variety of ways.

5

ITALY, *ii*: 1560–1600

Noel O'Regan

DEVELOPMENTS in Italian music during this forty-year period were to prove crucial to the direction Western art music was to take in the following two centuries. In both sacred and secular music, Italy in the late sixteenth century served as a powerhouse for experiments in texture, in harmony, and in vocal and instrumental technique, all of which laid the foundations for stylistic change throughout Europe and beyond. In sacred music this was primarily due to a newly revitalized and centralized Catholic church, which in the wake of the Council of Trent looked to Rome in particular and Italy in general for models; this influence was to spread into other confessions too, especially in Lutheran Germany. In secular music the madrigal continued to dominate: by the end of the century it had moved well beyond its Italian roots to challenge the supremacy of the French chanson on the European stage. In seeking an ever closer relationship between words and music, as well as adapting to the increasingly wide variety of contexts in which both madrigal and motet were performed, musical language developed in ways hitherto undreamed of. New developments in solo and small-group singing began in Naples and Rome and moved rapidly on to Florence and northern Italy; these, together with advances in instrumental writing, opened up a further range of stylistic possibilities.

All this happened in an Italy that, in the wake of the Treaty of Câteau-Cambrésis of 1559, enjoyed a period of relative stability, with rivalries between courts played out on the cultural stage rather than on the battlefield. Spanish hegemony was a political reality, but in musical terms this was not hugely apparent, except for some interventions by Philip II and his representatives in the debate over the retention of polyphony during the Council of Trent and the subsequent reform of

For more detailed studies of the period, see Allan Atlas, *Renaissance Music* (New York and London, 1998); Howard M. Brown and Louise Stein, *Music in the Renaissance*, 2nd edn (Upper Saddle River, NJ, 1999); Tim Carter, *Music in Late Renaissance and Early Baroque Italy* (London, 1992); John Walter Hill, *Roman Monody, Cantata, and Opera from the Circles around Cardinal Montalto* (Oxford, 1997); Leeman L. Perkins, *Music in the Age of the Renaissance* (New York and London, 1999).

plainchant ordered by Pope Gregory XIII.[1] Indeed, musically, Spain was to gain much more from Italy than vice versa, with the Italian polychoral idiom in particular taking productive root in Spanish soil by the end of the century. The viceregal courts in Milan and Naples lacked the weight and continuity of personnel found in independent duchies, and they had an uneasy relationship with the older indigenous aristocracies; this meant that, on the whole, the most interesting musical developments happened elsewhere, though Naples, with its vibrant traditions in theatre and in aristocratic involvement in performance and composition, did make important contributions.[2]

In northern Italy the Venetian Republic continued to thrive on commerce, which included Europe's most developed music printing industry.[3] The naval victory by a Venetian-led coalition over the Ottoman Turks at Lepanto in 1571 represented the apogee of the Republic's expansionism and self-regard. State music made an ever greater contribution to Venice's self-promotion, accompanying the doge in a growing round of ceremonial visits and rituals, many of them celebrating feasts that coincided with days of political importance to the state.[4] The smaller duchies of Ferrara and Mantua also continued to spend significant amounts on culture, favouring music that was often experimental and trend-setting; their proximity and interconnectivity through Este–Gonzaga marriages ensured regular cultural exchange, while their position on travel routes within Italy and beyond guaranteed wider dissemination. In Florence the Medici propped up their still relatively new status as grand dukes of Tuscany by lavish musical display, particularly at dynastic wedding celebrations.[5] The translation of Ferdinando I from Roman cardinal to grand duke in 1588 promoted Roman–Florentine musical interaction and ushered in a period of artistic ferment which encouraged the "new" music of c. 1600.[6] In Rome and the Papal States a newly vigorous papacy, epecially that of Sixtus V Peretti-Montalto (r. 1585–90), revitalized government, centralizing much in the process. This created an environment in which both sacred and secular music could flourish in chapels, confraternities, and the palaces of princely cardinals

[1] Philip's intervention was encouraged by Fernando de las Infantas, an aristocratic Spanish composer living in Rome. See Michael Noone, "Philip II and Music: A Fourth Centenary Reassessment," *Revista de Musicología*, 21 (1998), 447–48.

[2] Donna G. Cardamone, *The Canzone Villanesca alla Napoletana and Related Forms, 1537–1570* (Ann Arbor, MI, 1981).

[3] Richard J. Agee, "The Venetian Privilege and Venetian Music-Printing in the Sixteenth Century," *Early Music History*, 3 (1983), 1–42; Jane Bernstein, *Print Culture and Music in Sixteenth-Century Venice* (Oxford, 2001); Mary S. Lewis, *Antonio Gardano, Venetian Music Printer, 1538–1569: A Descriptive Bibliography and Historical Study*, 2 vols. (New York, 1988–97).

[4] Iain Fenlon, "Venice: Theatre of the World," in idem, ed., *Man & Music*, II: *The Renaissance: From the 1470s to the End of the 16th Century* (London, 1989), 102–32; idem, "Music and Ceremonial Space in Early Modern Venice," in Fiona Kisby, ed., *Music and Musicians in Renaissance Cities and Towns* (Cambridge, 2001), 28–44.

[5] John W. Hill, "Florence: Musical Spectacle and Drama, 1570–1650," in Curtis Price, ed., *Man & Music*, III: *The Early Baroque Era: From the Late 16th Century to the 1660s* (London, 1989), 121–45.

[6] Tim Carter, *Music in Late Renaissance and Early Baroque* (London, 1992), ch. II.

such as that of Sixtus' great-nephew Alessandro Montalto and his younger brother Prince Michele Peretti or Clement VIII's nephews, Cardinals Cinzio and Pietro Aldobrandini.[7]

Sacred Music

IN sacred music this period was dominated by the final session of the Council of Trent (1562–63) and its aftermath. The Council's rather generalized pronouncements on liturgical music were gradually pinned down to specifics in individual dioceses, especially Rome and Milan.[8] The result was a change of emphasis, with the text coming more to the fore, and technical mastery, as foregrounded by northern European composers and their Italian disciples such as Costanzo Festa and the young Giovanni Pierluigi da Palestrina, receding somewhat in prominence. Not that contrapuntal skill disappeared—far from it: a simplified but revitalized contrapuntal style, later labelled the *prima pratica* or *stile antico*, was to remain one of the choices open to composers, particularly for Mass ordinary settings and for office hymns and Magnificats. The key point, however, was that by 1600 it was just one among a number of styles available to composers, depending on genre, text, and liturgical context.

Papal Rome and Spanish Milan took the lead in pushing through liturgical reform, with the increasingly single-minded Cardinal Carlo Borromeo playing a leading role in both cities. In Rome the Cappella Pontificia was reauditioned *en masse* in 1565, with a wholesale weeding out of singers on both vocal and moral grounds;[9] in the same year Borromeo and Cardinal Vitelozzo Vitelli organized a sing-through of masses by members of the Cappella Pontificia to test the intelligibility of the text; whether or not Palestrina's *Missa Papae Marcelli* was one of those tested, this mass soon came to symbolize the whole reform movement in sacred music.[10] It was published in 1567 in his Second Book of masses, in the foreword of which the composer, recently appointed *maestro di cappella* at the newly-founded Roman Seminary, spoke of adorning the holy sacrifice of the Mass "in a new manner." That same year saw the publication by Palestrina's main competitor in Rome, Giovanni Animuccia, of his First Book of masses for four to six voices, in which the composer spoke of writing "in such a way that the music may disturb the hearing of the text as little as possible, but nevertheless . . . that it may not be entirely devoid

[7] James Chater, "Musical Patronage in Rome at the Turn of the Seventeenth Century: The Case of Cardinal Montalto," *Studi musicali*, 16 (1987), 179–227; Claudio Annibaldi, "Il mecenate 'politico': Ancora sul patronato musicale del Cardinale Pietro Aldobrandini (1575–1621), *Studi musicali*, 16 (1987), 33–93; 17 (1988), 101–78.

[8] Craig Monson, "The Council of Trent Revisited," *Journal of the American Musicological Society*, 55 (2002), 1–37.

[9] Richard Sherr, "Competence and Incompetence in the Papal Choir in the Age of Palestrina," *Early Music*, 22 (1994), 606–29.

[10] Lewis Lockwood, ed., *G. P. da Palestrina: Pope Marcellus Mass*, Norton Critical Scores (New York, 1975).

of artifice and contribute in some degree to the listener's pleasure." It seems logical to equate Palestrina's "new manner" with Animuccia's more extended description. Certainly both composers used extensive homophony in the wordier Gloria and Credo movements, while keeping imitative polyphony to a greater or lesser degree in the rest. Palestrina succeeded Animuccia as *maestro di cappella* of the Cappella Giulia in St Peter's in 1571 (he had preceded him in 1551–54), keeping his role as papal composer while churning out a whole series of liturgical cycles (hymns, Magnificats, Lamentations) as well as litanies, motets, and a large number of masses that secured his position as the standard-bearer for the Tridentine musical reformation. These cycles were to replace those already produced by Animuccia, so that it was Palestrina rather than the Florentine Animuccia whose name was to be forever associated with the new style.[11]

Even before moving back to Milan in 1565, Cardinal Carlo Borromeo had issued instructions to the *maestro di cappella* at the duomo, Vincenzo Ruffo, that he should compose masses in which the words should be as intelligible as possible. The results are clear in the strongly homophonic masses that Ruffo published in 1570 "in accordance with the decrees of the Council of Trent."[12] Ruffo moved on from Milan in 1572, and subsequently, whether because of the heavy hand of church authority or the lack of a strong and rich central patronage source, Milan did not attract the very best composers. Ruffo's successors at the duomo included Simon Boyleau, the theorist Pietro Ponzio, and Giulio Cesare Gabussi, while Orfeo Vecchi had some very productive years at S. Maria della Scala, the one-time ducal church that maintained the ancient Ambrosian liturgy.[13] Being more than two hundred years old, the Ambrosian Rite was allowed to continue in use after Trent, though largely confined to the Milanese duomo, to S. Maria della Scala, and to a few other churches. In Mantua, Duke Guglielmo I Gonzaga sought and obtained papal approval for a unique rite in his ducal chapel of S. Barbara. For this he commissioned Palestrina to compose a series of Mass ordinaries, based on *alternatim* settings of plainchants unique to that chapel.[14]

An important result of the post-Tridentine reform process was the issuing of a new *Breviarium romanum* in 1568 and a *Missale romanum* in 1570. These ration-

[11] Animuccia's compositions in 1568, and very likely his First Book of masses as well, were composed "according to the form of the Council of Trent and of the new service." See Jeffrey J. Dean, "The Repertory of the Cappella Giulia in the 1560s," *Journal of the American Musicological Society*, 41 (1988), 488. Giovanni Animuccia's brother Paolo had also put himself forward in January 1566 for the task of reforming the music of the Cappella Pontificia, but his offer was ignored. See Richard Sherr, "A Letter from Paolo Animuccia," *Early Music*, 12 (1984), 75–8.

[12] Lewis Lockwood, *The Counter-Reformation and the Masses of Vincenzo Ruffo* (Venice, 1970). The 1570 masses are edited by Lockwood in Part II of Vincenzo Ruffo, *Seven Masses*, Recent Researches in the Music of the Renaissance, 22–23 (Madison, WI, 1979) where they can be compared with Ruffo's pre-Tridentine masses in Part I.

[13] Robert Kendrick, *The Sounds of Milan* (New York, 2002), 116 ff.

[14] Iain Fenlon, "Patronage, Music and Liturgy in Renaissance Mantua," in Thomas F. Kelly, ed., *Plainsong in the Age of Polyphony* (Cambridge, 1992). Palestrina's masses can be found in Giovanni Pierluigi da Palestrina, *Le opere complete*, ed. Raffaele Casimiri (Rome, 1939–87), XVIII, XIX.

alized the church's calendar, suppressing many feasts as well as all tropes and most sequences, and created a demand for new settings of specifically liturgical music such as Magnificat and hymn cycles for Vespers. They were complemented by the issuing of the *Caeremoniale episcoporum* in 1600, which codified much of the Tridentine ritual, including the use of organ. These books stabilized the Roman Catholic liturgy internationally for centuries to come, making it more attractive for composers to write for what was a much broader market than before. The afternoon office of Vespers, coinciding as it did with the *passeggiata* or daily walk in streets and piazzas, increasingly came to dominate as the most musically elaborate service, and by the end of the century composers were providing large-scale settings of the psalms most commonly set for first and second Vespers on major feasts, as well as of the Magnificat and the four Marian antiphons, one of which normally concluded the service.

Among the first to provide such large-scale settings of Vespers psalms and Marian antiphons was the composer who, perhaps above all others, embodied the spirit of the Catholic Reformation in his entirely sacred output: the Spaniard Tomás Luis de Victoria, who spent his most productive years in Rome (*c.*1565–*c.*1585); his music is at least as much Roman as Castilian in its inspiration. In a string of publications from 1572 onwards, he supplied a comprehensive series of liturgical settings and motets that combined fidelity to the text and its intelligibility with musical artifice of the highest order. The opening piece of the 1572 collection, the four-voice motet *O quam gloriosum est regnum* for the feast of All Saints, has long been seen as emblematic of Victoria's approach. The initial "O" is spread over three chordal breves forming a brief circle of fifths that leads the ear onwards to the phrase's initial climax on the penultimate syllable of "gloriosum"and further to the keyword "regnum" (the kingdom [of heaven]). Thereafter the style is largely imitative, with fast rising scales for "gaudent" (rejoice), and the words "sequuntur Agnum" (they follow the Lamb) illustrated by a particularly apt series of falling suspensions.[15] The same series of opening chords had been used by Palestrina in the six-voice *O magnum mysterium* from his First Book of motets for five to seven voices of 1569, one of a number of pieces in that publication that launched a new relationship between words and music in Palestrina's motets in the wake of the Council of Trent.[16]

Victoria later published a "parody" mass or *missa ad imitationem* based on *O quam gloriosum.* Composers increasingly used their own motets or those of others in this way as the basis for mass composition, largely avoiding the secular models previously used. Victoria was the first *moderator musicae* at the Roman Collegio Germanico, founded in the wake of the Council of Trent to educate priests for the German mission and run by the Jesuit order. It quickly developed a reputation for musical excellence after 1573, when Pope Gregory XIII granted it the ancient church of S. Apollinare in which to train its seminarians in liturgical practice.[17] Subsequent *moderatores musicae* included Annibale Stabile, Ruggiero

15 Felipe Pedrell, ed., *Thomae Ludovici Victoria Opera omnia*, I (Leipzig, 1902), 1–2.

16 Palestrina, *Le opere complete*, V.

17 Thomas Culley, *A Study of the Musicians Connected with the German College in Rome*

Giovanelli, and Asprilio Pacelli, all of whom used the College's considerable resources and student choirs to experiment, especially with the polychoral idiom.[18]

This idiom was one of the most important legacies of the period in the sacred sphere. It had originated in northern and central Italy in mid-century, particularly for *cori spezzati* Vesper psalms by composers such as Adriano Willaert and Jachet of Mantua,[19] but its potential was only fully realized in the wake of the Council of Trent when it was found to provide just the right balance of text-intelligibility with musical interest. Full-blown polychoral music first appeared in Rome in Palestrina's Third Book of motets of 1575 and Victoria's First Book of masses, psalms, and Magnificat settings of 1576, taking to its logical conclusion the ever-changing kaleidoscope of textures found in works such as the six-voice *Missa Papae Marcelli* (indeed Francesco Soriano was to take that work's implicit polychorality to the full in his reworking for double choir, published in 1609).[20] Giovanni Animuccia, while not writing for full *cori spezzati*, came close in his 1570 Second Book of *laudi*, which contained pieces, including dialogues in Latin and Italian, written for the oratory of St Philip Neri. In his foreword Animuccia made an explicit connection between the attendance of the upper classes at these oratory devotions and the embryonic *concertato* polychoral style; he also summed up the deliberate use of music in targeting the nobility and rich middle classes undertaken by the Oratorians and Jesuits in particular:

> the said oratory having been expanded . . . with a concourse of prelates and of the most important gentlemen, it seemed to me appropriate in this second book to increase the harmony and the number of voices in concert, varying the music in diverse ways, now with Latin words and now with vernacular; now with more voices, now with fewer; sometimes with one type of verse, other times with another; interfering as little as possible by means of imitation or inventions, so as not to obscure the meaning of the words in order that their effectiveness, with the aid of the harmony, might penetrate more sweetly the hearts of those who listened.

During the 1580s and 1590s, the volume of polychoral music grew exponentially in Rome with composers like Palestrina, Victoria, Felice Anerio, Giovanni Andrea Dragoni, Ruggiero Giovanelli, Giovanni Maria Nanino, Asprilio Pacelli, and Annibale Stabile setting psalms, Marian antiphons, litanies, and motets. Some of these composers also set polychoral Mass ordinaries: both Palestrina and Victoria

during the 17th Century and of Their Activities in Northern Europe: Jesuits and Music 1 (Rome, 1970).

[18] Noel O'Regan, "Roman Polychoral Music: Origins and Distinctiveness," in *La scuola policorale romana del Sei-Settecento: Atti del convegno internazionale di studi in memoria di Laurence Feininger, Trento 4–5 ottobre 1996* (Trent, 1997), 43–64.

[19] These psalms can be found in a modern edition in *Adriani Willaert Opera omnia*, ed. Hermann Zenck and Walter Gerstenberg, CMM 3 (American Institute of Musicology, 1972), VII.

[20] For an edition of Palestrina's *Missa Papae Marcelli* see n. 10 above. Soriano's arrangement can be found in *Two Settings of Palestrina's Missa Papae Marcelli*, ed. Hermann J. Busch, Recent Researches in the Music of the Baroque Era, 16 (Madison, WI, 1973).

used the double-choir idiom in this way, and the triple-choir *Missa "Cantantibus organis Cecilia,"* which survives in manuscript, was a joint composition by members of the Compagnia dei Musici (recognised by Pope Sixtus V in 1585), probably for performance at their patronal feast-day celebration.[21] Such corporate endeavour was emblematic of the new spirit of urban devotion—both real and politically motivated—that swept Rome and other Italian cities in the late sixteenth century. This had its most visible face in the mushrooming of lay confraternities throughout Italy in the post-Tridentine period.[22] Some of these grew out of existing trade guilds; others were devoted to more specific charitable works such as the care of the sick and dying, the visiting of prisoners, or the comforting of those condemned to death. In Rome, each of the foreign nationalities had its confraternity, while eventually each parish also organized a Blessed Sacrament confraternity in an attempt at greater church control of these organizations. Public visibility was an important feature, with regular processions accompanied by musicians and the lavish celebration of one or two patronal feast-days with Mass and both sets of Vespers; extra singers and instrumentalists were hired, with polychoral settings the preferred means of making a *bella figura*. Devotion became fashionable, and the competition that developed between these groups was very much to the advantage of musicians, leading, in the case of cities like Rome, to a great increase in the amount of available work and in the number of active musicians in the later decades of the century.

Processions provided the most visible form of musically accompanied religious participation, particularly those accompanying the Blessed Sacrament on the Feast of Corpus Christi or those held during the increasingly popular Forty Hours' devotion, in which the Sacrament was publically displayed in elaborate theatrical sets (*sepolcri*) in commemoration of Christ's forty hours in the tomb.[23] There were occasions when whole cities seemed to go in procession, such as on Holy Thursday evening in Rome or the great procession which accompanied the relics of St Gregory Nazianzen from the Campo Marzio to their new resting place in the newly completed Cappella Gregoriana in St Peter's in 1582; other such urban joint civic-religious occasions included processions in Venice and in Milan to pray for deliverance from plague in 1576. Such processions were occasions when state, city government, church, religious orders, and lay confraternities all came together for a common purpose. The existence of a number of sets of printed and manuscript partbooks labelled for use during processions attests to the performance of

21 The mass, based on Palestrina's motet, can be found in Palestrina, *Le opere complete*, XXXI.

22 Jonathan Glixon, *Honoring God and the City: Music at the Venetian Confraternities, 1260–1807* (Oxford and New York, 2003); Noel O'Regan, *Institutional Patronage in Post-Tridentine Rome: Music at Santissima Trinità dei Pellegrini, 1550–1650*, Royal Musical Association Monographs, 7 (London, 1995).

23 Noel O'Regan, "Processions and Their Music in Post-Tridentine Rome," *Recercare*, 4 (1992), 45–80.

polyphony on these occasions, as well as psalms and litanies in plainchant and in *falsobordone* (simple, often improvised, harmonization of plainchant).[24]

In Venice both Andrea Gabrieli and his nephew Giovanni wrote large-scale polychoral music for performance in the ducal basilica of S. Marco and in the city's other churches and institutions.[25] In developing their particular brand of state music, both Gabrielis were influenced by the music written in Munich by Orlandus Lassus: both had spent time in the Bavarian capital in the 1560s and 1570s. In 1587 Giovanni Gabrieli organized the posthumous publication of his uncle's *concerti* as well as some of his own. Those by Andrea (who had died in 1585) included the eight-voice motet *Benedictus Dominus Deus Sabaoth*, written to celebrate the victory at Lepanto, *O crux splendidior*, probably performed at the laying of the foundation stone of Palladio's church of the Redentore, and a series of four movements from the ordinary of the Mass for twelve to sixteen voices, which may well have been performed during a visit to Venice by some Japanese princes in June 1585.[26] In 1597 Giovanni Gabrieli published his *Symphoniae sacrae* for up to sixteen voices; the larger-scale works such as *Plaudite, psallite* or *Jubilate Deo* for twelve voices or *Omnes gentes, plaudite* for sixteen were clearly written for use on major celebratory occasions.[27]

As in Rome, the larger Venetian confraternities or *scuole grande*, such as S. Marco, S. Rocco, or S. Teodoro, proved important institutional patrons of large-scale festal as well as smaller-scale devotional music.[28] The doge's palatine basilica of S. Marco employed a growing instrumental ensemble from 1568, and instruments were regularly used to accompany or substitute for voices. Polychoral music was essentially written for choirs of solo voices, though often either with one choir consisting of a number of singers on each part, or with one or more choirs being doubled by *ripieni* choirs. By the end of the century, particularly in Venice, the music for the more virtuosic solo voices, the *cori favoriti,* became more elaborate. Their verse structure meant that psalms, Marian antiphons, and canticles lent themselves to the sort of contrast of textures first alluded to in 1570 by Giovanni Animuccia. The foundations of the *concertato* style, in which verses for solo or few voices alternated with tutti, with plainchant, or with verses in quasi-improvised *falsobordone*, were laid during the final decade of the sixteenth century by composers such as Emilio de' Cavalieri in Rome and Florence, Giovanni Gabrieli in Venice, Felice Anerio, Giovanni Maria Nanino, and Paolo Quagliati in Rome.

Sacred music in Italian cities other than Venice and Rome has been given less attention by historians, and yet it is clear from the wide geographical spread of

24 Murray Bradshaw, "Falsobordone," in Stanley Sadie, ed., *The New Grove Dictionary of Music and Musicians*, 2nd edn (London, 2001).

25 Denis Arnold, *Giovanni Gabrieli* (London, 1974); David Bryant, "The 'Cori Spezzati' of St Mark's: Myth and Reality", *Early Music History*, I (1981), 15–186.

26 Modern editions in *Edizione nazionale delle Opere di Andrea Gabrieli*, XI, ed. David Bryant (Milan, 1989).

27 Modern editions in Giovanni Gabrieli, *Opera Omnia*, CMM 12, II, ed. Denis Arnold (Rome, 1959).

28 Glixon, *Honoring God and the City.*

maestri di cappella with at least one publication to their name that similar practices were going on in every major city. Major patronal feast-days were celebrated with polychoral music, particularly at Vespers, while churches, monasteries, and convents (both male and female) relied on a staple diet of plainchant peppered with some polyphony depending on the availability of singers and instrumentalists, including an organist. Huge quantities of psalms, Magnificats, and other litugical items as well as motets survive in prints and manuscripts. The sacred music of composers such as the Flemish Giaches de Wert at Mantua, the Brescian Luca Marenzio in Rome, or Luzzascho Luzzaschi at Ferrara, has not received anything like the attention of their secular music, despite the evident quality of much of it. Wert in particular produced fine motets such as the six-voice *Ascendente Jesu in naviculam*, in which the rocking of the boat during the storm at sea is vividly depicted in the complex syncopated rhythms of the music.[29] Marenzio's only surviving sacred publication during his lifetime, his *Moteta festorum totius anni* of 1585, concentrated on lucid four-voice motets based on Magnificat antiphon texts for all the major feasts of the church year. Words and music are very closely bound together, as when the blood of the martyrs literally spills out ("sanguinem suum fuderunt") in rushing downward short-note scales in *Gaudent in coelis*.[30]

Marenzio was unusual in avoiding institutional employment until his move to the Polish royal court towards the end of his life: he enjoyed something of a freelance career, though heavily dependent on a succession of cardinals and ducal patrons.[31] Like almost all other composers at the time, Wert's stable employment was as *maestro di cappella* in a chapel, in his case the ducal chapel in Mantua, where he served from 1565 until ill health forced him to resign the post to Giacomo Gastoldi in 1592.[32] Among the religious orders, an occasional composer emerged from the general anonymity. One such was the conventual Franciscan friar Costanzo Porta, who studied with Adriano Willaert in Venice before following an itinerant career that covered much of northern and central Italy.[33] After thirteen years at Osimo Cathedral (where he first obtained patronage from the Della Rovere family of Urbino) he moved to the Basilica of St Anthony at Padua in 1565, then two years later to the Duomo at Ravenna to 1574, followed by six years at the Shrine of the Virgin at Loreto, during which time he published the first printed collection of Marian Litanies (Venice, 1575). He turned down attempts by Carlo Borromeo to lure him to Milan and returned to Ravenna in 1580 and, in 1589, to his final position once more at the Basilica of S. Antonio in Padua. Along the way he composed a thirteen-voice *Missa ducalis* for Cosimo I de' Medici to celebrate the chapter of

[29] Giaches de Wert, *Collected Works*, ed. Carol MacClintock and Melvin Bernstein, CMM 24 (American Institute of Musicology, 1961–77), XVI: 23.

[30] Luca Marenzio, *Opera omnia*, CMM 72, ed. Roland Jackson (American Institute of Musicology, 1976), II.

[31] Marco Bizzarini, *Luca Marenzio: The Career of a Musician between the Renaissance and the Counter-Reformation*, trans. James Chater (Aldershot, 2003).

[32] Iain Fenlon, *Giaches de Wert: Letters and Documents* (Paris, 1999).

[33] Lilian F. Pruett, "Constanzo Porta," *New Grove*^{2}. Porta's music can be found in Costanzo Porta, *Opera omnia*, ed. S. Cisilino (Padua, 1964–70).

his order held in Florence in 1565, and dedicated his Third Book of motets to Pope Sixtus V, who was a fellow Franciscan. Della Rovere and other patronage allowed Porta to publish a large amount of both sacred and secular music. Such frequent moves were not uncommon for musicians who followed work and patronage, seeking to better themselves in more prestigious and richer establishments. While many were celibate clerics, others had families: the married Palestrina's career, for example, both benefited and suffered from the vicissitudes of papal favour; in his case commercial interests in wine and fur, as well as free-lance work for Roman confraternities, supplemented his income as *maestro di cappella* at a succession of Roman institutions.[34]

Secular music

By 1560 the madrigal was long established as the pre-eminent form of serious secular music in Italy; the final four decades of the century saw that form and its musical language come to a flowering that made it the model for composers all over Europe. Madrigals served a wide variety of purposes and performance situations: amateur singers gathered around a table, performances by professional singing and instrumental virtuosi for whom the print or manuscript could often be just the starting point for ornamentation, ducal soirées, literary and musical academies, theatrical productions, state celebrations and weddings. There was a gradual shift in the balance of performance conditions over the period from musically literate amateurs singing for their own pleasure—perhaps in the company of professional musicians—to essentially concert performances by virtuoso singers and players for members of the nobility. Dedicated to princes or other aristocrats, or to members of the newly sprouting literary academies, the madrigal print was as important for career advancement as its sacred equivalent. Madrigal anthologies were especially widely circulated, playing a key role in dissemination within Italy and further afield, as, for example, the 1591 *Giardino de' musici ferraresi* in which twenty-one composers resident in Ferrara were represented.

During the 1560s and 1570s Venice retained much of the pre-eminence it had enjoyed in the time of Willaert and Rore, largely owing to the madrigals of Andrea Gabrieli, who, as we have seen, returned from spending some years with Orlandus Lassus in Munich to provide music for a wide variety of public and private occasions. Gabrieli used great stylistic variety and anything from three to twelve voices to provide textural contrast and colour in response to his chosen texts. These were not just the serious poetry of Petrarch and his imitators but often more popular lyrical texts with a pastoral bent, or encomiastic texts referring to the city of Venice and its ruling families. His Second Book of madrigals of 1570 included *Felici d'Adria*, an eight-voice madrigal written for a visit by Archduke Charles of Austria to the city in 1565 or 1569, while the eight-voice *Hor che nel suo bel seno* and the

[34] Noel O'Regan, "Palestrina, a Musician and Composer in the Market-Place," *Early Music*, 22 (1994), 551–72.

twelve-voice *Ecco Vinegia bella*, both composed for the visit of Henri III of France to Venice in 1574, were printed in the posthumous *Concerti* of 1587. Contrapuntal writing contrasted or merged with a more popular homophonic texture imported from lighter forms (see below) in what is often referred to as a "hybrid" style. The emphasis was very much on providing an appropriate musical response to each phrase and word of the text, the pastoral imagery of much of the poetry finding a ready musical counterpart in high-voice roulades and lightly bouncing rhythms, as in his *Vaghi augelletti, che per valli e monti*.[35] A similar approach is found in the works of Gabrieli's north-Italian contemporaries and successors, such as his nephew Giovanni, Claudio Merulo, and Marc'Antonio Ingegneri.

An analogous process took place in Rome, where the increasing number of composers attracted to the city by opportunities in the sacred field found a ready market for their madrigals among the households of cardinals and other aristocrats. The 1574 anthology *Il quarto libro delle Muse* showcased the work of a generation of Rome-based composers: Palestrina, Giovanni Maria Nanino, Francesco Soriano, and Giovanni Antonio Dragoni. This corporate activity was to result in a further two anthologies (*Dolci affetti* of 1582 and *Le gioie* of 1589), now with the addition of younger composers such as Felice Anerio, Marenzio, and Giovanni Battista Moscaglia, as well as in the formation of the Compagnia dei Musici as a confraternity both for spiritual benefit and for the regulation of the profession.[36] These Roman madrigals were characterized by clarity of contrapuntal writing combined with lyricism and continuity of flow: the classic example is Palestrina's five-voice *Vestiva i colli*, much anthologized in its day. The composer who most came to embody the particularly Roman secular idiom was the Brescian Marenzio, who served a succession of cardinals, most notably Luigi d'Este, and who turned out a large number of collections of finely-crafted madrigals before trimming his sails to the winds of change in the later 1580s. Typical is *Che fa oggi il mio sole* from his First Book of madrigals for five voices of 1580, which uses a different texture for each word or phrase and highlights words like "sole" or "canto" with roulades while also containing seeds of the declamatory style with repeated chords, which was to gain favour in the late 1580s.[37]

In northern Italy the adjacent courts of Mantua and Ferrara were to serve both as custodians of a tradition of setting serious texts and as centres of experimentation in word-setting. After Wert settled in Mantua in 1565 he remained in the vanguard of composition, setting passion-laden texts using a variety of expressionistic devices such as extremes of range, large leaps, sudden silences, and contrasts of tempo or texture. Each phrase, often each word, could conjure up a very different musical conceit, ranging from strict counterpoint to declamatory recitation. Typical are

[35] *Vaghi augeletti* and *Felici d'Adria* can be found in modern edition in *Edizione nazionale delle Opere di Andrea Gabrieli*, III, ed. David Butchart (Milan, 1996).

[36] Nino Pirrotta, ed., *I musici di Roma e il madrigale* (Rome, 1993); Remo Giazotto, *Quattro secoli di storia dell'Accademia di S. Cecilia* (Rome, 1970); William J. Summers, "The Compagnia di Musici di Roma, 1584–1604: A Preliminary Report," *Current Musicology*, 34 (1982), 2–25.

[37] See Alec Harman, ed., *The Oxford Book of Italian Madrigals* (London, 1983), 193.

his settings of Petrarch's *Solo e pensoso* or Tasso's *Giunta alla tomba*.[38] Wert spent almost as much time in Ferrara as Mantua, both in the company of the Mantuan heir-apparent Vincenzo Gonzaga and because of a personal interest in one of the court singers there, Tarquinia Molza. Both courts pioneered performances by professional women singers, the *concerto delle donne*, who achieved quasi-aristocratic status by virtue of their skills as virtuosi. Their performances were exclusively given to the dukes and members of their families or favoured guests; the music performed, together with its methods of elaboration, was often jealously guarded from wide dissemination.[39]

This was the case with the highly mannered music of Luzzascho Luzzaschi at Ferrara, written as *musica segreta* for the *concerto* of Duke Alfonso II, whose reign of nearly forty years was to prove the last by a member of the Este family in that city. His death without a legitimate heir in 1597 saw the end of Ferrara's glory days when much of the duchy was integrated into the Papal States; at the same time this allowed for the publication of Luzzaschi's madrigals for one to three voices with accompaniment (now dedicated to the papal nephew Cardinal Pietro Aldobrandini) in 1601. In an attempt to amuse his young fourth wife Margherita Gonzaga and encourage her to produce the much needed male heir, Alfonso had held almost nightly entertainments in which three solo ladies were accompanied by male singers such as the Neapolitan nobleman Cesare Brancaccio and by Luzzaschi at the keyboard. Luzzaschi experimented with mild chromaticism, encouraged no doubt by the presence in Ferrara of Nicola Vicentino, who as both theorist and practical musician was concerned with rediscovering the three Greek *genera*: diatonic, chromatic, and enharmonic. Vicentino had an *arcicembalo* built with thirty-one notes to the octave, which allowed him and Luzzaschi to move freely around tonal space in good intonation. Such experiments caught the imagination of the Neapolitan prince Carlo Gesualdo, who came to Ferrara in 1594 to marry Alfonso's niece Leonora. Gesualdo's brooding personality found in Ferrarese music an idiom that he exploited to often extreme lengths in both sacred and secular music, perhaps nowhere more than in his highly chromatic *Moro, lasso, al mio duolo*.[40] On his accession as duke of Mantua in 1587, Vincenzo Gonzaga set up his own *concerto delle donne*, which performed regularly on Friday evenings. As well as Wert (who died in 1596), the young Claudio Monteverdi wrote regularly for this group, with the early results printed in his first three books of madrigals, published before 1600. Typical is the five-voice *O primavera, gioventù dell'anno* from the Second Book (1592), setting a pastoral text with a sting in its tail from Battista Guarini's "tragicomedia pastorale" *Il pastor fido*.[41]

[38] Wert, *Collected Works*, VII.

[39] Anthony Newcomb, *The Madrigal at Ferrara, 1579–1597*, 2 vols. (Princeton, 1980).

[40] Published in 1611. An edition is given in Carlo Gesualdo, *Sämtliche Werk*, VI, ed. W. Weisman and Glenn Watkins (Leipzig, 1987), repr. in Allan Atlas, ed., *Anthology of Renaissance Music* (New York and London, 1998), 367–70. The piece is discussed in Allan Atlas, *Renaissance Music* (New York and London, 1999), 564–65.

[41] Modern edition in Claudio Monteverdi, *Opera omnia*, IV, ed. Maria Teresa Rosa Barez-

A tendency towards seriousness of purpose and experimentation affected virtually all madrigal composers in the late 1580s and 1590s. The change was perhaps most pronounced in the work of Luca Marenzio, who after a silence of six years moved to a more declamatory and dissonant style in settings of texts from Guarini's *Il pastor fido* in his Sixth Book of madrigals for five voices of 1594. Wert and Monteverdi, too, turned to *Il pastor fido* for intensely expressive texts such as *Cruda Amarilli* or *Ah, dolente partita*, while other composers used specially commissioned texts by lesser poets that provided a sufficient pool of contrasting images in a minimum number of words. There was a new vogue too for cycles of madrigals based on texts taken from a single source such as *Il pastor fido*. An example is the poetic cycle *Mentre ti fu sí grato* by Luigi Alamanni, set in collaboration by six Roman composers headed by Giovanni Maria Nanino, published in their *Dolci affetti* of 1582.[42]

Various explanations have been put forward for this move to seriousness, including simple boredom with the successions of word-painting "madrigalisms" that tended to characterize the music of the 1570s and 1580s. Another factor may have been the influence of the Catholic church, now reformed in the wake of Trent and increasingly on the offensive. Philip Neri's follower Giovenale Ancina was an extreme campaigner against what he saw as the lasciviousness of all madrigals and *villanelle*—he famously cut up in the composer's presence some newly printed madrigals by Jean de Macque in Naples—and collections and manuscript copies of *travestimenti*, spiritual contrafacta of secular madrigals, began to abound. The fifteenth-century *laude spirituale* re-emerged with gusto with Serafino Razzi's First Book of *laudi spirituali* (Venice, 1563). The form was taken up particularly by the Florentine Philip Neri in his informal indoor and outdoor oratory gatherings in Rome, and for the rest of the century a stream of *laude* publications fed an ever-growing market. Popular, too, were the collections of *madrigali spirituali* with Italian texts, among them settings of Petrarch's cycle of *Vergine bella* poems, initiated in 1548 by Rore. These were much closer in style to the madrigal than to the motet, and examples in the genre were published by major composers such as Animuccia (1565), Palestrina (1581 and 1594), Marenzio (1584), and Felice Anerio (1585).[43]

One of the most splendid occasions for musical celebration in the period was the wedding of Grand Duke Ferdinando I of Tuscany to Christina of Lorraine in 1589. The centerpiece was the performance of a five-act comedy, *La Pellegrina*: as usual this was essentially a vehicle for a series of six *intermedi* sandwiched between the acts, in which music, costumes, highly elaborate stage machinery, and dancing all combined to aggrandize the ducal couple and the golden age they hoped to initiate. Humanist imagery based around the Harmony of the Spheres and other Greek mythological tales involving music was the inspiration for a series of

zani (Cremona, 1988), and in Claudio Monteverdi, *Tutte le opere*, ed. Gian Francesco Malipiero (Asolo, 1926–42), III.

42 Pirrotta, *I musici di Roma e il madrigale*.

43 Katherine Powers, "The Spiritual Madrigal in Counter-Reformation Italy: Definition, Use and Style" (PhD diss., University of California, Santa Barbara, 1997).

dazzling pieces for a huge variety of vocal and instrumental combinations, ranging from solo monody to seven choirs, by a group of composers including Marenzio, Cristofano Malvezzi, Jacopo Peri, Giulio Caccini, and the entertainment's supervisor, the Roman nobleman Emilio de' Cavalieri.[44] Cavalieri himself composed the vocal "ballo" *O che nuovo miracolo* that forms the climax to the final intermedio (as the *aria di Fiorenza* it became a favorite subject for ground-bass variation in the seventeenth century[45]); it has a sandwich structure in which sections for a concertino of three dancing female singers alternate with a five-voice ritornello involving all the singers and instrumentalists. The subsequent importance of this set of *intermedi* rests particularly with the fact that they were published in great detail, including instructions for instrumentation, by Malvezzi in 1591.[46] There were many other occasions in Florence and elsewhere graced by intermedii and theatrical music, including the "favola boscareccia" *I fidi amanti*, composed specially for Gesualdo's wedding in Ferrara in 1594 by Ercole Pasquini.

Such use of music, and that in Ferrarese productions of Guarini's and Tasso's pastoral dramas, foreshadowed the development of opera in Florence in the 1590s. This grew out of discussions in two successive gatherings of Florentine noblemen and musicians hosted by Count Giovanni de' Bardi in the 1570s and early 1580s and by Jacopo Corsi in the 1590s. These were underpinned by the researches of Girolamo Mei into ancient Greek drama. The composers involved, Peri, Caccini, and Cavalieri as well as Vincenzo Galilei, produced a number of works in the dying years of the century, music that sought to reproduce ancient Greek declamatory practices by developing the *stile recitativo.*

At the other end of the spectrum, lighter forms of secular music flourished in the later years of the sixteenth century. The Neapolitan three-voice *villanesca* continued to enjoy great success while becoming more refined, both textually and musically, in the hands of northern Italian composers such as Giovanni Ferretti, who moved between Ancona and Loreto in the Marche, Cremona, and Friuli. In the 1560s and early 1570s he published a series of *canzoni* or *canzoni alla napolitana*: while based on the three- or four-voice *canzon villanesca alla napolitana*, Ferreti's *canzoni* were set for five or six voices in a style that came closer to the lighter hybrid-style madrigal of Venetian and Roman composers, making use of pseudo-polyphonic figuration to avoid the monotony of continuous homophonic writing. As a result, these pieces enjoyed great success both at home and abroad. Anthologies of three-voice *villanelle*, *villotte*, or *canzonette*, as these more refined versions were usually called, appeared regularly from the 1560s by many composers, including Marenzio, Ghinolfo Dattari, and Ascanio Trombetti, the latter two from Bologna. Their basic texture remained that of two high voices and one lower, the upper voices working largely as a pair with much writing in parallel thirds

[44] Warren Kirkendale, *Emilio de' Cavalieri "Gentilhuomo Romano": His Life and Letters, his Role as Superintendent of all the Arts at the Medici Court, and his Musical Compositions* (Florence, 2001).

[45] See Warren Kirkendale, *L'Aria di Fiorenza, id est Il ballo del Gran Duca* (Florence, 1972).

[46] Howard Mayer Brown, *Sixteenth-Century Instrumentation: The Music for the Florentine Intermedii*, MSD 30 (American Institute of Musicology, 1973).

and sixths. Similar popular success attended the three- and five-voice *balletti* of Giacomo Gastoldi, based at the Mantuan court. Probably intended to be danced, these were also structured around two high voices and one lower, with the inner parts filled out in the case of the five-voice pieces.

These lighter forms, through their appearances in Flemish anthologies in particular, were to have a strong influence on the English madrigal and ballett of the 1590s. Gastoldi's ballett *A lieta vita* appeared largely unchanged, though with some additions to the "fa la" refrain, as Thomas Morley's *Sing we and chant it* in that composer's *First Booke of Balletts* of 1595.[47] Equally important, as John Hill has shown, the common practice, originating in Naples and spreading to Rome and later Florence, of performing *canzonette* and *villanelle* with solo voice accompanied by chord-playing instruments such as lute, guitar, or harpsichord, was to have a formative influence on developing monody.[48] Two related styles seem to have been prevalent in Naples from at least the 1560s: an extensively-ornamented cantillational style and a much simpler and syllabic *aria in stil recitativo*, the latter expounded by the Neapolitan Scipione della Palla. Writing in 1628, the Roman nobleman Vincenzo Giustiniani dated the move to solo singing to around 1575 in Naples and particularly Rome.[49] It seems clear that, while printed versions of madrigals and *villanelle* continued to have all parts texted, in practice professional performers often preferred to sing them alone with instrumental accompaniment.

By the end of the century the tendency towards solo or small group singing was also taking root in the sacred sphere. This was driven partly by the needs of smaller institutions, which often struggled to provide the four or preferably five singers needed for standard polyphony, partly by the recognition that the solo voice was the ideal vehicle for declamation of the text, and partly by the same increased professionalism and virtuosity as was found in secular music. While the first publications of such music did not appear until the turn of the century, it is clear from contemporary documentation that the practice of small-scale *concertato* singing had been developing in various centres since the 1580s. Composers such as Asprilio Pacelli in Rome, Ludovico Grossi da Viadana, also in Rome as well as in Mantua and Cremona, and Gabriele Fattorini in Faenza experimented in different ways with music for three or fewer voices accompanied by organ.[50]

Also highly significant for the development of music was the further growth of an indigenous repertory for instruments in Italy. Composers like the Gabrielis and Claudio Merulo in Venice or Jean de Macque in Naples brought a whole new way of thinking to forms such as the ricercare, canzona, and toccata and fed an

[47] Both pieces are given in Atlas, *Anthology of Renaissance Music*, nos. 99a, 99b.

[48] John W. Hill, *Roman Monody, Cantata, and Opera from the Circles around Cardinal Montalto* (Oxford, 1997).

[49] Vincenzo Giustiniani, *Discorso sopra la musica* (Rome, 1628), Eng. trans. Carol MacClintock, MSD 9 (American Institute of Musicology, 1961).

[50] Noel O'Regan, "Asprilio Pacelli, Ludovico da Viadana and the Origins of the Roman Concerto Ecclesiastico," *Journal of Seventeenth-Century Music*, 6/1 (2000) (http://sscm-jscm.press.uiuc.edu/jscm/v6/no1/Oregan.html); Murray Bradshaw, ed., *Gabriel(e) Fattorini: I sacri concerti a due voci (1600)* (American Institute of Musicology, 1986).

ever-expanding market with regular publications of keyboard music.[51] Cornett and sackbut (and, by the end of the century, the violin) regularly accompanied large-scale church music throughout the peninsula. The employment of a permanent instrumental ensemble at the basilica of S. Marco in Venice from 1568 ensured Venetian primacy in instrumental writing. While these instruments by and large improvised parts based on the vocal lines, with few instrumental parts surviving before 1600, the stage was set for the appearance of instrument-specific parts in the early years of the next century, by Giovanni Gabrieli in particular.

That Italian composers and performers achieved so much during this period is a testimony both to their own creative powers and to the support of those who patronized them. The multiplicity of centres of patronage and of opportunities encouraged both mobility and competitive innovation. Dukes and princes used music for relaxation but also to impress their subjects and visitors with their *magnificentia*. Dynastic weddings, as in Florence, were particular occcasions for show, but also for both collaboration and competition between composers and performers. Following an initial period of uncertainty after the end of the Council of Trent in 1563, the Church recognized the important role music could play in turning minds and hearts to God, and composers were harnessed to the work of propagating the Catholic faith. Most people's experience of art music was in church, where the offices articulated the rhythms of the day, providing a basic diet of plainchant and *falsobordone* spiced up with polyphony on feast-days. Outside of church, processions—both sacred and secular—were always accompanied by music, as were devotional services in the oratories of confraternities and the more informal gatherings of Philip Neri and his followers.[52] The singing of *laudi spirituali* helped encourage the spread of Christian doctrine, while periods such as Carnival saw regular performances of secular music on the street and in palaces. In all of this activity Italian composers used every opportunity to make their mark and in the process left a hugely significant legacy.

[51] Willi Apel, *The History of Keyboard Music to 1700*, trans. Hans Tischler (Bloomington, IN, 1972); Alexander Silbiger, ed., *Keyboard Music Before 1700* (New York, 1995).

[52] Howard Smither, *A History of the Oratorio*, I: *The Oratorio in the Baroque Era: Italy, Vienna, Paris* (Chapel Hill, NC, 1977).

6

ITALY, *iii*: 1600–1640

Tim Carter

FOR many historians, Italy in the Baroque period presents a rather sorry sight. During the Renaissance, the peninsula had been a major political, economic, and cultural force: by the mid seventeenth century, Venice, Florence, and Rome were seen more as just essential stops on the tourist trail of the "grand tour." It is generally assumed that the broad factors affecting the "decline" of Italy in the early seventeenth century included the shift of trade from the Mediterranean with the opening up of new routes to the Orient and the New World, a series of economic crises (particularly in 1619–22) and plagues (about a third of the population of Venice died in 1630–31), and the dulling effects of generally reactionary systems of government (for the most part, hereditary duchies). Italy was still an acknowledged haven for the arts and sciences, at least when they could avoid the heavy arm of the Church censors. But there was—and is—a distinct feeling that world events were now being played on a different stage.

Of course, this could have its advantages. The city-states of Italy had long been pawns of the three European "superpowers" of Spain, France, and the Empire—England was only on the distant horizon—but a new political realism now lessened the threat of foreign domination. So, too, did the cohesive force of the Catholic Counter-Reformation. Spain certainly reacted sharply to Florence's apparent attempts to woo the French with the marriage of Henri IV, king of France, to Maria de' Medici in October 1600, building a fortress on the island of Elba just off the Tuscan coast. But Grand Duke Ferdinando de' Medici took the message, and in 1608 he wedded his eldest son and heir, Cosimo, to Maria Magdalena, Archduchess of Austria and sister of the Queen of Spain. The War of Mantuan Succession between the French and the Habsburgs on the death of Vincenzo II Gonzaga in 1627 had much less happy results, with the horrific sack of the city of Mantua by Imperial troops in July 1630. These troops also brought the plague to Italy (and the entourage of the Mantuan court counsellor and librettist of Monteverdi's *Orfeo*, Alessandro Striggio, carried it to Venice as he pleaded for assistance from the doge). But for the most part, Italy was troubled only by relatively minor territorial disputes, such as the annexation by the papacy of Ferrara (1598; the Este family moved to Modena) and Urbino (1631), or the squabbles between Mantua and Savoy over the long-disputed duchy of Monferrato. If there was any major threat, it perhaps came more from the East than from beyond the Alps: Duke Vincenzo I Gonzaga's three military campaigns against the Turks in Hungary in 1595–1601 were gloriously chivalric—he took to heart Tasso's vibrant epic of the First Crusade, *Gerusalemme liberata*—but ultimately futile, and Venice increasingly lost Mediterranean ground to the Ottoman Empire as the republic's renowned victory at the Battle of Lepanto in 1571 faded into a distant (if annually revived) memory.

How all this affected the arts is open to debate. Supporters of the "crisis scenario" for the period 1550–1650 that has gained some favour (but also dissent) in recent decades would be happy to project such notions of crisis onto the languid virtuosity of Mannerist art (Pontormo, Rosso Fiorentino) and literature (especially Marino), or the seemingly conflicting tendencies towards ecstatic emotionalism and austere authoritarianism characteristic of the Baroque (the Carracci, Bernini).[1] Nor have historians and critics always been sympathetic to a post-Renaissance age that in both spiritual and intellectual terms seems somewhat alien to the modern world. Certainly the apparent decline of Italy had its effects: for example, the high levels of disposable income among the merchant and upper classes available for conspicuous consumption in the arts—arguably a driving force in the Renaissance—perhaps had fallen by the 1610s as fiscal common sense shifted in favour of "safe" investments (for example, land). But even if the commercial economy weakened, this may have been compensated in some areas (e.g., Venice) by a shift in favour of producing "luxury" goods.[2] Moreover, both Church and court still needed the arts for liturgy, ceremony, and entertainment, these functional demands placing an additional premium on what continued to be seen as a civilizing and instructional force.[3] For the educated classes, too, the arts remained both a source of pleasure and a symbol of social distinction and cohesion. Business, as it were, carried on as usual.

A genre-by-genre, composer-by-composer account of music in the early seventeenth century, and the common tendency to separate out its seemingly "conservative" and "progressive" threads, invariably does scant justice to the rich musical fabric of the period.[4] One might question whether our own priorities in discussing this music—the birth of opera and solo song, the formation of the *seconda pratica*, the rise of idiomatic instrumental styles, the new resources for large-scale liturgical and ceremonial music—square with contemporary perceptions. For example, the *Discorso sopra la musica* (*c.*1628) by the Roman dilettante Vincenzo Giustiniani locates the birth of a new style (what he calls "an air new and grateful to the ear")

[1] For the "crisis" of the 17th century, and its potential association with Mannerism and Marinism, see the comments (and references) in Ch. 3 above.

[2] This is the revisionist scenario presented in Richard Tilden Rapp, *Industry and Economic Decline in Seventeenth-Century Venice* (Cambridge, MA, 1976).

[3] Cf. Janet Southorn, *Power and Display in the Seventeenth Century: The Arts and their Patrons in Modena and Ferrara* (Cambridge, 1988).

[4] The following discussion draws on, and develops, the more extended discussion of these issues in Tim Carter, *Music in Late Renaissance and Early Baroque Italy* (London, 1992).

not in the Florentine "new music"—the normal focus of modern historians—but instead in works from the 1580s, particularly the light madrigals and villanellas of Luca Marenzio. Giustiniani said that this "air" existed in music both for several voices and for solo voice and instrumental accompaniment, and that modern composers had varied the style only in matters of ornament and not in substance.[5]

Such comments suggest that the boundaries of style and genre were more fluid than we tend to think. Monteverdi was happy to write a piece for solo voice and continuo, "but if later on His Highness orders me to rearrange the air for five voices, this I shall do":[6] indeed, his *Lamento d'Arianna*, the solo-voice lament that is all that survives of his opera *Arianna* of 1608, appears in a five-voice polyphonic version in Monteverdi's *Sesto libro de madrigali a cinque voci* of 1614, and then as a sacred contrafactum to a Latin text (the "Pianto della Madonna," *Iam moriar mi fili*) in his *Selva morale e spirituale* of 1640–41. Similarly, the introit of Monteverdi's 1610 "Vespers" (*Domine ad adiuvandum*) is a flamboyant reworking of the "toccata" opening his opera *Orfeo* of 1607; and his most erotic madrigals were also published with spiritual texts in Latin guaranteed to save the blushes of the devoutest nun.[7] Nor did new genres and styles always fare as well as the textbooks would have us believe. Opera had a somewhat patchy career in the north Italian courts: Florence was not alone in retaining a preference for the old-fashioned comedy with *intermedi* or for other kinds of courtly entertainment that enabled active participation (*balli*, tournaments) rather than passive observation.[8] Giulio Caccini's pioneering collection of monodies, proudly called *Le nuove musiche* ("New Songs"; 1602), did not immediately establish a trend. And despite Monteverdi's introduction of the basso continuo to the madrigal in the last six pieces of his Fifth Book (1605)—he was anticipated by the madrigals with intabulated accompaniment for chitarrone published by his Mantuan colleague Salamone Rossi in 1600, 1602, and 1603—the traditional five-part madrigal retained a creditable standing in printers' outputs until the late 1610s, particularly in more ostensibly conservative centres such as Rome and Naples (doubtless under the influence of Gesualdo). Indeed, for some composers, the basso continuo was an irrelevance—as with

5 Giustiniani's treatise is edited in Angelo Solerti, *Le origini del melodramma: testimonianze dei contemporanei* (Turin, 1903; repr. Hildesheim, 1969), 98–128; an English version is in *Hercole Bottrigari: "Il Desiderio . . ."; Vincenzo Giustiniani: "Discorso sopra la musica"*, trans. Carol MacClintock, MSD 9 (American Institute of Musicology, 1962), 63–80. I have discussed the issues from an analytical perspective in Tim Carter, "'An Air New and Grateful to the Ear': The Concept of *Aria* in Late Renaissance and Early Baroque Italy," *Music Analysis*, 12 (1993), 127–45.

6 Monteverdi to Alessandro Striggio, 24 Aug. 1609, in Denis Stevens (trans.), *The Letters of Claudio Monteverdi* (rev. edn, Oxford, 1995), 57. For another example, see Tim Carter, "Giulio Caccini's *Amarilli, mia bella*: Some Questions (and a Few Answers)," *Journal of the Royal Musical Association*, 113 (1988), 250–73.

7 Aquilino Coppini published three books containing *contrafacta* of madrigals by Monteverdi and others in Milan in 1607, 1608, and 1609; see Margaret Ann Rorke, "Sacred Contrafacta of Monteverdi Madrigals and Cardinal Borromeo's Milan," *Music & Letters*, 65 (1984), 168–75. The practice is also observable in northern Europe.

8 Tim Carter, "The North Italian Courts," in *Man & Music*, III: *The Early Baroque Era: From the Late 16th Century to the 1660s*, ed. Curtis A. Price (London, 1993), 23–48.

instrumental "basso seguente" parts, following the lowest sounding voice—or even a downright nuisance (witness the complaints in Cesare Zoilo's *Madrigali a cinque il primo*, 1620).

For that matter, a statistical survey of printer's outputs casts doubt on the common emphasis on secular music as a whole in early Baroque Italy.[9] We know of 29 prints of sacred music and 66 prints of secular music published in Italy in 1585; for 1620, the proportions are almost exactly reversed (62 sacred prints to 30 secular). Despite the obvious dangers of such crude statistics, the picture seems clear enough: from the early 1600s onwards, Italian music printers significantly reoriented their output away from secular music in favour of sacred music (motets, psalms, Masses, etc.). New styles of secular music were not well suited to that mainstay of the sixteenth-century music trade, the amateur of moderate abilities wanting madrigals to sing round the table. And the present stability of the Church and its liturgies—in contrast to the mid sixteenth century—meant that printers could hope for a large, fixed market for their wares. Add to that the Counter-Reformation predilection for devotional music (motets, spiritual madrigals) used outside liturgical contexts—in confraternities or domestic settings—and the new emphases of the period become clear.

Sacred music was not necessarily reactionary: the Church soon latched on to the most modern trends—not least because of their rhetorical and emotional power—to the extent that contemporary audiences may well have come into contact with the "new music" more in sacred contexts than in secular ones. Emilio de' Cavalieri was quick to produce a sacred opera, the *Rappresentatione di Anima, et di Corpo*, performed at the Oratorio di S. Maria in Vallicella in Rome in February 1600 (it was published that same year), and his example was followed by Agostino Agazzari's *Eumelio*, performed at the Roman Seminary in 1606, and by the sacred dialogues of Giovanni Francesco Anerio's *Teatro armonico spirituale* of 1619. Similarly, Gabriele Fattorini noted in 1600 that

> although it can in no way be denied that, at great celebrations, choral groups which are harmonious and well endowed with various kinds of musical expression provide the greatest delight and are most suitable, nevertheless when one voice sings the divine praises skilfully and sweetly, or when at the very most two voices sing on occasion accompanied by the organ, experience teaches over and over again that the flagging spirits of the singers are restored, the fervent attitudes of the listeners improved, and their minds seized with heavenly love.[10]

The point is made still clearer in Ottavio Durante's *Arie devote* (1608), containing

[9] Angelo Pompilio, "Editoria musicale a Napoli e in Italia nel Cinque–Seicento," in *Musica e cultura a Napoli dal XV al XIX secolo*, ed. Lorenzo Bianconi and Renata Bossa (Florence, 1983), 79–102; Tim Carter, "Music Publishing in Italy, c.1580–c.1625: Some Preliminary Observations," *Royal Musical Association Research Chronicle*, 20 (1986–87), 19–37.

[10] From the dedication of Fattorini's *I sacri concerti a due voci* (Venice, 1600); trans. Christopher Wilkinson, "Gabriele Fattorini: Rival of Viadana", *Music & Letters*, 65 (1984), 330.

solo songs directly inspired by Caccini (the debt is acknowledged in Durante's preface).

Older styles still had their part to play, particularly (for historical and functional reasons) in Mass music. Palestrina was dutifully imitated by many of his Roman followers (Giovanni Francesco Anerio, Asola, Giovanelli, Soriano), and indeed his most famous work, the *Missa Papae Marcelli*—reported in 1607 to have "saved" music from banishment by the Council of Trent (a myth, but a remarkably potent one)[11]—was reworked for eight voices by Francesco Soriano in 1609, and for four by Giovanni Francesco Anerio in 1619. When Monteverdi moved to Venice in 1613 as *maestro di cappella* of St Mark's Basilica—which lay at the heart of the city's ceremonial and liturgical life—he restocked its library with polyphonic masses by Palestrina, Soriano, and Lassus, among others,[12] and himself contributed two *a cappella* polyphonic masses to the repertory (published in his *Selva morale e spirituale* of 1640–41 and the *Messa . . . et salmi* of 1650); his first such mass, parodying a motet by Nicolas Gombert, had been included in his *Sanctissimae virgini missa . . . ac vespere* of 1610. Adrian Willaert's double-choir psalm-settings from the mid sixteenth century were also still being performed in St Mark's in the second decade of the seventeenth century, providing a continuity of tradition and a powerful evocation of Venice's past glories.[13]

It seems clear that the shifting preferences for "old" and "new" styles in sacred music were determined less by geography than by genre and function: Monteverdi's own spectacular combination of old and new in the *Sanctissimae virgini missa . . . ac vespere*—the six-voice *Missa "In illo tempore"* on a Franco-Flemish model contrasting with the *concertato* styles and modern virtuosic vocal writing of the "Vespers"—was not necessarily aimed at Rome and Venice respectively. Similarly, *concertato* techniques came late to the Mass, long after they had been accepted in Vesper psalms and motets: Monteverdi's *Gloria a 7. voci*, perhaps written for the celebrations marking the liberation of Venice from the plague in 1631, is a special example,[14] although there are precedents. Monteverdi was only one of many who could adopt different styles and techniques as the need arose, confounding the attempts of modern historians to pigeon-hole composers and their music. After all, this was a skill expected of any serious *maestro di cappella*.

[11] The story first appears in Agostino Agazzari's *Del sonare sopra 'l basso con tutti li strumenti e dell'uso loro in concerto* (Siena, 1607), trans. in Oliver Strunk, *Source Readings in Music History*, rev. edn, IV: *The Baroque Era*, ed. Margaret Murata (New York and London, 1998), 113–20; see p. 120. For the broader issues, see Gino Stefani, "Miti barocchi: Palestrina 'Princeps musicae,'" *Nuova rivista musicale italiana*, 8 (1974), 347–55.

[12] Paolo Fabbri, *Monteverdi*, trans. Tim Carter (Cambridge, 1994), 132–33.

[13] James H. Moore, "The *Vespero delli Cinque Laudate* and the Role of *Salmi spezzati* at St. Mark's," *Journal of the American Musicological Society*, 34 (1981), 249–78.

[14] James H. Moore, "*Venezia favorita da Maria*: Music for the Madonna Nicopeia and Santa Maria della Salute," *Journal of the American Musicological Society*, 37 (1984), 299–355; but compare Jeffrey Kurtzman and Linda Koldau, "Trombe, Trombe d'argento, Trombe squarciate, Tromboni, and Pifferi in Venetian Processions and Ceremonies of the Sixteenth and Seventeenth Centuries," *Journal of Seventeenth-Century Music*, 8/1 (2002), § 43 (http://sscm-jscm.press.uiuc.edu/jscm/v8/no1/Kurtzman_V.html#43).

These wide-ranging demands for music within and outside the liturgy had their effect on the staffing of ecclesiastical institutions. The choir of the Cappella Sistina in Rome was fixed at thirty-two singers in 1625, and when he arrived at St Mark's, Monteverdi could count on some thirty singers and six instrumentalists, although another sixteen instrumentalists were regularly imported for special services (well over twenty times a year). Lesser churches clearly were more constrained: this was a market for which Lodovico Grossi da Viadana specifically catered with his small-scale *concerti ecclesiastici*, avoiding, Viadana said, the need for small ensembles to perform cut-down versions of larger-scale polyphony, omitting one or more parts to the detriment both of the texture and of the text.[15] But even a relatively provincial centre such as Bergamo (in the Veneto) sought to maintain a significant musical establishment: in August 1614, the church of Santa Maria Maggiore employed a *maestro di cappella* (Giovanni Cavaccio), two organists, five sopranos, three altos, three tenors, two basses, and seven instrumentalists, and in 1627 it secured the services as *maestro* of Monteverdi's most distinguished colleague at St Mark's, Alessandro Grandi.[16]

Secular institutions could be no less well provided. In the first decade of the seventeenth century, the Medici court in Florence paid salaries to some fifteen singers and thirteen instrumentalists (wind, string, and keyboard players, lutenists, and two French violinists), including specialized groups such as Giulio Caccini's *concerto di donne* (his wife, daughters Francesca and Settimia, and pupils), the *concerto de' castrati* (two castratos and a director/accompanist), and the Franciosini, a wind band (although individual members played other instruments).[17] Such ensembles inevitably determined the resources available for specific occasions: the point is obvious in a work such as Monteverdi's *Orfeo* (1607), which was designed precisely for the ten or so male singers employed at the Mantuan court.[18] But again, when it came to special events more musicians could be brought in: for example, in Florence the last of the 1608 *intermedi* celebrating the wedding of Cosimo de' Medici and Maria Magdalena of Austria had thirty-six singers and thirty instrumentalists (as well as fifteen dancers) on stage, including two virtuosos imported from Rome, the soprano Ippolita Recupito and the bass Melchior Palantrotti (he had already performed in Peri's *Euridice* in 1600).[19] Recupito was in the service of Cardinal Montalto, who himself maintained a significant musical establishment and encouraged music in sacred, secular, and theatrical contexts.[20]

[15] Carter, *Music in Late Renaissance and Early Baroque Italy*, 225–26.

[16] Jerome Roche, "Music at S. Maria Maggiore, Bergamo, 1614–1643," *Music & Letters*, 47 (1966), 296–312. The musical establishment fluctuated due to economic and other pressures, but in 1620 it had nine singers, two organists, and four instrumentalists (two violins, cornett, trombone).

[17] Warren Kirkendale, *The Court Musicians in Florence during the Principate of the Medici, with a Reconstruction of the Artistic Establishment*, Historiae musicae cultores Biblioteca, 61 (Florence, 1993).

[18] Tim Carter, "Singing *Orfeo*: On the Performers of Monteverdi's First Opera," *Recercare*, 11 (1999), 75–118.

[19] Tim Carter, "A Florentine Wedding of 1608," *Acta musicologica*, 55 (1983), 89–107.

[20] John Walter Hill, *Roman Monody in the Circle of Cardinal Montalto*, 2 vols. (Oxford, 1997).

Clearly, performing virtuosity was at premium. Vittoria Archilei and Francesca Caccini were highly prized as sopranos in Florence, and the Neapolitan singer Adriana Basile was lured to Mantua in 1610 (with her poet brother Giovan Battista) by the promise of lavish remuneration and recognition.[21] The Roman castrato Francesco Severi published a collection of *Salmi passaggiati . . . sopra i falsi bordoni di tutti i tuoni ecclesiastici* (1615), displaying the spectacular techniques of embellished singing employed within the papal chapel. These techniques were also carried over into instrumental music. The lutenists Alessandro Piccinini in Bologna and Johann Hieronymus Kapsberger in Rome were renowned virtuosos in their field, as was Ippolita Recupito's husband Orazio Michi on the harp and the Brescian Biagio Marini on the violin. The organist Girolamo Frescobaldi may have been the butt of Giovan Battista Doni's typical disdain for performers: "he is a very coarse man, although he plays the organ perfectly and may be excellent for composing fantasies, dance music, and similar things; but for setting the words, he is extremely ignorant and devoid of discrimination, so that one can say he has all his knowledge at the ends of his fingers."[22] But Frescobaldi was secure in his post as organist of the Cappella Giulia in St Peter's from 1608 until his death in 1643 (with spells in Mantua in 1615 and Florence in 1628–34). For performers with talent—and the right patron—the rewards were great indeed.

Court composers may have had a harder time. Sigismondo d'India was born in Palermo, Sicily, and spent the first years of his professional career as a touring singer and composer, passing through Florence (?1600), Mantua (1606), Florence (1608), Rome and Naples (?1608), and then Parma and Piacenza (1610) before being appointed director of chamber music at the lavish court of Carlo Emanuele I, duke of Savoy, in 1611. But malicious gossip forced him to leave Turin in May 1623, whereupon he resumed a peripatetic career between Rome and the Este court in Modena (where there was, he said, "a gathering . . . of the best singers to be heard in Europe").[23] Claudio Monteverdi was trained in Cremona and moved to the Gonzaga court in Mantua as a string-player in 1590 or 1591. His career under Duke Vincenzo was not untypical: he was initially attached to the instrumentalist Giacomo Cattaneo, married his daughter, the singer Claudia (such arranged marriages were common between court musicians, not least to keep the wife active in court service), and worked his way up the ranks by service and publication to the position of the duke's *maestro della musica di camera*. But despite his achievements in Mantua—including three books of madrigals (added to the two already

[21] Tim Carter, "Finding a Voice: Vittoria Archilei and the Florentine 'New Music,'" in *Feminism and Renaissance Studies*, ed. Lorna Hutson (Oxford, 1999), 450–67; Suzanne Cusick, "Of Women, Music, and Power: A Model from Seicento Florence," in *Musicology and Difference: Gender and Sexuality in Music Scholarship*, ed. Ruth Solie (Berkeley and Los Angeles, 1993), 281–304; Alessando Ademollo, *La bell'Adriana ed altre virtuose del suo tempo alla corte di Mantova* (Città di Castello, 1888).

[22] For Doni's remark on Frescobaldi (made in a letter to Marin Mersenne, 22 July 1640), see Frederick Hammond, *Frescobaldi* (Cambridge, MA, 1983), 85.

[23] The comment is made in the dedication (to Isabella d'Este) of d'India's *Ottavo libro de madrigali a cinque voci* (Rome, 1626).

published), two operas, and various sacred and occasional works—he found the city oppressive and court life increasingly frustrating as he was overworked and underpaid by the duke. His peremptory dismissal by Duke Francesco Gonzaga in 1612 was only the last in a series of unhappy events encouraging the composer to seek employment elsewhere. The vacancy at St Mark's came at an opportune time, and although the Gonzaga made several attempts to lure Monteverdi back to Mantua, he remained in Venice, where, he said, his duties were regular, his salary was paid, and free-lance opportunities were ripe for the picking.

The careers of both d'India and Monteverdi might suggest that the north Italian courts were losing their creative force by the second or third decades of the century. Although Monteverdi still wrote music for Mantua, and more spectacularly for the wedding of Odoardo Farnese and Margherita de' Medici in Parma in 1628, his most significant courtly connection seems to have been with the Habsburgs in Vienna (the fruits are clear in his Eighth Book of Madrigals, the *Madrigali guerrieri, et amorosi* of 1638).[24] Some historians have painted a dismal picture for Florence in the 1620s when, on the death of Grand Duke Cosimo II in 1621, his wife Maria Magdalena and mother Christine of Lorraine acted as regents for the young Ferdinando II. But such anti-court prejudice may not be justified: in the case of Florence, for example, the regency opened up new spaces for women—including Francesca Caccini, whose opera-tournament *La liberazione di Ruggiero dall'isola d'Alcina* (based on Ariosto) was performed in 1625—and also produced a healthy number of religious dramas (often concerning female saints) sponsored by Florentine confraternities such as the Compagnia dell'Arcangelo Raffaello, with music by Marco da Gagliano and his brother Giovan Battista.[25]

Nor was Rome a last bastion of conservatism. Its sacred music was more varied than has tended to be assumed, with its polychoral music for voices and instruments vying with the reputation normally granted to Venice in this medium.[26] Opera may have had a rather fragmented history in the Holy City, but particularly after the election of Maffeo Barberini as Pope Urban VIII in 1623, it gained some stability. The Barberini were staunchly committed to the arts—not just for political ends—and the performance of Stefano Landi's *Sant'Alessio* (the first of several hagiographical works) at the 3,000-seat theatre within the Barberini's Palazzo alle Quattro Fontane in Carnival 1632 initiated a regular series of operas performed under their aegis.[27] The Barberini also supported the noted Florentine theorist,

24 Steven Saunders, "New Light on the Genesis of Monteverdi's Eighth Book of Madrigals," *Music & Letters*, 77 (1996), 183–93. There is here, however, a Mantuan connection, given the marriage of Eleonora Gonzaga to Emperor Ferdinand II.

25 Kelley Harness, "'Amazzoni di Dio': Florentine Musical Spectacle under Maria Maddalena d'Austria and Cristina di Lorena (1620–30)" (PhD diss., University of Illinois, Urbana-Champaign, 1996); eadem, "Chaste Warriors and Virgin Martyrs in Early Florentine Opera," in *Gender, Sexuality, and Early Music*, ed. Todd Borgerding (New York, 2002), 71–121.

26 Graham Dixon, "The Origins of the Roman 'Colossal Baroque,'" *Proceedings of the Royal Musical Association*, 106 (1979/80), 115–28; Noel O'Regan, "Sacred Polychoral Music in Rome, 1575–1621" (DPhil diss., University of Oxford, 1988).

27 Frederick Hammond, *Music and Spectacle in Baroque Rome: Barberini Patronage under Urban VIII* (New Haven and London, 1994).

Giovan Battista Doni (whose invention of a new instrument on Classical lines, the "lyra barberina," paid direct homage to his patrons); and composers associated with the Barberini and other Roman families, not least Luigi Rossi and Marco Marazzoli, had a significant influence on the emergence of new genres of secular music, in particular the cantata. Moreover, we now know that musicians variously associated with Rome were closely involved in the emergence of "public" opera in Venice in the late 1630s, such as the composer and singer Francesco Manelli and the poet, composer, and lutenist Benedetto Ferrari, both of whom provided the first operas staged at the Teatro S. Cassiano in Venice, *Andromeda* (1637) and *La maga fulminata* (1638).

Reading contemporary comment from the late 1620s onwards, there is a clear sense that change was in the air, and not always to the good. Vincenzo Giustiniani ended his survey (*c.*1628) of music in his lifetime on a rather ambivalent note, lamenting the decline of the polyphonic madrigal and the increasing emphasis on music as a listener's art (for all the delights of contemporary singing) rather than one in which learned connoisseurs could actively participate; like many Romans, he also doubted the merits of the new recitative, which often, he claimed, tended to boredom. For the madrigal, he was followed by Giovan Battista Doni in 1635 ("the madrigalian art is understood only by the experts") and the composer Domenico Mazzocchi in 1638 ("today few are composed, and fewer are sung, given that to their misfortune they seem more or less banned from the Academies").[28] Perhaps the most extreme example is the Florentine monk Severo Bonini, who in his *Discorsi e regole sovra la musica* (*c.*1650) said with heavy heart:

> Do you not see that today one is only concerned with composing little arias for one and two voices concerted with harpsichords or similar instruments? Madrigals to be sung at the table without instruments have been sent to oblivion, as is church music, all of which are too composed, and so little by little one will carry on losing this art, because today hard work seems somewhat unhealthy, having given the boot to the rules of Zarlino and to however many books one finds by rule-givers, with [musicians] acting according to their whim, believing in this idiotic maxim, that he who composed the rules is a man like the others.[29]

The poet and *letterato* Tommaso Stigliani also seems to sum up a general feeling of aesthetic world-weariness:

> At one time, readers contented themselves with readings that were not bad, then they wanted excellence, then they desired marvels, and today they look for stupors; but after having found them, they hold them boring and aspire to amazements and to astonishments. What must we do in so indifferent a time,

[28] Carter, *Music in Late Renaissance and Early Baroque Italy*, 241–42. Mazzocchi's comment comes from the preface to his *Madrigali a cinque voci, et altri varii concerti* (Rome, 1638).

[29] Carter, *Music in Late Renaissance and Early Baroque Italy*, 242.

> and so *delicata* and *bizzarra* an age, whose taste is so calloused and so obtuse that by now it no longer feels anything?[30]

But the Olivetan monk Secondo Lancellotti had little truck with those who moaned about life "hoggidì" (today):

> So many sufferings, so many complaints against the actions and the customs of the present, so many praises, so many damaging encomiums to the century already past, that they fill the surrounding air and deafen human ears almost more than the cascades of the Nile. "HOGGIDI" this is not done, "HOGGIDI" this is not said. "Once it was done," "once it was said," "The world is in a bad state, the world goes from bad to worse." "One can no longer live HOGGIDI."

Lancelloti's *L'hoggidì, overo Il mondo non peggiore nè più calamitoso del passato* (Venice, 1623) sought to prove that the world was no worse, nor more calamitous, than the past.[31] Pietro della Valle made much the same claim in his *Della musica dell'età nostra che non è punto inferiore, anzi è migliore di quella dell'età passata* ("Of the music of our time, which is not at all inferior but, rather, is better than that of the past age"; dated 16 January 1640).[32] Italian music of the first half of the seventeenth century had certainly changed significantly, but whether for better or for worse was for posterity to decide.

[30] Stigliani's letter of 4 March 1636 is given in Robert R. Holzer, "'Sono d'altro garbo . . . le canzonette che si cantano oggi': Pietro della Valle on Music and Modernity in the Seventeenth Century," *Studi musicali*, 22 (1992), 253–306, at 269. The present discussion owes a significant debt to Holzer.

[31] See ibid., 282–5. Lancellotti published a second *L'hoggidì* volume, *L'hoggidì, overo Gl'ingegni non inferiori à' passati* (Venice, 1636). Here the focus is on "intellects not inferior to those of the past."

[32] Della Valle's text is given in Solerti, *Le origini del melodramma*, 148–79, and is partially trans. in Strunk, *Source Readings in Music History*, IV: 36–43.

7

MUSIC FOR THE MASS

Allan W. Atlas

THE polyphonic mass of the Renaissance—especially the cyclic variety in which a single melodic or multi-voice "theme" cuts across and thus unifies all five liturgical "movements": Kyrie, Gloria, Credo, Sanctus, and Agnus Dei[1]—presents a paradox in terms of its reception. While the conventional musicological wisdom of our own day (beginning in the mid nineteenth century with August Wilhelm Ambros and developed in such landmark studies as those by Peter Wagner and Manfred Bukofzer)[2] has generally granted the cyclic mass "masterwork" status on the grounds of its organically unified structure, the few fifteenth- and sixteenth-century writers who addressed the matter viewed it in a different light. Thus Johannes Tinctoris and Paolo Cortese praised the mass for its social-religious function, calling it "cantus magnus" and "propitiary song," respectively,[3] while the Nuremberg publisher Hans Ott emphasized the opportunity that the cylic mass afforded for the display of compositional *varietas*, as composers constantly dressed the recurring cantus firmus—or even an entire multi-voice fabric—in new polyphonic garb, and so avoided the potential "boredom" (*fastidium*) of

For their help with various aspects of this essay, I am grateful to Professors Richard Charteris, Barbara Hanning, and Mark A. Pottinger, as I am to Lawrence Shuster, a doctoral candidate in the PhD program in Music, The Graduate School, The City University of New York.

[1] Each of the five portions of the Mass Ordinary is subdivided into two or more sections that correspond to the main articulations in the text: Kyrie–Christe–Kyrie; Gloria in excelsis Deo (intoned as chant by the priest)–Et in terra pax–Qui tollis peccata mundi, etc.

[2] Ambros, *Geschichte der Musik*, II (Leipzig, 1864; 3rd edn, ed. Heinrich Reimann, 1891), III (Leipzig, 1868; 3rd edn, ed. Otto Kade, 1893); Wagner, *Geschichte der Messe* (Leipzig, 1913); Bukofzer, "*Caput:* A Liturgico-Musical Study," in his *Studies in Medieval and Renaissance Music* (New York, 1950), 217–310. It was Wagner, in fact, who coined the term "cycle" (*Zyklus*) in connection with the Mass. My exposition of the paradox leans heavily on Andrew Kirkman, "The Invention of the Cyclic Mass," *Journal of the American Musicological Society*, 54 (2001), 1–47.

[3] Tinctoris, *Terminorum musicae diffinitorium* (*c.*1472–73); see the Latin–English edition in *Dictionary of Musical Terms*, ed. Carl Parrish (New York, 1963; repr. 1978), 40–41; Cortese, *De cardinilatu* (1510), in Nino Pirrotta, "Musical and Cultural Tendencies in 15th-Century Italy," *Journal of the American Musicological Society*, 19 (1966), 142–43, 150, 154–55, 159–60.

the repeated material.[4] Ott, then, expressed the sixteenth-century point of view in the clearest of terms: it was the Aristotelian concept of variety within unity—not merely the sense of unity alone—that distinguished the cyclic mass.

Yet despite the different vantage points—both within the Renaissance itself and between that period and ours—it seems clear that, with the development of the cyclic mass at the hands of the English circa 1430,[5] the polyphonic mass in general and the cyclic variety in particular did acquire a position of prestige, one that grew steadily during the fifteenth century and then—except where buffeted by religion and politics—continued to hold its own throughout the sixteenth. Only around 1600, under the pressure of sweeping changes that affected virtually every aspect of elite (and thus church) music—from the stylistic/aesthetic to the strategies of marketing both music and musicians—did the mass begin to relinquish its central position as a "masterwork" (again, our term) and adopt a more functional role.

Our survey of the shifting fortunes of the mass is divided into six sections: (1) the years around 1520, (2) the two decades from around 1530 to circa 1550, (3) the second half of the sixteenth century, (4) a discussion of various aspects of performance practice that cuts across the preceding periods, (5) the early seventeenth century, and (6) a concluding note.

Circa 1520

It was around 1520 that the generation of Josquin des Prez, Jacob Obrecht, Henricus Isaac, and Pierre de la Rue reached its end. With respect to music for the Mass, they and their contemporaries mark a turning point of sorts, as they synthesized past traditions and carved out new procedures that would influence the genre's development for the remainder of the century.

In the broadest of terms, Josquin and his contemporaries cultivated two different types of masses: one in which there is a sense of cyclic unity across the movements and which, in effect, may be said to constitute a central tradition, and another in which such unity is eschewed, whether for special liturgical reasons or as a legacy of local traditions.

[4] Ott, preface to *Missae tredecim quatuor vocum* (Nuremberg, 1539); for the original passage and translations, see Kirkman, "The Invention of the Cyclic Mass," 14–15, and Royston Gustavson, "Hans Ott, Hieronymous Formschneider, and the *Novum et insigne opus musicum* (Nuremberg, 1537–1538)," (PhD diss., University of Melbourne, 1999), II: 562–65.

[5] Attributions to three composers intersect with four masses: John Dunstable, *Missa "Gaudiorum premia"*; Leonel Power, *Missa "Alma redemptoris mater"*; and two Masses with conflicting attributions: *Missa "Rex seculorum"*, attributed to Dunstable and Power, and *Missa sine nomine*, ascribed to Dunstable, Power, and John Benet. For modern editions of these and all other Masses cited, see the first part of the Bibliography to this chapter.

The central tradition

Masses in which all the movements were based on the same model could follow one of three different procedures in terms of borrowed material and the way in which it was treated. The most archaic of these—though still full of life—was the straightforward cantus-firmus mass in which a pre-existent monophonic melody, or a single voice part from a secular song (usually the tenor of a French chanson), or a newly invented melody—short, sharply etched, and often treated in quasi-ostinato fashion—was placed primarily (if not exclusively) in the tenor, where it generally rolled out in note values that were longer than those in the surrounding parts and served as a scaffold-like anchor from one movement to the next. Josquin's *Missa "L'homme armé" super voces musicales*, Obrecht's *Missa "Fortuna desperata"*, and Josquin's *Missa "Hercules dux Ferrariae"* are cantus-firmus masses built respectively upon the three different types of models.

Rather freer in its treatment of the model is the so-called "paraphrase" (a modern term) mass. Here a single, pre-existent melody, propelled by the new style of pervading imitation, wends its way through all the voice parts, now in the same flowing rhythm as the other voices, and with melodic embellishment that ranges from the lightly ornamental to that so lavish as to make the original melody difficult to hear. Josquin's *Missa "Pange lingua"*, based on the hymn for Vespers of Corpus Christi, stands as a textbook example of the type.

Finally, there is the mass that was based not on a single melody, but on a pre-existent polyphonic complex as a whole. And while this type had its roots in procedures already developed during the third quarter of the fifteenth century, composers of the Josquin generation gave it a new twist. Unlike their predecessors—one thinks of Ockeghem, Johannes Martini, and Vincenet du Bruecquet, among others—who would draw on a polyphonic model that had its own structural tenor (a three-voice chanson, for example), alluded to the polyphonic whole at the beginning of a movement, but then continued by drawing mainly on the structural tenor alone (in cantus-firmus or paraphrase style), composers such as Jean Mouton and Antonius Rycke (known as Divitis) looked to a different kind of polyphonic model altogether for their *Missae "Quem dicunt homines"*: a motet by a younger contemporary, Jean Richafort, that is itself permeated by pervading imitation (in which all voices obtain a degree of structural equality) and so lacks a structural tenor of its own. Thus when Mouton and Divitis borrowed from the model, they drew on "combinations" of voices, points of imitation and all: there is no structural tenor on which the mass can rest; there is no cantus-firmus style to which the composer can retreat. Best known to us today by the problematic term "parody" mass (see below), it was this type of setting, probably born at the royal court of France early in the sixteenth century, that would predominate in the decades that followed, and we shall look at it more closely in the following section on the mass circa 1530–1550.

Non-cyclic mass types

A number of important mass types eschewed cyclic unity. The *Missa de beata virgine* and Requiem mass did so for liturgical reasons. Here each polyphonic movement was based on a chant of its own type: polyphonic Kyrie on a Kyrie chant, and so on. They differed, however, in their degree of standardization. Whereas polyphonic masses in honor of the Blessed Virgin generally set the same (or nearly the same) chants and consisted of the movements of the Ordinary only (the Gloria with a series of textual tropes in honor of Mary),[6] the Requiem mass did not become standardized in terms of which chants it set until Pope Pius IV, following the reforms of the Council of Trent, issued a new Missal in 1570. Thus Pierre de la Rue's well-known Requiem draws on the tract "Sicut cervus" instead of the soon-to-become-standard "Absolve Domine" and omits altogether both the gradual (as did Brumel's Requiem) and the sequence "Dies irae" (which Brumel included).[7]

A sense of cyclic unity is similarly missing in two mass types that belonged mainly to a Central-European (German/Austrian) tradition and attained their high point in the works of Isaac. Thus both his so-called "plainsong" Ordinaries for specific saints' days and other feasts (normally set without the Credo and with alternation between polyphony and chant) and the liturgical cycles of Propers that make up the three volumes of his *Choralis constantinus* (completed by Ludwig Senfl and published by Hieronymous Formschneider at Nuremberg in 1550–55) parallel the *Beata virgine* and Requiem traditions in basing each polyphonic movement on a corresponding plainchant. Common to all of these mass types is either a straightforward cantus-firmus approach or the more florid "paraphrase" technique.

Still another type of mass that drew on multiple cantus firmi set the Ordinary only and did so without the one-to-one correspondence between polyphony and chant (that is, polyphonic Kyrie on a Kyrie chant, etc.). Thus Obrecht's *Missa "Sub tuum praesidium"*, based mainly on the eponymous Marian antiphon, piles up additional Marian chants in each of the last three movements until the Agnus Dei absorbs four such melodies simultaneously. Other examples of this mass type include Obrecht's *Missae de Sancto Donatiano* and *de Sancto Martini*, Matthaeus Pipelare's *Missa de Sancto Livino* (which draws on no fewer than twenty chants), and the closely related *Missa de Sancto Job* by La Rue, to name just a few that share a common provenance in the Low Countries and were transmitted in such a way as to

[6] The *Missa de beata virgine* customarily utilized Kyrie IX (occasionally IV), Gloria IX, Credo I, Sanctus XVII (occasionally IX or IV), and Agnus XVII (occasionally IX or IV), using the convenient numbering of the cycles of Ordinary chants in the *Liber usualis* (Tournai, 1961), 16–78. The Gloria tropes (in italics) are inserted as follows:

> Domine Fili unigenite, Jesu Christe. *Spiritus et alme orphanorum Paraclite.* Domine Deus Agnus Dei, Filius Patris. *Primogenitus Mariae virginis matris.* Qui tollis peccata mundi, miserere nobis. Qui tollis peccata mundi, suscipe deprecationem nostrum. *Ad Mariae Gloriam.* Qui sedes ad dexteram Patris, miserere nobis. Quoniam tu solus sanctus. *Mariam sanctificans.* Tu solus Dominus. *Mariam gubernans.* Tu solus altissimus. *Mariam coronans.* Jesu Christe . . .

[7] Although the Requiem Mass draws on both the Ordinary and the Proper of the Mass, two portions of the former—Gloria and Credo—were omitted both before and after the Tridentine reforms.

support the idea that they were perfomed polytextually. Finally, there were masses with multiple secular cantus firmi, among them Obrecht's two *Missae plurimorum carminum*[8] and Isaac's *Missa carminum*, which incorporates the well-known German song *Innsbruck, ich muss dich lassen* among others.

Despite the somewhat cautionary note (at the head of this essay) concerning the differences between sixteenth-century and modern views of the polyphonic mass, there can be little doubt that the mass held a certain *musical* pride of place around 1520: it was the grandest of the polyphonic genres, certainly in terms of sheer weight (though the five "movements" were spread out across the service, with only the Kyrie and Gloria sung without intervening chants, prayers, or action) and probably in terms of contrapuntal intricacy (as in, for example, masses that proceed in canon from beginning to end).[9] Yet perhaps there is something missing at times: a sense of intensity, a sense of expressing the explicit meaning and especially the emotional content of the text—in short, the influence of the humanist concern for the intelligibility and musical expression of the meaning and emotion of the word that was already making itself felt in the motet and even the secular music of the time. Indeed, the mass was beginning to display the emotional conservatism (relative to other genres) that would mark it for the remainder of the century.

Circa 1530–1550

During the second quarter of the sixteenth century, the homogeneity of the Franco-Flemish style, which had characterized sacred polyphony for approximately a century, began to splinter. Moreover, the fortunes of the mass would henceforth vary according to religious persuasions, as the genre became subject to the Catholic–Protestant conflicts that were to tear Europe apart for an entire century to come. Still, we can speak about a mainstream tradition—an outgrowth of the Franco-Flemish style—and a group of parallel traditions that ran alongside it.

The "parody" mass in the Netherlandish mainstream

The extent to which the "parody" (or "imitation") mass (on the terminology, see below) came to dominate what might be called the Netherlandish mainstream—which, in terms of mass composition, flowed out from the Low Countries to Italy, Spain, and those German-speaking territories that remained Catholic—can be seen by reviewing its prominence in the masses of six leading composers from both the second quarter of the century century and beyond (Table 7.1), most of whom distinctly favored this approach.[10] Only Cristóbal de Morales employed the parody

[8] The titles were devised by the editors of *The New Obrecht Edition;* see the entry for Obrecht in the first part of the Bibliography.

[9] For example, the *Missae ad fugam* by Josquin and Palestrina, or La Rue's *Missa "Ave sanctissima Maria"*, which is based on a motet that is itself canonic.

[10] The numbers are derived from the work-lists in *The New Grove Dictionary of Music and Musicians*, 2nd edn, ed. Stanley Sadie and John Tyrrell (London, 2001): Clemens, VI: 29 (Willem

Table 7.1: The prominence of the parody type among the masses of six composers.

	masses	parody type	model	
			sacred	secular
Clemens	15	13	7	6
Gombert	10	8	6	2
Morales	22	8	6	2
Palestrina	104	51	42	9
Lassus	64	46	24	22
Victoria	20	16	15	1

type for much less than a majority, and Palestrina only for about half, though both wrote more masses of that type than any other.

Morales's *Missa "Quaeramus cum pastoribus"* (Rome, 1544), based on a motet by Mouton, may serve as an example of the type. Example 7.1 (overleaf) superimposes the opening of Mouton's motet above that of Morales's Kyrie. On the largest scale, Morales expands the number of voices from four to what was becoming an increasingly popular five (there are six in the final Agnus Dei), as he adds a second bassus which thickens the texture. On a smaller scale—to focus on the reworking at the beginning of Kyrie I of Mouton's opening point of imitation—he adds a quickly moving countermotive in the lower voices, breaks down the symmetry provided by Mouton's strict paired imitation and its "tonic–dominant" alternation, alters the time intervals between entries, and extends the point of imitation with a fifth entrance (on the fourth degree of the scale, as if to emphasize this added entrance). Yet Morales retains an important feature of Mouton's motet: throughout the Kyrie (and the mass as a whole) he borrows and reworks only those motives that had functioned as structural pillars and "frames" of sorts in the motet, using them to similar purpose in his own work. Table 7.2 outlines the points of correspondence in the Kyrie, showing how mass and motet are related not only thematically but structurally as well.

Clearly, the art of parody technique lay not in simple quotation, but in thoroughly reworking the pre-existent model, connecting its motives to one another with newly composed music, and, in so doing, fashioning something new from something old.

If parody technique was kaleidoscopic in its possibilities, certain basic procedures nevertheless crystallized, enough so that the theorist Pietro Cerone could look back from the early seventeenth century and—leaning on an earlier formulation by Pietro Pontio—offer a set of rules for how to write such a mass in his

Elders and Kristine Forney); Gombert, X: 119–21 (George Nugent and Eric Jas); Lassus, XIV: 307–8 (James Haar); Morales, XVII: 87–89 (Robert Stevenson and Alejandro Enrique Planchart); Palestrina, XVIII: 948–49 (Lewis Lockwood, Noel O'Regan, and Jessie Anne Owens); Victoria, XXVI: 535–36 (Robert Stevenson).

Table 7.2: Points of structural correspondence in Morales's mass (Kyrie I) and Mouton's motet.

Mouton	Morales
opening of *prima pars* (= Ex. 7.1a)	opening of Kyrie I (= Ex. 7.1b)
end of first half of *prima pars* = "Noe" refrain	end of Kyrie I
opening of second half of *prima pars*	opening of Christe
end of *prima pars* = "Noe" refrain	end of Christe
opening of *secunda pars*	opening of Kyrie II
end of *secunda pars* = "Noe" refrain	end of Kyrie II

El melopeo y maestro of 1613. And though Cerone bases his prescriptions on the practice of Palestrina and his contemporaries, Morales already anticipates most of them a generation earlier:[11]

> (1) . . . in composing a mass, it is . . . necessary and obligatory that the inventions ["subjects"] at the beginnings of the first Kyrie . . . Gloria . . . Credo . . . Sanctus . . . Agnus Dei should be one and the same . . . in invention . . . but not in consonances and accompaniments [that is, all five movements should begin with a common "thematic" headmotif, which is varied on each appearance].
>
> (2) When the first Kyrie is finished, the Christe may be written upon some subsidiary motif . . . [or] the composer may here use some invention of his own . . . [Morales draws on a subsidiary motif].
>
> (3) The beginnings of the last Kyrie . . . are in every respect at the composer's pleasure. Nevertheless, there is nothing to forbid his borrowing some other subsidiary motif . . . [Morales does the latter].
>
> (4) The endings of the last Kyrie . . . should . . . be in imitation . . . [Morales ends the Kyrie by drawing on the motet].
>
> (5) . . . the endings of the Christe . . . may close on the confinal of the tone, provided two endings in succession do not close on the confinal . . . [Has Morales violated the rule by ending both Kyrie I and the Christe on the confinal?].
>
> (6) In the course of the mass, the more use one makes . . . of motifs from

[11] Quoted after Oliver Strunk, *Source Readings in Music History* (New York, 1950), 265–68. Although the revised edition of *Source Readings in Music History*, ed. Leo Treitler, III: *The Renaissance*, ed. Gary Tomlinson (New York, 1997), omits the Cerone passage, it does include the relevant excerpt from Pontio's *Ragionamento di musica* (1588), 195–97. There is an abbreviated, slightly altered version of Strunk's translation of Cerone in Piero Weiss and Richard Taruskin, *Music in the Western World: A History in Documents* (New York, 1984), 132–34.

Ex. 7.1 (*a*) Mouton, *Quaeramus cum pastoribus*, mm. 1–22
After *Van Ockeghem tot Sweelinck*, ed. A. Smijers (Amsterdam, 1956), VII

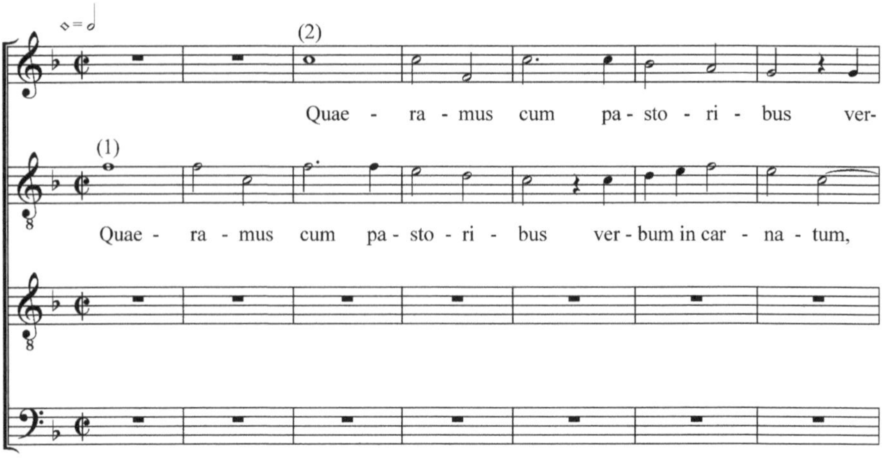

(*b*) Morales, *Missa "Quaeramus cum pastoribus"* (1544), mm. 1–22
Opera omnia, ed. H. Anglés, Monumentos de la música española, 11 (Rome, 1952)

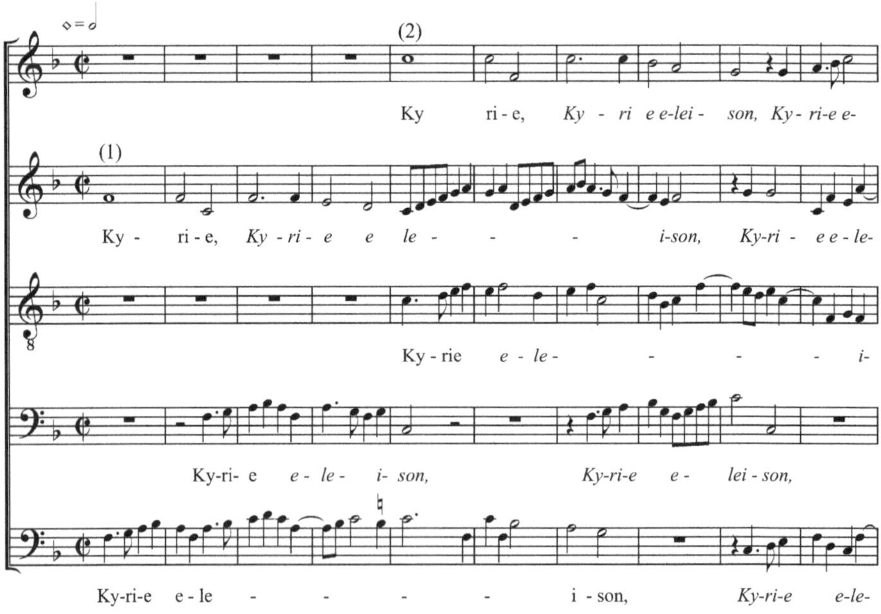

Quaeramus cum pastoribus verbum incarnatum, cantemus cum hominibus

Kyrie eleison

the middle or inside of the composition upon which the mass is written, the better and the more praiseworthy the work will be [Morales complies].

(11) And to conclude their work with greater harmony and greater sonority, composers usually write the last Agnus Dei for more voices . . . [Morales does so].

In all, it was the parody mass, virtually unlimited in the possibilities that it offered the creative composer—and nourished, perhaps, by humanist ideas about the virtues of *imitatio*—that became the standard for mass composition during the remainder of the sixteenth century.

The term "parody" calls for comment. During the sixteenth century, the simplest title for a mass consisted of the word *Missa* followed by the opening words of the model, as in *Missa "Quaeramus cum pastoribus"*. Beginning about the middle of the century, Italian sources sometimes added the term "super" between the two components, while the French came up with *Missa ad imitationem* . . . (in imitation of). Only in 1587 did the minor German composer Jacob Paix (more important for his organ music) publish a mass on a motet by Thomas Crecquillon with the title *Missa: Parodia mottetæ Domine da nobis auxilium*. And it is from this one instance of the term "Missa parodia"—with its use of the Greek "parodia," synonymous with the Latin "ad imitationem"—that we derive our customary modern term for the genre.

If the Netherlandish mainstream's major accomplishment was to establish the parody mass as the predominant mass type, it also added a notable twist to the overall structure of the mass, one that, as it gradually took hold over the course of this generation and the next, served to reduce the number of sections in both the Agnus Dei and the Sanctus. Increasingly the Agnus Dei became a two-part instead of three-part affair, while the Sanctus often lost its independent section for the "Pleni sunt caeli" and occasionally ended up as a single movement with no distinct subsections at all.

Other traditions

Though composers in France cultivated the parody mass, they reconciled the technique with their preference for a leaner surface style: a lighter, four-voice, more homophonic/syllabic texture that, with its often bouncy rhythms, seems to parallel the simplification so notable in their chansons. Perhaps nothing better illustrates this fondness for smaller-is-better than the opening Kyrie of Pierre Clereau's *Missa "In me transierunt"* (1544), which lasts all of six breves. It is also from France that we have a rare example of a parody mass based on more than one model: Claudin de Sermisy's *Missa plurium mottetorum*. Finally, in terms of quotation versus true reworking, perhaps the French lean at least slightly more in the direction of clear quotation than do their Netherlandish counterparts. Certainly, this is true of Janequin's *Missa super "La Bataille"* (1532), based on his own popular chanson *La Guerre* ("Escoutez, tous gentilz Gallois", also known as *La Bataille de Marignan*).

The polyphonic mass had a rather checkered career in those areas that fell under the sway of the Protestant Reformation. Calvin and Zwingli, of course, banned it altogether. The situation was more complex, however, among the followers of Luther, among whom there developed a tradition in which the musical boundaries between the traditional Roman and the newly minted Protestant liturgies were sometimes less than clear. This is evident, for example, from the publications of Georg Rhau, who, though he set for himself the task of providing the Lutheran church with an approved repertory of music, included in his *Opus decem missarum* (1541) settings of the Ordinary by, among others, Brumel, Isaac, and Senfl—Catholics all. Sometimes the boundaries are blurred within a single work. Thus there is a complete Protestant Easter mass by Johannes Hähnel (called Galliculus) that, while in Latin (which was still very much alive in Lutheran circles), defers to Protestant requirements by omitting the gradual, Credo (sung by the congregation), and offertory, abbreviating the Gloria, and setting the Gospel with its salutations intact. Moreover, the work, which was published by Rhau in his *Officia paschalia* of 1539, contains an alternatim sequence beginning with the words *Agnus redemit oves* (the second verse of *Victimae paschali laudes*), in which the tenor, sandwiched between three voices that sing the Latin text, introduces, in cantus-firmus fashion, the German chorale *Christ ist erstanden*, which is itself based on the Latin chant.

England presents another story. Having "invented" the cyclic mass around 1430, having established—with the anonymous *Missa "Caput"* of circa 1450—what long remained its standard four-voice texture, and having exported both to the Continent, English music turned in on itself, and cut itself off from developments in the Franco-Flemish mainstream. Settings of the Mass in particular seemingly vanished (they are absent from the Eton choirbook of 1490–1502). And when they come to the fore again at the hands of John Taverner, Robert Fayrfax, and Nicholas Ludford in the 1520s and 1530s, they do so in a manner that is almost archaic.

Whereas Continental composers were by now favoring the parody mass and drawing freely on both sacred and secular models, the English preferred the now old-fashioned cantus-firmus mass based on a monophonic melody, generally sacred in origin. Among the most impressive examples—though its model is secular—is Taverner's *Western Wind* mass, which is built on what seems to be a modified version of a popular tune, and eventually served as the model for masses by Christopher Tye and John Sheppard on the same tune. Further, English masses—Taverner's *Western Wind* included—typically omit the Kyrie (often troped and sung as plainsong), shorten the text of the Credo, and construct their four movements so that they are often equal, or nearly so, in length.

One mass type peculiar to England is that built "upon the square." Squares are monophonic melodies, extracted from the bottom voice of a polyphonic work and notated in mensural fashion, that stood outside the plainsong repertory and constituted a source of ready-made cantus firmi. This is how they work in no. 3 of the seven alternatim "Lady" masses—one for each day of the week—by Ludford, the most prolific of the English mass composers. After serving as the intonation of the opening Kyrie, the square is repeated at the bottom of the polyphonic setting that follows. The Christe then picks up the square at the point at which it left off in the Kyrie.

In all, England of the 1520s and 1530s produced a brilliant but short-lived mass tradition. With the coming of the English Reformation, such music became more than just superfluous, it was politically incorrect; and though Catholic composers continued to cultivate the mass, the polyphonic Ordinary largely gave way to the anthem of the Anglican liturgy.

In sum: with the second quarter of the sixteenth century, we reach the fifth generation of composers to cultivate the cyclic mass. And while the Netherlandish mainstream firmly established the predominance of the parody type, it added little else in terms of large-scale structure or compositional procedure. The mass had now settled comfortably—at least in those areas that remained loyal to Rome—into the conservative stance that it would maintain for the remainder of the century.

The Late Sixteenth Century

The "reform" mass

In answer to the rise of Protestantism—but also as part of what had been and would continue to be a long-term, on-going process of evolution—the Catholic Church embarked upon a series of reforms, reforms to which music and polyphonic settings of the Mass in particular were not immune.

On 10 September 1562, in what may be seen as a coming together of religious piety and humanist aesthetics, the Council of Trent proposed a draft calling for reforms in the celebration of the Mass. Canon 8 of the proclamation included the following ruling concerning music: "nothing profane should be intermingled . . . the entire manner of singing . . . should be calculated . . . so that the words may be comprehensible to all."[12] And though subsequent deliberations curtailed the pronouncement, the intent is clear enough: music for the Mass should avoid "creeping secularism," as Craig Monson has recently put it, and project the words as clearly as possible.

In addition, the Council later formed a committee, headed by Cardinals Carlo Borromeo (Archbishop of Milan) and Vitelozzo Vitelli, whose charge it was to invite composers to compose masses that fell into line with its recommendations. Among those invited was Vincenzo Ruffo, then choirmaster at the Cathedral of Milan, who seems to have responded with one or more of the masses that he eventually published—with the approval of the Church ("Missae . . . concinate ad ritum Concilii Mediolani")—in his *Missae Quatuor* of 1570. Example 7.2, the Credo from the *Missa octavi toni*, shows Ruffo's response at its most severe. Whatever else one might say about it, Ruffo's musical asceticism follows the letter of the law: there is no pre-existent model (secular or otherwise), and the words could not be set more intelligibly. And with further contributions by Costanzo Porta, the type, sometimes referred to as *Missa brevis*, enjoyed some popularity in northern

[12] Quoted after Craig Monson, "The Council of Trent Revisited," *Journal of the American Musicological Society*, 55 (2002), 9, which corrects some confusion about just what the Council eventually mandated and when it did so.

Ex. 7.2 Ruffo, *Missa octavi toni*, Patrem, mm. 1–9
After *Vincenzo Ruffo, Seven Masses*, ed. L. Lockwood (Madison, WI, 1979)

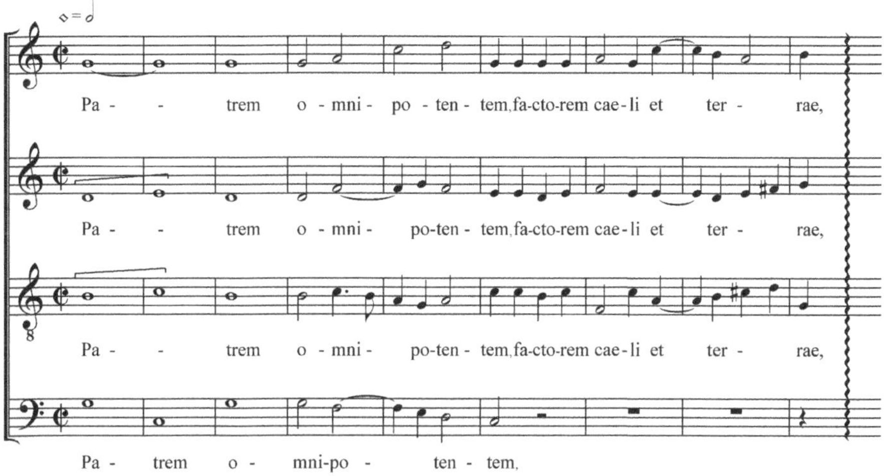

Patrem omnipotentem, factorem caeli et terrae

Italy, especially in the territories dominated by Milan and some of the smaller nearby courts.

Palestrina

No name looms larger in connection with the sixteenth-century mass than does Palestrina's. His 104 masses (more than by any other composer of his period) cut across the full spectrum of compositional types: parody, paraphrase, cantus-firmus, "free," canonic, and *alternatim*. As one might expect, it was the parody mass to which Palestrina turned most often, with the models upon which he drew for those fifty-odd works no doubt reflecting both his own tastes and those of the Roman church circles in which he spent virtually his entire career. Here Palestrina adopts a conservative stance: the overwhelming majority of models are sacred works (see Table 7.1 above), either his own or those of Netherlandish, French, and Spanish composers of the preceding generation who had found a home in the repertory of Roman and, especially, papal chapels. Thus there are masses based on the motets of Morales, Jean Lhéritier, Andrea de Silva, and Jacquet of Mantua, with which court and its duke, Guglielmo Gonzaga, Palestrina enjoyed close relations. No less indicative of his taste—or papal politics—are the major composers upon whose works he did not draw: those associated with Venice and the court of Charles V, including Willaert, Gombert, and Clemens non Papa, to name the three most obvious.

We might focus on three admittedly unrelated aspects of Palestrina's mass production. By far his most famous mass is the freely-composed *Missa Papae Marcelli* (published in his Second Book of masses, 1567, but probably composed in 1562/63), which, beginning with Agostino Agazzari in 1607 and continuing to

Hans Pfitzner's opera *Palestrina* of 1917, played a major role in developing Palestrina's mythic reputation as the "saviour of church music." Yet if large chunks of the Gloria and Credo deliver their texts in relatively intelligible fashion (no doubt the "new manner" to which Palestrina refers in the preface to the collection), the final Agnus Dei, with its seven voices—three of which, Bassus I, Altus II, and Cantus II, are in canon—wins no obvious prize in that respect.

By and large, Palestrina's treatment of parody technique accords with the recommendations eventually offered by Pontio and Cerone (see above): movements open with the model's opening and close with its cadential material, while a major subdivision will often begin, when the model is a motet, with its *secunda pars*. Between these main structural points, Palestrina usually proceeds in "chronological" order. At times, however, he jumps ahead or even backwards within the model. Thus in the Gloria of his *Missa "Dum complerentur"* (based on his own motet), the "Qui tollis" (m. 58) begins with the opening of the motet's second part, "Dum ergo essent" (motet, m. 85), but then backs up to the model's *prima pars* at "ad dexteram" (mass, m. 82 = motet, m. 41) and "Miserere" (mass, m. 88 = motet, m. 59), before returning to the *secunda pars* for "tu solus sanctus" (m. 96), which draws upon the motet's "sonus repente" (m. 102). After that point, mass and motet move in the same forward direction. And if the reason for going back to the *prima pars* is not entirely clear, perhaps Palestrina returned to the *secunda pars* when he did in order to match the phonic quality of the mass's "so*l*us" with the (unheard) "so*n*us" of the motet.

Despite the predominance of the parody type, there are among Palestrina's masses an interesting group of paraphrase and cantus-firmus settings based on plainsongs, particularly hymns and antiphons. These masses may well be related to the work that Palestrina (together with Annibale Zoilo) undertook on the revision of plainsong at the request of Pope Gregory XIII in 1577; and though Palestrina failed to see the project through to its completion, he was certainly involved in the production of the *Directorium chori*, a collection of hymns and antiphons, among other things, that was published in 1582. Together with his cycles of offertories, hymns, Magnificats, and Lamentations, then, perhaps these masses show Palestrina at his most "devotional"; and perhaps they are the masses in which he most explicitly expresses the Tridentine reforms and spirit of the Counter-Reformation.

Were we to place Palestrina and his masses on a continuum that runs from the innovative at one end to the synthesis-producing on the other, we should probably place him somewhere near the latter end, for in terms of the overall structure and design of the mass, he left things as he found them. Indeed, more than any other mass composer of his time, Palestrina sums up and in a sense brings to a conclusion the Renaissance tradition of a century and a half of mass production. In doing so, he came to be seen as a "classic," a model to emulate above all others (see below).

Venice

If, thanks largely to Palestrina, the mass held a central position at Rome, matters were very different at Venice, which followed an independent course both politically and artistically. There, as the century came to a close, the mass played a decidedly secondary role to the grand, multi-choir motet, which, however, must often have done extraliturgical duty during Mass on special feast days. The lack of Venetian settings of the Ordinary is striking. There are, to be sure, a handful by Giovanni Croce and Andrea Gabrieli, who at least in his earlier masses of 1572 was content to stay within the mainstream tradition. On the other hand, Giovanni Gabrieli struck a typically Venetian pose. He wrote only two masses, in both of which he follows the Venetian custom of setting only parts of the Ordinary: Kyrie–Gloria–Sanctus and Kyrie–Sanctus (in the *Symphoniae sacrae* of 1597 and 1615, respectively). And as one might expect, his masses—as well as Andrea's massive sixteen-voice Gloria, possibly written for the visit of a delegation of Japanese dignitaries in 1585 and published in the *Concerti* of 1587—exploit the antiphonal effects of S. Marco's *cori spezzati*. Moreover, Giovanni's masses forego the homogeneous sonority and smooth, floating lines of the Netherlandish style for a *concertato*-like mixture of colors—antiphonal choirs, solo voices, and instruments (see below)—rugged rhythms, sharply etched motives, and a *basso seguente* for the organ. The conclusion of the opening five-voice Kyrie (the Christe grows to eight voices and the Kyrie II to twelve) of the 1615 collection even peppers the uppermost voice (marked "voce" to indicate a soloist) with dynamic indications.

Venice, then, turned its back on the Netherlandish mainstream, both in general stylistic terms and with respect to the cyclic mass in particular.

Victoria, Lassus, and Byrd

The late sixteenth century produced three great mass composers aside from Palestrina: Tomás Luis de Victoria, Orlande de Lassus, and William Byrd, each of whom came to and cultivated the mass from a very different religious and political perspective.

Active in both Spain and Rome, Victoria was thoroughly enveloped by the orthodoxy of the Counter-Reformation. His sixteen parody masses (out of a total of twenty) are based almost exclusively on sacred models, the one exception being the *Missa pro victoria* (published in 1600 with an organ part), modeled on Janequin's *La Guerre*, which, by the end of the century, had become a true warhorse among models.[13] Victoria's greatest setting—and to my mind perhaps the most beautiful and deeply moving of the period—is undoubtedly the *Officium defunctorum ad matutinum* (1605), which, written to commemorate the death of the Dowager Queen Maria of Spain in 1603, includes a setting of the Tridentine-standardized

[13] Ironically, Janequin's chanson was one of the pieces that the Tridentine reformers seem to have singled out in prohibiting Masses based on secular models; see Monson, "The Council of Trent Revisited," 8.

chants for the Mass for the Dead (it is thus often referred to simply as a Requiem mass).

Working at the ducal court of Bavaria, which for a time did more than just tolerate Protestant reformers, and being no strong advocate of Tridentine reforms himself, Lassus, whose duties required him to provide music for morning services, was a prolific mass composer (at least sixty-some authentic works) and drew freely on both chansons and madrigals as models for his masses. And though modern scholarship has generally relegated Lassus's masses to a decidedly second place behind his motets, they were held in high regard during the late sixteenth and early seventeenth centuries.

Finally, Byrd was a Catholic in Protestant England. As such, his music for the Mass—three freely-composed settings of the Ordinary (one each for three, four, and five voices) and the last great cycle of Propers, the *Gradualia*—would have been sung behind closed doors. Indeed, when the settings of the Ordinary were published in the mid-1590s, they were issued without fanfare or title pages, while possession of the *Gradualia*, whose 1605 title page flaunted its allegiance to Rome, was reason enough for arrest.

For present-day listeners, the latter part of the sixteenth century marks the end of that simplistically proverbial "Golden Age of Polyphony." Both its style and some of its genres—the large-scale polyphonic mass in particular—were seemingly exhausted. And further attempts to cultivate them must, as we shall see in the section on the seventeenth century, be seen either as just old-fashioned or outright exercises in nostalgia (or, to put a positive spin on things: "historicism").

Aspects of Performance Practice

To discuss performance practice in connection with the sixteenth-century polyphonic mass is to deal more with questions than with answers. And it is on three questions that we focus briefly here.

Occasions

When were the large-scale cyclic masses by the likes of Josquin, Morales, or Palestrina sung? Apart from those institutions in which polyphony had become the norm, it was probably on occasions other than the "everyday," when, if Mass were sung at all, it was probably done in plainchant or quasi-improvised polyphony based on such techniques as falsobordone.

But even when polyphony was used, it is not always easy to link up an individual mass with a specific liturgical occasion. While a mass such as Palestrina's *Missa "Assumpta est Maria"* was obviously intended for the Feast of the Assumption, what are we to make of the many masses based on a chanson or madrigal that has no obvious liturgical association? What occasion was it, for instance, that inspired (or required) the composition of Jaquet of Mantua's *Missa "Chiare dolc'e fresch' acque"*? Jacquet based his mass on the first part of the five-part cycle with which Jacques

Arcadelt set Petrarch's eponymous canzone (no. 126 in the poet's *Canzoniere*). The poem is a lover's meditation on the vision of the "donna," who, "born in heaven" ("nacque in paradiso"), will intercede on the lover's behalf and "ask for mercy for [him]" ("che mercè m'impetre"). Surely, the cultivated Mantuans for whom Jaquet composed the mass would have required only a little hermeneutical ingenuity to allegorize the "donna" as the Virgin Mary. Could, then, the mass have served for some Marian occasion?[14]

Choir size

How big were the choirs that sang the masses? Again, things are murky. In 1568, the Bavarian court chapel over which Lassus presided numbered fifty-one singers: twenty sopranos (falsettists and boys), nine altos, ten tenors, and twelve basses (plus two organists and a body of instrumentalists).[15] But did all of them sing all the time? There is an instructive document about such matters from the fifteenth-century court of Burgundy. Although the court had twenty-three singers on its payroll in January 1469, an ordinance issued on the first of that month requires no more than fourteen of them to be present for the performance of polyphony.[16] Or, to give another example: though Cambrai Cathedral had thirty-four singers circa 1520, Dufay's now-lost Requiem mass was performed there by as few as five or six.[17] At times, perhaps, polyphony was even sung by just one singer on a part. Still, there were certainly occasions when a court's full complement of singers—however bloated the roster might have been—might well have been used, as when (to return to Munich, 1568, again) Lassus directed a choir of fifty-three singers for a performance of Brumel's 12-voice *Missa Et ecce terrae motus*.[18]

Finally, not only the size, but the very existence of a chapel was subject to economic-political fortunes. Again, Munich provides an example. In 1568–70, both Duke Albrecht V and his son Wilhelm maintained individual chapels. When this proved too costly, Wilhelm disbanded his group. And from then on, the remaining chapel grew now larger and now smaller until, in 1597, with the accession of Duke Maximilian, it shriveled into a nonentity.

[14] Arcadelt's madrigal appears in his *Opera omnia*, ed. Albert Seay, CMM 31 (American Institute of Musicology, 1969), VII, no. 54; and Alfred Einstein, *The Italian Madrigal*, trans. Alexander H. Krappe, Roger H. Sessions, and Oliver Strunk (Princeton, 1949), III, no. 52 (text, translation, and music). My suggestion for how the mass might have been interpreted is based on the reading of the poem in Robert M. Durling, *Petrarch's Lyric Poems: The Rime sparse and Other Lyrics* (Cambridge, MA: Harvard University Press, 1976), 125–29.

[15] Clive Wearing, "Orlandus Lassus (1532–1594) and the Munich Kapelle," *Early Music*, 10 (1982), 150.

[16] David Fallows, "Specific Information on the Ensembles for Composed Polyphony, 1400–1474," in *Studies in the Performance of Late Medieval Music*, ed. Stanley Boorman (Cambridge, 1983), 110–11.

[17] Craig Wright, "Performance Practices at the Cathedral of Cambrai, 1475–1550," *The Musical Quarterly*, 44 (1978), 303.

[18] Wearing, "Orlandus Lassus," 150.

Instruments

There is a broad consensus that fifteenth-century liturgical music—the polyphonic mass included—was customarily performed *a cappella* or, at most, with the support of an organ. No doubt, there were exceptions, as, perhaps, at the 1475 wedding of Constantino Sforza and Camilla of Aragón at Pesaro, where, according to a contemporary chronicler, Mass was celebrated by two choirs (sixteen singers), organists, piffari, trumpeters, and "tamburini," though just how the instrumentalists participated is anything but clear.

Already in the early sixteenth century the "exceptions" may no longer have been quite so exceptional, as documents that attest to the presence of instruments at Mass become more numerous. Among them are the 1503 description that notes the presence of sackbuts playing the gradual (with the singers? in monophonic fashion?) when the chapels of the Emperor Maximilian and his son Philip the Fair met at Innsbruck, or that of 1520 in which instruments are said to have joined and alternated with the singers of Henry VIII and François I when they celebrated Mass at the Field of Cloth of Gold. And Erasmus, writing about church music in England, complains bitterly about instruments encroaching upon the liturgy. Again, though, the descriptions are vague and could hardly serve as the basis for secure, modern-day "orchestrations." Finally, at least two prestigious musical establishments withstood the trend and continued an *a cappella*-only policy: the Sistine Chapel and the Cathedral of Notre Dame at Cambrai, neither of which even had an organ.

Instrumental participation—winds and strings—no doubt increased during the second half of the century, and may even have become the norm on lavish occasions at some establishments. For instance, the singer Massimo Troiano describes the situation at Munich in the late 1560s: "The wind instruments are played on Saturdays and feast days at Mass and Vespers in company with the singers."[19] And if Troiano is vague, a document of 1586 from the Cathedral of Seville (and nowhere, perhaps, did the participation of instruments become as well established during the sixteenth century as it did in Spain), probably prepared by Francisco Guerrero, is more explicit:

> Rojas and Lopez shall always play the treble parts; ordinarily on shawms. They must carefully observe some order when they improvise passages both as to places and to times ... the same Rojas and Lopez ... play on cornetts ... Juan de Medina ... shall ordinarily play the contralto part, not obscuring the trebles ... When ... his part becomes the top above the sackbuts ... he ... is free to add all the passages ... Alvanchez ... shall play tenors and the bassoon. At greater feasts there shall always be a verse played on recorders.[20]

[19] Quoted after Wearing, "Orlandus Lassus," 149.

[20] Quoted in Robert Stevenson, *Spanish Cathedral Music in the Golden Age* (Berkeley, 1961), 167; Weiss and Taruskin, *Music in the Western World*, 160–61.

And what Troiano and Guerrero describe verbally, the mass movements of Giovanni Gabrieli imply musically: instruments could double or even replace voices, even if the precise instrumentation was not yet indicated (but see below).

The Seventeenth Century

With the beginning of the seventeenth century, Italy took the lead in terms of both new directions and the preservation of the old, as three different traditions of mass writing took firm hold.

The "stile antico"

Known also as the *stile osservato*, *stile grave*, or *stile da cappella* (even when a continuo was added), this tradition—according to the composer-writer Marco Scacchi (writing *c.*1648)—looked back to the masses of Josquin, Lassus, and Palestrina. It was, however, with Palestrina's style in particular, now all but canonized by his Roman students and followers—the brothers Felice and Giovanni Francesco Anerio, Francesco Soriano, and Giovanni Maria Nanino, among others—that the style became identified. It is apparent in Soriano's six-voice (though four was the preferred number) *Missa super voces musicales*, which uses as its *soggetto* the hard hexachord on G.

To be sure, the *stile antico* filtered Palestrina's style through seventeenth-century ears: there was often a clearer sense of "tonality"; surface rhythm, harmonic rhythm, and barline began to coincide to a greater extent than before, and the continuo became the norm. And in the hands of Monteverdi, it could display real dramatic contrast, as in the progression from "Et incarnatus est" to "Crucifixus" to "Et resurrexit" in the Credo of his posthumously published *Messa a 4 voci da cappella* (1650), probably the last—and certainly the finest—of his three extant cyclic Ordinaries.

Finally, the *stile antico* kept the parody mass alive, and we have, among others, Monteverdi's *Missa "In illo tempore"* (1610, as part of the well-known *Vespers* collection) and Stefano Bernardi's *Missa super "Il bianco e dolce cigno"* (1615) on models by Gombert and Arcadelt, respectively.

When did the *stile antico*, in its Palestrina-style guise, become "antique"? When did it begin to be cultivated as a conscious effort at "historicism"? Certainly, the idea is apparent by the second decade of the century at the latest: in 1609, Soriano revived Palestrina's *Marcellus* mass, adding two voices to it (there is a record of Soriano's version being performed at St Peter's in 1618); it was in 1610 that, with his mass on Gombert's motet, Monteverdi took up the style for the first time; in 1616, twenty-nine of the thirty-three polyphonic Ordinaries sung in the Sistine Chapel on festive or solemn occasions were by Palestrina; and in 1619, Francesco Anerio engaged *Marcellus*, issuing it in a simplified, four-voice version (with added continuo) that was still being reprinted as late as 1662. Once established, the *stile antico* led a long if somewhat peripheral life, still making appearances as late as the nineteenth century, when it was considered an effective and immediate means of signifying religiosity.

The polychoral style

There was ample precedent for masses with multiple choirs. Venice had the Gabrielis—to whom the Germans, too, would turn—while Rome could look back to Palestrina's polychoral motets and imaginative use of antiphonal writing even within a single choir. And when, in Rome, the use of multiple choirs—pitted against one another spatially, but without the dramatic contrasts of sonority favored by the Venetians—was joined with the *stile antico*, there developed the so-called "monumental" (or "colossal") style, in which the number of voices was occasionally increased to as many as forty-eight. In treating such massive forces, the polychoralists , skilled contrapuntists though they were, tended toward a block-chord style much of the time. Ironically, the most famous work traditionally associated with the Roman polychoral school—the fifty-three-voice *Missa Salisburgensis*—does not belong to it. Long thought to have been written by Orazio Benevoli for the consecration in 1628 of the Cathedral of Salzburg, the mass is now dated from 1682 and at least tentatively attributed to Heinrich Biber (or Andreas Hofer).[21]

The concertato style

What the "monumental" polychoral mass was to Rome, the concertato mass was to Venice in particular, northern Italy in general, and non-Italian musical institutions that fell under Venetian sway. And if early examples of such masses—the earliest seems to be Lodovico Viadana's *Missa dominicalis* (1607), which does nothing more than add a continuo part to plainsong—were often content to limit their sense of contrast (or "working together") to a group of solo voices against a *ripieno* choir (with the now ever-present continuo), as in Alessandro Grandi's *Messa a 4 voci* of 1610, it was the "mixed" concertato mass with added instruments that soon came to the fore. One of the earliest of these is the mass in Giovanni Francesco Capello's *Motetti et dialoghi*, Op. 7 (1615), which actually draws upon pre-existent instrumental canzonas in its parody-style Kyrie and Gloria.

Two points may be made about the use of instruments in these mixed-concertato masses. First, although instrumental forces had already entered the mass repertory on what was probably a more-than-occasional basis in the late sixteenth century (see above), they seem to have been limited simply to doubling or replacing individual voices or groups thereof, so that the contrast they provided was, in effect, limited to matters of timbre; now, however, they began to take on a true *obbligato* role, often providing *sinfonia*-like ritornellos that contrasted with the voices stylistically and articulated the structure. Secondly, whereas past composers—Giovanni Gabrieli included—had been content to leave the "instrumenta-

[21] See Ernst Hintermaier, "The Missa Salisburgensis," *The Musical Times*, 116 (1975), 965–66.

tion" up to the choirmaster-arranger (who presumably anticipated the criteria that Michael Praetorius would describe in Book III of his *Syntagma musicum* of 1619), the younger Seicento composers chose instruments according to the clefs of the voice parts, and thus began to specify the instruments themselves. Thus Amadio Freddi supplemented the five-voice choir of his *Messa, Vespro e Compieta* (1616) with violin and cornetto, while Ercole Porta scored his *Messa concertata* of 1620 for five voices, two violins, and three trombones, and provided the instruments with an independent *sinfonia* in the Credo. In effect, we have the beginnings of the mass for voices and instruments.

The jewel among *concertato* masses of this period is undoubtedly Monteverdi's *Gloria a 7 voci*, which appears in the second edition of his *Selva morale* (1641) and which might have been written for the so-called "Mass of Thanksgiving"—for deliverance from the plague—celebrated at Venice in November 1631. Monteverdi calls for two violins and "quattro viole da brazzo overo 4. Tromboni quali anco si ponno lasciare se occoresce l'acidente." Thus while the violins, which may have been doubled by trumpets (*trombe squarciate*), were obligatory, the complementary violas or trombones were optional. Example 7.3 shows the opening of the work, with its independent interjections by the violins and play between soloistic and tutti choral writing.

Diverse as these three stylistic traditions were, they seem to have coexisted amiably with one another, at least at those institutions that had the requisite forces to mount them. Moreover, they coexisted at different hierarchical levels, between and even within works. Thus Giovanni Priuli's *Missae . . . octo novemque vocibus* of 1624 contains concertato masses—both with and without obbligato instruments—alongside rather more traditional polychoral masses, while Monteverdi composed alternate sections in concertato style as substitutes for the original "Cruxifixus," "Et resurrexit," and "Et iterum" sections of his *stile antico* mass in the *Selva morale*. Indeed, the concertato-style *Gloria a 7 voci* itself may have been conceived as a movement-long substitute for the original Gloria of that mass.

At times, instruments took center stage altogether. Although the seventeenth century produced no equivalent of Palestrina's *Offertoria totius anni* (1593)—that is, a cycle of settings of a single item from the Proper of the Mass (in fact, publication of such cycles ceased almost completely)—various new types of Proper "substitutes" came to be favored. And while the use of motets (not necessarily on a liturgical text) and organ elaborations (whether composed or improvised) already had a long history, the seventeenth century added a new possibility: pieces for instrumental ensembles, which, like the other types, would have been performed while the celebrant recited the liturgical item as if in a Low Mass. Thus sung movements of the Ordinary—in all three of the main traditions—would have alternated with the likes of canzonas, capriccios, and sinfonias, which replaced the gradual and communion, with ricercars, which did duty for the offertory, and with slow, chromatic pieces at the moment of the elevation.

Central Europe and France also continued to cultivate the mass, with those parts of Central Europe that remained within the Catholic fold generally looking to Venice for their inspiration, and often importing composers from the Venetian

Ex. 7.3 Monteverdi, *Gloria a 7 voci* (1641), mm. 1–11
Tutte le opere, ed. G. F. Malipiero (Vienna, 1967), XV

orbit. And when, in the second half of the century, German composers fully realized the potential of the "orchestral" mass, they did so with flair, as in Johann Kaspar Kerll's *Missa a 3 chori*, which supplements the voices with pairs of clarinos and cornetts, three trombones, strings, and continuo. As in Italy, though, all the mass types coexisted, with the *stile antico* continuing to be cultivated in southern Germany and Austria in particular.

Gloria in excelsis Deo

The French were less adventurous, content for the most part to steer a conservative path that looked back to the Netherlandish traditions of the preceding century. Thus the masses in Jean de Bournonville's *Missae tredecim* of 1619 are all for *a cappella* choir of four to six voices, each mass based on a single pre-existent melody.

The *doyen* of the seventeenth-century French mass was no doubt Eustache Du Caurroy, who, familiar with the music of Josquin and Willaert, was inclined to the teaching of Zarlino. Du Caurroy's *Missa pro defunctis* stands as a monument of French conservatism: written in 1606, performed at the funeral of Henri IV in 1610, and published by Ballard in 1636, it continued to be performed for the obsequies of French kings and princes at St Denis well into the eighteenth century. Perhaps Sébastien de Brossard summed up French conservatism best in his *Catalogue* of 1724 when he described the composer Artus Aux-Cousteaux, active at the Sainte-Chapelle from 1634 to 1651, as "never wish[ing] to hear of adding *Basses-continues* to his work."[22]

Concluding Note

By circa 1640, which marks the end of our period, the mass occupied a very different *musical* status than it had around 1520. The signs are everywhere. For example, whereas Obrecht and Josquin had written about 30 and 25 complete cycles respectively, and whereas Palestrina, Lassus, and Victoria added another 104, 64, and 20, Monteverdi composed but three. Likewise, the very format in which masses were published during the early seventeenth century underwent a telling change. In the sixteenth century, masses were customarily published in volumes devoted entirely to that genre; the early seventeenth century, on the other hand, usually issued masses in collections that cut across musical-generic boundaries and presented the mass together with music for one or another part of the liturgy for a particular feast. Three collections from as many decades may illustrate the point: Freddi's *Messa, Vespro e Compieta* of 1616, Francesco Bellazzi's *Messa, motetti, letanie* of 1622, and Giovanni Rovetta's *Messa, e salmi concertati* of 1639. Clearly, such a format emphasizes the polyphonic mass's liturgical function at the expense of its status as a privileged work of art. Finally, if many a sixteenth-century mass ranked among the masterpieces of its time, few of their early seventeenth-century counterparts could claim such distinction.

Why this shift in status and emphasis? First, perhaps, was the mass's innate conservatism, already evident as far back as the beginning of our period, and becoming more noticeable as the sixteenth century wore on. Certainly, it was not the genre in which composers developed their more "forward-looking" ideas (word painting, chromaticism, etc.) The mass was simply ill suited to the period's ever-increasing emphasis on the word and its musical expression, just as it was, perhaps, to the potential drama of the few-voice, concertato style. Second, as the late sixteenth century turned into the early seventeenth, the mass had to compete with an intense spirit of musical secularism, both inside and outside the Church. Especially in Italy, composers found that it was in opera that reputations were now to be made, while even within the Church, instrumental music challenged the traditional reliance on the choir. Third, there were economic forces at work. Not only could the fee for a single opera easily equal a year's salary in the church-music trenches, but smaller

[22] Quoted after James R. Anthony, *French Baroque Music from Beaujoyeulx to Rameau* (New York, 1974), 159.

churches were probably hard pressed to afford the choral forces needed to mount such large-scale works as polychoral masses. And even if they could afford them, the best singers were leaving the Church for the more lucrative opera stage. Finally, matters of patronage and personal taste could sometimes play a role: because Louis XIV (to reach beyond our period) preferred the *grand motet* as the major vehicle for liturgical music, a 200-year tradition—reaching back to Ockeghem—of polyphonic mass composition at the royal court of France effectively came to an end.

Peter Wagner opens his *Geschichte der Messe* with the following statement: "The mass, as a musical genre, is the most noble fruit of the prosperous relationship between liturgy and art."[23] To be sure, Wagner's judgment—if we preface the word mass with "polyphonic"—probably rings true for the period that began with the development of the cyclic mass in the early fifteenth century and continued, at least where Catholicism held fast, through the waning of the sixteenth. Yet the "prosperous relationship" is already called into question by the mid sixteenth century in places where Protestantism flourished, while the mass's "nobility" certainly comes to be tarnished, at least in purely musical terms, even in Catholic lands by the early seventeenth. In all, our period sees the polyphonic mass fall from a position of being what was arguably the dominant musical genre to one that, with some exceptions, can best be described as being not much more than functional in nature.

Bibliography

Masses cited (with modern editions)

BENET (*see* DUNSTABLE); BIBER (or HOFER): *Missa Salisburgensis*, in DTÖ XX, ed. Guido Adler (Vienna, 1903; repr. 1959); BERNARDI: *Missa super Il dolce e bianco cigno*, in DTÖ LXX, ed. Carl August Rosenthal (Vienna, 1929); BRUMEL: *Missa "Et ecce terrae motus", Missa pro defunctus*, in *Opera omnia*, CMM 5, ed. Barton Hudson (American Institute of Musicology, 1970), III, IV; BYRD: the three Ordinaries, in *The Collected Works of William Byrd*, ed. E. H. Fellowes (London, 1937), I; the *Gradualia*, ibid., VI–VII (1937), and *W. Byrd: Gradualia, Books 1 and 2*, Tudor Church Music, 7, ed. Percy C. Buck et al. (London, 1927); the *Gradualia* also appears in *The Byrd Edition*, V–VII, ed. Philip Brett (London, 1989–97); CAPELLO: *Missa ad votum*, in *Seventeenth-Century Italian Sacred Music*, ed. Anne Schnoebelen (New York, 1995), II; CLEREAU: *Missa "In me transierunt"*, Kyrie, in Peter Wagner, *Geschichte der Messe*, I (Leipzig, 1913; repr. 1963), 250–51; DIVITIS:

[23] "Die musikalische Form der Messe ist die edelste Frucht des segensreichen Bundes, der Liturgie und Kunst. . ." [v].

Missa "Quem dicunt homines", in *Collected Works*, ed. G. A. Nugent, Recent Researches in Music of the Renaissance, 94 (Madison, WI, 1993); DU CAURROY: *Missa pro defunctis*, in *Les Œuvres complètes*, I, ed. Blaise Pidoux, Gesamtausgaben, 9 (Brooklyn, 1975); DUNSTABLE: *Missa "Da gaudiorum premia"*, *Missa "Rex seculorum"* (also attributed to Power and Benet), in *Complete Works*, ed. Manfred Bukofzer, Musica Britannica, 8 (London, 1953; rev. edn by Ian Bent, Margaret Bent, and Brian Trowell, 1970); FREDDI: *Messa à cinque voci*, in *Seventeenth-Century Italian Sacred Music*, II; GIOVANNI GABRIELI: Kyrie–Gloria–Sanctus and Kyrie–Sanctus from *Symphoniae sacrae* (1597 and 1615, respectively), in *Opera omnia*, ed. Denis Arnold, II, IV, CMM 12 (American Institute of Musicology, 1959, 1962), to be re-edited by Richard Charteris, who is completing the edition and redoing that part of it issued by Arnold; GALLICULUS (*see* HÄHNEL); GRANDI: *Messa a quattro voci*, in *Seventeenth-Century Italian Sacred Music*, I; HÄHNEL: *Östermesse: Christ ist erstanden*, in Das Chorwerk, 44, ed. Friedrich Blume and Willi Schulze (Wolfenbüttel, 1936); ISAAC: *Constantinus choralis*, vols. I–II in DTÖ X, ed. E. Bezecny and W. Rabl; XXXII, ed. Anton von Webern (Vienna, 1898, 1909; repr. 1959); vol. III in *Heinrich Isaac's Choralis Constantinus Book III*, ed. Louise Cuyler (Ann Arbor, MI, 1950); *Missa carminum*, in Das Chorwerk, 7, ed. Reinhold Heyden (Wolfenbüttel, 1930); the "plainsong" Ordinaries, in *Opera omnia*, ed. Edward R. Lerner, I–IV, CMM 65 (American Institute of Musicology, 1974 , 1977), *H. Isaac: Messen*, Musikalischer Denkmäler, 7–8, ed. Martin Staehelin (Mainz, 1970–73), *H. Isaac: Five Polyphonic Masses*, ed. Louise Cuyler (Ann Arbor, MI, 1956); JACQUET OF MANTUA: *Missa "Chiare dolc'e fresch'acque"*, in *Opera omnia*, ed. Philip Jackson and George Nugent, CMM 54 (American Institute of Musicology, 1971), I; JANEQUIN: *Missa super "La Bataille"*, in Harry E. Gudmundson, "Parody and Symbolism in Three Battle Masses of the Sixteenth Century" (PhD diss., University of Michigan, 1976); JOSQUIN DES PREZ: *Missa ad fugam*, *Missa "Hercules dux Ferrariae"*, *Missa "L'homme armé" super voces musicales*, *Missa "Pange lingua"*, in *Werken*, ed. Albert Smijers: *Missen*, I–IV (Amsterdam and Leipzig, 1921–69; the four masses are currently numbered 12.1, 11.1, 6.3, and 4.3 respectively in the *New Josquin Edition* (Utrecht, 1986–); the *Missa "Pange lingua"* is also available in both Das Chorwerk, I, ed. Friedrich Blume (Wolfenbüttel, 1938), and *Missa Pange lingua: An Edition, with Notes for Performance and Commentary*, ed. Thomas Warburton (Chapel Hill, NC, 1977); LA RUE: *Missa "Ave sanctissima Maria"*, *Missa pro defunctus*, *Missa de Sancto Job*, in *Opera omnia*, I, III, V, ed. Nigel St John Davison, J. Evan Kreider, T. Herman Keahey, CMM 97 (American Institute of Musicology, 1990, 1992, 1996); the Requiem mass also in Das Chorwerk, II, ed. Friedrich Blume (Wolfenbüttel, 1931); the *Missa "Ave sanctissima Maria"* also in *P. de la Rue: Missarum*, ed. Antonio Tirabassi (Kassel, 1941), and Documenta polyphoniae liturgicae, ed. Laurence Feininger (Rome, 1950), 1st ser., B, I; LUDFORD: *Missa de feria III*, in *Collected Works*, ed. John Bergsagel, CMM 27 (American Institute of Musicology, 1963); MONTEVERDI: the three masses appear in *Tutte le opere*, ed. G. F. Malipiero, 2nd edn (Vienna, 1967–68), XIV–XVI, and Eulenburg Edition, Nos. 982, 990, 991, ed. Hans F. Redlich; the *Missa a 4 voci da cappella* and the *Gloria a 7 voci* have been ed. Jeffrey Kurtzman (Stuttgart, 1992), the latter also appearing as *Gloria concertata*, ed. John Steele, in Penn State Music Series, 18 (University Park, PA, 1968); MORALES: *Missa "Quaeramus cum pastoribus"*, in *Opera omnia*, ed. Higini Anglès, I, Monumentos de la música española, 11 (Madrid, 1952); MOUTON: *Missa "Quem dicunt homines"*, in *Opera omnia*, III, ed. Andrew C. Minor, CMM 43 (American Institute of Musicology, 1969); OBRECHT: *Missa de Sancto Donatiano*, *Missa de Sancto Martino*, *Missa "Fortuna desperata"*, *Missae plurimorum carminum I/II*, *Missa "Sub tuum praesidium"*, in *The New Obrecht Edition*, III, III, IV, X, XII, ed. Barton Hudson and Thomas Noblitt (Utrecht, 1984–92); PALESTRINA: *Missa Papae Marcelli*, *Missa ad fugam*, *Missa "Dum complerentur"*, *Missa*

"Assumpta est Maria", in *Le opere complete*, ed. Raffaele Casimiri, IV, IV, XXIV, XXV (Rome, 1939, 1958, 1968); the *Marcellus* mass also conveniently available in Lewis Lockwood, *Palestrina: Pope Marcellus Mass*, Norton Critical Scores (New York, 1975); PIPELARE: *Missa de Sancto Livino*, in *Opera omnia*, ed. Ronald Cross, CMM 34 (American Institute of Musicology, 1966–1967), II; PORTA: *Missa secundi toni*, in *Seventeenth-Century Italian Sacred Music*, II; POWER: *Missa "Alma redemptoris mater"*, in *Complete Works*, ed. Charles Hamm, CMM 50 (American Institute of Musicology, 1976), II; ROVETTA: *Messa à 5. 6. 7. con due violini*, in *Seventeenth-Century Italian Sacred Music*, V (1996); RUFFO: *Missae Quatuor*: nos. 1–2, in *Opera omnia*, ed. Giuseppe Vecchi (Bologna, 1963), I; nos. 3–4, in *Vincenzo Ruffo: Seven Masses*, ed. Lewis Lockwood, Recent Researches in the Music of the Renaissance, 32/ii (Madison, WI, 1979); SERMISY: *Missa plurium mottetorum*, in *Opera omnia*, ed. Gaston Allaire and Isabelle Cazeaux, CMM 52 (American Institute of Musicology, 1977), V; SHEPPARD: *Western Wind* mass, in *Complete Works*, ed. David Chadd, Early English Church Music, 17 (London, 1977); SORIANO: *Missa super voces musicales*, in *Selectus novus missarum*, ed. Carl Proske (Regensburg, 1857), I/2; TAVERNER: *Western Wind* mass, in *Four- and Five-Part Masses*, ed. Hugh Benham, Early English Church Music, 25 (London, 1989); TYE: *Western Wind* mass, in *Tye: The Latin Church Music*, ed. James Satterfield, Recent Researches in the Music of the Renaissance, 13 (Madison: A-R Editions, 1972), I; VICTORIA: *Missa pro victoria*, *Officium defunctorum*, in *Opera omnia*, ed. Felipe Pedrell (Leipzig, 1909; repr. 1965), VI; the Requiem mass also in *Tomás Luis de Victoria: Sacred Music*, ed. Michael Noone, Boethius Editions, 10 (Aberystwyth, 1990).

Suggested reading

(The bibliography is highly selective and focuses on the broader aspects of the mass at the expense of detailed studies of individual works.)

GENERAL. The classic study is still Peter Wagner, *Geschichte der Messe*, 2 vols. (Leipzig, 1913; repr. Hildesheim, 1963), which ends with the period around 1600; there are good surveys in *The New Grove Dictionary of Music and Musicians*, 2nd edn, ed. Stanley Sadie and John Tyrrell (London, 2001), XVI, and *Die Musik in Geschichte und Gegenwart*, rev. ed., ed. Ludwig Finscher (Kassel and Stuttgart, 1997), *Sachteil*, VI; for a more extended survey, see Finscher, "Die Messe als musikalisches Kunstwerk," in *Neues Handbuch der Musikwissenschaft*, III/1: *Die Musik des 15. und 16. Jahrhunderts*, ed. Ludwig Finscher (Laaber, 1989); for the argument that the privileging of the cyclic mass in particular is an invention of modern musicology, see the important article by Andrew Kirkman, "The Invention of the Cyclic Mass," *Journal of the American Musicological Society*, 54 (2001), 1–47.

CIRCA 1520. For surveys of the masses of Josquin, Obrecht, Isaac, and La Rue: Helmut Osthoff, *Josquin Desprez* (Tutzing, 1962), I; Gustave Reese and Jeremy Noble, "Josquin Desprez," in *The New Grove High Renaissance Masters*, ed. Stanley Sadie (London and New York, 1984), 40–56; *The Josquin Companion*, ed. Richard Sherr (Oxford, 2000), chs. 4–8 on the masses (by Bonnie Blackburn, Alejandro Enrique Planchart, M. Jennifer Bloxam, and Richard Sherr); Rob C. Wegman, *Born for the Muses: The Life and Masses of Jacob Obrecht* (Oxford, 1994); Martin Staehelin, *Die Messen Heinrich Isaacs*, 3 vols., Publikationen der Schweizerischen musikforschenden Gesellschaft, ii/28 (Bern and Stuttgart, 1977); and Honey Meconi, *Pierre de la Rue and Musical Life at the Habsburg-Burgundian Court* (Oxford, 2003); see also Edgar H. Sparks, *Cantus Firmus in Mass and Motet, 1420–1520* (Berkeley and Los Angeles, 1963). On the *Missa de beata virgine* and the Requiem mass, see Gustave Reese, "The Polyphonic *Missa de Beata Virgine* as a Genre: The Background of Josquin's Lady Mass," in *Josquin des Prez: Proceedings of the International Josquin Festival-Conference*, ed. Edward E. Lowinsky (London, 1976), 589–98; and Alec Robertson, *Requiem: Music of Mourning and Consolation* (New York: Praeger, 1968). One of the most exciting developments in recent research on the masses by composers of the Josquin generation has focused on associating individual masses with local liturgies; see especially the work of M. Jennifer Bloxam, "In Praise of Spurious Saints: The *Missae Floruit egregiis* by Pipelare and La Rue," *Journal of the American Musicological Society*, 44 (1991), 163–220, and "Sacred Polyphony and Local Traditions of Liturgy and Plainsong: Reflections on Music by Jacob Obrecht," in *Plainsong in the Age of Polyphony*, ed. Thomas Forrest Kelly, Cambridge Studies in Performance Practice, 2 (Cambridge, 1992), 140–77.

CIRCA 1530–1550. The seminal articles on the "parody/imitation" mass are by Lewis Lockwood: "On 'Parody' as Term and Concept in 16th-Century Music," in *Aspects of Medieval and Renaissance Music: A Birthday Offering to Gustave Reese*, ed. Jan LaRue (New York, 1966), 560–75, and "A View of the Early Sixteenth-Century Parody Mass," in *Queens College: Twenty-Fifth Anniversary Festschrift*, ed. Albert Mell (New York, 1964), 53–77; see also Quentin W. Quereau, "Sixteenth-Century Parody: An Approach to Analysis," *Journal of the American Musicological Society*, 31 (1978), 407–41; and René B. Lenaerts, "The 16th-Century Parody Mass in the Netherlands," *The Musical Quarterly*, 36 (1950), 410–21. On Morales in particular, see Robert M. Stevenson, *Spanish Cathedral Music in the Golden Age* (Berkeley and Los Angeles, 1961). The German tradition is covered in Friedrich Blume, *Protestant Church Music: A History* (New York, 1974). On England, see John Caldwell, *Oxford History of English Music*, I: *From the Beginnings to c.1715* (Oxford, 1991); Peter Le Huray, *Music and the Reformation in England: 1549–1660* (Cambridge, 1978); Hugh Benham, *Latin Church Music in England, c.1460–1575* (London, 1975); and Peter Phillips, *English Sacred Music: 1549–1649* (Oxford, 1991).

THE LATE SIXTEENTH CENTURY. On Ruffo, the Counter-Reformation, and the "reform" mass, see Lewis Lockwood, *The Counter-Reformation and the Masses of Vincenzo Ruffo* (Vienna, 1970), and "Vincenzo Ruffo and Musical Reform after the Council of Trent," *The Musical Quarterly*, 43 (1957), 342–71. On the Council of Trent, see Craig A. Monson, "The Council of Trent Revisited," *Journal of the American Musicological Society*, 55 (2002), 1–37; and, though only tangentially related to the polyphonic mass, Christine Getz, "Simon Boyleau and the Church of the 'Madonna of Miracles': Educating and Cultivating the Aristocratic Audience in Post-Tridentine Milan," *Journal of the Royal Musical Association*, 126 (2001), 145–61. The literature on Palestrina is vast; there are surveys in both Lewis Lockwood, "Giovanni Pierluigi da Palestrina," in *The New Grove High Renaissance Masters*, 104–19; and Jerome Roche, *Palestrina*, Oxford Studies of Composers, 7 (Oxford, 1971). On Palestrina's refashioning of his models (both polyphonic and plainsong), see Quentin W. Quereau, "Aspects of Palestrina's Parody Procedures," *Journal of Musicology*, 1 (1982), 198–216; the series of three articles by Johannes Klassen in *Kirchenmusikalisches Jahrbuch*, 37 (1954), 53–63; 38 (1954), 24–54; 39 (1955), 41–55; and Robert L. Marshall, "The Paraphrase Technique of Palestrina in his Masses Based on Hymns," *Journal of the American Musicological Society*, 16 (1963), 347–72. On Palestrina as "historicist" and as object of "historicism," see James Haar, "Palestrina 'historicus': Le due messe L'homme armé," and Stephen R. Miller, "Palestrina and the Seventeenth-Century Mass at Rome: Re-use, Reference, and Synthesis," both in *La recenzione di Palestrina in Europa: Fino dell'Ottocento*, ed. Rodobaldo Tibaldi (Lucca, 1999), 3–22, 67–104 (the former is a translation of Haar's "Palestrina as 'Historicist': The Two *L'homme armé* Masses," *Journal of the Royal Musical Association*, 121 [1996], 191–206). There is an especially perceptive discussion about the differences between Roman (Palestrina) and Venetian styles in Tim Carter, *Music in Late Renaissance and Early Baroque Italy* (Portland, OR, 1992), ch. 7. On Gabrieli, see Denis Arnold, *Giovanni Gabrieli and the Music of the Venetian High Renaissance*, rev. edn (Oxford, 1986). For surveys of the masses of Lassus and Victoria, see the articles by James Haar and Robert M. Stevenson in *The New Grove High Renaissance Masters*, 168–70, 300–303. On Byrd, see Joseph Kerman, *The Masses and Motets of William Byrd* (Berkeley and Los Angeles, 1981). For a glimpse into the cultivation of the parody mass in the New World, see Igor De Gandarías, "La misa de parodia en Guatemala: Aporte al studio de la música en Guatemala durante el siglo XVI," in *Pauta: Cuadernos de teoría y crítica musical*, 75–76 (2000), 166–80.

PERFORMANCE PRACTICE: There is a balanced account of the major issues in Christopher A. Reynolds, "Sacred Polyphony," in *Performance Practice*, ed. Howard Mayer Brown and Stanley Sadie, I: *Music Before 1600*, Norton/Grove Handbooks in Music (London and New York, 1989). For the knotty problems concerning the performance of Venetian music and the early concertato style in particular, see David Bryant, "The 'Cori spezzati' of St Mark's: Myth and Reality," *Early Music History*, 1 (1981), 165–86; and Richard Charteris, "The Performance of Giovanni Gabrieli's Vocal Works: Indications in Early Sources," *Music & Letters*, 71 (1990), 336–51. For arguments that set forth the possibility of singing one to a part, see Jean Lionnet, "Performance Practice in the Papal Chapel during the 17th Century," *Early Music*, 15 (1987), 4–15; and Richard Sherr, "Competence and Incompetence in the Papal Choir in the Age of Palestrina," *Early Music*, 22 (1994), 607–29. On the use of instruments in Spain, see Kenneth Kreitner, "The Cathedral Band of León in 1548, and When it Played," *Early Music*, 31 (2003), 41–62, and "Minstrels in Spanish Churches," *Early Music*, 20 (1992), 533–46.

THE SEVENTEENTH CENTURY: There is a survey in Lorenzo Bianconi, *Music in the Seventeenth Century*, trans. David Bryant (Cambridge, 1982). On Italy in particular, see Jerome Roche, *North Italian Church Music in the Age of Monteverdi* (Oxford, 1984); a number of the masses discussed by Roche have recently become available in modern edition in *Seventeenth-Century Italian Sacred Music*, ed. Anne Schnoebelen (New York, 1994–); see also Graham Dixon, "The Origins of the Roman 'Colossal Baroque,'" *Proceedings of the Royal Musical Association*, 106 (1979/80), 115–28. Jeffrey G. Kurtzman, "Monteverdi's Mass of Thanksgiving' Revisited," *Early Music*, 22 (1994), 63–84, is a good starting point for the Monteverdi masses, especially the *Gloria a 7 voci*. On the use of instruments during the Mass, see Stephen Bonta, "The Uses of the Sonata da Chiesa," *Journal of the American Musicological Society*, 22 (1969), 54–84; and Anne Schnoebelen, "The Role of the Violin in the Resurgence of the Mass in the 17th Century," *Early Music*, 18 (1990), 537–42, which refers to a number of the masses mentioned above. On the exportation of Italian styles to German-speaking lands, see Steven Saunders, *Cross, Sword, and Lyre: Sacred Music at the Imperial Court of Ferdinand II of Habsburg (1619–1637)* (Oxford, 1995). France is covered in James R. Anthony, *French Baroque Music from Beaujoyeulx to Rameau* (New York, 1974); on the relationship between the function of French masses and the formats in which they are preserved, see Jean-Charles Léon, "L'Art du maître de musique: Essai sur la function des sources musicales de la messe polyphonique en France aux XVIIème et XVIIIème siècles," *Revue de musicologie*, 86 (2000), 193–216.

8

THE MOTET

Anthony M. Cummings

WE begin with the problem of definition. To paraphrase William S. Newman and Philip Gossett, what is called a motet in the sixteenth and early seventeenth centuries *is* a motet.[1] I propose, therefore, to survey the characteristics of some representative pieces called motets in sources of the period in order to arrive at a conspectus of features that typify the genre and distinguish it from related genres. My premise is that, although contemporaries may on occasion have used the term inconsistently, they are likelier than we to have known what it meant; we, therefore, ought to use it in a way that is consistent with and respectful of their usage.

The term is found in various kinds of sources: music prints entitled, for example, *Motets of the Crown* or *of the Flower*,[2] manuscript materials that contain rubrics employing the term,[3] contemporary narrative accounts (diaries and chronicles)

For helpful and stimulating exchanges about many of the issues addressed in this paper, I am grateful to Professors John H. Baron (Tulane University), Margaret Bent (All Souls College, University of Oxford), Jennifer Bloxam (Williams College), John T. Brobeck (University of Arizona), Michele Fromson (then University of Washington), Peter Jeffery (Princeton University), Cristle Collins Judd (University of Pennsylvania), Patrick Macey (Eastman School of Music, University of Rochester), and Alejandro E. Planchart (University of California, Santa Barbara). None of these colleagues is to be held responsible for errors of fact or judgment that remain.

1 William S. Newman, *The Sonata in the Baroque Era*, 4th edn (New York and London, 1983), 6, 8, wrote that the scope of his study of the sonata was "defined by the range of meanings and uses that 'sonata' underwent as a musical title." Philip Gossett, "Communications," *Journal of the American Musicological Society*, 26 (1973), 175–77, esp. 175, invoking Newman's "position (what is called a sonata *is* a sonata)", argued that it "seems far more defensible than denying or ignoring the evidence of the [sources]."

2 *Motetti de la corona, Libro primo* (Venice: O. Petrucci, 1514), *Primus liber cum quatuor vocibus: Motteti del fiore* (Lyons: J. Moderne, 1532). Sigla for printed books of music cited in this study are from RISM B/I/1; the titles cited are RISM volumes 1514^{1} and 1532^{10}.

3 See, for example, the contemporary index to the manuscript *I-Rvat* Pal. lat. 1980–81, where the titles of the nine motets are preceded by the rubric "Motetti"; see Anthony M. Cummings, "Giulio de' Medici's Music Books," *Early Music History*, 10 (1991), 65–122, esp. 115–118.

of the professional activities of musical establishments (see the discussion below), contemporary correspondence, contemporary music-theoretical treatises (see the discussion below), and so on. The earliest music prints that employ the term in the title date from the first years of music printing. Later in the sixteenth century, it evidently came to offend the more refined linguistic sensibilities of printers influenced by Renaissance humanism, for whom the medieval term was characteristic of inelegant scholastic Latin usage. They accordingly began to entitle their prints *Liber XIII Ecclesiasticarum cantionum quinque vocum* (Antwerp: Susato, 1557), for example, or *Continuatio Cantionum sacrarum quatuor, quinque, sex, septem, octo, et plurium vocum* (Nuremberg: Catharina Gerlach, 1588), changes in nomenclature that cannot be said to be motivated by changes in the type of text set, for example. The titles of other prints reveal more clearly still the discomfiture of their editors concerning the medieval term: one late-sixteenth-century collection is entitled *Vincentii Ruffi veronensis musici praeclarissimi, Sacrae modulationes vulgo Motecta, quae potissimos totius anni festos dies compraehendunt, & senis vocibus concinuntur, nunc primum in lucem editae: Liber primus* (Brescia: Pietro Maria Marchetti, 1583).[4]

Several observations emerge from a rapid (and inevitably incomplete) survey of the vast repertory of pieces called motets. They are—almost without exception, to my knowledge—on Latin texts.[5] Moreover, their texts' subject matter—again, almost without exception—is sacred.[6] However, although almost invariably sacred,

The manuscript sigla used in this volume (see the list of abbreviations at the front) follow the system of library sigla used by RISM and the *New Grove Dictionary of Music and Musicians*, 2nd edn, ed. Stanley Sadie and John Tyrrell (London, 2001).

[4] See Lewis Lockwood, *The Counter-Reformation and the Masses of Vincenzo Ruffo*, Studi di musica veneta, 2 (Vienna, London, and Milan, 1970), 253, 256.

[5] I can point to one text that uses the term "'mottetto'" in reference to a work in a vernacular language: in 1585, on the occasion of the wedding festivities for Virginia dei Medici and Cesare d'Este, the Church of Santo Spirito was provided with elaborate stage machinery "che rappresentava un Cielo che s'aperse. Comparve una gran moltitudine d'Angeli cantando un mottetto, che cominciava: *O Benedetto giorno*." See Filippo Baldinucci, *Opere*, 14 vols. (Milan, 1808–12), VIII: 40–41. In this instance, of course, one cannot know whether the contemporary chronicler applied an inappropriate term to a piece in an unfamiliar genre or reported incorrectly on the text incipit.

I should add the important qualification that in considering the liturgical and paraliturgical uses of motets, I have limited myself to their relationship to the Catholic liturgy. However, there are clear reflections of the Latin motet tradition of the Catholic Church in the liturgical practices of the Lutheran Church, for example. On them, see, e.g., Lorenzo Bianconi's excellent book *Music in the Seventeenth Century*, trans. David Bryant (Cambridge, 1987), chap. 17, "The Music of the Lutheran Church: Heinrich Schütz," esp. pp. 134–35, 140, 142–43, 145.

[6] For one apparent exception, see Martin Picker (ed.), *The Motet Books of Andrea Antico*, Monuments of Renaissance Music, 8 (Chicago and London, 1987), 13, 38. The example in question, Jean Richafort's *Philomena previa*, is found in such sources as Antico's *Motetti novi libro secondo*, the *Motetti libro secondo* (Rome, 1521; RISM [1521][4]), and Attaingnant's *Motetz nouvellement composéz*; under no circumstances, therefore, can one argue that it failed to qualify in contemporary terms as a motet. The text of the *prima pars* ("Nightingale, harbinger of pleasant weather, / Who announces the cessation of rain and mud, / While you caress souls by your gentle song, / Most delightful bird, I beg you, come to me.") is the first stanza of a poem by

the texts are by no means always liturgical in origin. On the contrary, one regularly finds classical texts, devotional poetry taken from books of hours and not presently known to have been sanctioned by the Church for use within prescribed liturgical contexts, texts newly composed for specific occasions, composites within single pieces of liturgical and (apparently) non-liturgical texts, and so on.[7] Nonetheless, many motets are based on single texts drawn verbatim from the liturgy. A broad range of compositional techniques and practices available to the sixteenth-century composer is used; indeed, the most refined compositional procedures of the time are associated with the genre, as contrasted with other sacred vocal genres, which ordinarily employ a narrower range of simpler procedures (we shall consider this important point in greater detail below).

As I suggested in an earlier essay,[8] these internal characteristics, and much external evidence of various types, argue for a rough division of the sixteenth-century Latin sacred repertory into groups of "strictly liturgical" pieces (service music) and "quasi-" or "paraliturgical" pieces. In the first group are works that served precise liturgical purposes; they set entire texts drawn verbatim from the liturgy and were therefore appropriate to performance at the precise ritual moment from which their texts were drawn. Many such pieces are marked as well by distinctive musical characteristics: one is a compositional technique that seems to be a kind of written reflection of the practice known as *falsobordone*; another is *alternatim* treatment of the text, in which one verse is chanted and the next sung in homophony or simple polyphony, or the music for one verse sung and that for the next played on the organ. In the second group are motets and related genres. Such pieces may well make use of single liturgical texts and in some instances, therefore, would have been able to be sung in the ritual contexts from which their texts were taken. Often, however, motets have characteristics that make them unsuitable for such purposes: their texts may be composites of phrases drawn from several liturgical contexts and as such are imprecisely matched to a specific ritual context. In other cases, as suggested above, pieces demonstrably called motets in period sources were based on classical or newly-written texts. Finally, the compositional language associated with the genre in a sense made it less appropriate to precise liturgical purposes than service music, since the compositional freedom exercised by the composer in setting motet texts serves to some extent to lessen their intelligibility and thus loosen the connection with the liturgy (this argument will be developed more fully below). It is in this sense that motets are paraliturgical: their relationship to the ritual service, though demonstrable, is somewhat freer in a number of

John Peckham (d. 1292), a student of St Bonaventure in Paris and subsequently archbishop of Canterbury (see Picker, 38). Its content is indeed seemingly secular; or is it that our 21st-century sense of the distinction between the sacred and the secular is simply very different from the 16th century's?

[7] I say "apparently" because, here again, without an exhaustive investigation of period liturgical books documenting the liturgical traditions of specific centers, one cannot be certain that a text not at present known to be liturgical had the same status in pre-Tridentine Europe.

[8] See Anthony M. Cummings, "Toward an Interpretation of the Sixteenth-Century Motet," *Journal of the American Musicological Society*, 34 (1981), 43–59.

important ways. Indeed, one has the sense that the liturgical books were freely used as anthologies of sacred texts that the composers (or whoever furnished them with their texts) utilized for purposes that in some cases had little to do with their original function, just as collections of secular verse were similarly utilized. The motet, therefore, was a polyphonic work based on a sacred Latin text—sometimes liturgical, sometimes not—apparently selected to express sentiments of a particular type; the question of its use or function is a separate one.[9]

There is much external evidence supporting the interpretation advanced here, and we shall consider it in some detail. It is of several types, including (1) the testimony of contemporary narrative accounts and books containing directives that specify occasions when motets were, or were intended to be, performed; (2) the testimony of occasional motets; (3) the testimony of patterns of transmission in the practical sources, which in many instances relegate motets and service music to separate collections; (4) the testimony of music-theoretical treatises that devote separate discussions to motets and other types of sacred pieces, which suggests that to contemporaries there was a distinction.

The testimony of contemporary narrative accounts and books containing directives

Much of this first type of evidence was quoted and interpreted in an earlier essay (see n. 8 above), and here I shall limit myself to similar illustrative evidence not reviewed there. To summarize the material in the earlier piece: Sixteenth- and early-seventeenth-century diaries from the Cappella Sistina and other, similar sources specify occasions on which motets were performed and in many instances identify particular works, so that we can determine the precise relationship of their texts

[9] John Brobeck has drawn attention to an apparent instance of the use of the term "motet" in reference to a liturgical genre. In "Some 'Liturgical Motets' for the Royal Court: A Reconsideration of Genre in the Sixteenth-Century French Motet," *Musica disciplina*, 47 (1993), 123–57, Brobeck notes that Attaingnant published liturgical polyphony in the seventh in his series of thirteen volumes of motets (*moteti*, *moduli*, etc.) issued in 1534–35, *Liber septimus . . . musicales . . . modulos . . . habet* (RISM 1534[9]). In my view, however, this is a simple inconsistency, an anomalous usage that proves the general rule. Indeed, as Brobeck himself suggests (p. 142), "if the use of synonyms [like *moduli* and *cantiones*] and the mixed nature of his motet volumes indicate that Attaingnant found little cause to segregate works intended for liturgical and para-liturgical uses, *it also leaves the distinct impression that he was not entirely comfortable describing compositions intended for liturgical use as motets* [emphasis added]. In fact, the word 'motet' does not appear on the title pages of fully half of his collections devoted to 'motet-like' sacred works. . . . The printer's search on the title pages of his prints for other descriptive terms thus might be taken as evidence that he essentially was ambivalent about the meaning of the term 'motet.'" I must also say that I believe that Professor Brobeck has misunderstood the thesis advanced in my earlier article (see n. 8); rather than arguing for a narrower definition of the motet, I in fact argued for a broader, more flexible definition that took account of evidence documenting that motets, while sometimes used at the ritual moment from which their texts were taken, were often used in other kinds of contexts as well. The adjective "paraliturgical" connotes a broader view of the genre, not a narrower one.

to their ritual contexts.[10] In a great many instances, the motets were *not* sung at the point in the service from which their texts are taken (although they were almost always sung on the same feast day); rather, motets seem to have been performed in a small number of other contexts, such as during the celebrant's recitation of the Offertory text, or at the Elevation or Postcommunion. Thus the motet sung at the Offertory on a particular feast was ordinarily based on a text that was "calendrically" appropriate, in that it was a text for the office of the day, for example; it was *not*, however, a setting of the Offertory text *per se* for that day. What might seem to us to be a liturgical irregularity may have been regarded as such in the sixteenth century as well: Harold Powers has suggested, reasonably, that Palestrina's cycle of polyphonic settings of Offertory texts was composed in order to have polyphonic elaborations of texts proper to the Offertory available for performance at that point in the service, where motets had traditionally been performed;[11] to my knowledge, however, there is no evidence that Palestrina's settings were so used.

Let us now consider some representative references suggesting this general interpretation. The *Osservazioni per ben regolare il coro de i cantori della Cappella Pontificia* (Rome, 1711) of Andrea Adami da Bolsena (1663–1742)[12] is an early-eighteenth-century work documenting seventeenth-century practices. Although its testimony is thus late, it is absolutely consistent with sixteenth-century evidence, which may serve as yet further evidence of the rather extraordinary conservatism of the practices of the papal chapel, and the examples quoted here are perfectly consistent with those one could draw from sixteenth-century materials.[13] Adami's text is replete with directives indicating that specified motets were to be sung at the Offertory on particular feast days. At Mass on Ash Wednesay, for example, "The Offertory has to be said *andante* in counterpoint [*contrapunto*], so as to be able to say *adagio* Palestrina's motet *Derelinquat impius*, in Book no. 167, just the part on page 14." On the fourth Sunday of Lent, "The Offertory has to be said *andante*, because Matteo Simonelli's motet *Cantemus Domino* with its second part (Book no. 193, page 1) is very long." (This second reference helps clarify the meaning of the first; elsewhere Adami makes it clear that first or second parts of bipartite motets were sometimes performed without the other.) On Passion Sunday, "The Introit, Kyries, Graduale, and Tract are chanted; not so the Offertory, which is sung in

[10] One of the most important of the sources in question is the Sistine Chapel diary of 1616, edited by Herman-Walther Frey, "Die Gesänge der sixtinischen Kapelle an den Sonntagen und hohen Kirchenfesten des Jahres 1616," in *Mélanges Eugène Tisserant*, 7 vols., Studi e testi, 231–37 (Vatican City, 1964), VI: 395–437. For bringing this extremely important publication to my attention, and for much useful information about the liturgy of the church and ecclesiastical Latin usage, given with characteristic generosity, I am very grateful to Professor Peter Jeffery.

[11] Harold S. Powers, "Modal Representation in Polyphonic Offertories," *Early Music History*, 2 (1982), 43–86, esp. 49.

[12] See the facsimile edited by Giancarlo Rostirolla in the series Musurgiana, 1 (Lucca, 1988). Biographical and bibliographical information is contained in Rostirolla's introduction, pp. vii–xxi.

[13] That the interpretation of the motet advanced here is substantiated by 17th-century evidence is suggested as well by Bianconi's discussion of the genre in *Music in the Seventeenth Century*, esp. chap. 15, "Music in the Catholic Liturgy."

counterpoint, but *andante*, however, so as then to sing *a bell'agio* Palestrina's motet *Salvum me fac* (Book no. 177, just the part on page 8)."[14]

These references, representative of a great many others from sixteenth- and seventeenth-century sources as well as from elsewhere in Adami's own text, document that the Offertory was the principal ritual locus for performances of motets in the practice of the papal chapel. A later reference suggests that the Elevation also served as locus for such performances: "*Corpus Domini . . . The morning at Low Mass* . . . . The chapelmaster, at his pleasure, will have to choose five singers for the *concertino*, which has to follow the pope in the procession; and after the Elevation, these same sing a motet selected by the chapelmaster from the books, which the said singers carry in procession." A handwritten annotation in the copy of Adami's book published in facsimile by Rostirolla inserts before this: "after the Elevation the eight-voice motet *Sacerdotes*."[15] In its specification of Palestrina's eight-voice *Sacerdotes Domini*, the annotation thus supersedes Adami's directive, which specifies that five singers were to perform the Elevation motet; nonetheless, both references document that the Elevation, like the Offertory, accommodated performances of motets.[16]

There are, finally, references suggesting that motets were performed in ritual contexts at the end of mass. On Sunday, 12 May 1596, for example,

> at San Silvestro on Monte Cavallo, His Holiness said Low Mass, and he gave communion to twelve elderly maidens and twelve widows, who at the end of Mass went in procession to their convent, which stands opposite the aforementioned church. And while His Holiness was saying Mass, the reverend singers sang one motet at the conclusion of the *Credo*, another at the Elevation, and another while communion was being given; and at the end of Mass, His Holiness entered the sacristy, and the elderly maidens went in procession to the convent, and while they were passing by, the singers sang the *Te Deum laudamus*.[17]

[14] Adami, *Osservazioni*, 2: "L'Offertorio si de(v)e dire andante in contrapunto, per poter dire adagio il Mottetto *Derelinquat impius* del Palestrina nel Libro 167, parte sola a carte 14"; p. 28: "L'Offertorio si de(v)e dire andante, perche il Motetto *Cantemus Domino* di Matteo Simonelli con parte al lib. 193, carta 1 è molto longo"; ibid.: "L'Introito, i *Kyrie*, il Graduale, e il Tratto vanno detti in Canto fermo non così l'Offertorio, che va in contrapunto, ma però andante per cantar poi a bell'agio il Motetto *Salvum me fac* del Palestrina al lib. 177, parte sola carte 8."

[15] Ibid., 78: "*Corpus Domini . . . La Mattina alla Messa bassa . . .* Il Signor Maestro dovrà a suo piacere sciegliere cinque Cantori per il Concertino, che nella Processione deve andare dopo il Papa; e questi medesimi cantano dopo l'Elevazione un Motetto eletto dal Signor Maestro ne i libri, che i detti Cantori portano in Processione [*in marg.*: dopo l'Elevazione il mott.° ad 8. Sacerdotes]."

[16] There are several substantiating references for this assertion in Herman-Walther Frey, "Das Diarium der Sixtinischen Sängerkapelle in Rom für das Jahr 1596 (Nr. 21)," *Analecta musicologica*, 23 (1985), 129–204, which appeared after my earlier essay. I might observe that the references in Adami's text are interesting in that they state precisely where in the choirbooks the specified works were to be found; these references could perhaps be connected to an 18th-century library classification scheme.

[17] "a Monte Cavallo a san Silvestro, . . . nostro Sig[no]re ha detta Messa bassa, et ha

What these references suggest is a loose relationship between the text of the motet sung at the Offertory (or at the Elevation, Communion, or Postcommunion) on a particular feast and the specific textual provisions of that moment in the ritual service; the text of the Offertory motet, that is, is *not* the Offertory text. For example, the *Salvum me fac* sung at the Offertory on Passion Sunday, presumably the Palestrina *opus dubium* found in Cappella Sistina manuscripts 72 and 117,[18] is partly based on the responsory to the fifth lesson of Matins on Palm Sunday,[19] and is therefore only seasonally related to the occasion of its performance.

Although the currently available evidence from northern Europe is, to my knowledge, less abundant than Italian evidence, it nonetheless suggests that motets were performed in the same kinds of ritual contexts. On the "morning of the 22nd" of October 1532, for example, on the occasion of the meeting of François I and Henry VIII at Boulogne-sur-Mer, "[the two] having entered a church, one went to one chapel, the other to the other, and at the conclusion of Mass, they came together, [His Most Christian Majesty] having had a motet sung in his chapel, namely *Da pacem, Domine, in diebus nostris*."[20]

Motets demonstrably had non-liturgical uses as well. In my earlier piece, I cited much evidence suggesting that motets were regularly sung at the pope's table at dinner.[21] Colin Slim has drawn attention to a theatrical use: Joachim Greff, furnishing directions for a performance of *Lazarus vom Tode . . . erwecket* (1545), his versification of Joachim Sapidus's play *Lazarus redivivus* (1539), specified that "when the actors have . . . arrived on stage, one should begin to sing as a prologue the motet, *Haec dicit Dominus VI vocum*, the quintus of which begins with the

communicate 12 zitelle et dodici Vedove, le quali, finita la messa, sono andate processionalmente al Monasterio loro, che sta dirincontro alla detta chiesa. Et li Rev[eren]di SS.ri Cantori, mentre N[ost]ro sig[no]re diceva la messa, finito il Credo, cantorno un Motetto, un altro all'elevatione et un altro mentre si faceva la communione; et finita la messa, N[ost]ro sig[no]re è intrato in Sacrestia, et le zitelle sono andate in processione al Monasterio et mentre passavano, li Cantori hanno Cantato il *Te deum laud[am]us*." Quoted in Frey, "Das Diarium . . . für das Jahr 1596," 165.

[18] Knud Jeppesen, "Palestrina," in *Die Musik in Geschichte und Gegenwart*, X (Kassel and Basel, 1962), 658–706, esp. 678.

[19] See, e.g., Carl Marbach, *Carmina scriptuarum* (Strasbourg, 1907; repr. Hildesheim, 1963), 153.

[20] Marin Sanudo, *I diarii di Marino Sanuto (MCCCCXCVI–MDXXXIII)* (Venice, 1879–1903; repr. Bologna, 1969–70), LVII: col. 317. Richard Freedman, "Paris and the French Court under François I," in *Man and Music*, ed. Stanley Sadie, II: *The Renaissance: From the 1470s to the End of the 16th Century* (Basingstoke and London, 1989), 174–96, esp. 179–80, identifies the motet with Claudin de Sermisy's.

[21] Cummings, 'Toward an Interpretation," esp. 45–46 and nn. 5–6. There are many substantiating references to the singing of motets in the pope's quarters after mass in Frey, "Das Diarium . . . für das Jahr 1596." See also the reference to the singing of motets at the court of Duke Alfonso I d'Este in the same kind of context; a contemporary chronicler wrote that "il Prencipe stesso averebbe il verno innanzi cena suonate di Viuola, ma un cotal Cameriere, un Cappellano privato de' suoi, e passato quel tempo non solo avanti, ma anco dopo la cena, cantato dui o tre mottetti, Canzone Francese, ed altri, come spesse volte l'istate alla Villa ed al Boschetto mentre si cenava i musici averebbono cantato quattro o sei Canzone molto leggiadre." See *Atti e memorie della R. Deputazione di storia patria per le provincie di Romagna*, 3rd ser., 10 (1891/92), 182.

text, *Circumdederunt me dolores mortis etc.* Afterwards, in the first act: *Si bona suscepimus V vocum* by Philip Verdelot."[22]

The testimony of occasional motets

An interpretation of the motet as a paraliturgical genre is substantiated by the evidence of occasional motets. These are works based on non-liturgical texts, newly composed for specific occasions. That they are explicitly called motets in the sources and are compositionally indistinguishable from motets on liturgical texts suggests that, to contemporaries, they were as much motets as those based on antiphon, respond, or sequence texts. To take an entirely typical example: on 20 January 1540, on the occasion of the visit to Cambrai of the Holy Roman Emperor Charles V, there was performed *Venite populi terrae* by Jehan Courtois, chapel master of the Bishop of Cambrai, a piece explicitly called "ung motet" in a contemporary narrative account of the occasion.[23] Both the *prima pars* and *secunda pars* open with the familiar imitative entries generally characteristic of the compositional procedures associated with the genre throughout the century,[24] and the prevailing texture is imitative, although there are two instances of rather arresting shifts to stark homophony that serve to set important passages in sharp relief and thus make them especially intelligible (the words are "et civitas pacis conduce suo" and "Ave Caesar ave majestas sacra").[25] Another example is Francesco Corteccia's eight-voice motet *Ingredere*, performed by twenty-four singers atop the arch of the Porta al Prato in Florence during Eleanor of Toledo's triumphal entrance into the city in 1539.[26]

22 H. Colin Slim (ed.), *A Gift of Madrigals and Motets*, 2 vols. (Chicago, 1972), I: 100.

23 "ung motet d'excellente musicque composé par maistre Jehan Courtois maistre de la chappelle dudict seigneur Révérendissime." See *Declaration des Triumphantz honneux et Recoeul faictz a la maieste Imperialle a sa ioyeuse et premiere entree ... en la cite et duche de Cambray ...* (Cambrai, 1539 [1540]), fol. Cii, quoted by Nanie Bridgman, "La Participation musicale à l'entrée de Charles Quint à Cambrai, le 20 janvier 1540," in *Les Fêtes de la Renaissance*, ed. Jean Jacquot, II: *Fêtes et cérémonies au temps de Charles Quint* (Paris, 1960), 235–53, esp. 241.

24 For a masterful survey of stylistic developments in the 16th-century motet, written largely from the perspective of changes in constructional technique, see Leeman L. Perkins, "Motet" II: "Renaissance," in *New Grove*^{2}, XVII: 202–15, esp. 209–213.

25 See the edition of the piece in Bridgman, 'La Participation', [245–53].

26 See, most recently, Anthony M. Cummings *The Politicized Muse: Music for Medici Festivals, 1512–1537*, Princeton Essays on the Arts (Princeton, 1992), 76–79. Once again, the contemporary narrative account of the occasion makes explicit use of the term "motet": "i sonatori & Cantori ... Cantarono per mottetto quelle Parole che nel maggior fregio dello Arco ... si leggevano. INGREDERE." Quoted in Henry W. Kaufmann, "Music for a Noble Florentine Wedding (1539)," in *Words and Music, The Scholar's View: A Medley of Problems and Solutions Compiled in Honor of A. Tillman Merritt By Sundry Hands*, ed. Laurence Berman (Cambridge, MA, 1972), 161–88, esp. 165 n. 18.

The testimony of patterns of transmission in the practical sources

Even a random survey of sixteenth-century practical sources serves to document that motets were often transmitted with secular works, which suggests non-liturgical uses; indeed, why were they mixed with madrigals and chansons if not to afford opportunity for performance on the same, or same kinds of, occasions? In the early sixteenth century, for example, one finds prints entitled *Motetti e canzone libro primo* and *Fior de motetti e canzone novi*,[27] and manuscript sources that transmit motets and secular works alike.[28] Similarly, printed collections often (though not invariably, to be sure) are devoted either to strictly liturgical genres or to motets; the two repertories, that is, are frequently found in separate collections, which further suggests that to contemporaries there was a conceptual generic distinction between them. The non-mass sacred music of the Counter-Reformation composer Vincenzo Ruffo, for example, is transmitted in separate collections devoted to: (1) Magnificats (for example, *Li Magnificat breui et aierosi di Vincenzo Ruffo*); (2) Psalms (for example, *I sacri et santi Salmi che si cantano a Compieta dell'eccellente M. Vincenzo Ruffo*); (3) responsories and Lamentations for Holy Week (for example, *Li soavissimi Responsorii della Settimana Santa a cinque voci, dell'eccellentissimo musico M. Vincenzo Ruffo, con un Benedictus, & alcuni Miserere a 2 chori, doi Adoramus te Christe & tutti li otto toni in falso bordone, a cinque voci*); and, finally, (4) motets, which are found in prints entitled, for example, *Il primo libro de Motetti* and *Motetti, a sei voci*.[29] The careful generic distinctions implied by the contrasting contents of the different collections, and the contrasting attendant nomenclature, suggest something of the way in which contemporaries thought of the sacred literature.

The testimony of music-theoretical treatises

At least two comprehensive and important music-theoretical treatises of the late sixteenth and early seventeenth centuries, Pietro Ponzio's *Ragionamento* of 1588 and Pietro Cerone's *El melopeo y maestro* of 1613, devote separate discussions to the compositional procedures associated with motets and with strictly liturgical genres. This, like the evidence of patterns of transmission in the practical sources, suggests a contemporary conceptual distinction between the repertories.[30] Early in the sixteenth century, Pietro Aaron similarly devoted a separate chapter (Book II, chap. 19) of his *Toscanello in musica* of 1523 to "The Way to Compose Psalms and

[27] See, for example, Iain Fenlon and James Haar, *The Italian Madrigal in the Early Sixteenth Century: Sources and Interpretation* (Cambridge, 1988), 205–9.

[28] See Cummings, 'Giulio de'Medici's Music Books', 100–108, 113–18.

[29] See Lockwood, *The Counter-Reformation*, 243–44, 248–49, 251.

[30] As Lewis Lockwood and others have noted, however, Cerone's text borrows directly and liberally from its many sources, Ponzio's treatise among them; one therefore cannot assume the mutual independence of these theoretical discussions. See Lockwood, "On 'Parody' as Term and Concept in 16th-Century Music," in *Aspects of Medieval and Renaissance Music: A Birthday Offering to Gustave Reese*, ed. Jan LaRue (New York, 1966), 560–75, esp. 570–72.

Magnificats," a discussion that assumes *alternatim* performance and the particular compositional challenges it posed.[31]

We have considered the question of the quasi-liturgical character and function of the motet in such detail because, I would argue, they had such important implications for the genre's musical profile and explain its distinctive compositional characteristics. Its somewhat looser relationship to the liturgy, that is, apparently freed the composer to employ a different, more elaborate kind of musical treatment. This contrasts with settings of more strictly liturgical works, which were ordinarily clothed in simpler musical dress, so that the texts are more fully intelligible, and the pieces' ritual purposes are more effectively served. The stylistic features of service music—*alternatim* treatment of the text, the use of procedures reminiscent of *falsobordone*—are appropriate to texts performed at their proper place in the ritual service and serving specific liturgical purposes; the service's textual provisions, it might be said, are musically elaborated in more modest, limited, and circumscribed ways. Offertory motets, on the other hand, given that they were sung while the celebrant recited the proper liturgical text *sotto voce*, could be accorded different, more complicated musical treatment precisely because their relationship to the liturgico-textual provisions of the moment was freer, and their texts perforce were not expected to satisfy "local" liturgico-textual requirements.

Eustachius de Monte Regali Gallus composed two settings of Psalm 115, *Credidi propter quod locutus sum*, one in each tradition. Here compositional style is a function not of text type but of ritual usage; thus patently functional works elicited one kind of compositional treatment, motets another. One of Eustachius's settings exemplifies the tradition of the simple *alternatim* type, intended for liturgical use.[32] The piece opens with full harmonies, the four voices declaiming the text simultaneously, and the texture throughout is almost unrelieved homophony, although enlivened by brief, intermittent instances of contrapuntal writing. Some variety is also achieved through the structural use of contrasting vocal sonorities; verse 7, for example, is set off from the others by a reduced complement. In the contemporary psalm-motet on the other hand, Eustachius's musical design at the very least is more flexible than that exemplified by his liturgically determined piece, and often

[31] See Pietro Aaron, *Toscanello in Music*, trans. Peter Bergquist, 3 vols., Colorado College Music Press Translations, 4 (Colorado Springs, CO, 1970), II: 32–33. The compositional issues to be considered were tonal ones; the beginning, middle, and ending of the verses set polyphonically had to take careful account, in tonal terms, of the profile of the alternate verses to be chanted or played on the organ. The same concern is expressed in Aaron's *Trattato della natura e cognizione di tutti gli toni di canto figurato* of 1525, trans. in Oliver Strunk (ed.), *Source Readings in Music History*, rev. ed. Leo Treitler (New York, 1998), 423.

[32] There is an edition of the *alternatim* setting in David Crawford, "Vespers Polyphony at Modena's Cathedral in the First Half of the Sixteenth Century" (PhD diss., University of Illinois, 1967), II: 340–45. Eustachius's Psalm-motet *Credidi propter quod* is, to my knowledge, unpublished; it is found in *I-Fn* II.I.232, fols. 173^{v}–176. The implication in the work-list in *New Grove*^{2}, VIII: 447, that these two settings are the same is incorrect.

results in a refined intermingling of conventional contrapuntal writing with less complicated note-against-note homophony.

At the risk of redundancy, I feel it is important to describe this fundamental distinction in yet another way, precisely because it is so crucial to an understanding of the motet as a genre, specifically as it contrasts with other sacred genres. In polyphonic service music, the textual and musical elements of the Gregorian original are imported more or less directly. In the motet literature, on the other hand, it is more a matter of there being general "resonances" of the Gregorian original in the polyphonic elaboration.[33] Reluctant as one is to make very much of this kind of analogy, there is a reminder here of the Renaissance concept of *inventio*.[34] The composer's "sources"—the Gregorian models—furnished the basic materials, which were then elaborated by the composer, who was free to apply liberally his powers of *inventio* to the compositional task at hand. In this context, the concern stated in Aaron's discussion of the composition of Psalms and Magnificats—that in setting the alternate verses to be sung polyphonically, composers had to be attentive to the tonal substance of the verses to be chanted or played on the organ—may be seen as an expression of the kind of distinction argued here. There were no such strictures applied to the composition of motets, precisely because they had a different relationship to the liturgy, which in turn permitted a different attitude toward and treatment of the Gregorian materials serving as "sources." This interpretation leads, then, to a fuller consideration of the compositional procedures associated with the motet as a genre and as contrasted with other sacred genres.

In what ways are there resonances of the Gregorian tradition in the motet literature? In an important and provocative article, Oliver Strunk briefly described the distinctive musical profiles associated with particular text types in the Gregorian repertory (especially sequences, antiphons, responds, psalms, and canticles), and outlined the ways in which they are reflected in the sixteenth-century motet literature. For all its remarkable brevity and concision, Strunk's article remains the best statement of its thesis and bears quoting here *in extenso*:

> [The sequence's] chief characteristic is the parallelism inherent in its paired structure, a parallelism which invites a polyphonic treatment of alternate verses . . . , a setting as variation-chain . . . , or an antiphonal harmonization . . . . Not less important is its tendency to paraphrase the plainsong model . . . . Even when no paraphrase is present [in Palestrina's sequence-motets] . . . the characteristic parallel structure is as a rule maintained through alternations and combinations of two choirs. . . . One sees, too, that Palestrina connects certain definite procedures with the form—that, generally speaking, it is for him a large form, calling for a large and divided body of voices (normally the eight-part chorus) and for homophonic rather than polyphonic treatment;

[33] For the useful and suggestive term "resonances," I am very grateful to Professor Cristle Collins Judd.

[34] For a recent discussion of *inventio*, see Charles Dempsey, *The Portrayal of Love: Botticelli's "Primavera" and Humanist Culture at the Time of Lorenzo the Magnificent* (Princeton, 1992), 28 ff.

> that he relies for his effect less on complex combination than on beauty of line and accent; and . . . that . . . he tends . . . to elaborate rather than . . . invent.
>
> . . . Palestrina makes a sharp distinction between the old established [antiphon] texts on the one hand and the texts for specific festivals on the other. In setting such texts as *Alma redemptoris Mater* . . . , he carries paraphrase of the plainsong model even further than in the Sequence, going so far as to begin in some cases with the official intonation; when he sets the *Ave Regina coelorum* and *Salve Regina* the sequence-like structure of his originals induces a sequence-like structure in his motet and leads in half a dozen instances to the use of two choirs. . . .
>
> For the Office . . . , the Antiphon is . . . the typical small motet-form. The typical large form . . . is the Respond [or responsory]. Its characteristic feature . . . is its division into two sections, exactly reproducing the form of the plainsong Respond from which it takes its text. The . . . *Prima pars* . . . sets the text of the Respond proper; the . . . *Secunda pars* . . . sets the text of the Verse and concludes with a repetition of the concluding line or lines of the Respond; the whole, then, exhibits the form AB (*Prima pars*); CB (*Secunda pars*). The plainsong Respond . . . is a musical reply to the reading of a Lesson or Chapter, an elaborate and extended composition affording considerable opportunity for soloistic display. In keeping with this, the motet-setting . . . is usually an elaborate, extended, and brilliant composition. Palestrina, while he occasionally begins an Antiphon with full harmonies . . . , does not use this technique in Responds for four and five voices, which invariably open with imitations. What is more, . . . this motet-type calls in its full development for a relatively large body of voices. Among the Palestrina motets for four voices the Antiphon is the commonest type, among those for five it occurs less frequently . . . ; the . . . Respond occurs infrequently among the motets for four voices, more frequently among those for five . . . . among the motets of Palestrina [there is a] general rule that the Respond-motet does not paraphrase its plainsong model. . . .
>
> Motet-settings of the Psalms and Canticles (other than the Magnificat) call for still another mode of treatment. Here . . . the eight-part chorus is the norm, and the necessity for dealing with a relatively lengthy text without exceeding the usual bounds leads to . . . a homophonic or at best quasi-polyphonic texture and . . . an emphasis on sonority and rhythmic declamation. At the same time the parallel structure of the Sequence is lacking and the melodic interest less sustained.[35]

The selection of a particular text type, therefore—itself a fundamental precompositional choice—had related precompositional consequences for the composer, since in many cases it clearly suggested how to address and resolve such basic

[35] Oliver Strunk, "Some Motet-Types of the Sixteenth Century" [1939], repr. in idem, *Essays on Music in the Western World* (New York, 1974), 109–13.

compositional issues as the number of voices, large-scale formal procedure, melodic substance and style, and texture and constructional technique.

Strunk illustrated his argument principally by reference to the mid-sixteenth-century repertory, but I believe it is substantiated by other repertories as well. It is, for example, roughly substantiated by the motets of Josquin des Prez, who in an important sense stands at the very head of the entire sixteenth-century motet development (indeed, the genre appears to have appealed powerfully to his artistic temperament and imagination). Once again, I would say that the correspondences between the elements of the Gregorian tradition and their evocation in the motet literature are not always direct and are often inexact; indeed, in some instances they are essentially nonexistent. Nonetheless, there are frequently resonances of the type at issue here.

Jeremy Noble lists 79 authentic Josquin motets in his work-list for *The New Grove High Renaissance Masters*.[36] Of those, let us examine the 44 identified by Jacquelyn Mattfeld as settings of single, integral texts drawn more or less verbatim from the liturgy[37] and classified as antiphon, canticle, chapter, genealogy, Gospel, hymn, lection, prayer, Psalm, responsory, sequence, or tract.[38] The classification is

[36] *The New Grove High Renaissance Masters* (London and New York, 1980, 1984), 66–72. I have excluded: (1) Latin *contrafacta* of other works; (2) doubtful and misattributed works; (3) separate listings for parts after the first of multipartite works; and (4) the Magnificats. The worklist in *New Grove*², XIII: 242–46 (newly drawn up by Jeremy Noble and Jeffrey Dean) is somewhat differently organized. See n. 38 below.

[37] Jaquelyn Mattfeld, "Some Relationships between Texts and Cantus Firmi in the Liturgical Motets of Josquin des Pres," *Journal of the American Musicological Society*, 14 (1961), 159–83. The remaining motets discussed by Mattfeld are either: (1) settings of an excerpt or excerpts from a single liturgical text or of composites of texts drawn from several different liturgical contexts; (2) settings of composites of liturgical and *non*-liturgical texts; or (3) settings of non-liturgical texts (including one setting of a composite of biblical, but apparently non-liturgical, texts). In some important respects, of course, Mattfeld's pioneering work has been superseded. However, although her calendrical assignments can in some instances be challenged—a text identified as the antiphon for a particular feast, for example, is more accurately to be associated with a different feast—her classification by basic text type remains valid; an antiphon text, that is, is unlikely to be shown to have been a different type of text altogether. For this reason, therefore, her classification scheme remains sound and can be used for the present purpose of relating text type to musical style. For useful discussion and advice on this point, I am grateful to Professor Jennifer Bloxam.

[38] The classification scheme calls for a few words of clarification. If the principal text is a single, integral liturgical text, it determines the classification. For example, the text of *Sic Deus dilexit mundum/Circumdederunt me* is, strictly speaking, a composite of two liturgical texts; similarly, the text of *Stabat mater dolorosa/Comme femme desconfortée* is a composite of a liturgical and a non-liturgical text. However, they are classified as based on a single, integral liturgical text (a chapter in the first case, a sequence in the second) because their *principal* text may be so described. A multipartite work whose individual sections are each based on a single, integral liturgical text is classified as based on such a text, even though the text of the work is, strictly speaking, a kind of composite; such a work utilizes a very different sort of procedure, however, from those where the text is a patchwork of snippets of text from different sources. Thus *O admirabile commercium* is classified as based on an antiphon, and *O Domine Jesu Christe* is classified as based on a prayer, even though they are, strictly speaking, based on a *cycle* of antiphons and a *cycle* of prayers. Their procedure, however, is different from that of *Missus est*

illustrated in Table 8.1 (overleaf). When we examine the distribution of the 46 motets[39] across text type by number of voices, for example, we find that one of Strunk's observations is equally valid for this repertory. Of the 46 motets, 33 are for four voices or fewer, and 13 are for more than four voices. Although the counts in some categories are too small to be meaningful, we nonetheless find that of the nine sequence-motets, for example, five (56 %) are for five or six voices, very different proportions from those of the group of 46 motets as a whole, where only 13 (28 %) are for more than four voices. Among sequence-motets, that is, there is a disproportionate representation of works for a larger number of voices. The single responsory-motet is also for a larger than normal complement. On the other hand, the distribution of antiphons by number of voices mirrors almost exactly the proportions in the group of 46 as a whole; of the eight antiphon motets, five (63 %) are for four voices, and three are for more than four. The text of one of the eight, however, *Inviolata, integra et casta es, Maria*, is found in the sources as both an antiphon and a sequence. At the risk of a tautology, I might suggest that precisely because it is a five-voice work, it could be argued that it is more properly to be classified as a sequence-motet, since in Josquin's *œuvre* antiphon-motets are ordinarily four-voice works.[40] (Another exception to this general rule is the five-

Gabriel angelus, which is based on a patchwork of texts drawn from antiphons and a responsory from Lauds and Matins on the feast of the Annunciation.

I must add that the traditional attribution to Josquin of some of the works listed in the table has not altogether survived recent scrutiny. Indeed, the work-list by Jeremy Noble and Jeffrey Dean accompanying Patrick Macey's excellent article on Josquin in *New Grove*² eliminates any number of the motets listed by Noble in the 1980 edition of *New Grove*. On the inauthenticity of the Psalm-motets *Celi enarrant gloriam Dei* and *Levavi oculos meos in montes* in particular, see two persuasive studies by Macey: "*Celi enarrant*: An Inauthentic Psalm Motet Attributed to Josquin," in *Proceedings of the International Josquin Symposium, Utrecht 1986*, ed. Willem Elders (Utrecht, 1991), 25–44; "Josquin as Classic: *Qui habitat, Memor esto,* and Two Imitations Unmasked," *Journal of the Royal Musical Association*, 118 (1993), 1–43. On the status of *Sic Deus dilexit mundum/Circumdederunt me*, see John Milsom, "*Circumdederunt*: 'A Favourite Cantus Firmus of Josquin's'?", *Soundings* 9 (1982), 2–10; Martin Just, "Josquins Chanson 'Nymphes, napées' als Bearbeitung des Invitatoriums 'Circumdederunt me' und als Grundlage für Kontrafaktur, Zitat und Nachahmung," *Die Musikforschung*, 43 (1990), 305–35. In addition, on the precise generic status of the prayer-motet *Ave Maria, gratia plena . . . benedicta tu*, which, like the hymn-motet *Qui velatus facie fuisti* and the prayer-motet *O Domine Jesu Christe*, might more properly be considered part of a set of *motetti missales*, see Patrick Macey, "Josquin's 'Little' *Ave Maria*: A Misplaced Motet from the *Vultum tuum* Cycle?", *Tijdschrift van de Vereniging voor Nederlandse Muziekgeschiedenis*, 39 (1989), 38–53. If a consensus ultimately emerges that some of these motets are indeed not by Josquin and, further, if others are classified in different generic categories, the counts in some of the categories in the table will change. But whoever the composer of the disputed works, one can say that certain types of text seem to have been associated with attendant compositional strategies with respect to number of voices, for example, or use of paraphrase, which, as we shall see, is my principal point; the matter of who their composer is does not affect that point.

[39] I say 46 rather than 44 because two motets count in two different categories and therefore are listed twice in Table 8.1: (1) *Inviolata, integra et casta es, Maria* is found in Mattfeld's sources as both an antiphon and a sequence; and (2) *Liber generationis Jesu Christi* is found as both a genealogy and a gospel.

[40] This kind of argument reverses the order of the methodology employed up to this

Table 8.1*a*: Josquin motets classified by text type (see n. 38)

motet	number of voices
ANTIPHON	
Alma Redemptoris mater	4
Inviolata, integra et casta es, Maria	5
O admirabile commercium	4
O virgo virginum	6
Regina celi	4
Salve regina	4
Salve regina	5
Virgo prudentissima	4
CANTICLE	
Benedicite omnia opera Domini Domino	4
CHAPTER	
Sic Deus dilexit mundum/Circumdederunt me	6
GENEALOGY	
Factum est autem	4
Liber generationis Jesu Christi	4
GOSPEL	
In principio erat Verbum	4
Liber generationis Jesu Christi	4
HYMN	
Qui velatus facie fuisti	4
LESSON	
Responde mihi	4
Stetit autem Salomon	4
PRAYER	
Ave Maria, gratia plena . . . benedicta tu	4
O Domine Jesu Christe	4
Pater noster – Ave Maria	6
PSALM	
Celi enarrant gloriam Dei	4
De profundis clamavi	4
Domine, Dominus noster	5
Domine, exaudi orationem meam	4
Domine, ne in furore tuo (Ps vi)	4
Dominus regnavit	4
Jubilate Deo omnis terra	4

motet	number of voices
PSALM (*cont.*)	
Laudate, pueri, Dominum	4
Levavi oculos meos in montes	4
Memor esto verbi tui	4
Mirabilia testimonia tua, Domine	4
Miserere mei, Deus	5
Paratum cor meum	4
Qui habitat in adjutorio Altissimi	4
Usquequo, Domine, oblivisceris me in finem	4
RESPONSORY	
Homo quidam fecit cenam magnam	5
SEQUENCE	
Ave verum corpus	2–3
Benedicta es, celorum regina	6
Gaude virgo, mater Christi	4
Inviolata, integra et casta es, Maria	5
Mittit ad virginem	4
Praeter rerum seriem	6
Stabat mater dolorosa/Comme femme desconfortée	4
TRACT	
Domine, non secundum peccata nostra	4

Table 8.1*b*: Josquin motets: distribution of text types by number of voices

number of voices	6	5	4	2–3
antiphon	1	2	5	
canticle			1	
chapter	1			
genealogy			2	
Gospel			2	
hymn			1	
lesson			2	
prayer	1		2	
Psalm		2	13	
responsory		1		
sequence	3	2	3	1
tract			1	
totals	6	7	32	1

voice *Salve, regina*, one of the old, venerable concluding antiphons of Compline, and here one is reminded of Strunk's observation that Palestrina distinguished sharply between the old, established texts and the texts for specific festivals.) If one classifies *Inviolata, integra et casta es, Maria* as a sequence-motet, therefore, there are five antiphon-motets for four voices (71 % of the total of seven) and two (29 %) for more than four, proportions that are almost identical, as I indicated, to those of the entire group of 46. With respect to the size of the vocal complement, therefore, Strunk's observations seem to be borne out equally well by Josquin's *œuvre*.

Other features of the Gregorian categories as carried over into polyphonic elaborations are also observable in the motets of Josquin and his contemporaries.[41] Gustave Reese described how several of Josquin's sequence-motets exploit the parallelism of the double versicle structure.[42] And although there are some notable exceptions, four-voice settings are the norm among the antiphon-motets of Josquin *and* his contemporaries; in this respect, the early-sixteenth-century repertory anticipates later-sixteenth-century developments in which, in Strunk's words, the antiphon was "the typical small motet-form" for the Office. Moreover, the antiphon-motets in a representative early-sixteenth-century source (*I-Fn* II.I.232) paraphrase their Gregorian models without exception. Of Isaac's settings of antiphon texts in general, only one, *Sub tuum presidium*, fails to make use of paraphrase, and in Josquin's the tendency to paraphrase is equally pronounced.[43]

The musical characteristics of the entire corpus of Josquin's motets, further, suggest a rough division into one group comprising motets based on texts associated with a reciting tone (Gospels and Psalms, for example) and the other group comprising motets based on the other types of text.[44] The principal musical characteristic substantiating such a classification is melodic style; the length of Gospel and Psalm texts led in the Gregorian tradition to a fundamentally different kind of writing, in which the text is set to reciting-tone formulae, a melodic procedure that contrasts sharply with that of "composed" genres. In Josquin's motets on Gospel and Psalm texts, the reciting tone is almost invariably incorporated in some way, and in many instances there are related, attendant effects resulting from the dis-

point. Heretofore, we have attempted first to identify text type and only then describe the relationship between text type and musical style. In this case, where a single text is of two types, the musical characteristics of the piece might be used to classify the work according to text type. For helpful discussion of this point, I am very grateful to Professor Cristle Collins Judd.

41 Much of the remaining portion of the text is based on Anthony M. Cummings, "A Florentine Sacred Repertory from the Medici Restoration (Manuscript II.I.232 of the Biblioteca nazionale centrale, Firenze)" (PhD diss., Princeton University, 1980), 309–19.

42 Gustave Reese, *Music in the Renaissance* (New York, 1954, 1959), 250 ff.

43 Reference to the Gregorian models for the Isaac antiphon-motets may be found in Martin Just's excellent "Studien zu Heinrich Isaacs Motetten," 2 vols. (PhD diss., Eberhard-Karls-Universität, Tübingen, 1960); identification of Isaac's and Josquin's antiphon-motets may be found there and in Mattfeld, "Some Relationships."

44 On this issue, see especially Cristle Collins Judd, "Aspects of Tonal Coherence in the Motets of Josquin" (PhD diss., King's College, London, 1993). I am very grateful to Professor Judd for stimulating exchanges on questions of musical style in the Josquin motets.

tinctive melodic characteristics of the Gregorian original, "a homophonic or at best quasi-polyphonic texture and . . . an emphasis on sonority and rhythmic declamation," to quote Strunk's words once more.

Further, one can certainly find examples of early-sixteenth-century responsory-motets that are not built along the lines exemplified in Palestrina's settings, in which the polyphonic elaboration reproduces the form of the Gregorian model, a division into two parts with identical or similar conclusions. In addition, there are cases (Isaac's *Quae est ista*, for example) where the motets paraphrase their plainsong model and are thus an exception to the general rule that responsory-motets do not elaborate Gregorian melodic materials. Nonetheless, there are some distinctive procedures typifying Isaac's polyphonic treatment of the text type. While his antiphon-motets sometimes open with the full vocal complement, or establish it within the space of a single breve, his responsory-motets, with one exception, open with widely-spaced paired or through-imitations and thus employ an elaborate polyphonic design in keeping with the similarly elaborate character of the Gregorian responsory.[45] Other responsory-motets by Isaac's younger contemporaries exemplify the characteristics articulated by Strunk, in that they develop melodic materials that are freely invented independent of Gregorian models. Jean Richafort set the text *Sufficiebat nobis* in one part,[46] and the requirements of accommodating a borrowed secular melody in the superius (Hayne van Ghizeghem's *Mon souvenir*), in its entirety and essentially unchanged, precluded a treatment reflecting the form of the chant model. That Richafort nonetheless favored the customary formal procedure is evident from three of his other responsory-motets, in which both parts conclude identically, like the Gregorian originals: *Emendemus in melius*, *Non turbetur*, and *Christus resurgens*.[47] And Mouton, like Richafort (his younger contemporary at the French Royal Chapel), composed a number

[45] The classification according to liturgical type is based on Just, "Studien." The antiphon-motets *Argentum et aurum*, *Salve regina*, and *Veni Sancte Spiritus* open with full harmonies. *Cum esset desponsata mater* establishes the full vocal complement within the space of a semibreve and *Alma redemptoris mater* and *Ecce sacerdos magnus* within the space of a breve. The responsory-motets opening with through-imitations are *Discubuit Jesus*, *Judaea et Jerusalem*, and *Quae est ista*; the responsory-motet with paired imitations is *Accesit ad pedes Jesu*.

Editions: *Argentum et aurum* and *Ecce sacerdos magnus*, EDM, 1st ser., 33 (Kassel and Basel, 1960); *Salve regina* (ii), EDM, 1st ser., 77 (Kassel and Basel, 1990); *Cum esset desponsata mater* and *Quae est ista*, in Emma Kempson, "The Motets of Henricus Isaac (c.1450–1517)" (PhD diss., University of London, 1998); *Alma redemptoris mater*, in Martin Just, "Heinrich Isaacs Motetten in italienischen Quellen," *Analecta musicologica*, 1 (1963), 1–19; *Judaea et Jerusalem* (doubtful), in *New Obrecht Edition*, ed. Chris Maas et al. (Utrecht, 1983–99), XVIII: 1–8; *Accessit ad pedes*, in Martin Just, "Anschaulichkeit und Ausdruck in der Motette des späten 15. Jahrhunderts", in *Die Motette: Beiträge zu ihrer Gattungsgeschichte*, ed. H. Schneider (Mainz, 1991), 75–104. *Veni Sancte Spiritus* is doubtful, *Discubuit Jesus* is incomplete, and both are unedited; see the incipits in Just, "Studien."

[46] All Richafort's motets here cited are edited by Harry Elzinga, *Johannes Richafort: Opera omnia*, CMM 81 (American Institute of Musicology, 1979–99), II.

[47] A fourth Richafort responsory-motet, *Quem dicunt homines*, approximates "classical" form to the extent that the cadences to the two parts agree.

of responsory-motets adhering to "classical" formal procedure, *Congregatae sunt gentes*, *Jocundare Jerusalem*, and *Reges terrae* among them.[48]

An anonymous early-sixteenth-century motet, *Spem in alium*, effectively illustrates some of the ways in which the formal characteristics of the Gregorian responsory can govern the form of its polyphonic elaborations.[49] The piece adopts an unusual plan that clearly distinguishes the setting of the respond proper by concluding it with a "V–I authentic cadence" (on G). The composer elided the end of the *repetendum* and the beginning of the verse and closed the verse with a cadence on C. Alone among the sources for the work, one manuscript (*I-Fn* Magl. XIX 164–67) calls for a repetition of the music of the respond proper, set to the opening of the text of the lesser doxology, so that, musically if not textually, the two parts conclude in identical fashion.

We have considered the paraliturgical uses of the sixteenth-century motet repertory, the varied contexts in which motets were sung, and the evidently related matter of the somewhat free nature of the musico-textual "evocations" of Gregorian material. In some respects, the discussion up to this point of the musical characteristics of the genre has admittedly been abstract. One means of achieving some greater specificity is by taking a closer look at some representative examples of the genre, and we will conclude with a look at two settings of the sequence *Gaude, Barbara beata*, one for four voices by Mouton, the other for five by Palestrina.[50]

Gaude, Barbara beata is in honor of St Barbara, virgin and Christian martyr, who was beheaded in the fourth century; her feast day is December 4. The text of the sequence as transmitted independent of its polyphonic settings[51] displays

[48] The first two are edited in Picker, *The Motet Books of Andrea Antico*, 277–85, 385–97; the third in *Treize Livres de motets parus chez Pierre Attaingnant en 1534 et 1535*, ed. Albert Smijers and A. Tilman Merritt (Monaco, 1934–64), I: 16–24.

[49] The text is the responsory to the third lesson of Matins for the third Sunday of September; see, for example, the *Breviarium Lincopense*, 7 vols., ed. Knut Peters (Lund, 1950–58). The motet is found in a print, RISM 1512^1, and three manuscripts: *I-Fn* II.I.232, *Fn* Magl. XIX 164–67, and *D-Mbs* Mus. ms. 1516. In the contemporary index to *Fn* II.I.232 there is a composer ascription to 'Leo p[a]pa x' that has been partially erased. An edition of *Spem in alium* may be found in *Erhart Öglin: Liederbuch zu vier Stimmen, Augsburg 1512*, ed. Robert Eitner, Publikationen älterer praktischer und theoretischer Musikwerke, 9 (Leipzig, 1880).

[50] The sources for the Mouton motet are listed in Anthony M. Cummings, "A Florentine Sacred Repertory from the Medici Restoration (Manuscript II.I.232 [*olim* Magl. XIX.58; Gaddi 1113] of the Biblioteca nazionale centrale, Firenze): Bibliography and History," *Acta musicologica*, 55 (1983), 267–332. It was the model for imitation masses by Mouton's pupil Willaert and Morales.

Palestrina's piece may be found in Raffaele Casimiri's edition of the *Opere complete*, VII (Rome, 1940), 78–88. It was first published in 1572; see Casimiri's introduction, p. ix. Palestrina composed a second setting of the text, *a 4 voci pari*. It remained unpublished during his lifetime and was edited by Franz X. Haberl in his edition of the *Werke* (Leipzig, 1862–1903), VII: 70–72, from a manuscript in the library of the Collegio Romano dei PP. della Compagnia di Gesù. On the motet and the codex containing it, see Giuseppe Baini, *Memorie storico-critiche della vita e delle opere di Giovanni Pierluigi da Palestrina*, 2 vols. (Rome, 1828), II: 329 ff.; Siegfried Hermelink, *Dispositiones modorum: Die Tonarten in der Musik Palestrinas und seiner Zeitgenossen* (Tutzing, 1960), 24 n. 14.

[51] See *Analecta hymnica medii aevi*, 55 vols. (Leipzig, 1866–1922), XXIX: 97.

Table 8.2 : Text of the Mouton motet *Gaude, Barbara beata*

[*prima pars* of the motet:]

1a:	Gaude, Barbara beata, Summe pollens in doctrina Angeli mysterio;	A B C	Rejoice, blessed Barbara, most powerful in the mysterious doctrine of the angel;
1b:	Gaude, virgo Deo grata, Quae Baptistam imitata Es in vitae stadio.	A A C	Rejoice, Virgin pleasing to God, who imitated the Baptist in the theater of life.
2a:	Gaude, cum te visitavit Christus vita, et curavit Plagas actu proprio;	D D C	Rejoice, since Christ visited you in life, and he healed your stripes by his own act;

[*secunda pars*:]

2b:	Gaude, quia meruisti Impetrare, quod petisti, Dante Dei Filio.	E E C	Rejoice, since you have deserved to obtain that which you sought, the Son of God granting it.
3a:	Gaude, namque elevata Es in caelo et velata Nobili martyrio,	A A C	Rejoice, for you have been raised to Heaven and veiled with a noble martyrdom,
3b:	Te laudantem familiam Trahe post te ad gloriam Finito exilio.	F F C	Draw to glory behind you the family praising you, your exile completed.

[interpolated concluding couplet:]

	O Barbara, tam beata, Pro nobis Christum exora.		O Barbara, so blessed, for us prevail upon Christ.

some of the features generally characteristic of the type (see Table 8.2). It is divided into three pairs of versicles; the final lines of each of the six versicles rhyme. The concluding couplet found in both Mouton's and Palestrina's settings may have been newly added, since it apparently is not transmitted in the sources collated in the *Analecta hymnica*. Because the text comprises six versicles rather than four, for example, or eight, it presents something of a difficulty to a composer intent on setting the text in two roughly equal parts. He had little alternative but to set three of the versicles as the *prima pars* and three as the *secunda pars*; the second of the three pairs of versicles is therefore divided in two by the cadence at the end of the *prima pars*, and the textual pairing is in that sense disturbed. Nonetheless, this is precisely the solution Mouton adopted in his setting, so that the *prima pars* comprises versicles 1a, 1b, and 2a, and the *secunda pars* 2b, 3a, and 3b. One notes, however, that versicles 1b and 3a, the central versicle in each part, share a rhyme scheme (AAC), so that there is a poetic feature appropriate to the composer's bipartite division of the text, which reinforces the sense of symmetry between the two parts.

The clear impression one receives from the Mouton work (Example 8.1) is of

Ex. 8.1 Jean Mouton, *Gaude Barbara*, mm. 1–22, 32–43, 60–67, 179–88, 196–202. After Higinio Anglés (ed.), *Cristóbal de Morales: Opera omnia*, VI, Monumentos de la musica española, 21 (Barcelona, 1962), 133.

musical procedures loosely generated by considerations of text form, so that the polyphonic setting exploits the distinctive poetic structure of the plainsong original. That the piece is a D-tonality work is suggested not only by the root of the final triad but by a number of interior cadences as well. The motet unfolds as a series of paired or through-imitations corresponding to new text elements and concluding with cadences of contrasting types and weights. Cadences are of two general types: (1) those in which the movement into the cadential octave is by stepwise contrary motion, one voice approaching its cadential degree by a whole step, the other by a half step (when cadences of this type contain more than two parts, the additional voices function chiefly as harmonic filler); and (2) those involving 5–1 motion in

(*cont.*)

the lowest voice, which results in what is acoustically identical to a "V–I authentic cadence" in tonal music (these are ordinarily in four voices).

V–I authentic cadences in four voices serve principally to articulate major textual divisions. The first of these cadences occurs at m. 39 and defines the conclusion of the first half of the first double versicle (versicle 1a). Note, however, the identical melodic and rhythmic design of the tenor at m. 39, the altus at m. 40, and the bassus at m. 42, which serves to elide the close of versicle 1a and the opening of versicle 1b and thus to lessen the effect of the cadence. Appropriately enough, the first unequivocal point of articulation is reserved instead for the end of the first double versicle (paired versicles 1a and b), at mm. 66–67. This is marked not only by its pitch content but its rhythmic design as well: the superius and altus voices hold their pitches for the length of a breve, while the tenor and bassus hold theirs for a long. In a piece where the fundamental note motion is at the level of the minim, the cadence at m. 66 constitutes the first principal point of rhythmic repose. Within the first 67 measures, when subsidiary text divisions generate cadences at all, they occur on degrees other than the final or are obscured by overlapping entries.[52] A V–I authentic cadence on D at m. 163, and again at measures 176 and 180, articulates the end of the third double versicle (paired versicles 3a and b).

Finally, one notes that the last couplet, beginning "O Barbara, tam beata," is evidently an interpolation and therefore lies outside the paired versicle scheme. Accordingly, it invites a different treatment: the meter shifts temporarily from duple to triple, and the texture is prevailingly homophonic, with ornamented cadences.

If we attempt to summarize the overall formal plan of the work and describe the

[52] At m. 60, in the Phrygian cadence on E, where the composer set the first word of the following line of text (the "Es" of "Es in vitae stadio") to the final note of the cadence that properly concludes the setting of the previous line ("Quae Baptistam imitata"), the textual overlap is demanded by the enjambement.

Ex. 8.1 (*cont.*)

special structural role of cadences generated by major textual divisions, we see that with one exception (versicle 2b), the setting of each versicle concludes with a V–I authentic cadence in four voices; that the first, second, and last of these cadences (at the end of versicles 1a, 1b, and 3b) are on the root of the final triad (D); and that the third and fourth (at the end of versicle 2a—the end of the *prima pars*—and versicle 3a) afford variety by cadencing on contrasting degrees, specifically A (versicle 2a) and F (versicle 3a).

Had the composer adopted a formal plan that more closely followed the paired versicle structure, he might have chosen to set the text in three parts—one corresponding to each of the three pairs of versicles—and close the setting of versicle 2b with a more decisive cadence. As it is, that versicle is the only one that does *not* conclude with a V–I authentic cadence. Having decided to disturb the textual pairing of versicles 2a and 2b by placing the end of the *prima pars* at the end of versicle

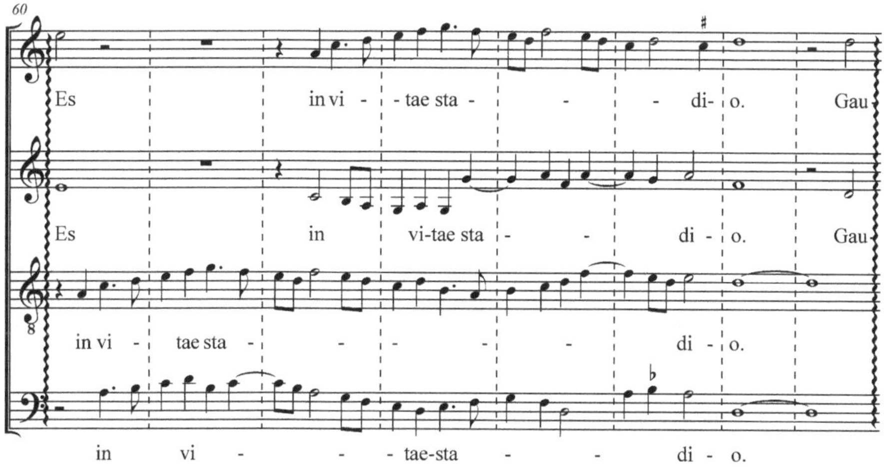

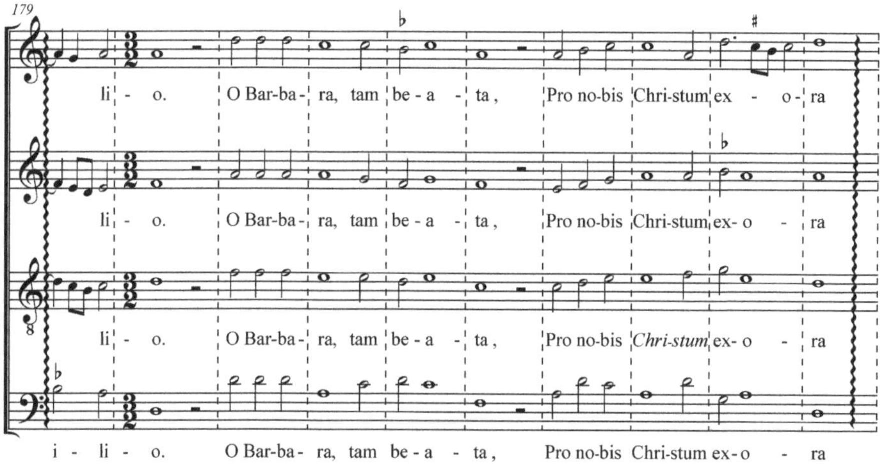

(*cont.*)

2a, it is as if he concluded that there was no need to respect the formal properties of the text by means of the cadential design at the end of versicle 2b. Moreover, having closed the settings of the previous two versicles with V–I authentic cadences, he may have chosen not to close versicle 2b in this way so as not to have three cadences of similar design in immediate succession. Of course, the work contains other V–I authentic cadences, generated by subsidiary text elements (ends of lines, for example, rather than ends of versicles); however, they are distinguished from those that close settings of versicles through use of overlapping entries that serve to make the cadence less decisive.

All of this is to say that the formal characteristics of the text do not, in a mechanical way, dictate the formal plan of the polyphonic setting; rather, they furnish

Ex. 8.1 (*cont.*)

Gaude, Barbara beata . . . Angeli mysterio; Gaude, virgo . . . Es in vitae stadio. . . . O Barbara, tam beata, Pro nobis Christum exora.

material that the composer then elaborates, very freely in some cases. What one *can* say is that the various textual and musical elements of the Gregorian original could guide the composer in making choices about such fundamental compositional matters as the large-scale formal plan and placement and design of cadences, meter, and constructional technique (as in the handling of the interpolated, "non-Gregorian" final couplet), melodic substance, and so on. In this respect, what evidence of compositional planning one can detect in the work is roughly consonant with such period descriptions of the compositional process as Zarlino's in Part III of his *Istitutioni harmoniche* of 1558.

The differences between Mouton's setting and Palestrina's may serve as a rough measure of the stylistic distance traveled between the beginning of the sixteenth-century motet development and its more mature phases, although absent a more complete survey of the entire literature, one cannot be certain that some are not due instead simply to differences between Mouton's and Palestrina's artistic personalities or, at another level still, to the distinctive characteristics of the two pieces as specific works rather than as expressions of more generic developments. In any event, there are many important differences in how the two works treat the sequence text, as one would expect. First, however, let us consider some similarities.

Palestrina's setting, like Mouton's, divides the text in two at the end of the third versicle; the *prima pars* thus comprises versicles 1a, 1b, and 2a, and the *secunda pars* versicles 2b, 3a, and 3c, as well as the interpolated concluding couplet found in both works. Also like Mouton, Palestrina decisively articulated the conclusion of the first and third double versicles (paired versicles 1a and b and 3a and b), although the precise means of articulation in the first case differs sharply from Mouton's: whereas Mouton concluded the setting of the first double versicle with a V–I authentic cadence and the rhythmic design described above, Palestrina chose to shift from duple to triple meter and from polyphony to homophony at the beginning of versicle 2a, so that the second double versicle is set off from the first by clearly audible metrical and textural means. (On the other hand, both composers treated the interpolated final couplet in roughly the same way, by means of a shift to triple meter and a greater use of homophonic writing; indeed, this similarity and the others noted may be evidence that Palestrina in some way modeled his setting on Mouton's, as may the similar, more homophonic handling of the words "dante Dei filio."[53]) There are other significant differences. That the pieces are of comparable length is owing to quite different compositional strategies with respect to text setting: Palestrina's is much more syllabic than Mouton's, and the comparable length of the two pieces is the result of a greater use of textual repetition in the later work. Moreover, whereas the distinctive formal characteristics of the poetic text are reflected in Mouton's setting in the design and systematic placement of cadences, the Palestrina work has a less sharply-chiseled effect, in that the cadences that conclude settings of individual lines are less decisive as a result of overlapping entries. It is almost as if, for Mouton, the triumph of pervasive imitation as a fundamental organizing principle was of too recent vintage for him to depart from the systematic presentation of a series of points of imitation, each precisely geared to a new text element and concluded with a more or less decisive cadence. Alternatively, it may be that the compositional strategy employed by Mouton in this particular work is simply a specific expression of his artistic personality in general, since it seems consistent with what we know of his style. In Howard Brown's words,

> Mouton wrote serene, smoothly flowing polyphony, with great technical finish and superb contrapuntal command . . . . The smooth flow of Mouton's melody stems in large part from the stately regular pace at which much of his music moves. Short notes are used primarily to break up this slow, regular motion rather than to offer genuine rhythmic contrast. The melodic contours themselves tend to be rather short-spanned, Mouton's penchant for clear, sharply profiled motives perhaps reflecting the rational and precise spirit of his specifically French rather than Flemish heritage.[54]

By Palestrina's time, the principle of syntactic imitation was less novel, so that composers felt freer to extend the range of compositional strategies employed in any given piece. In the Palestrina work, therefore, the distinctive properties and character of the Gregorian original are expressed less in the large-scale structural plan and systematic placement of points of articulation generated by text elements than in the use of a somewhat larger number of voices (five as contrasted with Mouton's

[53] I was not able to locate the original chant melody. In its absence, one cannot know whether the similarities between the two motets result from their common dependence on the chant or the dependence of Palestrina's setting on Mouton's. For assisting me in my search for the chant original, I am grateful to Professors Jennifer Bloxam and Alejandro Planchart.

[54] Howard Mayer Brown, *Music in the Renaissance*, Prentice-Hall History of Music Series (Englewood Cliffs, NJ, 1976), 176.

four) and the more syllabic text setting, which substantiates Strunk's point about Palestrina's sequence-motets generally.

Finally, there is evidence of the kind of sensitivity and responsiveness to the meaning of the text and to the individual words it contains that one would expect from a figure who was, after all, a madrigalist as well as a composer of sacred music: in the *secunda pars*, at the words "namque elevata es in coelo" (mm. 39–57 in the Casimiri edition), the melodic line rises by step on each of the four syllables of the word "e-le-va-ta" and in the superius part leaps at the word "coelo" to the highest pitch in the entire piece. Admittedly, the same pitch is used elsewhere in the piece, both earlier and later, and it is approached by leap elsewhere as well, but in the context of the setting of this particular line of text, the melodic writing is an especially successful instance of word painting. One notes, moreover, the florid treatment of the word "gaude" immediately before (mm. 32–40 in the Casimiri edition). The opportunities inherent in the text at this point were not similarly exploited by Mouton.

To sum up: the sixteenth-century motet was a polyphonic setting of a sacred Latin text, which in many instances was not derived verbatim from the Catholic liturgy. It was used in a variety of contexts, some liturgical, some not, and even when used liturgically was not often performed at the precise ritual moment suggested by its text. The liturgical books, therefore, appear in some instances to have been utilized by composers as sources of texts that appealed to them because of their power to express particular religious sentiments. The looser relationship to the liturgy—looser, that is, as contrasted with that of service music—permitted the composer to lavish elaborate treatment on motet texts, and the full range of compositional techniques available to the sixteenth-century composer is associated with the genre. The distinctive textual and musical properties of the Gregorian text types nevertheless guided the composer in making choices among possible compositional strategies, so that the polyphonic settings of a particular text type share some important characteristics that are reminiscent of the Gregorian original and serve to provide those settings with an identifiable musical profile. Finally, there is evidence of the kind of cross-generic stylistic influences found in Palestrina's *Gaude, Barbara beata*. As we have seen, there is some reason to believe that Palestrina, in composing polyphonic settings of Offertory texts, was seeking to provide pieces proper to the liturgical moment when motets had traditionally been performed. In the charged atmosphere of post-Tridentine Europe, many composers were increasingly moved to "purify" their output of madrigalisms, secular elements, and liturgical anomalies and fashion genres whose characteristics were more compatible with the objectives of the Counter-Reformation Church.

9

FRANCE, *i*: 1520–1560

Richard Freedman

PRE-EMINENTLY a perishable medium, music is compelled by its very nature to rely upon repetition for enduring effect. In this respect the history of any musical form is inseparable from the larger narrative of the institutions that made such repetition both possible and necessary. For Renaissance Europe this close connection between performance and circumstance seems especially important: in this age musical sounds were not only objects for aesthetic contemplation, they were also the necessary attributes of a civilized community, the persuasive instruments of spiritual enlightenment, and even symbols of social prestige. To retell the central musical developments in France during the middle years of the sixteenth century is consequently to rehearse the sweeping social, religious, and intellectual changes at work in Europe's most populous realm.

Music at Court

THE economic and political influence of aristocratic households played a central role in the formation of tastes and the production of music during the middle years of the sixteenth century. It was at court that patronage was distributed, an economic lure that attracted singers from provincial choirs and instrumentalists—not just from France, but Italy, too—to the seats of power. Thus the most powerful dynastic powers of sixteenth-century France—the Valois kings, the dukes of Lorraine and Guise, the French cardinals and bishops—were also among its most influential patrons of music. Their travels, and the subtle rivalry of consumption that their elevated social positions engendered, put into motion processes of musical production that had pervasive influence on musical life throughout the kingdom.[1] A musician working in the royal *maison* during the reign (1515–47)

[1] Courtly life and its relationship to artistic production has spawned a vast bibliography. Among recent works on the subject, see Richard Bonney, *The European Dynastic States, 1494–1660* (Oxford, 1991), and particularly Ronald G. Asch and Adolf M. Birke (eds.), *Princes,*

of King François I would by ancient convention have belonged to one of three separate departments of this vast (but surprisingly mobile) juggernaut of official attendants: a staff of domestic servants (the *chambre*), clerics and singers charged with the observance of sacred liturgy (the *chapelle*), and officials for public ceremony and military protection (the *écurie*).[2] Each of these administrative divisions carried with it an implied set of social circumstances, constraints whose operation can at times be detected in the music of those who sang and played at court.

What sorts of musicians and musical repertories were heard in the royal *chambre*? During the 1530s and 1540s the private household apparently included a small vocal ensemble and several instrumentalists, musicians who were above all prized as interpreters of the French chansons, dance music, and instrumental solos that served as musical entertainment for the king and his guests. Jeannet de Bouchefort, for instance, served as "valet de garde-robe" (an honorific title conferred upon valued professionals and some nobles, too) to successive French monarchs between 1530 and at least 1572. In addition to his duties as singer Jeannet also had skills as a composer: two polyphonic chansons by him appear among the music books issued by the royal printer Pierre Attaingnant. Bouchefort's career is remarkable for a curious detour it took during the 1530s: apparently a Protestant sympathizer, he exiled himself from court in 1535 following the Affair of the Placards, taking refuge among the Francophone entourage of Renée de France, duchess of Ferrara. He was tried there for heresy by local inquisitors but was eventually released and allowed to return to France, where he resumed his long career as a royal singer.[3] Bouchefort's musical life, in brief, can stand as an emblem of the stability of royal musical institutions, even in the face of the deepening religious rifts that divided French society during the decades before the Wars of Religion. It also stands as a reminder of the profoundly international character of musical life during the middle years of the sixteenth century, a time when French and Italian musicians were engaged in a particularly fertile dialogue.

Among the Italian musicians at the French court during this period, for instance, was the famous Mantuan lutenist Alberto da Ripa or Albert de Rippe,

Patronage, and the Nobility: The Court at the Beginning of the Modern Age (Oxford, 1991). On the French court and its organization during the early 16th century, see Robert Jean Knecht, "The Court of Francis I," *European Studies Review*, 8 (1978), 1–22; and Desmond Seward, *Prince of the Renaissance: The Life of François I* (London, 1974). On the court of Lorraine, closely allied to the royal court and its cultural policies at the time, see Richard Freedman, "The Chansons of Mathieu Lasson: Music at the Courts of Lorraine and France, ca.1530," *Journal of Musicology*, 8 (1990), 316–56; idem, "Le Cardinal Jean de Lorraine: Un Prélat de la Renaissance mécène de la musique," *Le Mécénat et l'influence des Guise: Actes du Colloque organisé par Centre de recherche sur la littérature de la Renaissance de l'Université de Reims, Joinville, May 31–June 4, 1994*, ed. Yvonne Bellenger (Paris, 1997), 161–73.

2 Concerning the musical organization and personnel of the French royal household during the 16th century, see Christelle Cazaux, *La Musique à la cour de François Ier*, Mémoires et documents de l'École des chartes, 65 (Paris, 2002).

3 For a detailed narrative of Bouchefort's career, see Cazaux, *La Musique à la cour de François Ier*, 344–46. For a detailed history of the *chambre* and its musicians, see ibid., 127–60.

whose contrapuntal skill and extraordinary sense for the sonorous qualities of his instrument were held in high regard by the princes and prelates for whom he played. But if Albert enjoyed a pre-eminent reputation among patrons and *literati* of the early sixteenth century, it was not until after both his death and the death of his royal patron that his music was made available to the general public, edited (with permission of the new king, Henri II [1547–59]) by Guillaume Morlaye, one of the great lutenist's pupils and a musical entrepreneur. In a dedicatory epistle to Henri, Morlaye justified the patent commercialism of the venture by offering lavish praise for French monarchs—including two of "the most noble, virtuous, and magnanimous kings in Europe" (namely François I and Henri II), who had until now carefully guarded Albert's music as a private domain.[4] Appropriating this formerly secret and socially restricted art as an object of profit and of public enjoyment, Morlaye's print hints at the growing interdependence of aristocratic patronage and bourgeois commerce. If printers came to rely on princes for protection from competition, rulers looked to the press for the ready means to promote the princely virtue of their sponsorship of private music.

For members of the nobility, the practice of music was no less important a sign of civility than its appreciation. When a young Mantuan prince, Lodovico Gonzaga, came to the French court during the 1550s as a companion to the Dauphin François II, singing and playing the viol figured in his daily routine, alternating with worship, military training, dancing, and, in the words of his guardian Leonardo Arrivabene, "altre scientie à Principi profittevoli."[5] Arrivabene does not say exactly how well young princes like Lodovico or François applied themselves to their musical studies, but they may well have avoided giving the impression of having practiced too thoroughly: for conversants of the most celebrated of Renaissance courtesy manuals, Castiglione's *Cortegiano* (1528; available in printed French translation in the 1530s), the cultivated *nonchalance* (or *sprezzatura*) with which one ought to perform was itself a means of social positioning. According to this code of conduct, a cultivated lack of interest in the demands of professional discipline would likely have earned Ludovico and François the esteem of their fellow aristocrats. In this respect the reputation of a French courtier resided less in the

[4] The original text reads: "Veritablement, Sire, si ce tant excellent Albert se sentant parvenu au sommet de ce que peut sçavoir un parfaict sonneur de Leut, se fust seulement contenté d'avoir donné contentement à deux, les plus nobles, vertueux, et magnanimes Roys de l'Europe . . . ." From the epistle printed in the *Premier livre de tabulature du leut dAlbert* [*sic*] *de Rippe* (Paris: Fezandat, 1553). Cited in Jacques-Gabriel Prod'homme, "Guillaume Morlaye, éditeur d'Albert de Ripe, luthiste et bourgeois de Paris," *Revue de musicologie*, 6 (1925), 163–64. Albert's fantasias and his arrangements of courtly chansons appear in Jean-Michel Vaccaro (ed.), *Œuvres d'Albert de Rippe*, 3 vols. (Paris, 1972–75). The problems of performing Albert's music are considered in Lyle Nordstrom, "Albert de Rippe, joueur de luth du Roy," *Early Music*, 7 (1979), 378–85.

[5] The description of Lodovico's daily activities appears in a letter written at Amboise on 14 Nov. 1552 to Lodovico's mother Margherita Paleologa in Mantua. For the text of this missive, see Alessandro Luzio, *Leonardo Arrivabene alla corte di Caterina de' Medici (1549–1559): Notizie e documenti* (Bergamo, 1902), 49–51.

music made (which was plainly paramount for de Rippe) than in the countenance one assumed while playing.[6]

If music in the royal *chambre* was directed principally at the creation of personal and private meanings for aristocratic audiences, that of the *écurie* was aimed at the ceremonial and political requirements of the monarchy as it faced a wide French public. The subtle blend of a small vocal ensemble or the quiet resonance of the lute had no place in this division of the royal *maison*. The musical forces of the *écurie* were chiefly outdoor instrumentalists: drummers and pipers attached to the military guard, plus trumpeters, shawmists, and a violin band (including some Italian instrumentalists) who played during large social dances and public processions.[7] These musicians could hardly have practiced a "secret" art of the sort that de Rippe's performances remained, for their task was to use ordinary music to extraordinary effect. Underscoring gesture and visual spectacle, their playing called attention in sound to the sort of flamboyant display that accompanied elevated status. When Henri II and Catherine de Médicis made their official entry into the city of Paris as king and queen of France in 1549, for example, the accompanying spectacle would have been the envy of any aristocratic couple. The procession from the Port Saint Denis to the Cathedral of Notre Dame and the nearby royal palace involved thousands of participants—cavalry, merchants, civic officials, scholars, courtiers, and princes—a parade watched in awe by more thousands of other Parisian citizens.

Official chronicles of the sort written to commemorate events such as this one are characteristically vague about the music heard during such events. One may read, for instance, that the Parisian ceremonial guard that met the king at the city gates was accompanied by "phiffres et tabourins," or that Henri's own band of "trompettes" rode near the head of his entourage. But exactly what sorts of music these bandsmen played is left largely unexplored.[8] For the chroniclers, it seems, what mattered was not the music itself but rather its effect on those who processed and watched. Transfixed by the range of official costume set out before them, impressed by the triumphal arches with their symbolic devices, and quite literally compelled by the "la diversité des instrumens qui sonnoyent lesdicts lieux durant tout le jour de ladicte entrée," courtiers and citizens alike were moved to assent "à haulte voix" to the obvious conclusion that Henri was the perfect monarch, ruling a perfect and harmonious realm.[9]

[6] On the problems of translating *sprezzatura* for 16th-century French writers, see Reinhard Klesczewski, *Die französischen Übersetzungen des "Cortegiano" von Baldassare Castiglione* (Heidelberg, 1966), 68, 168–69.

[7] On the personnel and history of the royal *écurie*, see Cazaux, *La Musique à la cour de François Ier*, 107–26.

[8] For a study of improvised repertories among wind bands of the period, see Keith Polk, *German Instrumental Music of the late Middle Ages: Players, Patrons, and Performance Practices* (Cambridge, 1992).

[9] The original text reads: "Le Roy passant en cest ordre, pompe, et magnificence, fut veu par les habitans de ladicte ville, avec une joye et allegresse incroyable, ainsi que en feirent foy les acclamations et prieres qu'ils luy faisoyent de lieu à autre, à haulte voix, de longue vie et prosperité, mesmes les estrangers surpris d'admiration de la singularité et richesse des choses

Church and State

In addition to his ensembles of public and private musicians, the French king seems to have had several church choirs in his direct service. By the 1530s François's own *chapelle* was by far the largest of his musical organizations, an institution boasting nearly three dozen adult singers (plus choirboys) divided between two specialist choirs—one for liturgical plainsong and another for *musique*, or polyphonic compositions.[10] The Sainte-Chapelle du Palais, not far from the royal Parisian residence, also had its own professional choir, an organization that like the king's chapel was very much at the center of musical life under the French monarchs. Many of the musicians active in these establishments were also the same composers who figured prominently in the early publications of the royal music printer Pierre Attaingnant. Claudin de Sermisy (*c.*1490–1562), for instance, had been a minor cleric at the Sainte-Chapelle long before his appointment to the rank of *sous-maître* in the royal chapel (in practice, he was the musical director, although the titular leadership of the group was in the hands of an aristocrat, Cardinal François de Tournon), where from the 1530s until his death he held a prestigious canonical post. Pierre Certon, a close contemporary of Claudin's, began musical service in Paris at the Cathedral of Notre Dame, but later joined the Sainte-Chapelle as a *clerc* and then *maître des enfants*, a post he held from 1536 until his death in 1572. Like Claudin, Certon enjoyed the favor of several French monarchs, who conferred upon him the title of *chantre de la chapelle du Roy* and *compositeur de musique de la chapelle du Roy*. Either or both of these positions may have been purely honorific, but the distinction suggests the prestige and enduring protection that French rulers lavished on their favorite composers and singers. Indeed, the pursuit of ecclesiastical offices for musicians prompted François I, like other French kings before him, to intercede with papal authorities on behalf of his singers in order to obtain for them benefices or other canonical appointments throughout the kingdom.[11]

Maintaining a staff of clerics and singers for the observance of divine worship, of course, had long been the practice of Catholic princes. But in addition to the chanting of plainsong and, at times, polyphonic settings of sacred texts, royal

cy devant descrites, et encores beaucoup plus de la presence d'un si vertueux, magnanime, et accomply Prince, faisoyent publiquement confession de sa grandeur. Et (qui ne semble moins decent que louable en si excellent Roy) de la grace, disposition, et adresse qui se representoit en sa personne, aussi perfecte que en autre Monarque qui ayt iamais esté." Quoted in the facsimile of the original printed text edited by Ian D. McFarlane as *The Entry of Henri II into Paris, 16 June 1549*, Medieval and Renaissance Texts and Studies, 7 (Binghamton, 1982), fols. 25^{v}–26^{r}.

10 Concerning the personnel and history of the royal *chapelle*, see Cazaux, *La Musique à la cour de François Ier*, 69–106; and John T. Brobeck, "Musical Patronage in the Royal Chapel of France under Francis I (r.1515–1547)," *Journal of the American Musicological Society*, 48 (1995), 187–239.

11 Further on the French kings and papal benefices, see Richard Sherr, "The Membership of the Chapels of Louis XII and Anne de Bretagne in the Years Preceding their Deaths," *Journal of Musicology*, 6 (1988), 60–82.

choirs were also called upon to provide music for state ceremonies—coronations, peace treaties, and victory celebrations—that marked the political and dynastic calendar of a reign. For the singers of the royal *chapelle*, ceremonial duties and the needs of statecraft were rarely far apart. In the summer of 1520, for example, the courts of France and England gathered near Calais for the meetings of the Field of Cloth of Gold; in honor of the occasion the two royal chapels of François I and Henry VIII sang in alternation the sections of a festive Mass.[12] And when the two monarchs met again at Boulogne-sur-mer in October 1532, one chronicler, whose report was later reproduced by the Venetian diarist Marin Sanudo, recounted that

> this morning, the 22nd, the most Christian king sent the English king the gift of a rich and beautiful gown, coat, and doublet, and the king clad himself in like manner. Entering into a church, one went to one chapel, the other to another, both of which were very richly furnished; and the Mass being ended, they joined company, and a motet was sung in [the king's] chapel [*a la sua capella*], namely, "Da pacem Domine in diebus nostris."[13]

A four-voice motet with this beginning, which combines the opening phrase of a well-known antiphon for peace with verses of Psalm 122, was soon thereafter issued by the French royal music printer Pierre Attaingnant, ascribed to Claudin de Sermisy.[14] Exactly what any musical reader of Attaingnant's print would have understood about the previous use of Claudin's motet remains elusive, but when one of Attaingnant's typesetters designated Mathieu Gascongne's *Christus vincit, christus regnat, christus imperat* "pro rege nostro," he was merely acknowledging in print what any French cleric would have already understood: this text, with its formulaic refrain and long litany of patron saints, was an ancient musical acclama-

[12] For a modern edition with commentary of the Anglo-French conclave of 1520, see Jean Dupebe and Stephen Bamforth (eds.), "The Field of the Cloth of Gold," *Renaissance Studies*, 5 (1991), 1–229. Concerning the respective French and English musical groups in attendance, see Paul Kast, "Remarques sur la musique et les musiciens de la chapelle de François Ier au camp du drap d'or," *Les Fêtes de la Renaissance*, ed. Jean Jacquot, II: *Fêtes et cérémonies au temps de Charles Quint* (Paris, 1960), 135–46; and Hugh Baillie, "Les Musiciens de la chapelle royale d'Henri VIII au camp du drap d'or," ibid., 147–59. Further on the musical dimension of the 1520 meetings, see Cazaux, *La musique à la cour de François Ier*, 204–7.

[13] The Italian original reads: "Questa mattina a di 22 il re Christianissimo ma[n]dò a donar al re inglese una vesta, una zimara e uno giupone riche et belle, e il re nostro uno simile, e intrati in una chiesia uno andò in una capella, l'altro in l'altra, quale erano molto ricamente apparate, e finita la messa si reduseno insieme, et fatto cantar un motetto a la sua capella, zoè *da pacem domine in diebus nostris.*" Cited in Marin Sanudo, *I diarii di Marino Sanuto (MCCCCXCV–MDXXXIII) dall'Autografo Marciano Ital. Cl. VII Cod. CDXIX–CDLXXVII*, 59 vols., ed. Rinaldo Fulin et al. (Venice, 1879–1902), LVII: cols. 317–19. I have based my translation for his passage on the one given in Rawdon Brown (ed.), *Calendar of State Papers and Manuscripts Relating to English Affairs, Existing in the Archives and Collections of Venice and in other Libraries of Northern Italy*, 38 vols. (London, 1871–1940; repr. Neudeln, Liechtenstein, 1970), IV: 336.

[14] A modern edition of Claudin's piece appears in *Treize Livres de motets parus chez Pierre Attaingnant en 1534 et 1535*, ed. A. Smijers and A. Tillman Merrit, 14 vols. (Paris, 1934–64), XI: 69–80 (a simpler three-voice setting of the antiphon text, also by Claudin, is in VII: 183–84). Further on Claudin's motet in the context of his musical output, see John T. Brobeck, "Style and Authenticity in the Motets of Claudin de Sermisy," *Journal of Musicology*, 16 (1998), 26–90.

tion in praise of the king. The "Laudes regiae," as they had been known since their inception in Carolingian times, were for François I highly political acts. Sung in church during coronation Masses, at festal crown wearings that were joined to sacred feasts, and to commemorate the king even when he was not in church, "they attempted," in the words of Craig Wright,

> to correlate the heavenly and earthly realms and thereby effect an apotheosis of the ruler. The analogue of the victorious Christ was, in the temporal sphere, the conquering Carolingian king. Through this divine equation he assumed the mantle of *rex christianissimus* and a claim to divine right to which the French monarchs subsequently held fast for more than a millennium.[15]

It seems no coincidence that so many of these ceremonial motets, with their musical and verbal allusions to princes and the beneficence of their reigns, were made readily available to a musical public through the efforts of a musical press specifically authorized and protected by the monarchy itself. If the esoteric performances of Albert de Rippe were purposefully kept away from the popularising stigma of print, music by composers like Claudin de Sermisy, Pierre Certon, and Mathieu Gascongne were actively promoted through this new medium. Publicly inscribing the music associated with central events in the monarchy's own history, the press lent legitimacy to an official view of the glories of the present regime.

Given the close connection between divine right and royal authority, it should not be surprising that French monarchs concerned themselves with the liturgy of the Catholic church. By the early 1520s, for instance, François had sought to reinstate the singing of *O salutaris hostia*, a versicle for the sacrament that had been imposed upon the Gallican church by his predecessor, Louis XII. A famous woodcut from a book of Mass settings issued by Attaingnant in 1532 apparently commemorates this royal interest in the sacrament, depicting François and his immediate peers as they watch the elevation of the host and listen to the versicle in question, which appears on the music book open before the choir. In 1540 Attaingnant issued another Mass book, this one with polyphonic settings of the ordinary and one of the *O salutaris hostia* settings by Claudin de Sermisy and Pierre Certon, two leading members of the king's musical establishments.[16]

[15] Craig Wright, *Music and Ceremony at Notre Dame of Paris, 500–1550* (Cambridge, 1989), 201–2. A modern edition of Gascongne's motet appears in *Treize Livres de motets*, II: 57–66. Further on the history of the text in question, see Ernst H. Kantorowicz, *Laudes Regiae: A Study in Liturgical Acclamations and Mediaeval Ruler Worship* (Berkeley, 1946). According to Edward Lowinsky, Jean Mouton composed a motet in honor of Pope Leo X using a similar "Laudes regiae" formula. On the text and probable destination of this piece, which is preserved uniquely in a fragmentary motet print from 1521, see Edward E. Lowinsky (ed.), *The Medici Codex of 1518: A Choirbook of Motets Dedicated to Lorenzo de' Medici, Duke of Urbino*, 3 vols., Monuments of Renaissance Music, 3–5 (Chicago, 1968), I: 39–40.

[16] Further on the king and his direct concern with the Catholic liturgy, see Wright, *Music and Ceremony*, 221ff., and John T. Brobeck, "Some 'Liturgical Motets' for the French Royal Court: A Reconsideration of Genre in the Sixteenth-Century Motet," *Musica disciplina*, 47 (1993), 123–57. The contents of the *Missarum musicalium quatuor vocum* are listed in Daniel Heartz, *Pierre Attaingnant, Royal Printer of Music: A Historical Study and Bibliographical*

The Musical Press and Its Audiences

The needs of the French monarchy seem to have been well served by church and press alike during the early sixteenth century. But clearly not all of the efforts of ecclesiastical composers or music printers were directed toward fulfilling the wishes of royal patrons. Attaingnant issued a wide range of sacred music (both plainsong and figural) to texts intended for a variety of liturgical purposes. His important series of motet volumes that appeared in 1534 and 1535, for instance, embraced not only political texts for the French court (Book 11), but also volumes with important concentrations of Marian texts (Books 4, 8, and 12), Easter and Nativity pieces (Book 2), motets for Passion week (Book 10), and a cycle of Magnificat settings (Books 5 and 6). Still other volumes of sacred music issued by Attaingnant point to his wide musical readership among church musicians in provincial France. In 1539, for instance, Pierre de Manchicourt dedicated a volume of motets to Remy Roussel, a canon and important dignitary at the Cathedral of Tours. And in 1545 Attaingnant issued another book of motets, this one containing works by another canon at the same church, Guillaume Le Heurteur.[17]

In the southern French city of Lyons, too, there appeared sacred music that was destined for Catholic devotion around the kingdom. Much of this material was issued by Jacques Moderne, who had set up shop here during the late 1530s, even while Attaingnant enjoyed a royal patent protecting him from close competition in Paris. The Cathedral of Lyons itself continued a long-standing aversion to figural polyphony throughout the middle years of the sixteenth century, but Moderne nevertheless found other markets for his prints. A number of the volumes that he produced seem to have been tailored to the devotional needs of Notre Dame de Confort, a Lyonnaise church patronized and supported by the large community of Italian bankers and merchants who lived in this cosmopolitan city. Moderne, himself an expatriate Italian, used as his editor the Florentine organist of this very church, Francesco de Layolle, whose musical tastes apparently extended widely

Catalogue (Berkeley, 1969), 307. The title woodcut from the *Viginti missarum musicalium* of 1532 appears ibid., pl. 8. The musical contents of the 1532 book provide still more evidence of the close ties between rite and rule: included here is Claudin de Sermisy's *Missa plurium motetorum*, a parody composition that borrows from Josquin, from Jean Conseil, from Claudin himself, and from Gascongne's *Deus regnorum*, a motet that calls for divine protection of King François. For a modern edition of the mass and its models, see Claudin de Sermisy, *Opera omnia*, 6 vols., ed. Gaston Allaire and Isabelle Cazeaux, CMM 52 (Rome, 1970–86), v: pp. ix, 59–84, 136–58.

[17] For a complete modern edition of the series, see *Treize Livres de motets*. A complete set of the 1534–35 motet series was once part of the chapter library of the Cathedral of Noyon, seat of Attaingnant's (and Jean Calvin's) native diocese in Picardy. The cathedral had in fact given the printer his very first commission, for liturgical books, in 1525. On Attaingnant and his connection with Noyon, see Heartz, *Pierre Attaingnant*, 38, 135–36. Manchicourt's preface to the volume of 1539 appears ibid., 178–81. A complete edition of Manchicourt's print appears as vol. XIV of *Treize Livres de motets*. The style and history of Attaingnant's motet production is considered in John T. Brobeck, "The Motet at the Court of Francis I," 2 vols. (PhD diss., University of Pennsylvania, 1991).

among the French and Italianate idioms of the day. Moderne's own series of motet books, the *Motetti del fiore*, was thus a suitably international publication, featuring not only music by some French composers, but also by northerners (especially that of Nicolas Gombert) and composers active in Italy, including Philippe Verdelot and Jacques Arcadelt.[18] All of this points towards the profound musical internationalism of the first half of the sixteenth century, a time when Italian instrumentalists played for northern princes, when northern polyphonists directed the most celebrated choirs of the Italian peninsula, and when the expatriate Florentine and Lucchese communities of Lyons moved easily between the French and Italian repertories of the day. This rich web of transalpine movement forms the necessary backdrop to any assessment of the stylistic development of instrumental music and of the emerging dialogue between chanson and madrigal during the middle years of the sixteenth century.[19]

By mid-century, Moderne's attentions turned from the production of collective volumes to the publication of music by individual composers, musicians whose works reflect an increasing concern for proper spiritual effect through precise musical presentation of sacred texts. When Moderne reprinted Christóbal de Morales's *Missarum liber primus* in 1545 (it had first been issued in Rome by Dorico a year before), he was careful to reproduce the composer's eloquent Latin dedication, a manifesto which advocated careful control of the potentially distracting sensuousness of musical expression, favoring instead a restrained idiom well suited "to praise immortal god and illustrious men."[20] So, too, when Pierre Colin dedicated the twelve masses of his *Liturgicon musicarum* to his fellow canons at the Burgundian Cathedral of Autun in 1554, he took pains to note that

> just as I have so arranged the matter that nothing harsh or forced is encountered here, but everything flows as it were of its own accord, so I have tempered the musical modulation in its modes so that not only each word of the sentence is clear, but so that anyone may easily hear even the complete sentences in such a way that the ears should be so affected by the charms of

[18] The publication history and contents of Moderne's eight-volume *Motetti del fiore* (issued 1532–42) are considered in Frank Dobbins, *Music in Renaissance Lyons* (Oxford, 1992), 217–28, and in Samuel F. Pogue, *Jacques Moderne: Lyons Music Printer of the Sixteenth Century* (Geneva, 1969), 17, 60–61.

[19] Further on the common language of chanson and madrigal repertories of the period, see Howard Mayer Brown, "Paroles et musique: Willaert, la chanson et le madrigal vers 1540," *La Chanson à la Renaissance*, 209–42. Brown's essay appeared in English translation as "Words and Music: Willaert, the Chanson, and the Madrigal about 1540," in *Florence and Venice: Comparisons and Relations; Acts of Two Conferences at Villa I Tatti in 1976–1977*, 2 vols. (Florence, 1979–80), II: 217–66.

[20] The dedication is transcribed in Cristóbal de Morales, *Opera omnia*, 8 vols., ed. Higinio Anglés, Monumentos de la música española, 11 (Barcelona, 1952–71), I: 48–49. On the surprising legal measures taken by the composer to assure himself editorial control over the original publication of the mass book, see Suzanne G. Cusick, *Valerio Dorico, Music Printer in Sixteenth-Century Rome* (Ann Arbor, 1981), 95–101. It is perhaps fitting that in reprinting the volumes Moderne should have slavishly copied even the smallest typographical details from Dorico's work. See Pogue, *Jacques Moderne*, 191–94.

> the voice that the soul may nonetheless be nourished by the very quintessence of the sense.[21]

In recognizing the close connection between sonorous forms and ethical effects, Colin's preface implicitly yields to his fellow composers a certain power (even a certain obligation) to shape the world in which they lived through the proper control of aesthetic means. But inasmuch as aesthetic propriety—in this case the correct relation between musical line and verbal sense—requires control over performance as well as over composition itself, this high aim is in many ways utterly dependent on the medium of print in order to guarantee convincing effect.

The French musical press of the sixteenth century, in sum, had important links with the state (a principal patron and protector) and the Catholic Church (a traditional training ground for composers and singers). But printers also enjoyed a growing readership among a musical public that stretched well beyond the confines of courts and cathedrals. Indeed, Attaingnant's royal privilege of 1531 explicitly acknowledges this very broad appeal, which it identifies as a worthy aim, authorizing Attaingnant alone to print

> many books and quires of Masses, motets, hymns, chansons, as well as for the said playing of lutes, flutes, and organs, in large volumes and small, in order to serve the churches, their ministers, and generally all people, and for the very great good, utility, and recreation of the general public.[22]

The printer had good grounds to seek royal protection for what the privilege called "the merit of his labors and the recovery of expenses," for he had apparently found a ready market among an increasingly literate urban populace. He did not, however, long remain the only music printer active in the realm. Jacques Moderne, as we have already seen, began issuing music books in Lyons even while Attaingnant's patent was still in effect. And when Henri II became king following the death of François I in 1547, Attaingnant's and Moderne's rather exclusive hold on French music printing was briefly loosened. In Paris Attaingnant was joined in the musical marketplace first by Nicolas du Chemin (in 1548) and later by Adrian Le Roy and Robert Ballard (in 1551). Moderne, too, was joined by local competitors starting in the late 1540s, when the Beringen brothers, Nicolas Granjon, and others began issuing music aimed at the cosmopolitan world of mid-century Lyons.[23]

[21] Translation quoted in Pogue, *Jacques Moderne*, 63. The Latin original appears on that page as n. 2.

[22] Translation from Heartz, "A New Attaingnant Book and the Beginnings of French Music Printing," *Journal of the American Musicological Society*, 14 (1961), 22–23. A facsimile of the privilege appears in Heartz, *Pierre Attaingnant*, pl. 10. On the history of royal printing patents, see Elizabeth Armstrong, *Before Copyright: The French Book-Privilege System, 1498–1526* (Cambridge, 1990). Musicologists have recently started to explore music printing as a cultural process that shapes repertories as well as simply preserves them. See, for a representative sample of this work, the essays assembled in *Music and the Culture of Print*, ed. Kate van Orden (New York and London, 2000).

[23] On the musical output of Le Roy and Ballard and that of Du Chemin, see François Lesure and Geneviève Thibault, "Bibliographie des éditions musicales publiées par Nicolas

Exactly who bought and used any of these books will remain a topic for continuing investigation. Among the books issued by Moderne and Attaingnant were volumes of sacred music conceived with audiences at court and in French regional churches clearly in mind. The Beringens, too, printed music books directed towards special audiences, in this case the Italian merchants and bankers of Lyons. But aside from these books, few of those issued by French printers give direct testimony as to their intended audiences. For clues as to the circulation of printed music we must thus turn to the physical design of the books themselves, to the likely musical tastes of their owners, and to the new didactic manuals that served to instruct amateurs in the conventions and techniques of music making.

We should recall first and foremost that if the business of music had wide geographical horizons, these were nevertheless public offerings destined in many instances for private domestic enjoyment. Du Chemin's first chanson series, for example, was printed with pairs of voices on facing pages of each of two partbooks, a design that naturally lends itself to use around a domestic table—Superius and Tenor facing Altus and Bassus.[24] Indeed, not long after its advent in France, printed music books were already to be counted among the most prized personal possessions of urban bureaucrats and merchants. At the time of his death in 1544, for instance, the personal library of Jean de Badonvillier, an official in the Paris *chambre des comptes*, contained a printed collection of masses, two of Attaingnant's chanson anthologies, and printed books of motets by Claudin de Sermisy and Johannes Lupi.[25] Exactly what Badonvillier and his fellow bureaucrats in sixteenth-century Paris thought of this repertory is difficult to determine. None of these books contain prefaces of the sort found in Pierre Colin's book of masses, which would have directed a reader's attention to the proper relationship between musical means and spiritual meaning. Nor do the books of motets carry rubrics of the sort found in Attaingnant's motet series of 1534–35, which carefully designated works intended for particular liturgical or political commemorations.

Chanson anthologies of the sort owned by Badonvillier present a particularly

du Chemin," *Annales musicologiques*, 1 (1953), 269–373; 4 (1956), 251–53; 6 (1958–63), 403–6; and idem, *Bibliographie des éditions d'Adrian Le Roy et Robert Ballard (1551–1598)* (Paris, 1955). Le Roy and Ballard, designated as royal printers of music following the death of Pierre Attaingnant, apparently had very close ties to the royal court, printing works by Pierre Certon, Claudin de Sermisy, and others favored by the king's household and aristocratic salons. The history of music printing in Lyons is considered in Laurent Guillo, *Les Éditions musicales de la Renaissance lyonnaise (1525–1615)* (Paris, 1991).

24 Du Chemin's series of *chansons nouvelles* has recently been issued in facsimile by the Centre de musique ancienne of Tours, France. See, by way of introduction to the volumes and their musical contents, Richard Freedman, "Du Chemin's *Second livre* of 1549 and the Commerce of the French Chanson," *Second Livre de chansons à quatre: Nicolas Du Chemin, 1549* (Tours, 1993), pp. v–xv.

25 On the musical possessions of this official, see François Lesure, "Un Amateur de musique au début du XVIe siècle, Jean de Badonvillier," *Musique et musiciens français du XVIe siècle* (Geneva, 1976), 79–81. The entire *inventaire*, prepared for the goods of "Jean de Badonvillier, seigneur d'Aulnay-la-rivière, maître ordinaire en la chambre des comptes," is discussed in Madeleine Jurgens, *Documents du minutier central des notaires de Paris: Inventaires après décès; Tome premier (1483–1547)* (Paris, 1982), 273.

varied menu of musical and poetic types, idioms that embraced a wide range of styles and themes. Such mid-century chanson volumes depend closely on the forms and ideals of elite culture, especially the aesthetic of serious love offered in the lyrics of poets like Clément Marot. The long metrical patterns and elegantly balanced *quatrains* and *huitains* of such lyrics lend themselves well to the refined melodic manner that is the epitome of the mid-century chanson, with its clear alignment of rhyme, prosody, and musical line. Alongside such serious chansons, however, are text types and musical settings that acknowledge a social landscape extending well beyond elite circles. These works, in contrast to the restrained lyricism and serious sentiments of the courtly songs, dwell instead in pastoral and ribald themes drawn from popular culture. These chansons also use poetic and musical language quite different from that just described. Avoiding the closed formal designs and long lyrical lines favored by composers like Claudin and Certon, composers who set these texts preferred instead a style that tends towards musical contrast and rhythmic animation to carry recitational dialogue and descriptive narrative. Imitations of everyday speech and satirical representations of the infidelities of clerics and of peasant lovers were simply not part of the serious aesthetic. All of this variety suggests a world in which music was used as a form of private entertainment, not just by the nobility, but by wealthy merchants and bourgeois too.[26]

Of course, the wide circulation of printed music books is unimaginable without the basic musical skills to read and perform the works they contain. Attaingnant did not issue any truly practical manuals for the performance of polyphonic vocal music (although he did issue a treatise on some more abstract aspects of musical thought by the royal mathematician, Oronce Finé).[27] Yet by the 1550s, the legacy of Attaingnant's chansonniers had provoked public demand sufficiently to justify the publication of music primers such as Claude Martin's *Elementorum musices practicae pars prior* (issued by Du Chemin in 1550 and in French translation in 1556) or Maximillian Guilliaud's *Rudiments de musique practique* (which was in fact little more than a French summary of Martin's *Elementa*, issued by Du Chemin in 1554). These modest treatises offer practical and theoretical observations about music that shed some light on the habits and competencies of the readers who used these new books of chansons.[28] Through them novice musicians could gain

[26] On the stylistic and cultural landscape of the chanson between about 1520 and 1560, see Lawrence F. Bernstein, "The 'Parisian' Chanson: Problems of Style and Terminology," *Journal of the American Musicological Society*, 31 (1978), 193–240; Leeman L. Perkins, "Towards a Typology of the 'Renaissance' Chanson," *Journal of Musicology*, 6 (1988), 421–47; Freedman, "Words and Tones in Du Chemin's *Sixiesme Livre*," *Sixiesme Livre de chansons à quatre: Nicolas Du Chemin, 1550* (facs. Tours, 1998), pp. v–xx; and Jean-Pierre Ouvrard, "La Chanson française du XVIe siècle, lecture du texte poètique," *La Chanson à la Renaissance: Actes du XXe Colloque d'Études humanistes du Centre d'Études Supérieures de la Renaissance de l'Université de Tours, Juillet 1977*, ed. Jean-Michel Vaccaro (Tours, 1981), 106–19.

[27] His *Epithoma musice instrumentalis* was issued in 1530. See Heartz, *Pierre Attaingnant*, 236.

[28] Du Chemin's treatises sought the stamp of official approval in the reflected light of eminent Parisian authorities: Martin's book was dedicated to a leading figure in the Parisian *Parlement*, while that of Guilliaud, who identifies himself as a member of the Collège de Na-

a basic understanding of the notation of rhythm, the tone systems of Renaissance polyphony, the rudiments of *solfège,* and even elementary composition. Such skills doubtless afforded a point of entry into the colloquy of urban society. Indeed, in his *Épitome musicale* of 1558, a book devoted to musical instruments and how to play them, the Protestant musician Philibert Jambe de Fer explicitly acknowledged this social dimension of music making. Advising his readers of the best way to tune their viols, "instruments with which gentlemen, merchants, and other men of virtue pass their time," Jambe de Fer implies that to be in disharmony with one's social peers would be a particularly unpleasant situation.[29]

For Jambe de Fer's readers the acquisition of musical skills was a basic requirement for anyone who aspired to civility. Other readers of sixteenth-century France, however, were urged to regard music not so much as a social grace or form of entertainment than as a means of spiritual edification. In his *Droict Chemin de musique* of 1550, Loys Bourgeois bitterly complained of the salaciousness of the secular music of his day, preferring instead "choses sainctes et divines," meaning in this case a Psalm or spiritual song ("d'un Pseaume ou cantique spirituel").[30] Indeed, a number of composers in mid-century France, including Certon, Clément Janequin, Didier Lupi, Claude Goudimel, the previously noted Philibert Jambe de Fer, and even Bourgeois himself, turned their attentions to Psalms and spiritual texts in French, producing great quantities of devotional music for domestic use by French Protestants. A number of Huguenot editors also brought out editions of secular chansons in which the poetic texts were rewritten to embrace spiritual rather than worldly themes.[31] Such enterprises traced their origins to attitudes already implicit in the first printed edition of the Genevan Psalter (in 1543), where Jean Calvin acknowledged that music "has a secret and almost incredible power to move our

varre, addresses itself to the leading musician of the French royal court, Claudin de Sermisy. See Maurice Cauchie, "Maximillian Guilliaud," *Festschrift Adolph Koczirz zum 60 Geburtstag*, ed. Robert Haas (Vienna, 1930), 6–8. A third musical treatise issued by Du Chemin, Michel de Menehou's *Nouvelle instruction familiere* of 1558, was offered to another illustrious figure of mid-century Paris, the Cardinal Guillaume du Bellay. All three of the treatises published by Du Chemin have been issued in facsimile (Geneva, 1981).

29 A complete facsimile edition of the *Épitome musicale des tons, sons et accordz, es voix humaines, fleustes d'Alleman, Fleustes à neuf trous, violes, et violons* (Lyons: Michel du Bois, 1556) appears in François Lesure, "L'*Épitome musicale* de Philibert Jambe de Fer (1556)," *Annales musicologiques*, 6 (1958–1963), 341–418. The comments on viol playing come from pp. 58 and 62: "donques si je m'efforce de vous donner à entendre le plus commode et plus facile que pour le jourd'huy à cours entres gentilzhommes, et marchants, il vous plaira n'estre fachéz, vous autres qui à ce n'accordez"; and "Nous appellons violes c'elles desquelles les gentilzhommes, marchantz, et autres gens de vertuz passent leur temps."

30 See Loys Bourgeois, *Le Droict Chemin de musique (Genf, 1550)*, ed. P. André Gaillard. Documenta Musicologica, ser. 1, 6 (Kassel, 1954).

31 See, by way of introduction to this vast musical repertory, Dobbins, *Music in Renaissance Lyons*, 264–67, and Marc Honegger, "Les Chansons spirituelles de Didier Lupi et les débuts de la musique protestante en France," (Doctoral thesis, Paris, 1970). On the place of literacy and Protestantism in Lyonnaise urban life during the 16th century, see Natalie Zemon Davis, "Printing and the People," *Society and Culture in Early Modern France* (Stanford, 1975), 189–226.

hearts in one way or another."[32] Yet along with this recognition of the spiritual potential of music came a simultaneous concern about its sensuous effects and how to control them. For Calvin, the solution was to be found not by discriminating the effects of one sound from another, but instead by making the potentially salutary effects of music upon the listener dependent on the kinds of verbal texts to which it was bound, for in this way he hoped "to moderate the use of music to make it serve all that is of good repute."[33] According to this view, music was a maker of moral fiber rather than principally a manifestation of worldly civility.

The history of music, as we have seen in this survey of France in the middle decades of the sixteenth century, is in many ways inseparable from the history of the institutions that produced it. As sponsors of lavish entertainment, refined vocal and instrumental chamber music, and impressive works for state ceremony, the musical needs of the ruling elites necessarily dominate much of our understanding of the stylistic history of the French musical Renaissance. Yet if aristocrats frequently directed music towards their own needs, they by no means held a monopoly on musical expression. The French musical press of the first half of the sixteenth century, although authorized and protected by the dynastic state, nevertheless made music available to a broad and newly literate public. Recognizing both the commercial opportunity and the essentially cosmopolitan implications of this new musical public, printers like Pierre Attaingnant in Paris and Jacques Moderne in Lyons thus promoted the musical ideals of the ruling elites while giving voice to the varied needs of an increasingly diverse culture. Important, too, in this survey, has been the recognition of the latent and very deep spiritual and social divisions that were to prove so destructive during the later wars of religion, diverging convictions about art and society reflected in the very different sorts of music advocated in Protestant and Catholic circles. In all its varied forms and settings, music was for Renaissance France both an ornament of daily life and a vital means of making plain the order of French society itself.

[32] The translation is in Oliver Strunk, *Source Readings in Music History*, rev. ed., ed. Leo Treitler (New York: Norton, 1998), 366. The original text reads: "Et de fait, nous experimentons qu'elle ha une vertu secrete et quasi incredible à emouvoir les cueurs en une sorte, ou en l'autre." Quoted from Calvin's preface as it appears in a Genevan book issued in 1551, Thédore de Bèze and Clément Marot, *Pseaumes octantetrois de David mis en rime françoise* (Geneva, 1551; repr. New Brunswick, NJ, 1973). For a survey of the sources and contexts of Calvinist thought on music, see H. P. Clive, "The Calvinist Attitude to Music, and its Literary Aspects and Sources," *Bibliothèque d'humanisme et de Renaissance*, 19 (1957), 80–102, 294–319; 20 (1958), 79–107. The classic studies of the French Psalter are Orentin Douen, *Clément Marot et le Psautier: Étude historique, littéraire, musicale, et bibliographique*, 2 vols. (Paris, 1878; repr. Amsterdam, 1967); and Pierre Pidoux, *Le Psautier huguenot du XVIe siècle: Mélodies et documents*, 2 vols. (Basel, 1962). More recently, see L. Guillo, "Le Psautier de Paris et le Psautier de Lyon: A propos de deux corpus contemporains du Psautier de Genève (1549–1561)," *Bulletin de la Société de l'histoire du protestantisme français*, 136 (1990), 361–420.

[33] Trans. from Strunk, *Source Readings*, 366. The original text (cited in Bèze, *Pseaumes octantetrois de David*) reads: "Si nous doit elle bien emouvoir à moderer l'usage de la musique, pour la faire servir à toute honesté."

10

FRANCE, *ii*: 1560–1600

Jeanice Brooks

LATE-SIXTEENTH-CENTURY France—the era of Ronsard and Montaigne—has long been a focus for literary scholarship; but for musicologists, this has been one of the least investigated areas of Renaissance music history. While some repertories from the period (the polyphonic chanson and *musique mesurée*, for example) received a certain amount of attention in the middle years of the twentieth century, others (liturgical music, *chanson spirituelle*, psalm translations) went virtually unstudied. Biographical details for many important composers and performers of the time have been scant, as well as information about those who purchased and listened to their music; the absence of basic information has been a significant obstacle to understanding musical life in France during this period. In recent years, however, there has been a renewal of interest in the French Renaissance, and several major studies have begun to address these gaps.[1]

Among the most striking features of the period was the near-complete domination of the music printing industry by the Parisian firm of Le Roy & Ballard. Unlike the more competitive environment that characterized Italian printing centers such as Venice, the increasingly centralized economy of France and its system of royal privileges created a condition of virtual monopoly. Le Roy & Ballard's printed repertory is the largest single body of evidence we have about musical practice, so that the market strategies of the firm and the needs, abilities, and tastes of its public inevitably color our understanding of the period. Another significant aspect of these years was the domestic unrest of the Wars of Religion; violence and disruption

[1] Howard Mayer Brown, "*Ut Musica Poesis*: Music and Poetry in France in the Late Sixteenth Century," *Early Music History*, 13 (1994), 1–63, furnishes a "state of the discipline" look at the problems and questions posed by the era; other essays in the same volume are aimed at addressing various concerns Brown raises. Recent full-length studies of the period include Richard Freedman, *The Chansons of Orlando di Lasso: Music, Piety, and Print in Sixteenth-Century France* (Rochester, 2000); Isabelle His, *Claude Le Jeune (v. 1530–1600): Un Compositeur entre Renaissance et Baroque* (Arles, 2000); Kate van Orden, "Vernacular Culture and the Chanson in Paris, 1570–1580" (PhD diss., University of Chicago, 1996); and Jeanice Brooks, *Courtly Song in Late Sixteenth-Century France* (Chicago, 2000).

affected the lives and careers of musicians, and the fostering of new views on the role of music in religious life and of new kinds of music for different religious factions had a significant impact on musical production. Finally, the particular directions taken by French humanist thinking had clear consequences for music. I have organized the discussion that follows around these three areas—music printing, religious controversy, and musical humanism—to illustrate some of the most distinctive aspects of French musical life in the second half of the century.

Le Roy & Ballard

Robert Ballard, who was related by marriage to several musicians in the royal service, and his "cousin germain" Adrian Le Roy, himself a lutenist following the court, obtained a privilege to print music in August 1551. Their first book, a collection of motets, songs, and dances intabulated for lute, was issued only two weeks later. In February 1553 they were awarded Pierre Attaingnant's former title of *imprimeur du roi en musique*; the office, bestowed by Henri II, was regularly renewed under succeeding kings and provided significant legal protection against competitors as well as commercially valuable prestige.[2] Competition from other printers was consequently very slender. After Attaingnant's operations (run by his widow after his death in late 1551 or early 1552) stopped in 1557, and Michel Fezendat ceased to print music in 1558, only Nicolas Du Chemin produced any rival publications in the 1560s.[3] The number of Du Chemin prints dwindled after 1570, leaving virtually the entire market to Le Roy & Ballard. Lyons, one of the European capitals of printing, remained a secondary center for music publishing. Yet after the cessation of Jacques Moderne's activity (much reduced after the death in 1540 of his principal editor, Francesco de Layolle), Lyonnais music prints were produced by general publishers rather than specialist music printers. Most seem designed to respond to religious and cultural circumstances particular to the region rather than to compete with the output of Le Roy & Ballard.[4]

Le Roy & Ballard's first prints seem intended to fill a niche in the market during the moment of relative freedom in the music printing industry that existed for a few years early in the reign of Henri II (r. 1547–60).[5] Between 1551 and 1554, the firm produced a series of books of lute and guitar tablature, containing abstract

[2] The standard source on Le Roy & Ballard remains François Lesure and Geneviève Thibault, *Bibliographie des éditions d'Adrian Le Roy et Robert Ballard (1551–1598)* (Paris, 1955). On the family connections of Robert Ballard, see also Brooks, *Courtly Song*, 76.

[3] On Du Chemin, see François Lesure and Geneviève Thibault, "Bibliographie des éditions musicales publiées par Nicolas Du Chemin (1549–1576)," *Annales musicologiques* 1 (1953), 269–373.

[4] Between 1540 and 1600, almost 100 editions of music were printed in Lyon. After 1560 these were principally devoted to psalm settings, reflecting Lyon's position in the religious controversy and the Protestant tendencies of its printing industry. A few prints of madrigals (by Regolo Vecoli and Mayo, for example) reflect the tastes of the large Italian community in the city. See Laurent Guillo, *Les Éditions musicales de la Renaissance lyonnaise* (Paris, 1991) and Frank Dobbins, *Music in Renaissance Lyons* (Oxford, 1992), 138–72.

[5] See Daniel Heartz, "Parisian Music Publishing Under Henri II: A Propos of Four Recently

pieces such as preludes and fantasies, intabulations of chansons and motets, and dances (many based on chansons). Most of the arrangements were by Le Roy himself, although music by the celebrated Italian lutenist Albert de Rippe, the darling of the French court under François I, appeared in the *Quart Livre de tabulature de luth* of 1553. This concentration on lute music in the early years seems an effort to capitalize on Le Roy's own reputation as a player, but also reflects the partners' ability to obtain new and fashionable music through their court connections. Royal patronage not only provided protection from competition, but also a steady supply of new music and a ready market for Le Roy & Ballard's prints. Like Attaingnant before them, Le Roy & Ballard published large amounts of music generated by court musical institutions, principally the polyphonic chapel (*chapelle-musique*) and the royal chamber (*chambre*). These divisions of the royal household, to which can be added the royal stable (*écurie*) were largely organized during the reign of François I (r. 1515–47), and continued to provide the nucleus of court musical activity under his successors. Though the polyphonic chapel's size and composition changed little, the chamber and stable in contrast underwent considerable expansion and reorganization in the second half of the century.[6] The changes reflect growth in the size of the court as a whole as it became a principal political instrument of secular monarchy, as well as the increasing value placed on secular music-making in contemporary courtly ideology.

Under Henri II's music-loving sons Charles IX (r. 1560–74) and Henri III (r. 1574–89) the relationship of the music printers to the court became especially close. By 1572, both Le Roy and Ballard had become paid members of the king's entourage, their names appearing on official lists of royal household servants; by 1578, Le Roy had become a pensioner of the chapel as well.[7] One of the most vivid musical documents surviving from the period is a 1574 letter from Le Roy to Orlande de Lassus describing a session in which Le Roy presented and performed new music to an enthusiastic Charles IX; the printer's account of the event shows him to have been on familiar and cordial terms with the monarch.[8] And courtly values appear to have had significant impact on Le Roy & Ballard's production. In the late 1550s, the firm spent a few years concentrating on prints of sacred music, producing folio editions of masses, principally by court composers such as Jacques Arcadelt, Pierre Certon, and Claudin de Sermisy, as well as several volumes of psalm settings by Claude Goudimel. These types of publication also continued to form part of the repertory of the company in later years, but they never again accounted for such

Discovered Guitar Books," *The Musical Quarterly*, 46 (1960), 448–67, for a discussion of this critical period.

[6] On the structures under François I, see Henry Prunières, "La Musique de la chambre et de l'écurie sous le règne de François I," *L'année musicale*, I (1911), 215–251; and Christelle Cazaux, *La Musique à la cour de François I* (Paris, 2002). On changes in the second half of the century, see Jeanice Brooks, "From Minstrel to Courtier: The Royal *Musique de Chambre* and Courtly Ideals in Sixteenth-Century France," *Trossinger Jahrbuch für Renaissancemusik*, I (2001), 39–49.

[7] Brooks, *Courtly Song*, 26–27.

[8] The letter is reproduced and transcribed in Lesure and Thibault, *Bibliographie*, 36–7.

a large percentage. The statistics compiled by Le Roy & Ballard's bibliographers Lesure and Thibault show that between 1551 and 1598, the firm published only 17 editions of instrumental music and 123 of sacred music, as opposed to 207 of secular vocal music. When these statistics are broken down further into the number of pieces in various genres, the contrast is even more striking: Le Roy & Ballard printed 52 masses, 491 psalms and *chansons spirituelles*, and 645 motets compared to nearly two thousand chansons and *airs*.

The secular vocal music that formed the staple of Le Roy & Ballard's repertory was usually published in numbered song anthologies in the tradition of Attaingnant. These were generally re-edited many times, with their contents shuffled and partially replaced to reflect changing tastes and availability of new pieces. For example, the *Tiers Livre de chansons*, first published in 1554, originally contained sixteen pieces for three and four voices by Arcadelt, two by De Bussy, two by Entraigues, and two by Didier Leschenet; when it was re-edited in 1557, one of the Leschenet songs was replaced by another Arcadelt chanson. In 1561, all of Arcadelt's three-voice pieces were dropped and replaced by new four-voice songs by the same composer, and new songs by Maillard were substituted for the remaining pieces by Leschenet and Entraigues. In 1567, two of the Maillard pieces disappeared and two new songs by Arcadelt were added. Other collections seem to have been sure sellers from the start, and underwent little change in editions after the first. The *Sesieme Livre*, consisting primarily of songs by the much-admired Lassus, retained its contents unchanged in editions of 1565, 1567, 1570, 1573, 1575, 1578, and 1579, before undergoing slight alterations in 1584 and 1593.

After 1560, like publishers in other centers of music printing, Le Roy & Ballard supplemented the song anthologies with an increasing number of volumes devoted to the music of single composers. They published considerable numbers of songs by Netherlandish composers, particularly by Lassus, who though working in Munich had close ties with the French court and particularly amicable relations with Le Roy; his music was enormously successful in France, and Le Roy & Ballard published a steady stream of his chansons starting in 1559 with the *Douziesme Livre de chansons*.[9] Volumes by other composers working in the northern song tradition included those of Philippe de Monte (1575) and François Regnard (1579). The polyphonic chanson was also cultivated by composers in the provinces; Toulouse, a city with an active humanist circle and home to several notable poets, emerges as an especially fascinating musical center, with volumes of songs by Anthoine de Bertrand and Guillaume Boni. Boni's *Premier Livre des sonetz de P. de Ronsard* (first published by Du Chemin, but rapidly re-edited by Le Roy & Ballard) was particularly successful, becoming the most often reprinted volume of chansons by any single French composer of the sixteenth century. Many of these song collections, by northerners as well as by provincial composers working in chanson styles closer to that of French composers of the Sermisy generation, were marketed through their settings of famous poetry, particularly verse by Ronsard. As well as

[9] For a recent overview of Lassus's relationship with the firm, see Annie Cœurdevey, *Roland de Lassus* (Paris, 2003), 174–99 and passim.

catering to their public's desire for new music, Le Roy & Ballard also published backward-looking collections that included the music of long-dead composers. From 1567, the firm had a privilege singling out Josquin, Mouton, and Richafort among others, and pieces by these composers were included in anthologies such as the *Tiers Livre de chansons à trois parties* of 1578. The enormous *Livre de meslanges* of 1560 contained works by Josquin and Pierre de la Rue alongside up-to-date pieces by Lassus. The inclusion of such pieces suggests that Le Roy & Ballard's clientele had a lively interest in music of the past, an interest perhaps related to a nascent sense of a canon comprising works of enduring value.[10]

Towards the end of the century the polyphonic chanson, which had accounted for the bulk of Le Roy and Ballard's secular vocal prints, gradually lost its place to the *air*. The term was used in a music print for the first time in Guillaume Costeley's *Musique* (1570), where it appeared at the beginning of a section of strophic songs in homophonic syllabic setting. Though they were printed as vocal polyphony, their melody-dominated texture and lack of contrapuntal complexity strongly suggests that they were most often (if not always) performed as accompanied song.[11] Similar pieces, such as those in Pierre Certon's *Premier Livre de chansons* (1552), had been published in the two previous decades, though they were printed under the rubrics "chanson" or "voix de ville" rather than "air." The earliest songs of this type employ regular meter and frequent rhythmic clichés, largely derived from either Italian *frottole* or, more often, dance music.[12] Soon after 1570 and the appearance of the label *air*, pieces so called began to differ from those known as *voix de ville*: the poetry was often more self-consciously literary, and the text could be set in additive rhythms in which strong syllables received long notes and weak syllables short ones, combining to produce phrases of varying lengths, often without regular metric divisions. At first the boundaries between the genres are not especially clear. Le Roy himself seemed to regard the difference as predominantly one of terminology when he wrote in the preface to his 1571 collection of airs, *Livre d'airs de cour miz sur le luth* (a collection of lute tablatures plus a separately notated vocal line in white mensural notation, mainly of songs first published two years before in a polyphonic vocal collection attributed to Nicolas de la Grotte), describing its contents as light songs "que jadis on appelloit voix de ville, aujourd'huy Airs de Cour" [that used to be called *voix de ville*, and today are called *airs de cour*]. Though Le Roy's term *air de cour* did not appear again in the title of a music print until the 1590s, its use here is telling; it refers not only to the courtly origin of the

[10] For a more detailed analysis of retrospective editions, see Kate van Orden, "Imitation and 'La musique des anciens': Le Roy & Ballard's 1572 *Mellange de chansons*," *Revue de musicologie*, 80 (1994), 5–37.

[11] See Jonathan Le Cocq, "French Lute Song, 1529–1643" (DPhil thesis, University of Oxford, 1997), for a detailed discussion of accompanied song practice in the period.

[12] On the genre's early history, see Daniel Heartz, "*Voix de ville*: Between Humanist Ideals and Musical Reality," in *Words and Music: The Scholar's View . . . in Honor of A. Tillman Merritt*, ed. Laurence Berman (Cambridge, MA, 1972), 115–35; Jane Ozenberger Whang, "From *Voix de ville* to *Air de cour*: The Strophic Chanson, c. 1545–1575" (PhD diss., University of North Carolina, 1981).

pieces (as we have seen, the majority of the music Le Roy & Ballard published was in some sense *de cour*) but to the role such songs could play in contemporary ideals of courtiership.[13] By the end of the century, the more declamatory *air* had become the principal genre of French secular music, a role it would retain under the absolutist rule of the Bourbons. It formed the backbone of Pierre Ballard's production between 1600 and 1642 in the same way the polyphonic chanson had supported the business of his father Robert and his partner Le Roy.

Le Roy and Ballard published few treatises on music. Those they did print, such as the *Traité de la musique pratique* by Jean Yssandon (1582) and the anonymous volume of 1583 (possibly by Le Roy himself) followed the "quick and easy" model of treatises published by Du Chemin in the mid-1550s. They were primarily aimed at teaching singing, presenting the rudiments of solmization and mensural notation. [14] There seems to have been no tradition in France of thoughtful and detailed technical treatises such as those by Zarlino, Vicentino, or Glarean, although references in poetry and prefaces to music collections confirm that treatises in Italian and Latin were read in France. As well as singing manuals, Le Roy and Ballard produced instructions for instruments—guitar, lute, mandora, and cistre—that complemented Le Roy's books of intabulations, which provided models of how to intabulate songs according to the rules of the instructions. Neither the treatises or the instructions were directed to professional musicians; they seem to have been intended for the college or university student and the amateur music-lover interested in acquiring skills increasingly seen as socially desirable.

Religious Conflict and Sacred Music

THE religious wars, which began in earnest in 1560 and did not finish until the accession of Henri IV (1589), the end of the Valois dynasty, and the eventual issue of the Edict of Nantes (1598), made this period one of violent outbreaks interspersed with times of uneasy peace.[15] Musicians were often involved in the conflicts between factions: Marin Mersenne claimed that when the Protestant composer Claude Le Jeune fled the capital during the siege of Paris (1590), his music was saved from being burnt only through the intervention of a fellow composer, the Catholic Jacques Mauduit; Anthoine de Bertrand, according to the Jesuit Michel Coyssard, was assassinated by Protestants because of his Catholic religious music; Claude Goudimel was killed in Lyons during the St Bartholomew's Day massacre of Protestants in 1572.

The conflict helped to create an atmosphere in which traditional religious and liturgical genres such as the motet and cyclic mass continued to flourish but

13 Brooks, *Courtly Song,* is a detailed investigation of the *air* and courtly values.

14 See Philippe Vendrix, "On the Theoretical Expression of Music in France During the Renaissance," *Early Music History*, 13 (1994), 249–73, and Brown, "*Ut Musica Poesis*," 50–54.

15 Good general introductions to the history of the Wars of Religion include Mack P. Holt, *The French Wars of Religion, 1562–1629* (Cambridge, 1995), and Robert J. Knecht, *The French Wars of Religion, 1559–1598* (London, 1989).

were accompanied by new kinds of music. The rapid proliferation of vernacular psalm settings from the middle to the end of the century is a case in point. The most influential French translation of the Psalms was that of Clément Marot and Théodore de Bèze; originating at the Catholic court of François I, where Marot was employed, the translations were eventually finished in Calvinist Geneva. The Marot/De Bèze psalms were initially favored by Protestants and Catholics alike. François I and Henri II were both said to enjoy the psalms, and courtiers sang them to popular tunes in the 1540s. The Marot/De Bèze translations gradually became associated with a repertory of melodies which appeared in Genevan publications starting in 1539. Loys Bourgeois, who wrote new melodies and revised old ones for the 1551 Psalter, was the only named composer to be involved; the composers who wrote and revised melodies for earlier publications of psalms with tunes, as well as for psalters after 1551, remain unknown. After numerous publications of parts of the Psalter with melodies, the final version containing the 150 translated psalms, two canticles, and their associated tunes—the "Geneva Psalter"—appeared in 1562.[16]

The Genevan Psalms became a principal emblem of self-identification for French Huguenots, used not only in worship but as marching songs for Protestant forces on the field of battle, as hymns of victory when they were successful, and as songs of defiance performed by Huguenots awaiting execution. The public singing of the Psalms was officially banned in 1558 by Henri II (who himself had sung Marot's translations at court when he was still *dauphin*); Protestant pampleteers were quick to condemn the king for substituting "silly, lascivious *chansons*," with texts by Ronsard and the like, for the holy songs of the Psalter.[17] Recognition of the symbolic weight and moral power of the vernacular psalms seems to lie behind the production of rival psalm translations by Catholic poets such as Jean de Baïf and Philippe Desportes, both of whom produced new French versions of the Psalter during the Wars of Religion.

Despite their Calvinist associations the Psalms and their tunes were initially exploited by composers on both sides of the religious controversy, and Janequin, Arcadelt, and Certon—all Catholics—wrote and published settings of the Marot/De Bèze psalms employing the Genevan melodies. After 1560, however, when Catholic and Protestant positions became more firmly entrenched and the identification of musical repertory with political and religious programs clearer, most Catholic composers turned to other texts, and polyphonic music based on the Geneva Psalter became the domain of Protestant composers. The most prolific of these was Claude Goudimel, who after writing a large number of psalm settings in the 1550s, produced two settings of the complete Psalter in the 1560s. These varied in style from note-against-note settings with the Genevan tune in the superius or tenor (*Les Cent cinquante pseaumes de David*; Paris: Le Roy & Ballard, 1564)

[16] The standard source on the Geneva Psalter is Pierre Pidoux, *Le Psautier huguenot du XVIe siècle*, 2 vols. (Basel,1962); see also *The New Grove Dictionary of Music and Musicians*, 2nd edn, ed. Stanley Sadie and John Tyrrell (London, 2001), s.v. "Psalms, metrical" by Nicholas Temperley et al.

[17] See Brooks, *Courtly Song*, 277–79, for an example of this kind of polemic.

to settings in more ornate animated homophony (*Les Cent cinquante pseaumes*, 1568); some of his earlier partial settings of the Psalter employ a more richly contrapuntal motet style. Other Protestant composers who published complete settings of the Geneva Psalter included Philibert Jambe de Fer, Richard Crassot, Jean Servin, Pascal de l'Estocart, and Claude Le Jeune.

Other new music generated by the religious ferment included the large numbers of *airs* and *chansons spirituelles* sharing the musical language of their secular counterparts. These could be sacred contrafacts, with new words adapted to existing music, such as the series of volumes published by the Parisian Jean Le Royer in Geneva between 1578 and 1580, in which the Protestant pastor Simon Goulart of Senlis fitted new devotional words to secular chansons by Bertrand, Boni, and Lassus.[18] In other cases they were settings of new texts, such as French translations or paraphrases of Latin hymns, or contemporary religious poetry such as the *Quatrains* of the Catholic chancellor Guy du Faur de Pibrac (set by Boni, Planson, Lassus, and L'Estocart) or the *Octonaires de la vanité et inconstance du monde* of the Calvinist pastor Antoine Chandieu (set by Le Jeune and L'Estocart). Like the polyphonic settings of the Psalter, these pieces were primarily intended for domestic performance and private edification rather than the ceremonial usage envisioned for prints of Mass settings. Motets, which continued to be published in France in reasonably large numbers (Lassus again accounting for the lion's share of Le Roy & Ballard's prints in this genre after 1564), seem to have encompassed different kinds of performing contexts. Used for state and religious ceremonial, motets could also be sung or played domestically, as the presence of motet books in the libraries of music-loving bourgeois attests.[19]

French Musical Humanism

As in Italy, musical culture in France was significantly marked by humanist ideas and ideals. Neoplatonic conceptions of music played a particularly important role in French intellectual life, and the period saw the translation into French of the principal Italian writings (such as Marsilio Ficino's commentary on Plato) as well as the production of new French works relying heavily on Neoplatonic and Pythagorean ideas. The poets of the Pléiade manifested a strong interest in the moral and spiritual aspects of music; Ronsard wrote a lengthy preface, which has been read as a miniature Neoplatonic treatise on music, to Le Roy & Ballard's

[18] Freedman, *The Chansons of Orlando di Lasso*, discusses these transformations and the religious and social needs they served.

[19] Books of motets by Lassus figured in the library of the Lyonnais merchant Justinien Pense, a Catholic who took an important organizational role in Henri III's penitential confraternities; they were included there with other volumes of private devotional material, such as books of hours and collections of sermons. See Jeanice Brooks, "Music by Jean de Castro in the Parisian Library of Justinien Pense," *Revue belge de musicologie / Belgisch tijdschrift voor muziekwetenschap*, 50 (1996), 25–34.

1560 *Meslanges*, and Pontus de Tyard's *Solitaire second, ou Prose de la musique* (1555) is a full-length philosophical dialogue on music's role in the universe.

Despite the lack of French-language treatises on modal theory, French composers showed particular interest in its applications; some composers wrote works that can be read as exemplars of beliefs about the structural and expressive possibilities of modal usage. For example, Anthoine de Bertrand's first books of Ronsard settings, *Les Amours de P. de Ronsard* (1576) contains a cycle of 35 sonnets describing the stages of an ultimately unsuccessful love affair; each group of chansons in the cycle shares a tonal structure chosen to illustrate the affect of the poems.[20] Claude Le Jeune's collection of psalm settings, the *Dodecacorde* (1598), has a title clearly referring to Glarean's treatise on the modes. It contains settings of twelve psalms, one in each mode following Zarlino's definition and ordering, and even includes a psalm in F without a B-flat in the signature as a representative of the Lydian mode.[21] These extremely self-conscious illustrations of modal thinking exist along with more utilitarian examples that seem more rooted in tradition and less tied to contemporary developments in modal theory and ideas about modal affect. For example, Le Roy & Ballard's publications, like Attaingnant's before them, were regularly organized by mode; Le Roy's treatise on intabulating music for the lute used modes to help in the intabulating process.[22]

French composers' interest in the modes was in many cases inspired by the desire to revive the legendary effects of ancient music, evoked in the prefaces to both the Le Jeune and Bertrand collections just mentioned. The most extreme manifestation of of this type of experimentation involved the poets and musicians of the Académie de poésie et de musique.[23] Founded by the poet Jean-Antoine de Baïf and granted a royal charter by Charles IX in 1570, the Académie attracted the collaboration of the composers Joachim Thibault de Courville and Claude Le Jeune; Fabrice Marin Caietain had some contact with the group, and later converts to its musical style included Jacques Mauduit and Eustache Du Caurroy. The goal of the Académie, expressed in its charter, was to revive the marvellous effects of ancient music by imposing classical meters on French poetry and then setting it

20 The structure is described in Jeanice Brooks, "'Ses Amours et les miennes tout ensemble': La Structure cyclique du *Premier Livre des Amours* d'Anthoine de Bertrand," *Revue de musicologie*, 74 (1988), 201–220.

21 On Le Jeune's use of modal theory, see His, *Claude Le Jeune*, 189–93, 278–96.

22 On the order of the Attaingnant books, see Howard Mayer Brown, "Theory and Practice in the Sixteenth Century: Preliminary Notes on Attaingnant's Modally Ordered Chansonniers," in *Essays in Musicology: A Tribute to Alvin Johnson*, ed. Lewis Lockwood and Edward Roesner (Philadelphia, 1990); Le Roy & Ballard follow similar patterns.

23 On the Academy, Frances Yates, *The French Academies of the Sixteenth Century* (London, 1947; repr. with foreword by J. B. Trapp, London, 1988), remains a central source; see also the influential work by D. P. Walker, particularly "The Aims of Baïf's Académie de Poésie et de Musique," *Journal of Renaissance and Baroque Music*, 1 (1946–47), 91–100; "The Influence of *Musique Mesurée à l'Antique*, Particularly on the *Air de Cour* of the Early Seventeenth Century," *Musica Disciplina*, 2 (1948), 141–63; and "Some Aspects and Problems of *Musique Mesurée à l'Antique*: The Rhythm and Notation of *Musique Mesurée*," *Musica Disciplina*, 4 (1950), 163–86. For a more recent perspective, see His, *Claude Le Jeune*, 243–307.

to music specially designed to reflect the poetry's metric patterns. As there was no system of quantitative meter for the French language, Baïf first devised a series of rules for determining long and short syllables and their combination into metric patterns drawn from Greek and Latin models. Poetry written according to this scheme, *vers mesuré à l'antique*, was set to music in which long syllables received notes exactly twice the duration of short syllables. The longs and shorts combine to produce the asymmetric rhythmic groupings that are the hallmark of *musique mesurée*; the rigidly homophonic texture of the pieces ensured that both the words and the metric groupings were clearly intelligible. Because of the draconian rules of secrecy imposed on musicians and listeners in the Académie, relatively little of its music was published before 1600. The musical style of the Académie nevertheless affected court spectacles produced in the last third of the century, particularly the *Balet comique de la Royne* (1581). It may also have had some influence on the rhythm of the *air de cour*, a genre in which some of the poets and musicians of the Académie also worked and one which shared some of the rhetorical and declamatory impulses of *musique mesurée*.

French musicians also showed considerable interest in experimental chromaticism, of the type derived from speculation about the *genera* of ancient theory as well as the expressive or coloristic use of chromatic alteration characteristic of late-sixteenth-century Italian madrigals. Costeley's "chanson spirituelle" *Seigneur Dieu ta pitié*, composed around 1558 but not published until 1570, uses an octave divided into nineteen tones rather than twelve.[24] Bertrand's *Ces liens d'or* (1576) is partially written in the chromatic *genus*, and his *Je suis tellement amoureux* (1578) employs the enharmonic, with microtone divisions.[25] Bertrand knew Nicola Vicentino's treatise *L'antica musica ridotta alla moderna prattica*, which he cites in the preface to his *Amours de P. de Ronsard* (1576). Vicentino's own chromatic music was performed at the court of Charles IX, and appreciated by the king himself. In the famous 1574 letter to Lassus mentioned above, Le Roy described how Charles IX listened with great enjoyment to a chromatic piece by Vicentino; Le Roy then presented the king with the Prologue to Lassus's *Prophetiae Sybillarum* to demonstrate the northern composer's ability to write similar music.

French humanism produced some fascinating and unique musical consequences, and it is hardly surprising that twentieth-century scholarship has often concentrated on its manifestations. It is a rare music history textbook that foregoes mention of *musique mesurée*, for example, although it could be argued that Baïf's experiment—despite the participation of at least one indisputably gifted composer, Claude Le Jeune—is less representative of late-sixteenth-century French musical culture than, say, the chansons of Guillaume Boni, the psalm settings of Goudimel, or the *airs* of Nicolas de La Grotte. Other features of the period I have not mentioned, but which deserve more scrutiny, include the formation of the

24 See Kenneth Levy, "Costeley's Chromatic Chanson," *Annales musicologiques*, 3 (1955), 213–63.

25 On Bertrand's sources and methods, see Jean-Michel Vaccaro, "Les Préfaces d'Anthoine de Bertrand," *Revue de musicologie*, 74 (1988), 221–35.

violin bands that regularly accompanied dancing at the French court in the second half of the century; the central role of the lute in social life and in literature; and the function of music in court and civic spectacle in the period. As more is learned about these musics and their milieux, a more nuanced vision of musical life in late sixteenth-century France, in all its richness and complexity, is bound to emerge.

Further Reading

Besides studies cited in the notes, the following are recommended:

BROSSARD, Yolande de. *Musiciens de Paris, 1535–1792: Actes d'état civil d'après le ficher Laborde de la Bibliothèque Nationale.* Paris, 1965.

CARPENTER, Nan Cooke. "Ronsard's Préface sur la Musique." *Modern Language Notes,* 75 (1960): 126–33.

CAZEAUX, Isabelle. *French Music in the Fifteenth and Sixteenth Centuries.* Oxford, 1975.

DELLABORA, Mariateresa (ed.). *"Une invention moderne": Baldassare da Belgioioso e il "Balet comique de la Royne".* Lucca, 1999.

DUROSOIR, Georgie. *L'Air de cour en France, 1571–1655.* Liège, 1991.

GRAHAM, Victor E., and William McAllister Johnson. *The Paris Entries of Charles IX and Elisabeth of Austria.* Toronto, 1974.

——. *The Royal Tour of France by Charles IX and Catherine de' Medici: Festivals and Entries, 1564–66.* Toronto, 1979.

LESURE, François. *Musique et musiciens du XVIe siècle.* Geneva, 1976.

TYARD, Pontus de. *Solitaire second.* Ed. Cathy M. Yandell. Geneva, 1980.

VACCARO, Jean-Michel. *La Musique du luth en France au XVIe siècle.* Paris, 1981.

——, ed. *La Chanson à la Renaissance.* Tours, 1981.

VAN ORDEN, Kate. "Cheap Print and Street Song Following the Saint Bartholomew's Massacre of 1572." In *Music and the Cultures of Print,* edited by Kate van Orden, 271–323. New York, 2000.

11

FRANCE, *iii*: 1600–1640

David Tunley

MUSIC in France during the seventeenth century, particularly during the first half, displays a character distinctly different from that of its artistic rival Italy, where at the turn of the century Jacopo Peri and others were creating the foundations of opera and where Giulio Caccini had developed a style of singing that could convey the passionate intensity of this new dramatic form. In contrast, French music appears decidedly conservative, despite the opportunity to embrace the Italian innovations afforded by the marriage of Henri IV of France to Maria de' Medici of Florence. After becoming queen of France, Maria de' Medici invited Caccini and other leading Italian musicians to Paris, where, however, only faint traces of their influence are apparent in the music written during or after their visits. Later political developments created such hostility towards Italian music that its cause in France stood no chance of success until near the end of the century when unexpected social changes opened the way for it again. Nevertheless, Mersenne in his *Harmonie universelle* (1636) urged French singers to study in Italy, or at least to read Caccini's *Le nuove musiche* (1601) and thereby "add that more pathetic quality of the Italians to the beauty, purity, and delicacy of ornamentation that our musicians perform with such grace when, having a good voice, they have learned to sing from the great masters."[1] What impact Italian music had upon French music in the early seventeenth century thus seems to have been largely in the field of performance rather than in composition, and even here it would seem that it did little to disguise the essential character of French music.

The focus of almost all significant artistic creation in early-seventeenth-century France was the court, which, in the period that concerns us, saw the short reign of the first of the Bourbon kings Henri IV (assassinated in 1610), the Regency of his widow Maria de' Medici and the beginning of the reign of their son Louis XIII, particularly troubled in the early years because of his mother's reluctance to allow him to govern. Although he is said to have enjoyed dancing, the soldier-king Henri was not overfond of the arts (his main leisure interests were violent physi-

[1] Marin Mersenne, *Harmonie universelle* (Paris, 1636), II: 357.

cal exercise, hunting, and gambling), but he nevertheless maintained the court's traditional patronage. Musicians, like many artists in those days, depended heavily upon the court for employment; since the time of François I near the beginning of the previous century, it had offered opportunities to many composers, singers, lutenists, and other chamber musicians as well as to those whose duties were to serve the royal chapel, or provide music for outdoor ceremonials and, of course, military maneuvers. It had been François I who had organized court music into the three departments of *chambre*, *chapelle*, and *écurie*, an administrative structure that was to last until the Revolution.[2] For the *musique de la chambre* Henri IV created the position of *surintendant* and gave to his new wife her own group of musicians, the *musique de la reine*. Lutenists, harpsichordists, and singers were the select musicians at court appointed to the *musique de la chambre*, as were the string players who by 1626 became known as the *vingt-quatre violons du Roy*, a title that probably formalized what had been a loosely grouped orchestra for some years.

It was an ambience that musicians outside the court might have envied. There seems to have been a close rapport between master and musical servant that sometimes led to members of the nobility acting as godparents to the children of court musicians.[3] Some musicians held additional appointments at court, such as *valet de chambre* or even *conseiller du roi*, and a number of chamber musicians gained the title of *honorable homme*. One has the impression of a somewhat closed musical world (particularly as families of court musicians often intermarried), so it is perhaps not surprising that much of the music of this period has a somewhat stylized and conventional expression. Yet it says much for the strong tradition of royal patronage in France that court music was able to flourish as it did in the politically turbulent years of the early seventeenth century.

Ballet de Cour

FRENCH lack of interest in opera in the first half of the century by no means indicated indifference to musical spectacle at court. A passion for lavish entertainment was as strong at the French court as it had been in Italy and as it was to be in Stuart England. The *ballets de cour* of the seventeenth century were merely an extension of the long tradition of Renaissance entertainments enjoyed by the Valois kings in which dancing, singing, and scenic display were joined (sometimes very loosely) through dramatic action. This reached a high point of dramatic unification in the celebrated *Circé, ou le Balet comique de la Royne* (1581), after which the *ballets de cour* were far more loosely organized for nearly thirty years.

A good example of the *ballet de cour* of the more dramatically unified kind is *La Délivrance de Renaud*, performed at court on Sunday 29 January 1617. Thanks

[2] See James R. Anthony, *French Baroque Music from Beaujoyeulx to Rameau*, 3rd edn (Portland, OR, 1997), for essential background to the period.

[3] As, for example, when Queen Marguerite de Valois (former wife of Henri IV) and the Duke of Nevers acted as godparents to the first child of the singer François Gallement in 1612. See Yoland de Brossard, *Musiciens de Paris, 1535–1792* (Paris, 1965), 130.

to a booklet describing the performance, published by Ballard that same year, and his publication of some of the vocal music, as well as Henry Prunières's reconstruction of the dances found in the Philidor collection, we can gain an idea of this event. Based upon an incident in Tasso's famous epic poem *Gerusalemme liberata*, recounting the legendary exploits of the medieval Crusaders who fought to liberate Jerusalem from the Saracens (a story to inspire a number of opera libretti set by Lully, Handel, and Gluck amongst others), the ballet tells of the rescue of the Christian warrior Renaud from the magic power of the princess Armide, a feat accomplished by two of his companions. Like all such works, it was done at royal command (in this case of the young Louis XIII, who was just beginning to assert his authority against that of his mother and the powerful clique surrounding her). The poet Estienne Durand was directed to co-ordinate the text, and it would seem that he wrote the 'narrative' part of the poetry (the *vers*). As was the custom at this time, the music was written by a team of composers: Philippe Guédron (who preferred to set his own words in this ballet), Gabriel Bataille, Antoine Boësset, and Jacques Mauduit. Not least amongst the creators of this theatrical event were the machinists who were called upon to provide spectacular scenic effects, particularly as this story dealt with magic. Altogether there were 92 singers and more than 40 instrumentalists. Because *La Délivrance de Renaud* was a *ballet du roi*, that is, coming from the King's Music, only men, almost all of them from the highest aristocracy, performed the dances and solo songs—unlike those ballets performed by the Queen's Music, in which women took the main roles. Thus the part of Armide was played by a man: in this case, not a member of the nobility but a celebrated court singer and dancer called Marais. The part of Renaud was taken by the King's favorite the duc de Luynes. An extract from Ballard's description best illustrates the event. The ballet commences as

> a great scene opening on to a palace and countryside. Music was heard, but the musicians were hidden from view. It would seem that this was a concert of birds that Armide had called up to give entertainment while she was absent. She had given them the power to imitate human voices. [They sang a choral work composed by Guédron.]
>
> The scene changed, a mountain appearing. Renaud (played by M. de Luynes) was lying on a flowery lawn in a grotto in the middle of the mountain. Above this and around the grotto was the King, accompanied by a dozen nobles, representing as many demons left by Armide to guard her beloved Renaud. . . . The King descended the steps of a little theatre to the accompaniment of 24 strings, each placed in a separate niche and representing as many spirits. . . . The King led Renaud to the middle of the room and danced with him until M. le chevalier de Vendôme (representing the Demon of the Waters) and M. de Mompoullan (as a Spirit of the Air) descended from the mountain to join them. Their *entrée* was embellished with dances so beautiful and diverse in steps, and so playful in action, that they left the impression that one could not see anything better.[4]

[4] Henry Prunières, *Le Ballet de cour en France avant Benserade et Lully* (Paris, 1914), 251ff.

The *entrée* mentioned in the extract above referred to a unified set of dances, songs, and action, subdivisions of an act (although 'acts' are not necessarily specified). Another term associated with the *ballet de cour* was *récit*, the technical meaning of which was a song sung at the beginning of an *entrée*. Nevertheless from 1611 onwards a number of songs called *récit* were published, many of which cannot be traced to any *ballet de cour*. Some tended to be somewhat declamatory in style, suggesting that the term was also sometimes associated with the Florentine innovations brought to French ears through the visits of Italian singers encouraged by Maria de' Medici, but unlike Italian *recitativo* they were usually strophic in structure. One of the *récits* from *La Délivrance de Renaud* has survived through a Ballard publication (see Example 11.1); it is by Pierre Guédron (*c.*1570–*c.*1620).

Like most French vocal music of the period, this *récit* was published by the royal printers, the Ballard family, whose domination of music printing in France commenced with Robert Ballard (*c.*1525–1588), who had gained the title of Printer to the King in the middle of the sixteenth century and whose descendants enjoyed the royal privilege for some two hundred years. Their reputation as one of the leading music publishers in Europe was eclipsed only in the eighteenth century when other firms in France embraced the newer technique of music engraving rather than that of moveable type employed by the Ballards. Particularly in the area of vocal composition, both solo and ensemble, the output of anthologies from the Ballard establishment is extraordinarily high. If one were to count each partbook separately, Ballard produced nearly 200 publications in the short period that concerns us. *Quel subit changement* was published in Book Seven of one of his most important collections of vocal music of the time: the 15-volume series *Airs de différents autheurs mis en tablature de luth* (1608–1632). Comprising just over 700 solo songs, the collection was initiated by the composer and lutenist Gabriel Bataille (*c.*1575–1630), who brought together most of the airs in the first six books (including some of his own), transcribing the melodies of various well-known composers—especially those by Guédron—and providing lute accompaniments for them. Many of these had originally been composed as ensemble pieces for four or five voices. Antoine Boësset (1586–1643) edited the series from Book Nine onwards and included a considerable number of his own airs, some volumes devoted entirely to them. Overall, the collection comprised solo airs and *récits* from the court ballets as well as independent songs, dialogues, songs to Spanish and Italian texts, *complaintes*, and some settings of Desportes' translations of the Psalms. It allows an unparalleled glimpse of French vocal music at this time.

Secular Songs

The earliest songs of the period were usually called *airs de cour*, a term that originated in the previous century. Then, the term meant music that was lighthearted and simple, of the kind that Adrian Le Roy (1571) said used to be called *voix de ville*. Nevertheless those airs were also polished and graceful, qualities taken by seventeenth-century composers to an even more refined degree. Such refinement

Ex. 11.1 Pierre Guédron, *Quel subit changement*, from *La Délivrance de Renaud* (1617) *Airs de différents auteurs* (Paris, 1608–32), VII (RISM 1617^{8})

may have come about through their courtly provenance, or perhaps even more by their association with salons such as Mme de Rambouillet's, which initiated a tradition of literary, musical, and intellectual gatherings that lasted until the final years of the nineteenth century. A song such as the anonymously composed *Douce beauté* published in Book Four (1613) of the *Airs de différents autheurs* is fairly typical. In this air (Example 11.2) those devices that lend a "popular tunefulness" to

Ex. 11.2 Anon., *Douce beauté*, from *Airs de différents auteurs*, IV (RISM 1613[9])

music—regular metre, repetition, sequences, and balanced phrasing—are largely missing, replaced by rather elusive rhythms and subtle figuration.

The texts of the *air de cour* were as stylized and refined as their music. This was largely the result of developments in French poetry at the turn of the century, initiated by François Malherbe (1555–1628) who "purged" the language of many words that had been introduced into it in the sixteenth century by Pierre de Ronsard and others, retaining only those he considered elegantly appropriate for the poetic art. He also introduced principles of rhyme, rhythm, and construction that were to rule classical French poetry up to the Romantic period. Further refinements came through Vincent Voiture (1597–1648), whose graceful poetry charmed his listeners in Mme de Rambouillet's salon. Some of the texts in Ballard's collection are called *vers mesurée*, a form inspired by Jean-Antoine de Baïf who had sought to reach the Platonic ideal of the unity of word and note by imitating the so-called quantitative measures of classical Greek and Latin poetry. He established rules to identify long and short syllables in the French language, encouraging composers to set them in the ratio of 2:1. The result was known as *musique mesurée*. Claude Le Jeune's works in this form appeared in publications towards the end of the sixteenth century, leaving a mark on the *air de cour*. One such song in Ballard's *Airs de différents autheurs* is *Eau-vive, source d'amour, de mon ardeur* (Book Three, 1611) to poetry by Baïf himself. There are very few examples of true *musique mesurée* in the collection, but many songs suggest its strong influence, not least in *Douce beauté*.

Often associated with the *air de cour* was the art of *diminutions* in which the simple vocal lines (and including the parts of the ensemble settings) were richly embellished, usually through improvisation. Exponents of this "art within an art" included the court singers Le Bailly, Moulinié, and Boësset. It is probably unlikely that their sophisticated and virtuosic style of ornamentation was widely adopted outside the court or salons. Some of the airs in Ballard's collection are already quite highly embellished and probably needed little more. Yet, in fact, the real attraction of the *air de cour* lay in what one English observer of the day, Edward Filmer, described as "their free Fant'sie of Air."[5] It is true that in Ballard's collections there are some songs that make considerable musical demands, but the majority are vocally quite simple (we have already seen that the songs in *La Délivrance de Renaud* were mostly written for aristocratic amateurs). Indeed, the remarkable success of Ballard's song publications can only be explained by their wide appeal to domestic performers. While in notation many of the songs seem to have a high tessitura, it can be shown how the tuning of the lute accompaniments brings the pitch of the songs to within an easy singing range,[6] and the lute part itself is also well within the scope of the amateur performer. Even as the century moved on to its third decade, lute accompaniments to the *air de cour* looked back to the past, at the same time as solo playing was exploring new tunings and techniques that were to take lute music in France to its highest level.

From 1627 Ballard also began publishing a 20-volume series entitled *Chansons pour danser et pour boire*, comprising very simple tunes, either unharmonized (as in the case of the dancing songs) or with a bass part (as in the case of the drinking songs). These and the much more highly-prized *airs de cour* were the main categories of song until the second half of the century.

[5] Edward Filmer, *French Court-aires, with the ditties Englished* (London, 1629), "To the Musicall User of this Booke."

[6] David Tunley, "Tunings and Transposition in the Early 17th-Century French Lute Air: Some Implications," *Early Music*, 21 (1993), 203–9.

Instrumental Music

The lute commonly used when accompanying the *air de cour* was a tenor lute (the others being a treble and a bass). It was a 10-course instrument, its six fingered courses tuned to g′–d′–a–f–c–G and the remaining four open "diapason" courses providing four notes beneath the deepest fingered course, tuned to whatever low notes were required by the harmony. This tuning, involving perfect fourths enclosing a major third, was known as *vieil ton* or "old tuning." It was also used for treble and bass lutes, but at pitches higher or lower than that for the tenor lute. Such tuning remained constant throughout Ballard's *Airs de différents autheurs*. For the solo repertoire, however, there was considerable diversity of tunings. From about 1620, the most popular tuning featured major or minor thirds, such as e′–c′–a–f–c–G. The "D minor" tuning (f′–d′–a–f–d–A) and its variants emerged, at least tentatively, in 1638 (with the lutenists Pierre Ballard and Pierre Gautier), although it was by no means universal until some years later.

Together with developments in tuning went developments in style and technique. Essential to solo lute playing was the so-called *style brisé*, a modern term used vaguely to describe a style in which melody and harmony are dissolved into a flow of single notes, thus helping to keep alive the rhythm and the sonorities of the instrument's quickly fading tone.[7] David Ledbetter points to the difference in *style brisé* figuration used in Renaissance practice and that of the seventeenth century.[8] Whereas the earlier style favored regularity of pattern, the later style (from the earliest years of the century) featured a more asymmetrical approach to the rhythmic patterns, one following another in a fanciful, unpredictable way. This is, indeed, similar in spirit to the examples of vocal ornamentation in the *air de cour* that have come down to us through Mersenne's *Harmonie universelle* (1636) and Millet's *L'Art de bien chanter* (which, while published as late as 1666, in fact looks back to practice earlier in the century). It raises the question, as yet unexplored, that this development in seventeenth-century lute style may have been the result of interaction between singer and lutenist (in many cases a single musician). French lute compositions in which the new trends can first be traced were by Antoine Francisque (*Le Trésor d'Orphée*, 1600) and by Robert Ballard (*Livres de tablature*, 1611 and 1614). The truly characteristic works of the seventeenth-century French lute school were to come from René Mesangeau, Pierre Ballard, Pierre Gautier, and the cousins Ennemond and Denis Gaultier. The forms they used were the unmeasured prelude (in which the lutenist improvises the rhythm and texture of the music from the chordal progressions set down in the tablature) and dances: allemande, courante, sarabande, chaconne.[9] In these works are to be found all the techniques of French lute playing, which in the hands of the virtuosi

[7] David Buch, "*Style Brisé*, *Style Luthé* and the *Choses Luthées*," *The Musical Quarterly*, 71 (1985), 52–67, discusses the usage of the term *style brisé*.

[8] David Ledbetter, *Harpsichord and Lute Music in 17th-Century France* (Bloomington, IN, 1987), 33–34.

[9] David Buch, "The Influence of the *Ballet de cour* in the Genesis of the French Baroque

of the day led to great subtlety of timbre, texture, and nuance. At this level, the secrets of the lutenist's art were kept between master and pupil. It is no wonder that in the hierarchy of musical appointments at court, lutenists were at the highest rung.

Amongst other highly regarded virtuosi belonging to the *musique de chambre* were the harpsichordists, whose keyboard techniques absorbed some of those of the lute (most notably the *style brisé*)—although why this should have happened in the seventeenth century when the techniques of the two instruments had remained distinctively different in the previous century is not clear. While examples of seventeenth-century French harpsichord music are evident from about 1626 (the Copenhagen manuscript), the true founder of the seventeenth-century French harpsichord school was Jacques Champion de Chambonnières (*c.*1601–1672) whose works, however, were not published until his declining years in 1670. He had been appointed to the court some forty years before, when his extraordinary talent caught the attention of some of the foremost connoisseurs of the time. They spoke of the beauty of his touch and his skill and taste in ornamentation. It would seem that he overshadowed all who came before him in France, but it is difficult to assess his predecessors and their compositions because of the paucity of sources in the early years of the century. Nevertheless, it is reasonable to assume that they pointed the way to his mastery. Over a hundred of his works are contained in the Bauyn Manuscript, as are works by some of his pupils—Hardel, Lebègue, and Étienne Richard.[10]

What Chambonnières was to the harpsichord, Jehan Titelouze (1563–1633) was to the organ. As in the case of the former, there is a lack of earlier sources that would enable us to see Titelouze's achievements in the light of his immediate predecessors. While his austerely polyphonic style undoubtedly stems from his Renaissance roots, unlike much sixteenth-century instrumental music it is idiomatic for the organ, calling upon registers and timbres characteristic of the instrument, although it was not until after our period that composers in France were writing music with specific tonal effects in mind.[11] The alluring, colorful sounds that we associate with the music of Couperin and others had to wait for the organ builders of the second half of the seventeenth century, who also were to develop a keyboard action that was light in touch, encouraging a transfer of harpsichord styles.

Amongst the favored instruments of the time were the viols. Whether played as a solo instrument or in ensemble, the viol retained its prestige in France long after it had given way to the violin and violoncello in Italy and other countries. In the early years of the century, composers in both England and France brought the ensemble fantasia to its height. Amongst French composers were Du Caurroy,

Suite," *Acta musicologica*, 58 (1958), 94–109, discusses how the ordering of the dance movements in the Baroque suite reflects the order in the *ballets de cour.*

10 On the Bauyn MS, see the facsimile edn, *Manuscrit Bauyn: Pièces de clavecin, c.1660 (B.n., Paris, Rés. Vm^7, 674–675)*, ed. François Lesure (Geneva, 1977); Bruce Gustafson, "Bauyn," *Die Musik in Geschichte und Gegenwart*, 2d edn, ed. Ludwig Finscher (Kassel, 1994), 1: cols. 1306–9.

11 Fenner Douglass, *The Language of the French Classical Organ* (New Haven, 1969), 19.

Claude Le Jeune, Guillet, and Métru, while players like Maugars were to inspire a long line of later virtuoso performers (Saint-Colombe, Hotman, Marin Marais, and others) stretching well into the next century.

Religious Music

The gap in extant repertoire of the first forty years of the century is wider in the field of sacred choral music than in instrumental music, despite evidence that much was being composed in cathedrals and churches throughout France. What has come down to us, such as the 23 motets by Eustache du Caurroy (1549–1609) were in the Renaissance tradition of northern Europe. The influence of Italian Baroque music had to wait until towards the end of our period, when Nicolas Formé (1567–1638) began to introduce more 'progressive' features—borrowed from earlier Italian practice—into his music, such as the concerted style, but only two of his double-chorus motets have survived. It would be difficult to deny their influence on Henry Dumont (1610–1684), whose motets set the seal on what was to become the characteristic French form, the *grand motet*, but his mature works date from the period after 1640.

Perhaps the most striking influence of the Italian Baroque in the first half of the century is to be found in the dramatically inclined motets of the Provençal composer Guillaume Bouzignac. However, because they remained unpublished, Bouzignac's music was undoubtedly limited in its influence, and it would seem that religious choral music in France generally retained a deeply conservative style for many years. We are told of considerable resistance to the idea of using the continuo bass, certainly until after the period that concerns us. Yet in the early repertoire are works that deserve to be more widely known and performed, such as the settings of the *Missa pro defunctis* by de Bournonville and by Moulinié (published in 1619 and 1636 respectively).

Despite the period of relative calm following Henry IV's Edict of Nantes in 1598, which granted religious tolerance to French Protestants after the Wars of Religion, there were few musical developments in the Reformed church to match those of the previous century. Even though a number of psalm settings by Claude Le Jeune appeared in the early years of the seventeenth century (including some in the style of *musique mesurée*), these were all posthumous publications that had been composed before 1600. Nevertheless, it must be said that his settings of the complete Huguenot Psalter (published 1602–10) remained popular in a number of countries, including France, Switzerland, Holland, and England, for nearly 200 years.

In comparison to Italian music of the same period, much early-seventeenth-century French music seems strikingly conservative, particularly in the realm of sacred music. Yet, in the field of secular music may be found those seeds of a tradition that were to lead to a distinctive style now usually known as the French classical style. It is characterized by suave and tender melodies that are seemingly unhampered by that regularity of harmonic rhythm and syntax that became the hallmark of Italian Baroque music. It would be left to the brilliant circle of musicians at the court of the next monarch, Louis XIV, to bring this style to full maturity.

Further Reading

GÉROLD, Théodore. *L'Art du chant en France au XVIIe siècle.* Strasbourg, 1921; repr. 1971.

ISHERWOOD, Robert M. *Music in the Service of the King: France in the Seventeenth Century.* New York, 1973.

BUCH, David. *Dance Music from the Ballet de cour, 1575–1651.* New York, 1994.

RANUM, Patricia M. *The Harmonic Orator: The Phrasing and Rhetoric of the Melody in French Baroque Airs.* Hillsdale, NY, 2001.

12

CHANSON AND AIR

Kate van Orden

THE chanson flourished in a startling array of forms. From city streets to courtly chambers and from beggars' songs to princely pastimes, chansons resounded throughout Europe in all circles of society. Squares in Paris, Antwerp, and Lyons had their mountebanks, who sang narrative verse to the accompaniment of a violin, cittern, or guitar. They stood on benches, hanging a painted sheet of paper or fabric behind them with illustrations of the story they sang, pointing to scene after scene with a long stick. In Paris, vendors at Les Halles hawked their wares in song, crying out "allumettes," "beaux choux blanc," or "sallade belle sallade" to the characteristic tunes immortalized by Clément Janequin in his "Cris de Paris," while the traffickers of cheap print sang the newsy songs they sold among the book vendors' stalls on the Pont Neuf. Town minstrels played dance songs at bourgeois weddings, and play-acting societies such as that of the law clerks in Lyons sang theatrical chansons during their morality plays and farces.[1]

At the upper end of the social scale, part-songs satisfied a pan-European public for vernacular polyphony. Here one should remember that written polyphony marked out a set of practices and a musical culture that stood apart from urban minstrelsy. Minstrels were primarily instrumentalists who controlled their repertory and employment through a guild system based on orality and secrecy. Masters taught monophonic chansons and dance tunes to their apprentices by rote, circumventing musical literacy and thereby preserving trade secrets. In contrast, polyphonic chansons were produced by composers or, as contemporaries would have called them, "musicians"—musicians trained at cathedral schools, where they learned to read and write polyphonic songs, masses, and motets. The separation between their world of written music and the music of minstrels was noted by Noël du Fail, who in 1549 set the two terms against one another when

[1] For studies of these and other urban repertories and performance practices, see especially Howard Mayer Brown, *Music in the French Secular Theater, 1400–1550* (Cambridge, MA, 1963); and Frank Dobbins, *Music in Renaissance Lyons* (Oxford, 1992). On a more general note, my heartfelt thanks go to Lawrence F. Bernstein and Leeman L Perkins for their invaluable comments on an earlier draft of this essay.

he described a series of songs as "chansons plus menestrières que musiciennes" ("songs more minstrel-like than musicianly").[2] The minstrel/musician distinction held for instruments as well: "the hurdy-gurdy [*vielle*] is for the blind, the rebec and viol for the minstrels, the lute and guitar for the musicians," the author of *La manière d'entoucher les lucs et guiternes* observed, reminding us of the gap between minstrelsy and composed polyphony that chordal instruments like the lute and keyboard might bridge.[3] Chansons sat squarely on the horizon shared by minstrels and musicians, and, as we will see, one of the broader histories to be told about the chanson between 1520 and 1640 is how minstrelsy and composed polyphony came to occupy much of the same terrain.

We should also note, here at the outset, the venerability of the polyphonic chanson tradition inherited by sixteenth-century composers. By 1500, polyphonists had been penning chansons for the delectation of European elites for centuries, everything from tokens of affection, such as the chansons filling the delightful heart-shaped Chansonnier Cordiforme (*F-Pn* Rothschild 2973) and the models of *amour courtois* Guillaume de Machaut included in his *Remede de Fortune*, to personal works such as the lament of Marguerite of Austria's parrot at the absence of his mistress. Indeed, Marguerite's chanson albums reflect individual connoisseurship at its best and beautifully exemplify private musical life among European nobles. Several songs in the albums reflect her sense of individual misfortune and were likely written for her by poets and musicians at court. Her refined literary taste and musical talents—she wrote poetry, sang, and played the clavichord—made her a discerning patron of chansons cast in a polyphonic language wholly accessible only to the musically literate.

The court culture that connected Europe through a web of marriages among ruling families proved fundamental to the production and transmission of the chanson. Although the term chanson is a catch-all designation for songs in French, the chanson's popularity was hardly limited to Francophone lands. Polyphonic chansons can be found, with and without their texts, in English, German, Italian, and Spanish sources. Chansons were particularly favored by Italians in the fifteenth and early sixteenth centuries before the native madrigal supplanted them there. One need only consider the Cappella Giulia chansonnier (*I-Rvat* C.G. XIII 27), the Braccesi chansonnier (*I-Fn* Banco Rari 229), or leaf through the pages of Ottaviano Petrucci's beautiful three-volume anthology of chansons, the *Odhecaton A*, *Canti B*, and *Canti C* (Venice, 1501–4), to see that at the turn of the sixteenth century chansons were not so much French imports as they were the foremost pan-European genre of secular song. The composers represented in these sources, men such as Alexander Agricola, Antoine Busnoys, Loyset Compère, Josquin des Prez, Johannes Martini, and Henricus Isaac, were Franco-Flemings who made their fortunes in Italy and brought their native chanson tradition with them. Thus, the chanson traversed the Alps into Italy just as surely as it was caught up in the daily lives of

[2] Cited in Howard Mayer Brown, "The *Chanson Rustique*: Popular Elements in the 15th- and 16th-Century Chanson," *Journal of the American Musicological Society*, 12 (1959), 18.

[3] Cited in Brown, *Music in the French Secular Theater, 1400–1550*, 71.

aristocrats and folk in France and Flanders. That the chanson supported such diverse cultural practices explains its many forms, from the oral minstrelsy behind the chansons of the bourgeois public theatre and court fête to the written tradition producing polyphonic chansons for the enjoyment of Europe's musical elite.

THE Renaissance chanson provided a musical "reading" of its text. Its style of declamation might range from a standard formula to a highly individual setting of the text to music, but no matter what the style, the relationship between poetry and music was a close one. This is to say, the text might be written to fit a standard musical mold, or, at the other end of the continuum, the text could control the flow of the music and generate the song's form. In every instance, however, chansons bound music and text in a reflexive relationship. Changes in poetic taste affected compositional styles and changes in musical taste revised the way poets penned their *poésie pour musique*. In France, these influences were largely reciprocal. Composers became increasingly attentive to the form and register of their texts, and poets such as Clément Marot and Pierre de Ronsard cast their verse in regular forms "so that the Musicians can accord [their music to] them more easily . . . for Poetry without instruments or the grace of one or more voices is hardly agreeable."[4] With the burst of interest in rhetoric as a way of organizing thought, speech, and art during the Renaissance, chansons quite naturally approached musical oration. Therefore, it is most revealing to write a history of the chanson in this period using developments in lyric poetry as a guide.[5] A history of *poésie pour musique* is a more useful point of departure than a history of great chansons, for individual chansons rarely reveal much about their own creation. Some songs, such as *Faulte d'argent* and *Mille regretz*, are monumental (and we will turn to the latter momentarily),[6] but the vast majority are stock, their texts or music exchangeable, anonymous, ordinary, and often reflective of oral poetry, minstrelsy, theatrical needs, a fad for dance, or an individual patron's taste in verse. Thus chansons describe a cultural history as much as a compositional one and a broad history of lyric practice as much as a history of the polyphonist's art.

Around 1500, a gradual transformation began to take place in the chanson, and we can characterize it in two ways, as a change in poetic taste and a change

[4] Pierre de Ronsard, *Abbrege de l'art poëtique françois* (Paris: Gabriel Buon, 1565; facs., Geneva, 1972), fol. 4[r]. The diverse settings of Marot's poetry suggest its particular suitability as *poésie pour musique*. See Annie Cœurdevey, *Bibliographie des œuvres poétiques de Clément Marot mises en musique dans les recueils profanes du XVIe siècle* (Paris, 1997).

[5] See especially Howard Mayer Brown, "*Ut Musica Poesis*: Music and Poetry in France in the Late Sixteenth Century," *Early Music History*, 13 (1994), 1–63.

[6] See Lawrence F. Bernstein, "Josquin's Chansons as Generic Paradigms," in *Music in Renaissance Cities and Courts: Studies in Honor of Lewis Lockwood*, ed. Jessie Ann Owens and Anthony M. Cummings (Warren, MI, 1996), 35–55; Jacques Barbier, "'Faulte d'argent': Modèles polyphoniques et parodies au XVIe siècle," *Revue de musicologie*, 73 (1987), 171–202; and Owen Rees, "*Mille regretz* as Model: Possible Allusions to 'The Emperor's Song' in the Chanson Repertory," *Journal of the Royal Musical Association*, 120 (1995), 44–76.

in polyphonic composition. In the first place, composers and poets began to turn away from the *formes fixes* that had dominated French lyric production since their codification by Guillaume de Machaut in the fourteenth century. The rondeaux and virelais that filled the pages of Petrucci's *Odhecaton* were the last breath of a dying art, and by 1550 the French poet Joachim du Bellay would vilify them as "fancies that corrupt the taste of our language and serve no purpose but to testify to our ignorance."[7] Such a vitriolic reaction was a bit unnecessary, since the *formes fixes* had fallen from favor decades earlier, but tradition was tenacious. The rondeau stayed in the repertory the longest, though its bulky refrains of four to six lines were eventually slashed to a mere half line, forming the *rondeau hemistiche*. Thomas Sébillet recommended the *rondeau hemistiche* to readers of his *Art poétique françois* (1548) because it conveniently did away with the "annoying long repetitions" of the old-fashioned rondeau, restriking the balance between stanza and refrain to favor the new material of the stanzas. Sébillet's dismissal of the *formes fixes* as cumbersome and rigid typified poetic tastes at mid-century, by which time the traditional lyric genres were all but completely abandoned. What had taken their place was a variety of freer verse forms: epigrams, narrative poems, and strophic poems known as *chansons*, each of which will be treated individually below.

The *formes fixes* had been just as prescriptive for composers as they were for poets, since rondeaux, ballades, and virelais bore conventional musical forms that matched the poetry. By contrast, the new verse forms that liberated poets left composers in need of a more flexible approach to lyric poetry that might still be coherent in the absence of the refrains that structured the *formes fixes* and provided their aesthetic logic. This new approach to text setting can be seen in the chansons of Josquin des Prez and his generation, and it proved to be a musical language that was malleable enough to sustain composers to the end of the century. Josquin's *Mille regretz* (Example 12.1, overleaf) will serve as our introduction to the sixteenth-century polyphonic chanson, not least because it was so enduring. It was known as "The Emperor's Song" throughout the Habsburg empire, and the story goes that Josquin made a gift of it to Charles V in 1520. It was printed and intabulated numerous times, emulated by the imperial composer Nicholas Gombert in his own *Mille regretz*, and honored in a parody mass by Cristóbal de Morales.[8]

Although anonymous, the poem can probably be attributed to the circle of Jean Lemaire de Belges at the court of Charles V and Marguerite of Austria. It is written in the form of a self-standing quatrain, one of the forms supplanting the *formes fixes* and precisely the simple form of text that Josquin preferred.

> Mille regretz de vous habandonner
> Et d'eslonger vostre fache amoureuse,
> J'ay si grand dueil et paine douloureuse,
> Qu'on me verra brief mes jours deffiner.

[7] Joachim du Bellay, *La Deffence et illustration de la langue françoyse*, ed. Henri Chamard (Paris, 1970), 238.

[8] See Martin Picker (ed.), *The Chanson Albums of Marguerite of Austria* (Berkeley and Los Angeles, 1965), 17; and Rees, "*Mille regretz* as Model".

[A thousand regrets to leave you, And to be far from your loving face. I suffer such deep sorrow and grievous anguish That soon I will end my days.]

The poem breathes the language of the *grands rhétoriqueurs*, poets who wrote in the tradition of *fin amour* or courtly love first perfected by the trouvères. So old was this tradition that its essence had been reduced to epigrammatic turns of phrase. Here the poet describes his unrequited love—the usual inspiration for song—as painful longing, separation, illness, and death. The decasyllabic lines each take a caesura after the fourth syllable, producing the epithets so characteristic of this kind of courtly verse—"Secourez moy," "Plus nulz regretz," "Cueurs désolez," and so forth.

Josquin marks the caesuras and line breaks with rests, cadences, and changes of texture, all of which give the setting a clarity consistent with that of its text. Weak cadences on A mark line breaks, deftly clarifying tonal and rhetorical structures without disrupting the flow of the polyphony (see Example 12.1, mm. 5, 22, 24, and 32). In the absence of cadences, changes of texture often set lines apart from one another. The largely homophonic texture of the first half of the chanson cedes to homophonic duets at m. 20. They, in turn, give way to points of imitation at the final line beginning in m. 24. This technique of composing a piece in differentiated segments presented polyphonists with a remarkably supple means of text setting. Music for each fragment of text could be conceived independently and then joined together in interlocking blocks of polyphony. Moreover, each bit of text could attain its own character by the use of contrasting head-motifs. Indeed, the effectiveness of *Mille regretz* lies largely in Josquin's recognizable motifs. The rising fourth of *Mille regretz* (superius, mm. 1–3) is countered with falling figures for "de vous habandonner" and "et d'eslonger," their contrasting contours made all the more pronounced by the rhythmic squareness of the opening (superius, altus, and bassus) and its undoing with motifs that begin off the beat and in staggered entrances.

The chanson's other principal motifs emphasize the half-step between E and F that gave the Phrygian mode its striking character. The opening figure in the bassus circles around the final almost obsessively (E–F–D–E), returning more audibly in the superius at "J'ay si grand dueil." The half-step from E to F is also used to set "et paine douloureuse" (altus and bassus), its poignant stress on F collapsing into a line that cascades downward a full sixth before coming to rest on A. The insistence on A—normal in Phrygian contexts—is prominent both in the piece's inner cadences and in the setting of "brief mes jours deffiner" at the end, where the bass rocks back and forth between A and E. Yet the tonality is never overstated. Josquin denies the listener closure by avoiding the usual fifteenth-century cadence formed by 7–8 motion in the superius and 2–1 motion in the tenor. Rather, here the bassus functions with the tenor to form cadences (on A in mm. 5, 24, and 32, and on E in m. 17), and the final cadence lands on an ambiguous triad that pits the Gs in the tenor and superius—voices that generally indicate the tonal orientation of the piece—against the E in the bassus that provides the fundament of the final sonority. The ending tempts modern listeners to hear the bassus as a structural voice in

Ex. 12.1 Josquin des Prez, *Mille regretz*
From *Werken*, ed. A. Smijers et al. (Amsterdam, 1921–69), *Wereldlijke werken*, no. 24

vertically conceived chords (an interpretation supported by the leaps by fourth and by fifth in the bassus), but it would seem that Josquin's unusual part-writing aimed instead to express the perpetual anguish of the poem with a tonally unresolved ending. By stressing imperfect sonorities in the structurally important superius and tenor voices, he subverts the conventional closing cadence of his day, thereby emphasizing the dwindling away of "brief mes jours deffiner" and the unsettled emotional state that pervades the entire poem.

Josquin scaled down his polyphonic writing in *Mille regretz* to match the brevity of the text, producing an exquisite miniature. The syllabic setting preserves a natural pace of declamation, while the melodies and rhythms attend to proper word stress. The musical phrases follow the poem's rhyme scheme, as we see in the parallels between "de vous habandonner" and "bref mes jours deffiner," and the rhythmically similar head motifs, too, create an inner coherence drawn from the words. Here we should recall Josquin's sojourns in Italy, where strong rhetorical training supported a culture of humanism that inflected secular music there in

myriad ways. Certainly one belief central to humanistic thinking was that the ancient Greeks and Romans sang their lyric poetry to music in a style of heightened recitation that respected the natural declamation of the verse and the audibility of individual words. If the text could shine through its brilliant musical garb, humanists believed, the poetry would achieve its greatest effect. The influence of Italian humanism cannot fully account for the transformation of the chanson between 1500 and 1530, particularly given the sheer number and variety of polyphonic chansons being composed and the popularity of the chanson across such a vast geographical area. Nonetheless, in the period before 1530, northern composers active in Italy wrote considerable numbers of chansons, and their remarkable sensitivity to the text hints at an emergent humanism in polyphonic song that may well owe much to the emphasis on good oratory in Italian *studia humanitatis*.

On French soil, the transformation of the polyphonic chanson culminated in the so-called Parisian chanson of Claudin de Sermisy (*c.*1490–1562), Pierre Sandrin (*c.*1490–1561), Clément Janequin (*c.*1485–1558), and Pierre Certon (d. 1572). The composition of songs in this style accelerated with the advent of music publishing in France, and it is to Pierre Attaingnant, royal printer of music from 1529 to 1551, that these *chansons nouvelles* owed their wide circulation. Attaingnant issued eight volumes of chansons in the first two years of his life-long collaboration with native chanson composers, beginning with the *Chansons nouvelles en musique a quatre parties* in 1528, which contained thirty-one chansons, over half of them by Claudin. Claudin became Attaingnant's principal composer, followed by Certon and Janequin, and it is relevant when we consider Attaingnant's role as an arbiter of taste in France to note that he favored royal musicians, for Claudin directed the Royal Chapel at the court of François I, and Certon was master of the children at the Sainte-Chapelle du Palais. Attaingnant's success thus depended upon not only his royal printing privilege but his association with royal institutions. He was not just the first music publisher in France but France's first national publisher of music; his chansonniers circumscribe a repertory of French chansons and the beginnings of a national style.

The chansons published by Attaingnant and by Jacques Moderne in Lyons (active 1529–1560) set texts by a transitional generation of poets who came after the *rhétoriqueurs* and before the Pléiade poets who began to write at mid-century. Clément Marot, Mellin de Saint-Gelais, and even François I penned the verses set by French composers in the second quarter of the century, their lyrics printed cheek by jowl with much anonymous song verse. Marot's mastery of lyric genres ran the gamut from the lofty *chant royal* to the epigram, *rondeau hemistiche*, and *chanson*, that quintessential form of *poésie pour musique*. The poetic genre called *chanson* consisted of strophes that might easily be sung to strophic musical settings, and its content, in an admixture of high and low, explored both courtly and profane love in plain-spoken French. Perhaps it was Marot's sensitivity to the vogue among musicians for simple song verse that inspired the unaffected language, brevity, and shorter lines of his poetry for music. Likewise, his attention to musical needs may have inspired the strophic form of his *chansons*, well loved by contemporary composers, who set all but five of his *chansons* to music. The majority of his rondeaux and epigrams were also graced with musical setting. All in all, a startling 234 musical settings of his texts were published in the sixteenth century.

Composers responded to the lighter verse typified by Marot's œuvre with the galant style that characterizes the so-called Parisian chanson. Like Marot's poetry, Claudin's chansons adapt some popular idioms to the courtly chanson. As Howard Mayer Brown has argued, Claudin's plainspoken melodies are indebted to the genre of *chanson menestriere* or *chanson rustique*, popular monophonic songs that had been all the rage at the court of Louis XII.[9] The term *chanson rustique* aptly describes the pastoral and carnivalesque themes so often treated in these songs, which were popular elements of the *sotties*, *farces*, and morality plays performed in the bourgeois theatre.[10] Not only do they tell stories of amorous shepherds and libidinous nuns and monks—thereby overturning the conventions of *l'amour courtois* expressed in chansons like *Mille regretz*—they are cast in forms that the *rhétoriqueurs* considered undistinguished, usually in strophes with refrains. Josquin, Antoine de Févin (*c.*1470–1511/12), Jean Mouton (*c.*1459–1522), and Adrian Willaert (*c.*1490–1562, a student of Mouton's *c.*1510–1515/16), had a true affection for monophonic *chansons rustiques*, and they arranged them as polyphonic chansons for three and four voices using a variety of techniques.[11] Brown posited that as *chansons rustiques* infused the polyphonic chanson with popular material, they fostered an interest in the direct idioms of traditional monophonic music, both in France and in Italy. Their appealing blend of polyphony and rustic simplicity may have inspired composers toward a lighter style in their freely composed chansons, producing chansons in which polyphonic complexities are reduced, melodies are trimmed down to the size of the text, repetitions mirror the rhyme schemes of the poetry, cadences are regular, and syllabic declamation enhances textual audibility. Although it seems that Claudin did not often work *chansons rustiques* into his polyphonic chansons—for this was a technique of his Parisian precursors—the immediacy and very singability of his songs suggest a *rustique* or minstrel influence that no doubt contributed to their astounding popularity.

One of Claudin's greatest hits—and perhaps the single most beloved chanson of the sixteenth century—was his setting of Marot's strophic chanson *Tant que vivray* (Example 12.2, overleaf). The opening of the poem strikes a courtly tone with its long lines and lofty diction, yet the short lines of the second half and its strophic form are both popularesque elements. The song's naïveté is exaggerated by the use of paired rhymes throughout, which sound particularly artless in the second half, where they follow one another quite quickly:

> Tant que vivray en aage fleurissant,
> Je serviray Amour le Dieu puissant,
> En faictz, en dictz, en chansons, et accords.
>   Par plusieurs jours m'a tenu languissant,
> Mais apres dueil m'a faict rejouyssant,
> Car j'ay l'amour de la belle au gent corps.

[9] Howard Mayer Brown, "The Genesis of a Style: The Parisian Chanson, 1500–1530," in *Chanson and Madrigal, 1480–1530*, ed. James Haar (Cambridge, MA, 1964), 1–50.

[10] Brown, "The *Chanson Rustique*"; idem, *Music in the French Secular Theater.*

[11] See esp. Lawrence F. Bernstein (ed.), *La Couronne et fleur des chansons a troys*, 2 vols. (New York, 1984).

Son alliance,
C'est ma fiance:
Son cueur est mien
Le mien est sien:
Fy de tristesse!
Vive liesse,
Puisqu'en Amours j'ay tant de bien!
(first of two stanzas)

[As long as life in me doth flourish, I shall serve Love, the powerful God. In deeds, in words, and harmonious songs. For many days he has held me in thrall, but after grief he has made me rejoice, for I have the love of a beautiful lady with a noble body. Her pledge Is all my faith, Her heart is mine, Mine is hers; Fie on sadness! Long live joy, Because in Love I have such delight!]

Claudin's setting emphasizes the turn from the high style of decasyllabic verse in the first two tercets to the patter of four-syllable lines that finish off each stanza. The song opens with a broad rhythm that Claudin often used to mark the caesura of decasyllabic lines (see Example 12.2*a*), while the short lines and chatty declamation in the second half of the stanza are matched with rhythmic diminution (see Example 12.2*b*). The melody elaborates a single fragment in ways that likewise relate to the form of the poem. The first four notes in the superius part present a descending third that is transposed down for the second line and inverted for the third line, then repeated ten times in quick succession in the second half of the chanson. Finally, the cadences also emphasize the division of the poem: strong cadences on F close each half of the chanson, while inner cadences are on C. The laconic sort of writing we find in *Tant que vivray* seems a beautiful illustration of the craft behind Claudin's simplicity. Yet how telling to discover, as Lawrence Bernstein has, that both Claudin's melody and Marot's poem are modeled on the anonymous monophonic chanson "Resjouissons nous tous loyaulx amoureux" included in the manuscript *F-Pn* fr. 12744.[12] Marot borrowed the form and diction of the anonymous poem, clarifying and personalizing its message, while Claudin extracted from the melody its essential gestures, streamlining and repeating them in his own superius line. *Tant que vivray*, then, illustrates not just the melodic charm and polyphonic transparency that made Sermisy's chansons so accessible, but how an older courtly chanson could be brought up to date by clarifying its melody and language.

While many of the songs printed by Attaingnant echo the charm of *Tant que vivray*, the term "Parisian chanson" has been applied to a repertory of huge variety. Composers such as Janequin and Certon drew differently upon the lyric traditions available to poets and musicians of the 1530s and 1540s. They set both courtly and

[12] Reported in Leeman L. Perkins, "Toward a Typology of the 'Renaissance' Chanson," *Journal of Musicology*, 4 (1988), 443. For a similar incidence, see Thomas D. Brothers, "Two *Chansons Rustiques* à 4 by Claudin de Sermisy and Clément Janequin," *Journal of the American Musicological Society*, 34 (1981), 305–24.

Ex. 12.2 (*a*) Claudin de Sermisy, *Tant que vivray*, mm. 1–8
From *Opera omnia*, ed. G. Allaire and I. Caseaux, CMM 52 (American Institute of Musicology, 1970–), IV: 99

carnivalesque verse, employing imitative counterpoint, chordal writing, or a mixture of the two. These many combinations of textual and musical style produced chansons ranging in tone from the *faux* rustic to ornate. While the Parisian chanson is well typified by Claudin's settings of Marot's lyric texts, Attaingnant printed chansons setting narrative texts as well, not to mention some highly imitative chansons and many chansons by provincial and Franco-Flemish composers who were, by definition, not Parisian at all.[13] Clément Janequin is a case in point, for

[13] For a critique of the "Parisian chanson" designation, see Lawrence F. Bernstein, "The 'Parisian Chanson': Problems of Style and Terminology," *Journal of the American Musicological*

Ex. 12.2 (*b*) *Tant que vivray*, mm. 13–16

his work is often considered exemplary of the Parisian style, yet he moved to Paris only in 1549, and his royal connections were frail at best. Nonetheless, his songs on ribald narratives and his famous descriptive chansons such as the *Chant des oyseaux* and *La Guerre* sustained the catalogues of Attaingnant and Moderne and helped jumpstart the printing venture of Adrian Le Roy and Robert Ballard when they devoted their *Verger de musique* to Janequin's onomatopoetic chansons in 1559.

Many other songs that ill fit the "Parisian chanson" designation played important roles in the musical life and times of Paris during the Attaingnant years. In the 1540s a craze for psalm-singing swept the court—even Henri II was said to be an avid participant—and the settings of Marot's versified psalm translations issued by Attaingnant undoubtedly helped along the general trend toward chordal types of writing. The queen, Catherine de Médicis, set another trend, for she introduced Florentine entertainments to the Valois household, welcoming Italian musicians such as the Ferrabosco brothers and Nicola Vicentino, Italian dance masters, and, later, *commedia dell'arte* players to the court. So pronounced became the Italian inclinations of the Valois that in 1575 Henri Estienne would accuse Catherine of ruining France with her Medicean tastes and Machiavellian politics.[14] One musical manifestation of this Italianism may be seen in the appointment of Mellin de Saint-Gelais as official court poet. Saint-Gelais had passed his youthful years in Italy, where he learned to sing, play the lute, and declaim verse to music in the manner of his Italian idol, the great Quattrocento improviser Serafino Aquilano. Saint-Gelais wrote his own *chansons* and sang them at court to high acclaim. Like Serafino, he probably never wrote down what he played, yet traces of his perform-

Society, 31 (1978), 193–240; for an overview of the pernicious problems of terminology and some solutions, see Perkins, "Toward a Typology of the 'Renaissance' Chanson."

[14] Henri Estienne, *Discours merveilleux de la vie, actions, et deportemens de Catherine de Médicis* ([Geneva], 1575), 62ff.

ances have been preserved in the work of contemporary polyphonists. Settings of his poems by Jacques Arcadelt, Pierre Certon, and Adrian Le Roy consistently employ the same melodies—most of them drawn from the dance—suggesting that Saint-Gelais sang his verse to dance music, a repertory that, as a lutenist, he would have known quite well. This practice of fitting new poetry to dance tunes or popular melodies produced the *voix de ville*, a genre whose very name relates to the Italian *villanella* and its ostensible roots in urban minstrelsy.[15]

In sum, the appellation "Parisian chanson" describes too narrow a repertory, since it refers primarily to Claudin's four-voice settings of Marotic verse and hardly captures the wealth of song styles prevalent in Attaingnant's Paris. Yet scholarship has not discarded the term because it offers a useful—though crude—way to distinguish the lighter and more homophonic chansons printed in France from the more imitative "Netherlandish" chansons written by contemporary composers to the North such as Clemens non Papa (*c.*1510/15–1555/6), Nicholas Gombert (*c.*1495–*c.*1560), and Thomas Crecquillon (before 1500–1557?). The term maps a stylistic distinction onto political boundaries that ill fit the pan-European currency of the chanson. [16]

Still, around 1550 national identity began to preoccupy French intellectuals in a way not wholly unlike the nineteenth-century nationalism that left us with the notion of "Parisian chansons." French poets and publishers began to draw up cultural boundaries with an intense focus on language as a defining factor and with specific attention to lyric poetry. Du Bellay's *Deffense et illustration de la langue francoyse* (1549) proposes a kind of culture-building using language as its foundation and the forms of classical lyric as its blueprint. The desire to remake "La France" in a classical mold rivaling Greece or Rome pulled the French language itself into the spotlight, and young poets made certain that lyric poetry was central to the cause by reiterating Plato's claim that wholesome songs could sustain the moral health of a republic. The seven most vociferous poets called themselves the Pléiade; they included Du Bellay, Pierre de Ronsard, Jean-Antoine de Baïf, and Rémy Belleau, the poet-philosopher Pontus de Tyard, the playwright Estienne Jodelle, and their teacher Jean Dorat.

The Pléiade's overhaul of French lyric began with attacks on the two genres of *poésie pour musique* most favored by musicians at the time: the *chanson* and the epigram. Du Bellay's *Deffense* threw down the gauntlet, warning young poets to avoid models like Mellin de Saint-Gelais's popular *chansons Laissez la verde couleur* and *O combien est heureuse*, which he condemned as "vulgar."[17] Rather, the poet should emulate the odes of Horace, *fons et origo* of classical lyric. In reality, there was no

[15] See especially Daniel Heartz, "*Voix de Ville:* Between Humanist Ideals and Musical Realities," in *Words and Music, The Scholar's View: A Medley of Problems and Solutions Compiled in Honor of A. Tillman Merritt*, ed. Laurence Berman (Cambridge, MA, 1972), 115–35; and Jean-Pierre Ouvrard, "Populaire ou savante: La *Chanson en forme de voix de ville* vers 1550 et le modèle italien de la *poesia per musica*," in *Meslanges pour le Xe anniversaire du Centre de Musique Ancienne* (Geneva, 1988), 77–89.

[16] See Perkins, "Toward a Typology of the 'Renaissance' Chanson."

[17] Du Bellay, *Deffence*, 115.

formal difference between the ode and the *chanson*, for both were strophic poems. The crucial difference was that the serious tone prescribed for the ode guaranteed its distance from the "vulgaire." The attack on Saint-Gelais and his *chansons* made much of the Pléiade's reinvention of the *chanson* under a new name, and it seems fairly clear that the *querelle* of the ode and the *chanson* was really part of a territorial war between the young and the old masquerading as a poetic revolution.[18] Indeed, many of the innovations the Pléiade would claim as their own—the use of new verse forms (the sonnet, eclogue, and epithalamium) and the imitation of Petrarch and Ovid—had already been introduced to France by Marot and Saint-Gelais.

Ironically, composers took little notice of odes, for they tended toward inflated Greek and Latin neologisms, labyrinthine syntax, and terrible length. A number of musical prints advertised odes in their titles, notably Pierre Clereau's two books of *Odes de Ronsard mis en musique à troys parties* (Paris, 1566), but they actually included few settings of odes. The positive significance of the ode was the way the term itself indicated a classical influence, the "tuning of the French lute to the sound of the Greek and Roman lyre," as Du Bellay said.[19] The Pléiade poets regularly spoke of the ode as poetry meant to be sung to the lute or lyre. In the preface to his first book of *Odes* (1550), Ronsard exclaims "I will revive again (if I can) the use of the lyre, today resuscitated in Italy, that lyre alone which should and can animate verses and give to them the just weight of their gravity."[20] Evidently, Ronsard hoped to cultivate Italian musical practices in France so that his odes would be performed as lute songs. Lutenists impressed poets as a sort of Orphic reincarnation, and poets, in turn, conferred an ancient mythology on the lutenist's art in France.

Notwithstanding the musical modes claimed for the ode, it was only when Ronsard began writing *chansons* that composers warmed to Pléiade poetry. Ronsard's *chansons* were the mainstay of his lighter verse, or the "style plus bas et populaire" he pursued later in his career. These poems perpetuate Marot's easy language while expanding the topos of pastoral love-making to include the courtly mistress as its object. That is to say, Ronsard's *chansons* bent the rules of *amour courtois* to allow for sexual satisfaction, and they did so using strophic texts as their vehicle, a form that appealed to composers. Many of Ronsard's *chansons* may have been inspired by closer contact with composers, for after he succeeded Mellin de Saint-Gelais as court poet in 1558, he began to work with musicians on material for fêtes, *magnificences*, and royal entries.

The first musical collection to contain a large number of Ronsard's *chansons* was Nicolas de La Grotte's *Chansons de P. de Ronsard, Ph. Desportes, et Autres* (Paris, 1569; five subsequent editions by 1580). La Grotte (1530–*c.*1600) served as organist to the future Henry III, and there is good reason to suppose that Ronsard collabo-

[18] For an overview of the *querelle* between the ode and the chanson, see Kate van Orden, "*La Chanson Vulgaire* and Ronsard's Poetry for Music," in *Poetry and Music in the French Renaissance*, ed. Jeanice Brooks, Philip Ford, and Gillian Jondorf (Cambridge, 2001), 79–109; and Donald Stone, *Mellin de Saint-Gelais and Literary History* (Lexington, KY, 1993).

[19] Du Bellay, *Deffence*, 112–13.

[20] Pierre de Ronsard, *Œuvres complètes*, ed. Paul Laumonier, 18 vols. (Paris, 1982), I: 48.

Ex. 12.3 Nicolas de La Grotte, *Quand j'estoy libre* (1569), mm. 1–8
From *The Sixteenth-Century Chanson*, ed. Jane Bernstein (New York, 1992), XX, no. 24

rated with him on some of the songs in the collection. Ronsard wrote *Autant qu'on voit aux Cieux* to be "played on the lyre" for the baptism of Charles de Villeroy, and we know it was sung at a banquet in January of 1567. *Je suis Amour* formed part of an intermedio for the comedy *La Belle Genièvre*, based on Ariosto, that was performed at Fontainebleau on 13 February 1564 and was most certainly sung. La Grotte's collection may recall the melodies used for those performances, placing them in the cantus with three strictly chordal accompanying voices below. Many of the chansons are cast in triple meter with hemiolas reminiscent of galliards. Take for instance *Quand j'estois libre* (Example 12.3), which is really just a *voix de ville* under the name of a *chanson*. Its strophic verse, Romanesca-derived bass (replete with step-wise descending soprano line), and slightly abstracted dance rhythms suggest that the Pléiade's revival of ancient lyric took shape after the model of

Saint-Gelais, despite their outspoken ambivalence toward the older poet. For better or for worse, the *voix de ville* must have remained a favorite at court even after the death of Saint-Gelais, and Ronsard's "revival of the lyre" in France seems to have been based partially on the Orphic practices of lutenist-poets like his great predecessor, who relied on stock bass patterns such as the Romanesca when declaiming their verse.

Strophic verse gained popularity with composers as the last third of the century wore on, but around 1560 composers still favored epigrams over all other types of poetry. Anonymous quatrains, cinquains, sixains, huitains, and dixains abounded in the chanson repertory. Du Bellay took epigrams to task in his *Deffense*, begging poets to "throw out these pleasant epigrams with their little punch lines."[21] In their place, he proposed the sonnet, a sort of overblown epigram made up of two quatrains and two tercets. Francesco Petrarca's *Canzoniere* was proclaimed the model, and French poets threw themselves into imitating the Trecento Tuscan. Du Bellay was not the first to recommend Petrarch as a model, for Pietro Bembo had called upon Italians to imitate Petrarch in his *Prose della volgar lingua* of 1525. And here we should recall that in Bembo's Venice, Petrarch's sonnets held a special cachet for madrigal composers, for whom they represented the highest possible register of lyric utterance. The *summa* of this impulse, Adrian Willaert's *Musica nova* (printed 1559 but composed much earlier), presents a wealth of Petrarchan sonnets in settings of motet-like expanse and imitative complexity. In France, Ronsard, for one, clearly hoped that chanson composers would embrace the sonnet in the same spirit, and to initiate the process, a musical appendix was published with his first sonnet cycle, *Les Amours* (1552). The six sonnet settings there, by Certon, Janequin, and Claude Goudimel (1514/20–1572), are for four voices and blend contrapuntal writing with homophony in the style of earlier chansons. The settings follow the rhyme scheme of the poetry, repeating the music of the first quatrain for the second (AA) and providing new music for the tercets that is either repeated or through-composed to produce the overall forms AABB or AABC. In short, they are typical chansons, not madrigals. They are not through-composed or rich with word-painting; rather, they deny the madrigal's aesthetic of close word–music relations, the more so because the settings were meant to be used as polyphonic "tunes" to which any of the sonnets in the collection could be sung by simply exchanging the words.[22]

The musical supplement crowns Ronsard's *Amours*, conjuring around his verse a group of admiring polyphonists meant to rival the madrigalists who accorded Petrarch such prestige and to announce his *Amours* as a French *Canzoniere*. But, except for the sonnet settings in *Les Amours*, composers would not comply: they found fourteen decasyllabic lines too imposing for song and the high diction of the sonnet too loaded with classical references. Only in the 1570s did composers

21 Du Bellay, *Deffence*, 110–11.

22 See Jean-Pierre Ouvrard, "Le Sonnet ronsardien en musique: Du *Supplément* de 1552 à 1580," *Revue de Musicologie*, 74 (1988), 149–64; and Sebastian Klotz, "Musik zwischen Supplément und Zitat: Zur musikalischen Poetik der Pléiade," *Renaissance-Hefte*, 2 (1993), 41–49.

and music publishers develop an interest in *Les Amours* and accept the musical initiative of its supplement. Two composers from Toulouse, Anthoine de Bertrand (1530/40–1580/82) and Guillaume Boni (d. after 1584), were foremost in this trend, collecting their settings of Ronsard's sonnets into cycles under titles such as Boni's *Sonetz de P. de Ronsard mis en musique* (Paris, 1575) and Bertrand's *Les Amours de P. de Ronsard mises en musique* (Paris, 1576). Bertrand's collection even recreated the cyclic structure of Ronsard's *Les Amours*, matching its loose narrative of love, desire, and denial with a modal cycle meant to portray the progress of love through ethical effect. (This resulted in a preponderance of chansons in the dark plagal modes owing to the unhappy outcome of Ronsard's love affair.)[23] Bertrand's experiments with mode owe much to the writings of Nicola Vicentino and show one way in which these French sonnets look toward Italy for appropriate musical language.[24] Both Boni and Bertrand borrow from the madrigal's array of expressive devices, including parallel major sixths, cross relations, and word painting, though they maintain the syllabic style and repetition schemes used by their countrymen in Paris. It would seem that the sonnet held special appeal for southern French composers such as Boni, Bertrand, and Jehan Maletty (d. after 1583), who tried to capture the difficult and "writerly" diction of the sonnet in music. Philippe de Monte (1521–1603), a Fleming at the imperial court, also set a considerable number of Ronsard's sonnets using the abstract and dense polyphony he employed in his other chansons.

What is telling about this brief appraisal is that Parisian composers never accepted the sonnet, while the "provincial" composers who did matched its high style with Italianate or highly imitative music. Composers closer to Paris and the court cultivated a more local style of musical rhetoric that coalesced around two poles: strophic poems set homophonically and epigrams set in an extension of earlier part-writing. Guillaume Costeley (*c.*1531–1606), organist to Charles IX, offers a prime example of Parisian tastes. His massive *Musique de Guillaume Costeley* (Paris, 1570) includes many chansons in the strictly homophonic idiom we have already encountered in the work of La Grotte. Alongside them one finds chansons written in a rich counterpoint that expands the style of Claudin and Janequin to five voices while preserving their affection for anonymous epigrams and rhythmic patter. The same can also be said for the chansons of Claude Goudimel—all penned, so the story goes, before his conversion to Protestantism—though some of his first works to come into print witness his close study of Josquin. His 1552 setting of Ronsard's famous ode to Michel de l'Hospital, *Errant par les champs*, employs motet-like writing, while later works include the madrigalesque *Allez, mes soupirs*, festive chansons that alternate between duple and triple mensuration, and four-voice chansons set in the style of the *voix de ville*. Before the Saint Bartholomew's Day massacre brought his life to an abrupt end in 1572, Goudimel

[23] See Jeanice Brooks, "*Ses amours et les miennes tout ensemble*: La Structure cyclique du *Premier livre* d'Anthoine de Bertrand (1576)," *Revue de Musicologie*, 74 (1988), 201–20.

[24] See Jean-Michel Vaccaro, "Les Préfaces d'Anthoine de Bertrand," *Revue de Musicologie*, 74 (1988), 221–36.

set the psalm translations of Marot and Théodore de Beze both simply and in the style of motets, showing how varied his compositional palette was, even when approaching the same texts.

Goudimel's Protestantism and his turn from the profane genre of the chanson to psalms is also a good reminder that song could be made to serve religious ends. The Reform's emphasis on psalmody for the masses enlarged the public for simple sorts of poetry and music, and arrangers rushed to "spiritualize" love songs by altering their texts. *Tant que vivray* offers a perfect case in point, for in more than one godly reworking, arrangers replaced "Amour" with "God," transforming it into a perfect expression of Christian piety: "As long as life in me doth flourish, I shall serve the Lord almighty in deeds, in words, and harmonious songs . . . ." In the 1570s and 1580s, as the Wars of Religion raged in France, Huguenot presses in La Rochelle issued whole volumes of polyphonic chansons that had been cleaned up for devout pleasure.[25] Catholics, too, participated in this trend. Anthoine de Bertrand, who had devoted himself to setting Ronsard's love poems, experienced an epiphany under the influence of the Jesuits in Toulouse and ultimately renounced the "chansons impudiques" he had composed on sonnets from *Les Amours*, many of which were subsequently published in spiritualized versions by Simon Goulart (Geneva, 1580). Bertrand's *Airs spirituels* (1582) were some of the first Catholic spiritual songs to be penned in France. The composer apparently died for his new convictions, martyred—according to the collection's preface—"by those who detest these ecclesiastical hymns."

The *chanson spirituelle* throws into relief the activity of publishers, who not only promoted new repertories with their own arrangements and commissioned works but shaped the careers of composers in print. Before 1570, only masses and motets had regularly been printed in fancy single-composer editions in France, but around that time, chansons grew surprisingly self-important in print, perhaps in conjunction with the new classicism claimed for vernacular lyric by the Pléiade, or perhaps in emulation of the forms in which the great Venetian presses issued their madrigals. Here again, *Musique de Guillaume Costeley* offers an excellent example of a new Parisian style, for it was a book of a very different nature from Attaingnant's *Chansons nouvelles* or *Trente et une chansons*. Its novelty hinged on publishing strategies that became regular features of the chanson prints issued by Adrian Le Roy and Robert Ballard, Attaingnant's successors as royal printers of music.

The first strategy was to devote an entire print to the chansons of a single composer or poet, naming him in the title. These prints were usually larger than chanson anthologies and more "motet-like" in their format and presentation; the opening pages of Costeley's *Musique*, for example, contained four panegyric sonnets from Costeley to the King, two to the Count and Countess of Retz, a sonnet from Belleau and two from Baïf in praise of Costeley, and a dedication to Costeley's friends.

The elevation of the composer through naming and encomia led to a second

[25] See Richard Freedman, *The Chansons of Orlando di Lasso and Their Protestant Listeners: Music, Piety, and Print in Sixteenth-Century France* (Rochester, NY, 2000).

standard marketing strategy, that of adding the name of a composer whose works sold well to the titles of their chanson anthologies, which Le Roy & Ballard had formerly issued in a numbered series entitled *Premier Livre de chansons, Second Livre de chansons*, and so forth. Even though the chansons of many other composers fleshed out the series, the names of individual composers were used to "authorize" these volumes. During the 1560s, a considerable number of Jacques Arcadelt's songs were printed in such series, and his name graced the *Livre de chansons* series beginning in 1561, its titles reading *Tiers Livre de chansons . . . par M. Jacques Arcadet & autres autheurs*, etc. Arcadelt (1507?–1568) had moved to France in 1551 to serve Charles de Guise, Cardinal of Lorraine, and his renown spread quickly thanks to Le Roy & Ballard. He died in 1568, and after this, if not before, Le Roy & Ballard began to promote Orlande de Lassus (1532–1594) as the newest marvel of their time. They filled the *Livre de chansons* series with his chansons, replaced "Arcadelt" with "Lassus," and issued five monumental editions devoted to his songs alone: the *Mellange d'Orlande de Lassus* (1570; revised edition, 1576), a luxurious quarto volume headed by five panegyric poems and a dedication to the Duke of Bavaria, and containing over 100 songs; the *Livre de chansons nouvelles a cinc parties avec deux dialogues a huict d'Orlande de Lassus* (1571); the *Continuation du Mellange d'Orlande de Lassus* (1584); and the *Meslanges de la Musique d'Orlande de Lassus* (1586). The stature of Lassus in France was uncontested. The king himself, Charles IX (r. 1560–1574), seems to have been genuinely infatuated with Lassus's music. In 1574 came a royal invitation for the composer to join the court, which Adrian Le Roy extended with the encouragement, "the king has a greater desire to have you than ever."[26]

The reception of Lassus in France and the way it was helped along in print cannot be separated from the concurrent push toward canonizing a gallery of French composers. The naming of classics and writing of a national history seem to have fascinated composers and publishers alike. Josquin came to be elevated as a model of a "classical" chanson style and imitated through musical borrowing by Willaert, among others. Meanwhile, Le Roy & Ballard obtained a special privilege to print the "historic" chansons of Josquin, already issued in impressive single-composer volumes by Susato (1545) and Attaingnant (1550). That Le Roy & Ballard strove to create a canon of chansons is nowhere more evident than in the retrospective *Mellange de chansons tant des vieux autheurs que des modernes* (1572), which drew its repertory from across the breadth of sixteenth-century chanson production, placing Paris at its center.[27] Ronsard's famous preface to the print constructs a genealogy of chanson composers beginning with Josquin and his "disciples" (in the order: Mouton, Willaert, Richafort, Janequin, Maillard, Claudin, Moulu, Jaquet, Certon, Arcadelt) and culminating in Lassus, who is said to have made "honey

[26] In a letter from Le Roy to the composer, printed in facsimile and transcribed in François Lesure and Geneviève Thibault, *Bibliographie des éditions d'Adrian Le Roy et Robert Ballard (1551–1598)* (Paris, 1955), 36–37.

[27] An earlier version of the collection was published in 1560 under the title *Livre de meslanges . . .*; 80 of its 120 chansons were reprinted among the 148 of the 1572 *Mellange*. Ronsard's preface first appeared in the earlier edition.

from all of the most beautiful ancient flowers." Le Roy dedicated Lassus's *Novem quiritationes divi Job* to Charles IX with the words "Your France doesn't concern itself with our vernacular music. Finally, to put it back on its feet and to soften the harshness of this troubling time, the necessary grace and harmony must come from Lassus." Here, Le Roy offers Lassus as a savior for song in France, yet the problem with the language of progress, retrospection, and self-conscious historicism applied to Lassus by the French is that the composer never lived there. Unlike Willaert, who received his training in Paris from Mouton, or Josquin, who served at the courts of René d'Anjou and (probably) Louis XII, Lassus only visited France once for a brief stay. That trip to Paris in 1571 produced a flurry of prints and the royal invitation mentioned above, but he was never to accept the offer.

Lassus's chansons perpetuate the international style of the chanson he inherited from an earlier generation. He favored pre-Pléiade poetry, often choosing epigrams that had been set by earlier composers, and employed a style of imitative polyphony lightened with chordal writing that took little notice of the strict homophony tacitly associated with ancient lyric by composers such as La Grotte who worked more proximately with the Pléiade poets. Yet while Lassus's taste in verse might be attributed to provincialism or the desires of his patrons and publishers, his musical style was right in fashion. Indeed, some of his more serious settings—that of Du Bellay's *La nuict froide et sombre*, for instance—pursue the affective style of *seconda pratica* madrigalists with distinctly un-Gallic chromaticism. His preference for five and more voices, deft control of this expanded musical space, lively rhythms, and ear for rich sonorities mobilizes his polyphony in the service of musical effect if not always in the service of the text. His frequent repetition of phrases of the text gives him the opportunity to revisit musical motifs more than it contributes to straightforward oratory, and no doubt one reason Lassus chose epigrams is precisely because they traded in brief epithets that translated nicely into motifs ripe for musical elaboration.

Claude Le Jeune (1528/30–1600), Lassus's great French contemporary, also favored larger numbers of voices and rich polyphony, both imitative and non-imitative. Like Lassus, Le Jeune was an internationalist, fluent in the language of the madrigal and *villanella*, whose traits inflect his chanson settings with their text-painting and active meters. Even while Le Jeune set Pléiade poetry with apparent enthusiasm, he, like Lassus, often turned to older chansons for inspiration: his five-voice setting of the "chanson rustique" *Allons, allons gay* may pay homage to Willaert's earlier three-voice setting, and his six-voice setting of *Je suis desheritée* and seven-voice setting of *Susanne un jour* both contributed new monuments to those venerable families of chansons.

Poetry from the time of François I may have elicited a sense of nostalgia for Le Roy & Ballard's public, recalling the "happier century and one less tainted by the vices which prevail in this Iron Age" that Ronsard described in his preface to the 1572 *Mellange*. A desire to revive France's golden age may have inspired the publication of songs such as Le Jeune's *Allons, allons gay* on an old theatrical chanson once set by Willaert (and another version by Jean de Castro), not to mention the dozens of three-part *chanson rustique* arrangements from the first decades of the century printed by Le Roy & Ballard in the 1570s. The three-voice chansons aimed to please a broad public, for it was always easier to find three able singers than four, as Antoine Cartier remarked in the preface to his *Vingt et une chansons nouvellement composée à trois parties* (Paris, 1557), and three partbooks are always cheaper than four or five. Didier Le Blanc even arranged a number of chansons by Lassus for two voices in his *Premier livre de chansons à deux parties* (Paris, 1578). They proceed in a simple fashion, stating a phrase from the model and repeating it with ornaments in a didactic mode. The proliferation of *bicinia* and *tricinia* suggest that—like Susato and Gardano—Le Roy & Ballard hoped to satisfy a growing number of musical amateurs amid the audience for print, an audience composed not just of singers but of instrumentalists as well. But we must not forget that the combination of three-voice textures and strictly homophonic part-writing was often associated with the Italian *villanella* in France, where Le Roy & Ballard saw fit to issue *Il primo libro di villanelle alla Napolitana novamente stampate a tre voci* in 1565. That the *villanella* of the 1530s and 1540s influenced the chanson is most evident in Arcadelt's œuvre, in which strophic texts consistently receive three-voice settings in the homophonic texture of the *villanella*. In fact, Arcadelt's *Je ne scay que c'est qu'il me fault* sets a "villanesque" by Saint-Gelais, replete with the *villanella*'s signature refrains at the end of each strophe, suggesting that the *villanella* inflected both French poetry and song. The *villanella*, more than the *voix de ville*, was a genre that captured the rustic idioms of guitar-playing popular singers in polyphonic chansons, the whole playing into an aesthetic prizing the natural grace of popular poetry rather than the artifice of complicated rhetoric. As Michel de Montaigne said, "popular and purely natural poetry has in it a certain naïveté and grace by which it may be compared with the principal beauty of poetry that is perfected by art, as we see in our Gascon villanelle and the songs that are brought to us from nations that have no knowledge of any science, nor even of writing."[28] The natural turn of French *villanelles* makes them like good "writerly" lyric, which is best when free of artifice. Montaigne argues that excessive subtleties can destroy a poem's effect, a criticism he levels against the overworked creations of Alexandrine poets in the same essay, "Des vaines subtilitez" (1: liv).

Montaigne's comments arise from a lively discourse about the chanson and its efficacy introduced in the 1550s by the philosopher-poet of the Pléiade, Pontus de Tyard. Tyard published two dialogues on lyric poetry, *Solitaire premier* and *Solitaire second*. The first explained how, when a poet wrote, he became infused with a *furor* or divine frenzy sent from the Muses, and how, when poetry written in this state was sung, the poetic furor enlivened the souls of listeners and transported them to heavenly realms. The second dialogue treated the elements of music and finished with the recommendation that poetry be sung as monody because "figured music [polyphony] most often yields nothing to the ears but a great noise, from which you feel no lively effect. But the simple and solo voice, gliding sweetly and continuously according to the dictates of a Mode chosen to the advantage of

[28] Michel de Montaigne, *Les Essais*, ed. Pierre Villey, 3 vols. (Paris, 1978), 1: 313.

the verse, ravishes you completely."[29] Here it is the music that must be "natural," and by freeing the poetry from the artificial "noise" of polyphony, the full effect of the verse can be gained. It is unclear precisely what Tyard meant by "Mode." He may refer to the tonal orientation of the melody, which could have been chosen according to its ethos to match the sense of the poem, but it is more likely that he uses "Mode" to indicate a rhythmic mode that paired the natural accents of the verse with rhythmic accents or long notes in the melody. This became the chief musical goal of the academy that developed from the Pléiade, and perhaps its most enduring musical achievement.

The *Académie de poésie et de musique* was established in 1571 by Jean-Antoine de Baïf and Joachim Thibault de Courville.[30] Letters patent issued by Charles IX guaranteed its royal patronage, and the list of academicians included members of the royal family and other nobles. The Academy musicians included Thibault de Courville, Eustache Du Caurroy, Jacques Mauduit (1557–1627), and Claude Le Jeune, who worked for the king's brother François, duc d'Anjou, until 1584 and after 1596 as *maistre de la chapelle* for Henry IV. The academicians set out to revive ancient music and its attendant moral persuasion, to create a kind of lyric based on what they could discern of classical practices and in so doing to achieve the magical effects attributed to song in Plato's *Republic* and Aristotle's *Politics*. The goal was to perfectly join the poetry to the music, and the key was rhythm. Baïf and his colleagues paired the stressed and unstressed syllables of French with long and short note values, attempting to give precise readings of the verse in music. But to do so, special poetry had to be written that deployed or "measured" the stresses according to regular patterns, and so Baïf penned a series of *chansonnettes mesurées à l'antique* for the Academy's secret weekly gatherings.

Only years after the Academy disbanded in 1574 did measured poetry and music surface in print, in Mauduit's *Chansonnettes mesurees de Jan-Antoine de Baïf* (Paris, 1586) and Le Jeune's *Le Printans* (1601). Both collections are written for four voices in a strictly homophonic style that produced the transparent texture Tyard had recommended. Le Jeune approached the notion of measure with two different rhythmic strategies: in some songs the slavish attention to long and short syllables produces what appears to be unmeasured music—since bar lines cannot be applied—while in other songs both poetry and music seem to have been themselves measured to dance rhythms.[31] *Voicy le verd et beau May* (Example 12.4a) is, roughly speaking, of the first type, while *Revoicy venir du printans* (Example 12.4b) is clearly based on the rhythms of a galliard. The dance-like chansonnettes certainly owe much to the *voix de ville* and even to the Italian *villanella*, for, as Jeanice Brooks has discovered, Baïf modelled the form and tone of several *chansonnettes*

[29] Pontus de Tyard, *Solitaire second*, ed. Cathy M. Yandell (Geneva, 1980), 214. On Neoplatonism in Europe at the time, see Gary Tomlinson, *Music in Renaissance Magic* (Chicago and London, 1993).

[30] Frances A. Yates, *The French Academies of the Sixteenth Century* (London, 1947; repr. 1988).

[31] Pierre Bonniffet, *Un Ballet démasqué: L'Union de la musique au verbe dans "Le Printans" de Jean-Antoine de Baïf et Claude Le Jeune* (Paris and Geneva, 1988).

Ex. 12.4 (*a*) Claude Le Jeune, *Voicy le verd et beau May*, mm. 1–4 (Dessus only)
From *Les Maîtres musiciens de la Renaissance française* (Paris, 1900–1901), XII

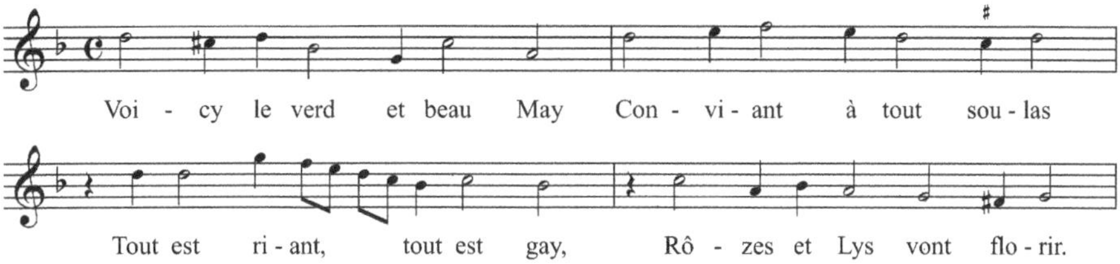

Ex. 12.4 (*b*) Le Jeune, *Revecy venir du printans*, mm. 1–2

on anonymous Italian *villanelle*.[32] This is an excellent reminder that no matter how esoteric humanistic projects presumed to be, poets and musicians usually cast about among the forms available to them to create the "new." And yet, *chansonnettes* like *Voicy le verd et beau May* did forge a link of lasting importance between poetry and music, one that ultimately typified the style not of the chanson, but of French recitative.

MANY of the trends we have been examining point toward the cultivation of monody in France: the superius-oriented texture of the so-called Parisian chanson and *voix de ville*, the strict homophony in settings like La Grotte's that creates a pseudo-monodic texture (Example 12.3), and the academic philosophy that prized textual audibility above polyphonic riches. We would be wise, in fact, to presume that monody was well established long before it shows up in print not only because minstrelsy was based on precisely the same texture of melody and accompaniment but because print itself presented the greatest obstacle to the publication of accompanied song. A space-efficient way to print standard vocal notation with lute tablature—the score—simply did not come to the fore before the end of the century. The four-voice versions of *voix de villes* and the guitar, cittern, and lute intabulations of the same songs are both representations of monodic practices that had been forced into the only standard print formats for secular song in the sixteenth century: tablature and partbooks. It should not surprise us to discover, then, that it was the lutenist-publisher Adrian Le Roy who produced one of the few sixteenth-century prints to place vocal melodies alongside intabulations, the *Livre d'airs de cour miz sur le luth par Adrian Le Roy* (1571). Le Roy not only issued his chansons in an unusual format, he presented them under the title of "airs de

32 Jeanice Brooks, *Courtly Song in Late Sixteenth-Century France* (Chicago, 2000), 293–315.

cour" for the first time, explaining that "one used to call these songs *voix de ville*, today [they are called] *airs de cour*."[33] These lute songs probably had their origin in a repertory of monophonic melodies, here represented by the solo line for voice, a supposition supported by their concordances with one of the few monophonic chansonniers to be printed in the sixteenth century, Jehan Chardavoine's *Recueil des plus belles et excellentes chansons en forme de voix de ville* (Paris, 1576). In the *Livre d'airs de cour*, the starkly homophonic accompaniment favors the clarity of the text to such an extent that Le Roy remarks "if the musical harmonies are not equal to the best, at least the words emanate from good forges like those of Ronsard, Desportes, and others of the century's finest poets." With the musical ken of beginners in mind, then, his "little opuscule of much lighter *chansons de la cour*" decks out court poetry in facile music. The volume was assembled for Catherine de Clermont, one of Le Roy's lute pupils, and his dedication to her rationalizes the songs as substitutes for the challenging intabulations of Lassus's chansons he had previously given her to play. But surely the collection supposed broad interest, and Le Roy's dedication to the countess functions doubly as personal address and public *avertissement* through which the purchaser of *Livre d'airs de cour* might participate in their exchange and learn the court's most popular songs. The new generic label, in fact, relocates the music's origin from the city (*voix de ville*) to the court (*air de cour*), conferring nobility upon these possibly common melodies. The new name and lighter style proved phenomenally popular, and by about 1595, most songs printed in France, whether for one, two, three, or four voices, were not "chansons," but "airs."

The shift was not merely terminological but registered the demise of chansons written in imitative counterpoint. Airs for several voices did prolong the polyphonic tradition *per se*, and only the advent of French opera in 1673 made polyphonic song truly obsolete. But airs cultivated chordal writing, not counterpoint or imitation. The art of the air lay in crafting limpid melodies that were then harmonized for several voices, sung as lute songs, or even circulated orally among the repertory of popular tunes. On its own, the term "air" meant tune or *timbre*, a stock melody to which new texts might be sung, and so to some extent, the *air de cour* evinced the same multiple forms of representation that we have encountered in one of its predecessors, the *voix de ville*. Yet the sobriquet rightly implies that the airs originated at court, even if minstrels and print trafficked them elsewhere. Pierre Guédron (1565–1621), Antoine Boësset (1587?–1643), and Étienne Moulinié (*c.*1600–after 1669), the principal composers of airs, were all in royal employ, and in 1608 Pierre Ballard, heir to the LeRoy & Ballard printing dynasty and its royal patent, would reinforce his sole right to use the words "Airs de cour" in titles.[34] *Airs de cour* poured from the lips of social climbers who purchased them in print,

[33] Preface reprinted in Adrienne Mairy, *Chansons au luth et airs de cour français du XVIe siècle* (Paris, 1934), pp. xxv–xxvi.

[34] A truly invaluable study of the *air de cour*, and one to which the following discussion is indebted, is Georgie Durosoir, *L'Air de cour en France, 1571–1655* (Liège, 1991). See also James Anthony, *French Baroque Music from Beaujoyeulx to Rameau* (New York and London, 1978); and Théodore Gérold, *L'Art du chant en France au XVIIe siècle* (Strasbourg, 1921).

but the designation still presumed some courtly authenticity. For example, the provincial anthologies published by Jacques Mangeant (1608, 1615) of what were essentially *airs de cour* never used that term in their title.

Court culture in the seventeenth century and its overriding concern for style decisively influenced the air. *Airs de cour* cultivated restrained melodic gestures meant to be embellished with precious ornaments that fit well with the understatement prescribed by genteel behavior, while conservative harmonies supported the top line in chordal writing that translated easily from partsong to solo song. Mersenne favorably compared the French air to Italian opera arias, dismissing the radical melodic leaps and dissonant harmonies of the Italian style thusly: "the French represent their passions with less violence. . . . Airs are composed particularly and principally to charm the mind and the ear and to enable us to spend our lives with a little sweetness amidst all the bitterness we meet with, . . . not . . . to excite anger and several other passions."[35] Thus, airs reflected the growing preoccupation in France with the civilization of manners that followed the ruder behavior so common during the Wars of Religion. One important site of the new *civilité* would be the Hôtel de Rambouillet and the *chambre bleue* held there by Catherine de Vivonne beginning in 1620. The softened gestures and purified speech pursued at her salon became a decisive model of refinement, and along with polite conversation, Catherine entertained her guests with literary games, comedies, serenades, and concerts that regularly included *airs de cour.*

The verse of airs recycled prefabricated affections that were easily captured in so subdued a musical style. Philippe Desportes, Ronsard's successor at court, was the first to fashion airs from the materials of Petrarchan language, distilling its already worn conceits to clear and imitable models. While the Pléiade poets had challenged and tried to best their classical sources, airs by poets such as François de Malherbe, Marc-Antoine Gérard de Saint-Amant, Vincent Voiture, and Honoré d'Urfé narrowed the range of lyric utterance, reworking models without reinventing them and abandoning the light-hearted pastoral or carnivalesque subject matter adored by sixteenth-century poets. This regularization of French verse constricted the tone, vocabulary, and topics of airs, rendering them highly stylized and even staid. Guédron, Le Jeune's successor as composer of the *Chambre du Roi* in 1601, was himself a poet, and his six books of airs for four and five voices published by Ballard between 1602 and 1620 helped standardize the formal parameters of the air. In these prints, his preference for octosyllabic or heterometric lines grouped into strophes of quatrains and sixains is amply apparent. His musical settings of each strophe took binary forms, either AB or, when text and music were repeated, ABB or AABB. The predilection for repetitions, particularly at the end of each strophe, appears already in the music of Guédron's principal forerunners, Pierre Bonnet (fl. 1585–1600), Jehan Planson (*c.*1559–after 1611), Guillaume Tessier (fl. *c.*1580), Charles Tessier (fl. *c.*1600), and Denis Caignet

[35] *Correspondance du P. Marin Mersenne*, ed. Cornelis de Waard (Paris, 1932), x: 236–49, cited in translation in D. P. Walker, "Joan Albert Ban and Mersenne's Musical Competition of 1640," *Music & Letters*, 57 (1976), 233–55.

(d. 1625), who published in the 1580s and 1590s. The pairing of the new French air in Tessier's *Premier livre d'airs tent François, Italien, qu'Espaignol* (Paris, 1582) with Italian *villanelle alla napolitana*, and the similar styles of the two genres, not to mention Le Roy & Ballard's simultaneous publication of the same print under the title *Il primo libro dell'arie Franzesi, Italiche & Spagniuole*, certainly suggest the air's initial ties to Italian *arie.* Among Guédron's airs one also occasionally comes upon measured verse penned to Greek and Latin verse types reminiscent of Baïf and Le Jeune's *chansonettes mesurées*, but in essence, Guédron's *airs de cour* bear little resemblance to sixteenth-century airs. Their limited range of note values resembles that of Le Jeune's measured chansons, yet rarely is it employed with Le Jeune's deftness and attention to text accent. Likewise, many seventeenth-century airs cultivate the dance-like quality of Le Jeune's isometric settings, yet destroy the prosody of their lyric texts, which were only rarely composed in *vers mesuré.* Only in his *récits*—a genre originating in the *ballet de cour*—does Guédron regularly combine rhythmic variety and good declamation with his refined melodies. In the end, airs shed the traits inherited from the *voix de ville* and *chansonnettes mesurées* early on or wed them to a new aesthetic prizing flexible vocal lines and elegant—if occasionally vapid—poetry.

Following the publication of Le Roy's *Livre d'airs de cour* for solo voice and lute in 1571, the French public waited over three decades for more collections of airs intabulated for the lute from Ballard's presses. The first series, by Gabrielle Bataille, appeared between 1608 and 1615. Bataille's six books gathered together *airs de cour* and *airs de ballets* along with the occasional psalm, *récit*, dialogue, and Spanish or Italian air. Bataille's intabulations ride the crest of Guédron's popularity at the time, honoring him with the lion's share of intabulations and a lengthy dedication in the 1608 book. Most of these airs by Guédron were published in polyphonic versions the same year, a fact that points up how Ballard thought of the audiences for prints of polyphonic airs and of airs for lute as two separate groups of consumers. The intabulations also initiated a trend of printing airs for solo voice and lute before the polyphonic versions. Intabulations marketed airs to a broader audience than that reached by polyphony, and in so doing they essentially vulgarized *airs de cour* for common consumption. Solo song proved less treacherous than polyphony, yet it also entailed a special need for ornaments. Ever mindful of his amateur readers, Bataille embellished the vocal lines slightly, hinting at the graceful turns expected in the style without altering the melodies too much out of "submission and respect" for Guédron. Only in 1637, with the publication of Marin Mersenne's *Harmonie universelle*, would the art of vocal embellishment finally be codified in a treatise. In "L'Art d'embellir la voix," Mersenne contrasts the ornaments of Italian singers, who aim to represent all the passions, both soft and violent, with the French, who "content themselves to flatter the ear and who seek a perpetual sweetness in their songs, which prevents energy in them."[36] Ornaments and diminutions helped mitigate the air's sobriety, yet in principle, the French style never

[36] Marin Mersenne, *Harmonie universelle, contenant la théorie et la pratique de la musique*, 3 vols. (Paris, 1636; facs., introd. François Lesure, Paris, 1963), II: 356.

succumbed to Italianate vocal excess. Chauvinistic in the end, Mersenne mines Italian sources such as Caccini's *Le nuove musiche* for ornaments, but finishes with the claim that vocal embellishment "has never before proceeded with such deftness and politeness" as in his France.[37]

Intabulations also served in the education of young nobles, since singing and playing the lute was commonly recognized as "honest exercise" that contributed to virtuous behavior. Montaigne's essay "De l'institution des enfans," François de La Noue's *Discours politiques et militaires*, and Thomas Pelletier's *La nourriture de la noblesse* all encourage learning to play the lute as part of a young nobleman's education. Pelletier understood that the lute could seem a frivolous enterprise in comparison with sword play, and music's detractors argued that playing the lute often led to a reclusive "humeur phantasque." Yet Pelletier encouraged young students to pursue lute lessons, and La Noue reminded his readers that Aristotle ordered musical instruction for young people to occupy their spirits honestly during leisure hours and to prevent bad thoughts.

Bataille's intabulations inaugurated a series of prints *chez* Ballard that would grow to 25 volumes by 1643, with Antoine Boësset carrying the torch after 1620. Boësset was very much Guédron's heritor at court, marrying the royal musician's daughter Jeanne in 1613, succeeding Guédron in the position of *Maître des Enfans de la Musique de la Chambre du Roy* that year, and rising to the rank of *Surintendant de la Musique du Roi* and finally *Conseiller* by 1634. While Boësset actively composed and intabulated airs for solo voice and lute, however, all of his single-author prints were of polyphonic airs, suggesting that polyphony still garnered admiration that lute songs could not. Within the parameters established by Guédron, Boësset expanded the *air de cour*'s musical idioms, including more varied rhythmic values, meters, and scoring in his nine books of polyphonic airs published by Ballard between 1617 and 1642. Another innovation found in his publications is an early form of basso continuo, in which untexted fragments of the bass line carry the indication "pour les luths," and, by the *VIIe Livre* of 1630, the more familiar label "basse continue pour les instruments." As court composer, Boësset contributed music for the principal genre of court spectacle, namely the *ballet de cour*, and scattered liberally among his printed works we also find *récits* and *airs de ballet* written in very much the same musical style as his other airs.

Étienne Moulinié, Boësset's younger contemporary, pursued a different career path, both at court and in print. He worked for Gaston d'Orléans, brother of Louis XIII, a dynamic man of letters who was more galant than his pious brother, whom he often schemed to depose. Moulinié made his debut in print with five books of airs for voice and lute (1624–35), concentrating on polyphonic airs only later (1635–39). This certainly reversed the emphasis placed on the four- and five-voice air by Guédron and Boësset. And Moulinié's predilection for the lute song may in some measure account for the metric surety and tonal focus of his style, even as he enhanced his direct musical language with varied textures and an extensive rhythmic palette.

[37] Ibid., II: 358.

Moulinié's taste for a new kind of air can be seen in the *airs à boire* for voice and lute or guitar he began to publish in 1629, a genre disdained by polyphonists for its symposiastic texts and vigorous rhythms. The immediacy of the *air à boire* eventually inspired innumerable drinking songs for one or two voices without accompaniment, making the genre a new fad with the ever-expanding public for print. Its success was helped along immensely by Robert Ballard (the younger), who took up the reins of the publishing house from Pierre in 1640. Robert popularized *chansons pour boire* and *chansons pour danser* at the expense of the polyphonic *air de cour*, which met its demise in print at the hands of the younger entrepreneur. Only a handful of *airs de cour* were published after 1640, a statistic that may also reflect the actual downturn of the court's social and political hegemony during the civil revolts known as the Fronde (1648–53), when drinking songs and *mazarinades* promoted disorder and rebellion. Another blow came from the court itself, where Mazarin vigorously promoted Italian opera rather than indigenous genres. But despite these trials, the *air* held on. The *airs* collected in manuscripts such as *F-Pc* Rés. Vm^7 501 and Rés. Vma 854 and in Bénigne de Bacilly's *Recueil des plus beaux vers qui ont été mis en chant* (1661) suggest that older *airs*—particularly those of Antoine Boësset—continued to enjoy performance in Parisian salons and noble circles into the latter part of the century. Only at that time did the taste for part-songs and lute songs finally gave way to more modern *airs* influenced by the Italian theater and the harmonic implications of melodies conceived with basso continuo accompaniment in mind.

Select Bibliography

Adams, Courtney, "Some Aspects of the Chanson for Three Voices during the Sixteenth Century," *Acta musicologica*, 49 (1977), 227–250.

——, "The Early Chanson Anthologies Published by Pierre Attaingnant (1528–30)," *Journal of Musicology*, 5 (1987), 527–48.

Anthony, James, *French Baroque Music from Beaujoyeulx to Rameau*. New York and London, 1978.

Barbier, Jacques, "'Faute d'argent': Modèles polyphoniques et parodies au XVIe siècle," *Revue de musicologie*, 73 (1987), 171–202.

Bartoli, Jean-Pierre (ed.), *Voix et instrument, parole et musique dans le répertoire musical du Moyen-Âge à nos jours, Analyse musicale*, 9 (1987).

Bernstein, Jane A., "Lassus in English Sources: Two Chansons Recovered," *Journal of the American Musicological Society*, 27 (1974), 315–25.

——, "An Index of Polyphonic Chansons in English Manuscript Sources, c.1530–1640," *Royal Musical Association Research Chronicle*, 21 (1988), 21–36.

BERNSTEIN, Lawrence F., "The Cantus-Firmus Chansons of Tylman Susato," *Journal of the American Musicological Society*, 22 (1969), 197–240.

——, "The 'Parisian Chanson': Problems of Style and Terminology," *Journal of the American Musicological Society*, 31 (1978), 407–41.

——, "French Duos in the First Half of the Sixteenth Century," in *Studies in Musicology in Honor of Otto E. Albrecht*, ed. John Walter Hill, 43–87. Kassel, 1980.

——, "Notes on the Origin of the Parisian Chanson," *Journal of Musicology*, 1 (1982), 257–326.

——, "Melodic Structure in the Parisian Chanson: A Preliminary Study in the Transmission of a Musical Style," in *Studies in Musical Sources and Style: Essays in Honor of Jan LaRue*, ed. Eugene Wolf and Edward Roesner, 121–89. Madison, WI, 1990.

——, "Josquin's Chansons as Generic Paradigms," in *Music in Renaissance Cities and Courts: Studies in Honor of Lewis Lockwood*. Ed. Jessie Ann Owens and Anthony M. Cummings, 35–55. Warren, MI, 1996.

—— (ed.), *La Couronne et fleur des chansons a troys*, 2 pts., Masters and Monuments of the Renaissance, 3. New York, 1984.

BLOCK, Adrienne Fried, "Timbre, texte et air, ou Comment le noël-parodie peut aider à l'étude de chanson du XVIe siècle," *Revue de musicologie*, 69 (1983), 21–54.

BOETTICHER, Wolfgang, *Orlando di Lasso und seine Zeit, 1532–1592*, 2 vols. Kassel, 1958.

BONNIFFET, Pierre, *Un Ballet démasqué: L'Union de la musique au verbe dans "Le Printans" de Jean-Antoine de Baïf et Claude Le Jeune*. Paris and Geneva, 1988.

—— (ed.), *Claude Le Jeune et son temps en France et dans les États de Savoie, 1530–1600: Musique, littérature et histoire*. Berne and New York, 1996.

BOSSUYT, Ignace, Eugeen Schreurs, and Annelies Wouters (eds.), *Orlandus Lassus and His Time: Colloquium Proceedings, Antwerpen, 24–26 August, 1994*. Peer, Belgium, 1995.

BROOKS, Jeanice, "Jean de Castro, the Pense Partbooks and Musical Culture in Sixteenth-Century Lyons," *Early Music History*, 11 (1992), 91–149.

——, *Courtly Song in Late Sixteenth-Century France*. Chicago, 2000.

BROTHERS, Thomas D., "Two *Chansons Rustiques* à 4 by Claudin de Sermisy and Clément Janequin," *Journal of the American Musicological Society*, 34 (1981), 305–24.

BROWN, Howard Mayer, "The *Chanson Spirituelle*, Jacques Buus, and Parody Technique," *Journal of the American Musicological Society*, 15 (1962), 145–73.

——, *Music in the French Secular Theater, 1400–1550*, 2 vols. Cambridge, MA, 1963.

——, "Words and Music: Willaert, the Chanson, and the Madrigal about 1540," in *Florence and Venice, Comparisons and Relations: Acts of Two Conferences at Villa I Tatti in 1976–1977*, II: *Il Cinquecento*, 217–66. Florence, 1980.

——, "Emulation, Competition, and Homage: Imitation and Theories of Imitation in the Renaissance," *Journal of the American Musicological Society*, 35 (1982), 1–48.

——, "Theory and Practice in the Sixteenth Century: Preliminary Notes on Attaingnant's Modally Ordered Chansonniers," in *Essays in Musicology: A Tribute to Alvin Johnson*, ed. Lewis Lockwood and Edward Roesner, 75–100. Philadelphia, 1990.

CŒURDEVEY, Annie, *Bibliographie des œuvres poétiques de Clément Marot mises en musique dans les recueils profanes du XVIe siècle*. Paris, 1997.

CURTIS, Stephen M., "La Technique de la parodie dans les chansons à cinq et six voix de Nicholas de La Grotte," *Revue de musicologie*, 72 (1984), 173–98.

DASCHNER, H., *Die gedruckten mehrstimmigen Chansons von 1500–1600: Literarische Quellen und Bibliographie*. PhD diss., Universität von Bonn, 1962.

DOBBINS, Frank, *Music in Renaissance Lyons*. Oxford, 1992.

DOBBINS, Frank, "Les Premières Mises en musique des chansons, des épigrammes et des rondeaux de Marot," in *Actes du colloque de Cahors*, 483–502. Paris, 1997.
DOTTIN, Georges, *La Chanson française de la Renaissance*. Paris, 1984.
DUROSOIR, Georgie, *L'Air de cour en France, 1571–1655*. Liège, 1991.
EGAN-BUFFET, Máire, *Les Chansons de Claude Goudimel: Analyses modales et stylistiques*. Ottowa, 1992.
FENLON, Iain (ed.), *Early Music History*, 13 (1994). [A volume devoted to music in late-sixteenth-century France.]
FREEDMAN, Richard, "The Chansons of Mathieu Lasson: Music at the Courts of Lorraine and France, ca.1530," *Journal of Musicology*, 8 (1993), 316–56.
——, *The Chansons of Orlando di Lasso and Their Protestant Listeners: Music, Piety, and Print in Sixteenth-Century France*. Rochester, NY, 2000.
GÉROLD, Théodore, *L'Art du chant en France au XVIIe siècle*. Strasbourg, 1921.
HAAR, James, "Orlando di Lasso, Composer and Print Entrepreneur," in *Music and the Cultures of Print*, ed. Kate van Orden with an afterword by Roger Chartier, 125–62. New York, 2000.
——, "Arcadelt and the Frottola: The Italianate Chanson, ca.1550," in *Res Musicae: Essays in Honor of James Worrell Pruett*, ed. Paul Laird and Craig Russell, 97–109. Warren, MI, 2001.
—— (ed.), *Chanson and Madrigal, 1480–1530*. Cambridge, MA, 1964.
HEARTZ, Daniel, *Pierre Attaingnant, Royal Printer of Music: A Historical Study and Bibliographical Catalogue*. Berkeley and Los Angeles, 1969.
——, "*Au pres de vous*: Claudin's Chanson and the Commerce of Publishers' Arrangements," *Journal of the American Musicological Society*, 24 (1971), 193–225.
——, "*Voix de Ville*: Between Humanist Ideals and Musical Realities," in *Words and Music, The Scholar's View: A Medley of Problems and Solutions Compiled in Honor of A. Tillman Merritt*, ed. Laurence Berman, 115–135. Cambridge, MA, 1972.
——, "The Chanson in the Humanist Era," in *Current Thought in Musicology*, ed. John W. Grubbs with Rebecca A. Baltzer, Gilbert L. Blount, and Leeman Perkins, 193–230. Austin, TX, and London, 1976.
HERTIN-LÖSER, Uta, *Die Tonarten in der französischen Chanson des 16. Jahrhunderts*. Munich, 1974.
HIS, Isabelle, *Claude Le Jeune (v. 1530–1600): Un Compositeur entre Renaissance et Baroque*. Arles, 2000.
JACQUOT, Jacques (ed.), *Musique et poésie au XVIe siècle*. Paris, 1954.
KLOTZ, Sebastian, "Musik zwischen Supplément und Zitat: Zur musikalischen Poetik der Pléiade," *Renaissance-Hefte*, 2 (1993), 41–49.
KOVARIK, Edward, "The Parody Chansons of Certon's *Meslanges*," in *Music and Context: Essays for John M. Ward*, ed. A. D. Shapiro, 317–51. Cambridge, MA, 1985.
LECLERCQ, F. (ed.), *Revue belge de musicologie*, 39–40 (1985–86). [An issue devoted to Lassus.]
LESURE, François, "Autour de Clément Marot et de ses musiciens," *Revue de musicologie*, 33 (1951), 109–19.
——, *Musicians and Poets of the French Renaissance*. New York, 1955.
——, and Geneviève Thibault, *Bibliographie des éditions d'Adrian Le Roy et Robert Ballard (1551–1598)*. Paris, 1955.
LEUCHTMAN, Horst, *Orlando di Lasso: Sein Leben*, 2 vols. Wiesbaden, 1976.
LEVY, Kenneth J., "*Susanne un jour*: The History of a Sixteenth-Century Chanson," *Annales musicologiques*, 1 (1953), 375–408.

——, "Costeley's Chromatic Chanson," *Annales musicologiques*, 3 (1955), 213–64.
Le Luth et sa musique. Paris, 1957; 2nd edn, 1980.
McClelland, John, "Marot et ses compositeurs: Coïncidences et interférences des langages poétique et musical," in *La Génération Marot: Poètes français et néo-latins (1515–1550)*, ed. Gérard Defaux, 169–89. Paris, 1997.
Massip, Catherine, "Le Mécénat musical de Gaston d'Orléans," in *L'Âge d'or du mécénat (1598–1661)*, ed. Roland Mousnier and Jean Mesnard, 383–91. Paris, 1985.
Maurice-Amour, Lila, "Les Poésies de Malherbe et les Musiciens de son temps," *Dix-septième Siècle*, 31 (1956), 296–331.
Musique et humanisme à la Renaissance, Cahiers V.-L. Saulnier, 10. Paris, 1993.
Ouvrard, Jean-Pierre, "Les Jeux du mètre et du sens dans la chanson polyphonique française du XVIe siècle," *Revue de musicologie*, 67 (1981), 5–34.
——, *La Chanson polyphonique français du XVIe siècle: Guide pratique*. Dijon and Paris, 1982.
——, "Populaire ou savante: La *Chanson en forme de voix de ville* vers 1550 et le modèle italien de la *Poesia per musica*," in *Meslanges pour le Xe anniversaire du Centre de Musique Ancienne*, 77–89. Geneva, 1988.
—— (ed.), *Revue de musicologie*, 74/2 (1988). [A volume devoted to the musicians of Ronsard.]
Packer, Dorothy S., "Les Chansons spirituelles de 1597: Une Anthologie protestant inconnue," *Revue de musicologie*, 65 (1979), 5–50.
Perkins, Leeman, "Toward a Typology of the 'Renaissance' Chanson," *The Journal of Musicology*, 4 (1988), 421–47.
Picker, Martin (ed.), *The Chanson Albums of Marguerite of Austria*. Berkeley and Los Angeles, 1965.
Pogue, Samuel F., *Jacques Moderne: Lyons Music Printer of the Sixteenth Century*. Geneva, 1969.
Rees, Owen, "*Mille regretz* as Model: Possible Allusions to 'The Emperor's Song' in the Chanson Repertory," *Journal of the Royal Musical Association*, 120 (1995), 44–76.
Suter, Louis-Marc, "Les *Amours* de 1552 mises en musique," in *Ronsard: Colloque de Neuchâtel*. Geneva, 1987.
Thibault, Geneviève, "Les *Amours* de P. de Ronsard mises en musique par Jehan de Maletty (1578)," in *Mélanges de musicologie offerts à M. Lionel de la Laurencie*. Paris, 1933.
——, "Anthoine de Bertrand: Musicien de Ronsard et ses amis toulousains," in *Mélanges offerts à M. Abel Lefranc*, 282–300. Paris, 1936.
Tiersot, Julien, *Ronsard et la musique de son temps*. Leipzig, 1902; Paris, 1903.
Vaccaro, Jean-Michel, *La Musique de luth en France au XVIe siècle*. Paris, 1981.
—— (ed.), *La Chanson à la Renaissance*. Tours, 1981.
——, *Le Concert des voix et des instruments à la Renaissance*. Paris, 1994.
Vanhulst, Henri, *Catalogue des éditions de musique publiées à Louvain par Pierre Phalèse et ses fils, 1545–78*. Brussels, 1990.
Van Orden, Kate, "Imitation and *la Musique des Anciens* in Le Roy & Ballard's 1572 *Mellange de chansons*," *Revue de musicologie*, 80 (1994), 5–37.
——, "Sexual Discourse in the Parisian Chanson: A Libidinous Aviary," *Journal of the American Musicological Society*, 48 (1995), 1–42.
——, "*Les Vers Lascivs d'Horace*: Arcadelt's Latin Chansons," *Journal of Musicology*, 14 (1996), 338–69.
——, "Street Songs and Cheap Print following the *Vespres Lyonnaises*," in *Music and the Cultures of Print*, ed. Kate van Orden with an afterword by Roger Chartier, 271–323. New York, 2000.

VAN ORDEN, Kate, "*La Chanson Vulgaire* and Ronsard's Poetry for Music," in *Poetry and Music in the French Renaissance*, ed. Jeanice Brooks, Philip Ford, and Gillian Jondorf, 79–109. Cambridge, 2001.

VERCHALY, André, "Desportes et la musique," *Annales musicologiques*, 11 (1954), 271–345.

——, "Gabrielle Bataille et son œuvre personnelle pour voix et luth," *Revue de musicologie*, 29 (1947), 1–24.

——, "Un Précurseur de Lully: Pierre Guédron," *Dix-septième Siècle*, 21–22 (1954), 383–95.

——, "Le Recueil authentique des chansons de Jehan Chardavoine (1576)," *Revue de musicologie*, 49 (1963), 203–219.

WALKER, D. P., "Some Aspects and Problems of *Musique Mesurée à l'Antique*: The Rhythm and Notation of *musique mesurée*," *Musica Disciplina*, 4 (1950), 163–86.

——, "The Influence of *Musique Mesurée à l'Antique*, Particularly on the *Airs de Cour* of the Early Seventeenth Century," *Musica Disciplina*, 2 (1948), 141–63.

——, "The Aims of Baïf's *Académie de Poésie et de Musique*," *Journal of Renaissance and Baroque Music*, 1 (1946), 91–100.

——, "Musical Humanism in the 16th and Early 17th Centuries," *Music Review*, 2 (1941), 1–13, 111–21, 220–27, 288–308.

——, *Music, Spirit, and Language in the Renaissance*, ed. Penelope Gouk. London: Variorum Reprints, 1985.

——, and François Lesure, "Claude Le Jeune and *Musique Mesurée*," *Musica Disciplina*, 3 (1949), 151–70.

WHANG, Jane Ozenberger, "From *Voix de Ville* to *Air de Cour*: The Strophic Chanson circa 1545–75." PhD diss., University of North Carolina at Chapel Hill, 1981.

YATES, Frances A., *The French Academies of the Sixteenth Century*. London, 1947; repr. 1988.

13

MADRIGAL

James Haar

IN the fifteenth century the French chanson dominated secular musical culture throughout Europe. For the first third of the sixteenth century this dominance was not seriously challenged; but as the century went on the Italian madrigal, nonexistent in 1500, was widely cultivated throughout the peninsula, then spread to the Netherlands, parts of Germany and Scandinavia, even France. At the century's end came a remarkable development, the sudden appearance and quick flowering of the English madrigal.

The chanson did not decline; on the contrary, French song flourished throughout the sixteenth century. But in the face of this the madrigal enjoyed a remarkable vogue, over a period of more than a century. It has been estimated that about 1,200 madrigal volumes (not counting reprints) were published between 1520 and 1630.[1] And it is not merely in quantity that the madrigal is remarkable; during much of its century of intense cultivation the madrigal was a genre in which experiments in rhetoric and style took place constantly, altering its musical character and influencing every sort of music, secular and sacred, across Europe.

Why all this should have been so is not an easy question to answer. It is not a matter of native Italian musicians suddenly coming to the fore; until about 1560 most of the best-known madrigalists were French or Flemish by birth, however Italianized they may have become as adults. Nor can one say that the madrigal drew from a font of popular poetry and song. It was from its beginnings a highly artificial genre, indeed more so than the contemporary chanson. The most important factor in the madrigal's rise to prominence was the extraordinary vogue of literary Petrarchism, starting in Italy about the second decade of the sixteenth century, continuing without serious challenge for a good half-century and frequently renewed thereafter, and spreading throughout Europe in the second half of the century. Petrarch (Francesco Petrarca, d. 1374) was not simply revived and

[1] Lorenzo Bianconi, *Music in the Seventeenth Century* [1982], trans. David Bryant (Cambridge, 1987), 2. If reprints and publications of concerted madrigals are added, the total is just under 1,900.

his vernacular poetry closely studied; his language was championed as the ideal for lyric verse by Florentine scholars and others, notably the poet-critic-theorist Pietro Bembo.[2] Petrarchan subject matter, vocabulary, imagery, and authorial persona were imitated by a host of *petrarchisti*, mostly amateur poets possessed of varying amounts of talent and skill but united in their adherence to one of the most enduring and all-embracing fashions in Western literary history.

Petrarch's *Canzoniere*, a kind of Bible for sixteenth-century poets, is chiefly made up of sonnets written in the form—fourteen lines of hendecasyllabic verse, organized into two quatrains followed by two tercets—made canonical by his example. It also contains *canzoni*, strophic poems of complex individual design; sestinas, successions of six-line stanzas with interlocking rhyme schemes recalling Provençal verse; a few single-stanza ballatas; and four madrigals, pastoral miniatures no two alike but consisting basically of three-line stanzas finished off by a ritornello couplet. Not included are *terza rima* stanzas, the verse type immortalized by Dante and used by Petrarch in his *Trionfi*, and demotic verse forms such as the strambotto or its sometimes more elevated cousin the *ottava rima* stanza, beloved of popular singer-poets throughout the Renaissance and the chosen form of the grandest of epic verse.

Musicians in early sixteenth-century Italy began to set Petrarch and especially his Cinquecento imitators. At first they were a bit shy of the sonnet, which may have been considered the property of singer-improvisers; but they made use of all the other Petrarchan verse forms, and turned readily to *ottava* stanzas as well; the Petrarchan-flavored stanzas of Ariosto's *Orlando furioso* (1516; definitive version 1532) offered a storehouse of usable verse.

The term madrigal is in this context something of a paradox. Applied during Petrarch's lifetime to a fairly well-defined strophic verse type employed by many Tuscan poets and set to music during the Trecento,[3] the word and the poetry it represented fell out of use in the fifteenth century. When the term was revived as part of a renewed attention to the literary past, it no longer had its old meaning but instead referred to a single-stanza poem of mixed seven- and eleven-syllable lines and a free rhyme scheme, sometimes loosely akin to the ballata or occasionally the old madrigal, more often resembling a single stanza of a canzone.[4] Amateur poets of a Petrarchistic bent enthusiastically cultivated this old-new verse form, which

[2] On Bembo, see Carlo Dionosotti, s.v., in *Dizionario biografico degli italiani* (Rome, 1960–). For his influence on the madrigal, see Dean Mace, "Pietro Bembo and the Literary Origins of the Italian Madrigal," *The Musical Quarterly*, 55 (1969), 65–89; but Mace's views have been variously challenged and are subject to qualification, especially with regard to the early madrigal.

[3] For the Trecento madrigal, see Kurt von Fischer/Gianluca d'Agostino, "Madrigal" 1, *The New Grove Dictionary of Music and Musicians*, 2d edn, ed. Stanley Sadie, 29 vols. (London, 2001), XV: 545–47.

[4] A standard work on 16th-century madrigal verse is Ulrich Schulz-Buschhaus, *Das Madrigal: Zur Stilgeschichte der italienischen Lyrik zwischen Renaissance und Barock* (Bad Homburg, 1969). On various subcategories of madrigal poetry as used by musicians, see Don Harrán, "Verse Types in the Early Madrigal," *Journal of the American Musicological Society*, 22 (1969), 27–53.

had the advantage of being a vehicle for succinct amorous complaint expressible in Petrarchan language without the challenge of meeting Petrarch in forms the master had himself cultivated.

The vogue for this poetry, Tuscan in language but not restricted to Florence and its environs, essentially replaced the craze for the *barzelletta*, *oda*, and *strambotto* of turn-of-the-century northern Italy and the antiquarian cultivation of the ballata in Florence. It is important to note that the poetic madrigal is quite unrelated in style and language to the strophic poetry set by the frottolists of Mantua, Ferrara, and the Veneto just before and after 1500; the poetic break is as evident as is the musical divide between frottola and madrigal. What unites them is that texts of both frottola and madrigal were conceived as *poesia per musica*, verses meant to be sung.

The Early Madrigal

In 1530 a set of printed partbooks bearing the title *Madrigali novi . . . libro primo de la Serena* appeared in Rome. This is the first music print to bear the new name; the new genre, if one takes it inclusively as with Petrucci's frottola volumes of the early sixteenth century (these contained *barzellette*, *strambotti*, etc.; madrigal collections included settings of sonnets, canzoni, ballatas, and the new poetic madrigal), was about ten years old. Printed collections of the 1520s used the term *canzoni*, which could mean "song" as well as the poetic form bearing that name; but after 1533, when the *Primo libro de madrigali di Verdelotto* was published in Venice, the word *madrigale* was firmly established in music as in poetry.[5]

Curiosity about the birth of an artistic genre is natural but is not easily satisfied. Gestation is easier, but for the madrigal it must be confessed that parentage is less than certain. The madrigal did not grow out of the frottola, occasional musical and poetic resemblances between the two notwithstanding. It seems instead to have been developed on the one hand from the ballata and related forms as practiced in Florence in the first two decades of the sixteenth century, and on the other from a particular kind of French chanson cultivated during the same period.[6] This chanson, with its chordal and fully vocal texture and its syllabic declamation, was the dominant gene; but there are early madrigals showing influence of a more florid polyphonic approach, that of Florentine music of the early Cinquecento. Settings of Petrarchan verse were made by composers such as Bernardo Pisano, a Florentine, and by Sebastian Festa and Elzéar Genet, *dit* Carpentras, active in Rome during the pontificate of the Medici Pope Leo X (r. 1513–1521).[7]

[5] For information on early madrigal prints, see Iain Fenlon and James Haar, *The Italian Madrigal in the early Sixteenth Century: Sources and Interpretation* (Cambridge, 1988).

[6] On Florentine music of the early 16th century, see the various editions and articles on the subject by Frank A. D'Accone listed in *New Grove*², VI: 629–30. For an attempt to explain the stylistic roots of the early madrigal, see James Haar, "The Early Madrigal: A Re-appraisal of its Sources and its Character," in *Music in Medieval and Early Modern Europe: Patronage, Sources and Texts*, ed. Iain Fenlon (Cambridge, 1981), 163–92.

[7] See Frank A. D'Accone, "Bernardo Pisano: An Introduction to his Life and Works,"

Philippe Verdelot, a French musician about whose training and early career we know little, was in Rome near the end of Leo X's reign. In 1521 he went to Florence, as a Medici protégé; and during the decade that followed Verdelot, together with a few other Florentine musicians such as Francesco Layolle, brought the madrigal into full-fledged existence.[8] Verdelot set a few Petrarchan texts; but most of his madrigals were written to contemporary verse, by Florentines such as Ludovico Martelli and Nicolo Machiavelli and by poets connected with Medicean Rome and thus known in Florence as well. Though a trained contrapuntist and a sober church musician (he was *maestro* at the Florentine Cathedral and Baptistry for most of the 1520s), Verdelot, if the much later testimony of Antonfrancesco Doni (who makes the composer an interlocutor in a free-ranging dialogue, *I marmi* [1551]) can be believed, may have been a boon companion as well, on friendly terms with the aristocratic *literati* of the last days of the Florentine republic. He set texts supplied him by these part-time poets, either for a specific occasion—such as the madrigals performed as *intermedi* between acts of Machiavelli comedies—or for social gatherings where poetry was discussed and music sung, the sort of meetings recorded in literary-musical form in the *Dialogo della musica* (1544) of the Florentine-born Doni. The dual purpose of the madrigal, for ceremonial or at least public occasions and for informal gatherings (later to be often identified with the academies that were springing up all over Italy) was thus already established.

Although Verdelot's madrigals show some use of imitative counterpoint and contain occasional melismatic passages, usually near cadences, their basic texture is chordal, their basic declamation syllabic. Verdelot wrote a number of pieces for five and six voices, but four-voice texture, designed for a female(?) soprano and male alto, tenor, and bass, is the norm for him and other early madrigalists. The pieces are in general through-composed, but internal repetition is found underscoring formal elements and rhyming lines, especially seven-syllable ones, in the text; and repetition of the final line, text and music, is common. A gentle melodic curve and a generally placid rhythmic flow, with many upbeat beginnings of phrases, give this music a quiet charm that closely matches the half-serious amorous complaints of its text. As an example, the opening of Verdelot's setting of an anonymous single-stanza ballata, *Afflitti spirti mei*, may be cited (Example 13.1).[9]

Madrigals such as this all but "sing themselves"; they, and the rather easy-going poetry they set, seem perfectly suited for the recreation of musically literate ama-

Musica Disciplina, 17 (1963), 115–35; Walter Rubsamen, "Sebastian Festa and the Madrigal," *Gesellschaft für Musikforschung: Bericht über den internationalen musikwissenschaftlichen Kongress Kassel, 1962* (Kassel, 1963), 112–26.

[8] The best account of Verdelot's career is that of H. Colin Slim, *A Gift of Madrigals and Motets*, 2 vols. (Chicago, 1972), 1: 41–65; see also Alexandra Amati-Camperi, "A Fresh Look at the Life of Verdelot," in *"Cantate Domino": Musica nei secoli per il Duomo di Firenze*, ed. Timothy Verdon and Annelisa Innocenti (Florence, 2001), 91–105. For Verdelot's arrival in Florence, see Richard Sherr, "Verdelot in Florence, Coppini in Rome, and the Singer 'La Fiore,'" *Journal of the American Musicological Society*, 37 (1984), 402–4.

[9] Verdelot, *Afflitti spirti mei* (*Libro primo* [1533], no. 11); the piece is also in the Newberry Library manuscript described and edited by Slim in *A Gift of Madrigals and Motets.*

Ex.13.1 Verdelot, *Afflitti spirti mei* (*Libro primo*, 1533, no. 11), mm. 1–11

Afflitti spirti mei / Non sperate gia mai d'haver più pace / Poi ch'a madonna sì il vostro mal piace

teurs. They circulated in manuscripts, a number of which survive, and in the 1530s were printed in Venice in the small oblong partbooks, priced within the reach of middle-class purchasers, that are so characteristic of sixteenth-century music. Verdelot's first madrigal book was also published in an arrangement for voice (the soprano) and lute, a favorite performance idiom for the whole century.

During the 1530s there are signs that the madrigal was being cultivated outside Florentine-Roman circles, in Ferrara, Venice, the Po valley. But Florence remained of central importance through the decade, chiefly because of the activity of Jacques Arcadelt, a Franco-Flemish musician who lived there for five years or so. We know from correspondence of the period that Florentines of substance commissioned

Arcadelt (and the papal singer Costanzo Festa) to set their own poetry or that of friends. There were many of these commissions, perhaps enough for Arcadelt, who had no ecclesiastical position, to live on; at any rate he produced a large number of madrigals, which like those of Verdelot circulated in manuscript partbooks. He was for at least part of his Florentine residence a salaried musican in the personal service of Alessandro de' Medici, the first duke of the new Florentine principate, and wrote some madrigals on occasional texts such as one honoring the duke's prospective bride.[10]

Arcadelt was said by a contemporary observer to have "followed in the footsteps" of Verdelot. So he did, chronologically and to some extent in manner of composition. His art is subtler and more varied than that of Verdelot, expanding the stylistic and expressive boundaries of the older composer's madrigals. By the time he left Florence (probably in 1537, after the murder of Duke Alessandro) Arcadelt had established a considerable reputation. In 1538 his *Primo libro*, to become the most often reprinted and longest-lived madrigal book in the history of the genre, was printed by Antonio Gardane, a Frenchman who settled in Venice and became one of the most prolific music printers of the century. In 1539, by which time Arcadelt had entered papal service in Rome, the First Book was reprinted and the Second, Third, and Fourth Books, the work of the "divino Arcadelte" in the printer's language, were published; a Fifth followed in 1544.[11] The obvious success of Arcadelt's music in print established the madrigal as real competition for the chanson repertory being printed by Pierre Attaingnant in Paris; the madrigal as represented by Arcadelt, Verdelot, Festa and a few of their contemporaries became the model for widespread cultivation of the genre.

Madrigals composed by Francesco Corteccia and other Florentine musicians served as sonorous backdrop for the wedding festivities of the new duke of Florence, Cosimo I, on his marriage to Eleanora of Toledo in 1539; the music was published, a rare occurrence for festival music in the sixteenth century.[12] Later in the century there were to be many more such occasions for which madrigals were written and composed, the Medici court festivals being particularly numerous and elaborate. Florence under the new regime seems however to have been less fertile ground for madrigal composition, though much poetry of madrigalesque nature continued to be written there; the center of musical acitvity moved elsewhere.

If we follow the peregrinations of Antonfrancesco Doni we can see something of this shift. Doni (1513–1574), one of those extraordinary sixteenth-century figures who wrote about everything under the Renaissance sun, was also a musician. On his departure from Florence in 1540 he went to Piacenza in the Po Valley, where

[10] See Warren Kirkendale, *The Court Musicians in Florence during the Principate of the Medici* (Florence, 1993), 57 n. On ceremonial texts set by Arcadelt, see Fenlon and Haar, *The Italian Madrigal*, 243.

[11] The lost first edition of Arcadelt's *Primo libro* was probably dated in the summer of 1538. See Thomas W. Bridges, "The Publishing of Arcadelt's First Book of Madrigals" (PhD diss., Harvard University, 1982), 70.

[12] See Andrew C. Minor and Bonner Mitchell, *A Renaissance Entertainment: Festivities for the Marriage of Cosimo I, Duke of Florence, in 1539* (Columbia, MO, 1968).

he found a congenial group of poets and musicians, among them the madrigalist Claudio Veggio. The first part of his *Dialogo della musica*, containing thirteen madrigals separated by whimsical bursts of conversation among the interlocutor/singers (all male), was written here. Next Doni went to Venice, where he managed to insert himself into musical circles and professed himself amazed at the quality of musical performance, unlike anything he had ever heard. Under the influence of this experience he completed the second part of the *Dialogo*, including a woman among the interlocutors (he had been very impressed by the singing of Polissena Pecorina, wife of a Florentine resident in Venice) and managing to get hold of two pieces by Adrian Willaert and one by Cipriano de Rore, the most important composers of the day active in Venetian and Veneto circles.[13]

Doni returned briefly to Florence, trying to establish himself as a musician and music printer there; but he had no success, and soon went back to Venice to pursue a chiefly literary career. His movements suggest something that other evidence confirms: the hub of Italian musical activity in the 1540s had moved north and especially to the Veneto. In Venice itself Adrian Willaert, who had been resident as maestro of St Mark's since 1527, had been composing madrigals for perhaps ten years; some of his early works were published along with those of Verdelot, and it was he who had arranged the madrigals of Verdelot for solo voice and lute. In the 1530s Jachet Berchem, presumably living in the Veneto, wrote madrigals close enough in style to those of Arcadelt to be published in the latter's volumes and only later attributed correctly. Florentine expatriates living in Venice, men such as Ruberto Strozzi and Neri Capponi, continued to be patrons of madrigal composition, and the renowned soprano Polissena Pecorina (one wonders whether it could have been for her that Willaert made the set of Verdelot arrangements) made a name for herself in Venetian circles.[14]

New currents were stirring in Venetian musical society. Pietro Bembo was a Venetian; in the 1530s he was living in the Veneto, and his theories of linguistic decorum were now bearing full fruit among Venetian academics. One result of this was a new wave of Petrarchism with renewed interest in the lyric poems of Petrarch himself. Among musicans in Venice (Willaert and a circle of his students) and elsewhere in the Veneto (the young Cipriano de Rore in Brescia) the result was adoption of a new stylistic decorum for the madrigal.[15] Choosing Petrarchan sonnets, including some of the darkest ones on the death of Laura, Rore and Willaert composed bipartite five-voice madrigals on a scale and of a complexity hitherto unknown in the genre. Precise declamation of the text in each voice formed a rich fabric eschewing simple chordal texture. Close attention to the poetic syntax rather than line-by-line setting of the text became of primary importance. These madrigals are as contrapuntally dense as any motet of the period; but they avoid

[13] There are two modern editions of the work: G. F. Malipiero (ed.), *Antonfrancesco Doni: Dialogo della musica* (Vienna, 1965); A. M. Monterosso Vacchelli, *L'opera musicale di Antonfrancesco Doni* (Cremona, 1969).

[14] See Richard J. Agee, "Ruberto Strozzi and the Early Madrigal," *Journal of the American Musicological Society*, 36 (1983), 1–13.

[15] See Martha Feldman, *The Madrigal and City Culture in Venice* (Berkeley, 1994).

exact fugal imitation and, in the case of Willaert, decorative melismas and assertive melodic invention. They represent a close, thoughtful reading of the text, in which purely musical values are deliberately held in check, the first of many attempts to set forth the primacy of words over music in the madrigal.

New Directions

In Venice, which had for at least a century been home to popularesque elements in music, a lighter form of madrigal was also cultivated, from the 1540s onward. The *villotta* with its easy-going four-voice polyphony and its incorporation of local folk tunes, popular in the 1520s, continued to exist in various guises. The new fashion was, however, for music from the South, the Neapolitan *canzone alla villanesca* or *villanella*. Three-voice pieces whose strophic verse often took the form of the strambotto with a refrain placed after every two lines of an eight-line stanza, villanescas were based on rustic, anti-Petrarchan themes. Their music, melodically and rhythmically crisp and pointed, adopted some "rustic" mannerisms such as parallel fifths in the counterpoint. Neapolitan composers, among them Giovan Tomaso di Maio and Giovanni Domenico da Nola, specialized in these pieces, which began to appear in print in 1537 and which clearly enjoyed popular success.[16] In Venice these pieces were picked up, dusted off to remove rusticities, and arranged for four voices (with the original soprano melody now in the tenor). The august Willaert wrote a lot of these, as did many other Venetian musicians. Later in the century specialized types using Germanisms (the *todescha*), Greek dialect (the *greghescha*) or the stuttering of comic old men (the *Giustiniana*) appeared. As these suggest, the villanesca found a home in popular theater and in the improvised art of *commedia dell'arte* actor-musicians.

Although madrigals patterned on the work of Verdelot and Arcadelt continued to be written, the 1540s saw the emergence of new musical fashions, chief among them the *note nere* or "chromatic" madrigal with its time signature of **C** as opposed to the more common **₵**, its many black (hence "chromatic", colored) notes, its nervous syncopations and strong contrasts of fast–slow motion.[17] It must have been the popularity of these pieces, published in anthologies through the 1540s, that led Doni to dismiss the madrigals of Arcadelt as "old-fashioned".[18] Another novelty was the madrigal *a voci pari* or *mudate* (equal or "changed" voices), scored for four male voices; this was the first of a series of departures, of which more will be said later, from the normal SATB texture of the madrigal.

[16] The best account of the villanesca is Donna Cardamone, *The Canzone Villanesca alla Napolitana and Related Forms, 1537–1570*, 2 vols. (Ann Arbor, 1981).

[17] James Haar, "The *Note Nere* Madrigal," *Journal of the American Musicological Society*, 17 (1965), 22–41.

[18] *Dialogo*, ed. Malipiero, 35, where Doni also refers to *note nere* pieces, calling them "canti turchi." Arcadelt wrote some *note nere* pieces himself, published along with madrigals of Claudio Veggio in 1540. Doni was referring to Arcadelt's earlier work, ten years old at the time the *Dialogo* was written.

By mid-century the madrigal was a genre in full growth, expanding variously in style and character. Rome in the 1550s was the center of composition and publication of the *madrigale arioso*, which emphasized freely speech-like declamatory rhythm in a basically chordal texture, perhaps reflecting a link with the improvisatory *arie* of singers still popular in the streets and in polite society as well.[19] In Rome and elsewhere musicians were creating large madrigal cycles, setting whole canzoni, sestinas, and chains of ottava stanzas. Cipriano de Rore, after his move from the Veneto to Ferrara, began experimenting with new chordal textures in place of the severe polyphony of the Venetian madrigal; along with other musicians such as Nicola Vicentino in Ferrara and Pietro Taglia in Milan, he started to employ chromatic (now used in the sense of pitch) progressions which gave new harmonic color to the tonal palette of the madrigal. The Venetian madrigal of the 1540s, like the Florentine one of the 1530s, began to appear dated; when in 1559 Willaert published his *Musica nova*, a collection of motets and madrigals, the music, magnificent as it is, was anything but new in style.

The Madrigal after 1550

In the early 1550s three young northern musicians, among the last to cross the Alps in search of a career, were all beginning to make a name for themselves: Orlando di Lasso (Orlande de Lassus), Philippe de Monte, and Giaches de Wert. All of them probably spent some formative years in Naples; Lasso and Monte were resident in Rome at mid-century, and Wert seems to have gone from Naples to northern Italy, where he began his career-long service to the Gonzaga family, dukes of Mantua and rulers of smaller adjacent principalities. All three turned to the madrigal under the influence of Rore, of practitioners (including the young Palestrina) of the *arioso* madrigal, and of the Neapolitan villanesca. Their subsequent careers illustrate much of the divided course of the genre in the second half of the Cinquecento.

Lasso returned to northern Europe in the early 1550s, living for a time in Antwerp. There his first published music, composed "after the new fashion of the Italians," as its title page proclaims, appeared in 1555. The next year he moved to Munich, recruited by emissaries of Duke Albrecht v of Bavaria. He remained there, a valued servant and personal friend of the duke and his successor, until his death in 1594.[20] Lasso fulfilled his duties in the ducal chapel, which he directed for some thirty years, in exemplary fashion, teaching, conducting, recruiting singers, providing music for religious and secular functions at court. He was one of the most prolific of Renaissance composers, active in producing masses, motets, miscellaneous liturgical works, chansons, even German lieder. His madrigals

[19] James Haar, "The 'Madrigale Arioso': A Mid-Century Development in the Cinquecento Madrigal," *Studi musicali*, 15 (1983), 203–19.

[20] Wolfgang Boetticher, *Orlando di Lasso und seine Zeit, 1532–1594* (Kassel, 1958); Horst Leuchtmann, *Orlando di Lasso*, 2 vols. (Wiesbaden, 1976–77).

(approximately 200 in number of titles, many of them multipartite cycles) range from gravely contrapuntal Petrarchan cycles through *arioso* textures and sunny chordal settings (used especially for occasional pieces in honor of the Bavarian ducal house) to incomparably witty villanescas. Lasso's directness, economy, and individuality of expression mark the madrigals as they do all of his music.

Until the last part of his career Lasso's madrigals were published in Venice (his chansons appeared mainly in Paris and the Low Countries, the lieder in Germany; the motets were printed in all these places); they surely had an international circulation, but Lasso seems to have wanted to make sure that his Italian music became known to Italians.[21] On the other hand he appears to have made no real effort, at least after the 1560s, to keep abreast of new developments in the madrigal; his poetic tastes were conservative, and his music developed along individual lines rather than in response to Italian madrigalian fashion.

Philippe de Monte also moved north of the Alps, first to Antwerp (with a brief period in England during the reign of Mary Tudor), then, after a second Italian sojourn, to the imperial chapel in Vienna and Prague. Here he settled into a quietly busy life marked by an impressively productive output; the most prolific of all madrigal composers, he published (entirely in Italy) about forty books of madrigals for three, four, five (the most common), six, and seven voices. Unlike Lasso, with whom he seems to have been on friendly terms, Monte wrote no villanescas. He did make some attempt to keep abreast of the times, setting newly fashionable poets such as Guarini and trying to rejuvenate what was by his later years a quite conservative style. How successful this effort was may be doubted; the Venetian publishers continued to issue his works (probably with imperial subsidies), but few of his later madrigals were reprinted. Monte's work is hard to assess because comparatively little of his vast output is as yet available in modern edition; but he clearly produced work of high technical finish and great beauty.[22] In general the level of compositional expertise in the madrigal of this period is remarkable, rarely if ever exceeded in the history of Western music.

Wert, unlike Lasso and Monte, remained in Italy, serving various members of the house of Gonzaga and in his later years spending a good deal of time at the court of Ferrara. His twelve books of madrigals were frequently reprinted (often with newly added works, enabling him to dedicate them as if they were first editions). Mantua and Ferrara were both centers of intense musical activity and of restless musical experiment. Wert contributed a good deal to this artistic culture, and his work changed more than that of Lasso or Monte. He cultivated stylistic aspects of the new canzonetta (of which more will be said); he set Tasso and Guarini in addition to Petrarch and Ariosto. Above all he develped the *arioso* madrigal of the 1550s into a supple declamatory style, mixed with athletic melismas and coun-

[21] The dedicatory letter of his *Libro quarto* of 1567, addressed to Alfonso II of (Ferrara, assures the duke that the Muses are being cultivated "in Germania."

[22] To date four books of Monte's madrigals have appeared in his collected works (Philippe de Monte, *Opera: New Complete Edition*, ser. D (Louvain, 1987–88). For a study of Monte as madrigalist, see Brian Mann, *The Secular Madrigals of Filippo de Monte: 1521–1603* (Ann Arbor, 1983).

terpoint based on short and dramatically contrasting motifs. The openings of two madrigals from Wert's seventh book (1581) show these two features (see Example 13.2, overleaf). In the second, a setting of a Petrarchan sonnet, the first line of the poem is divided, with separate motifs given each part of the line; this device was later to be much used by Monteverdi.[23]

After 1560 the madrigal can thus be seen to divide into conservative and experimental lines. The latter would seem to be exemplified by Wert, his mature madrigals showing alternations of virtuosic counterpoint with speech-like chordal declamation. Among new features in the period 1560–80 were, on the literary side, challenges to the pervading cult of Petrarchism; the rise of new religious poetry, set to music in the "spiritual" madrigal; and a renewed interest in strophic poetry. Each of these called forth new musical responses in the work of a young generation of Italian composers, including major figures such as Andrea Gabrieli in Venice, Wert in Mantua, and the Mantuan-born Alessandro Striggio in Florence, along with less famous composers of ability and interest such as Marc'Antonio Ingegneri in Cremona, Giovanni Ferretti, master of the new canzonetta, in Ancona, and Maddalena Casulana, the foremost woman madrigalist of the century, active mainly in northern Italy.

The sonnets and canzoni of Petrarch and stanzas from *Orlando furioso* continued to be set by composers; alongside them were new poems such as the *ottave rime* of Bernardo Tasso, and pastoral verse, some of it imitating that of Sannazaro's Arcadian eclogues of the beginning of the century. Petrarch was never completely supplanted, but Petrarchan forms and rhetoric were now only one, and not necessarily the dominant, choice for composers or their patrons. As Torquato Tasso's epic stanzas began to compete with those of Arioso, his pastoral poetry also began to be widely set. In the 1570s the star of Battista Guarini began to rise. His pastoral madrigals were often set, and by the end of the century verses from his *Pastor fido* became the rage with madrigalists. The vivid imagery, pointedly epigrammatic messages, and virtuosic elegance of the poetry, often in the freely varied form of the madrigal proper, were a perfect match for, if not indeed the cause of much of the new suppleness and wit of musical language beginning to be apparent by 1570.[24]

One of the earliest musical consequences of the Catholic Reform was a renewed cultivation of the *lauda*, simple (sometimes borrowed) settings of strophic devotional verse intended for congregational use outside the regular liturgy. In 1563 three volumes of Italian sacred music appeared in print: the *Laudi spirituali* collected by the Florentine monk Serafino Razzi, which make use of much older poetry and music; the *Primo libro* of *laude* by Giovanni Animuccia, a Florentine

[23] The two madrigals are in Wert's *Settimo libro de madrigali a 5* (1581); see Carol MacClintock (ed.), *Giaches de Wert: Collected Works*, VII (American Institute of Musicology, 1967). For a sensitive account of the careers of Lasso, Monte, and Wert as madrigalists, see Alfred Einstein, *The Italian Madrigal*, 3 vols., trans. A. H. Krappe, R. H. Sessions, and O. Strunk (Princeton, 1949), II: 477–519.

[24] For discussion of the new poetry, see Schulz-Buschhaus, *Das Madrigal*, §§ iv–v. Gary Tomlinson, *Monteverdi and the End of the Renaissance* (Berkeley, 1987), argues for direct and profound influence of poets on composers in the late 16th century.

Ex. 13.2 (*a*) Wert, *Voi volete ch'io muoia* (*Libro settimo*, 1581, no. 10), mm. 1–15

musician active in Rome and connected with the Congregazione dell'Oratorio of Filippo Neri, another transplanted Florentine; and the *Musica spirituale* collected by the Veronese Giovanni del Bene, containing settings of strophic poetry and of single poems, including religious texts by Petrarch, the music by north

Voi volete ch'io muoia / E mi date dolor sì crudo e forte

Italian composers including Vincenzo Ruffo and Giovanni Nasco. The *madrigale spirituale* differs from the lauda in that its texts, often religious transformations of secular poems, are not necessarily strophic and its music may be indistinguishable from that of a secular madrigal—in fact many "worldly" madrigals were "spiritualized" through alternation of their texts. New religious madrigal texts appeared, from poets such as Gabriele Fiamma and Luigi Tansillo. A number of composers, including Palestrina, Lasso, and Monte, were to set such texts, and many madrigalists, including Monteverdi, saw their work "spiritualized" by others.

Strophic poetry, at the core of the frottola repertory of the beginning of the sixteenth century, is absent from the serious madrigal but continued to be set in the villanesca. A new period for this genre began in the 1560s with compositions for five and six voices that blended the clear phrase structure and harmonic firmness of the older villanesca with some of the contrpuntal richness of the madrigal. The work of Giovanni Ferretti in the two decades after 1565 is particularly important here. Ferretti called his music *Canzoni alla napolitana* or simply *Napolitane*; but there is no real connection with Neapolitan music here, and the new genre gradually came to be called the canzonetta. Ferretti's music was popular and circulated widely, becoming known in Germany and later influencing the development of the madrigal in England. Many composers, including Marenzio and Monteverdi, were to take up the canzonetta, and characteristics of its style may be seen in the madrigals of Andrea Gabrieli and other Venetian composers.

Ex. 13.2 (*b*) Wert, *Gratie ch'a pochi il ciel largo destina* (*Libro settimo*, no. 11), mm. 1–5

The Late-Sixteenth-Century Madrigal

By 1580 madrigal composers thus had a variety of stylistic paradigms from which to choose, and they tended to mix them freely. The very fabric of the music was being altered; for instance, new combinations of range—emphasizing by its separateness the soprano, used for solos and duets and often elaborately ornamented—were chosen (this suggests a change in performance practice, with much greater emphasis on women singers, at a time when male castrati were beginning to be used in sacred music). Changes such as this mark a shift in taste away from the more severely linear aspects of contrapuntal writing, a shift confirmed by the frequent use of chordal declamation and by the renewed popularity of *arie* for one or two voices over a tenor/bass. Music historians used to be fond of looking for signs of "emerging tonality" in sixteenth-century music, adopting an evolutionary view that has been generally criticized.[25] We should not judge harshly on this matter; something was indeed happening, but it may be that texture and rhythm are as important as choice of vertical sonorities in the change. As for rhythm, the addi-

[25] Edward Lowinsky was a leading proponent of this idea. See his *Tonality and Atonality in Sixteenth-Century Music* (Berkeley, 1961).

Gratie ch'a pochi il ciel largo destina

tive flow of earlier melodic lines in Renaissance counterpoint was being gradually replaced by dance-song rhythms, still supple but basically following fairly regular divisions of the beat; this process affected even the speech-song rhythm of *arioso* style. Practitioners of the canzonetta such as Orazio Vecchi adopted the new textures and rhythms in the 1580s, and in the next decade Giovanni Gastoldi's *balletti*, literally dance-songs, achieved enormous international success.

An important heir to all the poetic and musical ferment that had been taking place in these years was the Roman madrigalist Luca Marenzio, whose early music, blending disparate elements into an amalgam of Mozartean brightness and charm, was immediately popular at home and abroad. During the two decades after 1580 Marenzio produced a large body of madrigals, including a number of volumes for five and six voices, one book *a* 4 and one for mixed number of voices, and several books of canzonettas and villanellas (now the preferred spelling of the term) for three voices. He made use of both old and new poetry, and is among the most distinguished of those to set stanzas from Guarini's *Pastor fido*. His ability to blend light pastoral style with more serious passages including—slightly moderated—the strongly profiled melodic gestures seen in Wert and featuring a good deal of chromatic color, all handled with unrivalled contrapuntal deftness, made his work a kind of summation of the late madrigal at its effective and affective best. Marenzio's late work is marked by a return to serious poetry—Petrarch and Dante—and a darker, more intense style.

Marenzio had connections with Mantua, Ferrara, and Florence; and he spent a brief period as *maestro* at the Polish court. For most of his career, however, he lived in Rome, not as a member of the papal chapel but in the private service of several wealthy cardinals, including Luigi d'Este and Cinzio Aldobrandini, the latter a nephew of Pope Clement VIII. His music, especially the early pastoral works, was often reprinted and very influential in Italy and abroad, notably in England.

Other madrigalist of stature were also working in Rome, among them Ruggiero Giovanelli and Giovanni Francesco Anerio. Cultivation of the madrigal remained strong throughout Italy; it was particularly intense and adventuresome in Ferrara, under the patronage of the music-mad Alfonso II, last of the Este dukes of that city. Ferrara could boast of a long history of musical distinction reaching back into the mid fifteenth century. Under Ercole I (d. 1505) such famous musicians as Josquin, Obrecht, Martini, and Brumel were in ducal service.[26] During the first half of the sixteenth century Willaert (until 1527), Maître Jhan, and members of the Dalla Viola family, including two madrigalists, Alfonso and Francesco, were in Estense employ. Cipriano de Rore spent some years before and after 1550 in Ferrara. Alfonso II, who just before his succession in 1559 sponsored the publication of Willaert's *Musica nova*, was the most dedicated patron of music of any Italian ruler, particularly in the latter part of his reign. In 1580 the duke instituted a regular—in fact, daily—concert life on the part of his *musica privata*. Wert spent much time in Ferrara in the 1580s, and the celebrated "singing ladies" of Ferrara, including Tarquinia Molza, Laura Peperara, Lucrezia Bendidio, Anna Guarini, and Livia d'Arco, brought the performance of women and of professional singers in general to new heights.[27] Alfonso's chief resident composer in this period was Luzzasco Luzzaschi, perhaps a student of Rore, a celebrated organist and a prolific madrigalist. It is to him (and to Wert) that the beginnings of a new period of experiment in the madrigal are owing. Luzzaschi wrote music, high in range and full of vocal ornament, for the court sopranos (it was very much Alfonso's private music and was not published until after the duke's death). He also wrote seven books of five-voice madrigals in which the move toward the style of the 1590s may be traced. Varied textures, use of contrast motifs, occasional employment of chromaticism and above all a tendency toward fragmentation—change of mood and style heading toward hair-trigger response to the affective message of the text—made of Luzzaschi's madrigals a model to be emulated, if possible to be surpassed.

The Ferrarese nobleman Alfonso Fontanelli, who published his madrigals *senza nome*, followed in Luzzaschi's path. So did one of the most curious characters among madrigalists, the Neapolitan Carlo Gesualdo, prince of Venosa. Gesualdo spent some time in Ferrara following his marriage (a second one, his first wife having been murdered by him or at his behest) to a princess of the Este family. He

[26] See Lewis Lockwood, *Music in Renaissance Ferrara, 1400–1505* (Cambridge, MA, 1984).

[27] Anthony Newcomb, *The Madrigal at Ferrara, 1579–1597*, 2 vols. (Princeton, 1978).

spoke openly of his wish to surpass Luzzaschi, and indeed Gesualdo's six books of madrigals, particularly the last four, are a kind of *ne plus ultra* of the polyphonic madrigal, alternating chordal writing of startlingly chromatic nature with canzonetta-like diatonic counterpoint. Gesualdo's madrigals are rather short—he chose brief epigrammatic verse to set—and their oddity is thereby more pronounced. In the hands of really expert singers these pieces are more effective than one might have imagined, but they mark a point beyond which no other madrigalist was to go.[28]

The Madrigal outside Italy

During the period 1570–1620 the writing of madrigals to Italian texts was practiced intermittently in the Netherlands, France, Germany, and Denmark, by composers most of whom spent short periods of time as students in Italy. Perhaps the most important figure among these musicians was Hans Leo Hassler (d. 1612), who studied briefly with Andrea Gabrieli in Venice and was then active in Augsburg and Nuremberg. Continental composers were of course attracted to the canzonetta, but a few cutivated the serious madrigal as exemplified by Marenzio and, later, Monteverdi.[29] The most extraordinary vogue of the madrigal outside Italy was in England, where poets and composers of a body of work written for the most part between 1590 and 1610 achieved a unique vernacular blend of English tradition with Italian literary and musical traits. This repertory, revived by antiquarian groups as early as the mid eighteenth century, remains popular today and for many amateur singing groups represents, despite its idiosyncratic character, the madrigal in general.[30]

The Reformation in England upset whatever musical cosmopolitanism had developed during the reign of Henry VIII. Things Italian were likely to be regarded as papist, even Jesuitical; and in any event the English tradition of solo song (with polyphonic accompaniment) was a sturdily resistant one. Some Italian musicians did visit and even live in England in the earlier years of Elizabeth's reign; chief among them was the elder Alfonso Ferrabosco, a Bolognese composer who wrote madrigals—to Italian texts—that gained some currency in England. The development of the madrigal in England was, however, to depend on the availability of English texts, for the insular aversion to speaking foreign tongues extended to singing as well.

An English brand of Petrarchism began to develop with the sonnet-writing of Thomas Wyat and Henry Howard, Earl of Surrey, in the last years of Henry VIII's reign. It took on new impetus with the work of Spenser and Sidney, some thirty years later, the beginnings of the great flowering of Elizabethan lyric, epic, and

28 See Glenn Watkins, *Gesualdo: The Man and his Music* (London, 1973).

29 Jerome Roche, *The Madrigal*, 2nd edn (London, 1990), ch. 7: "The Madrigal North of the Alps."

30 The best survey of the English madrigal is Joseph Kerman, *The Elizabethan Madrigal: A Comparative Study* (American Musicological Society, 1962).

dramatic poetry. Settings of serious English poetry were not, however, to be the mainstay of Elizabethan madrigalists. The immediate impulse to native composers seems to have been the success of several London-printed anthologies, the most celebrated being *Musica transalpina* (1588), of Italian madrigals in English translation. The works chosen (probably by way of Netherlandish anthologies of the early 1580s) were canzonettas and madrigals, including a number by Marenzio, in a light and bright canzonetta-influenced style. These, and the *balletti* of Gastoldi, served as models for English composers up to the turn of the century.

The most prolific and most successful of these composers was Thomas Morley, a member of the Chapel Royal, a music publisher, and a well-educated musician (he had studied with William Byrd) who wrote the most delightfully chatty of sixteenth-century music treatises, *A Plaine and Easie Introduction to Practicall Musicke* (1597). Morley knew Italian music fairly well, and borrowed freely from its lighter side. His canzonets and ballets and madrigals have a good deal of charm, though they tend to be schematic and to impose music on their often beguiling texts rather than to be composed out of verbal sound and meaning.

At the turn of the century a more serious vein in the English madrigal revealed itself in the music of composers such as John Wilbye and Thomas Weelkes, who wrote five- and six-voice madrigals of some complexity. Sometimes choosing verse loaded with imagery suitable for madrigalian conceits (the extreme is perhaps Weelkes' setting of *Thule, the period of cosmographie*, with its references to icebergs, volcanic fire, exotic bazaars, all in outlandish locales and all in the service of a Petrarchistic lover "whose heart with fear doth freeze, with love doth fry"), they managed to squeeze in a good many Italianate word-painting figures. At the same time they showed, within the generally rather narrow bounds of the genre, a command of contrapuntal skills that, as younger contemporaries of the great William Byrd, they might be expected to possess.

The Closing Years of the Madrigal

The last period of the Italian madrigal is dominated for us—perhaps a bit unfairly—by a single phenomenon, the continuo-accompanied monody, and by a single composer, Claudio Monteverdi. Unfairly because monody (a term not used during the period) is part of a larger subject, the development of explicitly scored concerted vocal music. And Monteverdi, a composer of indisputable stature, was not the only distinguished madrigalist of the early seventeenth century.

Participation of instruments in the performance of madrigals, apart from their complete intabulation as lute or keyboard pieces, must have been of common occurrence even if unaccompanied singing, one person to a part, was the assumed norm. Evidence for this participation is scattered, and in the domain of visual depictions of music-making, not especially reliable. Publishers did advertise on title pages of madrigal books the music's suitability for instruments ("da cantare o sonare" or the English "apt for voices or viols"). Festive madrigals such as those written for Medici celebrations in 1539, 1565, and 1589, were accompanied by a wide variety of instruments, as we are told in contemporary accounts.[31] In more intimate surroundings madrigals could be sung as solo songs with instrumental accompaniment made up of some form of the other vocal lines. But true concerted style, with parts written specifically for instruments, did not appear openly in the madrigal until the end of the sixteenth century (it was a notable feature of Venetian sacred music of the period).

Conservative attitudes in notating music, always strong even if our tendency is to view notation before 1600 as a series of breakthroughs and novelties, may be in part responsible, concealing developments that were taking place during the last quarter of the century. Emphasis on high soprano parts, particularly in duets widely separated from the lower voices, is a mark of both the lighter madrigal and the experimental Ferrarese style of the 1580s and 90s; this is surely an example of a Baroque texture *avant la lettre*, and there are others. Collections of *arie*, settings of strophic verse for one or two sopranos and a tenor/bass, were printed in all-vocal form but circulated as early as the 1570s as music for voice(s) and lute or a bass plucked string instrument.

The *aria*, music for strophic verse (ottava stanzas, *terza rima*, etc.), had already begun its long history as concerted solo song. Giulio Caccini's *Nuove musiche* of 1602 contains arias supported by continuo bass parts. The highly ornamented vocal lines may not be as original in style as Caccini claimed; the practice of using elaborate vocal diminutions was well established, if on the whole limited to professional singers. Caccini, by publishing his work, which itself was certainly not brand-new, implied that his *arie* were within the grasp of amateur singers (the continuo parts are indeed easy); one wonders if this could have been true. The whole climate for madrigal performance had changed; the best composers were writing for professional musicians, and the new monodic aria was created for performance before an audience.

Caccini's volume contains madrigals—non-strophic verse—as well as arias. Thus the solo continuo madrigal made its debut, and many composers began to cultivate it, notably in and around Florence but in northern Italy and in Rome as well. Not everyone did so; for Monteverdi the solo madrigal was not an important genre (the solo aria, in the early-seventeenth-century sense of the term, is of course a feature of his operas). Collections of madrigals and arias for varying numbers of voices supported by the new continuo bass, sometimes linked into proto-cantatas through use of refrains and instrumental ritornelli, appeared with increasing frequency, eventually pushing the unaccompanied polyphonic madrigal into the background, though not completely out of the picture.[32] Use of stereotyped bass patterns, the Romanesca, Ruggiero, etc., for concerted strophic variations became common, were a trademark of composers such as the Roman Antonio Cifra.

[31] See Howard Mayer Brown, *Sixteenth-Century Instrumentation: the Music for the Florentine Intermedi* (American Institute of Musicology, 1978).

[32] Madrigal anthologies in the 17th century, even when they are fully polyphonic, often come with *basso continuo* parts as a pure matter of fashion. Unaccompanied madrigals are often sets of *madrigali spirituali*; anthologies of secular madrigals are increasingly the work of provincial Italian publishers or of foreign, especially Flemish firms.

Prominent among madrigalists who wrote both polyphonic vocal music and concerted solo or few-voice pieces are the Florentine Marco da Gagliano and the Sicilians Antonio Il Verso and Sigismondo d'India, the latter active in various courts in northern Italy. Their work is of very high quality, and has in recent years begun to attract the attention it deserves. The judgement of posterity has however long been that the greatest madrigalist of the period is Claudio Monteverdi of Cremona, who served the Mantuan court from the early 1590s to 1612 and was *maestro di cappella* at St Mark's in Venice from 1613 until his death in 1643.

Monteverdi began precociously but conventionally for the time, with a set of spiritual madrigals (1583; he was born in 1567) and a set of three-voice canzonettas. His First Book of five-voice madrigals (1587) is less adventurous than the current work of Marenzio. With his Second Book of 1590 Monteverdi shows himself to be in full command of new madrigalian styles; here one sees use of contrast motifs, of sharply profiled rhetorical gestures, of soprano duet texture. Madrigals of strong individuality, such as the famous *Ecco mormorar l'onde* with its graphic mood-painting, stand out in this volume. In 1592 Monteverdi published his Third Book. He had now stopped calling himself "pupil of Ingegneri"; it is rather Wert, especially the latter's strongly declamatory chordal style, who is his model, Guarini and Tasso his poets, with more serious verse beginning to replace the pastoral mode so popular in the 1580s. The Third Book was successful and often reprinted.

Book Four did not appear until 1603, though some of its contents had been in circulation for several years previous to its publication. It is dedicated to a Ferrarese academy in a letter in which the composer laments his inability to present his work to Duke Alfonso (d. 1597). Guarini is again the favored poet, and again his more serious side is preferred. It is in this book, beginning with its opening piece *Ah, dolente partita*, that Monteverdi establishes himself as a "modern" composer, using fragmented textures, daring melodic intervals, some (never very extreme) chromaticism, and freedom of dissonance treatment. Much of this was inspired by Ferrarese experimentalism, but some of the rule-breaking dissonance treatment may derive from observation of monodic song.

This book and the closely following Fifth Book (1605) contain pieces singled out for criticism by the Bolognese theorist Giovanni Maria Artusi. Monteverdi's defense, hinted at in a letter appended to Book Five and outlined more fully in a "declaration" by his brother Giulio Cesare in the *Scherzi musicali* of 1607, took the form of announcing that Monteverdi followed a *seconda pratica* in which, without disrespect for the orthodox polyphony of the *prima pratica*, the sense and affective quality of the text justified transgression of contrapuntal rules. Much, perhaps too much, has been written about this subject.[33] Artusi admired Monteverdi's music as a whole, criticizing only details of the music considered apart from the text. And Monteverdi was in no way an extremist or a revolutionary. He was a good publicist on his own behalf, and the whole of the *seconda pratica* flap

[33] A solid and thoughtful treatment of the subject is that of Tim Carter, "Artusi, Monteverdi, and the Poetics of Modern Music," in *Musical Humanism and its Legacy: Essays in Honor of Claude V. Palisca*, ed. N. K. Baker and B. R. Hanning (Stuyvesant, NY, 1992), 171–94.

(Monteverdi's promised treatise on the subject was never written) is not a great deal more than effective self-advertising.

In the Fifth Book a continuo bass, "per il clavicembalo Chittarone od altro simile stromento," is added, optional for most of the volume since it is merely a *basso seguente*, reproducing the lowest-sounding vocal part; the last six pieces are however true concerted madrigals. So are many pieces in Book Six (1614), famous for its inclusion of the lament from Monteverdi's opera *Arianna* of 1608, here arranged for five voices, and for the sestina *Lagrime d'amante al sepolcro dell'amata*, an elegy for the Mantuan singer Caterina Martinelli. The Seventh Book (1619) is entitled *Concerto*. It contains several monodies, an extraordinary concertato solo work, *Con che soavità*, a number of concertato duets, and a *ballo concertato*, *Tirsi e Clori*, which had been performed in Mantua in 1616 (the volume is dedicated to the duchess of Mantua). Like Gagliano and other contemporaries, Monteverdi had now moved completely into the domain of the concerted style.

Not until 1633 did Monteverdi's eighth and final book (there is a posthumous Ninth Book of miscellaneous content), entitled *Madrigali guerrieri et amorosi*, appear. It is an extraordinary collection of small- and large-scale works written over a period of many years. In his preface Monteverdi speaks of the chief human emotions, "Ira, Temperanza, & Humiltà," and of three types of music, "concitato, molle, & temperata." Of these latter the *stile concitato*, to represent warlike anger, is his own invention; it consists largely of rapid repeated-note patterns played by strings. Monteverdi, the greatest dramatist among madrigalists, identifies several pieces in the Eighth Book as being in "genere rappresentativo"; one of these is the *Combattimento di Tancredi e Clorinda* (from Tasso's *Gerusalemme liberata*), which had been performed in Venice in 1624 and which introduced *stile concertato* for the first time. The book as a whole is a kind of testament of Monteverdi's later attitudes toward the madrigal.

Monteverdi's career as madrigalist has been described more fully than that of other composers not only because of his great achievement but because he sums up the whole final phase of the madrigal.[34] Born as chamber song for literary-minded musical amateurs, the madrigal ended as dramatic, even flamboyant concerted music for professionals to perform before an audience. The genre did not die; it transmuted itself into an almost unrecognizably distant relation when compared to its forebears. As a musical family it is second to none in vitality, breadth, and scope.

[34] A challenging consideration of Monteverdi as madrigalist is that of Tomlinson, *Monteverdi and the End of the Renaissance*. See also Eric Chafe, *Monteverdi's Tonal Language* (New York, 1992); Silke Leopold, *Monteverdi: Music in Transition*, trans. Anne Smith (Oxford, 1991); Paolo Fabbri, *Monteverdi*, trans. Tim Carter (Cambridge, 1994).

14

THE NETHERLANDS, 1520–1640

Kristine K. Forney

1520–1560

IN the sixteenth century, the Netherlands, or Low Countries, embraced the region including modern-day Belgium, Luxemburg, and the Netherlands, as well as, to the south, the French provinces of Artois and Hainault. These lands were drawn into the Habsburg Empire in the late fifteenth century through the marriage of Mary of Burgundy to Maximilian I (r. 1493–1519). During the era 1520–1560, Emperor Charles V (r. 1519–55) ruled the Netherlands from distant Madrid, placing regional authority with the regent of the Low Countries. Despite this regency, held by his aunt Marguerite of Austria (r. 1506–30) and his sister Mary of Hungary (r. 1531–55), the area was politically weak, divided by language and growing religious differences.

The revolt of the Netherlands against Spanish authority was brought on by complex religious, political, and economic issues that culminated in the outbreak of war in 1566. Lutheranism and Calvinism, introduced to the region by German and Swiss merchants, slowly gained sympathy and support among the free-thinking Netherlanders. The swift and violent response to the Protestant movement by Charles V only strengthened the Reform in the north, and many musicians were among those who converted to the new faiths.

The Netherlands was an urban culture in which musical activities were as strongly linked to cities as to the Burgundian-Habsburg courts. Ecclesiastical and civic support of the arts was manifested in the renowned choirs and thriving wind bands throughout the Low Countries. With the growing bourgeoisie, a new class of music consumers arose, who in turn supported the trades of music printing and publishing as well as instrument building.

In this era, important musical centers included, in the southern Netherlands, the cities of Antwerp, Brussels, Cambrai, Liège, Mechlin, Bruges, Ghent, and 's-Hertogenbosch, and in the northern Netherlands, Amsterdam, Utrecht, Leiden, and Haarlem. From the beginning of the sixteenth century, however, the cultural, artistic, and economic life of the Netherlands was focused in Antwerp.

The post-Josquin generation of Netherlandish composers

Northern composers living after 1520 generally took over and developed the compositional techniques of Josquin des Prez and his contemporaries. The Netherlandish or Franco-Flemish style, which had been the mainstream throughout Europe in the late fifteenth and early sixteenth centuries, flourished in the hands of a generation of musicians represented by Nicolas Gombert, Thomas Crecquillon, Jacob Clemens, and Adrian Willaert, as well as numerous lesser-known composers. Marked by pervading imitation and dense textures, often for five, six, or eight voices, this style was applied to most major genres: the mass, in which imitation was frequently coupled with parody technique; the motet, often characterized by broad, melismatic lines set imitatively; and the Franco-Flemish chanson, a relatively new national style based largely on points of imitation and various borrowing procedures. Following Josquin, northern composers grew increasingly aware of the expressive properties of music, striving for an ideal union of text and music. Some, like Adrian Willaert, Cipriano de Rore, and later Philippe de Monte, spent their productive careers in Italy, and thus infused the northern imitative style with a new expression while turning also to native Italian genres such as the madrigal. The diverse interests of Netherlandish composers in developing national styles paved the way for Orlande de Lassus (Orlando di Lasso), a truly European figure.

Nicolas Gombert (*c.*1495–*c.*1560), a native of Flanders, served the Madrid court of Emperor Charles V, first as a singer in 1526 and then as master of the children. He was later exiled from the court and may have retired to Tournai, in modern-day Belgium. Gombert's ten extant masses are mostly based on parody; two draw on his own motets, including the *Missa "Beata omnes"*, which unusually reduces the model's five voices to four. The *Missa "Sur tous regretz"*, on a chanson by the Netherlander Jean Richafort, may have been written for the 1530 coronation of Charles V in Bologna. The northern preference for many-voiced polyphony can be seen in Gombert's *Missa tempore paschali*, one of his two masses based on plainchant. This work's six-voice texture is expanded to eight for the Credo and to twelve for the Agnus Dei.[1]

Gombert also wrote over 160 motets, many of which set biblical or Marian texts. Among the latter are two settings (*a* 10 and *a* 12) of the antiphon *Regina caeli*. These works are typical of his style, characterized by a seamless texture made up of points of imitation at varied intervals. His four-voice *Salve regina*, which sets seven Marian antiphons, typifies the northern interest in symbolism.

Gombert's secular output includes some seventy chansons ranging from three to eight voices; a number of these further demonstrate the composer's interest in parody and other borrowing techniques. Several are modelled on Josquin chansons,

[1] The standard reference on Gombert is N. Schmidt-Görg, *Nicolas Gombert, Kapellmeister Karls V: Leben und Werk* (Bonn, 1938; rev. ed. Tutzing, 1971). On compositional techniques in Gombert's masses, see I. Bossuyt, "Nicolas Gombert and Parody," *Tijdschrift voor muziektheorie*, 8/2 (May 2003), 112–22; and C. A. Elias, "Imitation, Fragmentation, and Assimilation of Chansons in the Masses of Gombert, Clemens, and Crecquillon: A Kaleidoscopic Process" (PhD diss., University of Chicago, 1994).

including *Mille regretz* and *En l'ombre d'un buissonet*; Gombert set both chansons for six voices, the latter work using derived canonic techniques.[2] Most of Gombert's chansons are motetlike in texture, based on pervading imitation and variation techniques; several, including two programmatic works drawn from Janequin, are lighter in vein.

Thomas Crecquillon (*c.*1505/15–1557) was another Netherlandish master to work at the Madrid court, where he served as chapelmaster and later as chaplain. He also held a benefice in the north, at Dendermonde, and a canonicate at Béthune, where he retired in 1555. Most of Crecquillon's twelve masses demonstrate parody procedures; five of these works are based on his own motets and chansons. The remaining masses are, for the most part, for four voices and are modelled on widely known chansons, including Pierre Sandrin's *Doulce memoire*, Rogier Pathie's *D'amour me plains*, and Clemens's *Je prens en gré*.[3]

His motets, approximately 125 in all, are often structured on points of imitation for each new phrase, with smoothly flowing melodies and harmonies. Crecquillon also wrote more than 200 chansons, most of which were published by Antwerp and Louvain printers. Like his masses, Crecquillon's secular works depend heavily on parody technique; a number of them rework chansons by others, such as his three-voice *Content desir*, based on a Sermisy prototype. Some chansons display the composer's interest in the "response" phenomenon, in which sets of two or three works that are related textually, often in a dialogue, also share musical elements. Crecquillon wrote a number of these chanson groups himself, and he engaged in musical dialogue with other composers, including Josquin Baston and Tielman Susato.[4]

The career of Jacob Clemens (*c.*1510–*c.*1555/6) was much less public than those of his contemporaries Gombert and Crecquillon. He was a priest and church musician who held positions in Bruges, Ypres, and 's-Hertogenbosch, all in the Southern Netherlands. Clemens (enigmatically called "non Papa") is best remembered for his sacred music: fourteen parody Masses, a Requiem mass, about 230 motets, two Magnificat cycles, and over 150 Flemish devotional songs, called *souterliedekens* (see below, p. 253). His masses, set for four and five voices, depend largely on parody technique, using contemporary motets and chansons by Willaert, Gombert, Manchicourt, Hellinck, Lupi, Silva, and Sermisy as models. One work, the *Missa "Pastores quidnam vidistis"*, takes Clemens' own five-voice motet as its basis, reworking the model's lines into a prolonged imitative framework.[5]

His motets are generally on biblical or liturgical texts; most are freely composed and set in two large parts with a musical and textual refrain at the end of each

[2] See O. Rees, "*Mille regretz* as Model: Possible Allusions to 'The Emperor's Song' in the Chanson Repertory," *Journal of the Royal Musical Association*, 120 (1995), 44–76.

[3] Elias, "Imitation, Fragmentation, and Assimilation."

[4] K. Forney, "New Insights into the Career and Musical Contributions of Tielman Susato," in *Tielman Susato and the Context of Instrumental Music in Northern Renaissance Europe*, ed. K. Polk and J. Nussbaum (Hillsdale, NY, 2005), 1–44.

[5] Elias, "Imitation, Fragmentation, and Assimilation."

part. His seven-voice *Ego flos campi*, on a text from the Song of Songs, was written for the Marian Brotherhood of Our Lady at 's-Hertogenbosch, possibly upon his departure from that city; its seven-voice framework is undoubtedly symbolic of Marian numerology. This work, like many of Clemens' motets and Magnificats, has survived in the Leiden choirbooks, an important manuscript collection from the northern Netherlands that also includes works by Josquin, Willaert, and Crecquillon.

Many lesser-known northern masters contributed to the developing northern musical genres; these include Pierre Manchicourt, Cornelius Canis, Johannes Lupi, Benedictus Appenzeller, Jean Courtois, Josquin Baston, Hubert Waelrant, Lupus Hellinck, Jean Caulery, and Johannes Castileti (alias Guyot), all of whom held positions in either the courts or churches of the Netherlands and whose works, both sacred and secular, were disseminated throughout Europe from the presses of the Low Countries.

Netherlanders in Italy

Following the career path of many composers since the fifteenth century, Adrian Willaert and Cipriano de Rore both went to Italy as young men. Willaert (*c.*1485–1562) was in the service of the Este family by 1516 until 1527, when he was named choirmaster at St Mark's in Venice. During his thirty-five years there, he attracted many pupils, including Rore, Zarlino, and Jacob Buus. Willaert's large output of sacred music includes eight masses—several based on motets by Jean Mouton—170 motets, many psalm settings and hymns as well as two Magnificats. His double-chorus psalms are important contributions to the developing polychoral style that culminated in the works of Giovanni Gabrieli, and his motets, set for four to seven voices, display wide-ranging contrapuntal techniques.[6] A madrigal composer as well, Willaert's later Italian works display expressive features typical of the middle period of the genre. His collection *Musica nova*, published in 1559 but composed much earlier, contains 33 multipartite motets and 25 madrigals, the latter nearly all on sonnets by Petrarch.

Cipriano de Rore (*c.*1515–1565) traveled to Italy as a youth, where by 1546 he was appointed to the prestigious position of chapelmaster in Ferrara. Rore wrote five masses, several of which draw from Josquin's techniques and works. *Missa "Vivat felix Hercules"* is based on a *soggetto cavato dalle vocali*, much like the earlier master's *Missa "Hercules Dux Ferrariae"*. His motets, some eighty in number, reflect northern contrapuntal techniques coupled with Italian lyricism; some of these are on classical Latin texts, including the expressively chromatic *Calami sonum*. Rore's parody mass on his own chanson *Tout ce qu'on peut* also reflects the influence of his madrigal style in its notation *a note nere*. Some of his early madrigals employ this blackened, or *cromatico*, notation as well, and his first madrigal collection (1542) is

[6] A. Carver, "The Psalms of Willaert and His North Italian Contemporaries," *Acta musicologica*, 47 (1975), 270–83.

one of the earliest modally ordered music books.[7] Rore's five-voice *Da le belle contrade*, first published in 1566 and perhaps his most famous work, reflects his ability to set both the individual imagery of the words and ideas as well as the overall stark emotions of the anonymous sonnet.

Music printing and the dissemination of Netherlandish polyphony

Music printing was relatively late in coming to the Netherlands; by the 1520s, however, Antwerp was an established center for printed liturgical books, rivaling Paris in this trade. Christoffel van Ruremund, a Dutchman active in Antwerp from 1522 to 1531, issued publications for use at Utrecht and Brussels as well as a series of music books for the English, or Sarum, rite. The first music printing privilege in the Netherlands was granted to Symon Cock in 1539 to print "spiritual and devotional books." He issued two titles, including a highly popular collection of *souterliedekens*, or psalms set to popular tunes. Shortly thereafter, three significant music printing firms were established in the region: those of Tielman Susato and Hubert Waelrant & Jan de Laet, both in Antwerp; and that of Pierre Phalèse in Louvain.[8]

Tielman Susato (*c.*1515–*c.*1571) was the first to make a successful career of music printing in the Low Countries. A native of northern Germany, Susato worked as a music copyist and a city instrumentalist prior to the establishment of his printing shop in 1543. Over the next eighteen years, he issued 22 chanson books, 19 motet books, three mass books, and eleven Dutch-texted titles, including the well-known *Danserye* (1551), a collection of elegant dance settings, many of them arrangements of popular chansons.[9]

Susato's publications include works by major Netherlandish composers of the day, including Crecquillon, Gombert, Clemens, Pierre Manchicourt, and Orlande de Lassus, as well as many minor masters, among them Cornelius Canis, Johannes Castileti, Benedictus Appenzeller, Josquin Baston, and Susato himself. The motet prints were issued in two series: *Cantiones sacrae*, a four-book series for four and five voices, and *Ecclesiasticarum cantionum*, a large, modally organized series of 14 books, also for four and five voices. The motets, mostly built on through-imitative procedures, are identified in the prints by their biblical text citation or their liturgical occasion.[10] This repertory undoubtedly served as music for lay confraternal services as well as for the Mass and Office.

[7] Martha Feldman, "Rore's *Selva Selvaggia*: The Primo Libro of 1542," *Journal of the American Musicological Society*, 42 (1989), 547–603.

[8] On these firms, see E. Schreurs and H. Vanhulst, eds. *Music Printing in Antwerp and Europe in the 16th Century* [Antwerp, 23–25 Aug. 1995], Yearbook of the Alamire Foundation, 2 (Leuven and Peer, 1997).

[9] Susato's publications and compositions are discussed in various essays in *Tielman Susato and the Music of His Time*. On Susato as a printer, see K. Forney, "Tielman Susato, Sixteenth-Century Music Printer: An Archival and Typographical Investigation" (PhD diss., University of Kentucky, 1978).

[10] The five-voice motets from books 5–12 of Susato's *Ecclesiasticarum cantionum* are edited by R. Sherr in *The Sixteenth-Century Motet*, XV–XIX: *The Susato Motet Anthologies* (New York, 1995–96).

The chanson collections issued by Susato reflect the interest of northern composers in cantus firmus, paraphrase, and parody procedures. Many of these works set well-known texts of the day and draw on widely circulated chansons as musical models. Among the composers who employed musical borrowing techniques were Clemens, Crecquillon, Gombert, Canis, and Susato himself. Unlike the characteristically four-voice French chanson, these Franco-Flemish works are frequently set for large numbers of voices—in five, six, or eight parts.[11]

Susato's firm was particularly important for the transmission of Josquin chansons; the *Septième Livre des chansons* of 1545 includes 22 late works for five and six voices by the master, as well as three elegies on his death, written by Jeronimus Vinders, Benedictus Appenzeller, and Nicolas Gombert. This book, published 24 years after the death of Josquin, not only attests to the longevity of his works, but is the earliest printed source for many of the chansons. Susato's dedication explains his reasons for printing this retrospective repertory: "the present book of chansons for five and six voices, [was] composed by the late lamented Josquin des Prez, in his time most excellent and highly eminent in music knowledge.... I wanted to begin to print these works so that everyone would be able to keep them in perpetual memory as he well deserved."[12]

The Netherlandish polyphonic lied was also widely disseminated from Antwerp's presses. Two books of four-voice Flemish love songs, some with racy lyrics, were issued by Susato in 1551, and included works by Clemens, Josquin Baston, Lupus Hellinck, and Benedictus Appenzeller.[13] Baston's *Lecker Beetgen en Cleyn Bier* (Tasty Tidbit and Small Beer) draws largely on through-imitation and paired voicing to describe the nocturnal adventures of the shady characters personified in its title.

Pierre Phalèse opened his music publishing firm in 1545 in the university town of Louvain; he specialized at first in French lute intabulations and thereby cornered the market for solo instrumental music.[14] In 1554, Phalèse commenced a motet series including works by Clemens, Gombert, and Crecquillon, and beginning in

[11] *The Sixteenth-Century Chanson*, ed. J. Bernstein, XXIX–XXX: *Chansons Published by Tielman Susato*, ed. K. Forney (New York, 1994); K. Forney (ed.), *"Response" and "Replicque in the Franco-Flemish Chanson Publications of Tielman Susato*, Recent Researches in the Music of the Renaissance (Middleton, WI, forthcoming).

[12] See B. J. Blackburn, "Josquin's Chansons: Ignored and Lost Sources," *Journal of the American Musicological Society*, 29 (1976), 30–76; L. Bernstein, "Chansons for Five and Six Voices," in *The Josquin Companion*, ed. R. Sherr (Oxford, 2000), 393–422. Some scholars have questioned the attributions in this late publication.

[13] See T. McTaggart, "Susato's *Musyck Boexken* I and II: Music for a Flemish Middle Class" in *Music Printing in Antwerp and Europe in the 16th Century*, Yearbook of the Alamire Foundation, 2 (1995), 307–22; idem (ed.), *Musyck Boexcken, Books 1 and 2*, Recent Researches in the Music of the Renaissance, 108 (Madison, WI, 1997). On the Netherlandish polyphonic lied, see E. Schreurs, *Het Nederlandse polyfone lied* (Peer, 1986); B. Lenaerts, *Het Nederlandse polifonies lied in de zestiende eeuw* (Mechlin and Amsterdam, 1933).

[14] H. Vanhulst, *Catalogue des éditions de musique publiées à Louvain par Pierre Phalèse et ses fils, 1545–1578*, Académie royale de Belgique, Mémoires de la classe des beaux-arts, ser. 2, 16 (Brussels, 1990).

1556, he issued a series of ten parody masses by Jacob Clemens (*a* 4, 5, and 6), each based on a pre-existent motet or chanson.

Perhaps the most popular publication emanating from the Phalèse firm was the *Livre septième des chansons*, first issued in 1560 and reprinted more than thirty times over the next hundred years. This was a large, retrospective anthology of four-voice chansons by both Franco-Flemish and Parisian composers, many of which were already widely disseminated in Paris and Lyons as well as Antwerp. The volume was an immediate success with the musical public, and the longevity of the title was unparalleled by any other publication.[15] The Phalèse music printing house was the most prolific firm in the Low Countries, remaining in business in Louvain and then Antwerp until 1674.

One additional Antwerp printing firm resulted from a partnership (in the 1550s) between the composer Hubert Waelrant and the printer Jan de Laet.[16] Their first publications included a motet series dominated by the works of Jacob Clemens and Thomas Crecquillon. This firm also released three books of French psalm settings by Jean Louys, and the *Jardin musical* series, a four-volume anthology of chansons and *chansons spirituelles*—works with a religious or moralizing text. This chanson collection contained 97 works by, among others, Clemens, Crecquillon, Jean Caulery, and Waelrant himself.[17] The final publication of the Waelrant–de Laet firm was dedicated to five-part madrigals and chansons by Waelrant, an enigmatic composer who may have studied in Italy and whose works reflect careful attention to text expression. Waelrant's most progressive style is exhibited in his motets, which resemble those of Lassus published in Antwerp in 1556; his treatment of chromaticism led Edward Lowinsky to conjecture the presence of a "secret chromatic art" in certain of his motets.[18] Waelrant, like many northerners, showed sympathy for the growing Reform through his publications of works appropriate for Calvinist worship.

[15] See H. Vanhulst, "Un Succès de l'édition musicale: *Le Septièsme Livre des chansons à quatre parties*," *Revue belge de musicologie*, 32–33 (1978–79), 97–120; R. Rasch, "The Livre septième," in *Trasmissione e recezione delle forme di cultura musicale: Atti del XIV Congresso della Società internazionale de musicologia, Bologna, 27 viii – 1 ix 1987*, ed. A. Pompilio et al. (Turin, 1990), 1: 306–18.

[16] R. L. Weaver, *A Descriptive Bibliographical Catalog of the Music Printed by Hubert Waelrant and Jan de Laet*, Detroit Studies in Music Bibliography, 73 (Warren, MI, 1994); idem, *Waelrant and Laet: Music Publishers in Antwerp's Golden Age*, Detroit Monographs in Musicology/Studies in Music, 15 (Warren, MI, 1995).

[17] *The Sixteenth-Century Chanson*, I–II: *Chansons Published by Hubert Waelrant and Jean Laet*, ed. T. McTaggart (New York, 1992).

[18] Edward E. Lowinsky, *Secret Chromatic Art in the Netherlands Motet*, trans. Carl Buchman (New York, 1946). For a modern edition of his motets, see Hubert Waelrant, *Liber sextus sacrarum cantionum*, ed. Robert Lee Weaver, Recent Researches in the Music of the Renaissance, 125 (Middleton, WI, 2001).

The Reformation and music in the north

One of the most notable influences of the Reformation on music was the publication in 1540 of the first Dutch Psalter, a rhymed metrical translation of the Book of Psalms set to pre-existent melodies. Issued in Antwerp by printer Symon Cock, this collection, entitled *Souterliedekens*, was immensely popular, undergoing at least nine further editions printed by Cock, and another twenty editions by other Netherlandish printers. Although the Psalms had always held a privileged place in the Catholic liturgy, they acquired a renewed importance in this era, since Calvin preached that only the unaccompanied singing of the Psalms in the vernacular was appropriate to the Reformed liturgy.

Souterliedekens were sung to popular monophonic tunes of the day, mostly Dutch folk songs, many of which also appeared in the secular collection popularly known as the *Antwerps Liedboeck*, published in 1544 by Jan Roulans.[19] These same texts and tunes were set polyphonically by several Netherlandish composers, including Jacob Clemens, who composed 140 of the psalms for three voices. Clemens set the popular tunes as cantus firmi in the tenor, and occasionally the superius, voice. His *souterliedekens* are texted throughout in simple, syllabic settings that are occasionally imitative. These works were published in Antwerp in 1556–57 by Susato in a series that also included four books of settings by Clemens' disciple Gherardus Mes, issued in 1561.[20] Cornelius Buscop, an organist and composer active in Delft in the northern Netherlands, set fifty of the psalms for four voices, published in Düsseldorf in 1568.

The simplicity of these polyphonic psalm settings strongly suggests they were intended for home devotional use. Nevertheless, *souterliedekens* were soon associated with the Calvinist movement, and vernacular psalm singing in the Church was linked with the iconoclastic revolt of the 1560s, especially in the northern Netherlands.[21]

The earliest polyphonic psalm settings published in the Netherlands were not in Dutch, but in French. Jan Louys wrote three books of *Pseaulmes de David* for five voices, published in Antwerp in 1554–55; these used Clément Marot's French versification of the psalms and were set to tunes from the Genevan, or Huguenot, Psalter.[22] Unlike Flemish *souterliedekens*, the French settings are imitative and highly melismatic. As with other *chansons spirituelles*, these psalm settings may have originally been intended as devotional music for Catholics as well as Protestants;

[19] K. Vellekoop and H. Wagenaar-Nolthenius (eds.), *Het Antwerps Liedboek: 87 melodieën op teksten uit "Een Schoon Liedekens-Boeck" van 1544*, 2 vols. (Amsterdam, 1975).

[20] L. P. Grijp, "The Souterliedekens by Gherardus Mes (1561): An Enigmatic Pupil of Clemens non Papa, and Popular Song of the Mid-Sixteenth Century," in *From Ciconia to Sweelinck: Donum natalicium Willem Elders*, ed. A. Clement and E. Jas (Amsterdam and Atlanta, 1994), 245–54.

[21] H. Bruinsma, "The 'Souterliedekens' and its Relation to Psalmody in the Netherlands" (PhD diss., University of Michigan, 1949).

[22] H. J. Slenk, "The Huguenot Psalter in the Low Countries" (PhD diss., Ohio State University, 1965).

however, their use of the Genevan melodies linked them with Calvinism. A decade later, the Regent of the Low Countries banned a French psalter published in Antwerp based not on its vernacular texts but on its use of the heretical Genevan tunes.[23]

Both Catholic and Protestant composers contributed to the large body of *chansons spirituelles* published in the Low Countries. Many of them set texts by Clément Marot and Eustorg de Beaulieu—two poets sympathetic to the Reform—but most of these chansons do not use the Genevan tunes. One favorite text was *Susanne ung jour*, which is based on the Apocryphal story of Susanna and the Elders. The poem was written by the Huguenot poet Guillaume Guéroult with the intent to draw converts to the Reform. This text was set to music by some thirty composers, one of the earliest being Orlande de Lassus in 1560. Most composers, including Lassus, incorporated the tenor from the first musical setting, a *chanson spirituelle* by Didier Lupi published in 1548, into their own work. The extraordinary popularity of settings of *Susanne ung jour* among Catholic and Protestant composers, and with the public in general, is unparalleled, the appeal more sweeping even than Protestant ideology.[24]

One Netherlandish composer whose music reflects the influence of Lutheranism was Lupus Hellinck (*c.*1494–1541), a cleric at several churches in Bruges from 1519 until his death. Hellinck wrote eleven polyphonic settings of German chorale tunes, which were published posthumously by Georg Rhau in 1544. These works are imitative in texture, with the chorales set in the tenor voice. They suggest that he, although a priest, may have sympathized with the Reformation; this theory is supported by his participation in a controversial play, later banned by the Inquisition, that was presented at a rhetoricians' competition in Ghent in 1539.

The Church as patron of music

Despite growing Protestant sympathies throughout the Netherlands, the Roman Church remained a major musical institution and patron of Latin sacred music through the 1560s. Seats of dioceses were centered at Cambrai, Tournai, Utrecht, and Liège until an ecclesiastical reorganization of 1559 established Antwerp's Church of Our Lady as a cathedral, and named Cambrai, Mechlin, and Utrecht as seats of archdioceses. Singers were trained at the choir schools of the Netherlands, including Cambrai, Antwerp, Bruges, 's-Hertogenbosch, and Liège, and many collegiate and parish churches throughout the region supported choirs for the singing of polyphony. Choirs varied widely in size from as few as eight singers to as many as 24 for special occasions. Boys generally sang the top parts in sacred polyphony; in

[23] H. J. Slenk, "Christophe Plantin and the Genevan Psalter," *Tijdschrift van de Vereninging voor Nederlandse Muziekgeschiedenis*, 20 (1976), 226–48.

[24] K. Levy, "'Susanne un jour': The History of a 16th-Century Chanson," *Annales musicologiques*, 1 (1953), 375–408.

Antwerp, twelve positions were established for adult singers and twelve additional ones were endowed for choirboys.[25]

Many church musicians, including Jacob Clemens, were associated with confraternities, or lay devotional organizations. These groups held regular services, either weekly or daily, at private chapels or altars. Marian brotherhoods were popular throughout Europe in the fifteenth and sixteenth centuries: those at Bruges, Antwerp, Brussels, Bergen-op-Zoom, and 's-Hertogenbosch are known to be significant patrons of polyphonic music. Documents attest to the hiring of professional singers and instrumentalists for polyphonic masses and devotional services, and to the extensive copying of music for their use. The Marian confraternities at both 's-Hertogenbosch and Antwerp employed the famous Netherlandish court scribe Pierre Alamire to prepare manuscripts of sacred polyphony for their use.[26]

One manuscript from the Alamire workshop sheds light on the early musical history of Amsterdam. The Occo Codex (*B-Br* IV 922) is a retrospective collection of four-voice masses by Josquin, Mouton, Isaac, Divitis, and others, commissioned by the Amsterdam businessman Pompejus Occo and copied between 1526 and 1534. Occo's family loaned this manuscript to the Amsterdam Chapel of the Heilige Stede (Holy Place), where it was used from 1537 until 1566. Some of the music in this collection, including Josquin's *Missa "Pange lingua"*, can be linked to the chapel's theme of the Holy Sacrament, and was intended to be sung on the feast of Corpus Christi.[27]

In addition to Jacob Clemens, who was a member of the Marian brotherhood in 's-Hertogenbosch, many lesser-known composers were part of the musical establishments at the churches of the Netherlands. At Cambrai Cathedral, both Johannes Lupi (*c.*1506–1539), composer of two parody masses and approximately 37 motets, and Jean Courtois (fl. 1530–45), best known for his motets, carried on the esteemed musical tradition of the Du Fay era. At Antwerp, where both Johannes Ockeghem and Jacob Obrecht had once served, Antoine Barbe held the prestigeous position of choirmaster from 1528 to 1562; and Jean Castileti alias Guyot (1512–1588) was among the musicians associated with ecclesiastical music in Liège during this era.

Music at the Netherlandish courts

The courts of the Habsburg Empire were significant patrons of Netherlandish composers and polyphony. The Grande Chapelle of Charles V, Habsburg Emperor from 1519 to 1555, included some of the best known composers and musicians of the day. He engaged Nicolas Gombert and Cornelius Canis as successive *maîtres des*

25 K. Forney, "Music, Ritual and Patronage at the Church of Our Lady, Antwerp," *Early Music History*, 7 (1987), 1–58.

26 Ibid.

27 B. Huys (ed.), *Occo Codex*, Facsimilia Musica Neerlandica, ed. W. Elders, I (Buren, 1979).

enfans, responsible for the supervision of some ten choirboys. During Canis's years in Madrid (1542–55), the composers Thomas Crecquillon and Nicolas Payen as well as organist Johannes Lestainnier were part of the chapel.[28] Charles's son Philip II, king of Spain (r. 1559–98), had both a Spanish and a Flemish chapel in Madrid; Pierre de Manchicourt succeeded Payen as head of the latter and may also have served as master of the Spanish chapel.[29] Manchicourt had a connection in Arras and with that city's bishop, Antoine de Granvelle, a powerful statesman and great patron of the arts who was praised in the dedication of a Manchicourt motet print and in its opening motet, *O decus, o patriae lux*.[30] Both Canis and Manchicourt were active chanson composers whose works rank among the best of the Netherlandish masters of the era.[31]

The court of the regent was the most important musical establishment in the Netherlands. At Marguerite of Austria's court in Mechlin, the scribe Alamire and his workshop prepared sumptuous codices with compositions by court composers Pierre de la Rue and Alexander Agricola,[32] both contemporaries of Josquin. Among the next generation of composers, Benedictus Appenzeller and Roger Pathie served the Brussels court of Mary of Hungary. Appenzeller was master of the choirboys from 1537 to 1555, during which time he wrote some 59 chansons and motets as well as seven masses and twelve Magnificat settings. His secular works lean toward the French style in their syllabic, homorhythmic settings, while his sacred compositions are characterized by long melismatic lines in points of imitation. One occasional motet, *Musae jovis*, is an elegy on the death of Josquin. Rogier Pathie, who served the court as an organist and as treasurer from 1536 until 1565, wrote only a handful of works, among them one of the hits of the sixteenth century. His chanson *D'amour me plains* was published many times in both vocal and instrumental versions, and was the basis for a number of parody chansons and masses.[33] The Habsburg realm reached to Vienna as well, the site of the satellite court of Archduke Ferdinand I (r. 1521–63), brother of Charles V. Once an im-

[28] B. Bouckaert, "The Capilla Flamenca: The Composition and Duties of the Music Ensemble at the Court of Charles V (1515–1558)," in *The Empire Resounds: Music in the Days of Charles V*, ed. F. Maes (Louvain, 1999), 37–46.

[29] L. Wagner, "Music of Composers from the Low Countries at the Spanish Court of Philip II," in *Musique des Pays-Bas anciens: Musique espagnole ancienne (1450–1650); Actes du Colloque musicologique international, Bruxelles, 28–29-x-1995*, ed. P. Becquart and H. Vanhulst (Louvain, 1998), 193–214.

[30] *Liber quintus cantionum sacrarum vulgo motetta vocant, quinque et sex vocum a D. Magistro Manchicourt* (Louvain, 1554). Modern edition in Pierre de Manchicourt, *Opera omnia*, VII: *The Phalèse Motets*, ed. J. D. Wicks (American Institute of Musicology, 1999).

[31] *Chansons Published by Tielman Susato*, ed. Forney.

[32] M. Picker, *The Chanson Albums of Marguerite of Austria* (Berkeley and Los Angeles, 1965); H. Meconi, "Pierre de la Rue and Secular Music at the Court of Marguerite of Austria," *Jaarboek van het Vlaamse Centrum voor Oude Muziek*, 3 (1987), 49–58.

[33] G. G. Thompson, "Music in the Court Records of Mary of Hungary," *Tijdschrift voor de Vereniging van Nederlandse Muziekgeschiedenis*, 34 (1984), 132–73; eadem, "Mary of Hungary and Music Patronage," *Sixteenth-Century Journal*, 15/4 (Winter 1984), 401–18. On arrangements of Pathie's chanson, see J. Barbier, "*Damour me plains*: Remarques sur la tablature pour deux luths publiée par Pierre Phalèse en 1552," *Musique ancienne*, 22 (1987), 99–113.

pressive musical establishment under Maximilian I, Ferdinand's court at Vienna was dependent for musicians on the principal Imperial courts: his first Kapellmeister, Arnold von Bruck (*c.*1500–54), was trained as a choirboy in Madrid, and his second-in-command Pieter Maessens was sent to Vienna from Brussels by Mary of Hungary in 1543.[34] Bruck was an important contributor to the German polyphonic lied, and a teacher of the theorist Hermann Finck, author of *Practica musica* (1556).

Civic music and the rise of the instrumental ensemble

The most important civic institution throughout the urban centers of the Netherlands was the wind band, variously called *stad pijpers* (city pipers), *menestruels* (minstrels), *speellieden* (players), or *scalmeyers* (shawmists). An ensemble of four and occasionally five musicians, this group was much in demand for civic activities. The band's instrumentation varied little throughout the region: a four-person ensemble consisted of three shawms and a sackbut on the bass; a five-member ensemble added a second sackbut. All evidence suggests that the wind players in these groups were highly trained professionals who doubled on a number of instruments. A 1532 inventory of the Antwerp corp's instruments included 28 flutes and 19 crumhorns as well as two soprano shawms, two tenor shawms, three trombones, and a field trumpet.[35]

The duties of the town wind band included performing regular concerts, either from a church tower or at the town hall. In Bruges, the group was obliged to play on all sacred feast days; in other cities, such as Ghent, daily concerts were given. Their repertory included motets, chansons, and dance music. Prior to the sixteenth century, instrumentalists were skilled at improvisation, able to invent their own lines over a dance tenor. By the early sixteenth century, however, evidence supports the ability of instrumentalists to read notated polyphonic music.[36]

Wind players also participated in the Mass, particularly on high feast days such as Christmas and Easter, and played frequently for the devotional services of the lay confraternities and guilds. Evidence of their musical literacy is found in this context: in Antwerp, for example, motets were copied in 1508 for the city players to perform in the chapel of the Confraternity of Our Lady, and in 1530, the city player Tielman Susato was paid for copying a large songbook for use by the same confraternity.[37]

The city band, along with other instrumentalists, participated in religious processions throughout the Netherlands. Held on major feast days, these processions

[34] R. Lindell, "Music at the Imperial Court after Charles V," in *Le Concert des voix et des instruments à la Renaissance* (Paris, 1995), 273–86.

[35] K. Forney, "16th-Century Antwerp," in *Man & Music*, ed. S. Sadie, II: *The Renaissance: From the 1470s to the End of the 16th Century*, ed. I. Fenlon (Basingstoke and Englewood Cliffs, NJ, 1989), 361–79.

[36] K. Polk, "Ensemble Instrumental Music in Flanders, 1450–1550," *Journal of Band Research*, II (1975), 12–27.

[37] Forney, "Music, Ritual, and Patronage," 1–57.

brought out the clergy and trade and military guilds as well as town officials. German artist Albrecht Dürer described several events he witnessed during his travels in the Low Countries, including the splendid Antwerp Ommegang of Our Lady:

> On the Sunday after Our Dear Lady's Assumption at Antwerp, the whole town of every craft and rank was assembled, each dressed in his best according to his rank. And the ranks and guilds had their signs by which they might be known. In the intervals great costly pole-candles were borne and their long Frankish trumpets of silver. There were also in the German fashion many pipers and drummers. All the instruments were loudly and noisily blown and beaten.[38]

The city wind band frequently performed for special secular events, such as banquets and celebrations for visiting dignitaries. Paramount among these events were the so-called *joyeuses entrées*, or joyous entries. Two of the most famous were in honor of Emperor Charles V.[39] On 20 January 1540, a festive entry was held in Cambrai for Charles and his troops, for which the Cathedral's chapelmaster Jean Courtois wrote the four-voice motet *Venite populi terrae*. This work exemplifies the varied imitative procedures and shifting textural treatment that mark the Netherlandish motet style. A second joyous entry was held in Antwerp for Charles on 10 September 1549, on which occasion he formally introduced his son Philip to his northern subjects. Even more grandiose than the Cambrai procession, this event was accompanied by numerous pipers, trumpeters, and drummers, along with singers and instrumentalists performing polyphonic chansons.[40]

Instrumental music-making permeated many facets of secular life in the Netherlands. A number of cities had professional musicians' guilds that controlled the training of instrumentalists and established performance standards and conditions of employment. Professional players of all types of instruments found regular and occasional employment in dance halls, at private weddings and banquets, and with the varied trade and military guilds of each city. Some musicians worked for the chambers of rhetoricians, literary societies that sponsored poetic and dramatic competitions throughout the Netherlands. One such event held in Ghent in 1539 attracted guilds from cities across the Netherlands; plays presented on this occasion, frequently accompanied by music, were later judged to be heretical, smacking of Protestant ideology.[41]

The publication of music expressly for the growing instrumental ensemble

[38] A. Dürer, *Diary of his Journey to the Netherlands*, introd. J.-A. Goris and G. Marlies (Greenwich, CT, 1970), 94–95.

[39] E. Bowles, *Musical Ensembles in Festival Books, 1500–1800: An Iconographical and Documentary Survey* (Ann Arbor, 1989).

[40] Forney, "16th-Century Antwerp."

[41] P. Brachin, "La 'Fête de rhétorique' de Gand (1539)," in *Fêtes et cérémonies au temps du Charles Quint* (Paris, 1975), 255–79; A. Van Elslander, "Les Chambres de rhétorique et les fêtes du règne de Charles Quint," ibid., 281–85; K. Forney, "The Role of Secular Guilds in the Musical Life of Antwerp," *Musicology and Archival Research*, ed. B. Haggh, F. Daelmans, and A. Vanrie, Archives et bibliothéques en Belgique, 46 (Brussels, 1994), 441–61.

tradition is somewhat problematic. Clearly, northern musicians could perform instrumental renditions of the wide repertory of chansons and motets published locally and elsewhere. Only a handful of instrumental-ensemble books were issued in the Low Countries, however, and these, like Susato's *Danserye* of 1551, seem directed at an amateur rather than professional level. Susato's collection of four-part dance arrangements of popular chansons and dance tunes, arranged as basses danses, pavanes, galliards, branles, and rondes, may have served merely as a skeletal framework on which skilled improvisation was applied. The *Danserye* presents simplified settings of French chansons by Sermisy, Janequin, Jean Passereau, Jean Courtois, and Josquin; its repertory attests to the popularity of the Parisian prints of Attaingnant. Most of the basses dances are arranged from well-known serious chansons by Sermisy; Josquin's masterpiece *Mille regretz* is set homorhythmically as a pavane; and Janequin's erotic chanson *Il estoit une fillette* is almost literally transcribed as a branle. Some dances reflect local traditions, such as a branle entitled *Hoboecken dans*, named for a small town on the outskirts of Antwerp on the river Scheldt.[42]

Amateur music-making and the bourgeoisie

The economic prosperity of the Netherlands fueled the trades of music-book production and instrument building, and the growing middle and merchant classes were avid consumers of these products. Household inventories and iconographic evidence support the important role music-making played in family life—lutes and keyboard instruments were commonplace in the burgher home; these sources enhance an image of cultivated amateurs and music bibliophiles among the upper middle class.

Numerous avenues were open for acquiring a basic education in music; in Antwerp, elementary-level schooling, required of all children, included music skills, and singing and keyboard playing were highly desirable social traits for middle-class women in the Netherlands. Women studied the basics of reading, writing, arithmetic, and music at private schools or through tutorial arrangements; one such contract specifies that the daughter of an Italian merchant living in Antwerp should study a keyboard repertory of dances, including allemandes, galliards, passamezzos, and rondes. This rise in amateur performance and musical literacy provided a plentiful market for the exquisite virginals and spinets for which Antwerp became famous in the later sixteenth century.[43]

Sources for solo instrumental performance consist primarily of lute and cittern music, also popular instruments in the region. The Phalèse firm began publishing

[42] *Het derde musyck boexken . . . , daer inne begrepen syn alderhande danserye* (Antwerp, 1551; facs. Peer, 1987); modern edition in F. J. Giesbert, *Danserye*, 2 vols. (Mainz, 1936).

[43] K. Forney, "Music Patronage and the Rise of Bourgeois Culture in the Low Countries," in *Culturas musicales del Mediterraneo y sus Ramificaciones: Actas del XV Congreso de la Sociedad de Musicologia, Madrid 3–10/iv/1992, Revista de Musicologia*, 16 (1993), 607–10; eadem, "*Nymphes gays en abry du laurier*: Music Instruction for the Bourgeois Woman," *Musica disciplina*, 49 (1995), 151ff.

solo lute music in 1545, and in many such volumes included basic instructions for learning the instrument and the French tabulature system. One monumental collection for solo lute was *Hortus musarum*, issued by Phalèse in two volumes (1552–53) and containing solo fantasias as well as over a hundred arrangements of chansons, motets, and dances.[44]

Despite the popularity of keyboard instruments in the region, no music was printed in the Low Countries during the sixteenth century for this medium. French prints from the presses of Attaingnant and Moderne were surely available; however, the absence of any local keyboard publications raises an important issue: did amateur musicians prepare their own keyboard arrangements from vocal or instrumental ensemble prints? One popular treatise suggests this may have been the case. Sebastian Virdung's *Musica getutscht*, first issued in 1511 in Germany and republished in Antwerp in a French translation (1529) and in two Flemish editions (1554, 1568), demonstrates how to make a German keyboard intabulation of a vocal work. In the later Antwerp editions, the Flemish song *Een vrolic wesen* is substituted for Virdung's original example. The popularity and longevity of this source suggests its didactic role for the growing musical audience of the Netherlands.[45]

This new bourgeois audience represented the primary consumers of the instrumental, secular vocal, and sacred music prints of the era 1520 to 1560, often viewed as the golden age of Netherlandish polyphony. During these years, the post-Josquin imitative style dominated the music of the courts, churches, and towns of Europe, as northern composers held important posts across the continent. The ascendancy of Antwerp as the cultural center of the Low Countries was cut short during the turbulent decades of the later sixteenth century, allowing the northern Netherlands, and especially Amsterdam, to rise to musical prominence.

1560–1600

THE era 1560 to 1600 was a turbulent one for the Low Countries. Stripped of their democratic rights and suffering under religious persecution, Netherlanders—Protestants and Catholics alike—rose up against the Spanish domination of Philip II, beginning the Eighty Years' War in 1566. Philip responded swiftly, sending the powerful Duke of Alva to quell the rebellion. Under Alva's authority, Catholic statesmen such as Counts Egmont and Hoorn were executed during a period of severe repression. Alva built a citadel outside of Antwerp in order to establish Spanish domination in the region. In 1576, the Spanish troops sacked Antwerp in what was one of the bloodiest episodes in European history. Only a few years of peace, when the region was under Protestant control (1581–85), separated the decades of war. By the end of the century, the Northern Protestant provinces

[44] H. Vanhulst, "Édition comparative des instructions pour le luth, le cistre et la guitare publiées . . . à Louvain par Pierre Phalèse (1545–1570)," *Revue belge de musicologie*, 34–35 (1980–81), 81–105; idem, *Catalogue des éditions de . . . Phalèse*, 24–32.

[45] S. Virdung, *Musica getutscht: A Treatise on Musical Instruments* (1511), ed. and trans. by B. Bullard, Cambridge Musical Texts and Monographs (Cambridge, 1993).

had established their independence while the Southern Catholic region remained under Spanish rule.

The religious, political, and economic consequences of the troubled era had a harsh impact on the arts in the Low Countries. The iconoclastic destruction of the churches left many musicians without employment. Some fled the once-flourishing cultural centers of the southern region for the relative safety of the Northern Netherlands, Germany, England, and Scandinavia; a few found positions at the Habsburg Imperial courts of Ferdinand I and Maximilian II in Vienna and Prague, or, in the case of Orlande de Lassus, in Munich at the court of Duke Albrecht V. The Madrid-based Flemish Chapel of Philip II remained a major musical center, providing employment for a handful of the Low Countries' finest musicians. Many, too, went to Italy to work, as northern composers had done for decades, and some, like Giovanni di Macque, remained there for their entire productive careers.

In the Netherlands, the artistic domination of Antwerp began to wane late in the century as Amsterdam blossomed into the cultural and economic center of the Low Countries. Northern musical life flourished in Leiden and Utrecht too, as the region enjoyed relative political stability. Brussels was reinstated as a significant musical center in the southern Netherlands at the turn of the sixteenth century with the establishment there of the court of Duke Albert and his consort Isabella.

Church music in the Low Countries

This was an era of change for the church in the Low Countries. In 1559, an ecclesiastical reorganization had established fourteen new dioceses, with seats of archdioceses at Utrecht in the north, at Mechlin in Flanders, and at Cambrai in present-day northern France.

The elevation of Antwerp's Church of Our Lady to a cathedral in 1559 strengthened its thriving musical establishment. Its choir, with endowed positions for adult and boy singers, served the church's chapter as well as its many lay confraternities, who sponsored a complex cycle of daily and weekly devotional services.[46] The Antwerp church suffered a major blow in the image-breaking attack of 1566, and it fell to choirmaster Gérard de Turnhout (*c.*1520–1580) to rebuild its musical establishment. Turnhout oversaw the construction of new organs by the Mechlin builder Gilles Brebos; he replenished the library with new music manuscripts and prints; and he published in 1569 a collection of tricinia, including 20 motets possibly intended for the church's diminished musical forces.[47] This collection supports a trend of soloistic singing, leading toward Baroque monodic styles.

Many-voiced choral polyphony remained the standard, however, with one of the most widely-used collections being the famous *Octo Missae* of George de la Hèle (1547–1586). A Flemish composer, La Hèle was trained as a choirboy at Ant-

[46] Forney, "Music, Ritual, and Patronage."

[47] L. J. Wagner, Preface to Gérard de Turnhout, *Sacred and Secular Songs for Three Voices*, Recent Researches in the Music of the Renaissance, 9–10 (Madison, 1970).

werp, and held important musical posts at both Mechlin and Tournai in the 1570s before going to Madrid in 1580 as master of the Royal Chapel under Philip II. In 1578, the Antwerp firm of Christophe Plantin printed La Hèle's monumental book of eight parody masses for five, six, and seven voices, based on motets by Josquin, Lassus, Rore, and Crecquillon.

Plantin's presses also issued the motet collection *Cantiones sacrae* (1581) by Severin Cornet (*c.*1520–1582), Turnhout's successor as choirmaster at the Antwerp Cathedral. These are large-voiced works structured with pervading imitation. Polyphonic writing for five to eight voices was the standard too for Netherlandish Imperial court composers, as seen in the masses by Philip de Monte, Alard Gaucquier, and Jacob de Kerle, and the motets by Jacob de Brouck, all included in music prints issued by Plantin.[48]

The leading Netherlandish composer of sacred polyphony was Orlande de Lassus (*c.*1532–1594), who left the region in 1556 to join the court of Duke Albrecht V of Bavaria in Munich. A Catholic composer, Lassus's prolific output includes some sixty masses (including three Requiems), four Passions (to accounts of each of the Evangelists), over a hundred Magnificats, 18 sets of Lamentations, ten settings of *Nunc dimittis*, as well as a monumental number of motets—over 500 of these were published in his posthumous *Magnum opus musicum* of 1604.[49]

Lassus's masses are mostly parody settings for four to eight voices based on motets (many his own), chansons, and madrigals. Among his finest are the *Missa "In te domine speravi"*, on his own six-voice motet; *Missa "Doulce memoire"*, on a famous chanson by Pierre Sandrin; and his five-voice *Missa pro defunctis*. His *Missa "Susanne ung jour"* is a five-voice parody of his own setting of the well-known *chanson spirituelle*, and features a unifying head-motif derived from the chanson's initial point of imitation.[50]

Lassus's motets are highly varied in expression and musical construction; the early ones, such as *Gustate et videte* from a 1556 Antwerp collection, exhibit a command of counterpoint coupled with harmonic clarity and expressive text setting.[51] His motets were undoubtedly intended for the court chapel's celebration of the Mass and the Office, especially Vespers. They include many Marian as well as Gospel and Epistle motets; the six-voice *Cum essem parvulus*, on an epistle of St Paul, illustrates the master's consummate attention to the text. Some of Lassus's later motets are polychoral, such as the eight-voice *Osculetur me osculo* on a sensuous text from the Song of Songs; this work was the basis for an impressive polychoral

[48] On Plantin's music prints, see J. A. Stellfeld, *Bibliographie des éditions plantiniennes* (Brussels, 1949).

[49] See various essays on Lassus's music in *Orlando di Lasso Studies*, ed. P. Bergquist (Cambridge, 1999); *Orlandus Lassus and His Time* [Antwerp, 24–26 Aug. 1994], ed. I. Bossuyt, E. Schreurs, and A. Wouters, Yearbook of the Alamire Foundation, 1 (Peer, 1995).

[50] See R. Orlich, *Die Parodiemessen von Orlando di Lasso*, Studien zur Musik, 4 (Munich, 1985).

[51] E. Lowinsky, "Orlando di Lasso's Antwerp Motet Book and Its Relationship to the Contemporary Netherlandish Motet" (1933), trans. in *Music in the Culture of the Renaissance and Other Essays*, ed. B. J. Blackburn (Chicago, 1989), 283–431.

mass by the composer. Lassus's expressive chromatic writing surfaces in lush works such as the psalm motet *Timor et tremor* as well as in his famous *Prophetiae Sibyllarum*, a secular collection set to pseudo-classical humanistic verse. His vast output of sacred music was distributed and performed throughout the Netherlands and well beyond its boundaries.

Philippe de Monte (1521–1603) was another Netherlander who contributed significantly to sacred music. He went to Italy at an early age and returned to the north in 1567 to take the position of chapelmaster at the Viennese court of Maximilian II.[52] Monte wrote nearly forty masses, most using varied parody techniques. His six-voice *Missa "Benedicta es"*, published in Antwerp in 1579, thoroughly explores the possibilities of its Josquin model; seven additional masses, published in his *Liber primus missarum* (1581), are all motet parodies, one an eight-voice setting on Lassus's *Confitebor tibi Domine*.[53] Monte also used secular models for his masses, including Rore's famous *Anchor che col partire*, on which he based a four-voice work that systematically uses the madrigal's motifs.

Monte wrote some 260 motets as well, most of which were published in Venice. His style is largely contrapuntal, with melismatic lines and varied structural techniques. One of his earliest motets, the six-voice *Parce mihi Domine*, uses a short cantus firmus in a tenor voice that is repeated five times in the first section, then is treated in *cancrizans* in the second section. In some polychoral motets, Monte writes for seven voices in asymmetrical choirs of four and three. His motets, more than his masses, show his great sensitivity to text setting.[54]

Jacobus de Kerle (*c.*1531–1591) traveled extensively throughout his career, working in Italy, Germany, and the Low Countries. He wrote largely sacred music, including masses, hymns, Magnificats, psalms, and about a hundred motets. He is known for his *Preces speciales*, written in 1561–62 as a commission by the Council of Trent, and set to prayers for the success of the Council and of the Counter-Reformation movement. Implementing the recommendations of the Council, this work gives careful treatment to the text, maintaining audibility of the words within a largely polyphonic setting

The performance of Catholic church music ceased in some Netherlandish centers in the early 1580s, when the Calvinists briefly took political control. Already in the Northern Netherlands, churches had been stripped of their Catholic icons as cities embraced the Reform: first Leiden in 1572, followed by Amsterdam in 1578 and Utrecht in 1580. Organs were ordered removed from the churches, since accompanied psalm singing was forbidden in Calvinist services. Some cities, notably Amsterdam, refused the order, and established a civic use for the instrument.

After 1585, Catholicism returned to the Southern Netherlandish provinces. The Flemish composer Andreas Pevernage (1543–1591), newly appointed as choirmaster

52 Lindell, "Music at the Imperial Court after Charles V."

53 V. Franke, "Borrowing Procedures in the Late-16th-Century Imitation Masses and Their Implications for Our View of 'Parody' or 'Imitation,'" *Studien zur Musikwissenschaft: Beihefte den Denkmäler der Tonkunst in Österreich*, 46 (1998), 7–33.

54 On Monte's motets, see R. Lenaerts, "Philippus de Monte als Motettenkomponist," *Kirchenmusikalisches Jahrbuch* 66 (1984), 49–58.

at Antwerp Cathedral, continued the polyphonic tradition in his six masses, over 55 motets, and 34 spiritual chansons. Pevernage is also remembered for his *Laudes vespertinae*, a collection of Marian antiphons and sacrament hymns intended for Antwerp confraternity services. This book underwent a number of reprintings after his death in 1591 and introduced the first published examples of *cantiones natalitiae*, a genre of polyphonic Christmas carols developed by southern Netherlandish composers.[55]

Music for the Reformed church of the Netherlands remained simple, based on the Calvinist doctrine that considered polyphony a disturbance to worship. Thus, monophonic settings of the psalms provided the core of the Reform church's music, with polyphonic settings in French and Dutch intended for domestic use, possibly by Catholics and Protestants alike. Dutch-texted psalm settings, known as *souterliedekens*, were written near mid-century by Jacobus Clemens, his disciple Gerardus Mes, and the Delft composer Cornelius Boscop.[56] Among the Protestant composers who set the tunes of the French Genevan Psalter in polyphony was Jan Pieterszoon Sweelinck (1562–1621), organist at the Old Church in Amsterdam.

Composers at the Spanish court

Philip II inherited his father's taste for northern polyphonic music; thus he maintained, largely intact, the Flemish musical chapel that Charles V had established. Several Netherlandish composers headed Philip's Madrid-based chapel: these were Gérard de Turnhout, chapelmaster from 1572 to 1580; George de la Hèle, who held the same position from 1582 to 1586; and Philippe Rogier, who served the court from 1586 to 1596.[57]

Turnhout's connection with the court began in 1564, when he wrote a *Te Deum* for the grand entry into Antwerp of the new regent of the Low Countries, Margaret of Parma. Upon Turnhout's death in 1580, Georges de la Hèle, choirmaster at the Tournai Cathedral, was appointed to head the Flemish chapel. As noted earlier (see p. 261), La Hèle's parody masses appeared in *Octo Missae*, an elegantly printed collection published by Plantin in 1578; the masses are preceded by an alternatim setting of the introductory antiphon *Asperges me*, which intersperses phrases of chant between sections of imitative polyphony.[58] Records from the Royal Chapel in Madrid confirm that, while at court, La Hèle wrote various mass movements, motets, and a set of Lamentations; these works are, however, lost.

Philippe Rogier (*c.*1561–1596), a northerner from Arras, served the Madrid chapel as a choirboy under Turnhout and as assistant chapelmaster under La Hèle. Although he died young, a number of Rogier's masses were published posthu-

55 R. Rasch, *De cantiones natalitiae en het kerkelijke muziekleven in de Zuidelijke Nederlanden gedurende de zeventiende eeuw*, 2 vols. (Utrecht, 1985).

56 See J. Bonda, *De meerstemmige Nederlandse Liederen van de vijftiende en zestiende eeuw* (Hilversum, 1996), with English summary; Grijp, "The Souterliedekens by Gherardus Mes (1561)."

57 See Wagner, "Music of Composers from the Low Countries."

58 See Stellfeld, *Bibliographie des éditions plantiniennes*.

mously by his student and successor in the chapel, Géry de Ghersem (*c.*1573–1630). One of these is a tribute to Philip II: *Missa "Philippus Secundus Rex Hispaniae"* is a four-voice work based on a *soggetto cavato* theme drawn from the mass's title:

Phi-lip-pus Se-cun-dus Rex His-pa-ni-ae
mi mi ut re ut ut re mi fa mi re

The theme appears throughout in the tenor, treated with contrapuntal techniques including retrograde, augmentation and diminution. This work is reminiscent of Josquin's *Missa "Hercules dux Ferrarie"*, whose musical subject is similarly derived. Other Rogier masses include parodies of motets by Morales, Palestrina, Gombert, Crecquillon, and Clemens. Rogier's secular output includes more than seventy villancicos, reflecting his adoption of Spanish styles. He was eulogized by the Spanish poet Lope de Vega in 1630: "Rogier, honor, glory, and light of Flanders . . . left this life in the flower of (his) genius, depriving us of our sweet Orpheus."

The court of the regent of the Low Countries continued its Brussels-based musical establishment as well under Margaret of Parma (r. 1555–67) and by her successor, Alexander Farnese. However, the political instability of the region and the ensuing war overshadowed musical life at court, and many musicians fled to the safety of Germany, England, and the northern Netherlands.

Secular music in the Low Countries

The principal secular genres of the second half of the sixteenth century were the chanson, the Netherlandish lied, and the madrigal. Northern chanson composers furthered both the contrapuntal, many-voiced setting and the four-voice model more typical in France. Large retrospective collections such as the *Septièsme Livre des chansons*, first published in Louvain in 1560,[59] continued in popularity throughout the century, alongside settings of more contemporary poets by Orlande de Lassus and Jean de Castro among others. The most popular poets set to music in this era were Pierre Ronsard, Joachim du Bellay, and Antoine Baïf. Working in Antwerp in the 1570s, Castro (*c.*1540–*c.*1600) drew on the most direct and accessible of Ronsard's love poems, which he set in a contrapuntal style marked by homophonic passages and a careful line-by-line treatment of the text. Castro was a master of northern borrowing techniques; in particular, he favored three-voice settings based on pre-existent models, many by Lassus.[60] Castro's works were issued in modally organized collections that he edited himself. The chansons of the Antwerp composers Severin Cornet and Andreas Pevernage are generally imitative with overlapping phrases, set for five, six, and eight voices. Pevernage also wrote a number of motet-like *chansons spirituelles* on religious texts, and he parodied Lassus's work in his eight-voice setting of *Bon jour mon cœur*.[61]

59 Vanhulst, "Un Success de l'édition musical."

60 I. Bossuyt, "Orlando di Lasso as a Model for Composition as Seen in the Three-Voice Motets of Jean de Castro," in *Orlando di Lasso Studies*, 158–82.

61 G. Hoekstra, "An Eight-Voice Parody of Lassus: André Pevernage's *Bon jour mon cœur*," *Early Music*, 7 (1979), 367–77.

The most important chanson composer of this era was Orlande de Lassus, whose 150 works received wide distribution in many reprints and in intabulations for keyboard and lute. Lassus's chansons illustrate a wide diversity of styles, from the textual clarity and conciseness of his *Bon jour mon cœur*—a four-voice homophonic setting of Ronsard's charming poem of greeting—to the brooding and chromatic expressiveness of his setting of Du Bellay's *La nuict froide et sombre*. The constancy of unrequited love is seen in his five-voice setting of the epigram *Au feu, au feu* and its response *A l'eau, a l'eau*. Lassus's settings of popular poetry include drinking songs, such as the six-voice *Vignon, vignon*, and the lively and humorous *Il etait une religieuse*, an anecdotal story of a priest and a nun that satirizes the solemn *Pater noster* and *Ave Maria*. Many of Lassus's chansons were collected into two volumes entitled *Meslanges*, issued in Paris (1576 and 1584).[62] More than any other composer of the era, Lassus's chansons were frequently reworked as devotional songs.[63]

The Netherlandish polyphonic lied arose at mid-century and continued in popularity during this later era. Dutch-texted songs for four and five voices are included in a 1568 anthology of music by the Antwerp music teacher Noé Faignient, among them the table blessing *O hemelsche Vader*.[64] A later collection entitled *Een duytsch Musyckboeck*, issued by Phalèse in 1572, includes polyphonic Dutch songs for four, five, and six voices—many with moralizing texts—by Clemens, Faignient, Turnhout, Jan Belle, and Ludovicus Episcopius.[65] A choirmaster at Maastricht, Episcopius wrote a six-voice quodlibet, *Ic sou studeren in eenen hoeck*, that recalls the famous programmatic chanson by Janequin, *Les Cris de Paris*. Interest in preserving Dutch poetry led the Leiden composer Cornelis Schuyt (1557–1616) to publish his five-voice *Hollandsche Madrigalen* (1603); he claimed in the preface of this collection that he wished to prove his language capable of "expressing cheerfully in song the merriness that is demanded in music."

Some Netherlanders contributed to the German lied as well; paramount among them was Orlande de Lassus, who wrote nearly 100 German-texted works. Many of these were sacred pieces, some German psalms, suggesting their appeal as Lutheran devotional music. The Innsbruck court composer Alexander Utendal (*c.*1530–1581) was known for his polyphonic settings of German traditional songs.

The madrigal in the north

The Italian madrigal gained popularity in the north in the late sixteenth century, owing in part to the many composers who worked in Italy and also to the patronage of the large Italian merchant community resident in the Low Countries. The

62 On Lassus's chansons, see F. Dobbins, "Textual Sources and Compositional Techniques in the French Chansons of Orlando de Lassus," in *Orlandus Lassus and His Time*, 139–62.

63 See R. Freedman, *The Chansons of Orlando di Lasso: Music, Piety, and Print in Sixteenth-Century France* (Rochester, 2000).

64 See the facs. of Noe Faignient, *Chansons, Madrigales & Motetz* (Antwerp, 1568), ed. E. Schreurs (Peer, 1986).

65 See Bonda, *De meerstimmige Nederlandse liederen*.

first madrigals published in the north were by Orlande de Lassus; six villanesche, six madrigals, and a setting of a sestina were included in his so-called "Opus 1," issued in Antwerp in 1555.[66] These works were, however, probably written earlier, while Lassus was still in Italy. A collection of madrigals by the Antwerp composer Hubert Waelrant, published in 1558, included nine bipartite, five-voice works on texts by Petrarch, Ariosto, and Tasso. Northern composers, on the other hand, generally showed a preference for the lighter Italian forms: Severin Cornet published a book of villanesche in Antwerp in 1563,[67] followed shortly by Waelrant's book of *Canzone napolitane a 4* (Venice, 1565; now incomplete).

The vogue for the Italian style was furthered by the publication of a number of madrigal anthologies that included both Italian and northern composers. The first of these was edited by Jean de Castro in 1575 and contained thirteen of his own works as well as several of Lassus and Monte. The next decades saw the issue of four important anthologies from the Phalèse publishing firm, all of which underwent a number of reprints: *Harmonia celeste* (1583), edited by Andreas Pevernage; *Musica divina* (1583), edited by Pierre Phalèse; *Symphonia angelica* (1585), edited by Hubert Waelrant; and *Melodia olympica* (1591), edited by the English composer and organist Peter Philips.[68] These Antwerp publications were influential both in their repertory and format on *Musica transalpina* (London, 1588); this landmark collection of Italian madrigals with English texts included works by Netherlandish composers, among them Noé Faignient.[69]

Outside of Antwerp, the Netherlander Philippe de Monte was known throughout Europe for his more than 1,100 madrigals, including five books of *madrigali spirituali*. Monte was born in Mechlin, worked in Italy for several decades, then was appointed in 1568 as chapelmaster at the Imperial court in Vienna. His works are relatively progressive in style, featuring chromaticism and cross-relations for coloristic effects and a mixture of counterpoint interspersed with homophony for text declamation. Monte's madrigals are set to texts by Boccaccio, Petrarch, Bembo, and Tasso and to Guarini's *Il pastor fido* (1600).

Two additional northern composers who contributed significantly to the madrigal remained in Italy for their entire productive careers. Giaches de Wert (1535–1596), who was born near Antwerp, worked at the court of Mantua. His madrigals are often more homophonic and chromatic than those of his northern counterparts. Many are set to high quality verse, although he also wrote a number of villanelle. Wert dedicated some of his virtuoso madrigals to the famous *Concerto delle donne*, an ensemble of accomplished women singers at the court of Ferrara.

[66] On this collection, see K. Forney, "Orlando di Lasso's 'Opus 1': The Making and Marketing of a Renaissance Music Book," *Revue belge de musicologie*, 39–40 (1985–86), 33–60.

[67] See D. Cardamone, *The "Canzone villanesca alla napolitana" and Related Forms* (Ann Arbor, 1981).

[68] G. Hoekstra, "The Reception and Cultivation of the Italian Madrigal in Antwerp and the Low Countries, 1555–1620," *Musica disciplina*, 48 (1994), 125–87.

[69] On the madrigal in the Low Countries, see ibid.; K. Forney, "Antwerp's Role in the Reception and Dissemination of the Madrigal in the North," in *Trasmissione e recezione delle forme di cultura musicale*, 1: 239–53.

Wert's works were well known in the north, since several were included in the Flemish madrigal anthologies mentioned above.

Giovanni de Macque (*c.*1548–1614) was born in southern Belgium and trained at the Imperial Court in Vienna under Philippe de Monte. He then worked in Rome and in southern Italy, and is considered the leading composer of the Neapolitan school in the late sixteenth century. His early madrigals are generally conservative and some are in more popular styles. Two books of these *madrigaletti* and *canzonette napolitane* were reprinted in Antwerp in 1600, lending support to the northern interest in the lighter forms of Italian secular music. Macque's later works, written in Naples, explore pastoral themes and bold experiments in dissonance.

The continuing interest in the madrigal in the north is demonstrated by the Leiden composer and organist Cornelis Schuyt, who issued a book of Italian works (1600) that included a eulogy to his native city, *O Leyda gratiosa*. His second book, cited above, was set to Dutch texts in a style that blended northern and Italian characteristics.

The trades of music printing and instrument building

Music printing was centered in the southern Netherlands, especially Antwerp and Louvain, throughout the sixteenth century. The Phalèse firm, active in Louvain from 1545, was the region's most prolific music publisher. In addition to many chanson, motet, mass, madrigal, and solo lute prints, the firm issued its first liturgical music book in 1561, a *Cantuale* of chants for use in the Amsterdam churches. In 1570, Pierre Phalèse the elder formed a partnership with the Antwerp bookseller Jan Bellère that lasted until the latter's death in 1595.[70] Among the important prints issued by this business were the three volumes of Lassus's *Patrocinium musices* (1574–78), including motets, masses, and other sacred works, as well as four celebrated Italian madrigal collections (1583–91). All but one of these prints were issued by Pierre Phalèse the younger, who took over the firm after his father's death in 1576. One of the most significant lute publications from the Phalèse firm was *Pratum musicum* (1584), which included many chansons, madrigals, and Flemish songs arranged by the Antwerp lutenist Emanuel Adriaenssen.[71]

The Low Countries' most famous printer was Christophe Plantin, who settled in Antwerp in 1551, and who served as archtypographer to Philip II of Spain. In this position, Plantin held a monopoly for the printing of liturgical books, many of which included music. Although he originally had no plans to print polyphonic music, Plantin studied the craft, buying up type and equipment at the close of two of Antwerp's music printing houses. His first collection of polyphony was one of the most sumptuous and costly books of its day: *Octo Missae* of Georges de la Hèle,

[70] On this firm and its imprints, see Vanhulst, *Catalogue des éditions de . . . Phalèse.*

[71] See G. Spiessens, "Emmanuel Adriaenssen et son *Pratum musicum*," *Acta musicologica*, 36 (1964), 142–51; facs. of E. Adriaenssen, *Pratum musicum longe amoenissimum*, ed. K. H. Yong (Buren, 1977).

printed in 1578 and dedicated to Philip II. This large-format, elegantly printed mass book was widely disseminated throughout Europe at the very high cost of eighteen florins per copy.

Plantin's music output, very small compared to his other printing endeavors, consisted of ten additional books, including mass and motet collections by musicians from the Imperial court and five secular prints by Antwerp composers. These music prints sold well into the seventeenth century, owing to their high quality of craftsmanship and the longevity of the Plantin firm.[72]

Throughout the later sixteenth century, music printing houses sprang up in other cities as well, notably Douai and Ghent in the South and Leiden, Amsterdam, and Rotterdam in the North. The Douai shop of Jan Bogard was important for its motet volumes by Lassus, Jean de Castro, and Andreas Pevernage.

The art of engraving was applied to music during this era, with some of the most unusual and beautiful examples issued from Antwerp. Motets by both Pevernage and Cornelis Verdonck were engraved as part of elaborately decorated art prints; the earliest example is a 1584 Johan Sadelar engraving based on a Martin de Vos painting of *The Virgin and Child with St Anne* and including the four-part "picture" motet *Ave gratia plena* by Cornelis Verdonck. Similarly, in 1590, the printer Philip Galle issued his *Encomium musices*, a book with plates of Biblical scenes, each with accurate depictions of musical instruments and complete engraved musical scores. The most important early music engraver was Simone Verovio, who was born in the Southern Netherlands but worked his entire career in Italy; Verovio issued some twenty editions of engraved music in Rome between 1580 and 1608.

Instrument building was an important music trade in the Low Countries from the fourteenth century. Antwerp was home to makers of lute, viola da gamba, keyboard, and wind instruments in businesses that were often passed on within families from one generation to another. The city's elite artists' guild, dedicated to St Luke, inducted in 1557 a group of harpsichord and organ makers among its members. It was, however, the Ruckers family of keyboard builders that made Antwerp famous for this product. Founded in 1579 by Hans Ruckers the elder (*c.*1550–1598), the firm was active until 1665. Numerous instruments survive to document the fine craftsmanship and unrivalled sound that resulted from the sophisticated Ruckers design.[73] By 1580, the keyboard-making trade had burgeoned to include at least fifteen different workshops in Antwerp, each with its own master builders and apprentices.

Carillons originated in the Low Countries in the fifteenth century, the result of a long tradition of bell founding. Utrecht was a renowned center for bell casting, and Antwerp had one of the earliest known carillons, with a set of large tuned bells played from a keyboard and pedal board in the tower of the Church of Our Lady. Leiden's first carillon was installed in 1578 in the city hall tower, from which several concerts were played. By the seventeenth century, carillons could be heard

[72] See Stellfeld, *Bibliographie des éditions plantiniennes*.

[73] G. O'Brien, *Ruckers: A Harpsichord and Virginal Building Tradition* (Cambridge and New York, 1990).

throughout the cities of the Netherlands; many of these instruments are still played today.[74]

Civic instrumental music and private music-making

The civic band, or *stadspeellieden*, a four- or five-member ensemble of loud winds, was by this era an established institution in the Netherlands. In addition to regular concerts and ceremonial duties, its musicians generally doubled on soft winds and string instruments for performances at weddings, banquets, and dances. Instrumentalists also found occasional employment for church services and processions on high feast days, and with the many trade and military guilds of urban centers.[75]

Organ and carillon concerts were also civic-sponsored events. The onset of the Reform in the North and the ban of organ music in Calvinist services did not dampen the Netherlanders' love of the instrument; rather, city fathers hired musicians to play regular organ concerts, held directly before and after church services. Peter Swybbertszoon served first as church and later as city organist in Amsterdam, followed in 1580 by his more famous son, Jan Pieterszoon Sweelinck; the composer Cornelis Schuyt was appointed as city organist in Leiden in 1593.

Published instrumental music was intended largely for the growing amateur audience. Collections of four-part dance music were issued, containing simple arrangements of well-known tunes and vocal repertory "as appropriate for all instruments as for the voice." Many books of solo lute, guitar, and cittern music were printed by the Phalèse firm in Louvain, often with didactic prefaces, and the famed Antwerp lutenist and teacher Emanuel Adriaenssen published three books of French lute tablature between 1582 and 1600 with virtuosic arrangements of some fifty vocal works as well as many dances and five fugue-like fantasias. These works provide varied arrangements, some for voices and one or more lutes, of many of the best-loved chansons and madrigals of the day. The last of these publications contains directions for aspiring performers to intabulate polyphonic music. Adriaenssen, along with his brother, ran a school for lutenists in Antwerp, but ran into conflict there since neither were members of the powerful musicians' guild.[76]

Private music societies arose as well during this era. The composer Andreas Pevernage belonged to a St Cecilia society while working in Kortrijk, and as choirmaster at the Antwerp cathedral sponsored concerts in his own home to which he regularly invited music patrons. Both the university centers of Louvain and Leiden had private music groups that played a key role in the artistic life of these cities. Such organizations established a footing for the growing *collegium musicum* movement: as early as 1578, Leiden had a community ensemble, and by 1600, several Netherlandish cities had established groups of dilettantes and professional performers,

[74] A. Lehr, W. Truyen, and G. Huybens, *The Art of the Carillon in the Low Countries* (Tielt, Belgium, 1991).

[75] See Forney, "The Role of Secular Guilds."

[76] G. Spiessens, *Leven en werk van de Antwerpse luitcomponist Emanuel Adriaenssen*, 2 vols. (Brussels, 1974); facs. of Adriaenssen, *Pratum musicum.*

The natural marriage of music and verse placed the chambers of rhetoric in the forefront of music making. These literary guilds of amateur and professional writers, popular throughout the Low Countries, were an important force in the development of Dutch literature. Their verse was generally set to music, and presented in elaborate dramatic performances. One genre of Dutch lyric poetry, the *gezelschaplied*, presented the songs of the people, set to popular tunes of the day.[77]

The Low Countries continued to support a vital musical life during this tumultuous era, with both professional and amateur music making at its heart. The centers of creative activity gradually shifted, however, from the Southern Netherlands to the North, and to the Habsburg Imperial courts. Secular music—the chanson, lied, and madrigal—flourished during this time of religious turmoil, while church music advanced in the hands of a few Catholic composers.

1600–1640

By the early seventeenth century, the Low Countries were divided into two distinct and politically independent regions, the Northern and Southern Netherlands. The Eighty-Years' War against Spain, which began in 1566, was checked by a twelve-year truce beginning in 1606; this established the economic power of the newly formed, and largely Protestant, northern Dutch Republic. A blockade of the Southern Netherlands port of Antwerp allowed Amsterdam control of trade with southern Europe as well as the Baltic region. The European truce ended in 1618 with the onset of the Thirty Years' War, which pitted Germany and the Northern Netherlands against Spain. The struggle ended in 1648 with the Peace of Westphalia, which confirmed the independence of the northern Dutch Republic and its control of commerce as well as culture.

This polarization of North vs. South and Protestants vs. Catholics adversely affected the development of music during the era. Nevertheless, music was supported by the church, the state, and by the bourgeois class, whose life it permeated on a daily basis. Some of the best Netherlandish musicians were employed at the Brussels court of Archduke Albert and Isabella, who served as joint regents of the Low Countries (1599–1633), and at the Imperial courts in Vienna and Prague under Rudolf II (d. 1612) and Ferdinand II (d. 1637).

The most outstanding musician of this age was the Amsterdam organist Jan Pieterszoon Sweelinck (1562–1621), eulogized as the "Phoenix of Music."[78] His music was enriched by his knowledge of Italian and English styles, and through his friendship with composers John Bull and Peter Philips, both English recusants working in the Netherlands.

[77] On music and the chambers of rhetoric, see Forney, "The Role of Secular Guilds."

[78] J. van den Vondel, "Op Meester Joan Pietersen Sweling"; eulogy quoted in Henry A. Bruinsma, "An Introduction to Vondel and Music," *Tijdschrift van de Vereniging voor Nederlandse Muziekgeschiedenis*, 31 (1981), 100–101.

Sacred music

In this era, a discussion of Netherlandish church music must be divided between the Protestant North and the Catholic South. In the North, the sweeping Reform of Calvinism had impacted performance practices of sacred music through a declaration that instruments were heathen products that had no place in the church. The Dutch nevertheless preserved their beloved organs, using them exclusively for secular performance until around 1640. At this time, the musician/statesman Constantijn Huygens (1596–1687) anonymously published a tract advocating organ accompaniment of congregational singing, which he claimed had deteriorated to the point that

> it often sounds . . . more like howling and screaming rather than like human singing. . . . The tones sound as contrary as birds of different plumage, the meter is uneven like well-buckets, one rising as much as the other goes down. One yells at the top of his voice as if it were a matter of who can make the loudest noise and in this way would receive honors.[79]

This tract aroused an ecclesiastical dispute that was eventually resolved by the Calvinist church council's endorsement of the use of organ for the service.

The Northern composer J. P. Sweelinck contributed music for both Protestant and Catholic use. Probably a Protestant himself, he wrote a polyphonic setting of the complete Genevan Psalter, using the French metrical versions of Marot and Bèze. Published in four volumes between 1604 and 1621, his psalm settings range from four to eight voices; these works were likely intended for home devotions as well as for the Calvinist service. His setting of the original tunes varies from psalm to psalm: in some, he adopts a strict cantus firmus treatment with the tune in the Superius or Tenor, while in others he features the tune set in canon between two voices, in an echo effect. Some demonstrate antiphonal writing, while others are based on imitative counterpoint. Sweelinck's setting of Psalm 150, *Or soit lou, l'Éternel,* is a large, tripartite work for eight voices alternating between homophony and polyphony, and featuring quasi-canonic treatment between the two upper voices.

Sweelinck also published a collection of five-voice liturgical motets, *Cantiones sacrae* (1619), raising some question of his Protestant conversion. Unlike the psalm settings, these motets are freely composed, with more modern chromaticisms. They also feature a Baroque-style *basso seguente* that calls for an instrumental doubling of the lowest vocal part.

Polyphonic Dutch-texted psalm settings flourished during the seventeenth century. The first complete Dutch translation of the Genevan Psalter was *De Psalmen David* (1566) by Petrus Dathenus; his texts remained the official ones of the Dutch Calvinist Church well into the eighteenth century. In 1624, however, the Dutch poet and schoolmaster Dirk Rafaelszoon Camphuysen published his *Stichtelycke*

[79] C. Huygens, *Use and Nonuse of the Organ in the Churches of the United Netherlands* (Leiden, 1641), trans. and ed. E. E. Smit-Vanrotte (New York, 1964), 77.

rymen, om te lezen of te zingen (1624), intended as domestic devotional songs with accompaniment. Issued in many editions, this collection was first set to existing melodies, including some from Gastoldi's *balletti.* Although the Dutch Calvinist service used only rhyming psalms sung to the Genevan melodies, Camphuysen's collection opened the door for many new tunes and for freely-composed settings, the earliest of which appeared in 1652.[80]

During the early seventeenth century, Catholic church music was gradually shifting from multi-voiced imitative and polychoral settings to monody. Many Low Country composers were attracted to the new Italian style, among them Herman Hollanders (fl. 1626–37), one of the first in the north to employ the *stile concertato.* Jan Verrijt (*c.*1610–1650), organist at Rotterdam, continued the Italianate style in the North, publishing several concerted masses and a number of motets for two and three voices with basso continuo. The Dutch theorist Jan Albert Bannius (*c.*1597–1644) promoted the Italian monodic style through a system he called *musica flexanima*, or soul-moving music, in which the text was expressed musically through specific intervals, harmonies, and rhythms.[81] The Haarlem composer Cornelis Padbrué was the first in the North to exploit the *stile rappresentativo* in his Dutch motets set to texts by the Netherlandish poet laureate Joos van der Vondel.[82]

In the Southern Netherlands, Guillaume Messaus (1589–1640) functioned as choirmaster and schoolmaster at several Antwerp churches. His masses and motets feature both many-voiced settings, for up to twelve parts, as well as soloistic settings for two and three voices, all with basso continuo. Messaus also contributed to a new genre of polyphonic Christmas carols that developed in the Southern Netherlands during this era. Called *cantiones natalitiae*, these were sacred songs in Flemish or Latin, in simple, strophic four-part settings with figured bass. The composers of early seventeenth-century *cantiones natalitiae* were local church musicians of Antwerp, Brussels, and Ghent. The carols, mostly based on pre-existing songs, were sung in connection with Christmastide devotional services, especially the evening Marian *Salve* service. The earliest Flemish carols were published in the *Laudes vespertinae* of 1604 and 1629; among these was Messaus' *Een kindeken is ons geboren*, a popular tune that inspired three organ settings by the English keyboardist John Bull.[83]

80 J. de Bruijn and W. Heiting (eds.), *Psalmzingen in de Nederlanden van de zestiende eeuw tot heden* (Kampen, 1991).

81 On Ban and his theories, see Frits Noske, Introduction to *Joan Albert Ban: Zangh-Bloemzel (theoretical part) and Kort Sangh-Berich*, Early Music Theory in the Low Countries, 1 (Amsterdam, 1969).

82 B. van Asperen, "Padbrué's *Tranen*: De vroegste Noordnederlandse muziek in style moderno," *Tijdschrift voor oude muziek*, 2 (1987), 83–85.

83 Messaus was possibly the editor of a 1629 collection entitled *Cantiones natalitiae*; nearly half of the music in this book is by him. On this genre and for editions of Messaus, see Rasch, *De cantiones nataliatiae en het kerkelijke muziekleven.*

Catholic music at the royal courts

In Brussels, the court of Archduke Albert and Isabella attracted English Catholic musicians, including the composer and organist Peter Philips (*c.*1560–1628), who remained in their employment from 1597 until his death in 1628. While in Brussels, Philips published a number of liturgical music collections, including a book of five-voice motets for the principal feasts of the year and the common of the saints (1612); a book of eight-voice polychoral motets in the Roman tradition (1613); and, between 1613 and 1628, three sets of monodic motets for two or three voices and organ continuo. Philips also contributed to a repertory of French devotional songs intended as instruction for children; *Les Rossignols spirituels* of 1616 features new bass parts by Philips set to French popular tunes with religious verse.

The Brussels court composer Géry de Ghersem (*c.*1575–1630) served as a singer at the Madrid court of Philip II under its chapelmaster Philippe Rogier,[84] and headed the Archduke's chapel in Brussels from 1604 until his death in 1630. Much of Ghersem's music is now lost; a handful of surviving works demonstrate his commitment to the older polyphonic tradition in the mass and motet. His seven-voice *Missa "Ave virgo sanctissima"*, based on a motet by the Spanish composer Francisco Guerrero, was published with the masses of Rogier; his work continues the Flemish polyphonic tradition by setting a canon in the two upper voices. Ghersem shared his duties at court for a time with Jan van Turnhout (*c.*1545–*c.*1618), who wrote a mass for the joyous entry of Archduke Ernst into Antwerp in 1594.

The Imperial court in Vienna, politically linked to the Netherlands, drew its musicians from the region as well. Court composers Lambert de Sayve (*c.*1548–1614) and Carl Luython (*c.*1557–1620) continued writing in a conservative style.[85] Luython's short parody masses (all based on works by Monte) for manageable forces may reflect the weak financial position of the Vienna court during this era, while Sayve's large, modally-ordered motet collection *Sacrae symphoniae* (1612) features polychoral writing for eight, twelve, and sixteen voices.

The Netherlandish musical tradition at the Madrid court continued under Philip III (r. 1598–1621) and Philip IV (r. 1621–1665) with the engagement of Matheo Romero (born Mathieu Rosmarin in Liège in 1575) as chapelmaster in 1599. A member of the Flemish chapel in Madrid since his youth, Romero wrote polychoral Latin motets and Spanish villancicos; both genres look forward to the *stile moderno*. Pietro Cerone named him, in his monumental treatise *El melopeo* of 1613, as one of the most famous musicians of his era.[86] After Romero's retirement in 1638, the Madrid chapel was finally headed by a Spaniard.

[84] Wagner, "Music of Composers from the Low Countries at the Spanish Court of Philip II."

[85] See C. P. Comberiati, *Late Renaissance Music at the Habsburg Court: Polyphonic Settings of the Mass Ordinary at the Court of Rudolf II, 1576–1612* (New York, 1987).

[86] P. Becquart, *Musiciens néerlandais à la cour de Madrid*, Académie royale de Belgique, Memoires de la classe des beaux-arts, 13, no. 4 (Brussels, 1967), 205.

Secular vocal music

Secular music was fueled by the burgeoning *collegium musicum* movement and the rise of musical literacy among Netherlanders. The principal secular genres during this era were the chanson and the madrigal—the latter both Italian and Dutch. Paramount among chanson composers in the North was Sweelinck, discussed earlier, who published a collection of five-voice works of 1594, including a setting of the popular *chanson spirituel Susanne ung jour*. In this work, Sweelinck places the famous cantus firmus, taken from a sixteenth-century chanson by Didier Lupi, in slow moving notes in the Superius part. His later chansons are two- and three-voice works, with a more transparent texture and occasional canonic sections, set to texts by Desportes, Ronsard, and Marot. Sweelinck also wrote a number of Italian madrigals modeled on those of Marenzio, Ferrabosco, and Andrea Gabrieli. Curiously, he never wrote vocal works in his native Dutch language.

In this era of political upheaval, Northerners served the nationalist cause through their promotion of the vernacular. Thus, the Leiden composer Cornelis Schuyt's collection *Hollandsche Madrigalen* (appearing in 1603) was followed by the publication of many Dutch-texted secular works: among these was *Bruylofts-gesang* (1619), a collection of five-voice wedding songs by Nicolas Vallet, and *Kusjes* (Kisses, 1631) by the Haarlem composer Cornelis Thymanszoon Padbrué, set to Dutch translations of erotic Latin poetry by Janus Secundus (1511–1536). The Dutch writer Jan Albert Bannius demonstrated his theory of how to portray emotions through music in his collection *Zang-bloemzel* of 1642. In a more popular vein, the monophonic folklike songs of the *Nederlandtsche Gedenck-clanck* (1626) retold the political history of the war against the Spanish in the vernacular.

Music printing and the dissemination of styles

The printing firm begun by the archtypographer Christophe Plantin in the mid sixteenth century continued to issue liturgical and polyphonic music books well into the seventeenth century. After the death of Plantin in 1589, his heirs took over the prosperous business, which then had locations both in Antwerp and in Leiden. The northern branch of the firm issued four prints by the organist Cornelis Schuyt (1557–1616), among them a book of five-voice Italian madrigals (1600), a collection of large-voiced wedding madrigals (*Hymneo*, 1611), and a book of his instrumental ensemble dances (1611). Schuyt's personal music library reflects the strong interest among northerners in the Italian madrigal.[87] A volume of chansons and madrigals by Sweelinck, entitled *Rimes françaises et italiennes* (1612), was also issued in Leiden by Plantin's heirs.

The Antwerp branch of Plantin's firm focused on a more international market in issuing four sacred music books by Duarte Lobo, the most outstanding Portuguese composer of the early seventeenth century. The firm continued to print breviaries

[87] R. Rasch and T. Wind, "The Music Library of Cornelis Schuyt," in *From Ciconia to Sweelinck*, 327–53.

and missals and, by command of Pope Urban VIII, issued in 1644 a new and costly choirbook edition of Palestrina's hymns with updated liturgical texts.

Many sixteenth-century works were reprinted in the Northern Netherlands in the first decades of the 1600s, often with the addition of new Dutch-texted pieces or, in some cases, with Dutch translations of the earlier repertory. Among these is the very popular *Septième Livre des chansons*, first published in 1560 in Louvain, and reissued with added repertory in Amsterdam in some ten new editions, the last several released by Paulus Matthysz in Amsterdam at mid-century.[88] Matthysz also issued a number of instrumental music books, some for virtuoso solo recorder and others for ensembles. Some Low Country publishers, notably Phalèse in the Southern Netherlands, specialized in books geared toward dilettante tastes. Devotional music was also in vogue; thus numerous religious songbooks in French and in Dutch were issued for home use and for the instruction of children.

The turmoil of the Eighty Years' War inspired nationalistic and political songs that were published anonymously in the late sixteenth century and eventually collected in the famous *Nederlandtsche Gedenck-clanck*, issued in Haarlem by Adriaen Valerius in 1626. These songs, many set to well-known tunes, narrate the events of the war, particularly the victories of the Prince of Orange and of the rebellious Northern noblemen popularly known as the *geuzen* (beggars).[89] Valerius' collection presents the tune and text above an intabulation for lute or cittern. One of these tunes, "Wilt heden nu treden," is well known today as an American hymn of Thanksgiving ("We gather together to ask the Lord's blessing").

Instruments and instrumental music

Long renowned as a center for harpsichord and organ building, the Netherlands rose in fame for its composers of keyboard music. In 1610, the first Dutch keyboard publication appeared: a collection of psalm arrangements set in tablature by Hendrick Speuy (*c.*1575–1625), organist at Dordrecht.[90] The era saw a rise in organ music, when, beginning in the 1630s, organ playing was eventually restored to the Calvinist service as an accompaniment to psalm singing. Organs damaged during the Reform were rebuilt throughout the Netherlands, many by the Langhedul family, active from 1475 until 1635 and important to the development of the early Baroque instrument.

J. P. Sweelinck was the most famous organist of his day; his position at the Old Church (Oude Kerk) in Amsterdam required him to give daily recitals, before or after the service. Also renowned as a teacher, Sweelinck counted among his pupils

88 Vanhulst, "Un Success de l'édition musicale."

89 *Nederlandtsche Gedenck-clanck* (Haarlem, 1626; facs. Utrecht, 1968); modern edn in *De liederen uit Valerius' Nederlandtsche Gedenck-clanck*, ed. K. P. Bernet Kempers and C. M. Lelij (Rotterdam, 1941).

90 *De psalmen Davids, gestelt op het tabulatuer van het orghel ende clavecymmel met 2. partijen* (Dordrecht, 1610). On this collection, see Alan Curtis, "Hendrick Speuy and the Earliest Printed Dutch Keyboard Music," *Tijdschrift voor Nederlandse Muziekgeschiedenis*, 19 (1963), 143–62.

the German composers Samuel Scheidt and Heinrich Scheidemann. Sweelinck's keyboard works include over twenty sets of variations on Latin, English, Dutch, and German songs, as well as toccatas and fantasias. His style shows distinct English traits, undoubtedly influenced by his friendship with John Bull and Peter Philips, both resident in the Low Countries. Several works are modeled on English pieces, among them a *Pavana Lacrimae* based on the famous Dowland song *Flow, my teares* that inspired settings by Byrd and Morley as well. Sweelinck's variation technique reflects the influence of English virginalists, and in these works he sets secular songs as well as chorale melodies.[91] He adopts certain harmonic, melodic, and formal structures of pre-existent English pieces, imbuing them with Netherlandish polyphonic technique.

Sweelinck's free-form works—in particular, his toccatas and fantasias written in the Italian style—rank among his greatest achievements. The imitative fantasias, based on a single theme, are influential in the development of the monothematic fugue. The echo fantasias transfer a popular vocal technique to the keyboard idiom, and his well-known *Fantasia cromatica* manipulates a descending chromatic theme that became a cliché of seventeenth-century style.

In the Southern Netherlands, the court of Archduke Albert and Isabella employed a number of prominent keyboard composers, among them Peeter Cornet (*c.*1560–1628)—a composer of imaginative fantasias—as well as the Englishmen Peter Philips and John Bull. Peter Philips served the royal court for some thirty years as an organist; unfortunately, few of his liturgical keyboard works survive. His early keyboard pieces are included in the *Fitzwilliam Virginal Book* (copied 1609–19).

John Bull (*c.*1562–1628) served briefly as an organist at the Brussels court in 1613, after which he was employed at Antwerp Cathedral. Having left England amidst a scandal, Bull succeeded Raymond Waelrant, son of the publisher/composer Hubert Waelrant, in 1617 as the church's full-time organist, a position he held until his death in 1628. Much of Bull's keyboard music is extant only in manuscript, raising many questions of attribution; however, several sources can be associated with his years in Antwerp. These contain fantasias, canons (including a puzzle canon), dances, and variations on Flemish songs, three on the tune *Een kindeken is ons geboren*. His organ plainsong settings of *Salve regina* and *Salvator mundi* were clearly intended as liturgical works for use in the Antwerp church.

The carillon, which originated in the Low Countries during the fifteenth century, underwent significant technical improvements during this era. Utrecht was a center of bell founding, and its carilloneur, Jacob van Eyck (*c.*1589–1657), studied the acoustics of bells, working along with the Hemony family of bellfounders to refine and thus increase the purity of the instrument. Cities generally took pride in the size and quality of their carillon, which was heard in daily or weekly concerts. Repertory for the instrument was largely arrangements of all types of vocal or instrumental music.[92]

91 See A. Curtis, *Sweelinck's Keyboard Music* (London: Oxford University Press, 1969).

92 See Lehr, Truyen, and Huybens, *The Art of the Carillon in the Low Countries*.

The Netherlands saw the development of a school of lutenist composers in the early seventeenth century. Following the tradition established by the Antwerp lutenist Emanuel Adriaenssen (see p. 270), Nicolas Vallet, a French composer working in Amsterdam, published works in French tablature for solo lute as well as his *XXI Psalmen Davids* for solo voice with lute (1615) and several lute quartets. The Leiden composer Joachim van den Hove issued a collection of preludes for solo lute in 1616, and he intabulated or arranged many pieces for voice and lute, issued in two large anthologies (*Florida*, 1601; *Delitiae musicae*, 1612). These works, written for Renaissance lute, clearly served the growing amateur music-making public.

Cornelis Schuyt of Leiden continued the tradition of instrumental ensemble dances established by Susato and Phalèse in the mid-sixteenth century with a 1611 collection including twelve *padovane* and *gagliarde*, one set in each mode, along with several six-voice *canzone alla francese*. The earliest Baroque-style sonatas in the Low Countries were by Nicolas a Kempis, organist at the Brussels church of St Gudule, who wrote four volumes entitled *Symphoniae* (1644–47); these works, principally for strings, range from solo sonatas with continuo to works for six parts. Several important music collections for recorder were published in Amsterdam in the 1640s as well: Jacob van Eyck's *Euterpe* and *Der fluyten lust-hof* established a solo literature for the instrument that includes variations, some highly virtuosic, on popular melodies.[93]

The Southern Netherlands was a center for instrument building, notably strings and keyboards, throughout the sixteenth and seventeenth centuries. The Ruckers firm of virginal and harpsichord builders, established in Antwerp in the late sixteenth century by Hans Ruckers (*c.*1545–1598), continued to produce the most sought-after instruments of the day. These elaborately decorated instruments had a rich and resonant sound balanced across their full range. Joannes Couchet (1615–1655), a descendent of Hans Ruckers, built harpsichords and virginals similar in sound, design, and construction to those of Ruckers. A number of Ruckers and Couchet instruments survive today.[94]

Music and burgher life

Among professional musicians, the *stadpijpers* or city players remained an important urban institution throughout the seventeenth century; this ensemble of five or six musicians played weekly concerts and provided mid-day music to entertain the burghers as well as special performances for feast days and processions. In 1636, the city corps of instrumentalists played for the inauguration of the University of Utrecht and, after that, performed for all university ceremonies including promotions and orations. The city players also participated frequently in activities of their local *collegium musicum*, an association of professional musicians, academics, and

[93] On these instrumental works, see R. Rasch, "Some Mid-Seventeenth Century Dutch Collections of Instrumental Ensemble Music," *Tijdschrift voor Nederlandse Muziekgeschiedenis*, 22 (1972): 160–200.

[94] See O'Brien, *Ruckers*.

dilettantes that sprang up in cities throughout the region. Perhaps a response to the decline of church and court music in the North, the *collegium musicum* movement was vital to civic musical life in the Netherlands.[95] Amsterdam's Collegium was one of the earliest, begun in the 1590s; both Jan Tollius and Sweelinck dedicated music books to this organization. The Collegium Musicum Ultrajectinum of Utrecht, formed in 1631, was notable for its performances of instrumental music, which continued into the nineteenth century.

Education was important to the burgher middle class in the Netherlands, and music was central to the quadrivium-based curriculum.[96] Middle- and upper-class men and women were expected to be able to sing or play an instrument, and family music-making, well documented in paintings of the era, was a frequent entertainment. A series of salon concerts took place in the home of the writer Pieter Corneliszoon Hooft (1581–1647), at the castle of Muiden outside of Amsterdam; these events attracted an elite circle of nobility, poets, and musicians who met to play as well as listen to music. Among the participants of this group (the *Muiderkring*) was the Netherlandish poet Joost van der Vondel (1587–1679), who summed up the musical sounds he heard in Amsterdam:

> The town hall towers hold their beautiful bells; rich with sound, Hemoni [carillon makers] play a heavenly bell music. As fast as a lute, or like Sweelinck's organ pipes, and fleeting dulcimer, gripped with strong fingers, here trombone, cromhorn and flute blow out of the grand windows the great spirit of Orlando, to the glory of the city, and burgers promenade, refreshed by happy music . . .[97]

[95] See R. Rasch, "The Dutch Republic," in *Man & Music*, ed. S. Sadie, IV: *The Late Baroque Era: From the 1680s to 1740*, ed. George Buelow (Basingstoke and Englewood Cliffs, NJ, 1993), 398.

[96] See M. Medford, "The Low Countries," in *Man & Music*, ed. S. Sadie, III: *The Early Baroque Era: From the Late 16th Century to the 1660s*, ed. Curtis Price (Basingstoke and Englewood Cliffs, NJ, 1993), 209–10.

[97] J. van den Vondel, *Inwydinge van het Stadhuis te Amsterdam*, trans. in Bruinsma, "An Introduction to Vondel," 98.

15

MUSIC, PRINT, AND SOCIETY IN SIXTEENTH-CENTURY EUROPE

Iain Fenlon

DURING the second half of the fifteenth century, the reproduction of written texts of all kinds began to move from the copyist's desk to the printer's workshop. That the impact of Gutenberg's invention upon all fields of knowledge, learning, and information was profound is generally agreed, though the change was neither as immediate nor as wholesale as is sometimes claimed; throughout the sixteenth century and into the next, some categories of text continued to circulate in manuscript rather than in print. Older studies of the phenomenon tend to concentrate on the technical rather than the cultural aspects of early printing; the historiography of the early book is filled with studies of different aspects of printing processes and workshop practices, including considerations of type (and its migration), paper manufacture, imposition and presswork, elements of illustration and decoration, and patterns of production and selling. These subjects, sometimes approached on their own as a contribution to the history of the printed book seen as an aspect of the applied arts, have been combined in other cases with biographies and descriptive catalogues to form studies of individual printers and their output. More recently, and largely under the influence of French scholarship, the picture has gradually begun to change, and what one writer has called "the unacknowledged revolution" has begun to be studied as part of cultural history and to be concerned with the relationship of print culture to questions of literacy, the transmission and dissemination of texts, patterns of reading and book ownership, the propagandistic uses of print, and its relationship to orality and popular culture, in a richly textured approach generally known as "l'histoire du livre."

The traditional models evolved by specialists in the history of printing and related topics in the hand-press period have in turn largely determined the style and content of the study of early music printing. Here too the field has also been largely preoccupied with typography, bibliography, the study of press variants, and the operations of individual printers and publishers. The general picture is clear. As Francis Bacon, commenting on Gutenberg's invention and its consequences from the vantage point of the early seventeenth century, wrote, the coming of the printed book had altered "the appearance and state of the whole world."[1] And, we might add, its sound. By the middle of the sixteenth century, not only music itself but also treatises, textbooks, instruction manuals, and tutors were being produced in their hundreds and sometimes thousands to cater for the growing audience for music in the larger urban centers of Italy, France, Germany, and, some decades later, the areas served by the presses of Susato and Phalèse in northern Europe. In terms of the geographical distribution of this phenomenon it is perhaps useful to think of a center, roughly speaking bounded by Paris and Lyons to the west, Nuremberg and Frankfurt to the east, Antwerp to the north, and Rome to the south, together with a periphery, including Spain and Portugal, where the impact of printing was sporadic and much slower. In London, for example, local printing made little difference to established traditions of transmission until the late 1580s, and even then it continued to coexist with manuscript forms rather than replacing them, to a much greater degree than anywhere within the central area of production. A small number of music books (collections for vihuela and polyphonic choirbooks being two particular specialities) were printed in some of the larger towns and cities of the Iberian peninsula, but, as in England, Poland, and other places distant from the main centers, manuscript traditions continued and a great deal of music was imported. In general, by making copies of music available in such quantity, and throughout such a widespread geographical area, the press made a powerful impact on musical culture in general.

The first collection of polyphony to be printed anywhere was the *Harmonice musices Odhecaton A*, issued by Ottaviano Petrucci at Venice in 1501. This was evidently sufficiently successful in commercial terms to encourage Petrucci to reissue the book, and during the next decade in Venice he went on to print more than forty editions of chansons, *frottole*, masses, motets, *laude* and intabulations for lute.[2] By this time Venice had already become established as one of the most important European centers of the printing trade, rivalled only by Paris. The first book from a Venetian press had been issued in 1469, and within the next twenty years the city had gradually emerged as one of the major centers of the industry. By 1500 about a hundred and fifty printing shops had been set up there, and by the end

[1] For the cultural effects of print in general, see L. Febvre and H. J. Martin, *The Coming of the Book: The Impact of Printing 1450–1800* (London and New York, 1990), a translation of their classic study, *L'Apparition du livre* (Paris, 1958); E. Eisenstein, *The Printing Press as an Agent of Change: Communications and Cultural Transformations in Early-Modern Europe*, 2 vols. (Cambridge, 1979). An overview of the impact of music printing in Italy in the first half of the century is given in I. Fenlon, *Music, Print and Culture in Early Sixteenth-Century Italy* [The Panizzi Lectures, 1994] (London, 1995). The best technical account of early music printing and publishing can be found in the relevant parts of Edmund Poole's contributions (Part I) of D. W. Krummel and S. Sadie (eds.), *Music Printing and Publishing* (London, 1990), which is also useful as a general reference work on the subject.

[2] For Petrucci's output, see C. Sartori, *Bibliografia delle opere musicali stampate da Ottaviano Petrucci* (Florence, 1948), and its sequel, "Nuove conclusive aggiunte alla 'Bibliografia del Petrucci,'" *Collectanea historiae musicae*, 1 (1953), 175–210. Sartori provides further additions and corrections to his account of Petrucci's editions in his *Dizionario degli editori musicali italiani* (Florence, 1958), 117–20.

of the century they had produced between them some two million printed books. Since the total population of Europe was then about 55–60 million (of whom the majority were illiterate), it is easy to see that books printed in Venice formed the backbone of sixteenth-century collections, as surviving inventories confirm. As the richest and most cosmopolitan city in Italy, with a stable government and currency, lying at the confluence of major trade routes and at the heart of an established and extensive commercial network, Venice was at the center of an elaborate system of book production, sale, and distribution. The preservation of copies of early Italian printed music in places along the Istrian and Dalmatian coasts (then part of the Venetian Terra da Mar), or the impressive library of more than 450 printed editions and manuscripts put together by the Augsburg patrician Hans Heinrich Herwart (1520–1583), are just two examples that show how music travelled along established trade routes. Herwart, a member of a prosperous commercial family with business interests all over the continent, gathered his collection from different sources in a number of countries, and particularly from Venice.[3] With its domination of both a large overseas empire and its control of wealthy towns on the *terraferma* such as Brescia, Treviso, Vicenza, Verona, and the old university city of Padua, the Republic was able to command considerable markets both in Italy and beyond the Alps. It was the logical place for Petrucci to start his business.

From a purely technical point of view, the novelty of Petrucci's "invention" of music printing is more apparent than real. The printing of a book by sending the sheets through the press a number of times, adding an additional layer of symbols on each occasion (a process known as multiple-impression printing), had long been practiced to print the black and red layers of liturgical incunabula. A good number of these contain neumatic notation, and between 1476 and 1500 liturgical books with music, that is both notes and staves, had been produced by some 66 printers working in 25 towns and cities. In this sense, the technology that Petrucci used to produce his editions had been established in the trade, both in Italy and elsewhere, for some time.[4] Nor was he the first to print mensural music, since this is found in a small number of fifteenth-century printed books; the earliest, Francesco Niger's *Grammatica* (Venice: Theodor of Würzburg, 1480), contains sections on metre, rhythm, and harmony, the last of which is equipped with notation consisting of four lines of notes with a clef but without staves, printed by type. A decade or so later Michel de Toulouse, working in Paris, printed two pages of mensural notation using rather badly cast type in his edition of the anonymous *L'Art et instruction de bien danser* (undated, *c.*1496), and in 1499 Johann Emerich of Speyer included a mensural Credo, also printed by type, in his *Graduale*. Yet another incunabulum, the *Historia Baetica* (Rome: Eucharius Silber, 1493) written by the papal secretary Carolo Verardi, actually includes an anonymous Italian song for

[3] H. C. Slim, "The Music Library of the Augsburg Patrician Hans Heinrich Herwart (1520–1583)," *Annales musicologiques*, 7 (1964–77), 68–[109].

[4] The standard bibliography of 15th-century books containing music notation is K. Meyer-Baer, *Liturgical Music Incunabula: A Descriptive Catalogue* (London, 1962), now superseded for books printed in Italy by M. K. Duggan, *Italian Music Incunabula: Printers and Type* (Berkeley, 1992).

four voices printed by poorly cut woodblocks and arranged on facing pages in traditional choirbook format, in effect the first known instance of printed polyphony, predating the *Odhecaton A* by some eight years. Nevertheless, while on the one hand Petrucci's music printing did not involve any innovative processes as such, on the other it did establish new standards of artistic and technical performance in the design, layout, and presswork of music. For the first time, it also successfully introduced printed music as a distinct presence in the by now well-established trade of printing and publishing. Petrucci's real innovation was to have invented the concept of a printed book entirely devoted to music, influenced perhaps by Aldine's editions of the classics.

For the early volumes that Petrucci produced, the models in terms of format and design were, as is so often the case in the history of printing, the manuscript books that were already in use. At first he used the traditional choirbook arrangement for secular vocal music, but subsequently he changed to the partbook, which had come into vogue for manuscript music a little before the beginning of the sixteenth century and which was to become the favored method for the presentation of printed music in the following decades. This symbolic and practical change signals that these publications, directed to the competent amateur as well as to the professional performer, are filled with approachable music presented in a manageable and practical form. It is hardly surprising that, in order to make an impact on the market, Petrucci concentrated on producing collections devoted to the main international repertories of the day, music that had already established a considerable currency through its widespread dissemination in manuscript form. The other major area of the trade that Petrucci attempted to exploit was the largely institutional audience for sacred music. His volumes of masses, mass sections, and motets, essentially given over to the major repertories of the Josquin generation (and to a lesser extent those of his successors), represent a clear attempt to cater to the sizeable constituency for these repertories that had developed during the second half of the fifteenth century, in tandem with the considerable increase in both size and activity of the *cappelle* of princely and other institutions throughout the continent. All the signs are that Petrucci's business prospered, at least to judge by the wide distribution of his books both inside and outside Italy. A good number of his titles ran to second and even third editions, and his books found their way not only into the hands of professional scribes but also into those of buyers north of the Alps. As early as 1515 some English prelates were trying to obtain Italian *frottole*, presumably in Petrucci's printings.[5]

Petrucci's success with the printing of polyphonic music soon encouraged other printers both in Italy and elsewhere to try their hand. Erhard Oeglin entered the field as early as 1507 with his *Melopoiae*, a collection of 22 four-part settings of Horatian odes set by Petrus Tritonius, printed in Augsburg. This ran to a second edition, printed by Oeglin in the same year, which corrects the errors of the first and omits three settings of texts not by Horace. A few years later Oeglin followed

[5] R. Brown, *Four Years at the Court of Henry VIII* [1515–19]: *Selection of Dispatches Written by the Venetian Ambassador, Sebastian Giustinian*, 2 vols. (London, 1854), 1: 80–81.

this up with two further collections, mostly devoted to German songs written by Henricus Isaac and others connected with the court of Maximilian I. These are the first editions of music to be printed in Germany by using Petrucci's method of multiple impression, and Oeglin's example was soon followed by others in the area such as Peter Schoeffer of Mainz, whose father had been an associate of Gutenberg. Some of these northern productions are of considerable typographical complexity. Johannes Reuchlin's *De accentibus et orthographia linguae Hebraicae*, for example, issued in 1518, uses roman, Greek, and Hebrew fonts, includes three pages printed in both red and black, and finishes with nine pages of music presenting four-voice versions of scriptural cantillations. Highly professional though some of these books may be, music printing was not yet definitely established in the commerce of the trade north of the Alps.

Even in Italy, which lay at the heart of the book business, it was not until the arrival of an ambitious Istrian woodcutter, Andrea Antico, that Petrucci experienced any real competition in what was still a small, slowly developing and uncertain market. Antico's first edition, the *Canzoni nove con alcune scelte de varii libri di canto*, published in October 1510 in Rome in collaboration with the printer Marcello Silber and the woodblock cutter Giambattista Columba, inaugurated what quickly became a struggle for the still small audience for printed music. In terms of format and general appearance, the *Canzoni nove* is clearly indebted both repertorially and in appearance to Petrucci's *frottola* books, from which about half its contents, dominated by the work of Bartolomeo Tromboncino, are taken. Three years later Antico improved his position considerably by securing a privilege from Pope Leo X to print music in the Papal States with a ten-year copyright on the repertory that he issued. Just nineteen days later Petrucci, who had recently moved his business to his native Fossombrone in the duchy of Urbino, was granted a similar papal patent, which, in what seems to have been a clear challenge to Antico's entry into the market for keyboard music, also included the exclusive right to print organ tablature. These two papal licences put the two printers on an apparently equal commercial footing in Rome and the Papal States, and for the first time in the history of music printing and publishing genuinely competitive conditions now existed. Matters came to a head in 1516, when Leo withdrew Petrucci's right to publish organ tablature and assigned it to Antico instead, perhaps because Petrucci had failed to produce anything of the kind under the terms of his exclusive patent. Less than three months later Antico issued his *Frottole intabulate da sonare organi libro primo* (Rome, 1516), a collection of 26 organ arrangements of vocal pieces largely taken from his own collections. This is the first book of printed keyboard music.

In practice, the rivalry between Antico and Petrucci that developed during the second decade of the century was partly one of competing technologies. Throughout his career Petrucci had relied upon multiple-impression methods, at first sending the sheet through the press three times, a method that required highly accurate registration, but later reducing the number of impressions from three to two. For the rest of his career both the appearance of his books and his workshop practices remained largely unaltered, though both the quality of his printing and the condition of his typographical materials consistently deteriorated during the second half of his career. Worn type remained unreplaced, and the most elegant and ambitious book printed during his Fossombrone years was not music at all but the handsome folio of Paul of Middleburg's *De recta Paschae celebratione* (Fossombrone, 1513). This falling off in quality was accompanied by a lessening of interest in more recent composition and a reluctance to take new initiatives; in this context Petrucci's failure to exploit the possibilities of the papal privilege for the printing of organ tablature, which would have required investment in new fonts, is characteristic of his apparent determination to avoid undue financial risk and fresh capital investment. Following his move to Fossombrone he mostly concentrated on reprintings of earlier titles and on a narrower range of repertory. Something of a surprise comes with the interest in a new Roman-Florentine repertory indicated by the publication of Bartolomeo Pisano's *Musica* of 1520, and by the presence of three madrigals (including one by Verdelot) in the Fossombrone leaves; these fragments of a tenor partbook come from an otherwise unknown publication and may have been proofs of a book that was never completed. At the end of the 1530s Petrucci seems to have contemplated a return to music publishing. The evidence consists of two uncut sheets containing four leaves each of the tenor and bass partbooks of an edition of pieces from Moderne's *Motteti del fiore*, originally issued in 1532. The colophon carries the date 1538, Petrucci's name and printer's mark, and also the name of a business partner, Bartolomeo Egnazio, an engraver from Fossombrone.[6] Both Buglhat and Gardano had issued motet collections in 1538 before the date in the colophon of these leaves, and Petrucci may have felt the market to be too uncertain to bear yet a further collection; certainly no complete copy is known, and the book is not mentioned in sixteenth-century library inventories and bibliographies.

All of Antico's books are produced by combining woodblocks and type, a process that had a long ancestry. Simple block prints had first appeared at the end of the fourteenth century, usually as images printed on one side of single sheets of paper, and by the end of the fifteenth the technique by which texts are printed in type and blocks are used for initials and borders was being used in a wide range of books. The same procedure had also been used for printing musical notation, both neumatic and mensural, during the second half of the fifteenth century, albeit on a modest scale. By 1500 some dozen books containing woodcut music had been issued in Italy, including ten theoretical works that use blocks for diagrams and notated examples, the most accomplished of which is Franchino Gaffurio's *Practica musice*, first published by Johannes Petrus de Lomatius in Milan in 1496, and two missals, one of which includes 46 pages of monophonic music. The woodcut method continued to be used to print music in many parts of Europe during the early decades of the sixteenth century alongside the newer technology. So, as with Petrucci, Antico was not a technical innovator as such despite his claim (in the *Liber quindecim missarum* of 1516) that he was the first to cut notes in wood; rather, he was adapting printing methods that had already been tried and tested for some time, although with graphically different material. Antico's technical

6 T. M. Gialdroni and A. Ziino, "New Light on Ottaviano Petrucci's activity, 1520–38: An Unknown Print of the *Motteti dal Fiore*," *Early Music*, 29 (2001), 500–532.

achievements, like Petrucci's, were more to do with refinement than with novelty, for all that he was the first to produce whole books of music in this way rather than a few pages of incidental diagrams or examples incorporating musical notation in volumes otherwise given over to text.

In terms of production costs, the woodcut method does not seem to have been markedly cheaper than the multiple-impression process. Although the latter involved the labour of the paper going through the press a number of times, cutting blocks was obviously more time-consuming than setting type. Since the cost of paper and ink was a constant, it seems that the labour costs of the two printing methods more or less offset each other. This is not surprising, since the cost of paper was high and represented the single most expensive element in the economics of book production; although there are differences of opinion about the percentage of costs that paper represented, it is clear that it was the high price of paper rather than that of labour or other materials that largely determined the cost of books in general.[7] The argument is confirmed by what little is known about the prices of music books themselves. For example, Antico's *Canzoni nove* of 1510, a quarto of 42 folios closely and presumably intentionally modelled on Petrucci's publications, was bought in Rome in 1521 for 75 quatrines, a price close to that paid at about the same time for a Petrucci quarto lutebook of 56 folios.[8] Thereafter, with one notable exception, Antico seems to have restricted himself to the small octavo format, and using this he was able to produce modest collections that sold for between a third and a half of Petrucci's editions and were presumably intended to undercut his market.

The exception to the overall impression of Antico's cut-price operations is the *Liber quindecim missarum*, a heroic attempt, realized with formidable artistry and technical skill, to transfer the format, design, and visual effect of traditional deluxe illuminated manuscripts onto the printed page using his usual combination of woodcut and type. Both technically and economically this was a considerable undertaking. According to the contract, one of the few to have survived from this period, Antico was to divide the publication expenses with Ottaviano Scotto, an experienced member of an established Venetian dynasty of booksellers and printers. The third party to the agreement was the printer Antonio Giunta, a member of a Florentine family also well-established in the printing and publishing business with presses in Florence, Venice, and Lyons and bookshops in the major European cities. The *Liber quindecim missarum*, a time-consuming and therefore expensive book to produce (as Antico admitted in the preface), was in consequence costly to buy; the contract specifies that it was to be sold for 20 giulii retail, roughly

[7] According to P. Gaskell, *A New Introduction to Bibliography* (Oxford, 1972), 177, paper represented about 75% of the total direct costs of book production in the 16th century, and wages nearly all the rest. L. Voet, *The Golden Compasses: A History and Evaluation of the Printing and Publishing Activities of the Officina Plantiniana at Antwerp*, 2 vols. (Amsterdam, 1969), 1: 19 gives a figure of 60–65% rising to 75% for some large printings.

[8] The prices of Petrucci's and Antico's books are taken from C. W. Chapman, "Printed Collections of Polyphonic Music Owned by Ferdinand Columbus," *Journal of the American Musicological Society*, 21 (1968), 51.

equivalent to 480 quatrines; a price per sheet four times that of an average-sized Petrucci edition. More than a thousand copies of this luxurious folio were produced, but only a handful of examples now survives. Among early owners was the church of San Luigi dei Francesi in Rome, whose copy was evidently much used; an inventory of 1562 describes it as "tutto stracciato et senza coperta et sciolto" (all in shreds, without its cover and falling apart).[9] Once again, we are reminded that even the most expensive and elaborate music books were usually purchased for practical use.

This example raises an interesting series of connected questions relating to the buying public for books. What was the audience for printed music, and how did it change in the first half of the sixteenth century? How and why did the market for printed music grow during the first half of the sixteenth century? How did the dynamics of the music trade work? What was the relationship between composer, printer, and publisher? In short, is it possible to recover any sense of the complicated connections between the economics of music printing and publishing and the changing musical culture of the early sixteenth century? It should be said immediately that the answers to such questions are greatly hindered by a lack of crucial information about the books themselves. The casualty rate among editions of music has been high, perhaps as great as that for ephemera such as ballads, broadsides, almanacs, and prognostications with which they share an essentially utilitarian purpose. The problem is particularly severe for the early decades of the century. Few books printed before 1540 survive in more than one copy, and of many titles only a single example is recorded. Worse, many editions are lost completely, while others are often badly mutilated or are incomplete in the sense that only some of the partbooks of a complete set have been preserved. Occasionally we have the second book of a series but not the first one, and sometimes reprinted volumes imply original editions that have not survived, while in other cases the printer and place of publication cannot be determined at all. It is fair to say that the landscape of the earliest phase of the printing and publishing of polyphonic music is haunted, not only by the traditional bibliographical "ghosts" created by incorrect cataloguing, but also by the spectres of genuinely lost books, fragmentary leaves of otherwise unknown publications, undated volumes, missing colophons, and incomplete sets. Even for the second half of the century, when edition sizes were probably larger, often only one or two copies remain of what was probably a standard print run of somewhere between five hundred and a thousand copies, and in some cases there are no survivors at all.[10] It is symptomatic of the general picture that no copies are known of Valerio Dorico's edition of Palestrina's *Motecta festorum totius anni . . . liber primus* (Rome, 1563) which, it can be safely assumed, must have sold well, or that only a few leaves of the 1569 English translation of Adrien Le Roy's *Instruction*

[9] Quoted from L. L. Perkins, "Notes bibliographiques au sujet de l'ancien fond musical de l'Église de Saint Louis des Français à Rome," *Fontes artis musicae*, 16 (1969), 60.

[10] By comparing a number of 16th-century contracts from different countries, R. J. Agee, "A Venetian Music Printing Contract in the Sixteenth Century," *Studi musicali*, 15 (1986), 59–65, concludes that 500 copies was the usual print run for music. It seems more likely that edition size varied according to variables that allowed printers to estimate the size of the market.

. . . *for Gitterne* have been recovered from a binding, where they had been reused as strengtheners. It has been estimated that in general terms about 20 percent of all books printed before 1600 have been lost, and while this is obviously a crude average that includes widely different types of book, the rate of loss for music is probably greater still. Moreover, since the statistical sample of survivors is so restricted and only a small percentage of these copies contain any indications of original ownership or use, our ability to evaluate the size and nature of the buying public for early printed music is clearly inhibited.

Some help with the difficulties caused by such holes in the bibliographical record is provided by contemporary compilations such as Conrad Gesner's *Pandectae* and Anton Francesco Doni's *Libraria*, both of which refer to books or editions that have been lost. Of these two the first is by far the more reliable. A Swiss writer and naturalist of restless humanist disposition, Gesner published, as a sequel to his *Biblioteca universalis* of 1545, the first truly comprehensive bibliography of European literature, his monumental *Pandectarum sive Partitionum universalium libri XXI* of 1548; arranged systematically by subject matter, this lists some thirty thousand topical entries, each cross-referenced to the appropriate author and book, arranged under headings and subheadings traditionally associated with different branches of knowledge. The seventh book, devoted to music both practical and theoretical, contains extensive lists of contemporary editions; a number, including books printed by Attaingnant, Petrucci, Petreius, and Schoeffer, have not survived.[11] The second of these bibliographies, Doni's *La libraria* of 1550, is just one of many strange publications of an eccentric Florentine priest, poet, *novellatore*, letter writer, musician, traveller, and gossip. It is not perhaps surprising, particularly in view of his time in Venice in the 1540s, by which time Venice had definitively become the center of the Italian music printing trade, that most of the music titles listed in *La libraria* were printed in the Venetian workshops of Girolamo Scotto and Antonio Gardano, by then the foremost music printers working in the trade. Unlike Gesner, who was simply a tireless and precise collector of information, Doni was a performer who knew several important Venetian musicians including Jacques Buus, then organist at St Mark's Basilica. Doni clearly also had links with Scotto himself, since it was the latter who had published his *Dialogo della musica* of 1544, a series of witty dialogues interspersed with madrigals, presented as a picture of life in the musical and literary circles first of provincial Piacenza, then of Venice. Most of the editions cited in *La libraria* were printed in the years 1535–50, and although the list is far from systematically done and the entries are often infuriatingly vague, here also there are references to works no longer extant, and to a handful of editions printed in the first decades of the century.[12]

[11] For a general account of Gesner's work as a bibliography, see T. Besterman, *The Beginnings of Systematic Bibliography* (Oxford, 1936); L. Balsamo, *Bibliography: History of a Tradition* (Berkeley, 1990), 33–46. Gesner's references to printed music (and to music literature) are analysed and discussed in L. F. Bernstein, "The Bibliography of Music in Conrad Gesner's *Pandectae* (1548)," *Acta musicologica*, 45 (1973), 119–63.

[12] A lively account of Doni and his activities is given in P. F. Grendler, *Critics of the Italian World 1530–1560: Anton Francesco Doni, Nicolo Franco & Ortensio Lando* (Madison, WI, 1969).

If the *Libraria* can be taken as any sort of guide (and in common with all Doni's works it must be approached with considerable caution), then it would seem that many editions of music printed in the first decades of the century were no longer in circulation by 1550.

Knowledge of lost books from the first half of the century would be even more impoverished were it not for a handful of collectors. For the earliest phase of music printing, many unique copies and much information about prices and availability is the result of the extraordinary collection of one man, Ferdinand Columbus (Hernando Colón), illegitimate son of a more famous navigating and exploring father. It has been estimated that by the time of his death Colón's library contained some 15,370 volumes, and had it been preserved intact it would be without doubt the most important repository of early-sixteenth-century printed music (and of much other printed material) to have survived. Although only a fraction of the original donation now remains, Colón's meticulously kept records provide a good deal of useful information about his books and his methods of acquiring them.[13] They show that many of them were bought not only from booksellers and agents all over Europe, but were personally selected in the course of four extended trips to Italy and northern Europe that he made during the years 1512–35. Colón annotated many of these purchases with details of where they were bought and how much he paid, and similar information can also be extracted from the various handwritten catalogues of his collection that, with the loss of so much, are the only records of the true extent and contents of his library. Since he evidently owned a copy of nearly every Italian and French music book now known to have been published up to 1535 (together with a number published elsewhere), including a considerable number that have not come down to us, Colón's catalogues are invaluable for resolving some of the difficulties caused by the poor survival rate of the books themselves, and in this sense they are crucial for our understanding of the earliest phase of music printing in Europe. At the same time, it is clear that the collection of printed music assembled by Colón is unusual for its time, not only in terms of its size but also in being part of a very large general library put together on encyclopaedic principles. As such, and untypically for the period, it was intended to be consulted and studied rather than being put to practical use.

Among other "silent" readers of printed music were the authors of theoretical treatises. Most of the pieces quoted by Pietro Aron in his *Trattato della natura et*

The music listed in *La libraria* is discussed in J. Haar, "The *Libraria* of Antonfrancesco Doni," *Musica disciplina*, 24 (1970), 101–23.

[13] For the manuscript catalogues and related works that allow Colón's library to be reconstructed, see H. Harrisse, *Fernand Columb: Sa vie, ses œuvres* (Paris, 1872), 165–72; idem, *Excerpta Colombiniana* (Paris, 1887), 259–65. A. M. Huntingdon (ed.), *Catalogue of the Library of Ferdinand Columbus, Reproduced in Facsimile from the Unique Manuscript in the Colombina Library of Seville* (New York, 1905), reproduces *Registrum B*. Colón's music books are discussed in Chapman, "Printed Collections of Polyphonic Music." Recent years have seen the publication of *Hernando Colón: Abecedarium B y Supplementum, ed. facsímil de los manuscritos conservados en la Biblioteca Colombina de Sevilla* (Madrid, 1992); and especially *Catálogo concordado de la biblioteca de Hernando Colón, c.*10 vols., ed. T. M. Martínez, J. M. Ruiz Asencio, and K. Wagner (Madrid, 1993–), an analytical catalogue by accession number of all Colón's acquisitions.

cognitione di tutti gli tuoni (Venice: Bernardino de' Vitali, 1525), for example, come from seven identifiable Petrucci editions first published between 1501 and 1519, and most of the examples in his *Aggiunta del Toscanello* (Venice: Bernardino & Mattheo Vitali, 1529) are taken from an even narrower range of Petrucci editions comprising the three books of *Corona* motets, the *Odhecaton*, and the *Liber primus missarum Josquin*. Another writer about music, the Swiss humanist Heinrich Glarean, author of the influential *Dodecachordon* (Basel: H. Petri, 1547), bought Petrucci editions and perhaps other music books during his student days during the 1520s, at least in part for study purposes.[14] Yet despite such exceptions, printed music was mostly bought to be used in performance and was treated accordingly. Often stored unbound in cupboards and drawers rather than protected upon library shelves, most of it received hard practical wear until it finally fell apart. Hence the frequent absence of title pages and colophons.

It is clear that the identifiable buyers of music in the first decades of the century, and they are few in number, were then for the most part musically literate and bought with performance in mind. Bonifacius Amerbach, the Basel humanist familiar from his portrait by Hans Holbein the younger, is one clear example; he was an early and probably the first owner of the now unique copy of Antico's *Canzoni nove* of 1510 as well as a number of other music books. In the case of sacred music, purchasers were usually acting for institutions (mostly ecclesiastical) whose interest in buying music was utilitarian. The *maestro di cappella* of the Santa Casa at Loreto who bought "un libro contenente quindici messe in canto figurato" at the book fair at Recanati in 1516 must have acquired a copy (now lost) of Antico's recently published *Liber quindecim missarum*. Similarly, a group of ten Petrucci mass and motet volumes, all printed during his Venetian years, were almost certainly bought for the Gonzaga chapel in Mantua shortly after its foundation by Marchese Francesco Gonzaga in 1511.[15] Contemporary handwritten corrections and additions are the clearest evidence of use, and are to be found even in elegantly bound volumes. From the beginning purchasers bound up individual partbooks into larger sets, presumably to keep down the cost of binding, sometimes including extra gatherings of ruled music paper so that further additions could be made by hand.

The first music printers to work with type had sent the sheets through the press a number of times, which allowed them to print different elements of the printed page on each occasion. As a process this was clearly time-consuming, and the labour costs involved must have added to the price of a music book even though paper was clearly the most expensive single item of production. With the advent

[14] C. C. Judd, "Reading Aron Reading Petrucci: The Music Examples of the *Trattato della natura et cognitione di tutti gli tuoni* (1525)," *Early Music History*, 14 (1995), 121–51; the music examples in Aron's *Aggiunta* are discussed in M. Bent, "Accidentals, Counterpoint and Notation in Aron's *Aggiunta* to the *Toscanello in Musica*," *The Journal of Musicology*, 12 (1994), 306–44. 28 books from Glarean's library, including music, are identified in I. Fenlon, "Heinrich Glarean's Books," in J. Kmetz (ed.), *Music in the German Renaissance: Sources, Styles and Contexts* (Cambridge, 1994), 74–102.

[15] Further details of these and of some other individual copies preserving indications of original ownership are given in Fenlon, *Music, Print and Culture*, 13–14.

of single-impression printing, music notes and staves, clefs, indications of key, and words were printed together. Technologically this was achieved by adapting Gutenberg's invention of moveable type, casting each note and a fragment of a complete set of staff lines on the same type body. This important development, which gradually was to revolutionize the economics of the music trade, seems to have been first introduced not in any of the established centers of music printing but in London, where it was pioneered by the barrister and printer John Rastell, an author of a number of stage works as well as of a frequently reprinted compendium of legal terminology. Rastell's music type, reasonably elegant in design but poor in execution, was probably either imported from France, or was perhaps made by a foreign craftsman then living in London. Despite its evident technical shortcomings, it allowed him to produce staves, clefs, notes, directs, rests, and text all at one impression. Although this innovation is significant, the material that Rastell chose to print by this method was marginal in importance and local in impact; it includes a three-voice song in score which appears in the text of one of his own plays, *A New Interlude and a mery of the Nature of the iiij Elements* (this undated book has been assigned to *c.*1520), and a number of fragmentary broadsides printed both by him and later by his son William.[16] Following his death in 1536 music printing virtually stopped in England except for psalters and other liturgical material, until Vautrollier published an English edition of Lassus' *Receuil du mellange* in 1570. This was in turn something of a random event until William Byrd and Thomas Tallis were awarded a monopoly for music by Elizabeth I in 1575, which they honored by publishing their *Cantiones sacrae* in the same year, printed by Thomas East using a music font he had acquired from Vautrollier. This collection was a commercial failure, and it was not until 1588, when East brought out Byrd's *Psalmes, Sonets and Songs*, that English printers began to produce music in any quantity.[17]

The more influential printer who started to use the single-impression technique in the 1520s was Pierre Attaingnant, a printer working in Paris, whose earliest known book is a Noyon breviary issued there in 1525. After a number of years experimenting with mensural types, Attaingnant seems to have made use of the single-impression method for the first time in his *Chansons nouvelles* of 1527/8.[18] This was then quickly followed, within a year, by at least seven chanson volumes, all devoted to the latest Parisian style. From then until 1551, encouraged and protected by a series of royal patents that brought him the distinction of "imprimeur et libraire du Roy en musique," Attaingnant maintained a steady output of music that eventually totalled some 150 editions of music, containing several thousand

[16] The date of *A New Interlude* is discussed in A. H. King, "The Significance of John Rastell in Early Music Printing," *The Library*, 5th ser., 26 (1971), 197–214; see also idem, "An English Broadside of the 1520s," in F. W. Sternfeld, N. Fortune, and E. Olleson (eds.), *Essays on Opera and English Music in Honour of Sir Jack Westrup* (Oxford, 1975), 19–24. For the latest on Rastell, see J. Milsom, "Songs and Society in Early Tudor London," *Early Music History*, 16 (1997), 235–93.

[17] J. Smith, *Thomas East and Music Publishing in Renaissance England* (New York, 2003).

[18] See D. Heartz, "A New Attaingnant Book and the Beginnings of French Music Printing," *Journal of the American Musicological Society*, 14 (1961), 9–23.

compositions, printed initially in small octavo and then from the 1530s in a more attractive quarto format.[19] Nor did he restrict himself to anthologies of the latest chansons, popular though these proved to be. Beginning in 1532 Attaingnant began to print a series of seven folio mass volumes, each of which is illustrated with a woodcut showing the Royal Chapel and contains an astutely worded dedication. These choirbooks are a clear demonstration of the benefits of royal preferment; luxuriously produced, neat in execution, and authoritative in design, they are undoubtedly the most accomplished music books to have been produced anywhere in Europe since Antico's *Liber quindecim missarum* of some fifteen years earlier, which indeed Attaingnant may well have taken as a model. In common with Antico's book and Petrucci's volumes of masses and motets, Attaingnant's folios were primarily directed at church institutions, while the long series of chanson volumes was clearly destined for a largely domestic and amateur market. Elegant in design and reasonably priced, they set a new standard in terms of the market, not only in France but also south of the Alps. In addition to editions of music, Attaingnant also printed music paper, as did the anonymous craftsman who produced the *XX Songes* (London, 1530), something which the earliest Italian printers do not seem to have done.

In effect, Attaingnant was the first music publisher to cater for a wide public, or at least for a broader audience than Petrucci and Antico had been able to reach. His success in doing so was only partly to do with his business acumen, being to some extent dependent upon his privileged position as the recipient of royal patronage. While the commercial success of his enterprise coincided with the fashion for the new Parisian chanson, a vogue that François I may well have encouraged and that Attaingnant was quick to exploit, the music of the major composers of the new genre was readily available since they were all in royal service.[20] The patronage of the king was clearly decisive in harnessing Attaingnant's talents to the task of presenting this music in print, and it is noticeable that the compositions of the previous generation, much favored by Antico and Petrucci, are hardly represented at all in his editions. In other words, Attaingnant's activity was essentially that of a printer and bookseller whose primary role was to present the wider world with an image of the musical achievement and riches of a powerful patron, a propagandistic use of the music press that was to become increasingly common in the course of the century both in France and elsewhere. However, at this early stage commercial conditions in Paris stood in stark contrast to those in Italy, where patronage was less centralized and where no single ruling family or state, not even the papacy, had taken up the direction of music printing as wholeheartedly as had François I. Attaingnant's market for music seems to have been large by Italian standards; his press runs have been conservatively estimated at 1,000 copies, and his editions

[19] For further details, see D. Heartz, *Pierre Attaingnant, Royal Printer of Music: A Historical Study and Bibliographical Catalogue* (Berkeley and Los Angeles, 1969).

[20] For the connections between François I, the Royal Chapel, and Attaingnant's editions, see Heartz, *Pierre Attaingnant*, pp. xviii–xix, 90–104; J. T. Brobeck, "Musical Patronage in the Royal Chapel of France under Francis I (r. 1515–1547), *Journal of the American Musicological Society*, 48 (1995), 187–239.

were widely available abroad. Of the 63 music books that he issued in the first eight years of his career, Colón owned at least 37, one bought in Louvain in 1531 and the rest in Lyons four years later. Herwart, whose library was mostly put together after 1550, owned all 35 volumes of the *Chansons nouvelles* as well as a number of other Attaingnant prints, and Gesner, whose lists of practical music in the *Pandectae* are mostly confined to German and Italian editions, was nevertheless aware of 13 volumes from Attaingnant's motet series as well as a number of his other titles. One nearly complete set of the chansonniers printed during the years 1528–33 travelled to Germany about 1539, while a set of motet volumes found their way into the library of the Gonzaga court chapel in Mantua at about the same time.[21] Shortly after Attaingnant's death in 1552, the title of royal music printer was conferred upon Adrien Le Roy and Robert Ballard, who had obtained a privilege from Henri II and had started to print music some months earlier. The patronage of successive monarchs gave the firm a virtual monopoly of music printing in France during the second half of the century; other printers in Paris and Lyons (including Fezandat, Gorlier, and Granjon), issued only occasional publications, while its most serious rival (Nicolas du Chemin) published little after 1560. Altogether Le Roy & Ballard published more than 3,000 works in 350 editions between 1551 and 1598, among them a substantial repertory of chansons in serial publications. From their position in the French market, and with the considerable advantages of royal preferment and contacts with musicians at court, Le Roy & Ballard were able to exercise a decisive influence upon the formation of taste.[22]

In some of the larger urban centers of northern Europe, Attaingnant's single-impression printing methods were quickly copied, and the repertories which he published were pirated. Beginning with Jacques Moderne in Lyons[23] and Christian Egenolff in Frankfurt, printers working in the early 1530s seem to have acquired the types for printing single-impression music with considerable speed. Venice, Paris, and Nuremberg (to which Antwerp should be added with the arrival of Vissenaecken and Susato in the city in the early 1540s) were thus firmly established as major centers of music printing by the middle of the century. Italian printers were slower to adopt the new technique, partly because the shaky economic foundations on which so many of them were working must have discouraged the necessary investment in new fonts. The political and civil disruptions of the late 1520s, the "calamità d'Italia" that culminated in the Sack of Rome in 1527, did not encourage new initiatives, and although a number of attempts were made to establish workshops in both Rome and Venice during the 1520s, few of them achieved permanence. One that did was Valerio Dorico's press in Rome, which was set up shortly after the Sack and was to continue in business until the 1570s, but in general terms it

[21] The details are taken from Chapman, "Printed Collections of Polyphonic Music," 52–3. Other early owners of Attaingnant's books, including those mentioned here, are discussed in Heartz, *Pierre Attaingnant*, 126–36.

[22] F. Lesure and G. Thibault, *Bibliographie des éditions d'Adrien Le Roy et Robert Ballard (1551–1598)* (Paris, 1955).

[23] S. F. Pogue, *Jacques Moderne: Lyons Music Printer of the Sixteenth Century* (Geneva, 1969).

was not until Antonio Gardano began printing in Venice in 1538 that the production of music in Italy entered a new phase.[24] In business terms this dramatic entry into the music market must have required a considerable initial outlay for matrices and fonts; although the new method of printing was ultimately cheaper than either the multiple-impression technique used by Petrucci or Antico's woodblock process, it was expensive to set up. It was presumably in an attempt to recoup his initial outlay and to maintain a respectable cash flow that, right from the start of his career, Gardano capitalized on books devoted to the most successful amateur domestic music of the day, including the first four books of Arcadelt's madrigals and a sequence of collections containing Verdelot's music. Indeed, although he did publish other kinds of music, Gardano concentrated on the madrigal repertory in these early years, a body of music that was to be at the center of his printing and publishing operation throughout his career; it has been estimated that nearly three quarters of the 450 or so editions that he produced before 1569 are devoted to this genre.[25] From the early 1540s onwards Gardano settled into a rhythm of production that allowed him to issue an average of 15 or so new editions per year, produced in print runs of 500 or so copies. The whole nature of what rapidly became a successful business venture was based upon the rapid turnover of short print runs of new music interspersed with reprints of well tried and successful editions. As a strategy this approach seems to have worked well almost from the first, and for the first time in the history of Italian music printing the trade was not only secure but was much more responsive to the music that composers were currently writing. The most successful title of all was Arcadelt's *Primo libro de' madrigali*, first published in 1538 and destined to become one of the most popular books of printed music of the entire century; between then and 1654, 45 editions are known to have been issued, and there were evidently more, including the mysterious pirated first edition of which all traces are now lost.

Gardano's only true competitor in the Italian market was Girolamo Scotto, yet another member of a family that had been active and prominent in the publishing trade since the 1480s with a base in Venice and retail shops in a number of other large Italian cities. Scotto's various printing and publishing activities were established on a much more elaborate scale than those of Gardano. Unlike his major Venetian rival, Scotto printed other titles in a wide variety of subjects alongside his editions of music; in this way, with interests in a number of different areas of the trade, he was able to distribute to a more differentiated public and so minimize the risks of his financial outlay. Together with liturgical books, editions of the classics and commentaries upon them were one of the principal mainstays during Girolamo's early years in business. Although these non-musical works are generally unpretentious editions designed to appeal to a traditional market, some of them,

24 A brief account of music printing and publishing in Italy between Petrucci and Gardano is given in Fenlon, *Music, Print and Culture*, particularly Lecture II. The standard study and bibliography of Dorico's books is S. Cusick, *Valerio Dorico: Music Printer in Sixteenth-Century Rome* (Ann Arbor, 1981).

25 For Gardano, see M. S. Lewis, *Antonio Gardano, Venetian Music Printer 1538–1569: A Descriptive Bibliography and Historical Study*, 2 vols. to date (New York and London, 1988–97).

notably the 1545 Terence, which in turn seems to have been used as a model for other printers, were aimed at the wealthier buyer. Strange though it may seem, given the enormous amount of music that he produced, it was for his translations of and commentaries on Aristotle that Scotto was most respected by contemporaries; Gesner, for example, addressed his preface to the section on civic philosophy in his *Pandectae* of 1548 to Girolamo in recognition of his production in this field. Nevertheless, the production of music represented an important component of Scotto's business, and beginning in 1539 with seven editions of music, all printed with type struck from the same matrices that both Gardano and the Ferrarese printer Buglhat had also been using at the same time, he managed to maintain a steady output of some dozen or so music books for the next 33 years.[26] This average production rate of one music book per month contrasts strongly with the one or two music books *per annum* that had been issued by Antico and Petrucci and suggests a growing audience for printed music. Indeed, during the mid 1540s Scotto evidently took on too much music printing and, having been commissioned by a consortium of bookmen to publish a number of editions, was obliged to subcontract the work to other shops in Venice, some of whom borrowed Scotto's music font in order to do the job. Although the finished products appeared without the printer's name on the title page, a small number of them carry a distinctive typographical mark that features a salamander.[27]

It is often claimed that Gardano and Scotto were in fierce competition with each other, and that they were constantly pirating each other's editions in the search for the evidently insufficient supply of new repertory. This now seems to be fanciful, and the evidence suggests that the two printers operated in an atmosphere of friendly rivalry, and that at times they even co-operated. Together, Scotto and Gardano were able to virtually monopolize the Italian music trade for some thirty years, no doubt to their mutual financial advantage. Compared to the 750 or so editions that they produced between them, the output of Antonio Blado and the Dorico brothers in Rome, or that of Francesco Rampazetto who printed in Venice in the 1560s, or of the many printers who began to operate in the market elsewhere in Italy during the second half of the century, is indeed modest.

Most of the music books that they printed were directed at a domestic audience. By the middle of the sixteenth century, interest in music as a performed art rather than a body of scholastic knowledge had grown to such an extent that the ownership of music now extended to a larger constituency that included members of the merchant and professional classes, and even to those lower down the social ladder. This is clear from what is known about prices and the patterns of book ownership. To some extent this new emphasis on the cultivation of practical music was due to the influence of a growing and powerful body of literature, of which the most popular single title was Baldassare Castiglione's *Il cortegiano*, first published

[26] J. A. Bernstein, *Music Printing in Renaissance Venice: The Scotto Press (1539–1572)* (New York and Oxford, 1998).

[27] J. Bernstein, "The Burning Salamander: Assigning a Printer to some Sixteenth-Century Music Prints," *Notes* 42 (1986), 483–501, discusses 22 music books from the years 1545–47.

in 1527. Cast in dialogue form, it is usually described as a courtesy book, a manual of behaviour and practice for the Renaissance courtier, an attempt, as Castiglione himself puts it, "to make the perfect courtier through words." The fact that the subject of music is raised twice by Castiglione's courtiers in the course of their four days' conversations is an interesting reflection of progressive thinking about its function in contemporary society, based not merely upon an idealized conception, but also upon experience.[28] Castiglione's comments reflect the new emphasis upon music as a social accomplishment, as a form of entertainment, to be performed with a certain professionalism, but by amateurs. With the arrival of Castiglione's text the practice of music had become an aspect of manners; the widespread dissemination, in both edited and translated versions, and its enormous influence on other writers, did much to spread a new conception of the place of music in elite social life.[29]

In keeping with this changing status of practical music, editions of music now sometimes contain portraits of composers, much as theorists had been presented for some time in their publications. From the 1540s onwards the social connections and status of composers were advertised on title pages with ever increasing ingenuity, as new commercial attitudes took hold in a growing and increasingly prosperous market. As early as 1539 the publisher's dedicatory letter to an early edition of Arcadelt's *Primo libro* speaks of the composer as "divino," while in the same year Willaert was described by Scotto as "famosissimo." As *maestro di cappella* at St Mark's, and with a considerable reputation for both his teaching and his understanding of theoretical questions, Willaert was indeed well known certainly in Venice and probably throughout Italy, but Arcadelt's name could only have been known from his madrigals, which, together with those of Verdelot, had circulated in manuscript either as single pieces or in groups before being printed.[30] Throughout the 1520s and 1530s unpublished compositions by these composers had been eagerly sought after, as a letter of late 1534 written by Lionardo Strozzi in Lyons to his relative Ruberto in Venice reveals:

> Vincenzo tells me that you would like some *canzoni*, and though I think that I will fall behind in some things I don't want to fail to send you one of them which I got 8 days ago from Florence and [which] will be with this [letter]. And if it is already known there, accept my good intentions, and when I have a little time I'll make it up to you with some motets or something else that is new. Here we often meet either in your house or in the house of Niccolo Manelli to sing and we make good music . . . And, too, we have many new

[28] For a discussion of Castiglione's comments on music, see J. Haar, "The Courtier as Musician: Castiglione's View of the Science and Art of Music," in R. W. Hanning and D. Rosand (eds.), *Castiglione: The Ideal and the Real in Renaissance Culture* (New Haven and London, 1983), 165–89.

[29] P. Burke, *The Fortunes of the Courtier: The European Reception of Castiglione's "Cortegiano"* (Oxford, 1995).

[30] The manuscript circulation of the early madrigal repertory prior to its publication is described in detail in I. Fenlon and J. Haar, *The Italian Madrigal in the Early Sixteenth Century: Sources and Interpretation* (Cambridge, 1988).

> things from Florence. Let me know whether you wish me to send them to you. I'll do it often because I have a friend in Florence who, as soon as Arcadelt writes any pieces at all, is always the first to have them, and he sends them to me.[31]

It was in this way, as part of an elaborate network of diplomatic, commercial, and familial connections, that much new music was circulated. Remarkably, a number of these loose sheets, which were used to send fresh compositions from one place to another (usually enclosed in letters) have survived, as have a good number of more formal manuscripts containing madrigals by Arcadelt and others copied during the 1530s, before these pieces reached print. It was this music that Gardano and Scotto were so keen to acquire as soon as their businesses were securely launched in the early 1540s, so that they could profit from the established tastes of an already established audience.

In the changing circumstances of the trade which followed the adoption of the single-impression technique, there was also a perceptible growth in the importance of the editor. To a much greater extent than with older vernacular texts such as those of Petrarch, Boccaccio, and Dante, an area where editorial intervention was thought necessary from the very beginning of printing,[32] the presentation of an accurate version of a musical composition required highly specialized skills broadly analogous to those needed by the printers of classical Greek texts. For the most part music printers were businessmen and craftsmen and only rarely skilled composers; those who wished to achieve the highest reputations in the trade soon found it essential to develop a network of contacts with local musicians. Gardano, who was musically literate and published some of his own music right from the start of his career, had clearly established himself in Venetian intellectual circles by the late 1530s, when he could number among his close friends composers and musicians of the Willaert circle who could not only supply him with music but could also offer professional advice on grammatical matters.[33] We may be sure that editorial skill of this kind had been necessary from the very beginning of music printing, even if such assistance often remained unacknowledged at first by printers, as in the case of Petrus Castellanus, who worked for Petrucci in the preparation of the *Odhecaton A* and possibly some of his other titles.[34] The example of Andrea Antico is rather different; for one thing he was a cutter of woodblocks and as such a printer rather than a publisher, for another he was also a composer (he too published some of his own works) who could therefore edit, at least in the basic sense

[31] R. Agee, "Ruberto Strozzi and the Early Madrigal," *Journal of the American Musicological Society*, 36 (1983), 9.

[32] B. Richardson, *Print Culture in Renaissance Italy: The Editor and the Vernacular Text, 1470–1600* (Cambridge, 1994).

[33] M. S. Lewis, "Antonio Gardano's Early Connections with the Willaert Circle," in I. Fenlon (ed.), *Music in Medieval and Early Modern Europe: Patronage, Sources and Texts* (Cambridge, 1981), 209–26.

[34] B. J. Blackburn, "Petrucci's Venetian Editor: Petrus Castellanus and his Musical Garden," *Musica Disciplina*, 49 (1995), 15–45; S. Boorman, "The 'First' Edition of the *Odhecaton A*," *Journal of the American Musicological Society*, 30 (1977), 183–207.

of eliminating errors from a copy text or typographical ones from a set of proofs. In other cases it was the typesetters themselves who effectively acted as editors. Sometimes editorial functions could be carried out by composers who attended the press and corrected their own texts; this is true of Corteccia, whose music was published by both Gardano and Scotto in the 1540s with dedications that speak rather fiercely of the need to present correctly edited and attributed versions of the composer's music.

The importance attached to editorial intervention, whether it had been exercised or not, is clear from the way that, as competition between publishers grew more intense, there was a growing tendency to describe the contents of a book, most commonly on its title page, as being "corretti novamente." Indeed, the main reason that publishers of music employed editors at all was so that they could reassure buyers that the particular version of a work on offer was accurate and that it had been brought back to its pristine condition through the diligent activities of a knowledgeable musician. With increasing frequency and ingenious rhetorical urgency, printers and publishers did not hesitate to use title pages and dedicatory letters to emphasize, with varying amounts of honesty, their own role in returning to its original state a musical text that had been previously degraded by the carelessness, greed, and ignorance of unscrupulous interlopers. The Gardano 1550 reprint of Arcadelt's madrigals speaks of its contents as "ultimamente ristampati e corretti"; "corretti" or not, in this case they were at least "ristampati," but it was not unknown for printers to make such fraudulent claims even for first editions. This problem was obviously at its most intense in the case of music by well established and popular composers, where rogue printers were happy either to print poor versions or even to reattribute music by lesser men to established composers in order to gain a foothold in the trade.

The impact of music printing on its potential market was obviously gradual rather than immediate, but from the 1540s onwards the Italian market for music of all kinds greatly expanded. This is most obviously true for Italy, where a good deal of new music was being written, particularly by composers working in the major cities in the north, which stood at the heart of the system of production and distribution. From surviving copies it can be seen that by this stage there was a sizeable and growing public of individual purchasers for music among the professional classes—the doctors, lawyers, and administrators whose increasing power and wealth is such a notable feature of the economic and social demography of the period. It was precisely among this burgeoning sector of society that the earliest academies were founded. During the 1540s such gatherings, informal or formal, ephemeral or long-lived, began to appear everywhere in Italy, and by the second half of the century there were more than two hundred of them, many engaged in some form of musical enterprise if only on an occasional basis. The celebrated Accademia Filarmonica in Verona, founded in 1543 and primarily concerned with practical music, is an early and influential example of the type, though it is unusual in the accent that was placed upon music. Its founders included a composer, and within a few years the academy had engaged a permanent *maestro* and singing teacher, the Fleming Giovanni Nasco. Both the academy's collection of instruments (a reminder that from the start both madrigals and motets could be and were performed on instruments) and its extensive library of printed music and other books still survive in Verona, and the large number of editions dedicated to the Filarmonica in the second half of the century is indicative of a new and powerful form of collective patronage.[35]

By 1550 the music trade was sufficiently secure, at least in the major French and Italian centers of production, for new pieces rather than well established older repertory to be sought out by printers; from now onwards there was to be a considerable and expanding audience for music books, which had been made all the more affordable by the widespread adoption of single-impression printing. Members of the professional classes were now sometimes presented in painted portraits as musicians, surrounded by instruments and even open music books, whose sometimes legible notation can form an important element in reading the painting itself. Printed music now appeared in a more varied range of formats than before and carried a wider selection of music to an ever expanding market. These trends are reflected in the increasing numbers of separate editions of untexted instrumental music, keyboard scores, and lute tablatures, which began to appear from the 1540s onwards and which were evidently intended for domestic consumption. During the 1540s there is a noticeable increase in printed editions of lute music, some of which include instructions for playing and tuning the instrument, another clear indication of the nature of the market. It is no accident that these developments were accompanied by a heightened interest in music publishing by patrons. Dedications had been rare among Petrucci's publications (though this does not mean that subsidy had not been involved), but from the middle of the century onwards that characteristic nexus of relationships that bound together printer, composer, poet, and the hack writer employed to write a suitably flattering dedication to the patron (who had presumably provided some form of financial reward or might be expected to do so) became normal.

By this time Scotto and Gardano had begun to bring out collections of music composed by a large number of provincial musicians writing in a wide variety of styles and forms. Even at this level, the stimulation provided by the greater availability of printed music had a considerable impact on the growth of composition and performance. Comparatively low prices now made the acquisition of sizeable collections possible for a broad stratum of society. From the earliest account books of the Accademia Filarmonica we learn that the four partbooks of Gardano's *Motteti del frutto* of 1539 then cost one lira and four soldi, while six Gardano sets containing an average of four partbooks each were bought for a total of 6 lira and 11 soldi. Other groups of partbooks were purchased for about 1 lira each, a price that seems to have remained constant throughout the middle decades of the century. This makes music comparable in price to inexpensive editions of standard works of literature or the classics. In 1554, 1 lira would buy the vernacular translation of Cicero's *De oratore* in duodecimo, while later in the century it could even purchase an

[35] G. Turrini, *L'Accademia Filarmonica di Verona dalla fondazione (Maggio, 1543) al 1600 e il suo patrimonio musicale antico* (Verona, 1941).

illustrated edition of Tasso's *Aminta* in quarto. At the same time, a master mason or carpenter earned between 50 and 100 ducats annually, as did a schoolmaster, while a government official was paid 88 ducats (1 ducat = 6 lire) a year.[36] Prices of books obviously varied according to size and length (the cost of paper remained the single most important element of production costs), but the average set of five partbooks containing thirty or so compositions could clearly now be purchased by readers from a reasonably wide economic spectrum of society. These prices evidently refer to unbound copies.

The books that the Filarmonica bought are arranged and bound in a way which clearly shows that they were intended for performance. For the most part initial distinctions were made between secular and sacred music, even though the latter was performed in the domestic ambience of the Accademia's meeting-room. This kind of systematic organization also had the virtue of economy; costs were obviously reduced when several publications were combined within a single set of covers. To judge by the good number of such collections that survive in their original bindings, the practice was widespread throughout Europe from the 1530s onwards, encouraged by the ever increasing variety of music on offer at reasonable prices in the bookshops and stimulated by the publishers' commercially inspired fondness for issuing serial publications.[37] One interesting feature of some of these bound sets of partbooks is that motets and madrigals are often found together; as other collections bound in the period reveal, "sacred" music was often performed by amateurs in a domestic setting. Repertorial distinctions became even more hazy when chansons or madrigals travelled outside their immediate area of linguistic currency; the most common experience in such cases was for secular songs to be treated as instrumental music. While it is true that Italian madrigals could be and often were performed on instruments (or with voices and instruments) in Italy, once they were transported elsewhere they were more likely to surface either with changed literary texts (as in the case of Italian madrigals "Englished") or as purely instrumental music. The point is neatly demonstrated by many of the sixteenth-century manuscripts now in the University Library in Basel, originally copied for a fairly close-knit circle of prominent local citizens including members of the Amerbach, Iselin, and Hagenbach families. As might be expected, many of these books are substantially devoted to *Tenorlieder*, the principal repertory of native domestic music in German-speaking countries, but in addition the Basel manuscripts also contain untexted versions of Italian madrigals and motets and French chansons. Shorn of their original words and their musical (and in the case of sacred music also liturgical) functions, these "central" repertories of amateur song lived a second life outside their areas of origin in untexted versions for instrumental performance.[38] A similar process of reception can be observed in many contemporary manuscripts copied north of the Alps.

[36] The sources of these figures are given in Fenlon, *Music, Print and Culture*, 85–6.

[37] A number of such sets are listed in Lewis, *Antonio Gardano*, I: 123–62, II: 155–66; Bernstein, *Music Printing in Renaissance Venice*, 933–50.

[38] J. Kmetz, *Die Handschriften der Universitätsbibliothek Basel: Katalog der Musikhandschriften des 16. Jahrhunderts* (Basel, 1988).

The example of Italy, and above all the operations of Gardano and Scotto, established the music book in the commerce of the trade in a way that was without precedent, even taking into consideration Attaingnant's chanson series of the 1530s. During the second half of the sixteenth century, music printers proliferated throughout Europe, taking their workshop practices, distribution methods, and the format and design of their books from the examples of the early printers. Yet despite the growth of printing in this period, the market continued to be dominated by books printed in Venice and distributed through agents and booksellers abroad; in this sense the history of music printing in the period is essentially that of developments in Italy and of the imitation of those developments elsewhere, not only in terms in terms of book production and design but also in terms of repertory. The earliest surviving bookseller's catalogue, issued by Angelo Gardano in 1591, lists 345 items (mostly sacred and secular vocal music) and was presumably a means of advertising stock to individual customers as well as to bookshops both in Italy and elsewhere.[39] As a system, distribution of music by catalogue was certainly in existence earlier, and its effectiveness can be deduced from some of the surviving libraries of the time. The earliest editions in Georg Knoff's library in Danzig, for example, date from the 1570s, but the bulk of them were published between 1580 and the early 1600s. As he acquired them, Knoff arranged for them to be distinctively and elegantly bound in sets of ten or so books at a time, a systematic bibliophilia of the Colón kind albeit on a much smaller scale. Altogether Knoff bought 267 titles, the lion's share of which are books of Italian madrigals printed in Venice.[40]

Sometimes retaining the family name, and sometimes using that of Magni (the founder's grandson-in-law), Gardano's heirs played an important role in the popularization of the concertato style that became so fashionable after the appearance of Giulio Caccini's *Le nuove musiche* in 1600.[41] So too did a number of Venetian printers of a younger generation, principally Ricciardo Amadino and Giacomo Vincenti, who had briefly been in partnership in the 1580s but thereafter worked separately. The rapidity with which the Venetian trade took up the new style was just one more factor that enabled it to continue to dominate the international market, despite the temporary disruption caused by the plague and the minor impact made by incursions such as Tini's espousal of reformist repertories, notably the works of Vincenzo Ruffo, composed and printed in Milan as a local response to the decrees of the Council of Trent.[42] Similarly, the brief resurgence of music

39 O. Mischiati, *Indici, cataloghi e avvisi degli editori e librai musicali italiani dal 1591 al 1798* (Florence, 1984), 83–92.

40 M. Morell, "Georg Knoff: Bibliophile and Devotee of Italian Music in Late Sixteenth-Century Danzig," in Kmetz (ed.), *Music in the German Renaissance*, 103–26.

41 R. J. Agee, *The Gardano Music Printing Firms, 1569–1611* (Rochester, 1998).

42 L. Lockwood, *The Counter-Reformation and the Masses of Vincenzo Ruffo* (Venice, 1970); I. Fenlon, "Music and Civic Piety in Counter-Reformation Milan," in idem, *Music and Culture in Late Renaissance Italy* (Oxford, 2002), 67–92. For the most recent additions to the documentation, see M. Toffetti, "The Tini Family: Sixteenth-Century Music Printers in Milan," *Fontes artis musicae*, 46 (1999), 244–67.

publishing in Florence at the hands of Giorgio Marescotti and his heirs made little difference to the general shape of the market, for all that Marescotti's small number of handsome editions included the first scores of court opera (Caccini's *L'Euridice* and Peri's *Le musiche sopra L'Euridice*).[43] Elsewhere in provincial Italy printers occasionally took on music, usually by producing either collections devoted to the work of local composers (often dedicated to, and presumably paid for, by a local patron) or editions of established favorites. This is what happened in Umbria,[44] in a number of towns in the Veneto, notably Brescia,[45] and to some extent in Naples.[46] In this context it is worth noting that the reprint market for Arcadelt's *Primo libro*, dominated for much of its long history by the editions of Gardano and Scotto, is infiltrated from the middle of the sixteenth century onwards by the productions of minor Venetian printing houses as well as by editions published in Florence, Milan, and Palermo. Later still, editions were brought out in Bracciano, Naples, Perugia, and Rome, the latter (Paolo Masotti, 1627) allegedly but almost certainly spuriously "di nuovo ristampato e coretto in Venetia da Claudio Monteverdi." This pattern suggests that, notwithstanding the substantial holdings of Venetian stock by printers such as Tini in Milan and the heirs of Filippo Giunta in Florence (both of whom were also booksellers), printers in even moderately sized urban centers were able to rely upon a reasonable number of local sales of the music that they produced.

Although Venice remained at the center of the music printing and publishing industry throughout the sixteenth and well into the seventeenth century, just as it remained dominant in the book trade in general, the music that was published there could sometimes be transmitted in indirect ways. Traditional commercial patterns could profoundly affect musical taste, as is clear from the familiar example of English enthusiasm for the Italian madrigal at the end of the century, a taste substantially created by Thomas Morley's astute entrepreneurship.[47] Many of the versions copied into English manuscripts from the 1560s onwards, after the accession of Elizabeth I had secured both greater stability in the country and a more cosmopolitan cultural outlook, were taken from northern printed sources (particularly the anthologies produced by Phalèse in Antwerp) rather from Venetian editions.[48] Many of the Italian pieces copied into the so-called Tregian score of about 1620, for example, were taken from northern editions. In music, as in contemporary ar-

[43] T. Carter, "Music Printing in Late Sixteenth- and Early Seventeeenth-Century Florence: Giorgio Marescotti, Cristofano Marescotti and Zanobi Pignoni," *Early Music History*, 9 (1990), 27–72.

[44] N. Guidobaldi, "Music Publishing in Sixteenth-and Seventeenth-Century Umbria," *Early Music History*, 8 (1988), 1–36.

[45] L. Sirch, "Aspetti dell'editoria musicale bresciana dopo il Concilio di Trento," *Fonti musicali italiane*, 8 (2003), 7–30.

[46] K. Larsen and A. Pompilio, "Cronologia delle edizioni musicali napolitane del Cinque-Seicento," in L. Bianconi and R. Bossa (eds.), *Musica e cultura a Napoli dal XV al XIX secolo* (Florence, 1983), 103–39.

[47] J. Kerman, *The Elizabethan Madrigal: A Comparative Study* (New York, 1962).

[48] For Phalèse, see H. Vanhulst, *Catalogue des éditions de musique publiées à Louvain par Pierre Phalèse et ses fils, 1545–1578* (Brussels, 1990).

chitecture, the English taste for the Italianate was acquired at one remove, already sifted to accommodate the preferences of Antwerp merchants and consequently rather wary of progressive stylistic trends.

The gradual widening of the market for music in the course of the century is reflected in the proliferation of amateur repertories both vocal and instrumental, the continued popularity of publications such as Arcadelt's *Primo libro* and Gero's Duos (both of which had a didactic function) as well as in the growing market for basic theory books and other how-to-do-it manuals, the earliest of which had also been produced in Venice in the 1530s. By the middle years of the sixteenth century many men of substance and even a good many of more modest means owned a sizeable general library; as inventories and booklists show, from this date onwards it was increasingly the norm for members of the professional classes in France, Italy, and the German-speaking areas of Europe to own books, as also did a large proportion of chemists, barber-surgeons, and others in trade lower down the social scale. In view of the rather specialized character of musical literacy it is unlikely that the ownership of music penetrated as far as did that for books of history and law. Nevertheless, it is clear that both the size and nature of the public for music changed dramatically from the 1540s onwards. From the middle years of the sixteenth century onwards, music printers proliferated throughout Europe, taking their workshop practices and distribution methods and the format and design of their books from the example of the Venetian printers, though despite this growth the market continued to be dominated by books printed in Venice and distributed through agents and booksellers abroad. In this sense the subsequent history of music printing is essentially that of developments in Italy and of the imitation of those developments elsewhere, not only in terms of book production and design, but often in respect of much of the repertory that was printed.

16

CONCEPTS AND DEVELOPMENTS IN MUSIC THEORY

Karol Berger

TODAY'S understanding of what constitutes music "theory" in the years between 1520 and 1640 differs somewhat from that of sixteenth- and seventeenth-century musicians themselves. We tend to include under the heading "Theory, 1520–1640" all books about music written during the period. Contemporaries, however, would be much more likely to label this literature simply "music" (*musica*) and to consider "theoretical or speculative music" (*musica theorica/theoretica* or *speculativa*) to constitute only a part of "music," namely, the liberal-art part dedicated to the scientific contemplation of the universe of sound (what today we would call "acoustics"), that is, dealing principally with the measurement of intervals and closely related issues in the physics and metaphysics of music, the legacy of the Boethian curriculum of medieval universities. Following the Aristotelian distinction between "contemplating" (*theoria*) and "acting" (*praxis*), "theoretical music" was contrasted with "practical music" (*musica practica*) dedicated to various aspects of the craft of making music (what today we would call, in a curious reversal of the traditional usage, "music theory"), that is, dealing principally with the modal organization of the tonal material, counterpoint, mensural rhythm and notation, and closely related issues in the composition and performance of music, the legacy of the Guidonian curriculum of medieval cathedral choir schools. In 1537, a widely-read German theorist, Nicolaus Listenius, introduced a further category, that of "poetic music" (*musica poetica*), modelled on the Aristotelian notion of "making" (*poiesis*), to distinguish the theory of composition from that of performance. Poetic music, Listenius explained, "consists in making or producing, that is, in such labor that even afterwards, when the craftsman is dead, leaves a complete and fully finished work."[1] This usage gained considerable currency in Germany, where "poetic music" was considered to be either a third

Some of the material presented here has appeared in Karol Berger, *A Theory of Art* (New York and Oxford, 2000), chap. 3, §§ b, c.

[1] Nicolaus Listenius, *Musica* (Nuremberg, 1537), chap. 1: "Consistit enim in faciendo sive

subdivision of "music" (in which case "practical music" would refer to the theory of performance), or as a subordinated part of "practical music."

Both the "theoretical" and the "practical" doctrines transmitted in books on music interacted in complex and often unpredictable ways with the actual practice of composers and performers. On relatively rare occasions, theoretical research and speculation paved the way for new forms of music-making. Such was, most famously, the case of the intellectual work done mostly in Florence that made early monody and opera possible. More often, thinking about music developed in reaction to changes taking place in actual practice. Unexpectedly perhaps, this might happen even in the relatively esoteric world of acoustical and harmonic theory. One example is provided by the new tunings and temperaments that had to be worked out in response to the requirements of developing instrumental practices. Another important instance of theory catching up with what musicians had actually been doing for some time is furnished by the growing early-seventeenth-century recognition that it was the triad and not any single interval that was the fundamental unit of harmonic hearing.

The period from 1520 to 1640 witnessed massive shifts in the centers of gravity of musical practice. At the beginning of the period, the music that was artistically most ambitious, complex, and advanced, that exhibited most completely what art music was capable of at the time, flowed into the genres of the mass and especially the motet. This was music destined to embellish the most important public ceremonies of church and state. It was composed and sung by artists trained in their craft mostly in northern France and especially in the Low Countries, artists active both at home and abroad in the principal power centers of Italy, France, and the Habsburg lands. By 1600 none of this was any longer the case. It is not that mass and motet were forgotten, or that the Low Countries stopped training competent musicians, far from it. But the genres that engaged the attention of the most innovative composers were now in the first place the Italian madrigal and, a little later, opera. The court and the learned academy rather than the church had become the principal institutions supporting musical innovation. The function of even the most ambitious music was now as likely to be a more intimate and private sort of entertainment as it was the public celebration of important state occasions. To be sure, both madrigal and opera could have public—that is, political—uses, as well as private or semiprivate ones such as personal edification and social entertainment. But the fact that at least some of the composers' best efforts were directed toward the latter, private sphere represents an historically significant shift. The musicians themselves were increasingly likely to have been trained in Italy, which gradually became the net European exporter of musical talent. Venice might serve as the emblematic stage on which this change of guard, the passing of European musical hegemony from the Netherlanders to the Italians, was enacted, as San Marco's two great chapel masters from beyond the Alps, Willaert and Rore, gave way to native Italians, to Willaert's own pupil Zarlino and, later on, to Monteverdi.

fabricando, hoc est, in labore tali, qui post se etiam, artifice mortuo opus perfectum et absolutum relinquat."

The multiple causes of these fundamental shifts are discussed at various points in this volume. Our task will be to see how these shifts were reflected in the theory of the period. What did the theorists have to say on the subject of the aims of music making? And what means did they think music had to realize these aims?

The Aims of Music

From Prosdocimus de Beldemandis in the early fifteenth century through Marco Scacchi in the mid seventeenth, Italian musicians focused their theoretical thoughts best when engaged in polemics and controversies. When in 1600 the Bolognese canon Giovanni Maria Artusi, a pupil and follower of Gioseffo Zarlino, subjected to a critical analysis excerpts from several of Claudio Monteverdi's then still unpublished madrigals,[2] excerpts that he significantly presented without their poetic texts, he gave Monteverdi's supporters and the composer himself an invaluable opportunity to formulate and defend their artistic goals. A certain l'Ottuso Accademico responded with a letter (printed by Artusi together with his own answer in 1603).[3] Monteverdi himself reacted in the prefatory letter to his Fifth Book of madrigals of 1605, a text his brother Giulio Cesare glossed extensively in a "Dichiaratione" that appeared in Claudio's *Scherzi musicali* of 1607[4] and was in turn answered by Artusi (now under the pseudonym of Antonio Braccino da Todi) in his *Discorso secondo musicale* of 1608.[5]

To Artusi's accusation that some contemporary composers follow no other rule than "to satisfy their whims,"[6] Claudio Monteverdi responded "that I do not compose my works at haphazard" and that, like his predecessors, the contemporary composer also "builds upon the foundation of truth."[7] It is this foundation, however, that has shifted. The older "first practice" (*prima pratica*) was, as the composer's brother explained, "finally perfected by Messer Adriano [Willaert] with actual composition and by the most excellent Zarlino with most judicious rules."[8] The newer "second practice" (*seconda pratica*) "was first renewed in our notation

[2] Giovanni Maria Artusi, *L'Artusi, overo Delle imperfettioni della moderna musica* (Bologna, 1600), fols. 39^r–44^r; trans. in Oliver Strunk, *Sources Readings in Music History*, rev. edn, ed. Leo Treitler (New York and London, 1998), 526–34.

[3] Giovanni Maria Artusi, *Seconda parte dell'Artusi overo Delle imperfettioni della moderna musica* (Bologna, 1603).

[4] Claudio Monteverdi's letter and Giulio Cesare Monteverdi's "Dichiaratione" are trans. in Strunk, *Source Readings*, rev. edn., 535–44.

[5] Texts not cited in the notes are fully cited in the Select Bibliography to this chapter, where editions of manuscript texts are also given.

[6] Artusi, *L'Artusi*, fol. 16^r: "per scapriciarsi."

[7] Claudio Monteverdi, *Il quinto libro de madrigali a cinque voci* (Venice, 1605): "ch'io non faccio le mie cose a caso"; "fabrica sopra li fondamenti della verità."

[8] Giulio Cesare Monteverdi, "Dichiaratione della lettera stampata nel quinto libro de' suoi madregali," in Claudio Monteverdi, *Scherzi musicali a tre voci* (Venice, 1607): "perfettionata ultimamente da Messer Adriano con l'atto prattico, e dal Eccellentissimo Zarlino con regole giudiciosissime."

by Cipriano de Rore . . . , was followed and amplified, not only by the gentlemen already mentioned [i.e., "the Signor Prencipe di Venosa, Emilio del Cavaliere, Count Alfonso Fontanella, the Count of the Camerata, the Cavalier Turchi, Pecci, and other gentlemen of that heroic school"], but by Ingegneri, Marenzio, Giaches de Wert, Luzzasco, likewise by Jacopo Peri, Giulio Caccini, and finally by loftier spirits with a better understanding of true art."[9] The two practices differ primarily in their way of introducing and resolving dissonances, the second allowing licences that are prohibited by Zarlino's rules of strict usage. In a famous passage, Giulio Cesare explained how the foundation of truth shifted, making room for the new licentious compositional techniques: "By First Practice he [Claudio Monteverdi] understands the one that turns on the perfection of the harmony, that is, the one that considers the harmony not commanded, but commanding, not the servant, but the mistress of the words. . . . By Second Practice . . . he understands the one that turns on the perfection of the melody, that is, the one that considers harmony not commanding, but commanded, and makes the words the mistress of the harmony."[10] Quoting Plato's *Republic* (398D), Giulio Cesare understood by "melody" the union of "the words, the harmony [that is, the tune], and the rhythm." He also quoted Plato's opinion that it was apt "if the rhythm and the harmony follow the words, and not the words these,"[11] the opinion that was clearly a major source of his brother's celebrated slogan.

The slogan itself expressed with paradigmatic clarity and force the most fundamental opposition underlying our period's vision of what music was for, the opposition between the idea of music as a sensible embodiment of the intelligible harmony obtaining in the universe God created and the idea of music as an expressive medium enhancing the emotional power of the sung words. In both cases music was credited with a mimetic function. The object of imitation, however, was very different: on the one hand it was the imperturbable and eternal harmony of the superhuman cosmic order, on the other the impassioned and protean intonations of human speech. What was centrally at stake in the opposition was the status of harmony: on the one hand, harmony was understood to be the essence of music, autonomous and not subservient to anything else; on the other, it was subordinated to something more important, the expression of the passions of the singing character, passions whose nature and object was made clear through the text. It was not an accident that Artusi presented the excerpts from Monteverdi's madrigals without the text: autonomous harmony was all that mattered for him. And it was

[9] Ibid.: "è stato il primo rinovatore ne nostri caratteri il Divino Cipriano Rore, . . . seguitata, e ampliata, non solamente da li Signori detti, ma dal Ingegneri, dal Marenzo, da Giaches Wert, dal Luzzasco, e parimente da Giaccopo Peri, da Giulio Caccini e finalmente da li spiriti più elevati, e intendenti de la vera arte."

[10] Ibid.: "prima prattica intende che sia quella che versa intorno alla perfettione del armonia; cioè che considera l'armonia non comandata, ma comandante, e non serva ma signora del oratione, . . . Seconda prattica, . . . intende che sia quella che versa intorno alla perfettione della melodia, cioè che considera l'armonia comandata, e non comandante, e per signora dell'armonia pone oratione."

[11] Ibid.: "oratione, harmonia, Rithmo"; "quando-quidem Rithmus et Harmonia orationem sequitur non ipsa oratio Rithmum et Harmoniam sequitur."

not surprising that the composer found this abstraction of harmony from the text objectionable.

The Monteverdis clearly did not see the opposition of the two practices and the underlying opposition of harmony and passions as arising only in their own time. Rather, they traced its lineage a good half century back, to Willaert as the classic exponent of the First Practice and to his San Marco successors Rore and Zarlino as respectively the originator of the Second Practice and the codifier of the theoretical rules governing the First. Indeed, the dichotomy of harmony and passions was fully operative by the mid sixteenth century, and it remained in force long after the close of our period, at least until the mid eighteenth century. The individual terms of the dichotomy, the notion of universal harmony and the belief in music's ethical power, its ability to influence human character and emotions, were, of course, of ancient provenance. They remained well known to medieval theorists and were never in need of a humanistic revival. But it was only in our period that the passions began to be taken really seriously as an object of practical musical concern and not just as a topic to which one paid lip service; that it was regularly noticed that the demands of harmony and those of the passions did not have to coincide; that the two were often conceived in opposition to one another; that the primacy and autonomy of harmony began to be challenged.

Perhaps the earliest theorist to come unmistakably on the side of the passions was another pupil of Willaert, and, beside Zarlino, the most substantial figure in the music theory of the 1550s, Nicola Vicentino. In his *L'antica musica ridotta alla moderna prattica* (1555), Vicentino insisted repeatedly that music should express the meaning of the words, "show by means of the harmony their passions." The subordination of harmony to the passions was as clearly demanded by Vicentino as it was half a century later by Monteverdi: "music made upon words is made for no other purpose than to express the thought and the passions and their effects with harmony." The concept of imitation links the art of the poet and that of the composer, whom Vicentino calls, in an expression reminiscent of Listenius, the "musical poet."[12] A chain of imitation starts with the passions and leads through the words of the poet, the music of the composer, and the sounds of the singer, to the listener in whom the imitated passions are to be aroused.

In postulating the arousal of the passions as the most fundamental goal of music making, Vicentino was no doubt inspired by the classical reports of the miraculously powerful ethical and emotional effects that were supposedly achieved by means of music in antiquity, reports so widely known in his time that Vicentino could refer to them simply as "those effects that, as the Authors write, were made in ancient times"[13] and safely assume that his readers would know what precisely he was referring to. His aim, programmatically announced in the very title of his treatise, *Ancient Music Restored to Modern Practice*, was not an antiquarian restora-

[12] Nicola Vicentino, *L'antica musica ridotta alla moderna prattica* (Venice, 1555), fol. 48^{r}: "con l'Armonia dimostrare le sue passioni"; fol. 86^{r}: "la musica fatta sopra parole, non è fatta per altro se non per esprimere il concetto & le passioni & gli effetti di quelle con l'armonia"; fol. 94^{r}: "Poeta Musico."

[13] Ibid., fol. 6^{v}: "quelli effetti che scrivono gli Authori anticamente farsi."

tion of the stylistic and compositional resources of ancient music. It was rather the recovery for modern musicians of the miraculous power of ancient music.

In other words, what needed to be restored, Vicentino claimed, were not the means but the aims of music. As for the means, these required not restoration but further development, since their power to move diminishes as one gets used to hearing them. This point deserves our attention. In the period under discussion, the humanistically inspired reading of ancient pagan authors was, superficial appearances notwithstanding, likely to motivate progressive rather than conservative practice, development of new musical resources and styles rather than restoration of old ones. Those who wanted musical practice to proceed under the banner of the passions were likely to advocate stylistic change. The defenders of harmony were the defenders of the stylistic status quo. It is not difficult to see why this was the case. Harmony, whether cosmic, human, or instrumental, is immutable. Its laws may be progressively discovered and described, the musical practice embodying it may be perfected. But once it has been perfected (as, according to Giulio Cesare Monteverdi, it has been in Willaert's hands) and once its rules have been properly formulated (as they have been by Willaert's pupils, Zarlino in particular), stylistic history has come to an end. It can get motivated to move again only by a different ideal, that of passions. Thus it is not surprising to find that Ghiselin Danckerts, a singer in the papal chapel who opposed Vicentino's theories from the standpoint of practice guided by the ideal of harmony, argued in his unpublished *Trattato sopra una differentia musicale* (written, like Vicentino's own treatise, during the 1550s) against any novelty in composition and was, accordingly, most sceptical about the putative miracles worked by ancient music.

It was Gioseffo Zarlino, of course, who gave the most influential expression to the idea of music as harmony. His most important treatise, significantly entitled *The Harmonic Institutions* (*Le istitutioni harmoniche*, 1558), was generally recognized as the most authoritative statement of harmonic theory not only in its own time or in the time of Monteverdi, but even as late as the early eighteenth century, when it was admired by that era's great harmonic theorist, Jean Philippe Rameau. For Zarlino, modern music had reached a state of perfection that could hardly be surpassed and that itself far surpassed the achievements of the ancients. He compared innovators of the day to Herostrates, eager to gain fame through the destruction of traditional ways. The superiority of modern music rested on the perfection of its "harmony," simultaneous movement of parts regulated by the doctrine of counterpoint. Zarlino was aware of those who, like Danckerts, doubted the miraculous powers of ancient music, to whom "it does not appear believable that [ancient] musicians could have produced such various effects in human souls as are reported in the histories.... It appears even less believable, since today, when it has been brought to such perfection that one almost cannot hope for anything better, one does not see it have any of the effects mentioned above." As for himself, he found the reports credible, but thought that "also at the present time music is not deprived of the power to achieve such effects."[14] Since "also in our days ... music

[14] Gioseffo Zarlino, *Le istitutioni harmoniche* (Venice, 1558), part II, chap. 4, p. 62: "non

excites in us various passions as it did in ancient times,"[15] there is no justification to the calls to return to ancient practices.

It is thus that Zarlino deprives the reformers like Vicentino of their crucial argument. In themselves, the "effects," though valuable and important, are not the central aim of music making. Modern polyphony is superior to ancient monody not on account of any power to move it may have, but on account of its "harmony." Harmony is the essence of music: "speaking universally, . . . music is nothing but harmony."[16] The Boethian doctrine of resemblances, as fully assimilated by Zarlino as it was by most of his contemporaries, posited analogies between the macrocosmic harmony of the universe, the microcosmic harmony of the diverse components of the human body and soul, and the actually sounding harmony of music. The analogies were grounded in the fact that in all three harmonies the "concord of discords, meaning a concord of diverse things that can be joined together,"[17] as Zarlino defines harmony, could be conceived as a proportion expressible by a numerical ratio. In actual music, "improper harmony" ("harmonia non propia") arises out of consonant relations between two or more sounds and "proper harmony" ("harmonia propia")—out of consonant relations between two or more simultaneous melodies.[18] The superiority of modern polyphony over ancient monody lies precisely in that only in the former is the proper harmony possible. As for the musical imitation of the passions, Zarlino has nothing against that, provided it does not interfere with what matters essentially—harmony.

But, for all its well-deserved prestige, Zarlino's harmonic theory represented something of a rearguard action. The cause of the passions could no longer be suppressed. In the half-century between Vicentino and Monteverdi its main advocate was the Florentine lutenist Vincenzo Galilei. Galilei studied music theory with Zarlino in Venice in the early 1560s and after his return to Florence in 1572 played for two decades an important role as an authority on music theory in the discussions of musicians, poets, and amateurs who constituted the informal academy known as the Camerata of Count Giovanni de' Bardi, a group whose interest centered on a Vicentinian project of the revival of ancient Greek music. But unlike Vicentino, whose actual knowledge of ancient music theory was extremely limited, Galilei approached the task of understanding ancient music more seriously than any of his predecessors and was lucky enough between 1572 and 1582 to get expert advice from Girolamo Mei, a greatly learned Florentine philologist residing in Rome. By the time Galilei initiated the correspondence between the two, Mei was

par credibile, che i Musici potessero produrre ne gli animi humani tanti varij effetti, si come nelle historie si racconta: . . . Et tanto meno par credibile, perche essendo ella hoggidi ridutta a quella perfettione, che quasi di meglio non si può sperare, non si vede che faccia alcuno delli sopradetti effetti; . . . la Musica etiandio al presente non è priva di far cotali effetti."

15 Zarlino, *Le istitutioni harmoniche*, part II, chap. 9, p. 75: "etiandio a i nostri tempi . . . la Musica induce in noi varie passioni, nel modo che anticamente faceva."

16 Ibid., part I, chap. 5, p. 10: "in universale parlando . . . Musica non è altro che Harmonia."

17 Ibid.: "discordante concordia come sarebbe a dire, Concordia di varie cose, le quali si possino congiungere insieme."

18 Ibid., part II, chap. 12, p. 80.

already intimately familiar with virtually the complete corpus of ancient Greek music theory, and it was Mei's understanding of ancient music, as well as his arguments for its superiority over modern practice, that decisively influenced Galilei and turned him away from Zarlino. The result was Galilei's *Dialogo della musica antica, et della moderna* (1581), the Camerata's main theoretical statement.

Before his correspondence with Mei, Galilei believed with Zarlino that the aim of music was to provide pleasure by means of harmony. Mei showed him how a different aim for music might be envisioned, an aim giving music ethical significance and thus higher than mere sensuous pleasure, how modern practice might be criticized from the standpoint of ancient achievement. The music of the ancients, Mei claimed, aimed not just to delight the ear, like the modern one, but to arouse passions. On 8 May 1572, Mei wrote to Galilei:

> you are of the opinion that music should have as its object to delight the ear with harmony and that for this reason the same must have been the object of ancient music. Now if you mean the delight that is born from the sung air which when well accommodated, expressing the concepts it ornaments, and producing by its means . . . the affection, cannot but be pleasant to listen to, I easily agree with you. But since your words seem to be strongly determined in favor of the pure sense of hearing, . . . it occurred to me that you might see perhaps only this delight that today one sees as being openly proposed to our musicians as the goal which is only this delicacy . . . which does not have any other more profound goal than to satisfy purely the ear upon hearning . . . Now this I judge to be . . . completely opposed to the aim of ancient [music] . . . I believe that the proposed goal . . . was not the sweetness of the consonances to satisfy the ear . . ., but the complete and efficacious expression of everything he wanted to make understood.[19]

Having absorbed Mei's teaching, Galilei started to believe that the aim of modern practice would be suitable for instrumental music only, and that it was inferior to the ethical aim of ancient vocal practice. He wrote in the *Dialogo*:

> If the aim of modern practitioners is (as they say) to delight the sense of hearing with the diversity of the consonances, . . . let this goal of delighting

[19] Girolamo Mei, *Letters on Ancient and Modern Music to Vincenzo Galilei and Giovanni Bardi*, ed. Claude V. Palisca, MSD 3 (American Institute of Musicology, 1960), pp. 115–16: "voi havete oppinione che la musica debba havere per suo obbjetto il dilettare l'orecchio con l'harmonia, et che per ciò il medesimo dovesse essere quel de la antica. Or se voi intendete il diletto che nasce dal aria del cantare, la quale bene accomodata esprimendo acconciamente il concetto et facendo con l'ajuto suo . . . l'affetto, non puo essere se non gioconda ad udirsi, io agevolmente ne sono con esso voi. Ma perche le parole vostre appariscono molto resolute in favore de lo schietto sense del udito, . . . m'é venuto pensato che voi per ventura possiate haver solamente l'occhio à quel diletto che oggi apertamente si vede proposto per fine à nostri musici, che è quella sola delicatura, . . . la quale altro pju profondo fine non ha che il contentare schiettamente l'orecchio ne lo udirsi, . . . Or questo io . . . giudico che fusse in tutto e per tutto, . . . alieno de la mira de l'antica . . . io per tanto mi credo che il fine propostosi fusse . . . non la soavità de le consonanze per contentar l'orecchio . . . ma lo esprimere interamente et con efficacia tutto quello che voleva fare intendere."

> with the diversity of their chords be left to these instruments, since being deprived of sense, motion, intellect, speech, discourse, reason, and soul, they are not capable of anything else. But let men, who have been given by nature all these beautiful, noble, and excellent abilities, seek by their means not only to delight but, as imitators of the good ancients, also to be of use, since they have the ability to do this.[20]

"The practice of music," Galilei claimed, ". . . was introduced by men . . . first, . . . to express the conceits of the mind with greater efficacy in celebrating the praises of gods, geniuses, and heroes . . . and second, to impress them with equal force upon the minds of mortals for their benefit and comfort".[21] The "conceits" that music is to express and impress are, primarily, the passions of the words and their expression and impression aims at listeners' benefit, which is understood in the Horatian fashion not only as pleasure, but also as moral betterment, "not only as delightful to life, but also as useful to virtue".[22] These were the aims of ancient music and should be, but are not, the aims of modern practice too. Modern practice, which Galilei identifies with polyphony, got under way some hundred fifty years ago and, thanks to such of its "princes" ("Principi") as Zarlino, who codified its rules, or to Cipriano de Rore, "a truly unique musician in this manner of counterpoint," "from that time until today, . . . it has reached the highest pinnacle of perfection man could possibly imagine."[23] Nevertheless, "no man of understanding thinks that they have brought it back to its ancient state."[24] The reason for this is that modern practice treats counterpoint as the aim in itself, forgetting, in the words of Giovanni de' Bardi, that "just as the soul is nobler than the body, so the words are nobler than the counterpoint."[25] With regard to theory, Galilei thought, the task of restoring music to its ancient state has already been accomplished by Girolamo Mei. But the task of doing the same thing in practice remained to be accomplished.

With Galilei's *Dialogo*, the new Monteverdian aesthetic field, already outlined

[20] Vincenzo Galilei, *Dialogo della musica antica, et della moderna* (Venice, 1581), 86: "se il fine de moderni prattici è (come essi dicono) il dilettare con la diversità delle consonanze il senso dell'udito, . . . lascisi questo fine del dilettare con la diversità de loro accordi ad essi strumenti; perche sendo privi di senso, di moto, d'intelletto, di parlare, di discorso, di ragione, & d'anima; non sono di piu oltre capaci: ma gli huomini che sono dalla natura stati dotati di tutte queste belle nobili, & eccellenti parti, cerchino col mezzo di esse non solo di dilettare, ma come imitatori de buoni antichi, di giovare insieme, poiche acciò sono atti."

[21] Ibid., 81: "l'uso della musica . . . fu da gli huomini introdotto . . . principalmente . . . dall'esprimere con efficacia maggiore i concetti dell'animo loro nel celebrare le lodi de Dei, de Genij, & degli Heroi . . . & d'imprimergli secondariamente con pari forza nelle menti de mortali per utile & comodo loro."

[22] Ibid., 1: "non solo come dilettevole alla vita, ma ancora come utile alla virtù."

[23] Ibid., 80: "Musico in questa maniera di Contrapunto veramente singulare"; "da quel tempo sin'ad hoggi, . . . ella sia giunta à quel colmo di perfettione che l'huomo si possa imaginare."

[24] Ibid., 1: "non pare ad alcuni intelligenti, che l'habbiano resa all'antico suo stato."

[25] Giovanni de' Bardi, *Discorso mandato a Caccini sopra la musica antica e 'l cantar bene* (*I-Rvat* Barb. lat. 3990), fol. 10^r: "così come l'anima del corpo è più nobile, altresi le parole più nobili del contrapunto sono." Trans. Oliver Strunk, *Source Readings in Music History*, 1st edn (New York, 1950), p. 295.

in some detail by Vicentino, is fully mapped out. There are two musical practices, the modern and the ancient ones. The modern aims at "nothing other then the delight of hearing," and hence it is adequately served by means of polyphony, by what Zarlino called "harmony." The ancient, by contrast, wanted "to lead another to the same affection one feels oneself,"[26] to be ethically useful, and hence it could not treat harmony as an aim in itself, but had to subordinate it to the passions of the words. Since the aim of ancient practice, ethical education, is clearly nobler than the mere pleasure modern music aims at, the former is offered as an alternative, and higher, ideal for modern practice as well.

The two ideas of music, music as sensuous embodiment of the intelligible universal harmony and music as ethical imitation of human passions and characters, were both central parts of the European music's ancient Greek heritage. But in the century before the beginning of our period, the idea of harmony completely dominated musical practice. In the late sixteenth century, the balance between the two ideas shifted. The idea that in the middle of the sixteenth century stirred the imagination of isolated humanistically-inspired visionaries—the idea of music as a mimetic art, an art able to imitate passions—came to dominate opinion in more advanced circles by the last quarter of the century. It did so, however, without eliminating the idea of harmony altogether, so that from now on the two ideas had to coexist. And the tension between the two Monteverdian practices remained alive, basic to the aesthetics of music, long after the end of our period, at least through the middle of the eighteenth century. It can be strongly felt as late as Jean-Jacques Rousseau's polemic against Jean-Philippe Rameau.

Rameau's admiration for Zarlino, whom he regarded as his most important predecessor in harmonic theory, is well documented; the centrality of the idea of harmony to his thinking about music is announced in the very title of his seminal *Traité de l'harmonie* of 1722. What particularly provoked Rousseau was Rameau's Zarlinian identification of music's essence with harmony and the resulting subordination of melody to harmony. Rameau opened his treatise with these sentences:

> Music is the science of sounds; therefore sound is the principal subject of music. Music is generally divided into harmony and melody, but we shall show in the following that the latter is merely a part of the former and that a knowledge of harmony is sufficient for a complete understanding of all the properties of music.[27]

In his *Essai sur l'origine des langues* of 1754–61, Rousseau argued that music and language had their common origin in human moral needs and passions before they

[26] Galilei, *Dialogo*, 89: "non altro . . . che il diletto dell'udito"; "il condurre altrui . . . nella medesima affettione di se stesso."

[27] Jean-Philippe Rameau, *Traité de l'harmonie* (Paris, 1722), book 1, chap. 1, p. 1: "La Musique est la Science des Sons; par consequent le Son est le principal object de la Musique. On divise ordinairement la Musique en Harmonie & en Melodie, quoique celle-cy ne soit qu'une partie de l'autre, & qu'il suffise de connoître l'Harmonie, pour être parfaitement instruit de toutes le proprietez de la Musique, comme il sera prouvé dans la suite." Trans. Philip Gossett, *Jean-Philippe Rameau: Treatise on Harmony* (New York, 1971), 3.

separated so that language could express the ideas of reason and melody the passions of the soul. But "to the degree that language improved, melody, being governed by new rules, imperceptibly lost its former energy, and the calculus of intervals was substituted for nicety of inflection. . . . That is also when it stopped producing the marvels it had produced when it was no more than the accent and harmony of poetry and gave to it the power over the passions that speech subsequently exercised only on reason."[28] Having lost its intimate connection with speech and become identified with purely abstract harmony, music "found itself deprived of the moral power it had yielded when it was the twofold voice of nature."[29] It is imitation alone, Rousseau argued, that raises music to the level of a fine art, and what allows music to imitate the passions is not harmony, not pure sounds and their intervallic relations, which can provide no more than sensuous pleasure, but melody which follows the inflections of the impassioned speaking voice. Thus Rousseau's polemic against Rameau recapitulates at a distance of some 170 years the central themes of Galilei's strictures against Zarlino. (Similarities between Rousseau's and Galilei's positions are no less striking than the more overtly acknowledged indebtedness of Rameau to Zarlino. They extend to such mysterious details as Galilei's comparison, in his unpublished *Discorso intorno all'uso dell'Enharmonio*, of the function of vertical consonances in music to that of colors in painting, a topic Rousseau, who was unlikely to have read Galilei's discourse, developed in a most interesting way when he compared melodic lines with drawing and chords with coloring and claimed that in both music and painting only lines served the purpose of representation, while chords and colors provided mere sensuous pleasure.) The aesthetic agenda laid out in the late sixteenth century remained valid for almost two hundred years, to be challenged only in the late eighteenth century by the new German paradigm of "absolute music."

The legendary ethical power of ancient music is invoked by Rousseau no less than by Vicentino and Galilei to justify their advocacy of the ideal of music as a mimetic art, as imitation of the passions. But legends testifying to this miraculous power were never forgotten and constituted a standard repertory of the topic of *laus musicae* throughout the Middle Ages without anyone drawing serious practical consequences from them. What happened in the mid sixteenth century that allowed passions to challenge harmony in a serious and practical way for the first time? The causality involved in a profound shift like this one, a shift that reorganized the aims and means of the whole of musical practice, was necessarily complex.

[28] Jean-Jacques Rousseau, *Essai sur l'origine des langues, où il est parlé de la mélodie et de l'imitation musicale* (*CH-N* 7835), chap. 19; "A mesure que la langue se perfectionnait, la mélodie, en s'imposant de nouvelles règles, perdait insensiblement de son ancienne énergie, et le calcul des intervalles fut substitué à la finesse des inflexions. . . . Alors aussi cessèrent peu à peu ces prodigues qu'elle avait produit lorsqu'elle n'était que l'accent et l'harmonie de la poésie, et qu'elle lui donnait sur les passions cet empire que la parole n'exerça plus dans la suite que sur la raison." Trans. J. H. Moran in *On the Origin of Language* (New York, 1966), 68.

[29] Ibid.: "la musique se trouva privée des effets moraux qu'elle avait produits quand elle était doublement la voix de la nature." Trans. Moran, 72.

Without pretending to offer an exhaustive explanation, one might single out two important factors that caused the shift.

First, the sixteenth-century revolution in the natural sciences was making the idea of cosmic harmony, which music was supposed to embody, less and less secure. As Alexandre Koyré has pointed out,[30] modern science, with its implied separation of value and fact, was bound to undermine and eventually discard the use of value-concepts such as harmony, Johannes Kepler's and Marin Mersenne's powerful rescue efforts notwithstanding. Zarlino could still believe in the analogy of musical and cosmic harmony, because he understood the harmonious concord of diverse elements to consist in both cases in proportions expressible in similar numerical ratios. But, even as he wrote, scientists were beginning to challenge the traditional Ptolemaic cosmology and offering new views of the mathematical structure of the universe, transforming the closed pre-modern cosmos into the infinite universe of modern science. At the same time, empirical research into acoustics undertaken by the scientist Giovanni Battista Benedetti and later by Galilei demonstrated that the ratios of the just intonation on which Zarlino's view of musical harmony rested could not as a matter of fact be the basis of modern practice. The tuning, Ptolemy's syntonic diatonic, was greatly attractive to theorists of polyphonic harmony, since it made all consonances "just," whether perfect or imperfect; in the rival Pythagorean tuning, only perfect consonances were just, that is, only these were strictly consonant, which created a discrepancy with the practice that recognized thirds and sixths to be consonant. Ptolemy's syntonic diatonic tuning was rediscovered by the first real humanist among music theorists, Franchino Gaffurio, in his *De harmonia musicorum instrumentorum opus* (1518), and championed as the basis of contemporary practice by Giovanni Spataro in *Errori di Franchino Gafurio* (1521), Lodovico Fogliano in *Musica theorica* (1529), and Zarlino. Benedetti's proof, in a letter to Cipriano de Rore of *c.*1563 and in *Diversarum speculationum mathematicarum & physicorum liber* (1585), that the use of just intonation in polyphonic practice was bound to produce a lowering of pitch, deprived polyphonic harmony of its theoretical foundations. Thus, the credibility of the analogy between the celestial and musical harmonies was undermined on both ends. This "untuning of the sky" (to borrow John Hollander's paraphrase of Dryden's famous image) meant that music had to look for a new justification of its existence.

Second, just as scientific empiricism was beginning to deprive the idea of musical embodiment of the cosmic harmony of its credibility, humanist reverence for ancient ideas and practices provided music with a viable alternative ethical role based on the subordination of harmony to words. We have already seen how Giulio Cesare Monteverdi justified the Second Practice by invoking the authority of Plato. The same passage from Plato's *Republic* (398D) where the primacy of words over harmony and rhythm is asserted, had been used some 75 years earlier by Bishop Jacopo Sadoleto, a future member of the Council of Trent, in his *De liberis recte instituendis* (1533) to support his, and later the Council's, view that music should be guided by the text. (Sadoleto's book was known and quoted by Galilei.) The same

[30] *From the Closed World to the Infinite Universe* (Baltimore, 1957).

passage from Plato served as an inspiration to those who wanted to subordinate the autonomous "harmony" of the Netherlandish polyphonic tradition to words whether their main interest was in the reform of church or of secular music.

Two further developments reinforced the turn to the passions of the words. Late-fifteenth-century Florence witnessed in the writings of the Neoplatonist philosopher and magician Marsilio Ficino the birth of an influential and coherent theory explaining how music might achieve its powerful magical effects. In the words of D. P. Walker, the foremost student of Ficino's musical magic, Ficino

> is the earliest Renaissance writer I know of to treat the effects of music seriously and practically, and not merely as a constituent of the rhetorical topic of the *laus musicae*. By providing them with a rational explanation, he removes them from the status of more or less legendary marvels, makes them into exciting realities, and, by his astrological music, indicates ways of reviving them.[31]

Zarlino was aware of Ficino's theories, as was, more tantalizingly, Monteverdi's champion l'Ottuso Accademico, who quoted Ficino in his letter published by Artusi to explain how music influenced affections. By the middle of the seventeenth century, Descartes would provide the musical world with a new theory of the nature and mechanism of the passions in *Les Passions de l'âme* (1649).

At the same time, the steadily increasing influence of Aristotle's *Poetics*, generally available only since 1498 when Giorgio Valla's Latin translation appeared, reinforced this Platonic lesson by providing music, along with poetry, with a mimetic aim and by suggesting for it the role of a powerful amplifier of impassioned dramatic speech. We have noticed above Rousseau claiming the status of a fine art for music on the basis of its mimetic abilities. From Galilei through Rousseau, one took it for granted that music could and should represent passions and the dominant position of this idea remained unchallenged until the emergence of the new ideas of the "autonomous artwork" and "absolute music" in late eighteenth-century Germany. The Aristotelian notion of representation (*mimesis*) provided music with a ground on which it could be compared with poetry, allowing it by the eighteenth century to enter the emerging modern system of fine arts. Thus the shift from harmony to passions meant also that, increasingly, it was to poetics and rhetoric, rather than to the mathematical disciplines of the quadrivium, that music theorists looked for sources of useful concepts and ideas. Step by step, music ceased to be a premodern liberal art allied with the quadrivium and became a modern fine art allied with other fine arts.

31 D. P. Walker, *Spiritual and Demonic Magic from Ficino to Campanella* (London, 1958), 25–26.

The Means of Music

The shift in the aims of music, the emergence of a plurality of aims, could not but have an impact on the means by which these aims were realized and on their theoretical understanding. At the very end of our period, it began even to foster a new awareness of a plurality of styles and genres which we have already encountered in the Monteverdi brothers' notion of two practices. Influenced by the Monteverdis, the royal *maestro di cappella* in Warsaw, Marco Scacchi, proposed in his *Cribrum musicum ad triticum Syferticum* (1643) to distinguish *stylus antiquus* and *stylus modernus*, each with its own function and grammar. In his slightly later *Breve discorso sopra la musica moderna* (1649), Scacchi went on to group the genres of the actually practiced music into large functional families of church, chamber, and theater music (*Stylus Ecclesiasticus*, *Stylus Cubicularis*, and *Stylus Scenicus seu Theatralis*), to recognize the two Monteverdian paradigms (*ut harmonia sit domina orationis* and *ut oratio sit domina harmoniae*) operating within the first two classes, and to see that particular styles were chosen to suit particular genres of composition. Thus Scacchi offered an early theoretical recognition of the plural character of contemporary practices and a model of style classification to be imitated and elaborated for a century by such writers as Scacchi's pupil Angelo Berardi, Christoph Bernhard, Johann Joseph Fux, and Johann Mattheson.

But the shift affected also more traditional areas of music theory. As Giulio Cesare Monteverdi explained, the practice governed by the idea of autonomous harmony was given perfect theoretical description by Zarlino. Now, the two topics Zarlino discussed in depth in the practical part of his *Istitutioni harmoniche* were the modes and counterpoint. Evidently, he believed that mastery of these two subjects gave the composer what he needed to know if he wanted to ensure that his music be harmonious. The proper employment of the modes safeguarded the harmonic integrity of the melodic lines in a polyphonic composition, and the proper employment of the contrapuntal rules safeguarded the harmonic integrity of the polyphonic whole. These two central areas of theory went through profound development in our period, responding in part to their own internal logic and in part to the new aesthetic ideals.

The traditional theory of the eight church modes was something any even rudimentarily trained musician of our period would have had to master early on. In addition to its obvious classificatory and hence also mnemonic advantages for a church musician who had to memorize the large repertory of plainchant, the system offered any musician a set of concepts that allowed him to understand the coherence and unity of a well-constructed melody. An early attempt to apply the theory to polyphony was undertaken by Pietro Aaron in his *Trattato della natura et cognitione di tutti gli tuoni di canto figurato* (1525). A coherent melody represented, fundamentally, a single mode, that is, it projected a single step in the diatonic series, the final (*finalis*), as the most important point of arrival of the melodic motion at main moments of punctuation; it moved largely within a proper range of steps around the final (*ambitus* or *cursus*); and it emphasized in its progression a characteristic and often repeated interval (*repercussio*) between the final and the second most important step of the mode, the reciting tone (*repercussa*), for instance, by making the reciting tone the goal of some internal cadences and especially by projecting the *repercussio* at the beginning of individual phrases. The traditional theory also allowed for a discrete insertion of elements of other modes within the course of a melody (the *mixtio* of the authentic and plagal modes that share a common final, and the *commixtio* of modes with different finals), without endangering the coherence guaranteed by the fundamental mode.

A less widely taught alternative, originating with the eleventh-century Berno of Reichenau, was to understand modes primarily as octave species, that is, as octave segments of the diatonic series, composed of a species of fifth and a species of fourth, with the lowest step of the species of fifth serving as the final, and with the species of fourth taking the higher position if the mode was to be authentic, or lower if it was to be plagal. The coherence of a melody would in this case be assured, if it emphasized the appropriate species of fifth and fourth at the beginnings of its phrases and chose the final and the step a fifth above it as points of arrival at the principal moments of punctuation. The big disadvantage of this system was that it ignored some features of traditional practice, in particular the *repercussio*. In return, it offered some more systematically minded theorists a way of neatly removing the contradiction between the traditional system of eight modes and the diatonic series onto which it was projected. Realizing that the diatonic series makes possible seven different octave species, of which six can be divided into species of perfect fifth and fourth, the Swiss humanist theorist Heinrich Glarean proposed in his appropriately named *Dodecachordon* of 1547 to recognize four additional modes in addition to the traditional eight. (Glarean's attempt to formulate a modal theory that would be internally more consistent than the traditional one, and more responsive to contemporary polyphonic practice, has been followed up in our own time by the remarkably similar theories of Siegfried Hermelink and Harold Powers.)

For someone like Glarean, who was not professionally concerned with daily church services and thus could be relatively independent of traditional practices and doctrines, the alternative system offered the obvious advantage of being able to account for compositions centering on the finals of A and C without having to assimilate these to one of the four finals recognized by the system of eight modes, D, E, F, and G. (Since in practice the F-modes always used one flat in the signature to avoid automatically the tritone above the final, the C-modes could easily be assimilated to those; but the A-modes remained troublesome, since they had species in common with both the D- and E-modes. In sixteenth-century polyphony, D-modes pieces occasionally ended on a degree a fifth above the final, and E-mode pieces often ended on the fourth degree. Moreover, most E-mode pieces emphasized the fourth degree to such an extent that one has to ask whether E or A was experienced as the central pitch in such works. But modern scholarship can learn to ask questions of this sort only when it realizes explicitly that there is a distinction to be made between the way earlier musicians heard and the way they thought.) But for a church musician the reform was impractical, since it involved the use of two different modal systems, one for plainchant and one for polyphony. Numerous sixteenth-century collections of vocal and instrumental polyphony with individual compositions grouped according to modes leave little doubt that composers of polyphony no less than singers of plainchant thought in modal terms. Both systems were in use, though the traditional one remained by far the more popular.

Nevertheless, the species-based system offered one significant advantage to a composer of polyphony, an advantage that may account at least in part for Zarlino's decision to endorse it. In either system, the choice of the fundamental mode ensured the tonal coherence of a melody. But the traditional system of modes had no clear answer to the question of what modal features individual voices in a polyphonic complex should possess in order for the whole to be coherent. It did not make much sense to suggest that all voices should represent the same mode, since it was impossible to keep the ranges of all adjacent voices an octave apart from one another. And it did not make sense to suggest that the voices should share a common final, but move alternately within the authentic and plagal ranges, since the distinction between the authentic and its corresponding plagal involved not only the range, but also the *repercussio*. The great advantage of the system based on the species and disregarding the *repercussio* was, precisely, that it gave a clear and practical opinion on how the adjacent voices should be related: they should share the final, but represent alternately the authentic and plagal ranges, Zarlino advised, with the mode of the tenor traditionally defining how the piece would be classified. This way, not only the harmonic integrity of individual lines but also that of the whole was generally safeguarded.

The species-based system, minimizing as it did the distinction between the authentic and the corresponding plagal modes and encouraging their amalgamation into modal pairs, was only one symptom indicating that the long process of dissolution of the traditional modal system and of its transformation into the modern two-mode system of keys had begun. Another important symptom was the growing recognition that polyphonic practice minimized differences between some modal pairs. Specifically, the G-mode required in practice frequent sharpening of its seventh degree at cadences, thus assimilating it to the already identical F- and C-modes, while the D-mode often called for a flat sixth degree in order to avoid the non-harmonic relation with F, thus assimilating it to the A-mode. Zarlino was probably reacting to facts of this sort when he grouped all modes into two families (the family of C-, F-, and G-modes on the one hand, and the family of A-, D-, and E-modes on the other), because most of the imperfect consonances over the final and fifth degrees were major in one family and minor in the other, which accounted, he thought, for the contrasting affective characters, respectively cheerful and sad, of the two families.

Both the traditional and the species-based modal systems continued to be presented by theorists well into the eighteenth century, especially in Germany. But at the same time, a number of theorists after Zarlino recognized that the systems had to be modified if they were to describe contemporary polyphonic-harmonic practice adequately. Perhaps the most imaginative of these was the German theorist Johannes Lippius, whose *Synopsis musicae novae* (1612) may well represent the most important advance in harmonic theory since Zarlino. Building on his, and his immediate predecessors', recognition that it was the triad and not the single interval that constituted the most fundamental unit of harmonic thinking (see below), Lippius made the tonic triad rather than the species the basis of the modes and differentiated the modes by the major and minor tonic triads. Thus, he subtly subverted Glarean's system in a Zarlinian fashion: "Both species of legitimate modes are themselves trinities, the one—Ionian, Lydian, and Mixolydian; the other—Dorian, Phrygian, and Aeolian."[32] Lippius' slightly earlier *Disputatio musica tertia* (1610) was even more explicit: "Hence, we reduce these six [authentic] modes to two: one, which has the *naturalis* triad, the other which has the *mollis*."[33]

The step from Zarlino to the modern two-mode system was very short indeed. But the complementary gradual recognition of all 24 equally original keys was not to be completed until the early eighteenth century. It was preceded by a long period in which modes were identified less and less in terms of species and more and more in terms of specific finals combined with signatures (as when mode 2 was identified with G-final and one-flat signature), that is, a period in which modes were effectively transformed into keys. The practice seems to have originated in Adriano Banchieri's *L'Organo suonarino* (1605) as a theoretical recognition of what had been going on in practice for some time. Thus, for instance, even in late-sixteenth-century polyphony, the second mode practically never appeared untransposed, and its most common transposition was, in fact, by a fourth up with a one-flat signature.

Even in its species-based Zarlinian version, the theory of modes could account for the harmony of the polyphonic whole only in very general terms, simply by advising that all the voices should use predominantly the same species of fifth and fourth. For a micro-management of the harmony among the voices something more detailed was needed: the doctrine of counterpoint, which regulated the use of vertical harmonies by pronouncing on which ones were legitimate and how to move correctly from one to another. From its fourteenth-century beginnings through Zarlino and beyond, the doctrine was formulated in strictly intervallic terms, that is, it assumed that the interval was the most fundamental unit of harmonic thinking and that more complex harmonies were compounded of several intervals. But while the theory was entirely adequate as a pedagogical tool, its assumption of the primacy of the interval was incorrect in the sense that it did not correspond to the nature of harmonic hearing even in the fourteenth century, let alone in the sixteenth and seventeenth.

The theory rested on the classification of all legitimate intervals into three qualitatively differentiated classes of the dissonances, imperfect consonances, and per-

[32] Johannes Lippius, *Synopsis musicae novae* (Strasburg, 1612), sig. I1r: "Uterque Trinus est juxta Species Triadum: ille Jonicus, Lydius, & Mixolydius: hic Dorius, Phrygius & Aeolius." Trans. in Joel Lester, *Between Modes and Keys: German Theory, 1592–1802* (Stuyvesant, NY, 1989), 43.

[33] Johannes Lippius, *Disputatio musicae tertia* (Wittenberg, 1610), sig. D4r: "Hinc 6, Modos illos stringimus ad duos: unum, qui tenet Triadem Naturalem: alterum, qui Mollem." Trans. in Lester, *Between Modes and Keys*, 44.

fect consonances. Now, if it were true that the interval was the most fundamental unit of harmonic hearing, it would have to be the case that only one quality would attach to any specific interval. But this was not the case, not even in the fourteenth century. Long before our period, theorists recognized that the fourth was heard in some contexts as a perfect consonance (when there was a fifth below it), in others as an imperfect consonance (when there was a third below it), and in yet others as a dissonance (when there was nothing below it). Clearly, in this case the interval was not the ultimate unit of hearing, since its quality depended on something more fundamental yet, on the context in which it appeared.

It was only in the early seventeenth century that theorists began to realize what the nature of this context was: that the most fundamental unit of harmonic hearing was not the interval, but the root-centered and fully invertible triad. This momentous discovery would eventually make it possible to account for the nature of harmonic hearing better than the interval-based theory ever could, since it would allow one to derive the quality of a step (consonant or dissonant) from its relation to the triad: a step is heard to be consonant if it is heard to be a member of a triad and as dissonant if it is heard not to be a member of a triad. In his *Artis musicae delineatio* (1608), the German theorist Otto Siegfried Harnisch recognized the correlated facts that the root (*basis*) of a triad does not have to appear in its lowest voice and that a triad could appear in the root position and two inversions. Johannes Lippius went a step further (and, incidentally, coined the term *trias harmonica*), when he proposed to base the whole doctrine of harmony, both its modal and contrapuntal parts, on the triad. But Lippius himself was able to realize only a part of this program and to give modal theory as well as the theory of vertical harmonies a triadic basis. It was left to Rameau to realize fully the remaining part and to formulate a triadically based theory of chord progressions by conceiving those in terms of root progressions. Throughout the period 1520–1640, the progressions of vertical harmonies continued to be regulated by the intervallically based theory of counterpoint. A progression from one harmony to the next was intelligible not because it was governed by a consonant root progression, but because it involved a legitimate succession of two consonances, or the tendency of an imperfect consonance to move to the closest perfect consonance, or the tendency of a dissonance to resolve to a consonance. Musicians of our period may well have *heard* triadically, but, for the most part, they continued to *think* intervallically. Modern scholars have to learn to make this distinction if they are to do justice to the musical mind of the sixteenth and seventeenth centuries in its full complexity.

The practice of thoroughbass (*basso continuo*, a term coined by Lodovico Viadana in his *Cento concerti ecclesiastici* of 1602), the instrumental (mostly keyboard) accompaniment of vocal polyphony or monody from an unfigured or incompletely figured bass line, is very characteristic of this complicated state of musical consciousness. (The practice had its double roots in sixteenth-century Italian secular song and monody as well as the needs of church organists called upon to accompany choral music by doubling the voices in a simplified full score.) On the one hand, the practice encouraged vertical thinking, in terms of independent vertical harmonies —independent in the sense of not being the result of polyphonic interweaving of voices. On the other hand, however, it conceived of harmonies in intervallic, not triadic terms, since it made no distinction between the actually sounding bass note and the root. (Significantly, figures were already used to indicate intervals in some sixteenth-century counterpoint treatises.)

The strict *prima pratica* contrapuntal theory was given its classic formulation by Zarlino. By the late fifteenth century, all the fundamental conceptual issues of contrapuntal theory were resolved. Consonant progressions of the *contrapunctus simplex* had already been adequately described as early as the fourteenth century. In his *Liber de arte contrapuncti* (1477) Johannes Tinctoris presented the impressive conceptual breakthrough that allowed adequate description of the use of dissonances in *contrapunctus diminutus*, by showing that this required the introduction of metrico-rhythmic concepts into contrapuntal theory: the placement and length of dissonances could be regulated by relating them to the qualitatively distinct (strong and weak, or downbeat and upbeat) parts of the measure. Thus, what was required of Zarlino when he set out to write his contrapuntal *summa* was not so much intellectual innovation as attention to the actual practice of his predecessors and contemporaries, in particular to the practice of his revered teacher Willaert, as well as an in-depth treatment of special topics, such as various forms of imitation, invertible counterpoint, or text underlay.

Since dissonances presented the main threat to the consonant essence of "harmony," the core of the *prima pratica* had to lie in the strict regulation of dissonances—roughly speaking, by limiting the legitimate ones to passing notes and suspensions. Assuming that the normal duple measure (*tactus* or *battuta*) had the duration of a semibreve and consisted of a minim downbeat (*battere* or *positione*) and a minim upbeat (*levare* or *elevatione*), one might reduce Zarlino's most important rules of dissonance use to four. First, a dissonance has to be prepared by and resolved to a consonance. Second, the upbeat minim may be dissonant, if introduced and left by step. Third, the second and fourth semiminims in the measure may be dissonant, if introduced and left by step, but the third semiminim may be dissonant only if it is preceded by a minim or semibreve and followed by a stepwise descent. Fourth, a dissonant suspension is allowed on the downbeat, though it usually requires a consonant preparation and should always be resolved downward by step.

The core of the *seconda pratica* consisted in a relaxation of these rules, a relaxation understood, not as an abrogation whereby the strict rules would be simply pushed aside as irrelevant, but as an introduction of licences whose expressive sense could be grasped only against the remembered backgound of the strict usage. The Second Practice conceived of a dissonance not as a threat to "harmony," a threat that had to be strictly controlled and subordinated to consonances, but rather as an independent expressive means and expressive at least in part precisely because licentious. A systematic theoretical treatment of licences is, of course, not possible: one can list them, but one cannot, in principle, exhaust the list. This may be one of the reasons why Monteverdi never came up with the theory of Second Practice he had promised. The closest we get to such a theory is in Galilei's monumental and at the time unpublished *Trattato dell'arte del contrapunto* (1588–91). Of the many licences described by Galilei, three subverted the Zarlinian norms in a particularly striking fashion. First, of the four semiminims moving by step, any two (or even any three) can be dissonant. Second, dissonant suspensions can be resolved by downward leap, or by step to a new dissonance, or by step up, or simultaneously with a chromatically moving other voice; and several simultaneous suspensions are allowed. Third, a dissonance can be introduced on the downbeat even without a suspension, provided it is regularly resolved.[34]

Licences from the strict use of dissonances were analoguous to the figures of speech discussed in the "elaboration" or "decoration" (*elaboratio* or *decoratio*) division of rhetoric (the division concerned with the decoration of plain ideas of the oration with figures), since those also depended for their construction and rhetorical effectiveness on departures from normal usage. The analogy suggested the idea of musical-rhetorical figures representing particularly striking images and thoughts of the text, undoubtedly our period's most prominent adaptation of rhetorical concepts to music. Musical-rhetorical figures were in the main contrapuntal licences or madrigalisms, that is, musical gestures illustrating individual words of the text. The first attempt to codify them was made by the German theorist Joachim Burmeister in a series of treatises culminating in *Musica poetica* (1606). For a century and a half, Burmeister's attempt was widely imitated and developed by writers on music, and even though this remained a peculiarly German phenomenon, theorists often claimed that the use of figures characterized the music of Renaissance composers internationally. Lassus was particularly praised as the master musical orator, but composers as early as Dunstaple were included among users of rhetorical figures (thus Johannes Nucius in his *Musices practicae . . . praeceptiones* of 1613).

Incidentally, Burmeister's adaptation of rhetoric to music theory was not limited to the issue of musical representation of textual ideas and images. Already in 1563 another German theorist, Gallus Dressler, in his unpublished *Praecepta musicae poeticae*, proposed to think of the overall form of a musical composition in terms of the divisions of an oration, such as the *exordium*, *medium*, and *finis*. Burmeister developed the idea and illustrated it in a model analysis of Lassus' motet *In me transierunt*, which demonstrated the rhetorical division of form into periods or affections (*affectiones*) grouped into larger sections of introduction (*exordium*), the body of the piece (*corpus carminis*), and conclusion (*finis*) and described the figures deployed in individual periods. The idea that musical form might be described in oratorical terms continued to attract theorists as late as 1739, the date of Johann Mattheson's *Der vollkommene Capellmeister*.

Of the developments in theoretical understanding of musical means discussed so far, some, such as the development of modal theory or of the theory of vertical harmonies, were relatively independent of the underlying shift in the way the aims of music were conceived. Diminishing the importance of the distinctions between the authentic and plagal modes and between various modes in general, as well as

[34] All these details had been part of non-expressive normal usage before the mid-16th-century regulation of dissonance treatment; see Knud Jeppesen, *The Style of Palestrina and the Dissonance*, 2nd edn (London, 1946), *passim*. What is crucial in Galilei's formulation is their construal as licences, which empowers them to carry an expressive significance they had not had in the earlier styles.

the identification of the root-based and fully invertible triad, were processes and achievements that were likely to happen without any outside prompting, simply under the pressure of the internal developmental logic of polyphonic harmony. Other developments, however, and in particular the emergence of contrapuntal licences, represented new means that responded to new aims. In the case of licences and figures, theory was mostly following practice: Galilei and Burmeister were finding ways to describe what composers were already doing. In two areas, however, theorists took a more active and creative role, working side by side with composers, and occasionally even ahead of them, in developing new musical means.

One such area was that of radical chromaticism. For Vicentino, the most prominent early advocate of the subordination of harmony to passions, going beyond the confines of the diatonic system represented the best hope for a modern recapturing of the miraculous ethical power of ancient music. This was not so much because non-diatonic resources were used by ancient musicians, as because they were *not* used by modern ones and thus were fresh and able to produce strong effects. In his treatise, the theorist described a gamut that divided the octave into 31 equal parts, the constitution of the diatonic, chromatic, and enharmonic genera (the latter two modernized so as to divide by chromatic semitones and enharmonic dieses the entire octave and not only the lowest two intervals of the tetrachords, as the ancients did), the notation of non-diatonic steps, the construction and tuning of the *archicembalo* of two keyboards with three rows of keys each, and the ways in which all of these resources might be used to make non-diatonic music so as to express the passions of the words. Vicentino's book probably predated Lassus' *Prophetiae Sibyllarum* (*c.*1560), the most radical mid-century experiment in chromaticism, and it certainly predated the renewed interest in extreme chromaticism among the madrigalists around the turn of the century. But in the longer run, Vicentino's chromatic theories, like Gesualdo's chromatic practice, while interesting in their own terms, remained without lasting historical consequences: at the end of our period, music would have been no different even without them.

This certainly cannot be said about the other area of theoretical invention and initiative, that of monody. Like non-diatonicism, the turning away from Netherlandish polyphony was advocated by some late-sixteenth-century Italians in the spirit of a humanistic revival of ancient music and its ethical force. In the 1572 letter to Galilei already cited, Girolamo Mei affirmed that the aim of ancient musicians "was not the sweetness of the consonances to satisfy the ear (since there is no testimony nor any evidence by the authors about the use of these in their singing) but the complete and efficacious expression of everything he wanted to make understood . . . by means and through the aid of high and low sounds . . . accompanied with the regulated temperament of the fast and slow . . ."[35] Inspired by Mei, Galilei

[35] Mei, letter of 8 May 1572, in *Letters on Ancient and Modern Music*, 117: "fusse . . . non la soavità de le consonanze per contentar l'orecchio (conciosiache del uso di queste nel lor cantare non si truova ne testimonio ne riscontro alcuno appresso gli scrittori) ma lo esprimere interamente et con efficacia tutto quello che voleva fare intendere . . . per il mezzo et ajuto de la acutezza e gravità de la voce, . . . accompagnata con la regolata temperatura del presto et adagio."

and his Camerata friends concluded that, if modern vocal music was to abandon the aim of sensuous pleasure for the higher one of ethical efficacy, it had also to abandon polyphony for monophony. Passions were represented in a melody by appropriately chosen vocal range and rhythm and tempo. Polyphony not only made words difficult to follow but, worse, it set the same words in contradictory fashion, giving them different ranges and rhythms in different voices.

In the late discourses appended to his counterpoint treatise, Galilei modified somewhat this radically anti-polyphonic stance and began to advocate vocal melody supported by the accompaniment of instrumental consonant harmonies, the highest line of which doubled the melody. Instrumental consonances, he was now willing to concede, not only pleased the ear: "the musician, with variety of intervals and in particular of consonances communicates to the intellect all the passions of the soul, especially shaped appropriately by the text."[36]

In Italy, the ground for this sort of texture of instrumentally and chordally accompanied vocal melody was well prepared. Baldassare Castiglione advocated in his *Il cortegiano* (1528) solo song with viol accompaniment (*il cantare alla viola*) as the most appropriate form of courtly vocal music. But the reforms stemming from the Camerata circle were more far-reaching in that they went beyond a mere expression of preference for a particular mode of performance and resulted in viable new styles and genres of composition. Their permanent legacy was to provide even the most ambitious art music with a textural alternative to the classical equal-voiced polyphony of the high Renaissance, an alternative that assumed a functional differentiation between the soprano melody and the supporting chordal accompaniment as well as the polarization of the soprano and bass parts. Thus, the plurality of practices that was the most important achievement of our period involved not only a plurality of aims, but also a corresponding plurality of means and not the least among them, a plurality of textures. Given that the Orpheus myth illustrates the power of music to influence the passions and to suspend even the laws of nature, it is particularly fitting that the story of the singer with his lyre was the master-myth presiding over the simultaneous births of opera and of early modern music in general.

[36] Vincezo Galilei, *Discorso intorno all'uso dell'enharmonio* (*I-Fn* Galileiani 3 [1588–91]), fol. 17^{v}: "il Musico, con la diversità degl'intervalli et particolarmente de consonanti comunica al'intelletto tutte le passione dell'animo; et vie più informati con i mezzi debiti dall'oratione."

Select Bibliography

Sources

AARON, Pietro. *Thoscanello in musica*. Venice, 1523.

——. *Trattato della natura et cognitione di tutti gli tuoni di canto figurato*. Venice, 1525.

ARTUSI, Giovanni Maria. *L'Artusi, overo Delle imperfettioni della moderna musica*. Venice, 1600.

——. *Seconda parte dell'Artusi overo Delle imperfettioni della moderna musica*. Venice, 1603.

ARTUSI, Giovanni Maria. *Discorso secondo musicale di Antonio Braccino da Todi per la Dichiaratione della lettera posta ne' Scherzi musicali del Sig. Claudio Monteverde*. Venice, 1608.

BANCHIERI, Adriano. *L'organo suonarino*. Venice, 1605.

BARDI, Giovanni de'. *Discorso mandato a Caccini sopra la musica antica e 'l cantar bene*. MS, *I-Rvat* Barberinianus latinus 3990 [*c*.1578]. Ed. and trans. in Claude Palisca, *The Florentine Camerata: Documentary Studies and Translations*. New Haven, 1989.

BENEDETTI, Giovanni Battista. *Diversarum speculationum mathematicarum et physicorum liber*. Turin, 1585.

BERMUDO, Juan. *Declaración de instrumentos musicales*. Osuna, 1555.

BURMEISTER, Joachim. *Musica poetica*. Rostock, 1606.

CASTIGLIONE, Baldassare. *Il libro del cortegiano*. Venice, 1528.

CERONE, Pietro. *El melopeo y maestro*. Naples, 1613.

DANCKERTS, Ghiselin. *Trattato sopra una differentia musicale*. MS, *I-Rv* R 56 [3 drafts, *c*.1551–60].

DESCARTES, René. *Les Passions de l'âme*. Amsterdam and Paris, 1649.

DRESSLER, Gallus. *Praecepta musicae poeticae*. MS, *D-Bs* Mus. ms. autogr. theor. Dressler, Gallus [*olim* Theor. 4° 84], 1563–64. Ed. Olivier Tachier and Simonne Chevalier, Épitome musicale. Paris and Tours, 2001.

FINCK, Hermann. *Practica musica*. Wittenberg, 1556.

FOGLIANO, Lodovico. *Musica theorica*. Venice, 1529.

GAFFURIO, Franchino. *De harmonia musicorum instrumentorum opus*. Venice, 1518.

GALILEI, Vincenzo. *Dialogo della musica antica, et della moderna*. Florence, 1581.

——. *Trattato dell'arte del contrapunto*. MS, *I-Fn* Galileiani 1, [1588–91]. Ed. in Frieder Rempp, *Die Kontrapunkttraktate Vincenzo Galileis*, 7–76. Cologne, 1980.

——. *Discorso intorno all'uso dell'enharmonio et di chi fusse autore del cromatico*. MS, *I-Fn* Galileiani 3, [1588–91]. Ed. in Frieder Rempp, *Die Kontrapunkttraktate Vincenzo Galileis*, 163–80. Cologne, 1980.

GLAREAN, Heinrich. *Δωδεκάχορδον* [*Dodecachordon*]. Basel, 1547.

HARNISCH, Otto Siegfried. *Artis musicae delineatio*. Frankfurt, 1608.

KEPLER, Johannes. *Harmonices mundi libri v*. Linz, 1619.

LANFRANCO, Giovanni Maria. *Scintille di musica*. Brescia, 1533.

LIPPIUS, Johannes. *Disputatio musica tertia*. Wittenberg, 1610.

——. *Synopsis musicae novae*. Strasburg, 1612.

LISTENIUS, Nicolaus. *Musica*. Wittenberg, 1537.

MATTHESON, Johann. *Der vollkommene Capellmeister*. Hamburg, 1739.

MEI, Girolamo. *De modis musicis antiquorum*. MS, *I-Rvat* Vat. lat. 5323, 1567–73. Ed. Eisuke Tsugami. Tokyo, 1991.

MERSENNE, Marin. *Harmonie universelle*. Paris, 1636–37.
MONTEVERDI, Claudio. Letter introducing *Il quinto libro de madrigali a cinque voci*. Venice, 1605.
MONTEVERDI, Giulio Cesare. "Dichiaratione della lettera stampata nel Quinto libro de suoi madrigali." In Claudio Monteverdi, *Scherzi musicali a tre voci*. Venice, 1607.
NUCIUS, Johannes. *Musices practicae, sive De compositione cantus praeceptiones absolutissimae*. Neisse, 1613.
PONTIO, Pietro. *Ragionamento di musica*. Parma, 1588.
PRAETORIUS, Michael. *Syntagma musicum*. 2nd edn. Wolfenbüttel, 1615–19.
RAMEAU, Jean Philippe. *Traité de l'harmonie*. Paris, 1722.
ROUSSEAU, Jean-Jacques. *Essai sur l'origine des langues, où il est parlé de la mélodie et de l'imitation musicale*. MS, *CH-N* 7835 [*c*.1754–61]. Ed. Charles Porset. Bordeaux, 1968.
SADOLETO, Jacopo. *De liberis recte instituendis*. Venice, 1533.
SALINAS, Francisco de. *De musica libri septem*. Salamanca, 1577.
SCACCHI, Marco. *Cribrum musicum ad triticum Syferticum, seu Examinatio succinta psalmorum*. Venice, 1643.
——. *Breve discorso sopra la musica moderna*. Warsaw, 1649.
SPATARO, Giovanni. *Errori di Franchino Gafurio da Lodi*. Bologna, 1521.
TIGRINI, Orazio. *Il compendio della musica*. Venice, 1588.
TINCTORIS, Johannes. *Liber de arte contrapuncti*. MS, 1477. Ed. Albert Seay in *Johannes Tinctoris: Opera theoretica*, MSD 22, II. American Institute of Musicology, 1975–78.
VANNEUS, Stephanus. *Recanetum de musica aurea*. Rome, 1533.
VIADANA, Lodovico. *Cento concerti ecclesiastici*, Op. 12. Venice, 1602.
VICENTINO, Nicola. *L'antica musica ridotta alla moderna prattica*. Rome, 1555.
ZACCONI, Lodovico. *Prattica di musica*. Venice, 1592.
ZARLINO, Gioseffo. *Le istitutioni harmoniche*. Venice, 1558.

Literature

BERGER, Karol. *Theories of Chromatic and Enharmonic Music in Late 16th-Century Italy*. Studies in Musicology. 10. Ann Arbor, MI, 1980.
BLACKBURN, Bonnie J., Lowinsky, Edward E., and Miller, Clement A. (eds.). *A Correspondence of Renaissance Musicians*. Oxford, 1991.
CARTER, Tim. "Artusi, Monteverdi, and the Poetics of Modern Music." In Norma K. Baker and Barbara R. Hanning (eds.), *Musical Humanism and Its Legacy: Essays in Honor of Claude V. Palisca*, 171–94. Stuyvesant, NY, 1992.
CROCKER, Richard. "Discant, Counterpoint, and Harmony." *Journal of the American Musicological Society*, 15 (1962), 1–21.
DAHLHAUS, Carl. *Untersuchungen über die Entstehung der harmonischen Tonalität*. Kassel, 1968.
——. "Seconda pratica und musikalische Figurenlehre." In Ludwig Finscher (ed.), *Claudio Monteverdi: Festschrift Reinhold Hammerstein*, 141–50. Laaber, 1986.
HAAR, James. "*Musica mundana*: Variations on a Pythagorean Theme." PhD diss., Harvard University, 1960.
——. "The Frontispiece of Gafori's *Practica musicae* (1496)." *Renaissance Quarterly*, 27 (1974), 7–22.
HERMELINK, Siegfried. *Dispositiones Modorum: Die Tonarten in der Musik Palestrinas und seiner Zeitgenossen*. Tutzing, 1960.

HOLLANDER, John. *The Untuning of the Sky: Ideas of Music in English Poetry, 1500–1700*. Princeton, 1961.

KOYRÉ, Alexandre. *From the Closed World to the Infinite Universe*. Baltimore, 1957.

LESTER, Joel. "Root-Position and Inverted Triads in Theory around 1600." *Journal of the American Musicological Society*, 27 (1974), 110–19.

——. "Major–Minor Concepts and Modal Theory in Germany: 1592–1680." *Journal of the American Musicological Society*, 30 (1977), 208–53.

——. *Between Modes and Keys: German Theory 1592–1802*. Styuvesant, NY, 1989.

MEIER, Bernhard. *Die Tonarten der klassischen Vokalpolyphonie: Nach den Quellen dargestellt*. Utrecht, 1974.

——. *Alte Tonarten dargestellt an der Instrumentalmusik des 16. und 17. Jahrhunderts*. Kassel, 1992.

PALISCA, Claude V. *Humanism in Italian Renaissance Musical Thought*. New Haven, 1985.

——. *The Florentine Camerata: Documentary Studies and Translations*. New Haven, 1989.

——. *Studies in the History of Italian Music and Music Theory*. Oxford, 1994.

——, (ed.). *Girolamo Mei: Letters on Ancient and Modern Music to Vincenzo Galilei and Giovanni Bardi*. MSD 3. American Institute of Musicology, 1960.

PIRROTTA, Nino. *Music and Culture in Italy from the Middle Ages to the Baroque*. Cambridge, MA, 1984.

POWERS, Harold S. "Tonal Types and Modal Categories in Renaissance Polyphony." *Journal of the American Musicological Society*, 34 (1981), 428–70.

——. "Is Mode Real? Pietro Aron, the Octenary System, and Polyphony." *Basler Jahrbuch für historische Musikpraxis*, 16 (1992), 9–52.

REMPP, Frieder. *Die Kontrapunkttraktate Vincenzo Galileis*. Cologne, 1980.

SPITZER, Leo. *Classical and Christian Ideas of World Harmony: Prolegomena to an Interpretation of the Word "Stimmung."* Baltimore, 1963.

STRUNK, Oliver. *Source Readings in Music History*. New York, 1950. Rev. edn ed. Leo Treitler. New York, 1998.

TOMLINSON, Gary. *Music in Renaissance Magic: Toward a Historiography of Others*. Chicago, 1993.

VICKERS, Brian. "Figures of Rhetoric/Figures of Music?" *Rhetorica* 2 (1984), 1–44.

WALKER, D. P. *Spiritual and Demonic Magic from Ficino to Campanella*. London, 1958.

——. *Studies in Musical Science in the Late Renaissance*. Ed. Penelope M. Gouk. London, 1978.

WILSON, Blake. "*Ut Oratoria Musica* in the Writings of Renaissance Music Theorists." In Thomas J. Mathiesen and Benito V. Rivera (eds.), *Festa Musicologica: Essays in Honor of George J. Buelow*, 341–68. Stuyvesant, NY, 1995.

17

GERMANY AND CENTRAL EUROPE, *i*: 1520–1600

Peter Bergquist

1520–1560

GERMAN polyphony in the decades before 1520 was dependent on styles and devices from the Dufay–Binchois, Busnois–Ockeghem, and Josquin generations. Its national identity was expressed most notably in the instrumentalists who had been prized throughout Europe during the fifteenth century[1] and in the polyphonic lied, especially those by Paulus Hofhaimer, Heinrich Finck, and Henricus Isaac. The presence of the eminent Netherlander Isaac in this list is symptomatic of strong external influences on German music that continued into the seventeenth century. The tension between distinctive native elements and the eager absorption of external features remained typical of German music well past 1600. Key social and political events that shaped the development of German music between 1520 and 1560 were the Lutheran Reformation, the death of Maximilian I in 1519, and the subsequent dissolution of the Imperial Chapel in 1521. Monophonic songs continued to be written in sixteenth-century Germany, notably the *Meistersang*, but these repertories had little influence on polyphonic music and remained isolated.

The polyphonic lied

The earliest polyphonic lieder, mostly for three or occasionally two voices, are transmitted in the Lochamer, Schedelsche, and Glogauer Liederbücher (*c.*1452–60, 1460s, and *c.*1480 respectively). In them the leading melody, often pre-existing, is in the tenor voice, which however can be the highest of the three. Textures varied among simple note-against-note settings and duets for discant and tenor with a filling contratenor. The latter procedure resembles the contemporary chanson, which exerted an influence on the lied, but a native influence is also apparent in

[1] On these musicians, see Keith Polk, *German Instrumental Music of the Late Middle Ages: Players, Patrons and Performance Practice* (Cambridge, 1992).

the textures that appear to be derived from the improvisatory practice of German instrumentalists, notably the chains of parallel tenths moving against the tenor's cantus firmus. Early in the sixteenth century the published lied collections of Erhard Oeglin (Augsburg, RISM B/1/1 1512^{1}), Peter Schöffer (Mainz, 1513^{2}), and Arnt von Aich (Cologne, 1519^{5}) show a new stage of development in which four-voice texture is the norm, with the tenor melody now regularly in the tenor register as cantus firmus, surrounded by discantus, altus, and bassus, moving in shorter rhythmic values. In these publications usually only the tenor was texted; this may have been the publisher's as much as the composer's choice, but it does reflect the abstractly instrumental character of most of the music. Expression of the text is not a concern.

The cantus-firmus principle remained in force in the *Liederbücher* published in the 1530s and 1540s, which represent the high point of the genre. After a hiatus of fifteen years following Arnt von Aich's publication, a flood of new editions containing some 1,300 compositions appeared in quick succession. The first was Johann Ott's *Hundert und ainundzweintzig newe Lieder* (Nuremberg, 1534^{17}), followed by Christian Egenolff's *Gassenhawerlin* and *Reutterliedlin* (Frankfurt am Main, 1535$^{10\text{-}11}$), the *Fünff und sechzig teütscher Lieder* of Peter Schöffer and Mathias Apiarius (Strasburg, 1536^{8}), the five parts of *Frische teutsche Liedlein* of Georg Forster (Nuremberg, 1539^{27}, 1540^{21}, 1549^{37}, 1556$^{28\text{-}29}$), and another collection of *Hundert und fünfftzehen guter newer Liedlein* by Ott (Nuremberg, 1544^{20}). These collections by and large continue the tradition of the earlier books as seen in the lieder of Hofhaimer, Finck, and Isaac; indeed, these composers are represented in the retrospective portions of the newer books, along with younger men such as Ludwig Senfl (*c.*1486–1542/3), Arnold von Bruck (*c.*1500–1554), Caspar Othmayr (1515–1553), and Sixtus Dietrich (*c.*1493–1548). Of these the most significant was Senfl, a few of whose lieder had already appeared in the Oeglin and Schöffer collections. His works formed the backbone of both Ott collections, and he was well represented in the others as well.

Senfl's 260-odd lieder sum up the possibilities of the genre as it had developed up to that time. The poems range from courtly love songs to devotional or moralizing texts to popular, even ribald, doggerel. The cantus firmus appears most often in the tenor, occasionally in canon with one other voice but very frequently in imitation that involves all the other voices. In extreme cases this texture resembles that of the contemporary motet (Example 17.1). Homorhythmic texture governs some lieder, with the cantus firmus either in the tenor or the discant (Example 17.2). Senfl a few times throughout his career set multiple cantus firmi as a quodlibet, most notably in some six-voiced lieder .

Senfl, Othmayr, and their contemporaries brought the polyphonic cantus-firmus lied to a stylistic high point that was also a dead end. It could not develop further along the lines it had followed for over a century, and only through abandoning its distinctly German traits was it able to thrive as a secular genre past the end of the century. The sacred lied, however, gained new life and vigor in the Lutheran church, and in this friendly environment it retained its national character while also becoming the foundation for a rich new repertory of vocal and instrumental music.

Ex. 17.1 Ludwig Senfl, *Es wollt' ein Maidlein Wasser hol'n*, mm. 1–9
Senfl, *Sämtliche Werke*, IV, ed. A. Geering and W. Altwegg (Wolfenbüttel and Zurich, 1962), 66

Music of the Reformation

From its beginnings, the Lutheran Reformation prized music as an integral part of worship and home life. Martin Luther himself on many occasions expressed the highest esteem for music, as in his preface to Georg Rhau's *Symphoniae iucundae* (Wittenberg, 1538[8]):

> next to the word of God, music deserves the highest praise. She is a mistress and governess of those human emotions—to pass over the animals—which as masters govern men or more often overwhelm them. . . . Thus it was not

Ex, 17.2 Ludwig Senfl, *Leut' seltsam sind*, mm. 1–10
Senfl, *Sämtliche Werke*, IV: 63

> without reason that the fathers and prophets wanted nothing else to be associated as closely with the Word of God as music. Therefore, we have so many hymns and Psalms where message and music join to move the listener's soul, while in other living beings and [sounding] bodies music remains a language without words.[2]

The most distinctive Lutheran music was of course the chorale, and the Reformer himself contributed significantly to the new repertory, both as poet and composer.

[2] Martin Luther, "Preface to Georg Rhau's *Symphoniae iucundae*," in *Luther's Works*, LIII: *Liturgy and Hymns*, ed. Ulrich S. Leupold (Philadelphia, 1965), 323.

The most recent edition of Luther's hymns includes 60 melodies that appeared in his lifetime in association with his 37 chorale texts; nine other melodies or formulas were associated with liturgical texts, that is, German equivalents of portions of the Latin Mass or Office.[3] Of the chorale melodies, 14 are now ascribed with fair certainty to Luther himself, as many as 13 others were arranged by Luther from earlier sources, and ten were traditional melodies that remained unchanged when the new poems were adapted to them. Eight of the melodies for liturgical texts were also composed by Luther. Most of the remaining melodies were composed or arranged by Johann Walter.

The new hymns easily took root in the fertile soil that had been prepared by a strong tradition of vernacular hymns that had developed in German lands since the ninth century. Many of these hymns were translations of Latin hymns, antiphons, and sequences, while others were non-liturgical poems, either translated or originally written in German. Luther and his followers adapted many of these German texts for the sake of familiarity and continuity, adjusting their content to the changed belief. He additionally translated some Latin poems anew. Not many sixteenth-century chorale texts were completely new.

Many of Luther's hymn melodies were also adaptations from earlier sources, though seldom simple contrafacta. His skill in this enterprise and his sensitivity to the stress and meaning of the texts can be seen in the three different chorales he based on the Latin hymn *Veni Redemptor gentium* (Example 17.3).[4] Even when a chorale melody was apparently freely composed, it was typically based on a stock of standard melodic formulas and types common to much music of the time. For instance, the major mode and octave descent of *Ein feste Burg* can also be seen in Hans Sachs's "Silber Weiß," composed in 1513.

The first years of the Lutheran church, from 1517 to 1523, have been called the "songless period," before the development of a distinct liturgy and music. This development was fostered on the one hand by the composition and spread of the new chorale repertory. The chorales circulated rapidly in print, in the earliest years as broadsheets, then in small books, and eventually in more comprehensive collections that by the end of Luther's life had established a central repertory of some eighty poems and melodies. The other part of the development was the construction of new liturgical forms. In 1523 Luther published a reformed Latin Mass and in 1526 a German Mass, the latter in response to the more radical preachers among his followers; his own preference remained for Latin, and both languages were freely used in the sixteenth century, with Latin falling only gradually out of use. Luther did not change the structure of the Latin Mass but adjusted it to the new beliefs, with some of the Propers, notably the gradual, Alleluia, and communion, omitted or replaced by chorales. The German Mass required more extensive revision, in part because the Latin melodies were not always suitable for the vernacular. The

[3] Martin Luther, *Geistliche Lieder und Kirchengesänge*, ed. Markus Jenny, Archiv zur Weimarer Ausgabe der Werke Martin Luthers, 4 (Cologne and Vienna, 1985), 5.

[4] The example is suggested in Robert Marshall/Robin Leaver, "Chorale," 5: "Luther's melodies," *New Grove Dictionary of Music and Musicians*, 2d edn, ed. Stanley Sadie and John Tyrrell (London, 2001), IV: 315.

Ex. 17.3 (*a*) *Veni redemptor gentium*
Monumenta Monodica Medii Aevi: Hymnen I, ed. B. Stäblein (Kassel, 1956), 217

(*b*) Martin Luther, *Nun komm der Heiden Heiland*
Luthers Geistliche Lieder, ed. M. Jenny (Cologne and Vienna, 1985), 202

(*c*) Luther, *Verleih uns Frieden gnädiglich*
Luthers Geistliche Lieder, 274

(*d*) Luther, *Erhalt uns Herr bei deinem Wort*
Luthers Geistliche Lieder, 304

Propers were much less emphasized, and portions of the Ordinary were replaced by German texts, such as the Credo by "Wir glauben all an einen Gott" and the Sanctus by "Jesaja, dem Propheten, das geschah."

Luther put both of his Masses forward as guides, not prescriptions. Local use and preference could vary greatly, with languages freely mixed within a given service. The chorales early on found their place in the service as substitutes for or additions to the basic elements of the service. They served widely as substitutes for Propers, with care taken that the texts were appropriate to the particular feast; and, as noted, some chorales could replace items of the Ordinary. The congregation could increase its participation in the service through singing chorales, though choirs when present tended to take them over, to the consternation of some of the reformers. The congregations in fact were not used to singing in church, so opposition had to be overcome in order to develop that custom. They did not sing from the songbooks; these were used by cantors and pastors, and Luther in fact forbade the congregations to use them. The books found fundamental employment in the schools, with the result that the children learned the chorales and led the singing. It was the new generation in which congregational singing became the norm.

The congregations when they participated sang in unison. Several important collections of polyphonic settings of chorales and Latin hymns were published in the early decades of the Reformation, but these were addressed in the first place to schools and also to choirs for *alternatim* use in services. The earliest and probably most important such collection was Johann Walter's *Geystliche gesangk Buchleyn* (RISM B/VIII 1524[18]), the popularity of which is attested by the series of expanded and revised editions that continued to 1551. The style of Walter's and other polyphonic settings was based on the polyphonic lied tradition. Walter's earlier settings tend towards a texture in which the tenor melody was clearly distinguished from the other voices; he later moved towards a style based on Isaac, Stoltzer, and their contemporaries, with similar rhythm in all voices, clear phrase endings, and few melismas. The 1551 edition saw an increasing tendency to place the chorale melody in the discant, the pattern that became the norm in the *Cantional* style of the later sixteenth century.

The most important collection of polyphonic chorales after Walter was the *Newe deudsche geistliche Gesenge . . . für die gemeinen Schulen* (RISM B/I/1 1544[21]) of Georg Rhau. The 123 pieces from both older composers and contemporaries, Protestants and Catholics, show no appreciable stylistic advance over Walter's earliest publications. Balthasar Resinarius (Hartzer; *c.*1485–1544) is most generously represented with 30 pieces, all quite conservative in style, even including some pieces in three voices and several with the under-third cadence typical of fifteenth-century lieder. Most of the collection is more up to date, with numerous examples of cantus firmi in the tenor, just as in secular lieder. Only a few have the cantus firmus in the discant .

Almost fifty pieces were by Catholic composers, including Bruck, Senfl, Stephan Mahu, Thomas Stoltzer, and Lupus Hellinck. The few settings of Latin texts even include a *Pater noster – Ave Maria* motet by Bruck (no. 45), which hardly conforms to Lutheran preferences, though its cantus-firmus technique mirrors that of the Lutheran pieces. Stoltzer's settings date from before the beginning of the Reformation and are best seen as reflecting the older tradition of vernacular hymns. Settings by the younger Catholics may have reflected a degree of sympathy with Reformation ideals, but their employment at Catholic courts precluded overt expressions. It is probable that Rhau solicited settings from these composers simply to broaden his collection, since music remained largely interconfessional through this period, standing apart from the strife between Catholics and Reformers.

This is shown even more clearly by the other items in Rhau's series of publications between 1538 and 1545, which provided music for the Lutheran Mass and Office as well as other liturgical and non-liturgical music, mostly with Latin texts. The music was often adjusted to Lutheran usage, but much of it could equally well have been used in Catholic services, as it included settings of Ordinaries and Propers by contemporary composers such as Senfl and also earlier figures like Stoltzer. The numerous anthologies of Latin motets issued in Nuremberg and Augsburg up to 1560 were similarly not in a specifically Lutheran style but collected the best music from all sources. In Germany throughout the sixteenth century, settings of Latin sacred texts were published in much larger quantities than settings of German ones; the resultant increasing use of Latin in Lutheran services was eventually addressed in new reforms undertaken late in the century.

Music in Catholic areas

The Reformation at first threatened to overwhelm the German portions of the Empire, and only the organization of determined resistance by the Emperor Charles v prevented that outcome. The tensions engendered by Luther and his followers found full resolution only in the Thirty Years' War a century later. The courts that remained Catholic in the 1500s of course continued their musical establishments, though their relative importance shifted from one center to another.

The death of Maximilian I in 1519 initiated one of the most important of these shifts, since it resulted in the dissolution of the Imperial Chapel at Vienna in 1520, by order of Charles v. A number of excellent musicians were thereby set adrift, among whom one of the most notable was Ludwig Senfl. Senfl first traveled to Augsburg, where in *Liber selectarum cantionum* (1520^4) he published a collection of motets from the repertory of the Imperial Chapel, including works by Isaac, Josquin, and himself. The main purpose of his visit to Augsburg, however, was to gain the ear of Charles v and obtain a renewed appointment to the Imperial Chapel, but this enterprise was unsuccessful. After a few more years of traveling that are not well documented, in 1523 he obtained appointment to the Bavarian court chapel as "composer," not music director as sometimes stated. There he remained until his death, which occurred between 2 December 1542 and 10 August 1543.

Senfl was already an established composer when he settled in Munich. He had been the student, copyist, and collaborator of Henricus Isaac from 1509, and his own music had been published as early as 1512. He brought with him to Munich some of the music he had worked on with Isaac, notably the cycle of Mass Propers later published as the *Choralis Constantinus* (Nuremberg, 1555, 1560; RISM A/I

189, 190). Senfl expanded this collection into a new cycle for the Munich Hofkapelle, contained primarily in four court manuscripts (*D-Mbs* Mus. ms. 35–38), which Senfl titled *En opus musicum festorum dierum*. His intention probably was to publish this collection, though he eventually decided instead to combine both Isaac's and his own settings in a single publication, a plan realized only incompletely after his death. Other Propers by Senfl are contained in another Hofkapelle manuscript (*Mbs* Mus. ms. 52),[5] and after Senfl's death the cycle was expanded further by his successors, Matthaeus Le Maistre and Ludwig Daser.

Other Munich manuscripts contain masses and motets composed there by Senfl. Of the six surviving masses, five use a somewhat old-fashioned technique with Ordinary chants as cantus firmi in long notes, while one is in imitation of his own motet *Nisi Dominus*.[6] The *Missa dominicalis super "L'homme armé"* is notable for combining the secular cantus firmus in the tenor with lightly paraphrased chants in the discant. Some of Senfl's motets were printed in anthologies from 1520 and later, while others are transmitted only in manuscripts. They range in style from cantus-firmus pieces through cantus-firmus paraphrases to works in which the complete range of textures found in Josquin's generation is employed: full-fledged points of imitation, voice pairs, and note-against-note setting. Some of these motets rank among the finest of their period from any part of Europe.

Ferdinand I, the younger brother of Charles V, was given the German realms by Charles upon the death of Maximilian I, and in 1527 he was able to re-establish an Imperial Chapel in Vienna. His first *Kapellmeister* was the aging Heinrich Finck, who after six months was succeeded by Arnold von Bruck. Bruck's assistants were Stephan Mahu (1480/90–*c.*1541) and Pieter Maessens (*c.*1505–1563); the latter became *Kapellmeister* on Bruck's retirement in 1545. The repertory of Ferdinand's chapel and that of St Stephen's in Vienna from this period have not survived, but other music of these composers show them to be highly competent followers of Josquin.

Other Habsburg courts at Graz, Innsbruck, and Prague also had large musical establishments. Archduke Maximilian, the son of Ferdinand I and his successor in 1564 as Maximilian II, brought another Netherlander, Jacobus Vaet (*c.*1529–1567) to be his *Kapellmeister* in Prague. Vaet in his short lifetime produced a significant amount of music, of which some 76 motets, nine Masses, a cycle of eight Magnificat settings, and three chansons survive. His music moves away from the pervading imitation of Gombert to the variety of texture favored by his own generation. Vaet was especially interested in parody or imitation techniques, which are found frequently in his motets as well as his masses.

The names of the composers just mentioned show clearly how the Catholic courts sought out Netherlandish musicians to build the quality of their chapels and

[5] David Crook, *Orlando di Lasso's Imitation Magnificats for Counter-Reformation Munich* (Princeton, 1994), 41–47, argues convincingly on liturgical grounds that *D-Mbs* Mus. ms. 52 was copied and composed in Munich, not in Vienna as previously believed.

[6] The *Missa per signum crucis* published in Ludwig Senfl, *Sämtliche Werke*, I: *Sieben Messen zu vier bis sech Stimmen*, ed. Edwin Lohner and Otto Ursprung, EDM 5 (Leipzig, 1937), 92, is more reliably ascribed to Ludwig Daser in *D-Mbs* Mus. ms. 18.

bring them up to date stylistically. The most striking success among these acquisitions was the arrival of Orlando di Lasso (1530/2–1594) at the court of Albrecht V in Munich in 1556 as tenor and composer.[7] Lasso was born in Mons, Hainault, now in Belgium, and received his early training there. He was said to have been kidnapped three times as a boy on account of his beautiful voice, and the third time his parents agreed to let him join the chapel of Ferrante Gonzaga, Viceroy of Sicily. Between 1544 and 1554 he resided in Milan, Naples, and finally in Rome, where in 1552 or 1553 he became choirmaster at St John Lateran. Called home by the illness of his parents in 1554, he arrived only after they had already died. He is said to have made a short visit to England, after which he settled in Antwerp for two years until the call came from Munich. During the Antwerp years, his music began to appear in print, and his reputation quickly became established throughout Europe.

Much remains to be clarified about Lasso's early years. It has recently been suggested that he served as a low-level informer for Imperial factions in Italy,[8] which could have some bearing on his failure to return to Rome and his acceptance of a position at what was after all a rather provincial court in Munich compared to the circles in which he had previously moved. Recently discovered letters to and from Lasso establish that he was by no means content in Munich at first,[9] but he stayed there the rest of his life despite several offers from other courts. In his first years there he composed some music for the exclusive use of Albrecht's court, notably the *Penitential Psalms*, the strikingly but atypically chromatic *Prophetiae Sibyllarum*, and the first setting of *Lectiones ex propheta Iob*, all of which were withheld from publication for some years. His international fame grew with publications in France, Italy, and the Netherlands; by 1560 he had composed a significant quantity of chansons and madrigals and quite possibly a number of the motets that first appeared in print between 1562 and 1566. Only in 1562 was he named *Kapellmeister*, succeeding Daser, and thereafter his output of liturgical music increased substantially.

[7] Lasso was probably named Orlande or Roland de Lassus originally, but no documentary evidence establishes his birth date or name. By the time he reached Munich he had Italianized his name, and thereafter he used that form most often, though by no means consistently. His descendants were known under the family name "di Lasso." American and German writers now prefer to use the name he adopted for himself, while the English and French prefer the hypothetical French version. This and other aspects of Lasso's life are discussed most authoritatively in Horst Leuchtmann, *Orlando di Lasso: Sein Leben* (Wiesbaden, 1977).

[8] Donna Cardamone Jackson, "Orlando di Lasso and Pro-French Factions in Rome," in *Orlandus Lassus and His Time: Colloquium Proceedings, Antwerpen 24–26.08.1994*, ed. Ignace Bossuyt et al. (Peer, 1995), 23–47.

[9] Ignace Bossuyt, "Lassos erste Jahre in München (1556–1559): Eine 'Cosa non reuscita?'" in *Festschrift für Horst Leuchtmann zum 65. Geburtstag*, ed. Stephan Hörner and Bernhold Schmid (Tutzing, 1993), 55–67.

Instrumental music

As mentioned above, German instrumentalists were pre-eminent throughout Europe in the fifteenth century and into the sixteenth. Though musicians of other nationalities increasingly challenged this dominance after 1500, the vigorous roots of instrumental music in German soil continued to produce new fruit, even if it was increasingly crossbred with imported products. German instrumental music from 1520 to 1560 is documented primarily in keyboard and lute tablatures. The music of instrumental ensembles had been predominantly improvised; written ensemble music is thus preserved only sporadically, in sources that contain mostly vocal or keyboard music.

The most substantial German sources of keyboard music before mid-century were compiled by students and followers of Paul Hofhaimer (1459–1537), the organist to Maximilian I. These collections include the manuscripts of Hans Kotter (*CH-Bu* F.IX 22, 1513–32), Leonhard Kleber (*D-Mbs* Mus. ms. 40026, 1520–24), Fridolin Sicher (*CH-SGs* 530, 1525), and the *Fundamentum* of Hans Buchner (*CH-Zz* 284b, *c.*1530).[10] A slightly later Central-European source in the same tradition is the tablature of Jan z Lublina (Johannes of Lublin; *PL-Kp* 1716, 1537–48).[11] The repertory of all these sources is in part retrospective, reaching back in some cases well before the turn of the century. In addition to the treatises in the Buchner and Lublin manuscripts, the contents include ornamented intabulations of sacred and secular vocal works, settings of liturgical chants, freely invented polyphonic pieces, *praeambula*, and dances. Buchner's *Fundamentum* includes a systematic discussion of imitation, and his tablature, like most of the others, employs this technique extensively, in intabulations as well as in the original compositions. The *praeambula* follow fifteenth-century examples such as those of the Buxheim Organ Book in principle, but are more carefully constructed, frequently alternating passages in block chords with rapid scales. As Gustave Reese remarked, "Here, in embryo, is the toccata."[12] Kotter's tablature contains the earliest example of a *fantasia* for keyboard, in which imitative and prelude styles are combined. The dances in Kotter and Kleber are the earliest known for keyboard, most probably intended for a stringed instrument rather than the organ. Six of their nine dances are built on the *La Spagna* tenor (placed in the bass), and the styles range from written-out improvisations *supra librum* to elaborately ornamented polyphony. The Lublin tablature includes 36 dances from various national sources, many of which are paired as *Tanz* and *Nachtanz*, in the equivalents of $\frac{4}{4}$ and $\frac{3}{4}$ meter respectively.

Since the lute was the most popular instrument for house music in Germany as

[10] Editions: Kotter, in *Die Tabulaturen aus dem Besitz des Basler Humanisten Bonifacius Amerbach*, ed. Hans Joachim Marx, Schweizerische Musikdenkmäler, 6 (Basel, 1967); Kleber, *Die orgeltabulatur des Leonhard Kleber*, ed. Karin Berg-Kotterba, EDM 91–92 (Frankfurt, 1987); Hans Buchner, *Sämtliche Orgelwerke*, ed. Jost Harro Schmidt, EDM 54–55 (Frankfurt, 1974).

[11] Johannes of Lublin, *Tablature of Keyboard Music*, ed. John Reeves White, 6 vols., CEKM 6 (American Institute of Musicology, 1964–67).

[12] Gustave Reese, *Music in the Renaissance*, rev. edn (New York, 1959), 664.

elsewhere during the sixteenth century, manuals and collections of music could be printed with commercial success, so that fewer of the main sources of lute music are manuscripts. Among the most significant lute sources before 1560 are the collections by Hans Judenkünig, *Ain schone kunstliche Underweisung* (Vienna, Brown 1523_2); Hans Gerle, *Musica teusch* (Nuremberg, 1532_2), *Tabulatur auff die Laudten* (Nuremberg, 1533_1), and *Eyn newes sehr künstlich Lautenbuch* (Nuremberg, 1552_1); and Hans Newsidler, *Ein newgeordent künstlich Lautenbuch* (Nuremberg, 1536_6). Most of these books include instructional material, and the music itself is often printed in ascending order of difficulty. The contents include intabulations of sacred and secular vocal music, preludes, and dances. Since the books were largely directed towards amateur players, the intabulations were only moderately embellished, and imitation was usually confined to the initial presentation of a motif. Most of the music was arranged rather than newly composed, and indeed Gerle's *Newes sehr künstlich Lautenbuch* is almost entirely reprinted from Italian lute books originally published by Scotto and Gardane, transcribed from Italian into German lute tablature.

1560–1600

By 1560 the Empire had become nearly nine-tenths Protestant. However, Counter-Reformation activities thereafter regained much territory, led even more by the Jesuits than by political leaders. A process of education and religious renewal, together with political and military efforts, saved Austria and portions of Germany for the Roman Church, establishing the confessional boundaries that have continued with little change to the present day. The shift of momentum from Lutherans to Catholics was mirrored in music as well, a process in which the achievements of composers in Catholic courts were the most notable of the late sixteenth century. The musical aims of Lutherans and Catholics still coincided strongly in areas such as the desire for intelligibility of the text, and their repertories continued to overlap, though the Lutherans, under increasing pressure from the Counter-Reformation, moved more and more by the end of the century to German rather than Latin in their services.

Music in Catholic areas: Lasso and Monte

Around mid-century the German Catholic courts increasingly sought out Netherlanders to staff their chapels. Among them were the succession of *maestri di cappella* at the Imperial court in Vienna: Petrus Maessens from 1546 to 1560, Jacobus Vaet from 1564 to 1567, and Filippo di Monte from 1568 to 1603. Orlando di Lasso at the Bavarian court in Munich was the most outstanding and influential of all. Lasso and Monte both spent their formative years in Italy and adopted Italianized forms of their names, reflecting the other major movement of foreign musicians into German courts, the influx from Italy. By the end of the century, the preference of the courts had shifted decisively in that direction, and native German musicians had begun the pattern of study visits to Italy that continued with Schütz, Handel, Mozart, and Mendelssohn.

The Bavarian court was a major center of the Catholic Counter-Reformation, in some ways even more than the Imperial court, which was constrained by financial pressures of defense against the Turks in the east. The Bavarian dukes Albrecht V (r. 1550–79) and Wilhelm V (1579–97) were able to patronize the arts lavishly, though they were not without their own financial problems. Lasso was a principal object of this patronage, and despite whatever difficulty he had adjusting to Munich, he served those dukes faithfully for almost forty years, producing a body of music that in its era is second to none in quality, as well as impressive in its quantity. This estimate was emphatically shared by Lasso's contemporaries, who made Lasso by far the most popular composer of his time. His music was published frequently throughout Europe, in quantities far larger than that of any other composer. It has been estimated that during the 40 years during which he issued his own works for publication, 1555–95, on average one publication including Lasso's music appeared every month somewhere in Europe.[13] His chansons and lieder were assembled in collected editions during his lifetime, and soon after his death his sons brought out similar editions of his motets and Magnificat settings.

Lasso's motets, which number 525 or more, are the most representative and substantial part of his output. They stand in his production somewhat as the symphonies do for Joseph Haydn, as a genre in which he produced regularly throughout his career, even while his attention may have been focused elsewhere for a time. In them his imagination, expressive power, and technical prowess may be seen at their peak. The majority of the motets have religious texts, over a third of them from Psalm verses or complete Psalms. There are quite a few Gospel and epistle texts, an Offertory cycle, a number of Marian antiphons and other liturgical texts, and various biblical and other texts with no specific liturgical source. How or indeed whether this music might have been used in services at the court or elsewhere remains to be established. The motets with secular texts are variously ceremonial, didactic, hortatory, humorous, or classicistic.

Some other compositions with Latin texts are similar to the motets in style and purpose, including the *Penitential Psalms*, *Prophetiae Sibyllarum*, the *Lectiones* from Job, and the two Lamentation cycles. The latter have a specific liturgical function, and this is true of many other Latin settings, including the more than 50 masses and the over 100 Magnificat settings. The majority of the masses imitate polyphonic models; they range in size from perfunctory *Missae breves* to large-scale ceremonial pieces. No other composer is known to have approached even remotely Lasso's output of Magnificat settings. Almost all are *alternatim*, many using one of the eight Magnificat tones as cantus firmus. Forty imitate polyphonic models, a procedure that Lasso was apparently the first to apply to this genre. Both cantus-firmus and imitation techniques are also employed in Lasso's 13 settings of the *Nunc dimittis*. He composed large quantities of service music in the 1580s and 1590s, apparently to supply settings of the Tridentine texts that were supplanting

[13] Leuchtmann, *Orlando di Lasso*, 44.

the local Freising rite as part of Duke Wilhelm's efforts on behalf of the Counter-Reformation. This music includes the Lamentations, a cycle of *alternatim* hymns for the church year, responsories, litanies, and *falsobordoni*.

Lasso's settings of vernacular texts are less numerous than his Latin settings, but no less important. Four books of madrigals for four and five voices and the villanellas were composed in Italy prior to his move to Munich, while four more books, including his *opus ultimum*, the cycle of spiritual madrigals for seven voices, *Lagrime di San Pietro*, were composed in the north. Though Lasso did not pursue the more radical stylistic trends manifested in madrigals of the 1580s, his own madrigals are nonetheless among the finest of their time in their expressive and technical strength, true descendants of the art of Cipriano de Rore. The earlier works were especially popular, as their numerous contemporary reissues demonstrate.

A majority of the 150-odd chansons were published in 1576 or earlier. The earliest editions appeared in Antwerp or Louvain, but the most important edition is the comprehensive *Mellange d'Orlande de Lassus* published by Le Roy & Ballard in Paris in 1570 and enlarged in 1576. Though the chansons were mostly published in French-speaking territory, they would also have been prized at the Bavarian court, for which many of them were undoubtedly originally composed. Lasso's chansons incorporate both the "Parisian" and contrapuntal styles as well as a madrigal-like seriousness that stems from Rore.

Lasso's first lieder were published in 1567, after he had been in Munich long enough to have absorbed the new language. The Tenorlied tradition of Senfl would still have been alive there, but Lasso's lieder brought it to an end with an infusion of madrigal and chanson styles. Ludwig Finscher evaluates his achievement thus: "Orlando di Lasso's first lieder publication must have served as a signal, entirely like his first chanson print—the astonishing role of this one man in the history of musical genres is still by no means sufficiently appreciated."[14] Finscher goes on to observe that the Munich court provided the sympathetic and fertile environment in which Lasso was able to pursue this renewal.

Any brief description of style in an output as large as Orlando di Lasso's is necessarily limited. His music became more condensed and concise through the years; for instance, the average length of his six-voice motets decreased by one third from the works of the 1560s to his 1594 Graz motet book. He was always concerned with musical embodiment and expression of the text, and the text determined the form of the music, not any abstract musical scheme imposed from without. In effect his music was always through-composed. The melodic motives themselves and their treatment were generated by the text, as Example 17.4 shows. Both the general mood and specific details of the text would be conveyed by music. One of Lasso's most powerful means to accomplish this was rhythm. The speed and character of rhythmic activity can change drastically within a few measures in response to a new idea in the text. Chromatic inflection is another powerful tool in Lasso's kit,

[14] Ludwig Finscher, "Volkssprachige Gattungen und Instrumentalmusik," in *Neues Handbuch der Musikwissenschaft*, ed. Carl Dahlhaus and Hermann Danuser (Laaber, 1990), III/2: 552.

Ex. 17.4 Orlando di Lasso, *Tristis est anima mea*, mm. 35–44
Lasso, *The Complete Motets*, ed. P. Bergquist, IV (Madison, WI, 1996), 91

which he normally used with considerable restraint, although occasional colorful patches are provoked by the text and stand out all the more sharply in the prevailing diatonic context (Example 17.5). These examples are taken from Latin-texted sacred works. The source of much of this technique in secular music, especially

Ex. 17.5 Orlando di Lasso, *Lamentationes Jeremiae Prophetae*: *Lamentatio secunda Tertii diei*, mm. 7–14
Lasso, *Sämtliche Werke*, new ser., XXII, ed. P. Bergquist (Kassel, 1992), 230–31

the madrigal, is obvious, and Lasso simply extended that practice into the realm of church music, with telling effect.

The tonal structure of the music is not easy to define. Lasso nominally adhered to the traditional system of eight modes, and most of his music can be classified as representing one of those modes according to the external markers of clef combination, signature of *mollis* or *durus* species, and final. How the music itself expressed one of these modes needs to be explored further. His bass parts, for instance, frequently move in fourths and fifths, providing harmonic support such as became the norm later in major–minor tonality, and a full explanation of Lasso's tonal structures must encompass this trait.

Next to Lasso the most eminent Netherlander among those who occupied major positions in the north was Filippo de Monte.[15] Like Lasso, he spent many years as a young man in Italy and Italianized his name, which originally was probably something like Philippus van den Berghe. He was born in 1521 in Mechlin (Mecheln, Malines) and in the early 1540s is known to have been in Naples. He alternated between Italy and the north for 25 years, at Cambrai Cathedral in 1547–49, probably in Rome prior to 1554, then in Antwerp in 1554 and 1555, during which years he also spent a short time in the chapel of Philip II in England. From 1556 to 1568 he was mostly in Italy. Documentation is sparse, since he seems to have held no permanent position; he was in Rome in 1558, probably in Naples in 1562, and in Florence in 1566. Finally in 1568 he was appointed Kapellmeister at the imperial court of Maximilian II in Vienna. He held this position until his death in 1603. After Rudolph II became emperor in 1576, the court was increasingly located at Prague, where Rudolph gradually retreated from the world into his Hradčany castle.

Monte published 35 or 36 books of madrigals, the largest known production by a single composer. The earlier books were the most popular, being reprinted several times each. After 1580 the reprints ceased as his popularity waned. Monte throughout his life was slow to adopt the latest styles, and despite the high quality of his later music, the novel tastes passed him by, as they did Lasso also. At the beginning of his career, Monte did not at first absorb the innovations of Rore, and later he only gradually came to terms with the lighter canzonetta styles. He never published canzonettas as such, but his madrigals from the late 1580s on achieve an effective synthesis of that idiom with his own basically serious style. He was one of the great composers of Petrarch settings, which were his major achievement in his first ten years in the Imperial court.

The court appointment dramatically increased Monte's productivity. Prior to 1568 he had published no more than four madrigal books, but from then on they appeared regularly, almost one a year through 1600. Almost no sacred music was published before his arrival in Vienna, after which ten motet books appeared. His numerous masses remained largely in manuscript. They show considerable ingenuity and imagination in their imitation of a wide variety of secular and sacred models. Both the motets and masses favor polyphonic over chordal textures, and their restrained expressivity, while highly effective, seems to fall short of the imaginative heights often reached by Lasso. A thorough evaluation of all of Monte's music awaits completion of the collected edition.

Both Lasso and Monte had distinguished composers as members of their chapels, though no such composer remained in the Bavarian chapel for long. Andrea and Giovanni Gabrieli both served in Munich for periods of five years at most, in the 1560s and 1570s respectively. On the other hand, Carl Luython was organist in the Imperial chapel through all of Monte's tenure, and Jacob Regnart and Jacob de Kerle also had long associations with the chapel. Prominent musicians at other Habsburg courts include Lambert de Sayve, chapel master for Archduke Karl II

[15] This biographical summary is based primarily on Brian Mann, *The Secular Madrigals of Filippo de Monte, 1521–1603* (Ann Arbor, MI, 1983), chap. 1.

at Graz, and Regnart, who held the same position with Archduke Ferdinand II at Innsbruck. Other composers at these courts included Annibale Padovano and Lodovico Zacconi at Graz and Alexander Utendal, Christian Hollander, and Tiburtio Massaino at Innsbruck.

Lutheran music

Music in the Calvinist churches throughout Europe was confined essentially to congregational singing of hymns and psalms; in Germany it was the Lutheran churches that used artistically elaborated music. Lutheran music was nonetheless significantly influenced by the Calvinist Psalters, since these simple, largely note-against-note settings became important models for the later German songbooks. Goudimel's strophic settings published in 1565 were the most significant, especially when they were published in Königsberg in 1572 with Ambrosius Lobwasser's translation of the Geneva Psalter. Many of these homophonic settings placed the melody in the superius, and this disposition was increasingly taken up in German songbooks as well. Sigmund Hemmel's *Der gantze Psalter Davids* (Stuttgart and Tübingen, 1569; RISM A/I H 5020) was one of the first influential publications to spread the new cantional style. His settings still placed the melody in the tenor (which as Blume observed makes no real difference, since only the melody was sung[16]), but Lucas Osiander's *Fünfzig geistliche Lieder und Psalmen mit vier Stimmen* (Nuremberg, 1586; O 142) established the cantional pattern that was followed thereafter (Example 17.6): the chorale melody was in the superius; the setting was in four parts, largely note-against-note; the melody was sung by the congregation with women and men in octaves; the organ or other instruments could have accompanied the melody using the other parts of the setting. Osiander was not a musician himself, and he in fact excused his clumsy part-writing in his preface.[17] Nonetheless, his book remained the model for Protestant hymnody thereafter. A large series of cantionals followed in Germany. The most musically distinguished in southern Germany was that of Hans Leo Hassler, *Kirchengesänge: Psalmen und geistliche Lieder* (Nuremberg, 1608; H 2332). By far the largest compilation was Michael Praetorius's *Musae Sioniae*, parts VI–VIII (Wolfenbüttel, $1609^{9\text{-}10}$, 1610^{12}; P 5353, P 5355, P 5357), which included much new material in its collection of some 450 hymns in over 750 settings. It exemplified different versions of melodies and texts as used in various German courts and towns, and it remains an invaluable testimony of Lutheran practice around 1600.

The more elaborate chorale settings continued to be sung in schools and by choirs. In these the chorale could be interpreted, not simply stated or presented. The composer did not simply proclaim the word of God but tried to stir the feelings of the individual, an attitude exactly parallel to that of the Catholic artists of the Counter-Reformation. In the development of the Lutheran motet, which

16 Friedrich Blume, *Protestant Church Music: A History* (New York, 1974), 134.

17 Finscher, "Volkssprachige Gattungen," 561, which includes a quotation from Osiander's preface.

Ex. 17.6 Lucas Osiander, *Gelobet seist du Jesu Christ*, mm. 1–8
Antiqua Chorbuch, ed. H. Mönkemeyer (Mainz, 1951–52), I: 146

includes settings of chorales as well as biblical and other devotional texts, the key influence was Lasso, whose music was sung as widely in Protestant as in Catholic areas. His lieder and motets in particular were the model and point of departure for new manners of treatment of the texts, and his pupils were among the leaders in these developments.

Johannes Eccard (1553–1611) was born in Mühlhausen, Thuringia, and spent most of his career in central and northern Germany, except the years 1571–73 when he served in Lasso's Hofkapelle. His notable settings of German texts include the *Geistliche Lieder auff den Choral* (Königsberg, 1597; E173, E174), which were based on Osiander's cantional style, but with settings in five parts and more active voices that suggest polyphony, although the parts have no real independence. Blume remarks that "Bach's chorales are unthinkable" without the precedent of Eccard.[18] Eccard's chorale motets are his most outstanding achievement, especially the posthumous *Preussische Festlieder* (Elbling, 1642; Königsberg, 1644; RISM B/VIII 1642^{15}, 1644^{17}) for between five and eight voices.[19]

Leonhard Lechner (*c.*1553–1606), born in the South Tyrol, was among Lasso's choirboys from around 1564 to 1568 and soon after was in the chapel of Prince Wilhelm (later Wilhelm V) at Landshut. Lechner traveled widely, probably to Italy, in the early 1570s and thereafter held positions at Nuremberg, (*c.*1575–84), Hechingen (1584–85), and Stuttgart (1585–1606). Born a Catholic, he converted to Lutheranism at age 17, and thus had difficulties at the Catholic court of Hohenzollern-Hechingen, where he stayed only a year. Lechner has traditionally been considered a follower of Lasso, which is certainly true by his own testimony, but recent German scholarship has stressed the ways in which he went beyond his

[18] Blume, *Protestant Church Music*, 152.
[19] Examples are published ibid., 152–53.

mentor, in part as a result of his Italian experiences, which included direct contact with Luca Marenzio. At its best, Lechner's music can be more personal and inward than Lasso's. His earlier settings of sacred German texts published in 1577 and 1582 move increasingly towards the intensity found in his *Neue geistliche und weltliche teutsche Gesang* (Example 17.7), preserved in a manuscript of 1606.[20] Another major composition within Lechner's sacred music on German texts is his *Historia der Passion*, which was probably published in 1594 but survives only in a 1593 manuscript.[21] It is one of the finest early German Passions, in four voices, through composed, with the traditional Passion tone as a migrating cantus firmus.

Hans Leo Hassler (1562–1612) was one of the first in a long succession of German composers who studied in Italy, with Andrea Gabrieli in 1584–85. While in Venice, Hassler formed connections with other Italian musicians, notably his fellow student Giovanni Gabrieli. Hassler was in the service of Octavian II Fugger in Augsburg from 1586 to 1600. In 1601 to 1605 he was director of town music in Nuremberg, then in 1607 became a citizen of Ulm, though not holding a position there. He joined the electoral kapelle in Dresden in 1608, and by the time of his death in 1612 he had become its leader. Because of his position with the Catholic Fuggers, his earlier sacred music was presumably written for Catholic use. His main Protestant works are the *Psalmen und christliche Gesänge, auf die Melodien fugweiss componiert* (Nuremberg, 1607; RISM A/I H 2328) and the 1608 *Kirchengesänge* mentioned above. The former, like some of his settings of Latin texts, are motets in an almost anachronistic old style from which the *seconda pratica* is totally absent.

Like Hassler, most other German Protestant composers frequently set Latin as well as German texts, and their Latin motets have no specifically Protestant characteristics, belonging rather to the general history of the motet in the sixteenth century. Latin motets continued to be widely used in Lutheran services through the end of the century, since their texts were mostly common to both faiths. The Latin motet anthologies published by Berg and Neuber in the 1550s and the collections that followed them from Formschneider, Lindner, Schadaeus, and Bodenschatz were probably intended to be used by both Churches. Though issued in Protestant areas, their contents were predominantly by Catholic composers, notably Lasso, who was as much a presence in Protestant as in Catholic music in Germany. Music by Germans took second place in these collections to that of the Italians, French, and Netherlanders.

Hassler's Latin motet collections are the *Cantiones sacrae* (Nuremberg, 1591; rev. and enl. Nuremberg, 1597; H 2323, H 2324)[22] and the *Sacrae concentus* (Nuremberg, 1601; rev. and enl. Nuremberg, 1612; H 2328, H 2329).[23] The earlier collection, organized around the principal feasts of the church year, tends more often to use the traditional imitative polyphonic style, while the later one is much more

20 Leonhard Lechner, *Werke*, XIII, ed. Walter Lipphardt (Kassel, 1973).

21 Ibid., XII, ed. Konrad Ameln (Kassel, 1960).

22 Hans Leo Hassler, *Sämtliche Werke*, I, ed. Hermann Gehrmann, DDT 2 (1894), rev. C. Russell Crosby jr (Wiesbaden, 1961).

23 Ibid., V/VI, ed. Joseph Auer, DDT 24/25 (1906), rev. C. Russell Crosby jr (Wiesbaden, 1961).

Ex. 17.7 Leonhard Lechner, *Deutsche Sprüche von Leben und Tod*, 14. Teil, mm. 1–10
Lechner, *Werke*, XIII, ed. Walter Lipphardt (Kassel, 1973), 34

often homophonic. Both contain a large number of polychoral pieces that clearly show Hassler's exposure to the music of the Gabrielis. As a whole, these books contain some of the finest motets by German composers of their period, less subjective and better balanced than those of Lechner. Lechner's earliest published work was the *Motectae sacrae* for four, five, and six voices (Nuremberg, 1575; L 1286),[24] soon followed by another set of Latin motets, the *Sacrarum cantionum liber secundus* for five and six voices (Nuremberg, 1581; L 1295).[25] These motets clearly follow Lasso's

[24] Lechner, *Werke*, I, ed. Ludwig Finscher (Kassel, 1956).
[25] Ibid., VI, ed. Konrad Ameln (Kassel, 1982).

stylistic example and also his frequent practice of including a few secular texts in a motet book.

After 1570 Protestant composers less frequently set the standard Latin liturgical texts. The Latin Mass and Magnificat continued to be used in the Lutheran church, but settings of these texts were readily available and accepted from Catholic sources, even post-Tridentine ones. Hassler and Lechner among others each composed and published a few masses, but their output in this genre is small compared to a Lasso or a Palestrina. Magnificat settings by German Protestant composers followed the models established in Lasso's *Magnificat octo tonorum* of 1567.

The secular lied

As mentioned above, Lasso made the decisive break with the older cantus-firmus tradition in the polyphonic lied by moving towards a style similar to that of the madrigal and chanson. The younger composers of his time pursued this direction further by incorporating the lighter Italian styles, the villanella and the canzonetta, into their lieder. The first and most influential example of this process was Jacob Regnart's *Kurtzweilige teutsche Lieder, nach art der Neapolitanen oder welschen Villanellen* for three voices (Nuremberg, 1576; *Der ander Theyl*, 1577; *Der dritter Theyl*, 1579; R742, R746, R749).[26] These enormously popular compositions were in a simple, artless style, including the typical parallel fifths of their models; the poetry was similarly Italianized, departing altogether from German tradition, and frequently erotic. Lechner sought to make Regnart's lieder more artful by reworking some for five voices, presumably suiting them better to the conservative tastes of the Nuremberg public.[27] However, Lechner himself was not hostile to the lighter style, since he published his own set of three-voice lieder in villanella style, as well as a later set of four-voice lieder in canzonetta style.[28] His other secular lieder appeared in the same three books with the sacred lieder. The majority of these pieces build on the example of Lasso's lieder, though quite a few of them are strophic settings more closely resembling the lighter Italian forms.

Lechner also composed some Italian madrigals, and Hassler in 1596 published an entire madrigal book.[29] Though its texts are relatively serious, its style nonetheless has much of the canzonetta about it. Hassler also published a collection of can-

26 *Jakob Regnart's deutsche dreistimmige Lieder nach Art der Neapolitanen: nebst Leonhard Lechners fünfstimmiger Bearbeitung*, ed. Robert Eitner, Publikation älterer praktischer und theoretischer Musikwerke, 19 (Leipzig, 1895; repr. New York, 1966).

27 Lechner, *Neue teutsche Lieder mit fünff Stimmen* (Nuremberg, 1579; RISM A/I L1293); Lechner, *Werke*, v, ed. Konrad Ameln (Kassel, 1970).

28 *Neue teutsche Lieder, nach art der welschen Villanellen* (Nuremberg, 1576; L1288); Lechner, *Werke*, II, ed. Uwe Martin (Kassel, 1969). *Neue lustige teutsche Lieder nach art der welschen Canzonen* (Nuremberg, 1586; L1301); Lechner, *Werke*, IX, ed. Ernst Franz Schmid (Kassel, 1958).

29 *Madrigali* (Augsburg, 1596; H2339); Hassler, *Sämtliche Werke*, III, ed. Rudolf Schwartz, DTB 19 (Jg. II/I), rev. C. Russell Crosby jr (Wiesbaden, 1962).

zonettas[30] as well as a book of lieder that cited the madrigal and canzonetta in its title as models.[31] The lieder are all strongly chordal in texture and sectional in form. Hassler's best known collection of lieder is the *Lustgarten neuer teutscher Gesäng, Balletti, Gaillarden und Intraden* for 4–8 voices (Nuremberg, 1601; H2340),[32] which achieves a synthesis of Italian and German styles that became a model for his contemporaries and successors.

Instrumental music

Hassler's *Lustgarten* includes eleven instrumental pieces along with its 39 vocal works. The mixture of medium within a single publication is unusual, although a precedent exists in Lasso's *Novae aliquot . . . ad duas voces Cantiones* (Munich, 1577; L9002, Brown 1577_2), which contains twelve texted and twelve untexted duos, the latter in an instrumental rather than a vocal idiom. Another notable collection of pieces for instrumental ensemble are the *Intradae* for five and six parts (Helmstedt, 1597_{11}; O126) by Alessandro Orologio (*c.*1550–?1633), an Italian cornetto player in the imperial service who traveled widely in German lands. These relatively isolated publications look ahead to the great upsurge in instrumental ensemble music in Germany in the seventeenth century.

Late-sixteenth-century German keyboard composers are often lumped under the heading "colorists," because their intabulations of vocal music often tend toward routine, predictable, and over-elaborate "coloration" of the original. Though this generalization contains some truth, it says nothing about the interesting dance music published along with the intabulations, and the latter can themselves be more varied than a single catch-phrase would suggest. This is clear in the work of Elias Ammerbach (*c.*1530–1597), the organist at the Thomaskirche in Leipzig from 1561 to 1595. His *Orgel oder Instrument Tabulatur* (Leipzig, 1571_1; rev. and enl. Nuremberg, 1583_2)[33] is the earliest known German printed keyboard music. Some of Ammerbach's intabulations of lieder, both sacred and secular, are relatively free from ornamentation, while later in the book coloration is elaborate and continuous. A number of the dances are paired; most are uncolored except for some of the passamezzos. Ammerbach's *Tabulatur* is the first source to use the "new German" keyboard tablature, in which pitches are designated by letters, with rhythmic signs placed above them. Other important keyboard sources from this period are *Zwey Bücher einer neuen kunstlichen Tablatur* (Strasburg, 1577_6) by Bernhard Schmid the elder (1535–1592), organist at Strasburg cathedral, and *Ein schön nutz unnd*

30 *Canzonette* (Nuremberg, 1590; H2335); Hassler, *Sämtliche Werke*, II, ed. Rudolf Schwartz, DTB 8 (Jg. 5/2), rev. C. Russell Crosby jr (Wiesbaden, 1962).

31 *Neüe teütsche Gesang nach art der welschen Madrigalien und Canzonetten*, 4, 5, 6, and 8 v. (Augsburg, 1596; H2336); Hassler, *Sämtliche Werke*, II.

32 Hassler, *Sämtliche Werke*, IX, ed. C. Russell Crosby jr (Wiesbaden, 1968).

33 Elias Nicolaus Ammerbach, *Orgel oder Instrument Tabulaturbuch (1571/83)*, ed. Charles Jacobs (Oxford, 1984). "Instrument" in the title seems to refer to any kind of stringed keyboard instrument or organ.

gebreüchlich Orgel Tabulaturbuch (Lauingen, 1583_4) by Jakob Paix (1556–*c.*1623), organist at St. Martin, Lauingen an der Donau.

The lute remained the favorite household instrument through the end of the century, and printed lute tablatures continued to appear. Important examples are the *Teütsch Lautenbuch* (Strasburg, 1573_1) of Melchior Neusidler (1531–1590), son of Hans Newsidler, and the *Lautenbuch* (Strasbourg, 1586_5) of Sixt Kargel. The contents of these and other lute books of the time are intabulations of both sacred and secular vocal works, dances, and improvisatory or preludial pieces. Though both Melchior Newsidler and Kargel published some of their work in Italian tablature, German lute tablature continued in use until its final appearance near the end of the century in Matthäus Waissel's *Lautenbuch* (Frankfurt an der Oder, 1592_{12}).

18

GERMANY AND CENTRAL EUROPE, *ii*: 1600–1640

David Crook

THE early seventeenth century has generally been viewed as a period of intense polarization and conflict for Germany and central Europe. Historians speak of an Age of Confessionalization, during which the three principal confessions—Catholicism, Lutheranism, and Calvinism—elaborated their separate professions of faith and thereby developed distinct ideologies and cultures. Most German states became confessional, embracing a single religion and regarding toleration as dangerous and destabilizing. Church and state joined forces to define and enforce correct belief and behavior through education, propaganda, and censorship. In this process, music, like the other arts, became both an instrument and an object of the confessional states' social disciplining.[1]

Following the outbreak of the Thirty Years' War, armed conflict as well as differing ideologies shaped the cultivation of music at many institutions throughout the Holy Roman Empire. The hostilities, which began in Bohemia in 1618, spread to the rest of the Empire, and eventually involved all the major powers in Europe, bringing Germany to the brink of total anarchy. Technological advancements in the manufacture of firearms and enormous increases in the size of armies gave rise to unprecedented slaughter and destruction. Armies lived off the land: cities were sacked, villages destroyed, peasants tortured and murdered. Agriculture foundered; starvation and disease followed. Germany lost thirty to forty percent of its population.[2]

The circumstances Heinrich Schütz encountered at the electoral court in Dresden, where from 1614 he served as organist and music director, demonstrate

[1] Scholars apply the terms "confessionalization," "confessional formation," "confessionalism," and "social disciplining" to a broader historical span than the 40 years covered here, usually to a period extending from the Peace of Augsburg (1555) to the Peace of Westphalia (1648). In the second and longest part of Friedrich Blume's classic *Protestant Church Music* (New York, 1974), "The Age of Confessionalism" covers musical developments from the second half of the 16th century to the death of Johann Sebastian Bach. On the historiography of the aforementioned terms, see John W. O'Malley, *Trent and All That* (Cambridge, MA, 2000), chap. 4.

[2] Michael Hughes, *Early Modern Germany* (Philadelphia, 1992), 109.

the horrible consequences the hostilities could have for musicians and the institutions that supported them. At the time of Schütz's arrival in the Saxon capital, the Hofkapelle had 27 members (16 singers and 11 instrumentalists), a number that increased slightly in subsequent years. Following Saxony's entry into the war in 1631, however, the situation at court deteriorated dramatically, and between 1634 and 1639 the number of musicians dropped from 30 to 10.[3] By 1641 war, plague, and unpaid salaries had reduced the Kapelle to a state that, in Schütz's own words, resembled "a patient in the throes of death." And despite some efforts on the part of Elector Johann Georg I to ameliorate the situation, conditions worsened. In 1645, at the age of 59, an apparently exhausted and exasperated Schütz requested permission to retire from active duty as *Kapellmeister* on the grounds that the Kapelle had "gone completely to ruin in these perilous times," and he in the meantime had "grown old." (Schütz made a similar request again in 1651, but only in 1657, following the death of the elector the previous year, was he relieved of his daily responsibilities, provided a pension, and granted a semi-retired status that required his presence at court only several times a year.) In Dresden, as in many other parts of the Empire, improvements came slowly even after the Peace of Westphalia in 1648. In an oft-quoted letter of 1651, Schütz drew attention to the poverty the musicians continued to endure, citing the example of one singer who "lives like a sow in a pigsty, has no bedding, lies on straw [and] has already pawned his coat and doublet." The following year, Schütz confessed that owing to the "present wretched state of the electoral musicians the desire to work with them has been totally soured within me."[4]

But all was not war and misery. The vast geographical expanse of the empire, which bordered Poland in the east, France in the west, Denmark to the north, and various Italian states in the south, encompassed a patchwork of hundreds of individual states, and thus the effects of the war could vary considerably from one location to the next. In contrast to the appalling situation at Dresden, for example, the city of Hamburg, which employed a series of distinguished organists, including Hieronymus Praetorius and Heinrich Scheidemann, and cultivated brilliant polychoral music in the Venetian style, enjoyed a period of relative peace and prosperity. Hamburg and other wealthy trading cities had become important centers of musical activity by the seventeenth century, rivaling royal courts and

[3] Eberhard Schmidt, *Der Gottesdienst am Kurfürstlichen Hofe zu Dresden* (Göttingen, 1961), 163; Joshua Rifkin, "Schütz—Weckmann—Kopenhagen: Zur Frage der zweiten Dänemarkreise," in *Von Isaac bis Bach: Festschrift Martin Just zum 60. Geburtstag* (Kassel, 1991), 182–85; Moritz Fürstenau, *Zur Geschichte der Musik und des Theaters am Hofe zu Dresden* (Dresden, 1861–62; repr. 1971), 23. The assertion found in much of the secondary literature that the Hofkapelle included as many as 39 persons in 1632 evidently stems from a typographical error in Moritz Fürstenau, *Beiträge zur Geschichte der Königlich Sächsischen musikalischen Kapelle* (Dresden, 1849), according to which the Kapelle "bestand 1632 aus 39 Personen." The inventory of specific names immediately following and in support of that statement, however, lists not 39 but 29 musicians.

[4] Quotations from Schütz's letters of 7 March 1641, 21 May 1645, 19 Aug. 1651, and 26 June 1652; Erich H. Müller, *Heinrich Schütz: Gesammelte Briefe und Schriften* (Regensburg, 1931), nos. 48, 56, 81, 84.

employing some of the period's finest composers and organists. Schütz's friend, Johann Hermann Schein, for example, held the position of *Kantor* in the city of Leipzig. In this capacity, he directed the choral music in the city's *Nicolaikirche* and *Thomaskirche* and taught singing and Latin grammar in its *Thomasschule*. Samuel Scheidt, also a friend of Schütz and Schein, encountered difficulties both as a court *Kapellmeister* and as a civic music director in his native Halle. From 1609 as court organist and from 1619 or 1620 as *Kapellmeister*, Scheidt served Margrave Christian Wilhelm of Brandenburg. But in 1625, when the margrave went off to fight with the Protestant forces in the war, Scheidt ceased to draw his salary. Three years later the city created for him the position of *director musices* with responsibility for music in Halle's main church. But in 1630, following a bitter dispute with the *Rektor* of the Gymnasium concerning supervision of the choirboys, Scheidt was forced to relinquish his position. Indeed, both Scheidt and Schein became embroiled in disputes with local authorities similar to those that plagued Johann Sebastian Bach during his tenure as Leipzig's *Kantor* and music director approximately a hundred years later.

The tendency to view this period in German music as the age of Schütz, Schein, and Scheidt—a historiographical tradition that extends all the way back to Wolfgang Caspar Printz's *Historische Beschreibung der edelen Sing- und Kling-Kunst* (Dresden, 1690)—has never been seriously questioned.[5] Nevertheless, the privileged status awarded these three composers has tended to obscure the achievements of distinguished and prolific contemporaries like Christoph Demantius, Melchior Franck, Johann Stadlmayr, and especially Michael Praetorius, whose three-volume *Syntagma musicum* (1614–20) stands as the most important German treatise of the first half of the seventeenth century.

Italian Music in Germany

The traditional emphasis on Schütz, Schein, and Scheidt also reflects the relatively marginal role the southern Catholic institutions have played in histories of seventeenth-century German music. Nothing illustrates this more vividly than the newly emerging view of music at the Imperial court itself. For over a century scholars had accepted Ludwig Köchel's conclusion that the Thirty Years' War had forced Emperor Ferdinand II shortly after his election in 1619 to dismiss most, if not all, of his musicians. Recent research, however, has shown that the Imperial

[5] In his 12th chapter, "Von Denen Berühmtesten Musicis, so in dem siebenzehenden Seculo nach Christi Geburth bekannt worden," Printz writes, "Um eben diese Zeit ist berühmt worden Samuel Scheit, Organist zu Halle in Sachsen, welcher einer von denen dreyen gewesen, derer Nahmen von dem Buchstaben S. anfangen, und die man zu dieser Zeit für die besten drey Componisten in Teutschland gehalten. Diese drey berühmte S. aber seyn gewesen Schütz, Schein, Scheit." Wolfgang Caspar Printz, *Historische Beschreibung der edelen Sing- und Kling-Kunst* (1690), fasc. ed. Othmar Wessely (Graz, 1964), 137.

court maintained a large and vibrant musical organization notable for its cultivation of modern Italianate music north of the Alps.[6]

Whatever their differences, whether Catholic or Protestant, most German musicians and patrons of the early seventeenth century shared the Imperial court's enthusiasm for Italian music. One indication of that enthusiasm comes from collections of Italian music issued by German publishers. Nuremberg appears early on to have played an important role in this respect. Between 1585 and 1591 the Nuremberg printer Catharina Gerlach published a series of eight anthologies devoted almost entirely to works by Italian composers. According to the preface of one of these volumes, many of the composers had personally sent their music to Gerlach's editor, Friedrich Lindner, who from 1574 had also served as Kantor of the city's *Egidienkirche*.[7] In addition to such anthology volumes, Nuremberg publishers issued prints devoted to single composers, such as Orazio Vecchi's canzonettas for three and four voices (1597, 1593), Giovanni Gastoldi's balletti for three and five voices (1600), and Luca Marenzio's madrigals for four, five, and six voices (1601, 1603, 1608). The defensive assertion of Johann Staden, the leading musician in Nuremberg by the 1620s, that "the Italians do not know everything; the Germans are also capable of something," tacitly acknowledges the degree to which all things Italian had captured the German musical imagination.[8]

When it came to publishing their own music, German composers made a point of advertising the extent to which it observed Italian conventions and innovations. Title pages tell us, for example, that the sacred concertos contained in the first volume of Schein's *Opella nova* (1618) were "composed according to Italian invention" and that the settings of German sacred texts for five and six voices with optional basso continuo contained in his *Fontana d'Israel* (1623) display an "uncommonly graceful Italian-madrigal manner." In the preface to his *Psalmen Davids* (1619), Schütz drew attention to the fact that he had composed the psalms "in the Italian manner," utilizing the "*stylus recitativus*, almost unknown in Germany up to now." And Michael Praetorius published his *Polyhymnia exercitatrix* (1619–20) "with a view to giving choirboys practice in singing, and accustoming them to the new Italian manner."[9]

Hand in hand with the publication of Italianate music came the desire for musicians with firsthand knowledge of Italian practice. Already in the sixteenth

[6] Ludwig Ritter von Köchel, *Die kaiserliche Hof-Musikkapelle in Wien von 1543 bis 1867* (Vienna, 1869; repr. Hildesheim, 1976), 9; Steven Saunders, *Cross, Sword, and Lyre: Sacred Music at the Imperial Court of Ferdinand II of Habsburg (1619–1637)* (Oxford, 1995), 4.

[7] See Franz Krautwurst, "Lindner, Friedrich," *New Grove Dictionary of Music and Musicians*, 2nd edn, ed. Stanley Sadie and John Tyrrell (London, 2001), for titles of anthologies edited by Lindner; Royston Gustavson, "Gerlach," *Die Musik in Geschichte und Gegenwart*, 2nd edn, ed. Ludwig Finscher (Kassel and Weimar, 1994–), *Personenteil*, VII, for lists of Gerlach's music publications and relevant literature.

[8] Maxim attributed to Staden by Johann Andreas Herbst in his *Musica moderna prattica* (Frankfurt, 1653); see Harold E. Samuel, *The Cantata in Nuremberg during the Seventeenth Century* (Ann Arbor, MI, 1982), 64, 294 n. 477.

[9] Michael Praetorius, *Syntagma musicum II: De organographia, Parts I and II*, trans. and ed. David Z. Crookes (Oxford, 1986), 17.

century a tradition of recruiting foreign, mainly Netherlandish, musicians was well established. During the second half of the century, a preference for Italian performers emerged at the larger and more influential German centers, among them the Bavarian court in Munich under Orlande de Lassus, the Saxon electoral court in Dresden under Antonio Scandello, and especially the Styrian court of Archduke Karl II in Graz. In 1598, less than two years after acceding to the throne, Karl's successor Ferdinand II journeyed to Rome by way of Venice, where he attended Vespers at St Mark's, met Giovanni Croce, and heard Giovanni Gabrieli perform on the organ. This experience must have affected him deeply, for the Venetian polychoral style and especially Gabrieli's music assumed a position of central importance at Ferdinand's court in Graz and later in Vienna following his election as Emperor in 1619. At least three of his four chapel-masters—Simone Gatto, Pietro Antonio Bianco, and Giovanni Priuli—came from Venice, and other musicians in his service were sent to that city for training.

Gabrieli's Venice became the preferred destination for many German musicians sent to Italy by their patrons to acquire training in the latest styles and practices. Already in the 1580s Hans Leo Hassler had travelled from his native Nuremberg to study with Giovanni's uncle Andrea Gabrieli, and Gregor Aichinger with the support of the Fugger family of Augsburg had become one of the first German pupils of Giovanni himself. In 1599, King Christian IV of Denmark sent a group of musicians, which included Melchior Borchgrevinck, Hans Nielsen, and Mogens Pedersøn, to Venice to study with Gabrieli.

It was Heinrich Schütz's first patron, Landgrave Moritz of Hessen-Kassel, who in 1609 proposed and financed a trip to Venice that allowed the young composer to study with Gabrieli. Schütz, like Nielsen, Pedersøn, and other Gabrieli students, composed as a result of his first studies with the maestro a book of five-voice madrigals. Published in Venice in 1611, this *Primo libro de madrigali* bore a dedication to Landgrave Moritz. Whether or not his second journey to the *Serenissima Repubblica* in 1628 brought Schütz into personal contact with Monteverdi remains unclear.[10] There can be little doubt, however, that the new music he encountered at that time had a profoundly invigorating effect on the 43-year-old composer. He wrote back to Germany that Venetian music had changed dramatically since his first sojourn, and in the preface to his first volume of *Symphoniae sacrae*, which he published in Venice prior to his return to Dresden in 1629, he noted that the compositions contained therein reflected these new developments.

[10] According to an elegy by the Dresden court poet David Schirmer, "the noble Monteverdi guided him with joy and happily showed him the oft-sought path" (quoted in Hans Joachim Moser, *Heinrich Schütz* [Kassel, 1936], 609). Nevertheless, the biographical section of Schütz's funeral sermon, published in Dresden in 1672, although it mentions both trips to Italy and describes his studies with Gabrieli, says nothing about Monteverdi (Robin A. Leaver, *Music in the Service of the Church: The Funeral Sermon for Heinrich Schütz (1585–1672)* [St. Louis, 1984], 57, 59). Schütz's letters from Venice also make no mention of Monteverdi.

Categories of Musical Style

Expressions like Schein's "Italian-madrigal manner" and Schütz's "*stylus recitativus*" also reflect a heightened sensitivity to style distinctions characteristic of the period. The notion of diverse but equally valid styles was neither new nor uniquely German—one need only think of the stylistic profiles of genres in Pietro Pontio's *Ragionamento di musica* (1588) or the distinction drawn between *prima pratica* and *seconda pratica* by Claudio Monteverdi in the preface to his fifth book of madrigals (1605)—but during the seventeenth century, Germans pursued questions of style with unprecedented enthusiasm. The common antinomy of old style versus new style (*stylus antiquus* versus *stylus modernus*, *prima pratica* versus *seconda pratica*, and so on) arose in the first place from the continuing viability not only of sixteenth-century style but of sixteenth-century compositions themselves. Erhard Bodenschatz's huge two-volume anthology *Florilegium Portense* (Leipzig, 1618–21), which included motets by Lassus, Jacob Handl, and other sixteenth-century composers (albeit with a basso continuo part added by the editor), still formed part of the repertory performed at Leipzig's *Thomasschule* during Johann Sebastian Bach's tenure there. And hymn cycles by Lassus and Palestrina continued to be performed in Munich and Vienna up until the early eighteenth century.[11]

The true significance of the old style, however, derived from its maintenance as a legitimate category of new composition, especially in music for the Church and other solemn contexts. Perhaps nothing indicates more strikingly the status of the old style than a request by Schütz concerning the music for his own funeral. According to Johann Mattheson (*Grundlage einer Ehren-Pforte*, 1740), the aged composer asked his former pupil Christoph Bernhard to compose a piece "in the Palestrina style of counterpoint." The composition, receipt of which Schütz acknowledged in a letter of 1670, does not survive, but in a treatise written in the 1650s, Bernhard singles out Palestrina as the composer most worthy of emulation in the *stylus gravis* or *stylus antiquus*, which he sets in opposition to the *stylus luxurians* or *stylus modernus*. As with Monteverdi's *prima pratica* and *seconda pratica*, the distinction between Bernhard's antique and modern styles turns primarily on text setting and dissonance treatment: the antique style uses few kinds of dissonances and "does not consider text as much as it does harmony," whereas the modern style uses more kinds of dissonances and melodies that "agree with the text as much as possible."[12]

But writers did not always distinguish old from new according to the same criteria, and in some cases the whole question of historical precedence was incidental or irrelevant to the real distinction they wished to draw. Accordingly attempts to collapse the various stylistic distinctions from the period into a single opposition between old and new can scarcely do justice to the subtlety and diversity of those

[11] Marie Louise Göllner, Introd. to Orlando di Lasso, *Sämtliche Werke, neue Reihe*, XVIII: *Das Hymnarium aus dem Jahre 1580/81* (Kassel, 1980), p. vii; Saunders, *Cross, Sword, and Lyre*, 52–53.

[12] Walter Hilse, "The Treatises of Christoph Bernhard," *The Music Forum*, 3 (1973), 35.

distinctions. When Schein, for example, drew attention to the "Italian-madrigal manner" of the settings of German sacred texts in his *Fontana d'Israel,* he invoked the quintessential genre of the *stylus modernus,* and it seems reasonable to see in his designation the desire to contrast the style he adopted in those pieces with the *stylus antiquus* traditionally associated with the motet. To read his description as a mere label for the modern style, however, would be grossly reductive: at the very least the "Italian-madrigal manner" of the *Fontana d'Israel* also invites comparison with the equally modern and fashionable "italian-villanellische Invention" that he had advertised two years earlier on the title page of his *Musica boscarrecia.*

In the preface to his *Psalmen Davids* (1619), Schütz employed the term *stylus recitativus* to draw attention to a particular approach to text setting. According to his economical formulation, in the recitative style, "owing to the abundance of the words, one always recites without manifold repetitions." The simple forward-driving declamation of these pieces, so appropriate to the lengthy texts of the Psalms as Schütz pointed out, sets them apart not only from the *stylus antiquus* but also from many progressive compositions like those contained in Schein's *Fontana d'Israel.*

Rise of the Basso Continuo

With the publication of the *Geistliche Chor-Music* in 1648, Schütz intended to make a very different point. In his preface to this collection of 29 settings of German biblical and ritual texts for 5–7 parts, the composer distinguishes between two styles: one with basso continuo, the other without. Acknowledging at the outset what he sees as the completely justified popularity of the "concerting style with basso continuo," he goes on to express the hope that in issuing this collection he will encourage composers—"especially the younger generation of Germans"—to dedicate themselves to the style without basso continuo and thereby acquire the "foundations of a just counterpoint before progressing to the concerting style." His primary point involves the need for contrapuntal skill in both styles: in the polyphonic style (without continuo) where composers cultivate it most keenly, and in the essentially harmonic style (with continuo) where composers too often neglect it. But his formulation of the problem is telling, for in making his point about counterpoint he also confronts the two most significant developments in German music of the preceding half-century.

Schütz neatly encapsulates these two innovations—the basso continuo and the process of "concerting"—in his designation of the new style as "der über den *Bassum Continuum* concertierende *Stylus.*" The German verb *concertieren* (or *konzertieren*), with its noun *Concert,* paralleled the Italian *concertare* and carried the same general meaning as the English verb *concert,* "to act in harmony or conjunction." A concerting or concerted style brought heterogeneous elements into a state of harmony, balance, or agreement. In early seventeenth-century musical discourse, these terms refer especially to the bringing together of vocal and instrumental forces. Schütz speaks thus of a style in which voices concert together with the instrumental basso continuo.

Michael Praetorius, in his discussion of the concerto (*Syntagma musicum*, III, chap. 2), describes two types of pieces in which composers bring about such a conjunction of voices and instruments. The first type, the concerto for few voices and basso continuo, corresponds to Schütz's "concerting style with basso continuo" and takes as its model Lodovico Viadana's three volumes of *Concerti ecclesiastici* (Venice, 1602, 1607, and 1609) for 1–4 voices and basso continuo. At Frankfurt am Main, Nikolaus Stein reprinted Viadana's first two volumes in 1609 and his third volume in 1610, only a year after it had first appeared in Venice. A complete edition of all three volumes issued by Stein in 1613 and reprinted in 1620 and 1626 attests to the enthusiastic reception these pieces enjoyed in Germany. This complete edition provided a German translation of Viadana's preface with its valuable performance instructions, and a variety of German publications from Gregor Aichinger's *Cantiones ecclesiasticae* (1607) to Schein's *Opella nova* (1618) gave instructions that derived from Viadana's preface or referred the reader to it for further information and instruction. In an extensive chapter "De Basso Generali seu Continuo" (*Syntagma musicum*, III, chap. 6), Michael Praetorius quoted extensively from Viadana's preface and Agostino Agazzari's *Del sonare sopra 'l basso* (1607).

Already at the close of the sixteenth century a tradition of accompanying vocal polyphony at the organ was well established, and during the early seventeenth century organ parts that facilitated such an accompaniment became very popular for both old and new music. In 1604, for example, Lassus' sons had issued the *Magnum opus musicum*, a huge edition of their father's motets in six vocal partbooks. In 1625 Johann Volmar published a *bassus ad organum* part for the collection, prepared by Caspar Vincentius, organist at Würzburg cathedral. Demand for such parts also influenced the publication of new music: Schütz stated in the preface to his four-voice *Cantiones sacrae* of 1625 that he had provided a basso continuo part only because his publisher had insisted on it. And even the *Geistliche Chor-Music*, Schütz's paradigm of the style without basso continuo, was published with an optional *bassus generalis*. These parts, however, merely double the lowest sounding vocal part and are thus more properly what Adriano Banchieri called *basso seguente*. What defined the "style with basso continuo" for Schütz was the presence of a contrapuntally independent and indispensable continuo part like those in Viadana's concertos.

The first German publication to employ such a part, Aichinger's *Cantiones ecclesiasticae* of 1607, contains 16 compositions for three voices and a *bassus generalis et continuus* (four four-voice pieces without continuo and an instrumental canzona complete the collection). In these pieces, however, the continuo generally follows the lowest sounding voice in the manner of a *basso seguente* and only sparingly pursues an independent line. A more independently conceived continuo emerges in collections by Rudolph de Lassus, Johann Staden, and others published in southern Germany in 1614–16.[13] The sacred concertos of Schein's *Opella nova* (1618) reveal a complete adoption and mastery of the new style.

[13] Heinrich Pfender, *Delli motetti* (Graz, 1614); Rudolph de Lassus, *Virginalia eucharistica* (Munich, 1615); Philipp Zindelin, *Symphonia Parthenia* (Augsburg, 1615); Urban Loth, *Musa*

The Concerto

The second type of concerto described by Praetorius is characterized by the interplay of two or more choirs of voices and instruments set in opposition to each other. The earliest publication that uses the term *concerto* in its title, the *Concerti di Andrea, et di Gio. Gabrieli* (1587), and the influential *Sacrae symphoniae* of Giovanni Gabrieli (1597) both contain concertos of this second type. (Musicians, as Praetorius himself pointed out, called the types of pieces he described as concertos by a variety of names including *concerto, concentus, cantio, motetta*, and *symphonia.*) In these publications, as in the 101 polychoral *Geistliche Concert-Gesänge* contained in the first four volumes of Praetorius's own *Musae Sioniae,* all parts are texted and without explicit indications of instrumental performance. Title pages and prefaces refer to performance by a combination of voices and instruments, but the choice of which parts to perform instrumentally and which instruments to use is left to the performer.

Praetorius's concept of the concerto, as Carl Dahlhaus has pointed out, was "a musical manner in transition from a performance practice to a mode of composition." His second type of concerto in particular emerged as a way of performing polychoral pieces according to which vocalists sing some parts and instrumentalists play others. In *Syntagma musicum,* III, chap. 7, Praetorius demonstrates how "every concerto and motet with few or many choirs can be arranged quickly and without particular difficulty for all kinds of instruments and voices." The specific scorings that he suggests for several compositions—ranging from Lassus' seven-voice *Laudate pueri* to Giovanni Gabrieli's sixteen-voice *Omnes gentes*—show that the procedure was not simply a matter of instrumental doubling: in each case some parts are taken exclusively by instruments.

During the first two decades of the seventeenth century, composers throughout the empire adopted the polychoral concerto, which reached a climax in 1619 with the publication of Praetorius's *Polyhymnia caduceatrix* and Schütz's *Psalmen Davids.* In these two collections, the concerto's central principle of harmonious contrast expands to embrace contrasts not only between instruments and voices but also between solo voices and choral forces, between texted passages and purely instrumental *sinfonie,* and between sections for solo voices with independent basso continuo and sections for the full ensemble with doubling *basso seguente.* The scoring of individual parts generally remains unspecified, although in some pieces the use of extreme registers, the absence of text, and occasionally explicit designations like *cornetto* or *violino* indicate instrumental performance.

With their dramatic contrasts of timbre and texture and their lavish arrays of instrumental and vocal forces, such large-scale polychoral concertos provided composers with a genre of unprecedented magnificence. As such they became expressions of the wealth and prestige of the institutions that cultivated them and

melica (Passau, 1616); Johann Staden, *Harmoniae sacrae* (Nuremberg, 1616). See Anne Kirwan-Mott, *The Small-Scale Sacred Concertato in the Early Seventeenth Century,* 2 vols. (Ann Arbor, MI, 1981), I: 55–65.

appropriate adornments of the most important ceremonies of church and state. During the celebrations at Dresden in 1617 marking the hundredth anniversary of the Reformation, Schütz directed a series of compositions for 2–7 choirs.[14] And Giovanni Valentini apparently intended the three compositions in his *Messa, Magnificat et Iubilate Deo a sette chori concertati con le trombe* (Vienna, 1621) as commemorations of three major political events in the life of his patron: the coronation of Ferdinand II as king of Hungary in 1617, his Imperial coronation in 1619, and the victory of Catholic forces at White Mountain in 1620. The monumental scale of these pieces, the use of seven choirs as a symbol of the Empire's seven electors, and the prominent employment of trumpets with their royal and military connotations combined to create a *musica politica*—to use a term coined by the seventeenth-century theorist Athanasius Kircher—that mirrored the power and authority of the emperor and his court.[15]

In the 1620s and 1630s, as the effects of the Thirty Years' War spread through the empire, composers had fewer and fewer opportunities to write large-scale concertos—a fact Schütz lamented in the preface to his first volume of *Kleine geistliche Concerte* (1636)—and as a result turned their attention increasingly to the small-scale concerto for few voices with basso continuo. Between 1618 and 1648 German composers produced a distinguished series of sacred concertos for 1–6 voices with continuo that includes Schein's *Opella nova* (2 vols., 1618, 1626), Valentini's *Sacri concerti* (1625), Scheidt's *Newe geistliche Concerten* (4 vols., 1631, 1634, 1635, 1640), and Schütz's *Kleine geistliche Conzerte* (2 vols., 1636, 1639). Most of the compositions in these collections call only for solo voices with basso continuo. Other concertos of the period achieve a kind of rapprochement of the large-scale polychoral concerto and the few-voice concerto with continuo. All of the fifteen pieces contained in the first volume of the *Symphoniae sacrae*, which Schütz published at the end of his second Venetian sojourn in 1629, have at least one obbligato instrumental part in addition to the voice parts and basso continuo. The well-known *O quam tu pulchra es*, for example, calls for tenor and bass voices with two violins, and in the magnificent *Fili mi Absalon* a quartet of trombones accompanies a solo bass voice. In addition, a tendency to employ contrasts between passages for solo voices with continuo and passages for large choral forces appears already in some of the pieces of Schütz's *Psalmen Davids*, such as *Alleluja! Lobet den Herren*, and culminates in several pieces like his dramatic masterpiece *Saul, Saul, was verfolgst du mich?*, published after the war in the third volume of the *Symphoniae sacrae* (1650).

[14] Some of the pieces performed may be preserved in the *Psalmen Davids*. See Christhard Mahrenholz, "Heinrich Schütz and das erste Reformationsjubiläum 1617," in *Musicologica et liturgica: Gesammelte Aufsätze von Christhard Mahrenholz* (Kassel, 1960), 196–204; Matthias Hoe von Hoenegg, *Parasceve ad solemnitatem evangelicam* (Dresden, 1617), trans. Carol MacClintock in *Readings in the History of Music in Performance* (Bloomington, IN, 1979), 138–39.

[15] Saunders, *Cross, Sword, and Lyre*, chap. 5.

Church Music

The primary liturgical contexts for music in both Catholic and Lutheran churches remained the celebration of Mass and Vespers. In Catholic institutions, the Latin Mass Ordinary and the Magnificat retained their central position, and composers like Giovanni Priuli and Giovanni Valentini in Vienna and Johann Stadlmayr in Innsbruck composed many settings in styles both antique and modern. Mass Propers received far less attention, although they occasionally appeared in comprehensive collections like Christian Erbach's settings of the introits, Alleluia verses, and communions for the most important feasts of the Church year (*Modi sacri tripertiti*, 1604–6) and the *Communiones totius anni* and *Offertoria totius anni* (both 1611) of Mikołaj Zieleński, organist and music director to the archbishop of Gniezno in Poland.

Vespers developed into a service of considerable importance and musical splendor at some institutions. The confessor of Ferdinand II maintained that the Emperor would rather ride a horse to death than miss Vespers, which at the Imperial court was sung on Saturdays, Sundays, feast days, and their vigils and could last two or three hours.[16] Composers provided polyphonic settings of not only the Magnificat but also the Psalms, hymns, Marian antiphons, and the Litany of Loreto, which was appended to the end of the service. They sometimes set Psalm and Magnificat antiphons for major feasts, although these items were more commonly sung in plainchant or replaced by organ music or motets. The latter could also replace the offertory at Mass.

Lutheran composers concerned themselves to a far lesser degree than their Catholic contemporaries with settings of liturgical texts and instead focused primarily on settings of chorales, Psalms, and other Bible verses. Such settings assumed a variety of positions within the Lutheran services. At Mass, for example, chorales could appear both in place of the traditional liturgical items (e.g., as substitutes for the introit or gradual) and as free interpolations (e.g., before the sermon or during communion). Performance of the chorale could alternate verse by verse between congregation, choir, and organist. The traditional unison and unaccompanied congregational singing of chorales gave way in the late sixteenth century to the so-called cantional settings—simple, mainly homophonic settings for four or five voices with the chorale tune in the top voice. Some of these settings join the chorale poetry to a newly composed melody; others preserve a traditional tune. Such settings, which made it easy for the congregation to sing the chorale melody to an accompaniment provided by the organist, instrumentalists, or singers of the *Kantorei*, became very popular and inspired a series of early-seventeenth-century *Cantionale* that included Hans Leo Hassler's *Kirchengesäng, Psalmen und geistliche Lieder . . . simpliciter gesetzt* (1608), Schein's *Cantional oder Gesangbuch Augspurgischer Confession* (1627), and Schütz's settings of Psalm paraphrases by Cornelius Becker (1628, revised and enlarged 1661).

[16] Ibid., 43.

The trained singers and instrumentalists of the *Kantorei* performed more complex chorale-based compositions such as the four-voice chorale motets of Melchior Franck's *Contrapuncti compositi deutscher Psalmen und anderer geistlichen Kirchengesäng* (1602) and Hassler's *Psalmen und christliche Gesänge* (1607) and the chorale concertos of Schein's *Opella nova* (1618) and Scheidt's *Newe geistliche Concerten* (4 vols., 1631–40). The largest and most diverse collection of chorale compositions from the period, Michael Praetorius's *Musae Sioniae* (9 vols., 1605–10), includes *bicinia* and *tricinia* "for church and home," cantional settings, single-choir motets, and magnificent polychoral concertos—a total of over 1,200 compositions. In his preface to the fifth volume, Praetorius describes how vocal and instrumental forces can be varied from verse to verse and how the elaborate polyphony can alternate with simple congregational singing.

Organ Music

Alternatim performance of hymns, Magnificat settings, and other items within the Catholic and Lutheran liturgies also provided a context for much of the organ music that survives from the period. Sets of organ Magnificat verses, for example, were composed by Hassler, Scheidt, the Augsburg organist Christian Erbach, and the Hamburg organists Hieronymus Praetorius and Heinrich Scheidemann. In addition, Hassler, Erbach, and their south-German contemporaries produced a substantial body of ricercares (both monothematic and polythematic), canzonas, and toccatas. Among Protestant composers for the instrument, the chorale maintained a central position. Some organ chorale settings—Michael Praetorius's *Ein feste Burg* and Jacob Praetorius's *Vater unser im Himmelreich*, for example—took the form of the chorale ricercare, with each phrase of the chorale presented as a point of imitation. But Scheidt and Scheidemann, the period's two most important composers for the instrument, favored chorale variation sets, in which each variation presents a different polyphonic setting of the complete chorale melody. Both Scheidt and Scheidemann were students of the Dutch organist Jan Pieterszoon Sweelinck, who had adapted the variation techniques of the English virginalists to the Protestant chorale, and together they made the chorale variation the dominant genre of their generation. In most sets, the individual variations form self-contained sections that organists could incorporate into *alternatim* performances.

The many manuscript sources of Scheidemann's music testify to both the period's normal manner of transmission for organ music and the esteem he enjoyed among his contemporaries. Scheidt's *Tabulatura nova* (1624), on the other hand, is one of only six extant collections of organ music printed in Germany between 1600 and 1640.[17] It is also the first German organ publication devoted to the works of a single composer since Arnolt Schlick's *Tabulaturen etlicher lobgesang* (1512) and the first in open score (with each contrapuntal part on a separate five-line

[17] John Caldwell, "Sources of Keyboard Music to 1660," *New Grove*².

staff) rather than the letter notation of German organ tablature. The 58 pieces contained in it include variations on chorales, Latin hymns, the Magnificat tones, and secular tunes, as well as other types of pieces such as canons and dances.

Occasional Music and Dance Music

THROUGHOUT the Renaissance, European courts had commissioned special music for important events such as royal weddings. In the early seventeenth century, especially in Lutheran Germany, the desires of patricians and wealthy members of the aspiring bourgeoisie to mark important events in their own lives in similar fashion gave rise to an unprecedentedly large number of occasional compositions. In 1623, the Jena tax collector and financial advisor Burckhard Grossmann published *Angst der Hellen und Friede der Seelen* in fulfillment of a vow he had made following his deliverance from an unnamed calamity in 1616.[18] The overall plan of this extraordinary collection—16 settings of Psalm 116 by Schütz, Schein, Demantius, Michael Praetorius, and a dozen other composers—alludes to the year of Grossmann's "wunderliche Errettung." Compositions for weddings and funerals—the most common commissions, by far—customarily appeared in separate prints commemorating the events for which they were written, although they might appear subsequently in anthologies intended for wider commercial distribution. Schütz, for example, published *Das ist je gewisslich wahr*, a funeral motet for his friend and fellow composer Schein, in January 1631, three months after Schein's death, and later revised it for inclusion in *Geistliche Chor-Music* (1648). Schütz's most famous funeral music, the *Musikalische Exequien* for the funeral of Prince Heinrich Posthumus von Reuss in 1636, is exceptional in its length—approximately 30 minutes of music—and in the intricate theological program that Schütz's text shares with the funeral oration and 22 chorale verses and biblical passages inscribed on the deceased's coffin.

Wedding celebrations were also an important source of income for the instrumentalists of Germany's towns and cities. In the Hanseatic cities of Hamburg and Lübeck, the social status of the families involved determined the size and splendor of the wedding. For each level of society, civic ordinances stipulated the number and type of compositions and instruments allowed, set the amount of fees payable to the musicians, established penalties for overpayment, and required families that desired no wedding music to pay a compensatory fee. In Hamburg, the instrumentalists divided into two groups. The eight *Ratsmusikanten* played for various civil ceremonies and received a small salary from the city council in addition to what they earned performing at the weddings of the city's patrician families. Fifteen *Rollmusikanten*, who were not on the council's payroll but were expected to fill in for the *Ratsmusikanten* as needed, generally played for the city's middle and lower classes. Members of both groups provided music for the wedding ceremony itself,

[18] Ed. Christoph Wolff with Daniel R. Melamed, *Anguish of Hell and Peace of Soul*, Harvard Publications in Music, 18 (Cambridge, MA, 1994).

for the banquet that followed, and finally for dancing, which according to one ordinance was not allowed to continue after two o'clock in the morning.

For such wedding celebrations, for the entertainment of princes at table, and for informal gatherings of amateurs, German composers produced a rich body of dance music. During the first three decades of the century, over a hundred large collections of ensemble dance music issued from German presses. (About 1630, publication of dance music dropped off dramatically—presumably another casualty of the war.) The most common dance types were the pavan, galliard, intrada or *Aufzug*, allemande (sometimes designated simply *Tantz*), and courante. Composers of the period not only continued the sixteenth-century tradition of grouping dances into musically related pairs, they expanded it to create suites of dances. In his *Newe Padouan Intrada Däntz unnd Galliarda* (1611), Paul Peuerl grouped the four dance-types listed in his title into suites unified by common tonality and similar thematic material. The 20 suites of Schein's *Banchetto musicale* (1617) contain, according to the composer's preface, "pavans, galliards, courantes, and allemandes arranged so that they correspond to each other in both *tono* and *inventione*."

The dance repertory, perhaps more than any other, reminds us that Italy was not the only country that influenced early-seventeenth-century German music. Publications such as Demantius's *Sieben und siebentzig newe außerlesene, liebliche, zierliche, polnischer und teutscher Art Täntze* (1601) and Valentin Haussmann's *Venusgarten, darinnen hundert außerlesene gantz liebliche mehrerntheils polnische Täntze* (1602) call attention to the repertory's Polish elements. And with the 312 pieces contained in his *Terpsichore* (1612), Michael Praetorius offered his German compatriots "sundry French dances" as they were "performed by the French dance masters." But the most important foreign influence on German instrumental music of the period came from across the Channel. The two volumes of *Außerlesener Paduanen und Galliarden*, which Zacharius Füllsack and Christian Hildebrand published in Hamburg in 1607 and 1609, present a large body of music by English composers including John Dowland, Anthony Holborne, and William Brade. Brade, who served several German courts as violinist, viol player, and composer and became leader of Hamburg's *Ratsmusikanten* in 1613, published five dance collections between 1609 and 1621.

Musical Societies

German society of the early seventeenth century expressed the breadth and depth of its love of music most tellingly perhaps in the *collegia musica* and other convivial music societies that enthusiastic amateurs founded throughout the Empire. Such associations, which appealed to members of both patrician and bourgeois social classes, provided the opportunity to perform vocal and instrumental music of various kinds. Nuremberg's famous Meistersinger guild, for example, promoted the cultivation of monophonic song and drew its members from the bourgeois artisan class. The various *Kränzleingesellschaften* in the same city, on the other hand, were composed mainly of young men of high birth who came together to perform polyphony.

Regular meetings of *collegia* and informal gatherings in the homes of amateurs created a steady demand for attractive and technically undemanding part music. Hans Leo Hassler's *Lustgarten neuer teutscher Gesäng Balletti Galliarden und Intraden* (1601), Christoph Demantius's *Convivalium concentuum farrago* (1609), Schein's *Musica boscareccia* (3 vols., 1621–28), and numerous similar collections suggest that songs in the strophic, homophonic style associated with villanellas, canzonettas, and dances enjoyed particular favor. Love songs predominate, although political songs and drinking songs also appear, especially in publications intended for student music groups such as Johannes Jeep's *Studentengärtlein* (2 vols., 1605–14), Erasmus Widmann's *Studentenmut* (1622), and Schein's *Studentenschmaus* (1626). For the pious there were collections like Johann Staden's *Hertzens Andachten, geistliche Gesänglein* (1631) and Schein's more ambitious and madrigalian *Fontana d'Israel* (1623).

Some sense of the function and operation of such amateur ensembles emerges from the statutes of a *collegium musicum* established at Prague in 1616, two years before the outbreak there of the Thirty Years' War.[19] Apparently of differing confessions, the eight men who signed the document pledged to avoid discussions of theology and politics (as well as the personal affairs of other people). They agreed to come together every 14 days to perform "motets, madrigals, other songs, and artful compositions." Membership was limited to twelve, although guests were welcome. The members took turns hosting the meetings, which in the summer months began between two and three o'clock and continued until six o'clock, after which the assembled dined together. In winter, meetings began with the meal at eleven o'clock, followed by music-making until three or four o'clock. Unexcused absences incurred a penalty. How long this *collegium* survived remains unclear, although we know that some of its members were forced to leave Bohemia following the Catholic victory at White Mountain just outside Prague in 1620. In any case, the group's statutes attest to the zeal and industry that could imbue amateur music-making and remind us of both the bellicose tenor of the times and the salubrious power of music.

[19] Ernst Rychnovsky, "Ein deutsches Musikkollegium in Prag im Jahre 1616," *Zeitschrift der internationalen Musikgesellschaft*, 6 (1904), 20–24.

Further Reading

The general introductions to German music of the early seventeenth century in Bukofzer 1947, Abraham 1968, Bianconi 1987, Palisca 1991, and Price 1993 complement the brief overview offered above.

Saunders's 1995 study of the imperial court in Vienna provides the finest introduction to Catholic music, liturgy, and patronage. Federhofer 1967, Leuchtmann 1980, and Antonicek 1993 provide additional information on Graz, Munich, and Vienna respectively. Buelow's informative essay on "Protestant North Germany" (1993) focuses on the Hanseatic cities of Hamburg and Lübeck, and Spagnoli 1993 offers a vivid portrait of the electoral court at Dresden during Schütz's tenure there. Although dated and not entirely reliable, Moser 1959 remains the most comprehensive study of Schütz's life and works. For a more up-to-date account of Schütz's life, readers should consult Joshua Rifkin's article on the composer in *New Grove*². Lutheran liturgical practice and its relationship to music form the subject of Moser 1954, Schmidt 1961, Liliencron 1970, and Leaver 1990.

Palisca 1971 examines a famous debate on musical style from the 1640s; Katz 1926 and Braun 1982 present more detailed accounts of seventeenth-century German style distinctions. Boyden 1957, Samuel 1967, and Dahlhaus 1978 discuss German use of the term "concerto." Kirwan-Mott 1981 provides a comprehensive study of the small-scale concerto in Germany, the compositional procedures employed in it, and the cultural milieu in which it developed.

Praetorius 1958–59 is a facsimile of all three volumes of the *Syntagma musicum*. Large portions of the treatise are available in English translation: vol. I, part 1 (on church music) in Fleming 1979; vol. II, part 1 (on instruments) in both Praetorius 1980 and 1986; and vol. III (on terminology, genres, and performance practice) in Praetorius 2004. Hilse 1973 translates the theoretical writings of Schütz's student, Christoph Bernhard.

In Butt 1995, readers will find an insightful overview of the period's keyboard music. Buelow 1993 and Gable 1994 present information on Lutheran wedding music and the town musicians who provided it. The standard work in German on Hamburg's musicians is Krüger 1933. On instrumental ensembles and their music, see Meyer 1934. Gattuso 1989 gives an excellent survey of amateur music groups in Nuremberg during the late sixteenth and early seventeenth centuries.

Abraham, Gerald (ed.). *The Age of Humanism, 1540–1630. New Oxford History of Music*, IV. London, 1968.

Antonicek, Theophil. "Vienna, 1580–1705." In *Man & Music*, III: *The Early Baroque Era: From the Late 16th Century to the 1660s*, ed. Curtis Price, 146–63. London and Englewood Cliffs, NJ, 1993.

Bianconi, Lorenzo. *Music in the Seventeenth Century*. Trans. David Bryant. Cambridge, 1987.

Boyden, David D. "When Is a Concerto Not a Concerto?" *The Musical Quarterly*, 43 (1957), 220–32.

——. *Die Musik des 17. Jahrhunderts*. Neues Handbuch der Musikwissenschaft, 4. Wiesbaden, 1981.

Braun, Werner. *Der Stilwandel in der Musik um 1600*. Erträge der Forschung, 180. Darmstadt, 1982.

Buelow, George J. "Protestant North Germany." In *Man & Music*, III: *The Early Baroque Era: From the Late 16th Century to the 1660s*, ed. Curtis Price, 185–205. London and Englewood Cliffs, NJ, 1993.

BUKOFZER, Manfred F. *Music in the Baroque Era*. New York, 1947.
BUTT, John. "Germany and the Netherlands." In *Keyboard Music Before 1700*, ed. Alexander Silbiger. New York, 1995.
——. *Music Education and the Art of Performance in the German Baroque*. Cambridge, 1994.
DAHLHAUS, Carl. "Über den Motettenbegriff des Michael Praetorius." In *Beiträge zur Musikgeschichte Nordeuropas: Kurt Gudewill zum 65. Geburtstag*, ed. Uwe Haensel, 7–14. Wolfenbüttel, 1978.
FEDERHOFER, Hellmut. *Musikpflege und Musiker am Grazer Habsburgerhof der Erzherzöge Karl und Ferdinand von Innerösterreich (1564–1619)*. Mainz, 1967.
FLEMING, Michael David. "Michael Praetorius, Music Historian: An Annotated Translation of *Syntagma musicum* I, Part I." PhD diss., Washington University, 1979.
GABLE, Frederick K. (ed.). *The Motets of Jacob Praetorius*, II. Recent Researches in the Music of the Baroque Era, 73. Madison, WI, 1994.
GATTUSO, Susan. "16th-Century Nuremberg." In *Man & Music*, II: *The Renaissance From the 1470s to the End of the 16th Century*, ed. Iain Fenlon, 286–303. London and Englewood Cliffs, NJ, 1989.
HILSE, Walter (trans.). "The Treatises of Christoph Bernhard." *The Music Forum*, 3 (1973), 1–196.
KATZ, Erich. "Die musikalischen Stilbegriffe des 17. Jahrhunderts." PhD diss., Albert-Ludwigs-Universität zu Freiburg im Breisgau, 1926.
KIRWAN-MOTT, Anne. *The Small-Scale Sacred Concertato in the Early Seventeenth Century*. 2 vols. Ann Arbor, MI, 1981.
KRÜGER, Liselotte. *Die Hamburgische Musikorganisation im XVII. Jahrhundert*. Sammlung musikwissenschaftlicher Abhandlungen, 12. Strasburg, 1933.
LEAVER, Robin A. "Lutheran Vespers as a Context for Music." In *Church, Stage, and Studio: Music and Its Contexts in Seventeenth-Century Germany*, ed. Paul Walker, 143–61. Studies in Music, 107. Ann Arbor, MI, 1990.
LEUCHTMANN, Horst. "Die Maximilianeische Hofkapelle." In *Um Glauben und Reich: Kurfürst Maximilian I*, ed. Hubert Glaser, 364–75. Munich, 1980.
LILIENCRON, Rochus von. *Liturgisch-musikalische Geschichte der evangelischen Gottesdienste von 1523 bis 1700*. 1893; repr. Hildesheim, 1970.
MEYER, Ernst Hermann. *Die mehrstimmige Spielmusik des 17. Jahrhunderts in Nord- und Mitteleuropa*. Heidelberger Studien zur Musikwissenschaft, 2. Kassel, 1934.
MOSER, Hans Joachim. *Die evangelische Kirchenmusik in Deutschland*. Berlin, 1954.
——. *Heinrich Schütz: His Life and Work*. Trans. from the 2nd rev. edn by Carl F. Pfatteicher. St Louis, 1959.
PALISCA, Claude V. "Marco Scacchi's Defense of Modern Music (1649)." In *Words and Music, The Scholar's View: In Honor of A. Tillman Merritt*, ed. Laurence Berman, 189–235. Cambridge, MA, 1971.
——. *Baroque Music*. 3rd edn. Englewood Cliffs, NJ, 1991.
PRAETORIUS, Michael. *Syntagma musicum*. 3 vols. 1615–19; facs. Kassel, 1958–59.
——. *The Syntagma musicum of Michael Praetorius: Volume Two, De organographia, First and Second Parts*. Trans. Harold Blumenfeld. New York, 1980.
——. *Syntagma musicum ii: De organographia, Parts I and II*. Trans. and ed. David Z. Crookes. Early Music Series, 7. Oxford, 1986.
——. *Syntagma musicum iii*. Trans. and ed. Jeffery Kite-Powell. New York, 2004.
PRICE, Curtis. "Music, Style and Society." In *Man & Music*, III: *The Early Baroque Era: From the Late 16th Century to the 1660s*, ed. Curtis Price, 1–22. London and Englewood Cliffs, NJ, 1993.

RYCHNOVSKY, Ernst. "Ein deutsches Musikkollegium in Prag im Jahre 1616." *Zeitschrift der internationalen Musikgesellschaft*, 6 (1904), 20–24.

SAMUEL, Harold E. "Michael Praetorius on Concertato Style." In *Cantors at the Crossroads: Essays on Church Music in Honor of Walter E. Buszin*, ed. Johannes Riedel, 95–109. St. Louis, 1967.

SAUNDERS, Steven. *Cross, Sword and Lyre: Sacred Music at the Imperial Court of Ferdinand II of Habsburg (1619–1637)*. Oxford, 1995.

SCHMIDT, Eberhard. *Der Gottesdienst am Kurfürstlichen Hofe zu Dresden: Ein Beitrag zur liturgischen Traditionsgeschichte von Johann Walter bis zu Heinrich Schütz*. Göttingen, 1961.

SPAGNOLI, Gina. "Dresden at the Time of Heinrich Schütz." In *Man & Music*, III: *The Early Baroque Era: From the Late 16th Century to the 1660s*, ed. Curtis Price, 164–84. London and Englewood Cliffs, NJ, 1993.

WOLFF, Christoph, with Daniel R. Melamed (eds.). *Anguish of Hell and Peace of Soul: A 1623 Collection of Sixteen Motets on Psalm 116 by Michael Praetorius, Heinrich Schütz and Others*. Harvard Publications in Music, 18. Cambridge, MA, 1994.

19

THE REFORMATION AND MUSIC

Robin A. Leaver

AT the end of the First World War, Karl Straube, the recently appointed *Thomaskantor* in Leipzig, wrote the following in a letter to the young musicologist Wilibald Gurlitt:

> I see hardly anything in Protestant art of the age of the Reformation that I could not also find in the musical masters of Catholic circles. At least, I can find no difference between Joh. Walter, Senfl, and Hassler (all more or less under Lutheran influence) on the one hand, and Orlando di Lasso or Gallus on the other hand. Only much later does the spiritually form-giving influence of Protestantism begin, perhaps starting with Sweelinck and Schütz and becoming sharply manifest in Bach. In regard to these three one can really speak of a distinctly Protestant essence. I have been able to find nothing of the sort among those musicians contemporary with Luther.[1]

Straube suggests that the impact of the Reformation on music was minimal and that the development of overtly Protestant music did not really occur until the era of Renaissance and Reformation had given way to the early Baroque. The implication is that not until after Catholicism had redefined itself at the Council of Trent, and the first-generation Reforming movement had been displaced by the second-generation Protestant establishment, that specifically Protestant music becomes distinguishable.

There is substance to this opinion in that, in purely musical terms, distinctions between Catholic and Protestant music in the sixteenth century are sometimes difficult to establish. But the situation was in fact more complex than Straube suggested. Part of the problem is the common assumption that the basic historical and theological impact of the Reformation was substantially antithetical to all that preceded it. But when this model is applied to the music of the period, the theory is often at variance with the evidence, since much of the music was used

[1] The letter, dated 10 Sept. 1918, is given both in facs. and trans. in Friedrich Blume (ed.), *Protestant Church Music: A History* (New York, 1974), 496–503 at 499.

interchangeably within worship on both sides of the Catholic /Protestant divide. There were, of course, strong antithetical elements in the Reforming movement, especially those influenced by Zwingli and Calvin, but the Reformation in general was a catalytic process of change rather than a cataclysmic programme of substitution. The Reformation movement as a whole was not simply the replacement of the old by the new (though it was often conceived of as such), but rather a complex process of connection and disconnection in which the old and the new were combined. Much of the music of the Reformation was thus a synthesis of continuity from the past with the discontinuity of the present.[2]

The first generation of the Reforming movement was marked by ecclesiastical ambiguity. Certainly there was an obvious theological difference between the biblicism of the German Reformers on the one hand and the juristic nature of pre-Tridentine Latin Catholicism on the other, but there was a sense in which both sides of the debate were concerned with maintaining the unity of the Church. Even though Luther had been condemned as a heretic at the Diet of Worms in 1521, he and other Reformers did not consider the matter closed. They saw themselves as reformers *within* the one catholic Church and persistently called for a General Council of the Church to resolve the matters in dispute. The concern of Luther and his colleagues at this early period was not to create a new Protestant Church, in contradistinction to the Catholic Church, but rather to reform the one Church. This ecclesiastical ambiguity continued while efforts were made to find a synthesis between the disparate theologies within the one ecclesiastical entity, such as at the colloquy of Regensburg of 1541. But this ecclesiastical ambivalence evaporated following the Peace of Augsburg of 1555, which effectively polarized the German territories into Catholic or Lutheran areas according to the principle "Cuius regio, eius religio," the religious affiliation of the rulers determining the religious confession of the areas over which they ruled. The uncompromising decrees of the Council of Trent (1545–63) further clarified the polarity between Catholicism and Protestantism as being both theological and ecclesiastical, and therefore the one could not accommodate the other.

In the ambiguous ecclesiastical climate of this pre-Tridentine period, musicians (among others) appeared to vacillate between Catholicism and Protestantism by accepting successive church or court appointments that involved them first in the unreformed rites of Latin Catholicism, then in the reformed Latin and German liturgies of Lutheranism, or vice versa. In this context, as Straube implied, the same polyphonic settings of the Ordinary of the Mass, as well as polyphonic antiphons and motets, were to be heard in both unreformed and reformed liturgical worship. It was very much a period of transition, in which there was uncertainty with regard to the future resolution of the controverted issues. There was therefore a commonality of music heard in the worship of both sides of the continuing debate, but

[2] This dialectic between continuity and discontinuity is explored in Robin A. Leaver, "Christian Liturgical Music in the Wake of the Protestant Reformation," in *Sacred Sound and Social Change: Liturgical Music in Jewish and Christian Experience*, ed. Lawrence A. Hoffman and Janet R. Walton (Notre Dame, IN, 1992), 124–44.

at the same time new elements had begun to appear that could only be identified with the theology and practice of the Lutheran Reformation. Contrary to Straube, "the spiritually form-giving influence of Protestantism" begins not with the music of the seventeenth century but with the music composed during the earliest years of the Reformation of the sixteenth century.

Consequences of Theological Change

As can be demonstrated from many different periods of ecclesiastical history, a theological shift will ultimately affect the immediate context and content of worship. For example, in the medieval Church there were two major theological developments that were to have far-reaching consequences for the liturgy of Catholicism. One was the intensification of devotion to the Virgin Mary in particular and to the saints in general, and the other was the sharpened emphasis on the doctrine of transubstantiation, which received its classic formulation in the later thirteenth century. The theological focus on the saints as sources of influence on the lives of believers led to the development of pilgrimage routes to and from shrines dedicated to particular saints, which criss-crossed the map of Europe. The growth of pilgrimages was paralleled by an expansion of monasticism, which provided the necessary hostels for food and shelter along the major pilgrimage routes. But these monastic institutions were more than hostels: they were primarily worshiping and working communities. As the pilgrimages brought more and more travelers, so the monasteries were expanded and larger churches were built. These impressive buildings provided the immediate context for the daily celebration of the Mass and the Offices. The arts flourished in these new churches. The plastic arts were employed for three-dimensional representations of the saints that were honored in these impressive structures (or whose mortal remains were housed within them), as well as being incorporated into the fabric of their pillars and vaulting. The cult of the saints was also given alternate visual form in numerous paintings, largely stylized images that usually included the symbolic artifacts that brought about the particular saint's martyrdom. Although many altarpieces still centered on the crucifixion of Christ, there was a marked visual emphasis on the Virgin Mary and her significance for the doctrine of the Incarnation, which undergirded the understanding of transubstantiation in the Mass.[3] Among the musical consequences of these theological developments was the growth of polyphonic masses and antiphons for the feasts of the saints, and especially for the feasts of the Virgin Mary and the daily Lady Mass. There was a particular intensification of vocal polyphony after the technique of stone-vaulting was mastered in the twelfth century. The new church buildings, with their choral foundations, attached to expanded monasteries along the pilgrimage routes, provided large and resonant spaces in which the music of the Offices and the Mass could soar in waves of overlapping sound, a development that

[3] See, e.g., Barbara G. Lane, *The Altar and Altarpiece: Sacramental Themes in Early Netherlandish Painting* (New York, 1984).

was to reach its climax in the Franco-Flemish polyphony of the late fifteenth and early sixteenth centuries. Liturgical music in this context became an aural embellishment to the celebration of the Mass and of devotion to the saints.

The theological shifts of the sixteenth-century Reformation, arguably more fundamental than those of the previous few centuries, created far-reaching changes in the context and content of worship. Many of these changes appeared to be reactionary, since the principal targets of the Reformers were the cult of the saints, the primacy of the Mass, the doctrine of transubstantiation, monasticism, and the music associated with them. The rejection of the cult of the saints led to an almost universal iconoclasm within various strands of the Reforming movement.[4] The exception was Lutheranism, which fostered a new approach to the visual arts as vehicles for proclaiming the biblical Gospel.[5] The ecclesiastical architecture of the previous centuries, which gave prominence to high altar, lofty arches, and a lively reverberant acoustic that encouraged a highly-developed polyphony, were all called in question by the new theological perspectives of the Reformers. For example, on 26 February 1538 Martin Luther is reported to have said:

> Extraordinary buildings [that is, large cathedrals] . . . aren't suitable for listening to sermons. Good, modest churches with low arches are the best for preachers and listeners, for the ultimate object of these buildings is not the bellowing and bawling of choristers but the Word of God and its proclamation. The cathedral of St. Peter in Rome and the cathedrals in Cologne and Ulm are very large but inappropriate.[6]

Luther was concerned with the function of liturgical buildings and the music heard within them. His fundamental criterion, therefore, was audibility, and he thought that church buildings and church music that produced an indistinct sound undermined the clarity of the proclamation of the Gospel.

[4] See Bryan D. Mangrum and Giuseppe Scavizzi (eds.), *A Reformation Debate: Karlstadt, Emser, and Eck on Sacred Images* (Toronto, 1998); Lee Palmer Wandel, "Envisioning God: Image and Liturgy in Reformation Zurich," *Sixteenth Century Journal*, 24 (1993), 21–40; and David Willis-Watkins, "The Second Commandment and Church Reform: The Colloquy of St. Germain-en-Laye, 1562," *Studies in Reformed Theology and History*, 2/2 (Spring 1994), 1–80.

[5] See Carl C. Christensen, *Art and the Reformation in Germany* (Athens, OH, 1979); John W. Cook, "Picturing Theology: Martin Luther and Lucas Cranach," in *Art and Religion: Faith, Form and Reform: 1984 Paine Lectures in Religion*, ed. Osmund Overby (Columbia, MO, 1986), 22–39. Straube, in his letter to Gurlitt in Blume, *Protestant Church Music*, 501, acknowledged that "the graphic arts . . . have a decidedly Protestant work of art in Dürer's figures of the Apostles."

[6] 26 Feb. 1538; *Luther's Works: American Edition*, ed. Jaroslav Pelikan and Helmut T. Lehmann (St. Louis and Philadelphia, 1955–86) [hereafter *LW*] LIV: 272; *D. Martin Luthers Werke: Kritische Gesamtausgabe* (Weimar, 1883–1983) [Weimarer Ausgabe; hereafter *WA*], *Tischreden* no. 3781.

Reservations About the Role of Music in Worship

Long before the Reformers expressed some hesitation about the function of music in worship, humanist scholars of the early sixteenth century had frequently been critical of the embellishments of much liturgical music, and were concerned for the audibility of the liturgical text, which, in their view, should not be compromised by musical complication. Although this was a natural outgrowth of their exploration of the "new learning," these Renaissance humanists were innovative on the one hand but on the other were also part of a long aesthetic tradition that was suspicious of the power and effects of music. For example, in the first half of the twelfth century Aelred, Cistercian abbot of Rievaulx Abbey in Yorkshire, wrote:

> How comes it that the Church also has so many organs and cymbals? To what purpose is that terrible blowing of bellows, imitating rather the clash of thunder than the sweetness of the human voice? One sings low, another high, a third higher still, while a fourth puts in every now and then some supplemental notes. . . . The whole body is agitated by theatrical gestures, the lips are twisted, the eyes roll, the shoulders are shrugged, and the fingers bent responsive to every note; and this ridiculous trifling is called religion, and where it is carried out most frequently, there it is maintained that God is served most honorably. . . . you would think they had come not to prayer, but to a spectacle, not to an oratory, but to a theatre.[7]

Similarly, the fourteenth-century reformer John Wycliffe frequently criticized elaborate liturgical music in his treatises and sermons, an attitude that was characteristic of Lollardy in general.

Among the humanists of the sixteenth century Erasmus of Rotterdam was clearly the most influential. He received part of his early education in Deventer from the Brethren of the Common Life, a reforming movement within Catholicism that laid great stress on education and the cultivation of individual spiritual life, the *devotio moderna*. This concern with inward religion tended to foster a critical stance with regard to what was seen as the hollow performance of outward rites and ceremonies. Thus, in his *Annotationes* on the New Testament, first published in 1516 and reissued with revisions until the final form of 1535,[8] Erasmus made the following comment on 1 Cor. 14: 19:

> We have introduced to the churches an elaborate, theatrical kind of music, a turbulent chattering of different voices, the like of which, in my opinion, was never heard in the theatres of the Greeks and Romans. Everywhere

[7] *Speculum charitas*, book 2, chap. 23; *Patrologia cursus completus: Patrologiae Latinae*, ed. Jacques-Paul Migne (Paris, 1844–1855), CXCV: 571; trans. Robert F. Hayburn, *Papal Legislation on Sacred Music 95 A.D. to 1977 A.D.* (Collegeville, MN, 1979), 19. Other similar citations can be found in Hayburn.

[8] On the publication history, see *Erasmus' Annotations on the New Testament: The Gospels*, ed. Anne Reeve (London, 1986).

> resounds with horns, trumpets, pan-pipes, harps, and with these, human voices contend.... Into a church—as if to a theatre—people rush for the sake of their ears' enchantment. And to this end huge salaries are paid out to support organists [*organorum opifices*], herds of boys whose whole youth is spent in thoroughly learning this sort of snarling while at the same time they learn nothing worthwhile .... Now those who are too dense to learn the musical art, think that a feast day is not given the attention it deserves unless they use the depraved sort of singing which they call Fauxbourdon.... Moreover, although sober music has been received into the church for this purpose [Gregorian chant], that the meaning of the words may flow more effectively into the minds of the hearers, some people think this is a fine thing too: if one or two people, mixed in with the rest, accomplish the result, by their resonant booming, that no word may be distinguished.[9]

This Erasmian influence was strongly felt throughout the Reforming movement across Europe over succeeding generations. For instance, early in 1522 a Latin pamphlet appeared in Wittenberg, reflecting more the views of Andreas Carlstadt than those of Luther, who was then in exile in the Wartburg. It bore the title *De veteri et novicio Deo*.[10] William Turner translated the work into English, published in 1534, in which is the following:

> O how goodly ministers and services are daily done to almighty God? How goodly shrill songs do sound daily? Here ye young musicians do sing songs in five parts ... they do strain their voices above their reach, as though they would be strangled. Within a little while after they do let their voice fall so low that thou wouldest ween that they did weep. One man singeth on his part, another singeth on another part, and by and by afterward they wax dumb. Anon after one beginneth to crow as it were a hen, which would lay eggs, and then followeth a sound of a full voice, as it were the sound of a drone or of a leaden pipe ... they do howl so piteously ... much like the howling of cats.... But what shall I say of the gospel when it is sung?[11]

[9] Desiderius Erasmus, *Opera Omnia*, ed. Joannes Clericus (Leiden, 1703–6), VII: 731–732; trans. Mechthild O'Mara, CSJ. See also Clement A. Miller, "Erasmus on Music," *The Musical Quarterly*, 52 (1966), 332–49; Helmut Fleinghaus, *Die Musikanschauung des Erasmus von Rotterdam* (Regensburg, 1984).

[10] *De veteri et novicio Deo, de veteri et nova fide doctrinaque, sive Origo idolatriae* (Wittenberg, [1522]), a trans. by Hartmann Dulichius of *Vom alten und neuen Gott, Glauben und Lere* ([Basel], 1521), by "Judas Nazarei," formerly attributed to Joachim Vadianus [von Watt] among others.

[11] *A Worke entytled Of ye Olde God [and] the Newe, of the Olde Faythe [and] the Newe* (London, 1534), sig. Miii^{r-v}; spelling and punctuation modernized. For the Latin, see *De vetero et novicio Deo*, sig. Fii^{v}. The work exercised a strong influence on early English Reformers, especially William Tyndale and Robert Barnes, who took over passages into their writings almost without alteration; see William A. Clebsch, *England's Earliest Protestants 1520–1535* (New Haven, 1964), 253. It also exerted an influence on other writings of its English translator, William Turner; see Celia Hughes, "Two Sixteenth-Century Northern Protestants: John Bradford and William Turner," *Bulletin of the John Rylands Library*, 66 (1983), 104–38, esp. 130–31;

But at least a generation earlier, around the beginning of the sixteenth century, the later style of Josquin des Prez had begun to mirror this humanist concern: the complexity of his earlier polyphonic style gave way to greater restraint and economy with regard to the declamation of the verbal text in his compositional technique. Adrianus Petit Coclico, who claimed to be a pupil of Josquin's, reported that this high regard for the text was also fundamental to his teaching:

> My teacher Josquin . . . never gave a lecture on music . . . but taught [his pupils] the rules in a few words through practical application in the course of singing. And as soon as he saw that his pupils were all grounded in singing, had a good enunciation and knew how to embellish melodies and fit the text to the music, then he taught them the perfect and imperfect intervals and the different methods of inventing counterpoint against plainsong.[12]

Given this emphasis on the text, Luther's high regard for the music of the northern French composer is understandable. For example, toward the end of 1531 the Reformer expressed the view: "God preached the Gospel through music, too, as may be seen in Josquin, all of whose compositions flow freely, gently, and cheerfully, are not forced or cramped by rules, and are like the song of the finch."[13]

Primary Reformation Concerns

The heart of Reformation theology was summarized by three brief Latin formulae: *sola scriptura*, *sola fidei*, and *sola gratia*. Together they encapsulated the Protestant understanding of the Christian Gospel, that is: a Christian's standing before God depends not on the authority of the Church but on the authority of *scripture*; that salvation is offered and received as a gift by *faith* and not as a reward for a worthy life; and that this salvation is from beginning to end the work of God's *grace*. A fourth dimension was added with the doctrine of the "priesthood of all believers," which was directly antithetical to the particular priesthood of Catholicism. These four theological concepts were translated into the practical concerns of providing Bibles, catechisms, liturgies, and congregational songs for emerging Protestantism, and each one had distinct musical consequences.

Whitney R. D. Jones, *William Turner, Tudor Naturalist, Physician and Divine* (London, 1988), esp. 137–97.

[12] Adrianus Petit Coclico, *Compendium musices* (Nuremberg, 1552; facs. ed. Manfred F. Bukofzer, Kassel, 1954), sig. Bi^{v}–Bii^{r}; trans. Patrick Macey, "Josquin des Prez," §9, *New Grove Dictionary of Music and Musicians*, 2nd edn, ed. Stanley Sadie and John Tyrrell (London, 2001), XIII: 228–29.

[13] *LW* LIV: 129–30; *WA*, *Tischreden* no. 1258.

The Bible

The *sola scriptura* principle gave rise to the explosion of vernacular Bibles, published in many European languages during the first half of the sixteenth century. Although the motives were different, this activity can be seen as the natural outcome of Renaissance humanism. The "new learning" of the humanists involved studying literary and other source documents in their original languages, which included the Hebrew and Greek Testaments. The Greek New Testament that Erasmus published in 1516 had a profound effect on the course of the Reformation, since Luther and other translators used it as a primary source for vernacular versions of the New Testament. The continuity of the Protestant *sola scriptura* principle with earlier humanism can be seen, for example, in Sebastian Virdung's *Musica getutscht* (Basel, 1511), a treatise founded on biblical authority in which biblical citations are given in German rather than Latin.[14]

Although the *sola scriptura* principle did lead to significant examples of discontinuity with the theology and practice of Catholicism, there was a significant continuity in the singing of biblical lections in the reformed orders of the Eucharist and daily Office in Lutheranism and Anglicanism. In the *Deutsche Messe* of 1526 Luther not only directed that the epistle and gospel should continue to be sung but also gave his own versions of the lectionary tones: the epistle in the eighth tone and the gospel in the fifth tone.[15] Similarly, in the order of Matins in the Anglican 1549 Prayer Book there is the following rubric: "And (to the end that the people may the better hear) in such places where they do sing, there shall the lessons be sung in a plain tune after the manner of distinct reading: and likewise the epistle and gospel."[16] Here the tradition of Catholicism, the ideals of humanism, and the theology of the Reformation coincide in the concern for the audibility of the sung biblical text, the only difference being the Reformers' use of the vernacular.

In contrast, the *sola scriptura* principle led to discontinuity from Catholic tradition with the abandonment of non-biblical (or abbreviated biblical) liturgical texts in favour of substantial use of scripture. In both Luther's *Deutsche Messe* (1526) and Cranmer's *Book of Common Prayer* (1549) the liturgical introit was replaced by a complete vernacular psalm, sung to the first psalm tone in the former,[17] and to the eighth psalm tone in Marbeck's musical version of the latter.[18] Similarly, in the Communion service of the 1549 Prayer Book traditional offertories and communions, with their references to the offering of the Mass, were replaced by biblical sentences exhorting almsgiving and faith. These were given in syllabic monody in

[14] See *Musica getutscht: A Treatise on Musical Instruments (1511) by Sebastian Virdung*, trans. and ed. Beth Bullard (Cambridge, 1993), 8.

[15] *LW* LIII: 72–78; *Evangelischer Gottesdienst: Quellen zu seiner Geschichte*, ed. Wolfgang Herbst (Göttingen, 1992), 78–82.

[16] Cited in F. E. Brightman, *The English Rite* (London, 1921), I: 136. The rubric was repeated in the 1552 Prayer Book.

[17] *LW* LIII: 69–71; Herbst, *Evangelischer Gottesdienst*, 76–78.

[18] See John Marbeck, *The Booke of Common Praier Noted, 1550*, facs. ed. Robin A. Leaver (Appleford, 1980), 65–66.

Marbeck's *Booke of Common Praier Noted* (1550)[19] and in simple four-part settings in the Wanley manuscript partbooks dating from the same period.[20]

The musical application of the *sola scriptura* principle also led, in the interests of audibility, to a simplified polyphony and an increasing tendency towards homophony, trends already evident in the first edition of Johann Walter's so-called *Chorgesangbuch* (Wittenberg, 1524), and, in later generations, continued in the Anglican anthem and Lutheran *Spruchmotette*, musical settings of (usually) biblical texts, frequently from the Psalms or the Gospels.

The catechism

The *sola fidei* principle led to the formulation of catechisms in which the basic tenets of Protestant faith were expounded. In the *Deutsche Messe* of 1526 Luther had registered the need for a basic catechism; three years later he published his *Large Catechism* for pastors and *Small Catechism* for laypeople, especially children (both Wittenberg, 1529). Other Reformation churches produced their own catechisms, such as that of Calvin (Geneva, 1541), the catechism preceding the order of Confirmation in the first Anglican Prayer Book (London, 1549), and the Heidelberg Catechism (1563). The common practice in Lutheran, Calvinist (or Reformed), and Anglican churches was for the respective catechism to be taught within the context of reformed Sunday Vespers, or the preaching service that had replaced Sunday Vespers. Thus the teaching of the essence of the Protestant faith was given within a service of worship that included some form of music. In Reformed churches the music was minimal, comprising simple, unaccompanied singing of vernacular metrical psalms. In most Anglican parish churches the practice was similar, except in cathedrals and perhaps some parish churches where an anthem and organ music might have been heard at these catechizing services of worship.

In contrast, the music associated with the teaching of the catechism in Lutheran churches was more expansive.[21] Luther wrote specific hymns which became associated with each of the six[22] parts of the Catechism:[23]

[19] Ibid., 68–69, 71.

[20] On the Wanley partbooks (*GB-Ob* Mus. Sch. e. 420–422), see James Wrightson, *The "Wanley" Manuscripts: A Critical Commentary* (New York, 1989).

[21] See Robin A. Leaver, "Lutheran Vespers as a Context for Music," in *Church, Stage, and Studio: Music and Its Contexts in Seventeenth-Century Germany*, ed. Paul Walker (Ann Arbor, MI, 1990), 143–61.

[22] There is some confusion over the number of main sections of the *Small Catechism*, in some sources cited as five and in others as six. Luther was not entirely consistent himself. The *Large Catechism* (1529) was published first and structured in five main parts: Commandments, Creed, Lord's Prayer, Baptism, Eucharist. The *Small Catechism*, issued later the same year, included an extra section on repentance/confession in between the sections on Baptism and Eucharist, a subject treated in an appendix to the Eucharist in the *Large Catechism*.

[23] See Robin A. Leaver, *"Goostly Psalmes and Spirituall Songes": English and Dutch Metrical Psalmes from Coverdale to Utenhove, 1535–1566* (Oxford, 1991), 10–11; idem, "Luther's Catechism Hymns," *Lutheran Quarterly*, 11 (1997), 397–421, 12 (1998), 79–98, 160–80, 303–23.

Ten Commandments	*Dies sind der heilgen zehn Gebot* (1524)
Creed	*Wir Glauben all an einen Gott* (1524)
Lord's Prayer	*Vater unser im Himmelreich* (1539)
Baptism	*Christ unser Herr zum Jordan kam* (1524)
Repentance	*Aus tiefer Not schrei ich zu dir* (1524)
Eucharist	*Jesus Christus unser Heiland, der von uns* (1524)

The melodies associated with these hymns formed the basis for many congregational, choral, and organ settings by Lutheran composers, from the sixteenth century onwards, for use at Vespers when the substance of the catechism was being taught.

The liturgy

The *sola gratia* principle led to a re-evaluation of the theological presuppositions undergirding worship in general and the Mass in particular. Traditional Catholic teaching referred to the Mass in terms of *sacrificium*, *opus bonum*, and *meritum* (sacrifice, good work, and merit), concepts that focused on human activity, the offering of the Mass to God by the priest on behalf of the Church. In contrast the *sola gratia* principle meant that the eucharist was seen in terms of *beneficium*, *testamentum*, and *donum* (favor, bequest, and gift), concepts that expressed divine activity, God's gracious gift of forgiveness offered and given to his gathered people. This was the central argument of Luther's treatise *De captivitate Babylonica ecclesiae* [On the Babylonian Captivity of the Church] (Wittenburg, 1520) in which he dismantled Catholic sacramental theology, arguing from scripture rather than from the councils and decrees of the Church. From this new theological position with regard to worship, two different courses of action were possible: reform of existing rites or the development of new forms of worship. Luther, with his great respect for the continuity of authentic Christian tradition, chose the former.

In the *Formula Missae* of 1523[24] Luther wrote:

> We therefore wish to first assert: It is not now nor ever has been our intention to abolish the liturgical service of God (*cultus Dei*) completely, but rather to purify the one that is now in use from the wretched accretions which corrupt it and to point out an evangelical use.[25]

His focus of attention was the Canon of the Mass:

> What I am speaking of is the canon, that abominable concoction drawn from the everyone's sewer and cesspool. The mass became a sacrifice . . . Whereupon the mass began to be a priestly monopoly . . . And what shall I say of the

[24] *LW* LIII: 19–40; *WA* XII: 205–20; the Latin, with Speratus' German trans. of 1524, is given in in Herbst, *Evangelischer Gottesdienst*, 16–49.

[25] *LW* LIII: 20; Herbst, *Evangelischer Gottesdienst*, 18.

> external additions of vestments, vessels, candles, palls, of organs and all the music, and of images?[26]

Luther is not here objecting to liturgical music *per se* but to music being utilized to undergird and embellish the medieval understanding of the Mass as a sacrifice, as enshrined in the Canon. His solution was to remove the Canon altogether, replacing it with the *Verba testamenti* or Words of Institution alone, and eliminating everything else that spoke of the eucharist in terms of sacrifice, especially the offertory.[27] But the remainder of the Mass was mostly left intact:

> Those who added the Kyrie eleison also did well . . . [and] the Angelic Hymn *Gloria in excelsis: et in terra pax*, the graduals, the alleluias, the Nicene Creed, the Sanctus, the Agnus Dei, and the *communio* . . . All these are unobjectionable, especially the ones that are sung *de tempore* or on Sundays.[28]

The retention of the Latin Ordinary in Luther's reformed Mass thus encouraged the continued use of mass settings composed for the unreformed rite.

The *Formula Missae* was translated into German, and from 1524 various reformed vernacular Masses, in which its influence is traceable, began to appear in such places as Strasburg and Nuremberg.[29] The role of music in these German Masses was generally fairly limited. An exception was the *Deutsch euangelisch Messze* (Allstedt, 1524), the work of the radical Reformer Thomas Müntzer, who made extensive use of Gregorian chant.[30] The *Deutsch euangelisch Messze* was a conservative revision accomplished by a fiery, left-wing Reformer. It is therefore an open question whether it represented Müntzer's final conclusions with regard to the liturgy or an interim form that would have been replaced by a more radical revision had he not been executed in 1525. What is certain is that the *Deutsch euangelisch Messze* was intended as a replacement for the unreformed Latin Mass, and its music was confined to unaccompanied monody.

Towards the end of 1525 Luther drew up a vernacular Mass, the *Deutsche messe* (Wittenberg, 1526),[31] but his intention was to supplement rather than replace the Latin *Formula Missae*.[32] The *Deutsche Messe* was designed for villages and small

[26] *LW* LIII: 21–22; Herbst, *Evangelischer Gottesdienst*, 18, 20.

[27] See Bryan Spinks, *Luther's Liturgical Criteria and His Reform of the Canon of the Mass* (Bramcote, 1982); Robin A. Leaver, "Theological Consistency, Liturgurgical Integrity, and Musical Hermeneutic in Luther's Liturgical Reforms," *Lutheran Quarterly*, 9 (1995), 117–38.

[28] *LW* LIII: 20–21; Herbst, *Evangelischer Gottesdienst*, 18.

[29] See Julius Smend, *Die evangelischen deutschen Messen bis zu Luthers Deutscher Messe* (Göttingen, 1896; repr. Nieuwoop, 1967); Friedrich H. Hubert, *Die Strassburger liturgischen Ordnungen im Zeitalter der Reformation* (Göttingen, 1900).

[30] *Thomas Müntzer: Deutsche Evangelische Messe, 1524*, facs. ed. Siegfried Bräuer (Berlin, 1988); *Thomas Müntzer: Schriften und Briefe: Kritische Gesamtausgabe*, ed. Paul Kirn and Günther Franz (Gütersloh, 1968), 161–206; see also Karl Honemeyer, *Thomas Müntzer und Martin Luther: Ihr Ringen um die Musik des Gottesdienstes* (Berlin, 1974).

[31] *Martin Luther: Deutsche Messe, 1526*, facs. ed. Johannes Wolf (Kassel, 1934); *LW* LIII: 61–90; *WA* XIX: 72–113, also in Herbst, *Evangelischer Gottesdienst*, 69–87.

[32] "It is not now my intention to abrogate or change this service [the *Formula Missae*]"; *LW* LIII: 62–63; Herbst, *Evangelischer Gottesdienst*, 70.

towns where there were neither Latin schools nor universities. The main differences between Luther's two liturgical orders, apart from language, were the expanded role of hymnody and the musical implications of the *Formula Missae* that were fully worked out with specific notation in the *Deutsche Messe*. But the traditional structure of the Mass remained much the same, although, like the *Formula Missae*, the content was theologically reinterpreted. The traditional five parts of the Ordinary were retained,[33] except that in the *Deutsche Messe* Luther developed the principle that hymnic versions of them could also be sung by the congregation. In the course of the following decades particular chorales came into almost universal use throughout Lutheran Germany:

Kyrie	*Kyrie, Gott Vater in ewigkeit* (Anon. Naumburg, 1537)
Gloria	*Allein Gott in der Höh sei Ehr* (Decius, 1522)
Credo	*Wir glauben all an einen Gott* (Luther, 1524)[34]
Sanctus	*Jesaja dem Propheten das geschah* (Luther, 1526)
Agnus Dei	*Christe, du Lamm Gottes* (Luther, 1525/28), or
	O Lamm Gottes, unschuldig (Decius, 1522)

In the same way that the catechism chorales were inspirations for composition, the melodies of these liturgical hymns were the basis for numerous choral and organ settings for eucharistic use. The Gloria hymn, *Allein Gott in der Höh sei Ehr*, was sung almost every Sunday, which accounts for the growing number of organ chorale preludes on the melody that appeared with the passing of time.

As the various regional Lutheran churches were brought into being across Germany, most of their church orders for towns and cities prescribed a macaronic liturgy, a conflation of the provisions of Luther's Latin and German liturgies. This fostered the formation of a diverse musical tradition in which much of the music of the "old" Church, choral settings of the Ordinary, continued to be sung alongside the music of the "new" Church, congregational hymnody and the music derived from it, a tradition that was in large measure made possible by the Lutheran retention of the structure of the Mass, and with it the various elements of the Ordinary.[35]

In the early Edwardian years in England there were strong similarities between Lutheran liturgical reform and the emergence of the Anglican *Book of Common Prayer*: both included revisions of the Catholic Mass. The first steps in English liturgical reform were more conservative than Luther's *Formula Missae*, a process that began with addition rather than subtraction. In the year following Edward VI's accession to the English throne, *The Order of the Communion* was published

[33] The Preface was omitted from the *Deutsche Messe*. The German Sanctus was therefore appointed to be sung at the beginning, and the German Agnus Dei at the end, of the distribution of communion.

[34] *Wir glauben* was also employed as a Catechism chorale (see above); Robin A. Leaver, "Luther's Catechism Hymns, 3: Creed," *Lutheran Quarterly*, 12 (1998), 79–88.

[35] Although the Ordinary was retained in Lutheran liturgies, not all five parts were included in every service. Only the Kyrie and Gloria, the Lutheran *Missa*, were regularly used; the Latin Credo, Sanctus, and Agnus Dei were sung less frequently.

(London, 1548). This was a brief liturgical rite in English—comprising exhortations, confession and absolution, scripture sentences, prayer, and words of distribution—inserted into the Latin Mass after the Canon, in between the Pax and Agnus Dei. The essential nature of the Mass was unchanged, and therefore polyphonic settings of the Latin Ordinary could continue to be sung.

Later the same year that *The Order of the Communion* was published, work on the new English liturgy was completed, and the first *Book of Common Prayer* began to appear in print from the early spring of 1549, being authorized for use from the following Feast of Pentecost, 9 June 1549. The eucharistic rite in the new vernacular Prayer Book, "The Supper of the Lorde, and the holy Communion, commonly called the Masse," like Luther's *Deutsche Messe*, used the vernacular throughout, but its structure and content represented a more conservative revision of the Latin Mass than Luther's *Formula Missae*. Major changes included the replacement of the traditional introit by a complete psalm, and the deletion of the gradual. Unlike Lutheran liturgies, the Canon was not replaced by the Words of Institution. Instead the new Prayer Book prescribed a substantial eucharistic prayer, akin to the Canon of the Mass, in which language relating to the sacrifice and oblation of the Mass was transmuted into expressions of self-offering and commitment on the part of the worshippers. Apart from these changes, the structure of the traditional Mass remained the same, and the Ordinary was retained intact. This meant that it was possible for earlier polyphonic masses, composed for the unreformed Latin Mass, to be adapted to the English texts of the 1549 Prayer Book and sung within the new vernacular liturgy. The Wanley partbooks contain two such adaptations of five-part Latin masses by John Taverner, the *Missa "Christe Jesu"* (or Small Devotion Mass) and *Missa sine nomine* (or Meane Mass).[36] Like many English Latin masses, these Taverner masses omitted the Kyrie,[37] a deficency that was supplied by the first item in the Wanley partbooks, a separate Prayer-Book Kyrie that could be sung with those adapted Latin masses that lacked a Kyrie. The Wanley partbooks also include three anonymous settings of the English text of the complete Ordinary that appear to have been composed in a basic homophonic style for the 1549 Prayer-Book Communion service.[38]

But before a basic corpus of English mass settings could be compiled, the English Prayer Book was reissued in a radical revision in which the traditional structure of the Mass was seriously disturbed: the 1552 *Book of Common Prayer*.

[36] Communion Service nos. 9 and 10, following the numbering of Wrightson, *The "Wanley" Manuscripts*, 8–12.

[37] There is another anonymous setting (Communion Service no. 2) in the Wanley partbooks that similarly omits the Kyrie and is probably another adaptation of an earlier but unidentified Latin mass.

[38] Communion Service nos. 3, 6, and 8. The Wanley partbooks also contain four further settings (Communion Service nos. 1 [Heath], 4, 5, and 7) that most likely predate the 1549 Prayer Book, since they employ the text of the Apostles' Creed from the *King's Primer* (1545) rather than the Nicene Creed; see further Wrightson, *The "Wanley" Manuscripts*, 71–78. The earliest record of a Mass in which the Gloria in excelsis, Creed, Sanctus/Benedictus, and Agnus Dei were sung in English was at the Mass celebrated at the opening of Parliament, Nov. 1547; see Charles Wriothesley, *A Chronicle of England* (London, 1875–77), I: 187, II: 2.

The 1549 eucharistic prayer was substantially abbreviated in the 1552 rite, leaving a sacramental prayer that was little more than the Words of Institution. The intercessions that had been included within the 1549 eucharistic prayer now followed the sermon and the reinterpreted offertory. Similarly, the prayer of oblation was excised and relocated in a position following the distribution of communion. The musical implications of these changes were minimal; other changes were maximal. The Ordinary was completely reordered: the traditional Kyrie was replaced by what amounts to troped Kyries, responses to the Ten Commandments that were now rehearsed as part of the penitential beginning to the reformed Eucharist; the Gloria in excelsis was transferred to the end of the rite, to be sung (or said) immediately before the blessing; the Nicene Creed and Sanctus were retained in their usual positions, except that the Benedictus was omitted from the Sanctus; the Agnus Dei was deleted altogether.

These radical changes meant that the Communion settings adapted or composed for the 1549 Prayer Book could not be used without some fairly substantial modification. There are signs that this was done. For example, Heath's simple Communion setting that appeared in the Wanley partbooks was laboriously reworked for the new 1552 Communion service.[39] Both the Wanley and Lumley partbooks[40] include settings of the 1552 troped Kyries, but the center of gravity of emerging Anglican liturgical music was moving from Communion to the Offices of Morning and Evening Prayer. Even though this developing tradition was put on hold during the Catholic reign of Mary Tudor (1553–58), when the Latin rites and their music were reintroduced, the English Reformation was begun again in the early Elizabethan years essentially from where it had been suspended on the death of Edward VI. The 1552 Prayer Book was reissued in a slightly modified form in 1559, and the liturgical music of the 1550s was reintroduced. A comparison between the Wanley partbooks with the slightly later Lumley partbooks, as well as the printed settings in John Day's *Certaine Notes* and *Mornyng and Evenyng Prayer* (1560, 1565), clearly demonstrates that the compositional shift was in the direction of providing settings of the canticles at Morning and Evening Prayer, together with appropriate anthems for the same Offices, rather than with settings of the Communion rite. It is a shift, one that characterized later Anglican church music, which originated in the changing liturgical and theological ideals that led to the 1549 Prayer Book being replaced by the 1552 Prayer Book.

[39] The 1552 version of Heath's Communion service was eventually included in John Day's *Certaine Notes*, on which work was begun *c.*1560 but which was not issued until 1565 as *Mornyng and Evenyng Prayer*, an anthology of music for the English Prayer Book, most of which was composed in the early 1550s; see John Aplin, "The Origins of John Day's *Certain Notes*," *Music & Letters*, 62 (1981), 295–99. Peter Le Huray's comment regarding the 1552 revision of Heath's Communion service is apposite: "That such unremarkable music was thought to be worth modifying so extensively suggests that music for the reformed rites was scarce"; "Heath, John (i)," *New Grove*^{2}, XI: 300.

[40] On the Lumley partbooks, see Judith H. Blezzard, "The Sacred Music of the Lumley Books (London, British Museum, Royal Appendix Manuscripts 74–76): An Edition and Critical Study" (PhD diss., University of Leeds, 1972); see also eadem, *The Tudor Church Music of the Lumley Books* (Madison, WI, 1985).

The deficiencies of the Roman Mass, when examined from the perspective of the *sola scriptura* principle, led Lutheran and Anglican Reformers to undertake respective revisions of the traditional liturgy. Other Reformers, notably those in Southwest Germany and Switzerland, took the view that the Roman Mass was so corrupt that it could not be revised or re-formed, and therefore new vernacular liturgical forms, drawn up according to the *sola scriptura* principle, were thus required to replace the Latin Mass.

Liturgical reforms in Strasburg were on-going[41] and influenced other parts of Europe. Hubert lists 44 individual Strasburg publications of vernacular liturgies and congregational song appearing between 1524 and 1561.[42] The 1524 liturgy was a German translation of a revised form of the Roman Mass,[43] but from 1525, when the Reformer Martin Bucer assumed the leadership role in the reform of the city and area, the traditional structure of the Mass was abandoned in favour of a simpler form: confession and absolution, metrical psalm or hymn, prayer before the sermon, scripture readings and sermon, Creed or metrical psalm, exhortation and general prayer, Lord's Prayer, Words of Institution, communion, concluding with a hymn or metrical psalm and blessing.

Although the traditional epistles and gospels remained optional, in practice consecutive reading (*lectio continua*) of scripture was preferred. Similarly, although simple monodic settings of the vernacular Kyrie, Gloria, and Creed continued to be included in most of the hymnals,[44] the preference was for other congregational songs, increasingly metrical psalms.

This somewhat limited role for music within worship was the product of Erasmian influences, combined with the view that elaborate music was so much part of the unreformed Mass that it was invalid for "true" Christian worship. For example, the wife of one of the Strasburg Reformers, Katharina Schütz Zell, brought out a hymnal in pamphlet form: *Von Christo Jesu unserem säligmacher . . . etliche Christliche Kostliche lobgesäng* (Strasburg, 1534–36).[45] In the preface she drew a distinction between a mother's household duties and incomprehensible choral singing in monastic houses, then added:

> A poor mother would so gladly sleep but at midnight she must rock the wailing baby, and sing it a song about godly things. That is called, and it is,

[41] See Gerrit Jan van de Poll, *Martin Bucer's Liturgical Ideas* (Assen, 1954); René Bornert, *La Réforme protestante du culte à Strasbourg au XVIe siècle (1523–1598)* (Leiden, 1981)

[42] Hubert, *Die Strassburger liturgischen Ordnungen*, pp. xi–xxxix. See also Miriam Usher Chrisman, *Bibliography of Strasbourg Imprints, 1480–1599* (New Haven, 1982), 345–46, 353–56; William Young, "Music Printing in Sixteenth-Century Strasbourg," *Renaissance Quarterly*, 24 (1971), 486–501.

[43] See Herbst, *Evangelischer Gottesdienst*, 59–68.

[44] See Christian Meyer, *Les Mélodies des églises protestantes de langue allemande: Catalogue descriptif des sources et édition criique des mélodies*, 1: *Les Mélodies publiées à Strasbourg (1524–1547)* (Baden-Baden, 1987).

[45] The hymnal was essentially a reissue of Michael Weisse's hymnal for the Bohemian Brethren, *Ein New Gesengbuchlen* (Jungbunzlau, 1531; facs., Kassel, 1957); see Elsie A. McKee, "Reforming Popular Piety in Sixteenth-Century Strasbourg: Katharina Schütz Zell and Her Hymnbook," *Studies in Reformed Theology and History*, 2/4 (Fall 1994), 1–82.

> the right lullaby (provided it is done in the faith) that pleases God, and not the organ or the organist. He [God] is no child, and you may not silence him with piping and singing! But silence yourself: he requires something else.[46]

Other Strasburg Reformers expressed a more positive role for music in worship. For example, in a series of propositions of 1545 on the book of Exodus, the Italian Reformer and colleague of Bucer in Strasburg, Peter Martyr Vermigli, submitted the following, on the basis of Exodus 15:

> 1. To celebrate the praise of God in songs is not only lawful, but should be maintained in the Church.
> 2. Music has power to arouse the affections of the faithful to piety.
> 3. We should give thanks to God and sing his praises not only with human voice; it is proper to add musical instruments.[47]

Jean Calvin, who had imbibed much of the spirit of Renaissance humanism,[48] was much influenced by the liturgical practices of the German churches in Strasburg while he was minister of the French congregation in the city between 1538 and 1541. During this time in Strasburg he produced a French version of the Strasburg German liturgy (Strasburg, 1540; no longer extant). On his return to Geneva Calvin issued a simplified form of his Strasburg liturgy, *La Forme des prieres et chantz ecclesiastiques* (Geneva, 1542), which became the model for Calvinist or Reformed liturgies throughout Europe, though there was a tendency to simplify further this already simple liturgical form so that what remained was essentially a sermon surrounded by prayers and psalm-singing.

The so-called "Radical Reformation," the Anabaptists in general and such groups as Mennonites and Swiss Brethren in particular, were suspicious of liturgical forms and promoted non-structured services of worship, comprising Bible-reading, prayers, and preaching, which had no music other than the ubiquitous, unaccompanied congregational song,[49] *the* distinguishing feature of all the Refor-

46 The complete preface is given in English trans., ibid., 65–67.

47 Peter Martyr Vermigli, *Early Writings*, ed. Mariano Di Gangi, Joseph C. McClelland, and Philip M. J. McNair, The Peter Martyr Library, 1 (Kirksville, MO, 1994), 133. Vermigli included extended passages concerning music and dancing in his *In librum Iudicum . . . commentarii* (Zurich, 1561), which was trans. into English as *Most Fruitfull & Learned Commentaries* [*upon the Book of Judges*] (London, 1564). Vermigli, Regius Professor of Divinity at Oxford between 1548 and 1553, was a formative influence on the development of the Edwardian Reformation, and his views, especially his cautionary words on dancing, were frequently cited during the later Elizabethan Puritan debates. For example, they were extracted in *A Brief Treatise, Concerning the Use and Abuse of Dauncing, Collected oute of Peter Martyr* (London, [1580?]), and in *A Book of Notes and Common Places* (London, 1581), ed. John Marbeck, the Windsor musician and composer, as well as being included in Vermigli's *Loci communes* in Latin (London, 1576) and in English (London, 1583); see Robin A. Leaver, *The Work of John Marbeck* (Appleford, 1978), 146–47, 151–52.

48 See William J. Bouwsma, *John Calvin: A Sixteenth-Century Portrait* (New York, 1988), 113–27.

49 Representative literature includes Rudolf Wolkan, *Die Lieder der Wiedertäufer: Ein Beitrag zur deutschen und niederlandischen Literatur- und Kirchengeschichte* (Berlin, 1903;

mation Churches in Europe, except those in Zurich and the churches within the sphere of influence of that city.

Congregational song

Vernacular religious song was not the invention of the Reformation era. There was a long European history of such songs,[50] including English carols,[51] Dutch *geestelijke liederen*,[52] Italian *laude spirituali*,[53] and German *leisen*.[54] Luther knew of and utilized the single-stanza, paraliturgical German *leisen* that were closely associated with the liturgy and the festivals of the church year. Examples include the fifteenth-century *Wir glauben all an einen Gott*, based on the Creed, the fourteenth-century *Gelobet seist du, Jesu Christ* (Christmas Day), the twelfth-century *Christ ist erstanden* (Easter Day), textually and musically related to the Easter sequence *Victimae paschali laudes*, and the thirteenth-century *Nun bitten wir den Heiligen Geist* (Pentecost)—all of which, with others, Luther revised and expanded. But whereas previous generations had sung these *leisen* extraliturgically, after Mass on the respective festivals,[55] Luther directed that his versions, together with newly-created strophic hymns, should be sung liturgically, within the reformed Mass, by the congregation at large. The congregation, according to Luther, was not a passive aggregation of individuals who witness worship, but rather an active, corporate body of involved people who together undertake the affairs of the parish, especially worship.[56] For Luther the liturgical imperative of congregational song

repr. Nieuwkoop, 1965); Rosella R. Duerksen, "Dutch Anabaptist Hymnody of the Sixteenth Century," in *A Legacy of Faith: The Heritage of Menno Simons (A Sixtieth Annniversary Tribute to Cornelius Krahn)*, ed. Cornelius J. Dyck (Newton, KS, 1962), 103–18; Martin Brecht and Hannes M. Aleman, "The Songs of the Anabaptists," *Mennonite Quarterly Review*, 59 (1985), 362–66; see also George H. Williams, *The Radical Reformation*, 3rd edn (Kirksville, MO, 1992), passim.

[50] On the general background, see Patrick S. Diehl, *The Medieval European Religious Lyric: An Ars Poetica* (Berkeley, 1985).

[51] See Richard Greene, *Early English Carols*, rev. edn (Oxford, 1977); John Stevens (ed.), *Medieval Carols* (London, 1952); idem, *Words and Music in the Middle Ages: Song, Narrative, Dance, and Drama, 1050–1350* (Cambridge, 1986); Hugh Keyte and Andrew Parrott, *The New Oxford Book of Carols* (Oxford, 1992); see also Rosemary Woolf, *English Religious Lyric in the Middle Ages* (Oxford, 1968).

[52] See Johannes Adrianus Nelinus Knuttel, *Het geestelijk lied in de Nederlanden voor de kerkhervorming* (Rotterdam, 1906; repr. Groningen, 1974); Jacobus Johannes Mak and Eliseus Bruning, *Middeleeuwse Kerstliederen* (Utrecht, 1948); Eliseus Bruning, *De middelnederlandse liederen van het onlangs ontdekte handschrift van Tongeren (omstreeks 1480)* (Antwerp, 1955).

[53] See Fernando Liuzzi, *La lauda e i primordi della melodia italiana* (Rome, 1935); Cyrilla Barr, *The Monophonic Lauda and the Lay Religious Confraternities of Tuscany and Umbria in the Late Middle Ages* (Kalamazoo, MI, 1988).

[54] See Johannes Riedel, "Leisen Formulae: Their Polyphonic Settings in the renaissance and Reformation" (PhD diss., University of Southern California, 1953).

[55] It is possible that some early-16th-century churches in Germany may have anticipated Luther by singing, e.g., the stanzas of *Christ ist erstanden* in alternation with the verses of *Victimae paschali laudes* at Mass on Easter Day.

[56] Luther's concept of "congregation" is conveniently summarized in Gert Haendler,

was undergirded both by theological principle and ecclesiastical precedent. The theological principle was the doctrine of the priesthood of all believers, and unison congregational song was a remarkably powerful means whereby the doctrine was given practical expression. Thus in different Reformation liturgies rubrics directed that this liturgical hymnody or psalmody was to be sung by the total worshipping community.[57] Ecclesiastical precedent for congregational song Luther found in the practice of the early Church. In the *Formula Missae* he wrote:

> I also wish that we had as many songs as possible in the vernacular which the people could sing during mass, immediately after the gradual and also after the Sanctus and Agnus Dei. For who doubts that originally all the people sang these which now only the choir sings . . . ?[58]

Before the end of 1523 Luther and his colleagues began creating a basic corpus of metrical psalmody and freely-written hymnody for Reformation worship, both ecclesiastical and domestic. In addition to reworkings of the old German *leisen*, Latin Office hymns were translated into German and their plainsong melodies modified for use with new vernacular texts; *contrafacta* were created from pre-existing religious folksongs, or folk melodies were were supplied with new "evangelical" texts; and newly created hymns were written, frequently in the *bar*-form of the "court song" (*Hofweise*) and narrative ballad. At first these "new" hymns appeared on broadsides, but, beginning with the so-called *Achtliederbuch*, a small hymnal of just eight hymns published in Nuremberg in 1524, an extraordinary number of hymnals were published, with and without music, in German-speaking lands. The bibliography *Das deutsche Kirchenlied*, which records only German-text publications with hymn melodies, reveals that during the four decades that spanned the beginnings of hymn-writing in Wittenberg at the end of 1523 and the publication of the complete French metrical psalter in Geneva—and the complete Sternhold and Hopkins psalter published in London—in 1562, around 400 publications were issued.[59] Further, of this number almost 20 percent appeared in the formative four years, 1524 to 1527. Almost as soon as the early Lutheran hymns appeared in Wittenberg, they were republished in Strasburg, often with new melodies composed or edited by Mathias Greiter and Wolfgang Dachstein, respectively cantor and organist of Strasburg cathedral, and hymns written in Strasburg, especially metrical psalms, were added to them. It was in Strasburg that Jean Calvin encountered German metrical psalms and was stimulated to create French metrical psalms that could be sung to the same melodies. These were published as *Aulcuns Pseaulmes et cantiques* (Strasburg, 1539), the forerunner of what was to become the French Genevan Psalter, completed in 1562.[59]

Luther on Ministerial Office and Congregational Function, trans. Ruth C. Gritsch, ed. Erich W. Gritsch (Philadelphia, 1981).

[57] See Robin A. Leaver, "'Then the Whole Congregation Sings': The Sung Word in Reformation Worship," *The Drew Gateway*, 60 (1990–91), 55–73.

[58] *LW* LIII: 36; Herbst, *Evangelischer Gottesdienst*, 42.

[59] The origins and spread of congregational song in the first generation of the European Reformation is summarized in the 1st chap. of Leaver, *"Goostly Psalmes,"* 1–54.

As second-generation Reformers began to exert their influence, the center of gravity of the European Reformation moved from Luther's Wittenberg to Calvin's Geneva. In consequence congregational song narrowed from the diversity of the Lutheran chorale to the almost monolithic Calvinist metrical psalm, which dominated the music of many churches with Reformation roots over the following centuries. But whether it was the Lutheran chorale, the Calvinist metrical psalm, or the Anabaptist martyr-song, the unifying musical element common to the worship of European Protestantism was congregational song.

Three Reformation Traditions

Although it is important to trace the common strands of similarity with regard to music through the different manifestations of the sixteenth-century Reformation, it is also necessary to take note of significant examples of dissimilarity, variance of practice that was mainly the product of different Protestant theologies, but partly conditioned by specific musical environments. Such dissimiliarity can be demonstrated by comparing the distinctive Lutheran, Reformed, and Anglican responses to the question of music in worship.

Lutheran church music[60]

The Lutheran tradition of church music has its roots in Luther's theology in general, his specific theology of music in particular, and the pre-existing practice of liturgical music in Wittenberg.

Although the *sola scriptura* principle was common to the Reforming movement as a whole, it was subject to different interpretations. For Luther the principle was all-embracing and positive. Whatever scripture forbids must be avoided, but everything else is possible, providing that clear scriptural principles are not undermined. Luther was therefore not on principle antithetically opposed to everything that the Roman Catholic Church stood for. If specific practices did not undermine scripture then they could continue. Thus in Luther's liturgical revision, although the Canon was removed, the structure and much of the content of the traditional Mass were retained, and with them much music composed for the unreformed Mass continued to be sung within the Lutheran evangelical Mass.

Luther's theology was one of continuity and tradition, not the continuity and tradition of the medieval Church but continuity with the biblical traditions of the early Church. He saw that throughout the generations, from the earliest period of the Church's existence, music was integral to worship. But, in contrast to other Reformers of the sixteenth century, Luther developed a specific theology of music.

Luther understood music as a *donum Dei*, a gift from God, rather than a human invention, and frequent references to the interconnections between music and

[60] For the background, see Robin A. Leaver, "Lutheran Church Music," *New Grove*^{2}, xv: 369–75, §§1–3.

theology can be found throughout his writings.[61] In his preface to Georg Rhau's *Symphoniae iuncundae* (Wittenberg, 1538), he wrote:

> I would certainly like to praise music with all my heart as the excellent gift of God which it is and to commend it to everyone . . . Here it must suffice to discuss the benefit [*usus*] of this great thing [music]. But even that transcends the greatest eloquence of the most eloquent, because of the infinite variety of its forms and benefits. We can mention only one point (which experience confirms), namely, that next to the Word of God, music deserves the highest praise.[62]

In a letter to the composer Ludwig Senfl, dated 4 October 1530, he wrote:

> I plainly judge, and do not hesitate to affirm, that except for theology there is no art that could be put on the same level with music, since except for theology [music] alone produces what otherwise only theology can do, namely, a calm and joyful disposition.[63]

In the *Tischreden*, verbatim reports of Luther's conversations at table and elsewhere, there are numerous references to music, such as: "I place music next to theology and give it the highest praise."[64] This positive theological understanding of music, which was also espoused by Luther's colleagues, especially Melanchthon,[65] promoted the formation of a rich tradition of liturgical music, which embraced the compositions of Catholic as well as Lutheran composers.[66]

Luther's theology of music was formed within the context of a particularly rich tradition of choral liturgical music in Wittenberg. Kathryn Duffy has demonstrated the extent of this liturgical music tradition in her study of the repertory of the Castle Church in Wittenberg during the early decades of the sixteenth century,[67] Duke Frederick the Wise, Elector of Ernestine Saxony between 1486

[61] The basic study in German remains Oskar Söhngen, *Theologie der Musik* (Kassel, 1967), in which Luther's understanding of music is contrasted with that of Zwingli and Calvin. See also the summaries, Lothar Steiger and Renate Steiger, *Sehet! Wir gehn hinauf gen Jerusalem: Johann Sebastian Bachs Kantaten auf den Sonntag Estomihi* (Göttingen, 1992), 11–14; Christoph Krummacher, *Musik als Praxis Pietatis: Zum Selbst-Verstandnis evangelischer Kirchenmusik* (Göttingen, 1994), 11–52. English studies include Walter E. Buszin, "Luther on Music," *The Musical Quarterly*, 32 (1946), 80–97, which is indebted to Karl Anton, *Luther und die Musik* (Zwickau, 1916; 3rd edn, 1928); Paul Nettl, *Luther and Music* (Philadelphia, 1948), which is deficient in documentation; Carl Schalk, *Luther on Music: Paradigms of Praise* (St. Louis, 1988); Robin A. Leaver, *Luther's Liturgical Music: Principles and Implications* (Grand Rapids, MI, 2006).

[62] *LW* LIII: 321, 323; *WA* L: 368, 370–71; see also Walter Blankenburg, "Überlieferung und Textgeschichte von Martin Luthers 'Encomion musices,'" *Lutherjahrbuch* (1973), 80–104.

[63] *LW* XLIX: 428; *WA*, *Briefwechsel*, V: 639.

[64] *WA*, *Tischreden* no. 7034; see also nos. 968, 3815.

[65] See Krummacher, *Musik als Praxis Pietatis*, 41–49.

[66] See the summary in Robin A. Leaver, "The Lutheran Reformation," *Man & Music*, II: *The Renaissance: From the 1470s to the end of the 16th Century*, ed. Ian Fenlon (Basingstoke and Englewood Cliffs, NJ, 1989), 266–74.

[67] Kathryn Ann Pohlmann Duffy, "The Jena Choirbooks: The Music and the Liturgy of

and 1525, was second in political rank only to the Emperor Maximilian. Duffy convincingly argues that Duke Frederick's intention was to rival Maximillian's *Hofkapelle*—which included, in succession, such musicians as Isaac, Senfl, and Hofhaimer—by establishing a significant musical foundation for the liturgical life of the Castle Church, Wittenberg. Between 1508 and 1520 this foundation was doubled, as 40 singers and musicians were increased to 81. They were responsible for singing almost 1,200 Masses throughout the year, as well as the daily Offices, to music by such prominent composers as Josquin, Isaac, and Obrecht among others. It was therefore against a rich experience of polyphonic liturgical music that Luther developed his theology of music, and also, with others, notably the composer Johann Walter, created patterns of worship-music for the Wittenberg churches that proved normative for the formation of the Lutheran tradition of liturgical music.[68]

In many music histories Johann Walter does not figure prominently because the criterion for major coverage has been determined by an individual composer's impact on the development of the forms and content of music. Compared with Josquin, for example, Walter has been portrayed as a derivative rather than an original composer. Although there is merit in the judgment, it nevertheless undervalues the contribution that Walter made to Protestant church music in general and to Lutheran church music in particular. For instance, his polyphonic settings of congregational hymns are intriguing compositions. Modeled on Franco-Flemish cantus-firmus compositions such as those of Josquin, the settings of Walter are notable for their conciseness and for the fact that, instead of being based on plainsong melodies (in augmentation), they are composed on the melodies of the "new" congregational hymns (in regular note values), with the cantus firmus usually in the tenor and imitative counterpoint in the other parts. Walter's chorale settings first appeared in part books issued as *Geystliche gesangk Buchleyn* (Wittenberg, 1524), the so-called "Chorgesangbuch,"[69] a work that was revised and expanded in subsequent editions of 1528, 1544, and 1550/51.[70] The settings can be classified into two basic types: one more homophonic and the other more contrapuntal.[71] Walter's homophonic settings of chorale melodies eventually led to the later "Cantional"

Pre-Reformation Saxony" (PhD diss., University of Chicago, 1994); see also Jürgen Heidrich, *Die deutschen Chorbücher aus der Hofkapelle Friedrichs des Weisen: Ein Beitrag zur mitteldeutschen geistlichen Musikpraxis um 1500* (Baden-Baden, 1993).

68 See Ronald Lee Gould, "The Latin Lutheran Mass at Wittenberg, 1523–1545: A Survey of the Early Reformation Mass and the Lutheran Theology of Music, as Evidenced in the Liturgical Writings of Martin Luther, the Relevant *Kirchenordnungen*, and the Georg Rhau *Musikdrucke* for the *Hauptgottesdienst*" (SMD diss., Union Theological Seminary, 1970); Victor H. Mattfeld, *Georg Rhau's Publications for Vespers* (Brooklyn, 1966); Bartlett Russel Butler, "Liturgical Music in Sixteenth-Century Nürnberg: A Socio-Musical Study" (PhD diss., University of Illinois at Urbana-Champaign, 1971).

69 See the facs. of the the Worms reprint of 1525, Johann Walter, *Das Geistliche Gesangbüchlein "Chorgesangbuch,"* ed. Walter Blankenburg (Kassel, 1979).

70 See Walter Blankenburg, *Johann Walter, Leben und Werk*, ed. Friedhelm Brusniak (Tutzing, 1991), 124–223.

71 See ibid., 196–202, 204–16.

style of simple four-part harmonizations, exemplified in Lukas Osiander's *Fünffzig geistlicher Lieder und Psalmen, mit vier Stimmen, auff Contrapunctsweise, für Schulen und Kirchen . . . also gesetzet, daß ein gantze Christliche Gemein durchaus mitsingen kann* (Nuremberg, 1586; the chorale melody appear in the upper voice rather than in the tenor), and Johann Hermann Schein's influential *Cantional, oder Gesangbuch Augspurgischer Confession* (Leipzig, 1627). Walter's more contrapuntal style of setting congregational melodies gave rise to the expanding tradition of polyphonic motets and other choral and vocal forms based on Lutheran chorales. The *alternatim* practice in which Walter's settings were performed within the Wittenberg liturgy, with improvised organ preludes and other instruments doubling the voice-parts,[72] ultimately resulted on the one hand in the distinctive Lutheran genre of chorale preludes, partitas, and variations for organ, and on the other hand promoted composition for voices and instruments within worship, establishing a practice that would eventually develop into the Lutheran sacred concerto of the seventeenth century and the church cantata of the eighteenth century.

Straube was of the opinion that the essence of Protestantism is not detectable in Lutheran church music until the seventeenth or even the eighteenth century. However, this fundamental use of congregational melodies by such composers as, among others, Sixt Dietrich, Benedictus Ducis, Wolff Heintz, Balthazar Resinarius, Ludwig Senfl, and Johann Walter—all contemporaries of Luther—clearly demonstrates that distinctive and definable Protestant church music was being composed from the time of the earliest introduction of congregational song into the reformed evangelical Mass.

Reformed church music[73]

The Reformed tradition of music in public worship, in contrast to both Lutheran and Catholic traditions, was severely limited.[74] It has its origins in the theology and experience of Jean Calvin, although some areas were more influenced by the theology and practice of Ulrich Zwingli. For Zwingli and Calvin, in contrast to Luther's open-ended approach to scripture, the *sola scriptura* principle was more circumscribed and negative. Individual and corporate Christian life was to be regulated by the direct commands of scripture. Without a direct command there can be no legitimate action. Since Old Testament imperatives relating to instrumental music were integral to the sacrificial system that had been made obsolete by the sacrifice of Christ, the Reformed tradition either restricted music to the unaccompanied unison of congregational psalmody or eliminated it altogether.

72 See Blume, *Protestant Church Music*, 105–13; Adolf Boës, "Die reformatorischen Gottesdienste in der Wittenberger Pfarrkirche von 1523 an die Ordnung der gesenge der Wittenbergischen Kirchen von 1543/44," *Jahrbuch für Liturgik und Hymnologie*, 4 (1958/59), 1–40, 6 (1961), 49–61.

73 For the background, see Andreas Marti, "Reformed and Presbyterian Church Music," 1, *New Grove*^{2}, XXI: 78–82.

74 See the survey by Walter Blankenburg, "Church Music in Reformed Europe," in Blume, *Protestant Church Music*, 507–90.

Ulrich Zwingli, probably the most musically gifted of the sixteenth-century Reformers,[75] excluded all music from the churches in Zurich. A principal reason for this action was Zwingli's theological understanding of the nature of worship.[76] Garside summarizes thus:

> Outward observance in worship was without value, because it was corporeal; true Christian discipleship meant the spiritual life, an almost exclusively inner experience, whose external expression in public worship was in itself relatively insignificant. . . . To all those who must first know the Word, the longing for knowledge and control of music can only be an obstacle.[77]

However, not all Zwingli's decisions with regard to liturgical revision were motivated by theological principle alone; indeed, many seem to have been the product of political objectives. The need for the creation of a specific Christian society in Zurich, a theocracy, in contradistinction to the medieval Catholic intertwining of Church and state, was the primary goal, and a form of worship was created from scriptural principles that was different from the Catholic Mass, a difference that was made more emphatic by the absence of all music.[78] In his liturgical provisions of 1525 Zwingli accepted the common principle that lay behind the hymnody sung in other Reformation Churches, but whereas they employed corporate song he called for corporate speech.[79] Zwingli intended that the Gloria in excelsis, Nicene Creed, and Psalm 112 should be corporately and antiphonally spoken by the men and women of the congregation. In the event Zwingli was overruled by the magistrates who directed that these portions of the liturgy be spoken by the minister alone.[80]

Zwingli's exclusion of music from corporate worship did not mean that he developed a totally anti-music stance.[81] Music was important in his own devotional

[75] On Zwingli's musical formation, see Hannes Reimann, "Huldrych Zwingli: Der Musiker," *Archiv für Musikwissenschaft*, 17 (1960), 124–41, esp. 124–26; Charles Garside, *Zwingli and the Arts* (New Haven, 1966), 7–10. See also the contemporary assessment of Zwingli's musicianship in *Die Chronik des Bernhard Wyss*, ed. Georg Finsler (Basel, 1901), 3–4; cited in English in Garside, *Zwingli*, 22.

[76] See, e.g., Markus Jenny, *Zwinglis Stellung zur Musik im Gottesdienst* (Zurich, 1966); Söhngen, *Theologie der Musik*, 32–53.

[77] Garside, *Zwingli*, 37, 75.

[78] See further Robert Cutler Walton, *Zwingli's Theocracy* (Toronto, 1967).

[79] *Aktion oder Brauch des Nachtmals* (Zurich, 1525), Corpus Reformatorum, ed. Karl G. Bretschneider et al. (Halle, 1834–) [hereafter CR], *Zwingli*, IV: 13–24; English trans. in Bard Thompson, *Liturgies of the Western Church* (Cleveland, 1961; repr. Philadelphia, 1981), 149–56.

[80] Ibid., 145; see further Fritz Schmidt-Clausing, *Zwingli als Liturgiker: Eine liturgiegeschichtliche Untersuchung* (Göttingen, 1952). Even before Zwingli was appointed people's priest in Zurich there appears to have been an anti-music lobby among the city's authorities, which might have been a significant influence on Zwingli's elimination of music from the worship of city churches; see the letter of Oswald Myconius to Zwingli, 3 Dec. 1518, CR *Zwingli*, VII: 107.

[81] See A. Casper Honders, "The Reformers and Music," in *Pulpit, Table, and Song: Essays in Celebration of Howard G. Hageman*, ed. Heather Murray Elkins and Edward C. Zaragoza (Lanham, MD, 1996), 46–52.

life, and he is known to have written both words and music for at least three religious songs: the *Pestlied*, Psalm 69, and the *Kappeler Lied*.[82] He also believed that music had important secular functions, especially in education. Like his medieval predecessors, he classified music among the mathematical disciplines. But nowhere did he advocate the elimination of the study of music from the curricula of the schools in the city. On the contrary, his reforms of the schools attached to the Grossmünster and other Zurich churches included the teaching of music. Education at the Grossmünster school was bipartite. The lower level was a grammar school from which the boys would graduate into the second level, which was a theological seminary for the training of pastors for Reformed churches.[83] Thus whatever his reservations about music in public worship might have been, Zwingli apparently regarded the study of music as an essential part of a pastor's education.

Notwithstanding Zwingli's somewhat ambivalent attitude towards music, the impact of his views was almost exclusively negative. In the churches of Zurich all music was excluded from worship for the remainder of the century,[84] and although Zwingli died in 1531, his non-musical ecclesiastical agenda was continued by his successor in Zurich, Heinrich Bullinger, who was particularly influential in the rise of Elizabethan Puritanism in England.

Jean Calvin, while working from similar biblical presuppositions, came to a different conclusion than Zwingli with regard to the role of music in worship. The numerous biblical injunctions to sing psalms could not be ignored, and therefore Calvin argued that a simple, dignified congregational psalmody was required for Reformed worship. But this psalmody was restricted to the corporate, unaccompanied unison singing of metrical psalms to tunes of appropriate gravity that were untainted by secular associations.[85] Thus in the first edition of his *Institutes* (Basel, 1536), *Articles* (Geneva, 1537), and *Ecclesiastical Ordinances* (Geneva, 1541),[86] Calvin advocated the practice, and in his psalter *Aulcun Pseaulmes et cantiques mys en chant* (Strasbourg, 1539), the no longer extant Strasburg liturgy of 1540, and *La Forme des prieres et chantz ecclesiastiques* (Geneva, 1542), he provided both the liturgical context as well as the necessary psalmody. But there was no question of instrumental accompaniment, because he considered it to be part of the ceremonial

82 See especially the three contributions by Markus Jenny: "The Hymns of Zwingli and Luther: A Comparison," in *Cantors at the Crossroads: Essays on Church Music in Honor of Walter E. Buszin*, ed. Johannes Riedel (St. Louis, 1967), 45–63; "Die Lieder Zwinglis," *Jahrbuch für Liturgik und Hymnologie*, 14 (1969), 63–102; *Luther, Zwingli, Calvin in ihren Liedern* (Zurich, 1983), 175–214.

83 See G. R. Potter, *Zwingli* (Cambridge, 1976), 220.

84 See Hannes Reimann, *Die Einführung des Kirchengesangs in der Zürcher Kirche nach der Reformation* (Zurich, 1959).

85 On Calvin's theology of music, see H. P. Clive, "The Calvinist Attitude to Music and its Literary Aspects and Sources," *Bibliothèque d'humanisme et Renaissance*, 19 (1957), 90–94; Söhngen, *Theologie der Musik*, 60–79; Ross James Miller, "John Calvin and the Reformation of Church Music in the Sixteenth Century" (PhD diss., Claremont Graduate School, 1971); and especially Charles Garside, "The Origins of Calvin's Theology of Music: 1536–1543," *Transactions of the American Philosophical Society*, 69/4 (Aug. 1979), 5–35.

86 See ibid., 8–10, 16.

of the old covenant of law that had been displaced by the new covenant of grace. Commenting on Psalm 92: 4, Calvin wrote:

> the Levites who were appointed . . . singers . . . employ their instruments of music—not as if this were in itself necessary, only it was useful as an elementary aid to the people of God in these ancient times. . . . now that Christ has appeared . . . it were only to bury the light of the Gospel, should we introduce the shadows of a departed dispensation.[87]

This became the common Reformed standpoint on the question of instruments. For example, the marginal comment alongside Psalm 33: 22 in *The Bible and Holy Scriptures . . . Translated according to the Ebrue and Greke* (Geneva, 1560), commonly known as the "Geneva Bible," reads: "To sing on instruments was part of the ceremonial service of the Temple, which doth no more appertain to us than the sacrifices, censings and lights."[88] The sixteenth-century Reformed tradition of music in public worship was therefore confined to the congregational unison of metrical psalmody.

Anglican church music[89]

The development of English church music in the sixteenth century followed the ambiguities and complexities of the English Reformation of religion as it veered, often violently, between Protestantism and Catholicism.

The English Reformation was set in motion by largely Lutheran influences in the 1520s and 1530s but then returned to moderate, or "reform," Catholicism in the late 1530s and 1540s. Following the death of Henry VIII in 1547, the Reformation became openly Protestant during the short reign of Edward VI in the late 1540s and early 1550s, being influenced more by the theology of Zwingli and Calvin than that of Luther. In the later 1550s overt Protestantism was replaced by overt Catholicism during the reign of Mary I, which was itself overturned by the moderate Protestantism of the Elizabethan Settlement of the 1560s and 1570s. As the century moved to its close, Anglicanism was increasingly disturbed by hyper-Calvinism, the Anglican/Puritan divide that eventually led to the Civil War and the temporary demise of Anglicanism during the Cromwellian Commonwealth of the seventeenth century.

Taken as a whole, the English Reformation moved from its beginnings in moderate Lutheranism to a more pronounced Calvinism by the final decades of the century. This changing theological climate had the effect of diminishing the

[87] John Calvin, *Commentary on the Psalms*, trans. James Anderson (Edinburgh, 1845–49; repr. Grand Rapids, MI, 1949), III: 494–95; Johannes Calvin, *Librum Psalmorum commentarius*, ed. August Tholuck (Berlin, 1836), II: 153. For further representative examples, see his comments on Psalm 71: 22, Psalm 81: 3, Psalm 149: 1, *Commentary on the Psalms*, III: 98, 312, V: 312 = *Librum Psalmorum commentarius*, I: 529–30, II: 76, 522.

[88] Cited by John Marbeck in *Notes and Common Places* (London, 1581), 543.

[89] For the background, see Nicholas Temperley, "Anglican and Episcopalian Church Music," §§ 1–4, 6, *New Grove*^{2}, I: 658–61, 663–64.

musical aspects of public worship, and at least three composers—John Taverner, John Marbeck (Merbecke), and Christopher Tye—appear to have given up composing for the Church in response to this theological shift.

A number of the theologians who later played significant roles in the progress of the English Reformation, such as Thomas Cranmer and Miles Coverdale, had studied the writings of Luther in the 1520s. In the early 1530s both Cranmer and Coverdale, among others, visited Germany where they had first-hand experience of Lutheran liturgical music. At the same period there were also German visitors to England, one of them the court painter Hans Holbein the younger, who in his painting *The Ambassadors*, completed in London in 1533, included the 1525 Worms edition of Johann Walter's *Chorgesangbuch* in the central still life between the two ambassadors.[90] Thus there was the possibility of English composers emulating their Lutheran counterparts in these years when an English Reforming movement had its beginnings. That possibility was increased in the middle years of the decade, 1535–36, when Henry VIII was reviewing the feasibility of a political and military alliance with the Lutheran princes of the Schmalkaldic league. During these years Lutheran theologians were in England, and English theologians were in Wittenberg. The Augsburg Confession and its Apology were published in English in London (1536), and Miles Coverdale issued his translations of (mostly) German Lutheran hymns, including the music of their associated melodies, in his *Goostly psalmes and spirituall songes* (*c.*1535). In the event Henry cooled towards the Lutheran princes and initiated a period of reaction in which much of traditional Catholicism was reinforced in direct opposition to Lutheran reforms. Henry nevertheless still had theologico-political problems to overcome. Having broken with the papacy and subdued the secular clergy into accepting the Act of Supremacy (1534), whereby he assumed temporal headship of the English church, Henry's national Catholicism was vulnerable to betrayal by the many monastic institutions throughout the country that owed direct allegiance to the pope. Thus between 1536 and 1540 Henry pursued a relentless dissolution of English monastic houses, which not only resolved the papal-allegiance problem but also brought vast riches into the royal coffers. Since many of these monastic institutions were also significant musical foundations, an unfortunate by-product of their dissolution was the elimination of a large segment of the musical life of the English Church.[91]

At the same time as the monasteries, together with their musical traditions, were being dissolved, attempts to simplify liturgical music, both chant and polyphony, were being made in accordance with humanist criticisms. Between 1540 and 1543

[90] See Markus Jenny, "Ein frühes Zeugnis für die kirchenverbindende Bedeutung des evangelischen Kirchenliedes," *Jahrbuch für Liturgik und Hymnologie*, 8 (1963), 123–28; Leaver, "The Lutheran Reformation," 268–69.

[91] See Peter Le Huray, *Music and the Reformation in England, 1549–1660*, 2nd edn (Cambridge, 1978), 2–3; see also Stanford E. Lehmberg, *The Reformation of Cathedrals: Cathedrals in English Society, 1485–1603* (Princeton, 1988), 76–81. The destruction of musical foundations was somewhat mitigated by the creation of cathedrals of the New Foundation (see Le Huray, *Music and the Reformation in England*, 14–15, and Lehmberg, *The Reformation of Cathedrals*, 81–91), but more musical institutions were lost than were reconstituted.

a committee of bishops reported on the Latin rites of the English church and decreed that all ecclesiastical singing should be "sober, discreet, and devout."[92] Archbishop Cranmer, in an oft-cited letter of 1544, wrote to Henry VIII expressing his view concerning the nature of liturgical music: "In mine opinion, the song . . . would not be full of notes, but as near as may be, for every syllable, a note; so that it may be sung distinctly and devoutly."[93]

This concern for simplicity was intensified after the accession of Edward VI in 1547 and was coupled with an anti-Catholic-music polemic. John Bale, who was to become the Edwardian bishop of Ossory, like Luther before him, saw the Catholic Church as fallen Babylon. Commenting on Revelation 18: 22, he wrote in *The Image of Bothe Churches* (1548):

> But be certain and sure, thou miserable church (saith the Holy Ghost), that . . . the merry noise of them that play upon harps, lutes, and fiddles, the sweet voice of musicians that sing with virginals, viols and chimes, the harmony of them that pipe in recorders, flutes, and drones, and the shrill sound of trumpets, waites and shawms, shall no more be heard in thee to the delight of men. Neither shall sweet organs . . . be played upon, nor the great bells be rung after that, nor yet the fresh descant, pricksong, counterpoint and faburden be called for in thee, which art the very synagogue of Satan.[94]

William Turner, the translator of *A Worke entytled Of ye Olde God & the Newe* (1534),[95] had expressed similar views in *The Huntyng and Fynding Out of the Romyshe Foxe* in 1543, a book that was soon banned. But now in Edward's reign such criticisms had official sanction. Turner became successively chaplain to the young king and dean of Wells Cathedral. Thomas Becon, a chaplain to Archbishop Cranmer, wrote in *The Iewel of Joye* (1553):

> There have been (would God there were not now!) which have not spared to spend much riches in nourishing many idle singing men to bleat in their chapels, thinking so to do God on high sacrifice . . . but they have not spent any part of their substance to find a learned man in their houses to preach the word of God, to haste them to virtue and dissuade them from vice . . . .[96]

Various diocesan visitation injunctions began to place restrictions on the type and

92 *The Rationale of Ceremonial, 1540–1543, with Notes and Appendices and an Essay on the Regulation of Ceremonial during the Reign of Henry VIII*, ed. Cyril Stephen Cobb (London, 1940), 14.

93 Marbeck, *The Booke of Common Praier Noted*, facs. ed., 77.

94 *Select Works of John Bale*, ed. Henry Christmas (Cambridge, 1849), 536.

95 See n. 11 above.

96 *The Catechism of Thomas Becon: With other Pieces Written by Him in the Reign of King Edward the Sixth*, ed. John Ayre (Cambridge, 1844), 429. A rare exception to the trend was Roger Hutchinson of Eton College, who in a sermon preached in 1552 expressed the view: "But though God do not here esteem the voice, but the heart; yet both song and instruments be laudable and approved ceremonies in God's church, as I would prove, but only because I will not be over-long"; *The Works of Roger Hutchinson*, ed. John Bruce (Cambridge, 1842), 285.

content of musical settings for the English Church. For example, in 1548 Lincoln Cathedral injunctions decreed that the choir

> shall from henceforth sing or say no anthems of our Lady or other Saints, but only of our Lord, and them not in Latin; but choosing out the best and most sounding to Christian religion they shall turn the same into English, setting thereunto a plain and distinct note for every syllable one: they shall sing them and none other.[97]

In 1550 Ridley, bishop of London, acting on the authority of Archbishop Cranmer, banned the use of organs in St Paul's Cathedral, and a similar ban was introduced the same year at St George's Chapel, Windsor Castle.[98] Music for the new English liturgy, *The Book of Common Prayer* of 1549, was therefore to be simple in nature and unaccompanied in performance.

Almost as soon as the first English Prayer Book appeared in print, voices were raised in criticism, especially from those who espoused a Zwinglian theology, such as John Hooper, who became bishop of Gloucester in 1550. Work on what was to become the 1552 Prayer Book was undertaken at the same time that Cranmer and others were also working on a reformed canon law for the Church of England. The Latin manuscript, *Reformatio legum ecclesiasticarum* (*GB-Lbl* Harleian 4526), was completed in 1552 and published twenty years later in 1571. The *Reformatio legum* therefore not only expresses the perspectives of the Edwardian Reformers but also of the framers of the Elizabethan Settlement, since it was employed as a foundational document in the reconstitution of the English Reformation after the death of Mary I. The fifth chapter of the section devoted to the ordering and appointment of worship records the following under the heading "The Reading of Sacred Lessons and the Chanting of Psalms":

> In reciting of the divine chapters[99] and in the chanting of Psalms the ministers and clerks should carefully consider the fact that not only should God be praised by them, but others also should be led to the same worship by their exhortation, example, and observation. For this reason, let them pronounce the words methodically and distinctly, and let their chanting (*cantus*) be clear and connected so that all things may attain to the feeling and understanding of the hearers. Therefore, it is determined that the vibrato and elaborate music, which is called *figurata*, be removed. It causes such disturbance to the ears of the multitude that it is often impossible to hear the very language of those speaking (*loquentem*). Furthermore, the hearers themselves are to have a part in the work together with the [singing] clerks and ministers. They will chant certain small parts of the divine services, the first of which will be the Psalms. The Creed will be added and the *Gloria in excelsis*, the Ten Commandments of God and other special points of religion of this kind which

[97] Cited in Le Huray, *Music and the Reformation in England*, 9; cf. the 1552 Injunctions for York Minster, cited ibid., 25–26.

[98] Ibid., 25–26.

[99] See the 1549/1552 rubric cited at n. 16 above.

> have the greatest importance to our common faith. For with these pious exercises and inducements of the divine worship, the very people will be aroused and possess a certain feeling for prayer. If this amounts to nothing but to listen quietly, the mind will be chilled and dulled in such a way that it will be able to form no ardent and serious thought about divine matters.[100]

The kind of music that was to be eliminated from the English church is described as "operosam musicam (quae figurata dicitur)."[101] *Musica figurata* is probably being used here in its normal usage, which covered polyphonic music generally. Yet it is just possible that only the more extravagant forms of polyphony were to be eliminated and that less complex music, such as that found in the Edwardian Lumley and Wanley partbooks and in John Day's *Certaine Notes* (1560/65), could be retained.

What is clear in this section of the *Reformatio legum* is the emphasis on the need for congregational participation in psalmody and in the singing of parts of the revised liturgy of the 1552 Prayer Book. Here are the seeds of the later Anglican dichotomy between the widespread metrical psalmody of parish churches and the choral tradition of cathedrals and collegiate chapels.

Congregational singing was reinforced in the experience of the English exiles in Germany and Switzerland, during the reign of Mary I, where they encountered Continental practices, mostly the Reformed/Calvinist tradition of metrical psalmody.[102] The exiles also engaged in polemics against the Latin liturgical music then being heard in England. Thus William Turner, who had been drawing attention to Continental vernacular singing since the later years of the reign of Henry VIII,[103] stated categorically, in a book published in Emden in 1555, that "Christ never commanded any pricksong or busy descant" for worship.[104] When such exiles returned to England in the early years of the reign of Elizabeth I, they promoted congregational psalmody to the exclusion of other forms of liturgical music. Thus the metrical psalm effectively became the only music of most parish churches throughout the country,[105] and choral music almost the sole preserve of cathedrals and other non-parochial places of worship.[106]

100 *The Reformation of the Ecclesiastical Laws of England, 1552*, trans. and ed. James C. Spalding (Kirksville, MO, 1992), 121; Latin in *Reformatio legum ecclesiasticarum*, ed. John Foxe, (London, 1571), fol. 43^{r-v}.

101 The MS, *GB-Lbl* Harleian 4526, fol. 71^{r}, uses parentheses where the later printed version employs commas to enclose the clause.

102 See Leaver, *"Goostly Psalmes"*, chap. 6, "Strangers and Exiles Abroad," 175–238; and Nicholas Temperley, *The Music of the English Parish Church* (Cambridge, 1979), 1: 26–38.

103 Jones, *William Turner*, 163.

104 William Turner, *A New Book of Spirituall Physick* ([Emden], 1555), sig. $Kvii^{r}$, cited ibid., 182.

105 See Temperley, *The Music of the English Parish Church*, 1: 39–49.

106 See Edmund H. Fellowes, *English Cathedral Music*, rev. Jack A. Westrup (London, 1969), 34–61; see also Lehmberg, *The Reformation of Cathedrals*, 182–225.

The End of the Sixteenth Century

At the end of the sixteenth century the era of Renaissance and Reformation was beginning to give way to emerging early Baroque. Post-Tridentine Catholic music was more closely related to its liturgical or biblical texts than had been the case at the beginning of the sixteenth century. Both Palestrina and Gesualdo were careful in their respective declamation of the verbal text, the former with conservative clarity and the latter with extravagant word-painting. The Lutheran churches had developed their own distinctive tradition of church music in which congregational, choral, and instrumental elements were part of an integrated whole, as is exemplified by the music of such composers as Demantius, Gesius, Schein, Scheidt, Schütz, and Michael Praetorius. Although the Reformed churches confined the music of public worship to the unaccompanied metrical psalm, notable composers nevertheless wrote significant settings, in four or more parts, for vocal and instrumental use in domestic worship, among them Bourgeois, Goudimel, Le Jeune, and Sweelinck.

Anglicanism developed two almost distinct traditions of church music. One was the parish church tradition, modelled on Reformed metrical psalmody, of which the highpoints are the four-part settings in the psalters of Parsons (1563), Thomas East (1592), and Ravenscroft (1621). The other was the cathedral church tradition with its choral settings of biblical anthems and Prayer-Book canticles as exemplified in the music of Tallis, Byrd, Morley, and Tomkins, among others. But it was a tradition that had a somewhat tenuous existence in the final decades of the sixteenth century. In the late 1570s the composer Thomas Whythorne, sometime master of music to Matthew Parker, archbishop of Canterbury, wrote in his manuscript memoir:

> Now I will speak of the use of music in this time present. First, for the Church, ye do and shall see it so slenderly maintained in cathedral churches and colleges and parish churches, that when the old store of musicians be worn out, the which were bred when the music of the church was maintained (which is like to be in a short time), ye shall have few or none remaining, except it be a few singingmen and players on musical instruments.[107]

[107] *The Autobiography of Thomas Whythorne: Modern Spelling Edition*, ed. James M. Osborn (London, 1962), 204.

20

RENEWAL, REFORM, AND REACTION IN CATHOLIC MUSIC

Craig Monson

IN recent decades historians have frequently questioned the appropriateness of the long-accepted term "Counter-Reformation" within a wider European and world context of Catholicism. Various shifts in terminology, away from "Counter-Reformation," which originated in northern-European historiography, where it seemed apt for German religious history, and toward Hubert Jedin's "Catholic Reformation," Eric Cochrane's "Tridentine Reformation," John O'Malley's "Early Modern Catholicism," all acknowledged late-sixteenth- and seventeenth-century Catholicism's greater diversity and more pluralistic character. In addition, Jean Delumeau has chronicled the process of religious reform back long before the Council of Trent, to the thirteenth century, and its continuation down even into the eighteenth century.[1]

All these approaches broaden the field to admit the wide variety that characterized the Catholic tradition of this period. They also recognize that the activities of the Council of Trent followed no clear agenda and were not all directed toward Protestant heresy; that much activity of the early modern Catholic Church was not simply a reaction to events in northern Europe, but focused on the south and the New World; that many important aspects of renewal and reform occurred outside the institutional Church, which had represented the Council's focus almost exclusively, and took place within less familiar, unofficial, or informal contexts,

[1] See especially Hubert Jedin, *Katholische Reformation oder Gegenreformation? Ein Versuch zur Klärung der Begriffe nebst einer Jubiläumsbetrachtung über das Trienter Konzil* (Lucerne, 1946); Eric W. Cochrane, "Counter Reformation or Tridentine Reformation? Italy in the Age of Carlo Borromeo," in John M. Headley and John B. Tomaro (eds.), *San Carlo Borromeo, Catholic Reform and Ecclesiastical Politics in the Second Half of the Sixteenth Century* (Washington, 1988), 31–46; John W. O'Malley, *Trent and All That: Renaming Catholicism in the Early Modern Era* (Cambridge, MA, 2000); Jean Delumeau, *Catholicism Between Luther and Voltaire: A New View of the Counter-Reformation* (London, 1977); and idem, *Le Péché et la peur: La Culpabilisation en Occident, XIIIe–XVIIIe siècles* (Paris, 1983).

apart from parochial structures, which remained the ecclesiastical hierarchy's chief preoccupation.

Such broader terminology also serves music more effectively, for post-Tridentine Catholic church music encompassed a remarkably wide variety of practices beyond the Palestrina style, often perceived as paradigmatic. Many of these practices continued older traditions from before the Council of Trent, whose particular impact on music was less restrictive than often perceived. The musical activities of the Council were also less clearly focused than sometimes imagined, and the implementation of its published decrees, which were less specific in their details than musician historians have commonly made them out to be, was inconsistent and frequently contradictory. The diversity of post-Tridentine music was due partly to this vagueness and flexibility of interpretation and implementation, but also to the fact that much "sacred" music developed and flourished outside the institutional Church.

IT is not surprising that music was eclipsed by more significant issues during the last sessions of the Council of Trent in 1562–63, a time of "crisis," when prelates remained chiefly preoccupied with major political and doctrinal matters involved in vexed questions such as episcopal residency, Curial reform, or the reception of both bread and wine at Communion. When music came up among "abuses of the Mass" in initial preparations for the twenty-second Session of the Council in late summer of 1562, the chief issues involved both the presence of inappropriately secular or "lascivious" elements and musical elaboration that obscured the hearing of the sacred words. But the canons and decrees finally published at the twenty-second session were much more general, attenuated, and imprecise than the preliminaries, and articulated the bare minimum in terms of specifics. Thus, a preliminary canon from the abuses of the mass, proposed for examination on 10 September 1562 and commonly cited by later music historians, was never actually approved and therefore never published in the Council's official decrees:

> Everything should indeed be regulated so that the Masses, whether they be celebrated with the plain voice or in song, with everything clearly and quickly executed, may reach the ears of the hearers and quietly penetrate their hearts. In those Masses where measured music and organ are customary, nothing profane should be intermingled, but only hymns and divine praises. If something from the divine service is sung with the organ while the service proceeds, let it first be recited in a simple, clear voice, lest the reading of the sacred words be imperceptible. But the entire manner of singing in musical modes should be calculated, not to afford vain delight to the ear, but so that the words may be comprehensible to all; and thus may the hearts of the listeners be caught up into the desire for celestial harmonies and contemplation of the joys of the blessed.[2]

[2] Translations of preliminary and final pronouncements from the Council of Trent appear in Craig A. Monson, "The Council of Trent Revisited," *Journal of the American Musicological*

What the prelates actually approved in the twenty-second session on 17 September 1562 and published as part of the decree "concerning the things to be observed and avoided in the celebration of the Mass" was much simpler and more succinct: "let them keep away from the churches compositions in which there is an intermingling of the lascivious or impure, whether by instrument or voice." That was all.

Further musical references published as part of the twenty-fourth session of 11 November 1563 were even less prescriptive about music. Most important, prelates left musical matters to be interpreted and enforced at the local level, a decision that had a great impact on the wide range of Catholic church-musical practices in later decades:

> Let them all . . . praise the name of God reverently, clearly and devoutly in hymns and canticles in a choir established for psalmody. . . . With regard to the proper direction of the divine offices, concerning the proper manner of singing or playing therein, the precise regulation for assembling and remaining in choir, together with everything necessary for the ministers of the church, and suchlike: the provincial synod shall prescribe an established form for the benefit of, and in accordance with the customs of, each province. In the interim, the bishop, with no less than two canons, one chosen by himself, the other by the chapter, may provide in these matters as seems expedient.

There was, however, one instance in which polyphony was seriously threatened at Trent and had to be "saved" at the last minute: the reform of female religious orders at the twenty-fifth session. A preliminary musical decree not only banned performances by outside musicians in convent churches, but also appears to have forbidden the nuns' polyphony in their own choir or in the monastery. When the proposal was debated in congregation, however, a few churchmen spoke against the ban, others insisted that all conventual reforms should be the concern of the nuns' direct superiors, and many took the Cardinal of Lorraine's position, that these matters should be left to provincial councils. In the concluding twenty-fifth session of the Council, finally celebrated on 3–4 December 1563, all references to nuns' music had been dropped. The practice of music in convents would become a surprisingly lively aspect of Catholic musical life throughout the early modern period, one largely overlooked until recently.

The Council of Trent thus offered a structural impetus in an ongoing process of renewal and reform, in which music was also swept along, but with minimal specific directives. The Council's ultimate impact depended upon the commitment to the reform enterprise, not only of the centralized ecclesiastical bureaucracy in Rome but also of diocesan hierarchies, provincial synods, and the laity as well. The reform of liturgical texts of the Breviary (1568) and Missal (1570), of special importance for music, took place almost immediately under Pius V. This pope was strongly committed to the implementation of the new Tridentine decrees as part of a program that also included the publication of the catechism (1566) and the

Society, 55 (2002), 1–37, which offers a thorough reconsideration of the effect of the Council and its immediate aftermath on music.

establishment of a commission to revise the Vulgate Bible (1569). Reform of chant, at the urging of Gregory XIII, Pius V's equally reform-minded successor, got under way in 1577, overseen for a time by Palestrina. It dragged on for 35 years before a badly bowdlerized chant repertory was finally printed in the Editio Medicaea of 1614/15.

The primary implementation of reform was carried out both by centralized bureaucratic institutions in Rome, created during the same period, and by powerful individuals at the local level. The results were particularly intriguing from a musical point of view. Most notable and familiar is Paul IV's commission of eight cardinals, created in August 1564, just a few months after Paolo Manuzio's hasty publication of the complete decrees of the Council. In April 1565 Cardinals Vitellozzo Vitelli and Carlo Borromeo, assigned to reform the papal chapel, extended their investigation to include the rehearsal of polyphonic works by members of the chapel in order to judge the intelligibility of their texts. The important issue of textual comprehensibility, which had been dropped from the official Tridentine decrees, was thus promptly returned to the fore. Vitelli's and Borromeo's efforts provide one of the best examples of the way imprecise Conciliar canons and decrees were subsequently particularized to reflect current humanistic attitudes, which in this case had been articulated in the preliminary deliberations at Trent, but then left vague in the decrees finally published.

In concurrent musical reforms within his own diocese of Milan, Carlo Borromeo again stressed textual comprehensibility, which he even claimed "as you know, is ordered by the Council," thereby conferring upon the intelligibility issue a level of "official" approval beyond what had been stipulated in the Tridentine decrees. Similarly, in his manuscript "Acts," intended for publication as an official history of the Council of Trent, Archbishop Gabriele Paleotti of Bologna eventually rewrote his description of musical legislation to stress textual intelligibility:

> Music in divine service . . . should by all means be retained . . . provided that it should be free of lasciviousness and wantonness, and provided that, so far as possible, the words of the singers should be comprehensible to the hearers.

It is not surprising, therefore, that within a few years of the Council's conclusion, the issue of textual comprehensibility had come to be understood as a key, oft-cited principle of "official" Tridentine reform, though it had in fact been deleted from the formal decrees.

Several enduring Curial bodies were created in the wake of the Council, such as the Sacred Congregation of the Council of Trent, the Sacred Congregation of Bishops and Regulars, and the Congregation of Sacred Rites, which all focused upon the institutional Church throughout the Catholic world. These centralized administrative organizations continued to oversee post-Tridentine reform, sometimes including musical matters, occasionally jogging the memory of diocesan clergy about the Council's ideals, demanding periodic reports from bishops, and interpreting reform doctrine in individual cases submitted to them. Whatever their goals, universality or uniformity certainly did not result. Although the effect of these bodies on music came to be felt more strongly later in the seventeenth century, their earlier activities established patterns and attitudes toward music, and prompted local responses, of a sort that continued throughout the early modern period. Significantly, the index of the Sacred Congregation of the Council of Trent's deliberations during its first sixty years contains but one inquiry concerning music. The fact that the cardinals returned the matter to the relevant bishop, for a decision at the *local* level—precisely as canon 12 from Trent's twenty-fourth session had stipulated—confirms the prevailing pattern of diversity of practice, within general guidelines, rather than universally followed or enforced principles.

Flexibility of interpretation is apparent in local responses to the *Caeremoniale episcoporum*, promulgated by the Congregation of Sacred Rites in July 1600, as a guide to the ritual use of music. By observing the letter of the law, musicians sometimes arrived at varied and creative solutions, working within, but also around, the law, and not entirely in accord with Rome's intentions. In responding to the *Caeremoniale*'s prohibition of the organ during Lent, for example, composers of music for Holy Week sometimes supplanted the organ with harpsichords, lutes, and archlutes. Indeed, while dutifully avoiding the organ, Giovanni Francesco Capello, in his *Lamentatione, Benedictus, e Miserere da cantarsi il Mercordì, Giovedì, e Venerdì Santo di sera à Matutino* (1612) even introduced the more colorful timbres of the concerted style in a choir of strings (violetta, viola, viola, violone) and another of *bassi* and chitarroni—but with no organ.

The Congregation of Sacred Rites' most important decree with general application to polyphony only appeared in 1643, as part of a reintroduction of more rigorous control of religious life and a repurification of ritual, of a sort the Congregations attempted periodically to implement. The ruling is significant for its emphasis, not on textual intelligibility, which had figured so prominently in the immediate years after the Council, but on textual *integrity*:

> 1. That in many churches, to serve the charm of music, the text of the Sacred Scriptures is notably altered, by mutilating, interchanging, and altering the words and their sense, and by adapting them to the modulation so that the music does not seem to be the slave of the Sacred Scripture, but the Sacred Scripture of the music.
>
> 2. That in the solemn Masses musical concerti that are irrelevant to the service are intermingled, and are so prolonged that the priests are distracted for a long time at the altar, and the order of ceremonies is changed so that the music does not serve the Mass, but the Mass the music. . . .
>
> His Excellency the Cardinal Vicar is urged to prohibit the aforementioned abuses, according as he shall judge it to be more expedient.[3]

The decree recognizes the gradual eclipse of late-sixteenth-century musical proper settings, first drawing upon the new Pian Breviary of 1568, by a stream of collections of "free" motets after 1600, often centos that combined diverse, scattered scriptural texts. A striking preoccupation with the Song of Songs gave way by the

[3] *Decreta authentica Congregationis Sacrorum Rituum ex actis eiusdem collecta eiusque auctoritate promulgata sub auspiciis SS. Domini Nostri Leonis Papae XIII*, I (Rome, 1898), 176–77.

third decade of the seventeenth century to a reliance upon more varied sources, or even upon non-scriptural models. Although many such motets were conceived for devotions outside the institutionalized Church, they also proved useful in strictly liturgical contexts because their more general texts could serve for several feasts. That motets also continued to serve the same functions long after the Congregation's ruling of 1643 on textual integrity is revealed by the fact that essentially the same decree had to be reconfirmed under Alexander VII in 1657 and 1665, and again under Innocent XI in 1675 and under Innocent XII in 1692.

The occasional rulings about music by the Sacred Congregation of Bishops and Regulars ranged widely, from matters of personnel to performance practice. To protect the dignity of the clergy, for example, the Congregation informed the bishop of Mantua in 1584 that cathedral chaplains should not be required to sing polyphony, a task better left to salaried musicians. Ten years later the Congregation told the vicar of Pusignano that clerics were not to be forced to pump the organ bellows. The Congregation's ruling in 1593, permitting the cornetto in church, offers an excellent illustration of the inherent contradictions that remained a post-Tridentine reality, for it directly contradicted the ban on all instruments but the organ formulated at some local synods, such as the council of Ravenna in 1568 and at Carlo Borromeo's own first Provincial Council of Milan in 1565.

It is important to recognize that the general decrees of the Council of Trent, as well as the subsequent interpretive rulings by the Congregations of the Curia, proved to be ideals rather than the reality some music historians have suggested. Such decrees were not even consistent with one another; nor were they always intended to be. When in 1593, for example, the coadjutor of Bologna, Alfonso Paleotti, requested a decree banning elaborate convent music, identical to one issued by the Congregation of Bishops and Regulars against the nuns of Naples, the secretary of the Congregation responded, "as to the reform in Naples, it was local, [issued] for particular reasons, wherefore it should not be extended into universal circumstances."[4]

The music of the institutional Church was clearly less homogeneous than it might once have appeared to historians, partly because it depended not only upon the reforming zeal of numerous popes, congregations, and commissions of cardinals in the *caput mundi*, but also upon other links in the chain of superiors, down through bishops of the dioceses to individual priests of parishes, as well as upon some religiously committed members of the patriciate. And when it came to music, many of them must have continued largely oblivious to Trent. The Council's determination to delegate many decisions to the diocesan and provincial levels, under the not-always-watchful eye of superiors in Rome, thus admitted diversity, not merely from diocese to diocese, but within a diocese, from one bishop to the next.

The Tridentine implementation at the local level is most familiar from Carlo Borromeo's efforts in Milan, which would help him win sainthood 25 years after his death. Less familiar, however, is the resistance that the future saint encountered

[4] Monson, "The Council of Trent Revisited," 27.

from clergy, the secular authorities, and the patriciate of the diocese, even resulting in Borromeo's attempted assassination by a disgruntled Umiliato in 1571. Such resistance was not necessarily the work of lax or lapsed Catholics, but could include religiously observant segments of the urban upper classes, such as the patriciate of Monza, who strongly opposed Borromeo's efforts to replace the Roman Use there with the Ambrosian Rite (requiring another contradictory special dispensation, since the Council had urged the uniform observance of the Roman Use).

Between Borromeo's death in 1584 and his canonization in 1610, his reforms came to be revised or ignored by his successor Gasparo Visconti and were partially supplanted by a broader-based and more open pastoral program under the saint's cousin Federico Borromeo, archbishop from 1595 until 1631.[5] The subsequent archbishops Alfonso Litta (r. 1652–79) and Federico Visconti (r. 1681–93) would ironically turn back to aspects of Saint Carlo's original, more severe paradigm.

The results achieved by Carlo Borromeo's friend, the equally committed reformer Gabriele Paleotti, archbishop of Bologna, also illuminate the realities of reform. Paleotti's stipulations on music were almost as vague as their Tridentine models, and generally less thoroughgoing than Borromeo's, except when it came to convents. Returning to the restrictions on nuns' music actually rejected at the Council, Paleotti removed organs from convent exterior churches, forbade performances at the grated windows of the public parlors, and banned outside music teachers.

Paleotti met with as much indifference and resistance as his friend Borromeo. As early as December 1569 Paleotti complained that some of the canons he had required to sing solemn Mass at the high altar of the cathedral "resist openly and lodge appeals, and they want to start litigation, disseminating many calumnies, despite the decrees of the Council and the bulls of His Holiness." In the chapters of the cathedral of S. Pietro and the collegiate church of S. Petronio, and likewise in the nunneries of Bologna, the archbishop's authority continued to be subverted by powerful noble and patrician families, by civil authorities, and even by the papal legates, all of whom limited his reform efforts. In November 1581 the exasperated Paleotti complained to the pope's nephew, Cardinal Filippo Boncompagni, of "incorrigible nuns" and of "insolent and seditious canons of the cathedral and some from the collegiate church of S. Petronio," and insisted that "if Your Reverence does not send me a breve with the formal statement that I can severely kick even canons of the cathedral and S. Petronio, who ignore the discipline I shall impose on them, I begin to fear some notable disorder."[6] If this represents the post-Tridentine reality under dedicated reformers, we should not expect greater conformity or widespread uniformity in the Catholic world as a whole.

Legislated Tridentine and post-Tridentine reforms would thus remain paradigms, like the Catholic saints themselves. Gregory Martin, the English Catholic

[5] See Robert Kendrick, *Celestial Sirens: Nuns and their Music in Early Modern Milan* (Oxford, 1996), and idem, *The Sounds of Milan, 1585–1650* (Oxford, 2002), for a thorough discussion of these contrasting reforms.

[6] *I-Ma* F63 inf., fols. 381^r–382^v.

exile and translator of the Rheims-Douay Bible, claimed to perceive the reform spirit throughout the churches of Rome by the late 1570s. It is unlikely, however, that Martin's pious guidebook *Roma sancta* (1581), conceived to balance the Protestant view of the papist "whore of Babylon," offers an entirely accurate record of how matters really stood. Rather, it probably reflects what the musical ideal of the Catholic reformation was meant to be—majestic and moving to devotion, as Geneva's cold austerities would never be, and also varied, but with every word clearly perceptible:

> Solemnitie of Divine Service. It is the most blessed variety in the world, where a man may go to so many Churches in one day, chose where he wil, so heavenly served, with such musike, such voices, such instruments, al ful of gravitie and majestie, al moving to devotion and ravishing a mans hart to the meditation of melodie of Angels and Saintes in heaven. With the Organs a childes voice shriller and louder then the Cornet or Sagbut, or such like above al other voices. Wherein this is singular and much to be noted, that they deliver every word and everie syllable so distinctly, so cleane, so commodiously, so fully, that the hearers may perceave al that is sung. And that Verse which the Organs doth playe, one of the quyre in the meane time with a bass voyce very leasurely, rather sayth then singeth which there is common, in other places I have not seene it.[7]

Vincenzo Ruffo's committed response to post-Tridentine musical ideals of intelligibility was directly prompted by Carlo Borromeo's elevation of textual clarity to the status of a Tridentine decree, as the composer acknowledged in the dedication of his Masses of 1570 and reiterated in later publications. Similar goals were mouthed in numerous publications by other composers, notably Palestrina's Second Book of Masses (1567), which claimed "to adorn the holy sacrifice of the Mass in a new manner," or Giovanni Animuccia's First Book of Masses (1567), composed so "that the music may disturb the hearing of the text as little as possible." Both composers thus put Tridentine ideals into practice in ways reminiscent of Ruffo's during the same years, and for comparable reasons. Animuccia, as *magister cantorum* of the Cappella Giulia in St Peter's Basilica, received several payments between 1566 and 1568 for the composition of hymns, motets, and masses "needed for the chapel and . . . according to the requirements of the Council of Trent and the new Office." Palestrina, in fulfilling a musical commission in 1568 for Guglielmo Gonzaga, Duke of Mantua, offered to compose "so that the words may be understood," though this was presented as just one possible option. Only one of Palestrina's Mantuan masses betrays a particularly declamatory, chordal style—not surprising, given the duke's enthusiasm for contrapuntal complexities, a useful illustration of the aesthetic impact of the religiously observant lay nobility, not entirely in agreement with post-Tridentine concerns.

In 1575 Giulio della Rovere, bishop of Ravenna, commissioned Costanzo Porta to compose masses that were "short and in a manner which would make the text

[7] Gregory Martin, *Roma sancta (1581)*, ed. George Bruner Parks (Rome, 1969), 96.

easily comprehensible." But Porta's insistently contrapuntal idiom regularly intrudes on a simpler declamatory style. And, when the masses appeared in print in 1578, parodies of madrigals such as Palestrina's *Vestiva i colli* and Rore's *Come havrà fin* still discreetly masqueraded behind the titles *Missa secundi toni* and *Missa tertii toni*. Palestrina also used a similar ploy, as did Orfeo Vecchi in his *Missarum liber primus* (1588), which claimed to conform "ad normam Conc. Prov. Mediolensis." It is ironic that chordal and declamatory secular chansons such as the model for Lassus's *Missa "Je ne mange poinct de porcq"*, unashamedly acknowledged in its Venetian printing of 1570 and reprinted in Milan in 1588, offered one of the clearest paradigms for the post-Tridentine ideal of textual intelligibility, borrowed from their decidedly secular or "lascivious" models.

Concurrently diaries of the Cappella Giulia record in 1568 the continued performance of masses by Pipelare and possibly by Compère on *L'homme armé*, very probably Févin's *Missa "Le villain jaloux"*, as well as a mass based on the secular model *La castagnia*. The inclusion in a Cappella Sistina manuscript (*I-Rvat* C.S. 22, *c.*1565) of the paradigmatic reform mass, Palestrina's *Missa Papae Marcelli*, in company with a *Missa "En doleur et tristesse"* and a *Missa "Ultimi mei sospiri"*, in violation of Trent's most obvious musical prohibition of "lascivious" elements, reveals just how contradictory Vatican musical practice could be in the years after Trent.

Catchwords such as "juxta decretum sacrosancti tridentini Concilii" on the title page of the Psalms of 1578 by Gian Matteo Asola of Verona heralded their simpler, comprehensible style, which had already characterized psalm settings before Trent, however. Similar wordings on the title pages of Asola's Masses of 1581 and 1586 ("facilitati, brevitati mentique sanctorum concilii Tridentini patrum accomodatae") and on other collections of the period may also represent a marketing strategy during a time of uncertainty about what the actual aesthetic impact of Trent would be. And what many title pages promised was not always what the prints contained. By the time the obscure Biagio Pesciolini published his masses "juxta formam Concilii Tridentinii" in 1599, fewer composers worried about the phrase any longer, or bothered to include it.

When it came to secular "impurities," the most clearly articulated Tridentine musical restriction, practical responses were similarly contradictory. Composers who followed the lead of populist reformers could find in secular vitality a means to religious renewal, particularly outside formalized liturgical structures. The singing of *laude* by thousands of once rampaging but now comparatively angelic *fanciulli* in the Florentine processions that had supplanted Carnival revelries during the upsurge of popular piety under Savonarola represent one of the most prominent and successful earlier "tamings" of the popular and the secular. The process found expression again in the post-Tridentine attitude that all means of persuasion, including literary, artistic, and musical, should be committed to spiritual renewal and reform. It is strikingly manifest in the year of the Council's conclusion, not only in the publication of Serafino Razzi's *Libro primo delle laudi spirituali*, the first *lauda* publication since Petrucci's two *lauda* prints of 1508, in which Carnival songs and *canzonette* were turned into pious contrafacta (e.g., Domenico da Nola's *Tre ciechi siamo* becomes *Tre virtù siamo*), and in Animuccia's Oratorian *Primo libro delle laudi*, but also by the appearance that same year of the first collection devoted exclusively to spiritual madrigals, *Musica spirituale* by the Veronese priest Giovanni dal Bene, "a utilità delle persone christiane."

In March 1565 a similar sanctification of the secular was endorsed by Carlo Borromeo, who commended the plan of his vicar in Milan "to make a collection of decent madrigals such that every good man can sing them." Apart from collections devoted exclusively to pious effusions in the vernacular, spiritual madrigals were also printed in collections devoted primarily to their worldly counterparts, where they had occasionally appeared before Trent. Indeed, in publications such as Lassus's *Quinto libro dei madrigali* (1585) "spiritual madrigals" could occasionally outnumber the secular works promised on the title page.

The use of the vernacular, not to mention secular originals, had not prevented the earlier use in church of such contrafacta, judging by their prescription on feast day evenings in the cathedral of Florence after 1501 and by Tarquinio Longo's remark, urging the replacement of notably lascivious models for contrafacta, "not the least because they have been sung in churches." The permeability of the boundaries between Latin and vernacular on the one hand and the liturgical and paraliturgical on the other characterized these post-Tridentine genres, which ranged from spiritual madrigals proper to specific religious festivals, published as early as Animuccia's collection of 1565, to Serafino Razzi's *Hymnario dominicano in cui si comprendono tutti gli hymni* (1583), translated from the Latin for devout patrician ladies, to verse paraphrases of the Litany of Our Lady of Loreto, included in Palestrina's *Madrigali spirituali . . . libro secondo* (1594), to Anerio's *Teatro armonico spirituale* (1619), quasi-liturgically organized for the oratory that continued at San Girolamo della Carità in Rome long after Philip Neri had moved to different quarters. That these genres also continued to find occasional liturgical use is revealed by a 1594 ruling of the *Concilium Avenionense* that songs in the vernacular could be sung in church at Christmas with prior episcopal license, by Cardinal de' Medici's approval of Florentine nuns' singing of "*laudi spirituali* and other pious things in the vernacular" *except* "in chapel, where they might be heard by the laity," and by instructions in 1657 from the Congregation of Sacred Rites to the bishop of Ternana that songs and hymns in Italian during the exposition of the Blessed Sacrament were specifically *not* permitted.

The admixture of pieces "now on Latin words, now in the vernacular," acknowledged in Animuccia's *Secondo libro* (1570), also continued in compendia such as Gasparo Costa's *Primo libro de motetti e madrigali spirituali a cinque voci* (1581), on down to Monteverdi's *Selva morale e spirituale* (1640/41), whose post-Tridentine diversity is especially unusual in its inclusion of five spiritual madrigals.

Perhaps the most striking expression of such merging of sacred and secular, Italian and Latin, spiritual madrigals and *travestimenti spirituali* appears in Aquilino Coppini's three books of *Musica tolta da i Madrigali di Claudio Monteverde, e d'altri autori . . . e fatta spirituale* (1607–9), prepared (if Adriano Banchieri is to be believed) at the urging of Carlo Borromeo's cousin and eventual successor in Milan, Cardinal Archbishop Federico Borromeo. Here madrigals, chiefly by Monteverdi and including almost all from his notorious Books 4 and 5, are turned into

Ex. 20.1 Aquilino Coppini, *O Jesu mia vita*; arranged from Monteverdi, *Si ch'io vorrei morire* (Fourth Book of Madrigals)

Il terzo libro della Musica di Claudio Monteverdi a 5 voci fatta spirituale da Aquilino Coppini (Milan, 1609)

Latin "motets." It was their "wonderful power to move the passions exceedingly," extolled by Coppini, that rendered these worldly works "equally commendable to God and to his saints in churches and private houses." The necessity for a reprint of the first book suggests that others must have shared Coppini's view. Adriano Banchieri, for example, judged these madrigals-made-motets on a par with motets by Lassus and Palestrina and urged that Coppini's contrafacta replace the latter at the pious Accademia dei Floridi, founded by Banchieri in Bologna in 1614. The use of these madrigals even in church, seemingly in contradiction to Tridentine stipulations, is also suggested by the presence of Coppini's first book in the musical archive of the duomo in Piacenza, which received a copy as a seventeenth-century donation. In Coppini's third book, Monteverdi's memorable, graphically enthusiastic glorification of carnal love, *Si ch'io vorrei morire*, is transformed into pious longing for the saviour as *O Iesu mia vita*, with the unforgettable "ahi baci, ahi bocca, ahi lingua" becoming "O Iesu, lux mea, spes mea, cor meum" (see Example 20.1). No example could better illustrate the post-Tridentine recognition of the utility of the most secular entertainments for the service of the Church.

One volume of Coppini's startling retextings of Monteverdi madrigals was dedicated to a musical nun at the convent of Sta Marta in Milan. This volume represents just one of dozens of sacred musical publications dedicated to talented convent musicians in the post-Tridentine period, to which may be added numerous sacred publications by nun composers themselves, all part of a dramatic expansion in convent music-making during the late sixteenth and seventeenth centuries, throughout the Catholic world. It is impossible to say how much this striking growth in convent music might have been a response to the severe standards of strict enclosure imposed upon female monastics after Trent, but the cultivation of music proved to be a significant means of bridging the convent walls that came to be a reality of life for nuns after the Council. In many Italian cities, such as Milan, Bologna, Venice, Siena, and Rome, convent churches became the sites of extraordinary music-making, drawing both locals and foreign visitors in great numbers to hear the relative novelty of virtuoso female singing in a respectable setting. In Milan some of the best, most up-to-date sacred music could be heard not at the cathedral but at convents such as Sta Radegonda. The church hierarchy, consistently in Bologna and also in Rome and Milan during certain periods, deplored such convent musical traditions as an inappropriate, worldly distraction for the nuns, and fought continual, but often losing, battles to control them. In cities such as Siena, where convent performances were perceived as an important contribution to civic prestige, nuns' music-making came to be regarded more benignly and was even encouraged. Convent music flourished throughout the seventeenth century and well into the eighteenth, in some instances right down to the Napoleonic suppression of the monasteries.

At a time when some in the Catholic hierarchy, such as Pius V, concentrated on combating Protestant heresy and others, such as Borromeo and Paleotti, were preoccupied with local institutional reform, still others, such as Philip Neri and Ignatius Loyola, continued an older process of spiritual renewal at a personal level, outside the regular parochial structures that had remained almost exclusively the concern at Trent. Theirs was not just a program of Christian renewal but also of Christian conversion, and not merely beyond European shores. Whether in the hinterlands of France, as Jean Delumeau has shown, or in Italian backwaters such as the Friuli, as Carlo Ginzburg has demonstrated, pagan mentalities and pre-Christian rites persisted remarkably long after the Council. During the second half of the seventeenth century a bishop of Autun recorded that his flock was "quite uneducated, hardly initiated in even the rudiments of faith, . . . [living] in crass and deeply rooted ignorance." This was no exaggeration, for as late as 1686 the local peasantry was still prepared to sacrifice a heifer to the Blessed Virgin for protection against the "plague."[8] Such paganism continued to flourish even into the eighteenth century, combatted most infamously by the Inquisition, as well as by Jesuits and Oratorians, familiar to music historians, but also by less familiar monastic and mendicant orders.

While both Protestant and Catholic hierarchies could be said to dehumanize Christianity by their reemphasis upon the sanctity of institutionalized worship and their suspicion of secular elements, St Philip Neri's Oratorians and St Ignatius Loyola's Jesuits reached out to the world, "taming" and incorporating aspects of popular culture for use in their sacred mission (cf., on the other side, Luther's oft-quoted if apocryphal "Why should the Devil have all the good tunes?"). In contrast with Calvin's deep distrust of music's allure in almost all its forms, these perpetuators of Catholic reform were ready—eventually, if not always initially—to turn music's attractive powers to their own advantage.

Philip Neri's Congregazione dell'Oratorio, officially established by Gregory XIII in 1575, had been at work in Rome since the 1550s. The Oratorians' musical exegesis of sacred texts has been interpreted as an acceptable way to mediate between the Bible and the laity, whose reception of scripture the Roman Church traditionally preferred to keep indirect. Indeed, in 1568, when Neri's Congregation permitted lay members for a time to preach the Gospel, it found itself under scrutiny by the Inquisition and had to be protected by Carlo Borromeo. On the other hand, the aesthetic character of Oratorian rituals was gradually transformed by their own artistic successes into forms that might have distressed the earlier reformers who had offered inspiration for the movement.

The influential advocate of the Congregation, Cardinal Cesare Baronius, the Catholic Church's official historian, recalling "the marvelous utility and consolation of the listeners" afforded by *lauda* singing at Neri's earlier meetings of the 1550s, concluded: "It seemed that, as much as the present times allow, the ancient apostolic manner had been renewed." Baronius's validation of the Oratorian style derived not from a humanistic revival of the relics of the classical world but from its restoration of the sources of early Christian antiquity, whose appeal to the public imagination had been further enhanced by the rediscovery of the catacombs in Via Salaria in 1578. The mixture of classic Christian sources and music is described by the sometime *lauda* anthologist Giovenale Ancina in May 1576:

[8] Delumeau, *Catholicism between Luther and Voltaire*, 175.

> Every day they offer the fairest sermons about the Gospels, of virtues and vices, of church history, of the history and life of saints; and thus every day there are four or five who preach. And distinguished personages, bishops, prelates, and the like, come there to listen. At the end they provide a little music to console spirits fatigued by the preceding discourses.

A more direct link to Neri's "apostolic simplicity" from the pre-Tridentine reform movement, not about to be acknowledged openly in the decades after Trent, had appeared in the work of Girolamo Savonarola in Florence during the 1490s; his influence continued long after his execution in 1498. The Dominican prophet, who had condemned elaborate polyphony because its appeal to the senses distracted from internal contemplation and because its complexity rendered words unintelligible, had fostered in polyphony's place the singing of simple *laude*. Although Savonarola had inveighed against secular vanities, the *laude* themselves, sung in the streets of Florence and also in the Duomo before his sermons, had often been based on secular originals. The wide diffusion of *lauda* singing in the sixteenth century is partly attested to by the subsequent publication of *lauda* collections, from Venice and Turin in the north of Italy to Naples in the south. If some aspects of the sixteenth-century *lauda* tradition remain more elusive than the Oratorian *lauda*, it may be because they flourished farther afield, where historians were not prompted to link them to an incipient oratorio tradition. In the particularly interesting case of Florentine *lauda* singing, a connection to the cult of the "martyred" Savonarola, practiced surreptitiously in Dominican monasteries of monks and nuns, helped to keep the elusive tradition alive.

Philip Neri himself had sung *laude* at Savonarola's old convent of San Marco in the 1520s, and continued to venerate the reformer. The singing of simple and accessible *laude* remained a prominent feature of Neri's Oratorian devotions, which encouraged the publication of several collections, including three by Giovanni Animuccia between 1563 and 1577, another five overseen by Francesco Sotto between 1577 and 1598, and others by Giovenale Ancina (1599) and Giovanni Arascione (1600).

Despite the Oratorians' initial goals of universality and simple accessibility, increased attendance by an upper class audience opened the way toward greater artifice as early as Animuccia's Second Book of *laude* of 1570:

> But since, by the grace of God, the following at the said oratorio continued to increase, with the attendance of prelates and the most elite gentlemen, it also seemed to me advantageous to increase in this Second Book the harmony and the melody, varying the music in diverse ways . . . sometimes with a greater number of voices, at other times with fewer, now with verse of one sort, then with another sort, weaving into the gaps when I could imitations and inventions, but not to obscure the comprehensibility of the words, so that by their effectiveness, aided by the harmony, they would more sweetly touch the heart of the listener.

This Oratorian espousal not only of the original simple musical ideal but also of subtler and more complex idioms for more refined audiences continued as the Oratorians' appeal expanded. By the end of the century the typical four or five sermons, at least in the winter months, had dwindled to one, hemmed in on both sides by more lavish music. By the early 1590s the Congregation was spending more to maintain a higher musical standard and consciously recruiting proficient musicians as members in order to exploit their talents. After another thirty years, the pursuit of the Oratorians' revised musical goals had proved so effective that the throngs attracted to services provoked "extraordinary disorders of tumults, insolence, and scandals to the point where God's word is obstructed." Subsequent attempts to limit music by outsiders and to banish *sinfonie* and all instruments but organ and harpsichord have an ironically familiar ring. As elsewhere, however, such measures proved an ideal rather than a lasting reality, for a dozen years later, if contemporary chroniclers are to be believed, the solemn ordination of Loreto Vittori in 1643 at the Congregation's Chiesa Nuova included music by Fabbri, Mazzocchi, Foggia, and Carissimi, sung by 150 singers divided into no less than six choirs.

Ignatius Loyola, founder of the Society of Jesus, did not embrace music with the same enthusiasm as his Oratorian counterpart. This other Counter-Reformation saint-to-be claimed a personal attachment to music in the liturgy, but he eschewed music in obedience to what he saw as the wishes of his own ultimate superior. The views of Ignatius, who was occasionally soothed in private by the singing or clavichord playing of his fellows, and the attitudes of his immediate successors as head of the Society, Laynez and Borgia, thus contrast with those of Neri and recall similar old patrician views about music-making, going back as far as Aristotle but most familiar from Castiglione's *Cortegiano*. In Ignatius' view, music should not waste the time of the Society's members, who should not indulge in it publically or in company with outsiders, or allow it to distract them from their important labors.

For the first few decades of the Society's history, music thus received scant encouragement, especially by contrast with Oratorian attitudes. This was particularly true in Italy, where the faith was least directly under attack. Modern apologists' claims that the Jesuits made the general populace "more receptive to music"[9] reverse the actual process. It was the public's receptivity to music that eventually attracted the Society's hierarchy, particularly in areas where Jesuits had to work to hold onto, reclaim, or expand the Catholic empire. Father Goisson, rector of the Jesuit college in Prague, was hardly alone in claiming that a lack of music hindered the Jesuits' mission, and in using this as an excuse to introduce music, without prior license from higher authority: "[Bohemians'] devotion and affection [to music] are such that they think we are a new race and unworthy of the priesthood or of the Christian religion—because we do not sing Vespers and Mass." Displeasure at Jesuit headquarters in Rome was directed as much against such acts of insubordination as against the music they had fostered. And this conflict between

[9] Max Wittwer, seconded by Thomas Culley in "Musical Activity in Some Sixteenth Century Jesuit Colleges, with Special Reference to the Venerable English College in Rome from 1579 to 1589," *Studien zur italienisch-deutschen Musikgeschichte*, 12 (1979), 2.

central authority and lesser decision-makers farther afield reflects the same patterns commonly repeated elsewhere in the post-Tridentine Catholic world.

On European fronts especially threatened by Protestantism, such as the Spanish Netherlands, South Germany and Austria, and parts of France, Jesuits embraced music both to bolster institutionalized ritual and for its utility in less formal contexts. The provincial council at Aquitaine in 1571, for example, while discouraging further expansion of music into new areas, specifically supported its continued use in cities such as Lyons, which represented the front line of the Catholic–Huguenot struggle. Early in the previous decade a letter from Edmond Auger in Lyons to Laynez made music's enlistment into the arsenal of Catholic militancy particularly clear:

> I wrote your Paternity that it seemed to me that a translation of the psalms should be done in French by Pierre Ronsard, . . . for singing at home, in shops and while traveling–against those which the adversaries go around mumbling. For the French love singing very much, and with this weakness the devil has won over a whole world of them. . . . Everyone who sees the situation of the times judges it necessary to cure opposites with opposites. . . . Thus the people, having Mass, sermons, catechism and holy psalms, will have no occasion to be led astray by any novelty.[10]

Music's role in Catholic England, the most tenuous European front of all, may seem more elusive, but it reflects this militant spirit even more emphatically. A solemn liturgy with processions, performed secretly at Mass centers scattered among English Catholic communities, represented a more potent and significant act than comparable services in other areas, less under siege. In the English mission these rituals offered an especially powerful means of fostering a sense of membership in a continuing community at home and of affirming bonds with the larger Catholic community on the Continent. William Byrd's replacement of the Sarum Use with the Roman Breviary provides one of the clearest symbols of music's role in this process and may represent a direct implementation of English Jesuit insistence "that all would follow the Romane use in their office and service as a thing commended to all the world by the Concell of Trent."

The fostering of music and the employment of musicians, some of whom found themselves out of work thanks to Puritan artistic depredations, offered a means not only to preserve the Old Religion but also to strengthen and link its scattered communities. It is impossible to say how many George Lingans there were, who "under colour of teaching on the virginals goeth from papist to papist, [and] is thought also to be a priest so made in Queen Mary's time." The composer who has come to represent them all is, of course, William Byrd, who was made into a hero of Catholic resistance even in his own time. An English recusant wrote to Byrd's early patron Sir Thomas Paget that "we take comfort in him as a lean-to by whom we are relieved upon every casual wreck," while Father William Weston claimed in his autobiography rather extravagantly that the composer "had sacrificed every-

[10] Thomas D. Culley and Clement J. McNaspy, "Music and the Early Jesuits (1540–1565)," *Archivium historicum Societatis Jesu*, 40 (1971), 224 (Goisson), 231 (Auger).

thing for the faith—his position, the court, and all those aspirations common to men who seek preferment in royal circles."

In many motets, especially from his 1589/91 *Cantiones sacrae*, Byrd put his art to work for the Jesuit cause in the same spirit as the many works of Catholic literary propaganda secretly printed during those same years. In these publications, several of the same scriptural texts set by Byrd are woven into arguments or even printed on title pages to foster an English Catholic identity and ideology. The text of Byrd's most striking "martyrdom motet," *Deus venerunt gentes* (the opening verses of Psalm 78) was quoted, paraphrased, or versified by papist pamphleteers commemorating Catholic martyrs such as Edmund Campion, executed at Tyburn in December 1581. Quotations from Psalm 78 were even uttered by later martyrs, such as John Cornelius on the scaffold in 1594. Most remarkable, perhaps, the pope reputedly granted an indulgence, at the request of Cardinal William Allen, founder of the college at Douai, to "all those that did devoutlie for the conversion of England say . . . the psalme 78, *Deus venerunt gentes*."[11]

Jesuits jettisoned any remaining reticence about music in the special circumstances of the Americas and the East, a new arena of Catholic activity hard to overlook, in the same spirit that tolerated greater flexibility about other aspects of missionary activity there. While prelates at Trent were urging the abandonment of secular or worldly elements in liturgy, and considerably before the sanctioning of some vernacular to meet challenges beyond "civilized" western Europe, Father Manuel da Nóbrega's Jesuit mission to Brazil had arranged for the Our Father, the Ten Commandments, and other prayers to be translated into the native Tupi and set to native-style tunes in the 1550s, a practice subsequently emulated in Mexico in the 1570s, using the native Nahuatl. Choirs of boy musicians from the Jesuit orphanage in Lisbon were also dispatched to New World missions, seven to Bahía (Brazil) in 1550 to attract native children with their songs. The following year another five were sent to "Japan" (India), because of their facility with languages, plainchant, and organ playing. The boys' enthusiastic "taming" of secular, "savage" culture met with considerable success, though it appalled the thoroughly European Pedro Fernandez, first bishop of Bahía, who viewed it through the (literally) parochial eyes of a member of the ecclesiastical hierarchy:

> The orphan boys, before I came, had the custom of singing every Sunday and feast day songs of Our Lady set to pagan tunes, and playing certain instruments these barbarians play and sing when they want to drink their wines and kill their enemies. . . . I was also shocked to learn that the boys wore their hair in a pagan way, which looked like that of monkeys.

Recalled to Portugal in 1556, Fernandez survived shipwreck on route, only to be captured and eaten by the natives of Caeté.[12]

[11] On Byrd, the Jesuits, and the Catholic cause, see Craig Monson, "Byrd, the Catholics, and the Motet: The Hearing Reopened," in *Hearing the Motet*, ed. Dolores Pesce (New York, 1997), 348–74.

[12] Culley and McNaspy, "Music and the Early Jesuits," 236–37.

Monuments of European Catholic musical culture were also imported into New World missions and taught there; the first music school opened in Brazil as early as 1553. Beside the more complex polyphony of Europeans such as Mouton, Morales, Guerrero, or Vittoria, which survives in cathedral and mission libraries of Guatemala, Colombia, Peru, and Mexico, imitations of the western-European example, simpler, more homophonic, and enlivened by rhythmic and melodic details of the indigenous musical idiom, sometimes in the local language or mingled with it, were created by emigrés such as Gaspar Fernandes (*c.*1570–*c.*1629), organist of Guatemala and Puebla Cathedrals, Hernando Franco (1532–1585), chapel-master at the cathedral in Mexico City, and Juan Gutiérrez (*c.*1590–1664), Fernandes's successor at Puebla. The vital spirit of these rituals is captured in the descriptions sent home from the field:

> After Mass there was a procession . . . and since the feast did not seem to be exclusively ours, many natives, full of fervor and dressed in their own style with much adornment, and with native instruments in their hands and shaking them, formed their own procession and joined ours. So the feast was celebrated with motets with organ and psalms well accompanied with voices, and even with the singing and dancing of those who did as much as they knew how. (Father Leonardo do Vale in Brazil, to Laynez, September 1561).[13]

Catholic music in the New World thus intensifies the same patterns of diversity and contradiction we have seen in the Old. The occasional musical paradigms attributable to renewal or reform, both authentic and (just as useful) legendary, such as Kerle's *Preces speciales* for the Council of Trent, Palestrina's *Missa Papae Marcelli*, Byrd's "political" motets and *Gradualia*, Gaspar Fernandes's *Xicochi xicochi conetzintle* for Oaxaca Cathedral, but also the less formal *laude*, spiritual madrigals, and *travestimenti spirituali*, illustrate the great variety of post-Tridentine music, which belies any notions of a "monolithic" Counter-Reformation.

Further Reading

Alaleona, D. "Le laudi spirituali italiani nei secoli xvi e xvii e il loro rapporto col canti profani." *Rivista musicale italiana*, 16 (1909), 1–52.

Banchieri, Adriano. *Cartella musicale*. Venice, 1614.

Barassi, Elena Ferrari. "Il madrigale spirituale nel Cinquecento e la raccolta Monteverdiana del 1583." In *Claudio Monteverdi e il suo Tempo*, ed. Raffaello Monterosso, 217–52. Verona, 1969.

[13] Culley and McNaspy, "Music and the Early Jesuits," 240–41.

BIANCONI, Lorenzo. *Music in the Seventeenth Century*, trans. David Bryant. Cambridge, 1987.

BORROMEO, Agostino. "La storia delle cappelle musicali vista nella prospettiva della storia della chiesa." In *La cappella musicale nell'Italia della Controriforma*, ed. Oscar Mischiati and Paolo Russo, 229–37. Cento, 1993.

BRETT, Philip. Preface to *The Byrd Edition*, v, pp. vii–xx; VIa, pp. vii–xii. London, 1989, 1991.

CARAMAN, Philip. *Henry Garnet, 1555–1606, and the Gunpowder Plot*. New York, 1964.

COCHRANE, Eric W. "Counter Reformation or Tridentine Reformation? Italy in the Age of Carlo Borromeo." In *San Carlo Borromeo, Catholic Reform and Ecclesiastical Politics in the Second Half of the Sixteenth Century*, ed. John M. Headley and John B. Tomaro, 31–46. Washington, 1988.

——. *Italy, 1530–1630*, ed. Julius Kirschner. London, 1988.

Concilium Tridentinum: Diariorum, Actorum, Epistularum, Tractatuum novi collectio. 13 vols. in 17. Freiburg, 1901–67.

CULLEY, Thomas, SJ. "Musical Activity in Some Sixteenth Century Jesuit Colleges, with Special Reference to the Venerable English College in Rome from 1579 to 1589." *Studien zur italienish-deutschen Musikgeschichte*, 12 (1979), 1–21.

——, and MCNASPY, Clement J. "Music and the Early Jesuits." *Archivium historicum Societatis Jesu*, 40 (1971), 213–45.

D'ACCONE, Frank. "The Musical Chapels at the Florentine Cathedral and Baptistry during the First Half of the Sixteenth Century." *Journal of the American Musicological Society*, 24 (1971), 1–50.

DEAN, Jeffrey J. "The Repertory of the Cappella Giulia in the 1560s." *Journal of the American Musicological Society*, 41 (1988), 465–90.

Decreta authentica Congregationis Sacrorum Rituum ex actis eiusdem collecta eiusque auctoritate promulgata sub auspiciis SS. Domini Nostri Leonis Papae xiii, I. Rome, 1898.

DELUMEAU, Jean. *Catholicism between Luther and Voltaire: A New View of the Counter-Reformation*. London, 1977.

——. *Le Péché e la peur: La Culpabilisation en Occident, XIIIe–XVIIIe siècles*. Paris, 1983.

FELLERER, K. G. "Church Music and the Council of Trent." *The Musical Quarterly*, 39 (1953), 576–94.

GARDELLINI, Aloisius (ed.). *Decreta authentica Congregationis Sacrorum Rituum ex actis eiusdem collecta*, I. Rome, 1856.

GINZBURG, Carlo. *The Cheese and the Worms: The Cosmos of a Sixteenth-Century Miller*, trans. John Tedeschi and Anne Tedeschi. Baltimore, 1980.

——. *The Night Battles*, trans. John Tedeschi and Anne Tedeschi. Baltimore, 1983.

HABERL, Ferdinando. "Jacobus de Kerle e le sue *Preci speciali* per il Concilio di Trento." *Quadrivium* 7 (1966), 31–37.

HABERL, F. X. "Die Cardinalskommission von 1564 und Palestrina's Missa Papae Marcelli." *Kirchenmusikalisches Jahrbuch*, 7 (1892), 82–97.

HARDING, Robert R. "The Mobilization of Confraternities against the Reformation in France." *Sixteenth Century Journal*, 11 (1980), 85–104.

HAYBURN, Robert F. *Papal Legislation on Sacred Music, 95 A.D. to 1977 A.D.*. Collegeville, MN, 1979.

JEDIN, Hubert. *Katholische Reformation oder Gegenreformation*. Lucerne, 1946.

——. *Papal Legate at the Council of Trent: Cardinal Seripando*, trans. Frederic E. Eckhoff. St. Louis and London, 1947.

——. *Geschichte des Konzils von Trient*. 4 vols.. Freiburg, 1950–75.

JEDIN, Hubert. *Crisis and Closure of the Council of Trent*. London, 1967.

KENDRICK, Robert. "Feminized Devotion, Musical Nuns, and the 'New-Style' Lombard Motet of the 1640s." In *Rediscovering the Muses: Women's Musical Traditions*, ed. Kimberly Marshall, 124–39. Boston, 1993.

——. "'Sonet vox tua in auribus meis': Song of Songs Exegesis and the 17th-Century Motet." *Schütz-Jahrbuch*, 16 (1994): 99–118.

——. *Celestial Sirens: Nuns and their Music in Early Modern Milan*. Oxford: Clarendon Press, 1996.

——. "Martyrdom in Seventeenth-Century Italian Music." In *From Rome to Eternity: Catholicism and the Arts in Italy, ca.1550–1650*, ed. Pamela M. Jones and Thomas Worcester, 121–42. Boston, 2002.

——. *The Sounds of Milan, 1585–1650*. Oxford, 2002.

KERMAN, Joseph. "The Elizabethan Motet: A Study of Texts for Music." *Studies in the Renaissance*, 9 (1962), 273–308.

——. *The Masses and Motets of William Byrd*. London, 1981.

LEMMON, Alfred. "Jesuits and Music in Mexico." *Archivium historicum Societatis Jesu*, 46 (1977), 191–97.

LOCKWOOD, Lewis. "Vincenzo Ruffo and Musical Reform after the Council of Trent." *The Musical Quarterly*, 43 (1957), 342–71.

——. *The Counter-Reformation and the Masses of Vincenzo Ruffo*. Vienna, 1969.

—— (ed.). *Giovanni Pierluigi da Palestrina: Pope Marcellus Mass*. New York, 1975.

MACEY, Patrick. "The Lauda and the Cult of Savonarola." *Renaissance Quarterly*, 45 (1992), 439–83.

——. *Bonfire Songs: Savonarola's Musical Legacy*. Oxford, 1998.

MANSI, Joannes Dominicus. *Sacrorum Conciliorum nova et amplissima collectio*, XXXIV. Paris, 1902.

MARTIN, Gregory. *Roma sancta (1581)*, ed. George Bruner Parks. Rome, 1969.

MCGRATH, Patrick, and ROWE, Joy. "The Elizabethan Priests, Their Harbourers and Helpers." *Recusant History*, 19 (1989), 209–33.

MISCHIATI, Oscar. "Il Concilio di Trento e la polifonia: Una diversa proposta di lettera e di prospettiva bibliografica." In *Musica e liturgia nella riforma tridentina*, ed. Danilo Curti and Marco Gozzi, 19–29. Trent, 1995.

MONSON, Craig. *Disembodied Voices: Music and Culture in an Early Modern Italian Convent*. Berkeley and Los Angeles, 1995.

——. "Putting Bolognese Nun Musicians in their Place." In *Women's Voices across Musical Worlds*, ed. Jane Bernstein, 118–41. Boston, 2004.

——. "The Council of Trent Revisited." *Journal of the American Musicological Society*, 55 (2002), 1–37.

—— (ed.). *The Crannied Wall: Women, Religion, and the Arts in Early Modern Europe*. Ann Arbor, MI, 1992.

MORANDI, Giambattista (ed.). *Monumenti di varia letteratura tratti dai manoscritti di Monsignor Lodovico Beccadelli arcivescovo di Ragusa*. 2 vols. Bologna, 1797–1804.

MORELLI, Arnaldo. "*Il tempio armonico*: Musica nell'Oratorio dei Filippini in Roma (1575–1705)." *Analecta musicologica*, 27 (1992), whole issue.

O'MALLEY, John W. "Was Ignatius Loyola a Church Reformer? Rethinking the Myths of Reform." *Catholic Historical Review*, 77 (1991), 177–93.

——. *Trent and All That: Renaming Catholicism in the Early Modern Era*. Cambridge, MA, 2000.

PESCE, Dolores (ed.). *Hearing the Motet: Essays on the Motet of the Middle Ages and Renaissance.* New York, 1996.
PRODI, Paolo. *Il Cardinale Gabriele Paleotti (1522–1597).* Rome, 1959–67.
——. "Lineamenti dell'organizzazione diocesana in Bologna durante l'episcopato del Card. G. Paleotti (1566–1597)." In *Problemi di Vita Religiosa in Italia nel Cinquecento,* ed. M. Maccarrone et al., 323–94. Padua, 1960.
——. "San Carlo Borromeo e il Cardinale Gabriele Paleotti: Due vescovi della Riforma Cattolica." *Critica storia,* 3 (1964), 135–51.
——. "Il binomio jediniano 'Riforma Cattolica e Controriforma' e la storiografia italiana." *Annali dell'Istituto storico italo-germanico in Trento,* 6 (1980), 85–98.
——. "Controriforma e/o Riforma Cattolica: Superamento di vecchi dilemmi nei nuovi panorami storiografici." *Römische historische Mitteilungen,* 31 (1989), 227–37.
REARDON, Colleen. *Holy Concord within Sacred Walls: Nuns and Music in Siena, 1575–1700.* New York, 2002)
REESE, Gustave. *Music in the Renaissance.* New York, 1954.
ROCHE, Jerome. *North Italian Church Music in the Age of Monteverdi.* Oxford, 1984.
ROMITA, Fiorenzo. *Ius musicae liturgicae: Dissertatio historico-iuridica.* Turin, 1936.
RORKE, Margaret Ann. "Sacred Contrafacta of Monteverdi Madrigals and Cardinal Borromeo's Milan." *Music & Letters,* 65 (1984), 168–75.
SCHROEDER, H. J., OP. *Canons and Decrees of the Council of Trent.* London, 1941.
SHERR, Richard. "From the Diary of a Sixteenth-Century Papal Singer." *Current Musicology,* 25 (1978), 83–98.
——. "A Letter from Paolo Animuccia: A Composer's Response to the Council of Trent." *Early Music,* 12 (1984), 75–78.
SMITH, Jeffrey. *Sensuous Worship: Jesuits and the Art of the Early Catholic Reformation in Germany.* Princeton, 2002.
SMITHER, Howard. *A History of the Oratorio,* I. Chapel Hill, NC, 1977.
STEFANI, Gino. *Musica e religione nell'Italia barocca.* Palermo, 1975.
STEVENSON, Robert M. "European Music in 16th-Century Guatamala." *The Musical Quarterly,* 50 (1964), 340–52.
——. "The First New World Composers: Fresh Data from Peninsular Archives." *Journal of the American Musicological Society,* 23 (1970), 95–106.
——. *Latin American Colonial Music Anthology.* Washington, 1975.
WEBER, Edith. *Le Concile de Trente et la musique: De la Réforme à la Contre-Réforme.* Paris, 1982.
WEINMANN, Karl. *Das Konzil von Trient und die Kirchenmusik.* Leipzig, 1919; repr. Hildesheim, 1980)
WESTON, William. *An Autobiography from the Jesuit Underground,* trans. Philip Caraman. New York, 1955.
ZARDIN, Danilo. *Riforma Cattolica e resistenze nobiliari nella diocesi di Carlo Borromeo.* Milan, 1983.

21

SPAIN, *i*: 1530–1600

Todd M. Borgerding
Louise K. Stein

DURING the sixteenth century, Spanish musical culture enjoyed a period of expansion unprecedented in peninsular history. Religious and secular institutions, buoyed by the wealth flowing in from the colonies in the New World, spent lavishly on expanding the vocal and instrumental ensembles that had been established in the fifteenth and early sixteenth centuries. Because the Church enjoyed immense political and economic power during this period, musical life flourished particularly in such great cathedral cities as Seville, Toledo, and Barcelona, where churchmen favorably inclined to music supported a large number of musicians in a liturgy richly adorned with music. The Spanish monarchs Charles V and Philip II maintained large royal musical establishments as well, and their patronage assured that Spanish music kept its place in the compositional developments of the European mainstream. Many notable musicians came to Spain to serve the royal court. The unwavering royal support of traditional doctrine played a part as well in the flourishing of cathedral music, although the favor bestowed on foreign-born composers made the royal contribution to indigenous musical development somewhat less significant. Finally, peninsular musical culture, both sacred and secular, was deeply imbued with the humanist tradition, and the intellectual and economic resources of the Church, the royal court, and noble families were directed toward promoting artistic and musical creativity.

Music in Religious Institutions

Cathedrals

Early modern Spanish musical culture has been accused of insularity and Spanish composers characterized as provincial for their reluctance to work outside Spain. In fact, the inventories of sixteenth-century Spanish musical libraries make clear that Spanish patrons and musicians lived in a cosmopolitan musical culture where the works of many foreign composers were performed and studied. Works by Agricola, Arcadelt, Brumel, Clemens non Papa, Compère, Févin, Gombert, Isaac, Josquin, Manchicourt, Mouton, Obrecht, Ockeghem, Palestrina, Richafort, Verdelot, Weerbecke, and Willaert can be found today in Iberian manuscripts, or once filled the shelves of Spanish and Portuguese libraries.[1] Printed collections, such as the vihuela books put together by Spanish composers and editors, testify to the fact that even non-professional musicians and listeners were familiar with many kinds of foreign music, both sacred and secular. On the other hand, Spain's richly endowed cathedrals provided native composers with such attractive incomes and excellent musical resources that relatively few Spanish composers during the sixteenth century pursued careers abroad.

Peninsular musicians were, however, were a mobile group, traveling across Europe on professional trips and moving across the peninsula from cathedral to cathedral as more attractive positions fell vacant. Francisco Guerrero (1528–1599), whose large and varied body of works made him one of the leading composers in Spain, spent most of his career in Seville but traveled frequently across Spain and to Italy. After a brief appointment as *maestro de capilla* in Jaén while still in his teens, Guerrero returned to Seville in 1554, where he served first as assistant to Pedro Fernández de Castileja (from whom he had received his musical education as a choirboy) and later as *maestro* until his death. Guerrero traveled to Italy on several occasions: he was in Rome in 1581–82 in order to supervise several large publications of his music and returned to Italy in 1588 in the retinue of the cardinal of Seville, Rodrigo de Castro. That trip was extended by a pilgrimage to the Holy Land, which Guerrero wrote about in his best-selling travelogue *Viaje a Jerusalem* (Valencia, 1590). More common than Guerrero's long tenure at Seville were the itinerant careers of musicians like Rodrigo de Ceballos (*c.*1530–1591), who was educated in Seville, moved to Córdoba in 1556, and then went to the *capilla real* of Granada in 1561. Juan Navarro (1528–1580), born near Seville, was a member of the choir at Málaga Cathedral (1553–55) and Jaén before becoming *maestro* at a succession of institutions, including the collegiate church of Valladolid (1562) and the cathedrals of Ávila, Salamanca (1566), Ciudad Rodrigo (1574), and Palencia (1578). Sebastián de Vivanco (*c.*1550–1622), held successive posts in Lérida (Catalonia), Segovia, and his native city of Ávila before moving on to Salamanca, where he served both as the cathedral's chapel master and professor of music at the University. Alonso Lobo (*c.*1555–1617), another composer from Andalusia, sang at Osuna and served as Guerrero's assistant in Seville before his election in 1593 to the prestigious post of *maestro* at Toledo Cathedral, where he stayed until the

[1] A great deal of information on the musical holdings of Spanish libraries is offered in Emilio Ros-Fábregas, "Libros de música en bibliotecas españolas del siglo XVI," *Pliegos de bibliofilia* 15–17 (2001–2, forthcoming). The contents of the choirbooks in the library of the Spanish royal chapel in the time of Philip II are given in Francisco Javier Sánchez Cantón, *Inventarios reales: Bienes muebles que pertenecieron a Felipe II* (Madrid, 1956–59), 139–59. The inventory of the enormous library of King João IV of Portugal, *Primeira parte do Index da livraria de música de El-Rei D. João* (Lisbon, 1649), has been reprinted in facsimile with an introductory study by Mário de Sampaio Ribeiro (Lisbon, 1967).

Seville chapter lured him south again in 1604. And Juan de Esquivel Barahona (*c.*1562–1625), trained in Ciudad Rodrigo, became chapel master in his late teens at Oviedo Cathedral before returning to his home city.

The cathedrals, which typically supported instrumental ensembles, choir schools, polyphonic choirs, organists, and special chant choirs made up of clergymen (*veyntenores*), were fertile ground for the development of musical culture. The history of these musical institutions during the sixteenth century is one of expansion and development, as cathedrals vied with each other to adorn their liturgies with performances by the best musicians. The system of musical education in cathedral schools, which included lessons in counterpoint and composition for adults and boys alike, produced talented performers whose services were in high demand. The effort that cathedral chapters expended in recruiting singers was an indication of the high value they placed on the performance of polyphonic music in their liturgies. The choirboys, under the tutelage of the *maestro de capilla*, performed some chants, and a select group of six older boys (called *seises* in Seville) joined in the performance of polyphonic works. Polyphonic music was sung by a *capilla* of between eight and twelve adult singers, designated bass, tenor, alto and *tiple*. The choir school never produced enough adult singers to meet the needs of the cathedral, so that *maestros de capilla* such as Guerrero were frequently sent on recruiting trips across the peninsula in search of skilled singers. Special prebends were created in the second half of the sixteenth century to attract singers; this was the case in 1560 when the canons at Seville voted to create additional half-prebends for singers. Canon Hernand Ramírez, who in 1560 donated his prebend to this end, summed up the circumstances:

> given the great necessity that this holy church has that its musical *capilla* be appropriate for the service of God and his divine office, and correspond to the decency and grandeur of such an illustrious church, and given the need that she has of able singers with fine voices in the necessary numbers, and since because of the vagaries of these times they must be given large and competent salaries, and since we have gone out over the entire kingdom looking for singers and none desired to come and serve in his holy church at the present salary, and since the cause of this is that many cathedral churches offer more prebends reserved for singers, which positions they esteem more since they offer not only perpetual salaries but also the honor of the prebend, and since such prebends do not exist in this church except for the organist and *maestro de capilla* . . . I petition the pope that he divide my canonry and prebend that I possess in this holy church into three portions which are to be given to three famous singers.[2]

The new positions were not instituted until Ramírez's death in 1574, and in the meantime the chapter had to resort to other tactics: in 1562 it wrote to the Archbishop of Seville, Hernando de Váldez (who was in Madrid in his capacity as

2 Seville, Cathedral Archive (hereafter ACS), Sec. IV, leg. 198, no. 1, fol. 1^{r-v}.

head of the Spanish Inquisition), begging him to use his influence to procure more singers.

> we understand that in Gaudix there is a good bass or tenor who we would like your lordship to send to us . . . or that you advise us of where we may find other such appropriate singers. All of which we ask be done with all possible haste so that we do not find ourselves mute this Christmas. Since we know your lordship to be a great aficionado and devoted to music we pray you to assist us in this matter. 12 November 1562.[3]

The machinations of the Seville chapter to procure singers reflect not only the fierce competition that existed between cathedrals for competent musicians, but, just as important, the high value placed on musical adornment of the liturgy.

These singers performed a repertory that stressed the work of Spanish composers, but also included works from the international canon of Franco-Flemish and later Counter-Reformation composers. An inventory from Seville cathedral drawn up in 1586, for example, lists printed books and manuscripts of music by Guerrero, Morales, Victoria, Josquin, and George de la Hèle.[4] In Granada a similar inventory from 1592 lists music of the local composer Juan de Aranda together with pieces by Guerrero, Victoria, Morales, Gombert, and Palestrina.[5] And the rich music library at Toledo Cathedral contains the music of Josquin, La Rue, Noel Bauldeweyn, Jachet Berchem, Nicolas Champion, Clemens non Papa, Compère, Festa, Févin, Gombert, Isaac, Mouton, Palestrina, Phinot, Richafort, and Willaert.[6]

Spanish cathedral choirs performed a rich repertory of sacred music in a variety of liturgical contexts beyond the strictly liturgical numbers for Mass and Office. The *Salve* service, a popular devotional exercise in early modern Europe, was celebrated with polyphonic music in Spain. The sixteenth-century historian Alonso Morgado made special mention of this devotion in his description of the Antigua chapel at Seville Cathedral:

> There one may see the venerated image, in the form of a well-proportioned woman, in a sumptuous chapel in the cathedral, where she is venerated with popular and continuous frequency by all the people of Seville. The chapel is illuminated by forty silver lamps, and in her presence many masses and fiestas are said in her chapel. Every Saturday the *Salve* [is sung there] in polyphony by the cathedral's entire musical establishment of voices and instruments.[7]

The typical *Salve* service consisted of the performance of a polyphonic *Salve regina*, prayers, a motet, and a choral "Deo dicamus gratias" response to the

[3] ACS, Sec. IX, lib. 163, fol. 8ʳ.

[4] ACS, Sec. O, lib. 53, fols. 56ʳ–57ʳ.

[5] José López-Calo, "El Archivo de música de la Capilla Real de Granada," *Anuario musical*, 13 (1958), 122.

[6] Felipe Rubio Piqueras, *Códices polifónicos toledanos* (Toledo, 1925). See also François Reynaud, *La Polyphonie tolédane et son milieu des premiers témoignages aux environs de 1600* (Paris, 1996), 345–71.

[7] Alonso Morgado, *Historia de Sevilla* (Seville, 1587; repr. Seville, 1887), 350.

dismissal. A measure of the importance of this service is that several manuscripts containing *Salve regina* settings, motets, and choral reponses survive at Seville and other peninsular and colonial religious centers.[8]

Music was accorded such a lofty place in Spanish cathedrals that the extraliturgical genres in Latin and in the vernacular were cultivated as they were perhaps nowhere else in Europe. As was the case in many European churches, the motet in Spain was performed during the Mass, but was largely restricted to the Elevation. It was sometimes used at the offertory, as suggested by a document that describes motets being sung at the offertory in Valencia,[9] but the weight of the evidence strongly points to the Elevation as the context for motets. Thus a 1604 ceremonial for Toledo Cathedral notes that for Masses on solemnities, polyphonic music included a "motet at the Elevation," and in similar documents at Seville, motets were restricted in the Mass to the Elevation.[10] Motets were widely performed in extraliturgical contexts, including not only the *Salve* services but also processions. Seville Cathedral possessed special partbooks containing motets for processions, and late sixteenth-century accounts of religious celebrations are rife with descriptions of the singing of motets in processions.[11] *Villancicos* or *chansonetas* with texts in the vernacular had a similar if more restricted function in the liturgy. These light, often dance-inspired works were the staple of processions, although they also were sung at Matins and Mass on such occasions as Christmas, Epiphany, and during the famous Corpus Christi celebrations.[12]

Liturgists and chapel-masters were also able to take advantage of a well-established Spanish tradition of singing improvised polyphony or *contrapunto.* Trained in composition and improvisation as choirboys, Spanish singers made a name for themselves for their skill at the art of vocal improvisation over a cantus firmus, and attained a high degree of refinement in their performances, to judge by the testimony of the theorist Juan Bermudo.

> There are men so expert in improvisation, of such account and erudition, that when they perform with many voices it is so correct and fugue-like that it seems like the most studied composition in the world. In the consummate chapel of the very reverend Archbishop of Toledo, Fonseca of blessed memory, I witnessed dexterous singers make counterpoint such that if it were written down it might be sold for good composition. In the no less religious than very learned royal chapel of Granada there are such great abili-

[8] Robert Snow, *A New-World Collection of Polyphony for Holy Week and the Salve Service*, Monuments of Renaissance Music, 9 (Chicago and London, 1996), 65–76.

[9] See José Climent, "La capilla de música de la catedral de Valencia," *Anuario musical*, 37 (1982), 61–65.

[10] "Memorial del estilo que se ha de guardar en esta santa yglesia de Toledo (1604)", *E-Mn*, 14.145(123), fol. 1^{r}; Sebastián Vicente de Villegas, "Norma de los sagrados rítos y ceremonias ... en esta santa iglesia metropolitana de Sevilla (1630)," ACS, Sec. III, no. 36, fols. 35^{r}, 44^{r}.

[11] Todd Borgerding, "The Motet and Spanish Religiosity, ca.1550–1610" (PhD diss., University of Michigan, 1997), 61–106.

[12] Summarized in Paul R. Laird, *Towards a History of the Spanish Villancico* (Warren, MI, 1997), 17–31.

> ties in counterpoint that ears more delicate than mine would be necessary to comprehend them, and another pen to explain them. Indeed, such are the wonders of counterpoint made in the churches and courts of our Spain; who could manage to describe them?[13]

At the end of the sixteenth century *contrapunto* was a regular feature of cathedral music. It is described in cathedral ceremonials at Seville and Toledo as being performed on such chants as the *Asperges* and responsories.[14] Indeed, the Spanish tradition of polyphonic responsories for the Office of the Dead had a long tradition of improvised performance.[15]

One hallmark of sixteenth-century Iberian religious music is the important role that instrumental ensembles played in church music. Ensembles made up of shawms, cornetti, sackbuts, recorders, and dulcians were integral to the performance of Spanish sacred polyphony.[16] Wind players added color and majesty to the music for Mass, processions, and *Salve* services, and during the sixteenth century they evolved from ad-hoc groups to standing, salaried ensembles. In 1553 the canons at Seville voted to create permanent salaried positions for instrumentalists, and their reasons were made clear in the official act that created the positions:

> it is a very decent thing and conforms to divine scriptures that the cathedral be served with all kinds of honest music such as that of the said instrumentalists. Being as it is such an illustrious and grand temple it has a great need of the sonority of the said music. Moreover, all of the other cathedral churches in Spain have such instrumentalists, even though their resources are less than ours. And more importantly, since the cathedral community goes out in procession on many solemn days of the year to parishes and monasteries of Seville, often for long distances, this music is appropriate because with it the processions proceed with more honor and authority and devotion, and the music incites more devotion in the people and moves them to accompany the processions and come to the divine offices in the cathedral.[17]

The oft-cited guidelines drawn up in Seville in 1586 to regulate the performance of the *ministriles* during the *Salve* services in the cathedral testify to a tradition of interaction between voices and instruments that featured improvisation by wind players.[18] In addition, the *bajón* (a sort of early bassoon) and even ensembles of *bajones* and *bajoncillos* in different sizes were played to support the singers in polyphony, especially in the singing of psalms. The *vihuela de arco* (viol) is frequently

[13] Juan Bermudo, *Declaración de instrumentos* (Osuna, 1555), fol. 138r.

[14] "Memorial del estilo", fol. 2r; Villegas, "Norma de los sagrados rítos," fol. 35r.

[15] George Grayson Wagstaff, "Music for the Office of the Dead: Polyphonic Settings of the *Officium* and *Missa pro defunctis* by Spanish and Latin American Composers before 1630" (PhD diss., University of Texas at Austin, 1995).

[16] For an excellent overview of this topic, see Kenneth Kreitner, "Ministrels in Spanish Churches, 1400–1600," *Early Music*, 20 (1992), 532–46.

[17] ACS, Sec. IV, lib. 324, fol. 166v.

[18] First brought to light in Robert M. Stevenson, *Spanish Cathedral Music in the Golden Age* (Berkeley and Los Angeles, 1961), 167.

mentioned in the documents as one of the instruments heard in the performance of *chançonetas* during festivals, including Corpus Christi.

Monasteries

The conservative tone of musical performance at the royal Hieronymite monastery of San Lorenzo at El Escorial is an extreme example of the restricted musical environment that characterized most Spanish monasteries and convents in the sixteenth century. The performance of polyphony by the religious orders was a highly contentious matter , since the complexity of polyphonic music was considered by some religious leaders to be detrimental to the task of reciting the divine hours. Musical complexity could be heard as a distractingly earthly artifice, and musical beauty was suspect for its potential as sensual temptation, as St Augustine had warned. The Dominicans had strong proscriptions against polyphony, the Jesuits viewed music with suspicion, and the austerity of the Franciscans precluded the development of a vibrant musical tradition in their convents. The ambivalence of attitudes toward music at monastic institutions contrasts strongly with the enthusiasm for music that drained the treasuries of cathedrals and made famous the excellence of the royal chapels. One early-seventeenth-century critic grumbled that "polyphony sullies the purity of the cloister," yet grudgingly allowed for music in cathedrals: "Let the secular brethren have their polyphony if they insist, but religious orders must aspire to higher ideals."[19] Manuscripts of sacred polyphony survive in the archives of the largest and richest monasteries, such as those at Ávila, El Escorial, Guadalupe, and Montserrat, but the contents of these sources indicate that the strictly liturgical genres, such as psalms and hymns, were the staple of musical performances there.[20]

This reticence about music, especially polyphonic music, was celebrated by Spanish painters, it would seem, in their depictions of the famous musical distraction suffered by an otherwise penitent St Jerome. In the standard telling, Jerome was distracted from his holy penitence by a vision offering naked women who danced and wiggled to tempt him—a shocking thing for one of the learned fathers of the Church to imagine. Of course, early-modern Spanish artists did not paint naked women, so they found other ways to depict the effects of lascivious music for this episode from the life of St Jerome. Juan Ribalta's *St Jerome* (1618) (Barcelona, Museo de Arte de Catalunya) turns as if to lend his ear to an unexplained musical interruption, and Alonso Cano's *Penitent St Jerome* (Madrid, Museo del Prado) suffers from a sudden trumpet blast into his ear. Francisco de Zurbarán's *Temptation of St Jerome*, painted around 1638–39 (Guadalupe, Real Monasterio de

[19] Quoted in Stevenson, *Spanish Cathedral Music*, 333–34.

[20] For studies of monastic repertories, see David Crawford, "Two Choirbooks of Renaissance Polyphony at the Monasterio de Nuestra Señora of Guadalupe," *Fontes artis musicae*, 24 (1977), 145–74; Samuel Rubio, *Catálogo del archivo de música del Monasterio de San Lorenzo el Real de El Escorial* (Cuenca, 1976); Alexandre Olivar, *Catàleg dels manuscrits de la biblioteca del Monestir de Montserrat* (Montserrat, 1977); Alfonso Vicente Delgado, *La música en el Monasterio de Santa Ana de Ávila* (Madrid, 1989).

Nuestra Señora) tells the story with a depiction of the most beloved of contemporary Spanish instruments. A realistically painted harp is played by a lovely young girl, one member of a serious and placid group of six female musicians who visit St Jerome's otherwise clean, erudite imagination to tempt him. Though Zurbarán's girls seem not only modestly attired, serious, and without visual artifice, the Saint immediately throws up his hands in an exclamation of horror. His reaction tells us that Jerome most likely heard the music of lascivious *bailes* in his mind's ear from the guitars and the harp. What Zurbarán painted was St Jerome's horrified rejection of "dishonest and ill-formed songs."

Given the enticing beauty of the music heard in many public places, as well as at church, it should not surprise us that the monastic orders attempted to sweep their halls clean of music's wayward influence, but it is not at all clear that convents of nuns practiced the same sort of abstinence from musical performance. Scholars have uncovered very little about the place of music in peninsular convents as yet, but Morgado provided a tantalizing glimpse into the musical lives of nuns in Seville when he described:

> the blessed nuns and their admirable harmony of instruments, harps, *vihuelas de arco*, instrumentalists, keyboard, and sung polyphony, and the celestial harmony, smoothness, joy, jubilation and sweetness with which night and day they celebrate as Christ's spouses his worthy praises, awaiting his arrival with the burning lamps of their pure religion.[21]

To be sure, the convent of Descalzas Reales in Madrid, where Victoria worked at the end of his life, maintained a large musical establishment of ordained priests and expert singers. But that convent was exceptional; it had been established with a royal endowment, became the retreat of the dowager Empress, and enjoyed not only the financial resources of the royal household but also the status of a Capilla Real.

Spaniards Abroad

Despite enticements to remain at home, a number of Spanish musicians made their careers abroad, many finding work in Roman ecclesiastical choirs.[22] Bartolomé de Escobedo (*c.*1500–1563) sang at Salamanca Cathedral until 1536 when he was recruited to the papal choir in Rome, where he joined his countryman Juan Escribano (*c.*1478–1557), who sang in Rome from 1502 until 1539. The substantial, continuous Spanish presence in the papal choir was distinguished later in the century by the tenure of Francisco Soto de Langa (1534–1619) who sang there from 1562 until his retirement in 1611. Gabriel Gálvez (*c.*1510–1578) served at Sta Maria Maggiore in Rome (where Pedro Guerrero, older brother of Francisco, also sang in

[21] Morgado, *Historia de Sevilla*, 475.

[22] On the history of this tradition, see Richard Sherr, "The 'Spanish Nation' in the Papal Chapel, 1492–1521," *Early Music*, 20 (1992), 601–9.

the 1560s) before returning to his native Cuenca in 1560 to become *maestro* there. Other composers who traveled did so because of the relocation of their patrons. This was the case of Mateo Flecha the younger (*c.*1530–1604), who moved to Vienna when his employer, the Infanta María, became the wife of Maximilian II in 1548.

The careers of these musicians in Rome reflect the more general influence of the Spanish Church in the religious life of sixteenth-century Europe. The careers of the two Spanish composers who rose to international prominence during their Roman sojourns, Cristóbal de Morales (*c.*1500–1553) and Tomás Luis de Victoria (1548–1611), provide further evidence for the strength of the Spanish Church and its musicians. Morales, a native of Seville, was *maestro de capilla* at Ávila cathedral from 1526 until 1528, when he moved to Plasencia, where he stayed until 1531. It was during his ten years as a singer in the papal choir (beginning *c.*1535) that Morales established himself as a composer of international importance. His most important publications were issued beginning in 1541, during the second of his five-year terms in the papal chapel. Morales's prolific musical output was published in Rome, Milan, and Venice, as well as Antwerp, Augsburg, Lyons, Nuremberg, and Wittenberg.

When he returned to Spain in 1545, Morales assumed the position of director of music at Toledo Cathedral, arguably the principal musical post in Spain and one in keeping with his high reputation. Morales's tenure at Toledo was plagued by administrative difficulties, however. He left after only two years and returned to his native Andalusia. He served as *maestro de capilla* to the Duke of Arcos at Marchena from 1548 to 1551, and then took the relatively humble position of *maestro* at the cathedral of Málaga. Shortly after his appointment, the expected problems arose with the singers, who were unaccustomed to his rigorous standards. Morales applied again for the post of *maestro de capilla* at Toledo in August 1553, but died in October of the same year, while the cathedral's administrators deliberated about his questionable management skills.

The career of Tomás Luis de Victoria has important parallels to that of Morales, although Victoria was less an ambitious musician and more dedicated to his strictly pious, charitable, and pastoral duties as a priest. He began his musical training as a choirboy at Ávila cathedral, where Morales had started his career. Once his voice changed, around 1565, he was sent to study at the German Jesuit College in Rome. He remained in Rome for about two decades, composing and holding various positions at the church of Sta Maria di Monserrato, the German Jesuit College, the Oratory of S. Filippo Neri, and S. Girolamo della Carità. Proof of Victoria's standing as Good Samaritan among clerics in Rome is the fact that in 1583 he was elected visitor to the sick and destitute among the Spanish residents in Rome under the jurisdiction of the Confraternity of the Resurrection. In the dedication of his *Missarum libri duo* (Rome, 1583) to King Philip II, Victoria wrote that he wished to return to Spain to lead a quiet life as a priest. Recognizing Victoria's service to the faith, Philip II named him chaplain to his sister, the Dowager Empress María, who had retired with her daughter, the Infanta Margarita, to the Descalzas Reales convent in Madrid. Victoria served the dowager Empress from

1587 until her death in 1603. He was then *maestro* of the convent's polyphonic choir (comprised of twelve chaplains who sang with four choirboys) until 1604 and subsequently organist until his death. At least two Spanish cathedrals, Seville and Zaragoza, had attempted to lure Victoria away from the royal service in 1587. But his position at the Descalzas Reales afforded Victoria a number of perquisites, among them the chance to lead an especially fine choir of trained singers without incurring the heavy administrative and pedagogical responsibilities that a cathedral post would bring with it. Moreover, at the Descalzas Reales convent, his own compositions were regularly performed at Mass for a devout congregation that included members of the royal family and the nobility.

The Spanish Royal Court

THERE is no doubt that the rulers who presided over Spain's musical Renaissance, Charles v and Philip ii, supported music and musical institutions, but the extent to which their personal tastes influenced the development of music and musical styles is more difficult to determine. Because the daily rituals and routines of the Spanish Habsburg monarchs were smoothly controlled by protocols and administrative and ceremonial traditions inherited from the courts of Burgundy, Castile, and Aragon, these kings were in some ways "prisoners of ceremony." Both kings maintained large musical establishments, but musical leadership was given over largely to non-Spaniards, in keeping with the Burgundian traditions that came to Spain with Charles v. The so-called "Spanish Chapel" did not function as a wholly independent unit, since its members worked under the directorship of the northern *maestro*, and the Spanish musicians who served in the royal chapel (singers, players of wind instruments, viol players, and lutenists) were undistinguished as composers, with the notable exception of the organist Antonio de Cabezón (1510–1566), who was recruited especially by Philip ii and who served this king for most of his career. [23]

Charles v, who ruled Spain as Carlos i from 1516 until 1555 and as Holy Roman Emperor from 1530 until his abdication in 1556, was responsible for the fact that the Spanish royal chapel became a very large and unwieldy unit in the early sixteenth century, in part because he maintained a chapel of northern singers and instrumentalists that he took with him on his many travels across Europe, while a smaller ensemble made up of Spanish singers remained behind in service to his regent, the Empress Isabella. The *maestros* in the *capilla flamenca* included some of the most important northern composers of the age—Nicolas Gombert, Thomas Crecquillon, and Philippe de Monte, who began a tradition of foreign leadership in the royal chapel that extended to the 1630s. During Philip ii's reign, Nicolas Payen, Pierre de Manchicourt, Jean Bonmarché, Gérard de Turnhout, George

[23] Luis Robledo, "La música en la corte madrileña de los Aústrias; Antecedentes: Las casas reales hasta 1556," *Revista de musicología*, 10 (1987), 753–96. See also Isabel Pope, "The 'Spanish Chapel' of Philip ii," *Renaissance News*, 5 (1952) 1–5, 34–38.

de la Hèle, and Philippe Rogier served as singers, directors, or composers in the chapel. The last Flemish *maestro* to rule the chapel was Matthieu Rosmarin from Liège, who had come to Spain as a boy chorister in 1586. Better known as "Mateo Romero" or "El maestro capitán," he retired in 1633.

Four hundred years after his death, historians no longer think of Philip II as a withdrawn and neurotic monarch, an intolerant religious fanatic who worked and worshipped in solitude, preferring the shadowy hallways of his monastery-palace at El Escorial to a more conventional Renaissance court. Ruler of an enormous and multifaceted empire, Philip II was not the one-dimensional hero of the "black legend." He sincerely and fervently defended his faith and his territories, keeping a close watch on administrative matters for most of his reign. When he established his court in Madrid in 1561, the Alcázar palace became the official royal residence, and its renovation and decoration were of immediate importance. The very construction of the monolithic monastery at El Escorial, an architectural wonder erected between 1563 and 1584 under the direction of the architects Juan Bautista de Toledo and Juan de Herrera, reminds us that Philip's great projects involved the arts, though his piety and sense of filial duty motivated him to build the Escorial with an imperial crypt for the body of his father Charles V at its center. This project was to be Philip's most enduring monument to his personal faith and his chosen role as a political leader of the Catholic cause.

In keeping with the tradition of Spanish monastic houses, the musical practice at El Escorial was characterized by a conservative emphasis on plainchant, which is clearly set forth in the monastery's statutes of foundation:

> And as for the other masses and hours and divine offices which have to be said and celebrated continuously in the said monastery, we wish that they be said and celebrated according to and in conformity with what is laid down in the Constitutions and customs of the Order, and of this it is neither our intention nor desire to alter anything except that they be said and celebrated with the solemnity, ceremonies, order and authority that is the custom, with which we desire and expressly order that they be said and celebrated in plainsong and that there be in no manner, neither in any day nor feast, polyphony, and that for the remainder they be said and celebrated with the greatest devotion and calmness that would be possible.[24]

This statute was not followed to the letter, however, since sung polyphony did have a place in the Escorial liturgy. The music with which the monk-singers at El Escorial adorned chant consisted largely of *fabordone* and improvised polyphony over a plainsong melody, or composed polyphony with a prominently heard liturgical cantus firmus. The cantus firmus pieces by Martín de Villanueva, one of the few composers at El Escorial whose works survive from this period, demonstrate that a carefully simplified, severe, solemn style of polyphony was chosen at El Escorial.

The shadows of El Escorial were dispelled by its splendid decoration with

[24] Translated in Michael Noone, *Music and Musicians in the Escorial Liturgy under the Habsburgs, 1563-1700* (Rochester, 1997), 87.

exquisite paintings by a dazzling array of Flemish, Italian, and Spanish masters. Magnificent gardens and fountains surrounded this other royal residence where songs, dances, and musical-theatrical entertainments were performed for the court and royal family. Philip's early education had included music and dancing—he was taught to participate in the same stately court dances that were the required repertoire of the aristocracy throughout Europe, and the Castilian musical and poetic form of the *romance* also played a special role in the prince's education. With their historical and heroic focus, the *romances* helped the prince to understand his inheritance and to learn about both classical and Castilian heroes and their deeds. The *romances* and the traditional figured dances held their place at court, although Philip was perhaps more devoted to his gardens, and architecture was his passion. Though he did not incorporate chamber musicians with fixed, stable places in his household, Philip II was an enthusiastic and informed patron who cared about the correct and punctual administration of his musical establishment. Like Charles V before him, he supported a large royal chapel of singers, players, and composers who were among the best in Europe. He did not substantially alter or expand the musical establishment that he had inherited (although he created new positions for organists), and in this sense he was a mostly passive patron. Although his own education was Castilian, he invested in tradition rather than innovation, and thus did not foster the development of particularly Spanish genres. The close alignment between Church and state in Spain, together with royal religious policies, led to a special and carefully designed musical conservatism.

Outside of the chapel, music at Philip's court and at the Escorial was governed by the same princely decorum and uncomplicated elegance that characterized the royal taste in painting and architecture. Musical entertainments included the sacred and the secular, the pious and the profane, the high and the low styles, the popular and the sublime, just as did the selection of paintings commissioned and collected by the king. Wind instruments were especially important in royal celebrations and ceremonial, so the court employed *ministriles* who played various sizes of shawms, *orlos*, sackbuts, and cornetti, as well as trumpeters and drummers in various administrative units. Viol and lute playing were part of the musical education of the royal children, and these instruments were also essential for dance music. The courtly figured dances (*danzas* as opposed to the popular and less decorous *bailes*) were reserved for courtly settings, such as the private dancing parties for the queen and the infantas, the royal entertainments prepared by the pages and dancing masters, and the court balls or *saraos* in which the royal family and invited members of the court danced to display their grandeur and elegance. The nature of the occasion and the physical setting for these dances—whether they took place outdoors or indoors, in a large hall or a small apartment—determined whether loud instruments (*instrumentos altos*) such as cornettos, shawms (*chirimías*), and sackbuts (*sacabuches*) or soft instuments (*instrumentos bajos*) such as viols (*vihuelas de arco*), lutes, recorders, harps, or vihuelas accompanied the dancers.

The Spanish Nobility

The musical life at the courts of the Spanish nobility has not been thoroughly studied, although the evidence suggests that they supported a number of important composers. The duke of Arcos, Luis Cristóbal Ponce de León (1518–1573), was praised, together with his father, for his qualities as a musician and patron by Francisco Guerrero in the dedication to his 1555 *sacrae cantiones*:

> I know that it has been a venerable custom in your family to devote such time as remained after serious pursuits to the enjoyment of music. For, not to mention earlier ancestors, one need not be reminded that your father nurtured you from your earliest years in all the subjects proper to the education of a truly noble prince such as you . . . he so enjoyed music that not only did he listen long and lovingly to skilled singers with beautiful voices, but also learned to sing well himself. . . . I could go on praising your father, but conclude with his having engendered so accomplished and courageous a prince as yourself, who are like him in every way.[25]

The duke of Arcos maintained a small chapel at the ducal seat in Marchena, and his household included at various times such musicians as Morales, Juan Navarro, and the theorist Juan Bermudo. It was perhaps because of the small size of such musical establishments that noble courts figured more prominently in the careers of Spanish vihuelists and instrumentalists than they did in those of composers of polyphony. Luis de Milán, musician, composer, writer at the court of the dukes of Calabria in Valencia until about 1538, is the best-known example of this close connection between Renaissance Spanish courts and composers of secular music. In addition to his book of vihuela music, he published a book on courtly behavior, the *Libro de motes de damas y cavalleros, intitulado El juego de mandar* (Valencia, 1535), and an account of life at the court in Valencia in his *El cortesano* of 1561, which was inspired by Castiglione. The duke and duchess of Calabria, Ferdinand of Aragón (d. 1550) and Germaine de Foix, had an excellent chapel, which in the years 1546 to 1550 employed some twenty singers, two organists, a harpist, three sackbut players, three or four shawm players, and two music copyists, one of whom was also a composer. Enríquez de Valderrábano, who published his book of vihuela music in 1547, worked at the court of Francisco de Zuñiga, count of Miranda. Alonso de Mudarra, famed for his vihuela book of 1546, served the dukes of Infantado, Diego Hurtado de Mendoza (1461–1531) and Iñigo López de Mendoza (1493–1566), before he took up a canonry in Seville in 1546.

The dukes of Alba had contributed to musical life in the late fifteenth and early sixteenth centuries through their support of such influential figures as the poet and composer Juan del Encina and the Fleming Johannes Urrede, who later led the chapel of Ferdinand the Catholic. In the sixteenth century the Alba courts welcomed their share of illustrious Spanish musicians. The viol player and improviser

[25] Francisco Guerrero, *Sacrarum cantionum quae vulgo moteta nuncupantur* (Seville, 1555), p. [iv].

Diego Ortiz was *maestro de capilla* of the chapel maintained at Naples by Fernando Álvarez de Toledo, 3rd duke of Alba (Viceroy of Naples 1556–58), and he continued to lead the chapel under Álvarez de Toledo's successor, the duke of Alcalá. The blind organist and musical humanist Francisco de Salinas (1513–1590) also served the duke of Alba as organist to his chapel in Naples from 1553 to 1558, although he had traveled to Italy some years before in the retinue of a Spanish cleric who became a cardinal. In the last decade of the sixteenth century, the singer, vihuelist, and composer Juan Blas de Castro worked as chamber musician to the 5th duke of Alba at his court at Alba de Tormes, where he became a close friend of the poet and dramatist Lope de Vega, who also served there. From references in Lope de Vega's *La Arcadia* of 1598, we know that Juan Blas de Castro sang and played at court festivities, though by 1596 he had been hired away for the royal court by the future King Philip III.

Music and the Spanish Humanist Tradition

In his *Libro de descripción de verdaderos retratos de illustres y memorables varones* of 1599, the late sixteenth-century painter and art critic Francisco Pacheco recognized the professional friendship between Francisco Guerrero and the poet (and sometime composer) Baltasar de Alcázar, noting that they both had "a close friendship with music and poetry."[26] This observation characterizes the music of most peninsular composers, whose works, both sacred and secular, reflect the vibrant humanistic culture of sixteenth-century Spain. This was a century unified by its quest for elegance and its dedication to the linguistic revolution. Spanish writers, and the composers who set their texts, were swept up in the two most prominent linguistic movements of the period—on the one hand, some poets turned to classical Latin rhetoric for their models, while others worked to create a vernacular rhetoric firmly based in the everyday. At the close of the fifteenth century, with the patronage of Queen Isabella, the Spanish scholar Antonio de Nebrija published his *Gramática sobre la lengua castellana* (Salamanca, 1492), the first Spanish vernacular grammar and the first such systematic manual published for any modern European vernacular. In 1496 in Salamanca, the famous poet and musician Juan del Encina published his *Cancionero*, the first published "collected works" of a Spanish poet and one of the very first monographic collections to be published in any European language. Nebrija held the newly created chair in rhetoric at Cardinal Cisnero's University at Alcalá; his humanist legacy was a rich one, reflected in the further development of rhetorical theory by such scholars as Juan de Maldonado, Juan de Valdés, and, later in the century, the great theologian, preacher, and humanist Luis de Granada. Granada's *Rhetorica ecclesiasticae* (1575) was widely read at seminaries and universities founded after the Council of Trent to train a new generation of Counter-Reformation preachers in the precepts of classical oratory and rhetoric.

Within this humanist tradition, Spanish musicians were among the first to

[26] See Miguel Querol Gavaldá, *Francisco Guerrero: Opera Omnia*, I (Barcelona, 1982), 18.

recognize and promote the view that music and words to be sung should coexist in a close relationship. In 1555 the Spanish theorist Juan Bermudo advised aspiring composers that

> one should imitate as far as possible in his composition everything that is said in the text. When setting *Clamavit Jesu voce magna* one should compose a rising line where it says *voce magna*; for *Martha vocavit Mariam sororem suam silentio* the music should become lower for the word *silentio* so that it can scarcely be heard. Where it says *ascendit ad celum* make the music rise. Moreover, one must put a B-flat where there is a sad word. Wherever there is an idea that commands attention such notes should be put down so that in everything they are very much in agreement with the text . . . In this matter, he who is a grammatician, poet, and rhetorician will understand best what I mean.[27]

Bermudo's theoretical marriage of text and music some fifty years before Pacheco's observation about the "close friendship" of music and poetry is important because it reveals the principle that guided the work of Spanish composers, who invariably reveal an intimate understanding of the texts in their musical settings. Indeed, so prevalent is this characteristic of Spanish music that it seems wholly a part of the incipient "second practice," something that Bermudo made clear in a Platonic phrase that resonates with the writings of Monteverdi from a half-century later:

> The composer who wishes to compose correctly must first understand the texts, and make it so that the music serves the text, and not the text the music. For the music must be made according to the text, and not the text for the sake of the music.[28]

Bermudo's views were taken up later in the century by the composer and theorist Francisco de Montanos, who summed up his list of what constituted a good composer by observing that

> the most essential skill of a good composer is to do what the text asks—happy or sad, grave or light-hearted, complex or simple, humble or elevated—so that the music causes the affect that the text asks to be raised in the souls of the listeners.[29]

Later theorists promote a similar relationship between music and text. Francisco de Salinas's *De musica libri septem* (Salamanca, 1577), although more concerned with theoretical speculation than with musical practice, is notable for its chapter on rhythmic theory, which drew on not only classical and patristic authorities, but also on Nebrija's *Grammatica* of 1492. Salinas's pupil Gaspar Stoquerus is nearly unique among Renaissance authors in devoting his attention to the subject of text underlay. Spanish musicians strove to bend their technical resources to the goal of

[27] Bermudo, *Declaración de instrumentos*, fol. 125^{r}.
[28] Ibid., fol. 134^{r}.
[29] Francisco de Montanos, *Arte de música teorética y práctica* (Valladolid, 1592), 27.

creating affectively charged settings. Even at its most contrapuntally complex moments, Spanish music displays a remarkable sensitivity to the text.

Music of the Church

Motets

When composing music for the Church, composers were faced with the problem of balancing a developing humanistic tradition with the demands raised by the upheavals in musico-liturgical practice in the years surrounding the Council of Trent, while at the same time remaining faithful to peninsular religious traditions. Indeed, Guerrero alluded to some of these tensions in the dedication to his *Motteta Francisci Guerreri in Hispalensi Ecclesia musicorum praefecti* (Venice, 1570). Addressing Pope Pius V, Guerrero began with a classically influenced recitation on the power of music:

> Those who would set sacred things to music certainly use the nature of this divine faculty correctly, for there is no smoother balm with which to calm the affects of body or soul, and likewise there is nothing more effective to purify more sacredly, as we say, our mind and to effect our union with celestial things.

Clearly aware of the recent deliberations at Trent, which had called into question the very place of polyphonic music in the liturgy, Guerrero changes his tone to launch a bitter verbal attack upon

> certain men with very depraved ideas [who] must be the more condemned as impious. They are the ones who, desiring the imposition of silence and a perpetual cessation of divine things, hope for nothing less than the exile of music from the churches. But such men are condemned by consent of humanity, . . . [and] these errors are valiantly resisted by many men of rare doctrine and excellent genius. And I, following my profession, resolved to oppose myself, with the aid of your auspices, O Holy Father, to their damned detractions of holy song through the means of these religious compositions.[30]

The tension created by these often contradictory and conflicting demands was perhaps nowhere more brilliantly resolved than in the great motet collections produced by Spanish composers in the sixteenth century. The published collections of Morales and Guerrero set an example for other composers, and what developed was a particularly sensitive approach to the motet, its texts, and their meanings.

Spanish motet collections from the second half of the sixteenth century include settings of a variety of texts, from devotional prayers to Christ, the saints, and the Virgin to traditional liturgical texts and condensed gospel lessons. The most striking feature of these collections (both manuscript and printed) is the uniform

[30] *Motteta Francisci Guerreri in Hispalensi Ecclesia musicorum praefecti* (Venice, 1570), p. [ii].

appearance within them of cycles of motets for the penitential seasons of the church year. Guerrero's 1570 motet book, which has motets for the seven Sundays running from Septuagesima through Lent, provided the model for these cycles, although partial cycles are evident in his 1555 *Sacrae cantiones* as well as among Morales's motets and in manuscript sources for motets by Ceballos and Navarro. Using texts drawn from the gospels for each Sunday, Guerrero's four-voice motets in the Septuagesima–Lent cycle employ a relatively homophonic declamation of the text, unlike the highly imitative counterpoint on devotional texts in the collection.

Guerrero was not the first Spaniard to compose on such gospel texts: several motets by Morales fall into this category as well. Although Morales did not compose a complete cycle, several motets from Guerrero's 1555 motet book complement those of Morales to create a complete cycle.[31] The importance of the 1570 collection, then, was in Guerrero's consolidation of a new musical style for the gospel motets of the penitential seasons. Guerrero's example was imitated and developed by later Spanish composers such as Ceballos and Navarro, both of whom also adopted the four-voice texture used by Guerrero.

Nicasio Zorita's *Liber primus . . . motectectorum* (Barcelona, 1584) was the first peninsular publication to include an Advent cycle, and the motets in this cycle, like those in the Advent cycle in Guerrero's *Mottecta . . . Liber secundus* (Venice, 1589) exhibit the same textual and musical characteristics as the 1570 Septuagesima and Lenten motets. In fact, each motet book published by composers after Guerrero contains cycles for Septuagesima–Lent and Advent that set gospel texts with relatively conservative musical forces. Juan de Esquivel Barahona's *Motecta festorum et dominicarum* (Salamanca, 1608) is unique among Spanish motet publications in that each of its 70 motets is assigned to a specific feast or Sunday by rubric. The motets in this collection are arranged in three large sections corresponding to the feasts of the Sanctorale, the Common of the Saints, and the Advent and Septuagesima–Lent cycles of the Temporale. In general, Esquivel Barahona selected shorter texts than most peninsular motet composers, and these were mostly drawn directly from the revised Roman Breviary. Sebastián de Vivanco's *Liber motectarum* (Salamanca, 1610) marked the end of the era of printed motet collections in Renaissance Spain. Its 72 motets are arranged into six discrete groups in an organizational scheme more liturgically oriented than Guerrero's but less thorough than Esquivel's. Perhaps the most remarkable feature of Vivanco's motet book is its imposingly complete cycle of motets for the Septuagesima–Lent season, containing works not only for the Sundays but also the Wednesdays and Fridays of Lent.[32] The adoption of the Roman Rite in the 1570s caused a subtle change in

[31] Morales's motets for these Sundays appear in a variety of peninsular MS sources. See Reynaud, *La polyphonie tolédane*, 312–16; Eleanor Russell, "A New Manuscript Source for the Music of Cristóbal de Morales' 'Lost' *Missa pro Defunctis* and Early Spanish Requiem Traditions," *Anuario musical*, 33–35 (1978–80), 38–39; and López-Calo, "El Archivo de música," 112–14.

[32] Evaluations of the size of Vivanco's Septuagesima cycle have been confused by erroneous observations. Robert Stevenson, "Spanish Polyphonists in the Age of the Armada," *Inter-American Music Review* 12 (1991–2), 100, failed to point out that Vivanco's Septuagesima cycle

the content of the Spanish motet cycles for the Sundays of Septuagesima–Lent. In Spanish missals and breviaries before the 1570s, the gospel for the second Sunday in Lent (Matt. 15: 21) was the source of motets on the text *Clamabat autem mulier*, which was set by Morales, Guerrero, and Ceballos. The revised liturgy replaced this reading with the account of the Transfiguration (Matt. 17), and this was the text used in the cycles by Zorita, Rimonte, Esquivel Barahona, and Vivanco. It is striking, then, that Guerrero's final motet book, the *Motecta Francisci Guerreri* (Venice, 1597), signals an allegiance to the traditional Spanish liturgy by reprinting the motet *Clamabat autem* from his 1570 Septuagesima–Lent cycle. In general, Spanish composers residing outside Spain did not participate in this peninsular tradition: Victoria's motet collections, for example, published in 1572 during his time in Rome, followed the church calendar but did not include Advent or Septuagesima–Lent cycles.[33]

In all of their motets, Spanish composers took pains to create musical settings that would aptly illustrate the ideas and states of emotion in their texts. A variety of musical devices employed to this end are evident in a comparison of settings of *Clamabat autem mulier* by Morales, Ceballos, and Guerrero. This text narrates the account of a Canaanite woman pleading with Christ to cure her daughter; her plea is captured in the repeated exclamation "Domine adiuva me." Morales set this phrase by giving the text "At illa venit" over to the three lower voices, and introducing the *tiple* with the cry "Domine adjuva me." Here the highest voice declaims the text with a melodic line that descends through the modal octave, at once realistically painting the cry and tracing a sort of musical obeisance. Ceballos sets the phrase "At illa venit" homophonically, the top voice dropping out to paint a musical genuflection for the words "et adoravit eum." The soprano re-enters, as in Morales's setting, with the words "Domine adjuva me," now beginning on the upper limit of the modal octave and tracing a descending motif that, as in Morale's setting, affectively expresses the anguished cry.

Guerrero too presents a musical genuflection on the text "At illa venit" by having all of the voices drop to the bottom of their registers. Then, after a straightforward declamation of "Domine adiuva me" that neatly cadences on D, he repeats the text. This time the highest voice rises through the modal octave, but presents it in two chromatically altered segments, and gives it a modally-disorienting harmonic dress that hints at cadences, only to slip away with chromatic inflections. This composer's expressive use of harmony here captures the emotional distress of the Canaanite woman, even as it reminds us of his distinctive, individual musical voice.

includes motets for the Wednesdays and Fridays of Lent, but Snow, *A New-World Collection of Polyphony*, 65, errs in the other direction when he mistakenly states that the collection includes a motet for each weekday of Lent.

[33] Victoria's motets were published numerous times during his lifetime; the principal editions are *Motecta* (Venice, 1572), *Motecta* (Rome, 1583), and *Motecta festorum totius anni* (Rome, 1585). Victoria's biography and works are the topic of Robert M. Stevenson, "Tomás Luis de Victoria: Unique Spanish Genius," *Inter-American Music Review*, 12 (1991), 1–100. For a study of Victoria's motets, see Higinio Anglés (ed.), *Opera omnia de Tomás Luis de Victoria*, Monumentos de la música española, 26, 31 (Rome, 1965, 1968).

Indeed, in 1599 the Sevillian painter and theorist Francisco Pacheco singled out Guerrero's motets for special mention in his *Libro de retratos*:

> He [Guerrero] published many motets which, for their propriety and sound, will be eternally esteemed. And by itself his *Ave Virgo sanctissima* has sustained and given fame to an infinite number of Spanish musicians.[34]

Mass settings

The masses of Morales, Guerrero, Victoria, Esquivel Barahona, and Vivanco represent some of the highest achievements in this genre during the sixteenth century. The 21 masses by Morales make him one of the most prolific composers of his generation in this genre, and the wide variety of technical resources he employed places his masses among the most attractive of the century. Morales's masses appeared in print, along with works of Jachet, as early as 1540 in *Quinque misae Moralis Hispani ac Jacheti musici excellentissimi* (Venice, 1540) but were not published as a unified group until four years later, when they were printed in two volumes: *Christophori Moralis Hyspalensis missarum liber primus*, and *Christophori Moralis . . . missarum . . . secundus liber* (Rome, 1544); four other masses are preserved in manuscript form. All of his masses probably date from his years in Rome (1535–45).

Morales's masses are without exception based on pre-existent material from a wide variety of sources. In his imitation masses he most often looked to motets by Franco-Flemish composers such as Mouton, Verdelot, Richafort, and Gombert. Many of his cantus-firmus masses are based on Marian hymns, including the *Missa "Ave Maria"*, *Missa "Ave maris stella"*, and the two *Missae de beata Virgine*, although a substantial number drew upon secular cantus firmi, including popular Spanish songs like *Dezilde al cavallero* and *Tristezas me matan*, or the immensely popular tune *L'homme armé*, which shows up in two different settings by Morales. In the *Missa "Mille regretz"*, Morales extracts the cantus from Josquin's setting, the famous *canción del Emperador* intabulated by Narváez.

Most of Guerrero's eighteen masses appeared in his *Liber primus missarum* (Paris, 1566) and *Liber secundus missarum* (Rome, 1582). Like those of Morales, are all based on pre-existent material and include both parody and cantus-firmus techniques. A striking feature of Guerrero's masses is his propensity for incorporating extraliturgical texts. In his *Missa "Sancta et immaculata"* the textual incipit of Morales's motet appears in the tenor part of the Benedictus; in the Sanctus of the *Missa "Beata mater"* the superius sings a Marian intercession; the Kyrie I of the *Missa "Ecce sacerdos"* has the entire antiphon *Ecce saccerdos magnus* in the tenor voice, and so on. Guerrero treated the Mass text as if it were a madrigal, employing melodic word-painting, varied textures and meters, changing rhythms, and affectively charged harmonies in order to provide a musical reading of the Mass. A section of his four-voice *Missa de beata Virgine* shows Guerrero at his best (Ex-

[34] Francisco Pacheco, *Libro de descripcieon de verdaderos retratos, de ilustres y memorables varones* (Seville, 1599; repr. Seville, 1881–85), unpaginated.

ample 21.1, overleaf), with slow-moving homophony on "et homo factus est" giving way to the reduced imitative texture that introduces the Crucifixus. Wild upward leaps paint the words "et ascendit in caelum," and from "cum gloriam" a melismatic motif in imitative polyphony bubbles forth.

Victoria's published mass collections span the course of his career; they both trace his movement from Rome to Spain and show marked originality of development. His *Liber primus* (Venice, 1576) dates from the middle of his time in Rome, while the *Missarum libri duo* (Rome, 1583) marked the end of his Roman period and includes in its dedication to Philip II an expression of Victoria's desire to return to his homeland. The 1592 *Missae*, which includes a group of settings of the antiphons *Vidi aquam* and *Asperges* arranged for the church year, appeared shortly after Victoria took up his post at the Convent of the Descalzas Reales in Madrid but was published in Rome, showing that he had not completely severed his ties with that city. Finally, the liturgical compendium *Missae, Magnificat, motetcta, psalmi, et alia quam plurima* was published in Madrid in 1600. Victoria based eleven of his 20 masses on his own motets or polyphonic settings of liturgical works such as Marian antiphons or psalms. Four draw on motets or chansons by Morales, Janequin, Guerrero, and Palestrina. In addition he wrote four masses on plainsongs; only the *Missa quarti toni* (Rome 1592) is free-composed. In his later masses Victoria introduced several unconventional stylistic techniques that set him apart from other peninsular composers. The eight-voice *Missa "Alma Redemptoris mater"* is based on material from both of his own polyphonic settings of the antiphon; it and the other masses in his 1600 mass book are some of the earliest examples by a major composer to include organ accompaniment. Like Guerrero, Victoria's parody technique in his later works often departed from standard procedure by presenting borrowed material without regard to the order in which it appeared in the model. Moreover, Victoria's later masses offer less borrowed material in proportion to new material than do his earlier works.

Victoria's contemporary and friend Alonso Lobo published his only book of masses in Madrid in 1602. Three of these, *Prudentes virgines*, *Beata Dei genetrix*, and *Maria Magdalena*, are based on motets by Lobo's teacher at Seville, Francisco Guerrero. In addition, he composed an eight-voice *Credo romano* that remained in use at Seville Cathedral long after his death. Lobo's masses, which call for four to six voices, use more conservative forces than those of Victoria's 1600 mass book and are permeated with learned contrapuntal devices. In the Osanna I of the *Missa "Prudentes virgines"* the cantus II bears the canon *Cantus secundus vadit et venit, sed de minimis non curat*—that is, that this voice is realized by singing only the semibreves of the cantus I part followed by a retrograde statement. In that same movement the Tenor sings the realized cantus II voice an octave lower in cancrizans. The Osanna II of the same mass has the tenor and bass singing a mensural canon at the fifth. His *Missa "O Rex gloriae"* on Palestrina's 1563 motet presents a motif from the motet as a sequencing ostinato in the tenor performed in rhythmic diminution, and features a canon at the eleventh in the final section of the Agnus Dei.

When Juan de Esquivel Barahona composed his only published book of masses (Salamanca, 1608) he also relied heavily on Guerrero for source material. The first

Ex. 21.1 Francisco Guerrero, *Missa de beata virgine* a 4, Patrem, mm. 56–89
Guerrero, *Opera omnia*, ed. V. Garcia et al. (Barcelona, 1955–), V: 51–52

mass in this collection is a five voice setting based on Guerrero's famous motet *Ave virgo sanctissima*, and the four-voice *Missae "Ductus est Jesus"* and *"Gloriose confessor Domini"* also rework musical elements from Guerrero's motets. Taking Guerrero's two-voice canon in *Ave virgo sanctissima* as a cue, Esquivel presents unison canons in the top two voices of his mass throughout his setting. Canon also appears in the

Missa "Gloriose confessor Domini": the Osanna has a double canon, between alto and cantus and between tenor and bass. Most of Sebastián de Vivanco's masses (Salamanca, 1608) are unusual in their avoidance of parody technique, but eight of them use single melodic lines from the composer's own motets or chants, some of which have not been identified. [35]

Other liturgical music

Spanish composers distinguished themselves in settings of the Magnificat. Morales's Magnificat settings first appeared in two volumes printed in Venice in 1542 and 1545 and became the most popular and highly regarded examples of this genre in sixteenth-century Europe. They were also performed widely in the Hispanic Americas. They were issued in 16 editions between their first printing and the year 1619, and praised by such sixteenth- and seventeenth-century writers as Lodovico

[35] See Enrique A. Arias, "The Masses of Sebastián de Vivanco (circa 1550–1622): A Study of Polyphonic Settings of the Ordinary" (PhD diss., Northwestern University, 1971); idem, "Canonic Usage in the Masses of Sebastián de Vivanco," *Anuario musical*, 41 (1986), 135–43.

Zacconi and Adriano Banchieri.[36] Palestrina later added *si placet* voices to some of Morales's Magnificat movements in a manuscript copy used by the Cappella Giulia. The *Magnificat cum quatuor vocibus Moralis Hispani aliorumque authorum* of 1542 contains settings by Morales of all 16 verses (this, rather than the usual *alternatim*, was customary in the papal chapel) for tones I, II, IV, VI, and VII, with the remaining tones accounted for with music by Jachet, Richafort, and Tugdual. The Magnificat collection of 1545 added Morales's settings for Tones III, V, and VIII, presenting all eight Magnificat settings arranged in order of their mode. Around this same time, another prestigious composer of Morales's generation, Pedro de Pastrana (d. after 1559), a chaplain of Charles V from 1527, who had served as *maestro de capilla* to the duke of Calabria in Valencia and became chapel master to Prince Philip at the royal court in 1547, composed several Magnificat settings.[37] Eight Magnificat settings for tones I–IV by Bernardino de Ribera (*c.*1520–*c.*1571) survive in a manuscript at Toledo cathedral, and Magnificat settings by Andrés de Torrentes (d. 1580) are preserved in another manuscript at Toledo as well.

Morales's polyphonic Magnificat settings were praised by Banchieri because of their "fidelity to the plainchant."[38] Morales typically quotes the plainsong Magnificat formula in one of the vocal parts, either verbatim or in paraphrase, and uses the formula in canon in the final verse (except in settings in Tones IV and VI). Quite often the plainsong is also the source for melodic motifs in passages of imitative polyphony, but this is not always the case. More telling, with regard to Morales's fidelity to the chant, is the fact that he was one of the first composers to end each verse of his Magnificat settings with a cadence on the final tone of the chant formula.[39] These features also characterize the Magnificat settings of Juan Navarro, published posthumously in the compendium *Joannis Navarri Hispalen[sis] Psalmi, Hymni, ac Magnificat* (Rome, 1590), which contains nine settings of the even-numbered verses and nine settings of the odd-numbered verses of the canticle. Navarro, however, took on a greater contrapuntal challenge than Morales had, since the Gloria Patri of each of the first eight (of nine) Magnificat settings in this set not only contains a canon, but a canon whose interval corresponds to the number of the Magnificat tone: a unison canon for the Tone I setting, a canon at the second for the Tone II setting, and so on. A similar canonic scheme is at work in Sebastián Aguilera de Heredia's *Canticum Beatissimae Virginis Deiparae Mariae octo modis, seu tonis compositum* (Zaragoza, 1608); in each odd-numbered Magnificat verse, canons at successive intervals appear in each of the six verses. Esquivel de Barahona's Magnificat settings in his *Psalmorum, hymnorum, Magnificarum, et Mariae quatuor antiphonarum de tempore, necnon et missarum tomus secundus* (Salamanca,

[36] Stevenson, "Spanish Polyphonists," 81.

[37] Three of Pastrana's Magnificat settings are found in *E-TZ* 4, and one was inventoried in the chapel library of Philip II in 1597; see A. Andrés, "Libros de canto de la Capilla de Felipe II," *Música sacro-hispana*, 10 (1917), 124, 156; Pedro Calahorra, "Los fondos musicales en el siglo XVI de la Catedral de Tarazona, I: Inventarios," *Nassarre* 8 (1992), 9–56.

[38] Adriano Banchieri, *L'organo suonarino* (Venice, 1605; facs. Bologna, 1969), 89.

[39] Stevenson, *Spanish Cathedral Music*, 83–86.

1613), employ canonic devices in the final movements of the odd-verse settings.[40] Vivanco's *Liber Magnificarum* (Salamanca, 1607) includes alternate Glorias for seven of its 18 settings, with extra voices and virtuoso canons that combine inversion, augmentation, and *cancrizans* technique. The eight-voice Gloria of the Tone IV Magnificat does not use canon but instead presents an overwhelming *tour de force* of quodlibet composition. While the superius I and II, and tenor I and II sing the proper text of the Gloria, the alto sings a paraphrased *Ave Maris stella*, the Bass I the *Ave Maria* in long notes, and the Bass II paraphrases the Marian hymn *O gloriosa Domina*. At the same time, the Tenor II sings a melodic line that strings together the chant formulas for Magnificat settings I–VIII. When composing liturgical music for the Office, Spanish composers demonstrated their fidelity to liturgical tradition with clear modal organization, while at the same time taking advantage of the unassailable liturgical validity of the texts by indulging in contrapuntal complexities that never appear in their motets.

Spanish composers quite often gathered music for the Office into a single volume containing psalms, hymns, Magnificat settings, and Marian antiphons. In addition to the volumes by Navarro, Vivanco, and Esquivel Barahona cited above, Francisco Guerrero contributed a *Liber Vesperarum* (Rome, 1584) comprising seven psalms, 24 hymns, ten Magnificat settings, and four Marian antiphons. Guerrero's hymn settings, like Navarro's, typically set alternate verses, and quote the plainchant hymn tune in one or the other of the voices. Esquivel's 31 hymns in his 1613 collection follow the earlier publications by presenting the settings according to the calendar of feasts of the church year. These collections largely correspond to the requirements of the post-Tridentine Roman liturgy, but retain Spanish liturgical tradition in their settings of *more hispano* melodies, such as those for *Vexilla regis prodeunt* and *Pange lingua gloriosi.* Guerrero, for example, provides a setting of the Spanish *Pange lingua* in his 1584 book of Vespers music, as does Navarro, who also provides both a Spanish and a Roman version of *Vexilla regis* in his 1590 collection. Victoria's *Hymni totius anni secundum Sanctae Romanae Ecclesiae* includes, in spite of its title, the Spanish version of *Pange lingua*.

The expansion of the popular Holy Week processions in sixteenth-century Spain inspired the composition of elegant polyphony for the solemn Offices of Holy Week. Many collections of Lamentations and lessons have survived only in manuscripts, suggesting that local composers and local customs were favored for these services. Ambrosio de Cotes (*c.*1550–1603) left a group of Lamentations for the Capilla Real de Granada,[41] and Lamentations by Vivanco for Holy Saturday survive in a manuscript choirbook at the Hieronymite monastery at Guadalupe. Even published collections of Holy Week music seem to have been designed with Spanish traditions in mind, since most of them do not adhere to the Roman Rite. Morales's *Lamentationi a quatro a cinque et a sei voci* (Venice, 1564) set texts for the last three days of Holy Week, but according to a pre-Tridentine formula;

[40] Robert J. Snow, *The 1613 Print of Juan Esquivel de Barahona*, Detroit Monographs in Musicology, 7 (Detroit, 1978), 36.

[41] López-Calo, "El Archivo de música," 112–13.

nevertheless, these largely homophonic settings were sung throughout Spain during the sixteenth century.[42] Like other Spanish composers, Victoria incorporated Spanish cantus firmi in many of the items in his large collection of Holy Week music, the *Officium Hebdomadae Sanctae* (Rome, 1585), which includes Lamentations and responsories together with two Passion settings, several motets, and other liturgical items. Unlike Navarro and Guerrero, who introduced canons and a striking level of compositional virtuosity in the final stanzas of their hymns, Victoria's hymn settings are simpler, without such contrapuntal artifice.

Vernacular Genres

GIVEN the importance that religious institutions had in the lives of cities, towns, and courts in the Hispanic world, it is not surprising that so much of the music that was copied into manuscripts or published in sixteenth-century collections was Latin-texted sacred music. The church possessed not only the wealth and the skilled manpower to make sure that this music was copied out, but the practical motivation for encouraging the development of a literate musical culture that could include all churchmen and church musicians across Europe and into the New World. The extant sixteenth-century repertory of religious song in Spanish, however, is a small one. Neither Morales nor Victoria produced a significant amount of secular music. Guerrero composed only eleven secular songs and published only one volume in Castilian, his *Canciones y villanescas espirituales* (Venice, 1589), with settings of devotional poetry. This is not to say that secular song was somehow a neglected art in Hispanic lands, but it does point out that few composers expected to build careers as masters of vernacular song.

Nonetheless, just as the sixteenth century witnessed an explosion of secular song elsewhere in Europe, within the genres of the chanson, the madrigal, and the villanesca, for example, so the exploration of the possibilities of exquisitely elegant and expressive vernacular genres in Spain produced a new repertory of *romances* and *villancicos*. In essence, a romance is a strophic ballad that typically is laid out in quatrains of octosyllabic poetry and is usually narrative in its content. The sixteenth-century romances tend to treat historical themes and episodes from Spanish or regional histories. A number of musical and poetic traits in the romances suggest an earlier and now lost unwritten tradition of singing, but the preserved examples are surely just the idealized, highly valued versions that were considered especially worthy of being written down. No single description of their vocal style fits the diversity of their melodies. It is safe to say that the melodies of both romances and villancicos are generally consonant and conjunct, with repeated notes and some degree of recitation. The romances generally set their texts in a declamatory, mostly syllabic fashion, in duple meter. The overwhelming majority of extant Spanish songs from the fifteenth and early sixteenth centuries are villancicos, though the

[42] Glenn Watkins, "Three Books of Polyphonic Lamentations, 1549–1564" (PhD diss., University of Rochester, 1953).

term *villancico* has several meanings in the early modern period. Before about 1600 villancicos were essentially songs with a refrain, while in the seventeenth and eighteenth centuries the term *villancico* did not necessarily point to a fixed form but was applied only to religious songs in the vernacular, including the many thousands of elaborately polychoral pieces composed for cathedrals across Spain and Hispanic America. The repertory of sixteenth-century villancicos seems in some ways more affectively expressive than that of the romances. The villancico absorbed a broader range of moods and topics, sacred or secular, amorous or spiritual. The villancicos are strophic, but they tend not to extend to the many strophes of narration that were typical of the romance. A standard form for a villancico strophe is ABBA, in which the first A is called the *estribillo* (refrain), the Bs represent the statement of the music for the *copla* (stanza) twice (as *copla* and *mudanza*), and the return of the *estribillo* as the *vuelta*.

Most of the extant sixteenth-century romances and villancicos are preserved in two kinds of sources—a few manuscript and printed songbooks known as *cancioneros*, and the printed vihuela books that contain songs and instrumental pieces in tablature for the vihuela. The oldest of the sixteenth-century songbooks (*E-Bbc* Ms. M.454), whose repertory looks back toward the fifteenth century, mixes a small proportion of Spanish secular songs into a compilation of sacred works by foreign and native-born composers. The same can be said of the Cancionero de Segovia at the Segovia Cathedral, which contains some villancicos in addition to Latin sacred music. The Cancioneiro Musical d'Elvas (also known as the Cancioneiro Musical e Poético da Biblioteca Públia Hortênsia), copied around 1550 and now kept at the municipal library in Elvas, Portugal, contains Spanish and Portuguese songs exclusively; they are all anonymous in the manuscript, but some are known to have been composed in the late fifteenth century by composers such as Juan del Encina and Pedro de Escobar. The printed cancionero of the duke of Calabria, also known as the Cancionero de Upsala, published in Venice in 1556 with the title *Villancicos de diversos autores*, also belongs with the early group of backward-looking anthologies, despite its late date. Some of its villancicos in 2–5 parts (including one by Nicolas Gombert, the only composer named in the collection) were doubtless composed many years before its publication, and all of them fall squarely into the earlier stylistic and formal tradition. Most of these early Spanish cancioneros, like their counterparts in other countries (French *chansonniers* and German *Liederbücher*) include various kinds of music, and testify to the fact that peninsular musicians and patrons were not isolated—they performed and collected music of local and regional production as well as both sacred pieces and secular songs in non-Spanish genres.

Among the printed vocal anthologies, Juan Vázquez (d. after 1560) contributed two collections, the *Villancicos y canciones* (Osuna, 1551) for three and four voices and the *Recopilación de sonetos y villancicos* (Sevilla, 1559/60) for four and five voices. Mateo Flecha the Elder (1481–1553) had several works published posthumously in *Las ensaladas de Flecha, maestro de capilla que fue de las Serenissimas Infantas de Castilla* (Prague, 1581), and his nephew Mateo Flecha the Younger (*c.*1530–1604) published a *Libro primo di madrigali* (Venice, 1568) as well as three *ensaladas* in his uncle's 1581 volume. Other composers, such as Rodrigo de Ceballos and Juan Navarro, composed some secular pieces, but in numbers that pale in comparison to their sacred works. The remaining printed sources for Spanish songs are not exclusively "vocal" in orientation, because they are anthologies and tutors published for the benefit of skilled amateurs who wished to learn the art and practice of the *vihuela de mano*, or *vihuela española*. In these books, songs are included to demonstrate how the vihuela could serve to accompany a solo singer or how the vihuelist might accompany himself. The songs with sacred and secular texts in Spanish, French, Italian, and Latin as arranged by the vihuelists tell us a good deal about the performance practice of the time, because they are notated in tablature. Although the first of the vihuela books, *El maestro* (Valencia, 1535/36) by Luis de Milán (*c.*1500–*c.*1561), was the product of the refined courtly atmosphere of the ducal court in Valencia, the last of them, Esteban Daza's *El Parnaso* (Valladolid, 1576), was more likely produced for the use of lesser nobles and the middle-class gentlemen who emulated them.

In their secular works peninsular musicians display their awareness and interest in both native and Italian poetic forms. The villancico, which held immense importance during the fifteenth century, continued to be used by composers such as Juan Vázquez, but, while sacred villancicos increased in importance and became the most widespread vernacular genre in the Hispanic world during the seventeenth century, the secular villancico, with its fixed form and asymmetrical arrangement of poetic and musical materials, all but disappeared. Romances and villancicos survive in arrangements for many voices in the polyphonic songbooks and as solo songs with accompaniment in the vihuela books. The repertory of the romance grew with the contributions of a new generation of poets and composers in the late sixteenth century. Though the poetic sources that have survived through to our time far outnumber the musical sources, scholars agree that the romance texts circulated widely in manuscripts and in printed editions large and small. Poets and musicians alike perfected the art of *glosas* and *diferencias* (glosses and variations) and invented new settings based on the well-known tunes and texts.

The development of Spanish song, for all of its strong connection to a centuries-old tradition of improvised ballad-singing and recitation, was not untouched by the highly controversial wave of Italian influence that sparked debate in sixteenth-century literary circles. Clearly, some composers and anthologizers responded to the new demand for fashionable italianate or pseudo-classical poetry and music. Mateo Flecha the Younger's book of madrigals reflects an interest in foreign forms. Juan Vázquez and the vihuelists included musical settings of Italian and Spanish sonnets in their publications, and among the works in Guerrero's 1589 book are sonnets, madrigals, and villanescas. Vázquez's 1560 collection begins with the statement that his compositional goal was to "dress the spirit of the Words with the Music that best suits it."[43] But while Vasquez's music, which is relatively free of madrigalisms, indicates that he understood this to mean a special attention to text declamation and the general tone of the poem, Guerrero's Castilian-texted music is

[43] Eleanor Russell (ed.), *Juan Vásquez: Villancicos i Canciones* (Madison, WI, 1995), p. xi.

filled with madrigalesque features. In his villancico *Pastores, si nos queréis* (Example 21.2, overleaf), the text "¡O, qué mudança!"(Oh, what a change!) occasions not only a change from triple to duple meter but also harmonic sonorities that shift from minor to major.

The two fashionable currents that dominated literary circles in Spain in the last third of the sixteenth century also show their influence in the songs copied into the latest group of sixteenth-century Spanish manuscript songbooks. In these sources, settings of romances based on what were probably well-known tunes are copied in beside Spanish part-songs that might be classified as Spanish madrigals—they set poetry in the classicizing "Petrarchan" meters and employ a kind of madrigalesque polyphony that is, nevertheless, graver and more restrained in its approach to the texts than the Italian models. The late-sixteenth-century sources also indicate that the romances and *madrigales* had all but banished the old-fashioned villancico, with its fixed refrain pattern, from the musical landscape. The most important late-sixteenth-century manuscript source, the Cancionero Musical de Medinaceli, is a rich collection of sixteenth-century Spanish songs in polyphonic arrangements.[44] These demonstrate how the romance was transformed by the application of madrigalesque imitative counterpoint and the addition of a longer, freer, and more affectively-charged *estribillo*.

Instrumental Music

Despite the fact that Spain was known in the sixteenth century as the home of many a skilled musician and the source of fashionable new styles of instrumental performance, only music for solo instruments was published in Spain in the period. No music for instrumental ensembles was printed, nor do manuscript collections of purely instrumental music survive. The ensemble pieces that are preserved in manuscript collections are, for the most part, untexted versions of vocal polyphony. A large part of what was performed by ensembles in the sixteenth century, especially by the cathedral *ministriles*, was based on vocal models. On the other hand, the legacy of music collected and published by Spanish vihuelists, organists, and violists might contain some clues as to the nature of the instrumental ensemble repertory. Their works, published from the 1530s to the end of the sixteenth century, reveal a fecund musical imagination that sought out new ways to manipulate purely instrumental sounds, and they disseminated vocal works through intabulation and arrangement. The relative scarcity of dance music in these publications is puzzling, but does not mean that the Spaniards were uninterested in dance—descriptions of the court balls, the dancing parties of the nobility, and the use of popular *bailes* in the theater and in many other contexts, along with the famous dancing choirboys at Seville Cathedral and the choreographed dances performed in Corpus Christi processions, all tell otherwise. Most likely, the music

[44] *E-PA* Medinaceli 13230; pieces from this MS are transcribed in Miguel Querol Gavaldá (ed.), *Cancionero musical de la Casa de Medinaceli (siglo XVI)*, 2 vols. (Barcelona, 1949–50).

Ex. 21.2 Francisco Guerrero, *Pastores si nos queréis*, mm. 1–23
Guerrero, *Opera omnia*, 1: 86–87

that accompanied dances was improvised and not considered the sort of thing that anyone needed to collect in written form.

The plucked and strummed instruments—vihuelas, harps, and guitars—were the favorite accompanimental instruments in Spain and Latin America and pro-

vided the realization of the basso continuo or *guión* for dances, solo songs, and polyphonic works both sacred and profane. As for the dances whose harmonic patterns, rhythmic character, and bass lines infiltrated the repertory of Spanish songs in texted versions, those called *bailes* (the *chacona*, the *zarabanda*, the *folía*, the *zarambeque*, the *canarios*, and so on) were enjoyed by all social levels and were performed just about everywhere in the Hispanic world.

Although three surviving manuscripts from the early-seventeenth-century collection of the Duke of Lerma contain music for *ministriles* (wind bands), these pieces are almost all instrumental versions of motets and other polyphonic pieces by Flemish composers. The extant repertory of sixteenth-century Spanish instrumental music is confined to music for vihuela, solo viol, keyboard instruments, or Renaissance harp. Spanish vihuelists and organists in particular left a rich legacy of instrumental music that, in its own way, reflects the humanistic nature of peninsular music and the expertise in the art of improvisation that Spanish musicians were famous for. Their works, which appeared in a series of publications that span the mid-sixteenth century, explore the idiomatic textures, sonorities, and techniques of these instruments.

The 40 fantasias notated for vihuela in Luis de Milán's *El maestro* (Valencia, 1535/36; Brown 1536_3) juxtapose passages of homophony, imitative polyphony, and virtuoso display. They are also among the first examples of music to include tempo indications. The fantasias are sophisticated examples of idiomatic music for the vihuela and demonstrate that this instrument already in the early sixteenth century had its own improvised repertory and characteristic pedagogy with a highly developed technique. Milán described his fantasias as the products of his own "imagination and industry;" it is clear that he first discovered them in the course of his own improvisations and only later wrote them down. *El maestro* contains the first tablature printed in Spain, and it is the first Spanish collection of independent solo instrumental music and accompanied songs. It also contains pavans, settings of Spanish and Portuguese villancicos, romances, and through-composed settings of well-known Italian sonnets.

Working in Castile, Luis de Narváez published his *Los seys libros del Delfín de música* (Valladolid, 1538_1), a collection of fantasias, variations, and intabulations. In the fantasias, Narváez brings to a virtuoso instrumental genre the pervasive imitative polyphony more closely associated with vocal music, even as he bends the limitations of genre by providing numerous intabulations of sacred and secular vocal works by Josquin, Gombert, and others, including his famous instrumental setting of the "Canción del Emperador," Josquin's *Mille regretz*. Like Milán, Narváez also included variation sets known as *diferencias* on the music of such popular Spanish songs as *Conde Claros* and *Guárdame las vacas*—tunes that attained immense popularity in the instrumental literature both in Spain and elsewhere. The florid ornamentation that Narváez applied to the vocal models in his intabulations only hints at the inventive mind that is revealed in full in his variation sets—the first such compositions to be published with the term *diferencias*.

Alonso Mudarra (*c.*1510–1580) published his *Tres libros de música en cifra* (Seville, 1546_{14}) in the same year that he became a canon at Seville Cathedral. Before this he had enjoyed an illustrious career at the courts of the dukes of Infantado, Diego Hurtado de Mendoza and Iñigo López de Mendoza (see above). His collection contains over seventy compositions, including 27 fantasias, three pavans, *diferencias* (again on *Conde Claros* and *Guárdame las vacas*), and intabulations of vocal works by Josquin, Gombert, and Willaert, in addition to settings of villancicos, romances, sonnets, and a few classical poems. Mudarra's humanist tendencies, like Milán's, are apparent in his settings of Petrarch. Mudarra also included texts by Ovid, Horace, and Vergil. Some of the pieces in Mudarra's anthology call for the kind of virtuosity that only a skilled professional instrumentalist would be capable of, and in this sense they are important as examples of a specifically "instrumental" repertory. Two special pieces from Mudarra's book are the first printed examples of specific repertory of pieces for harp. The first of these, the *Fantasía que contrahaze la harpa en la manera de Luduvico*, is a brilliant example of an exceedingly daring instrumental piece whose musical ideas are derived exclusively from virtuoso improvisation. This *Fantasía* is meant to sound like a free improvisation. It is a "fantasy" invented for vihuela but based on the playing techniques of the famous late-fifteenth-century Italian harp player Luduvico (or Ludovico). In particular, this piece captures his execution of trills and accidentals (chromatic notes) on the harp, and the way he spiced his improvisations with unexpected cadences and chords on notes outside the usual cadential points for the mode. This fantasia begins slowly and delicately with a simple chordal gesture that is intensified through repetition. The texture becomes rhythmically animated as it proceeds, especially if the performer takes advantage of the free approach to tempo and rhythm that were the norm in sixteenth-century practice. The piece is only about what the performer does to it, though Mudarra notated the syncopations and daring harmonies, including some forbidden *falsas* or cross-relations (such as F-sharp against F-natural).

Mudarra included this fantasia based on the virtuosity of a harp player most likely because the harp was such a popular instrument in all contexts in the Hispanic lands. By around 1600 the harp had become the instrument of choice for itinerant professional virtuosos and accompanists, and was considered absolutely necessary in large churches and cathedrals because of its resonant sound. Moreover, the instrumental pieces in the vihuela books, as well as those in other collections, were composed for performance on all of the polyphonic instruments, whether vihuelas, harps, or keyboard instruments (*instrumentos de tecla*) such as the organ, harpsichord, and clavichord.

The remaining vihuela books, Enríquez de Valderrábano's *Silva de Sirenas* (Valladolid, 1547$_5$), Diego Pisador's slightly less polished *Libro de música de vihuela* (Salamanca, 1552$_7$), Miguel de Fuenllana's *Orphénica lyra* (Valladolid, 1554$_3$), and Esteban Daza's *El Parnaso* (Valladolid, 1576$_1$) follow the pattern set earlier by including pieces that are conceived wholly for instrumental exploration—the fantasias and *diferencias*—in addition to intabulations of vocal models and arrangements of songs for solo voice and accompaniment. Sacred and secular works by an impressive number of composers, including Arcadelt, Gombert, Josquin, Layolle, Morales, Mouton, Vázquez, Verdelot, and Willaert, are included in intabulations or serve as points of departure for inventive glosses. Taken as a whole, the vihuela books provide a broad illustration of the kinds of music that were considered marketable and were accordingly made available to cultivated amateurs and professionals alike in Spain in the sixteenth century. They also provide essential information about performance practice on plucked-string instruments, and about the performance of secular songs and instrumental music in Hispanic contexts. Their contents mark an important stage in the emancipation of instrumental training, composition, and performance from vocal models.

It was not until after mid-century that volumes dedicated primarily to keyboard music were published on the Iberian peninsula, with Luis Venegas de Henestrosa's *Libro de cifra nueva para tecla, harpa, y vihuela* (Alcalá, 1557_2). Like the vihuela books of the time, Venegas's volume collected fantasias and *tientos* (another genre founded on improvisation) together with hymn settings, intabulations of Flemish masters, and 21 pieces from contemporary vihuela books. But this volume, which employed a new kind of tablature (used as well by Antonio de Cabezón), also contains much music that is more idiomatically suited to keyboard instruments. The most famous of Spanish keyboard composers was surely Antonio de Cabezón, a blind musician personally chosen by King Philip II to serve as his organist. Cabezón's music takes full advantage of the technical possibilities of the keyboard and of some of the idiomatic features of Iberian instruments. The first compilation of Cabezón's music was edited by his son, Hernando, as the *Obras de música·para tecla, arpa, y vihuela* (Madrid, 1578_3). Cabezón's rich and varied legacy includes liturgical pieces, such as hymn settings, Kyries, and psalm verses, tientos, and some magnificent *diferencias* on dances and popular songs. The fact that very few of Cabezon's pieces are intabulations of existing works is a tribute to his originality as a composer.

The Spanish vihuela and keyboard collections are not mere miscellanies: they were carefully planned as important manuals of musical pedagogy, and they are valuable didactic tools today. Many include discussions of the rudiments of instrumental technique, explanations of tablature, and, perhaps most importantly, models for ornamentation and improvisation. The florid passagework in a Narváez intabulation is a model for cadential formulae. Mudarra's fantasias point out the extent to which trills, rhythmic flexiblity, accidentals, and fast passagework could enliven a musical performance. The art and practice of inventing *glosas* and *diferencias* is demonstrated in the six vihuela books and in the music for *tecla, arpa y vihuela* by organists such as Cabezón and Venegas de Henestrosa. In books such as the *Tratado de glosas sobre clausulas* for bass viol (Rome, $1553_{5\text{-}6}$) by Diego Ortiz, improvisatory formulae are taught and applied in a systematic manner. Together with the explanations offered in Milán's *El maestro*, Juan Bermudo's *Declaración de instrumentos* (Osuna, 1555_1), and Tomás de Sancta María's *Libro llamado Arte de tañer fantasía* (Valladolid, 1565_5), the Spanish instrumentalists provide modern musicians and scholars with a unique treasury of information about how improvisation was taught and practiced, as well as the key to understanding the central place that it held in Spanish musical culture.

22

SPAIN, *ii*: 1600–1640

Louise K. Stein

ALTHOUGH the death of Philip II in 1598 marked the end of an immensely important era in political history, it is difficult to draw a firm line of demarcation around the year 1600 in the history of Spanish music, because so many of the genres and musical techniques of the late sixteenth century were essential to Spanish music through the early seventeenth century, and the social place of music stayed much the same as well. For example, the association between reserved imitative contrapuntal polyphony and sacred Latin texts continued to shape the work of composers within the Church, especially when they set the invariable texts of the Mass. New textures and techniques were developed within vernacular religious genres, whose overtly expressive style included sections of homophony and solo song along with imitative counterpoint. As the seventeenth century progressed, Spanish society was especially desirous of the novelty, invention, enigma, artifice, and magnificent spectacle that scholars tend to associate with the culture of the Baroque. Great formal flexibility, bold contrasts, clear harmonic organization, sensitive text expression, and careful attention to text declamation are notable characteristics of Spanish music from the mid seventeenth century, whether in large-scale sacred pieces for one or more choirs, romances for two or three voices, solo settings of romances, or clever theatrical songs with improvised accompaniment.

While the seventeenth century is accepted as a Golden Age for Spanish culture, music, however, held a subsidiary place next to theater and the visual arts. The century did not produce a long list of extraordinarily innovative Spanish composers, pages of heated musical debate, tomes of erudite speculative writings on musical theory, or libraries full of beautifully prepared and bound scores—the sort of written legacy that modern scholars accept as evidence of historical investment in other musical cultures. The musical repertories from seventeenth-century Spain survive largely in manuscript copies on cheap paper and as humble performing parts. Of course, two of the largest collections of music by court composers were lost through natural disasters: in the fire that destroyed the royal library and music archive of the Royal Palace in Madrid known as the Alcázar in 1734, and in the earthquake of 1755 that took with it the great library of King John IV of Portugal. Most of the surviving musical sources are undated, and printed ones are scarce, limited to a handful of practical or theoretical manuals, especially for organ, guitar, or harp. It would seem that few composers sought to publish their works, printers found little market for the sale of music in Spain during the seventeenth century, and the public was largely illiterate in musical notation (though many amateurs could surely read tablature and various kinds of *alfabeto* notation for guitar).

The fact that Spanish musicians left behind very few accounts of their lives, performances, or ideas concerning music, is a direct result of the musician's place in society and an important statement about how musicians were viewed and perceived themselves. Composers and performers were servants and artisans employed by the court, the Church, or the municipal theaters in the largest cities. Professional composers did not come from the upper reaches of society, and even the best could not rise to that level. Even at the royal court, opportunities for individual fame were restricted, and the names of composers and performers were only rarely given in the printed descriptions of royal entertainments or in the accounts of court copyists. The royal chapel-master who retired in 1634, Mateo Romero, known by his nickname "el maestro Capitán," was actually a Fleming from Liège (Mathieu Rosmarin) and perhaps because he was not Spanish he rose to the position of registrar of the Order of the Golden Fleece in 1621.[1]

While the royal court's painters fought to assure the status of painting as a liberal art (and not merely as an artisanal trade), music was accepted as a liberal art, but musicians faced an impossible climb toward the summit of the contemporary Mount Parnassus. The status of even the most valued of Spanish musicians was lowered by their need to earn a living through bringing pleasure to others. The invisibility of the Spanish composer is documented in eye-witness accounts of rehearsals and performances. For example, in his published description of *La selva sin amor* (1627), the first opera ever performed in Spain, the poet and librettist Lope de Vega did not even mention the name of the composer, although he praised Cosimo Lotti as the scenic designer.[2] Because so much of the surviving music from early-seventeenth-century Spain has come down to us without any attribution, and we know so little about individual composers, it is difficult to assess their contributions through the lens traditionally used in historical evaluation.

[1] See Louise K. Stein, *Songs of Mortals, Dialogues of the Gods: Music and Theatre in Seventeenth-Century Spain* (Oxford, 1993), 93–95.

[2] See Lope's dedication to *La selva sin amor* in Lope Félix de Vega Carpio, *Laurel de Apolo, con otras rimas* (Madrid, 1630), *E-Mn* R-177, fol. 103r; also in *Obras de Lope de Vega*, XIII, ed. Marcelino Menéndez y Pelayo, Biblioteca de autores españoles, 188 (Madrid, 1965), 187–98. Cosimo Lotti's work for a Florentine entertainment in March of 1618 (a pastoral with intermedii by Giacomo Cicognini) was praised by the composer-singer Giulio Caccini in a letter to Andrea Cioli, quoted in Angelo Solerti, *Musica, ballo e dramatica alla corte Medicea dal 1600 al 1637* (Florence, 1905; repr. New York, 1968), 126–29, as "l'architetto della prospettiva e delle macchine ... il quale con l'esempio delle cose passate, si e portato di maniera che, dato la parità del sito, non e stata punto inferiore alle passate, ne di vaghezza, ne di ricchezza, ne d'invenzione.... tutte queste cose suddette seguirono in atto con tanta squisitezza, che piu non si potea desiderare."

Instrumental Music and its Contexts

Spanish instrumental music in this period depended a great deal on improvisation, oral tradition, and conventional but unwritten aspects of performance. In the late sixteenth century, Spanish musicians had contributed in important ways to the emancipation of instrumental music from vocal models, and in the early seventeenth century this process produced an independent repertory of keyboard music with a brilliant, virtuoso character. Although the genre of the *tiento* had been explained first in the sixteenth-century by Luis de Milán and Alonso Mudarra, *tientos* were increasingly created as brilliant, difficult, and exuberant instrumental pieces, as far as we can tell from the surviving repertory of *tientos* by organist composers such as Sebastián Aguilera de Heredia and most especially Francisco Correa de Arauxo. Correa de Arauxo built extravagant ornamental figures and virtuoso figuration into the *tiento*'s traditional contrast between fast passages of sometimes dissonant figuration and consonant, chordal progressions, between *redobles* and *consonancias*. Correa's *tientos*, substantial in length and of both monothematic and polythematic types, preserve an underlying structure of correct counterpoint, yet their elaborate and highly-colored figuration (whether performed on organ, harpsichord, or *arpa doble*) reveals the improvisatory basis of the genre, thanks to rhythmic patterns infused with syncopation and hemiola. The Spanish predilection for contrasts of color and texture is demonstrated in these *tientos*, with their exploitation of the divided single keyboard of the Spanish organ—the *medios registros*, or *registros partidos*—and timbral contrasts between registers; the very high *tiples* against the low *registro bajo*. Correa included a corpus of 69 pieces (mostly *tientos* but also *canciones*, *glosas*, *diferencias*, and settings based on cantus firmus) in his didactic *Facultad orgánica* (1626), which has become an indispensable source for study of early seventeenth-century performance practice.

Although formal sets of variations were not typical of early-seventeenth-century collections for organ and harp such as Correa's, his elaborate *tientos* luxuriate in a constant process of elaboration and variation that seems altogether characteristic of Spanish music in this period. Among the practices that defined Hispanic music in the seventeenth century, improvisation, variation, and recomposition shaped the sound and transmission of music just as they had in the previous century. These techniques grew in importance especially because the preferred continuo instruments for Spanish vocal music were harps and guitars, whose idiomatically virtuoso repertory did not reach print until later in the seventeenth century.

Aside from instruction books and collections of music for keyboard, guitar, and harp, the paucity of musical sources for strictly instrumental music for this period of Spain's musical history is striking. In part, this can be blamed on the low social and economic status assigned to musicians, especially instrumentalists, in Hispanic society. But, again, it may have resulted from the emphasis that Spanish musical culture placed on improvisation. Much of the instrumental music that survives from this period can be heard as "performer's" art—music designed to display the talents of a virtuoso interpreter whose consummate skills included the mastery of the proper *aire* (performance style and gestures) not specified by the composer. Precisely because the unwritten tradition was so important, the extant sources for Hispanic Baroque music do not always tell modern-day performers all that they need to know. In addition, the lack of a vigorous industry of music printing caused a scarcity of printed music of all kinds. Although solo compositions for organ, harp, and guitar are preserved in both manuscript and printed sources, manuscript sources of instrumental ensemble music from Spain are scarce. Three early-seventeenth-century manuscripts containing music for the royal wind band from the time of Philip III and his prime minister the duke of Lerma preserve the only extant music for Spanish *ministriles*—the ubiquitous ensembles of shawms (*chirimías*), cornettos, and *bajoncillos* that are described in nearly all of the *relaciones* of royal and aristocratic events.[3] The pieces collected in these three books, however, are not newly composed independent works but rather instrumental arrangements of vocal polyphony by both Spanish and Franco-Flemish masters; the same kinds of pieces that were sung during this period by the royal chapel under the direction of its last Flemish master, Mateo Romero.

In spite of the Flemish orientation of the royal chapel and its repertory for *ministriles*, there are indications that the practice of Spanish instrumental ensembles might not have been so different from that of ensembles elsewhere in southern Europe. In his now famous *Discorso sopra la musica*, which was probably written around 1628, Vincenzo Giustiniani lauded the music-making at the Spanish court of the young King Philip IV, stating:

> in our times, music has become more noble and illustrious than ever, since King Philip IV of Spain and both his brothers take great pleasure in it and are accustomed frequently to sing and play Viols together, with a few other musicians to make up the necessary number, among these Filippo Piccinini Bolognese, a most excellent performer on the lute and the pandora. And further, the King and his brothers write compositions not only for their own pleasure but also to be sung in the royal chapel and other churches while the divine offices are celebrated. This inclination and pleasure of his Majesty will be the reason why many gentlemen still delight in it, and many others apply themselves to music.[4]

These comments are strikingly similar to those of a Florentine diplomat who actually spent considerable time at Philip IV's court and wrote that the king was a fine player of the bass viol and composed in counterpoint.[5] Philip IV garnered respect

[3] Some of these pieces are available in Douglas Kirk (ed.), *Music for the Duke of Lerma* (Watertown, MA, 2003).

[4] Vincenzo Giustiniani, "Discorso sopra la musica de' suoi tempi," written Rome, 1628, ed. Angelo Solerti, *Le origini del melodramma* (Turin, 1903), 111–12, trans. Carol MacClintock, MSD 9 (Rome, 1962), 71–72.

[5] In a letter of 1 July 1627, transcribed in Shirley B. Whitaker, "Florentine Opera Comes to Spain: Lope de Vega's *La selva sin amor*," *Journal of Hispanic Philology*, 9 (1984), 63, Averardo Medici, a member of the Florentine delegation, wrote from Madrid to Andrea Cioli in Florence: "il Re si diletta della musica et n'intende tanto che sa comporre di contrappunto et suona

as an amateur musician and patron, and even beyond his household other chamber ensembles at court served the queen, the infante Don Fernando, and the infanta María. The royal court was replete with excellent instrumentalists, some of whom had been recruited from abroad. The duke of Lerma had recruited Stefano Limido and an ensemble of violin players from Milan early in the reign of Philip III. The Bolognese lute and theorbo player Filippo Piccinini came from a distinguished family of virtuoso lute players and had served in Rome and Turin before coming to Madrid. Mateo Troylo belonged to the famous Venetian Troilo family of string players, and Luis and Tomás de As were members of an English viol-playing family. These musicians surely brought with them modern pieces composed for their instruments as well as stylish virtuoso performance techniques, and they most likely retained their contacts with musical centers outside Spain.

Since hardly a trace of the music that the Spanish instrumental ensembles played is known today, we must look to sources published outside of Spain for clues to its nature. The *Primo libro de canzoni, fantasie & correnti* (Venice, 1638) by Bartolomé de Selma y Salaverde is a printed collection of instrumental music by a Spanish composer working abroad. Selma y Salaverde (son of Bartolomé de Selma, instrument-maker to the royal court in Madrid) was a virtuoso player of wind instruments who served the archducal court at Innsbruck and may have traveled among the other Habsburg courts as well. His collection contains difficult, florid virtuoso music for both solo instruments and for small wind ensemble. Some of these pieces might be profitably compared to the organ *tientos* of a decade earlier, with their exploitation of lavish figuration and contrasts of register within a reliable contrapuntal framework. Two other important points of contact between Spanish instrumental practice and the pieces called *canzoni* and *sonatas* that were prolifically cultivated in Italy in the mid-seventeenth century are the compositions of Andrea Falconiero and Henry Butler. Falconiero spent some time in Madrid and served the Spanish court at Naples, where his collections were published. Butler was an English Catholic viol player and violinist who worked at court in Madrid from 1623 to 1652. The form of a multi-sectional sonata with sections based on successive points of imitation was most likely known and cultivated by Spanish musicians, if pieces by Falconiero and Butler may be taken as representative of what they composed and performed in Madrid.

The Romance: Songs for the Streets, the Chamber, and the Theater

The same combinatorial inventiveness characteristic of these sonatas, and of organ *tientos* and *diferencias* for vihuela, enlivened the performance of multistrophic romances, simple polyphonic settings of courtly poetry based on well-

franco il basso del violone; et ogni sera si trattengono Sua Maestà et gli Infanti suoi fratelli un'hora con un concerto di viole, che tuttiatre suonano, et con loro il maestro di cappella et un Italiano musico di camera della Maestà Sua che si chiama Filippo Piccinini."

known tunes, *villancicos* based on traditional harmonic patterns, and improvised continuo accompaniments for all kinds of music. The secular songs of the first half of the seventeenth century are almost exclusively romances, whose poetic content is less heroic and more amorous, pastoral, pseudo-popular, and courtly in nature, compared to the *romances viejos* of the fifteenth and sixteenth centuries. The romances are preserved largely in manuscripts called *cancioneros*—bound anthologies of polyphonic songs in partbooks or in choirbook format, dating from the first half of the seventeenth century. Two printed sources, the *Libro segundo de tonos y villancicos a una dos tres y quatro voces, con la zifra de la guitarra española a la usanza romana* of Juan Arañés (or Arañies) (Rome, 1624), which contains settings of 31 Spanish songs with *alfabeto* and mensural notation, and the *Método mui facilíssimo para aprender a tañer la guitarra a lo español* by Luis de Briceño (Paris, 1626), attest to the popularity of the Spanish guitar and of Spanish romances among cultivated amateurs outside of Spain as well. Briceño's book includes Spanish *bailes* (*españoleta*, *chacona*, *villano*, and *zarabanda*), and the texts of romances given with a shorthand number notation for the guitar chords. Spanish songs borrowed or adapted from a widely circulating courtly repertory also appear in other collections.[6] In Italy and in France, *alfabeto* notation and tablature facilitated the spread of the romances along with the vogue for the Spanish guitar, which also fueled the fashion for Hispanic dances of a non-courtly nature based on repeated patterns and characteristic rhythms, such as the *canario*, the *chacona*, the *folía*, the *seguidilla*, and the *zarabanda*. Some of these *bailes* originated in the Americas; for example, the *chacona* and the *zarabanda* were brought from sixteenth-century Peru to the Iberian peninsula and thus to Europe.

Music by the court composers who worked in Madrid in the early seventeenth century dominates the repertory of the manuscript *cancioneros*, which are the primary musical sources for secular songs.[7] Many songs in the manuscript *can-*

[6] Spanish-texted songs performed in the *Ballet de la Folie* at the French court were published in Gabriel Bataille's *Airs de differents autheurs*, V (1614) for voice with French lute tablature. Étienne Moulinié included five Spanish-texted songs with strummed guitar accompaniment in his *Airs de cour avec la tablature de luth*, III (Paris, 1629), and at least one of these may draw material from a pre-existent Spanish song. The song "Vuestros ojos dama / tienen no se que . . ." (also found as "Vuestros ojos tienen de amor no se que"), which appears in a number of non-Spanish sources, illustrates the extent to which a handful of Spanish songs circulated widely in courtly circles in France, Italy, and even England. "Vuestros ojos dama" is found in Bataille, *Airs de differents autheurs*, II (Paris, 1609), fols. 62v–63r; *F-Pn* espagnol 390 (Corbie 55), fol. 38r ("Libro de villanelle spagnuol' et italiane et sonate spagnuole"); Robert Dowland, *A Musicall Banquet* (London, 1610); *GB-Lbl* Add. 36877 (compiled by Giovanni Casalotti), fols. 51v–52r; *I-Rvat* Chigi L.VI.200, p. 17 ("Libro de cartas y romançes españoles," copied for Isabella Gonzaga, Duchess of Traetta in 1599); *I-MOe* 2, song 6; *I-Fr* 2774, 2793, 2804, and 2951. See John H. Baron, "Secular Spanish Solo Song in Non-Spanish Sources, 1599–1640," *Journal of the American Musicological Society*, 30 (1977), 20–42; Stein, *Songs of Mortals*, 354–60, 397. The Italian MSS are described as well in Giovanni Maria Bertini and Cesare Acutis, *La romanza spagnola in Italia* (Turin, 1970); Cesare Acutis, *Cancioneros musicali spagnoli in Italia, 1585–1635* (Pisa, 1971); John Walter Hill, *Roman Monody, Cantata, and Opera from the Circles around Cardinal Montalto*, 2 vols. (Oxford, 1997), I: 70–75.

[7] The *cancioneros* include (listed in roughy chronological order): *P-La* 47-VI-10/13, "Can-

cioneros are presented without attribution, but a number of recognized composers are represented as well. Mateo Romero served as maestro of the Real Capilla until his retirement in 1633. Carlos Patiño, a master of strictly contrapuntal polyphony and the first Spaniard ever to lead the royal chapel (to 1675), also contributed settings of romances and *tonos humanos* to the repertory of the *cancioneros*, as did other court musicians serving Philip III and Philip IV in Madrid: Miguel de Arizo, Juan Blas de Castro, Gabriel Díaz (maestro at Lerma and later at the royal chapel of the Monasterio de la Encarnación), Diego Gómez, Manuel Machado, Juan de Palomares, and Álvaro de los Ríos. Juan Arañés (who accompanied the duke of Pastrana in 1623–24 when he served Philip IV as Spanish ambassador in Rome), Valencia's justly famous Juan Bautista Comes, and Juan Pujol, *maestro de capilla* in Barcelona and Zaragoza, also contributed to this repertory, as did a number composers or arrangers about whom little is known at present.

Although scholars tend to associate the music of the manuscript *cancioneros* from the early seventeenth century with musical life at court and in the most elite contexts, it is likely that their polyphonic settings were based on songs and refrains that might also have been familiar to people who were not of the elite. The transformation of pre-existent material was a common and pervasive creative process in the early seventeenth century. Musical materials circulated freely and rapidly in the oral tradition and were accessible to performers and listeners of all social classes. Poets and playwrights used refrains and sayings from popular lore as the basis for elegant poetic glosses, and borrowed each other's texts as well as texts from earlier repertories. Musicians and composers fashioned sets of variations and glosses on well-known tunes, dances, or harmonic patterns, and wrote crisply inventive polyphonic settings of pre-existent and well-known tunes. Rarely do two settings of the same song-text show exact musical concordance, though different settings of the same text often reveal that the polyphonic songs were based on well-known tunes or standard harmonic or rhythmic patterns. The art of exquisite counterpoint graced the settings for two to four voices, while solo performances of the same songs were tempered by the "sweetness" of the well-known tunes in improvised and mostly chordal accompaniments for guitar or harp.

cionero de Ajuda"; *I-Tn* R.I-14, "Cancionero de Turín"; *E-Mn* M-1370/1372, "Romances y letras a tres voces"; *I-Rc* 5437, "Cancionero Casanatense"; *E-PA* Medinaceli 13231, "Cancionero de Medinaceli – B" or "Tonos Castellanos – B"; *D-Mbs* Mus. ms. E.(200), "Cancionero de Sablonara" (1625); *E-Mn* 21741; "Cancionero de Onteniente" (1645); *E-OL* I–VIII, "Cancionero de Olot"; *E-Mn* M-1262, "Libro de Tonos Humanos" (1655–56). Poetic manuscripts with *alfabeto* notation for guitar include *I-Fr* 2774, 2793, 2804, 2951, 2973; *I-Rvat* Chigi L.VI.200 (1599); *I-MOe* 2 (P.6.22), 3 (R.6.4.), 115 (Q.8.21); *I-Nn* XVII.30; *GB-Lbl* Add. 36877, "Villanelle . . . per sonare, et cantare su la chitarra alla Spagnola"; *F-Pn*, espagnol 390 (Corbie 55).

Music in Court and Public Theatres

The extant polyphonic songs that are demonstrably based on well-known tunes present adaptations of popular material, but the carefully copied musical settings attributed to court composers (or included in manuscripts that were copied at court) are probably at least one step removed from the performance of the same tunes and texts in the public theaters. The Madrid public theaters, the *corral de la Cruz* and the *corral del Príncipe* (opened in 1579 and 1582 respectively) were important venues in the circulation of the new romances, just because so many playwrights worked in Madrid and wrote new plays for performance before the insatiable and varied public at the *corrales*, although by the close of the sixteenth century commercial theaters were also operating in several other major Spanish cities including Seville, Valencia, and Valladolid.[8] The theaters provided an essential source of revenue for the municipal hospitals and charities, and almost daily performances became an economic necessity. The growth of this business created a demand for new plays, so that an enormous number of new plays were written and performed in Madrid throughout the seventeenth century.[9] Although we know the names of many of the musicians who worked in the troupes and must have improvised, performed, composed, and arranged music for public theatrical performances, the extant song-books do not seem to preserve any of their songs.

While it is unlikely that the court composers would have worked for the public theaters, there are a few mentions of their participation in private performances known as *particulares*. The case of *El vergonzoso en palacio*, a widely-performed play by Gabriel Téllez (1583–1648), known by his literary pseudonym Tirso de Molina, is typical. Scholars know almost nothing about the performances of Tirso's play in the public theaters before it was published in his prose collection *Cigarrales de Toledo* of 1624. The text as published in the *Cigarrales* does not contain any song-texts, nor does the list of characters or *reparto* specify any musicians except for *un tambor*. Nevertheless, Tirso described the musical components of a performance of his play when he published it:

> Thus, six performers came onstage to sing with a variety of instruments, four musicians and two women. So as not to make this book a vexing tome, I have not included the song-texts, dances, and *entremeses* here . . . but let the reader be assured that they were excellent, citing as the authors of the songs Juan Blas, unique in this material; Álvaro, who if not the first is not second either; and the *licenciado* Pedro González, his equal in all things.[10]

[8] Norman D. Shergold, *A History of the Spanish Stage from Medieval Times to the End of the Seventeenth Century* (Oxford, 1967), 177–208; Othon Arroniz, *Teatros y escenarios del siglo de oro* (Madrid, 1977), 50–99.

[9] Shergold, *A History*, 177–78; J. E. Varey and N. D. Shergold, "Datos históricos sobre los primeros teatros de Madrid: Contratos de arriendo, 1587–1615," *Bulletin Hispanique*, 60 (1958), 73–76.

[10] *Cigarrales de Toledo compuestos por el Maestro Tirso de Molina* (Madrid, 1942; orig. pubd Madrid, 1624), 1: 136–37: "Salieron, pues, a cantar seis con diversidad de instrumentos: cuatro

The performance described in this passage from the *Cigarrales* was privately organized for a select audience of the aristocracy of Toledo, probably in the summer of 1620, and was given on the country estate known as the *cigarral de Buenavista*, where the late archbishop Don Bernardo de Sandoval y Rojas had sponsored several other such events. [11] The *entremeses* (short comic skits) staged with *El vergonzoso en palacio* were by Antonio Hurtado de Mendoza, a court poet who became secretary to Philip IV and was one of Tirso's competitors. The composers, Juan Blas de Castro and Álvaro de los Ríos, served Philip III as chamber musicians. They probably provided musical settings of well-known romances for many theatrical and musical entertainments at court. They may have been permitted to write or arrange music for the private, aristocratic performance of Tirso's play at the Toledo estate, and their songs could have been the source for further borrowing and improvisation.[12]

Plays known as *comedias* were written on a wide array of subjects; they could be tragic or comic in effect, and they dominated the Spanish public stage in the seventeenth century, although partly-sung masques, festival plays, and spectacle plays were also performed for small audiences at court and at country houses and estates. Many *comedias* were performed with songs drawn from the repertory of the *cancioneros*. Several conventions for music were developed through the practice of musicians in the public theaters within the genre of the *comedia*, which also affected the performance of music in courtly spectacles. Within *comedias*, music was mainly used in realistic ways or to reinforce the theatricality of a scene, what is sometimes called "diegetic music." Songs were most frequently incorporated in scenes that called for real-life music making—a wedding song to be sung during a wedding scene; serenades sung by musicians or by an aspiring *galán* from below a lady's window; rustic laborers sing and dance to a traditional *serrana* as they celebrate the harvest; servant-musicians sing to alleviate their mistress's melancholy; Moorish characters sing and dance a *zambra*; and so on. But songs were also used as a theatrical device or audible prop—as when angels sing in religious plays while they ascend to heaven or descend to earth as divine messengers, or anonymous choirs of mysterious voices sing to warn the protagonist of impending danger (as in the famous scene from Lope de Vega's *El caballero de Olmedo*). However elaborate or simple the theatrical setting and function of songs in the *comedias*, their basic musical materials were invariably those of the well-known repertory of the romances.

músicos y dos mugeres. No pongo aquí — ni lo haré en las demás — las letras, bayles y entremeses, por no dar fastidioso cuerpo a este libro ni quebrar el hilo al gusto de los que le tuvieron en ir leyendo sucessivamente sus Comedias. Baste para saber que fueron excelentes el dar por autores de los tonos a Juan Blas, único en esta materia; a Alvaro, si no primero, tampoco segundo, y al licenciado Pedro González, su igual en todo."

[11] Ruth Lee Kennedy, *Studies in Tirso*, I: *The Dramatist and his Competitors, 1620–26* (Chapel Hill, NC, 1974), 152–58, 169–71.

[12] Luis Robledo has explored the influence of theatrical music in chamber songs by Juan Blas in "Música de cámara y música teatral en el primer tercio del siglo XVII: A propósito de Juan Blas de Castro," *Revista de musicología*, 10 (1987). 489–99.

Comedias were performed frequently at the royal court and at the estates of the aristocracy, but they were not the only kind of theatrical entertainment seen at the court. As had been true in earlier periods, court balls, known in Spain as *saraos* or *máscaras*, were much favored among the aristocracy, but pageants and spectacle plays were also performed on important occasions. At the Spanish royal court a special concern for decorum shaped the royal entertainments, and some aspects of their protocol were specified in the Etiquetas de Palacio. Thus in June of 1585 Philip II had instructed the *mayordomo mayor* of the infanta Catalina Micaela (duchess of Savoy):

> In the court balls and parties attended by the infanta, the accustomed form and order must be observed, and no *bailes* or dances that might be considered indecent and inappropriate for a royal setting should be allowed; and neither in these fiestas nor in those that take place in public should any person be allowed to talk with the court ladies, except those who are there to accompany them.[13]

Some years later, the patriarch or chief administrator of the royal chapel, Diego de Guzmán, who was also the biographer of Queen Margarita de Austria (wife of King Philip III), wrote that his queen in fact disliked public fiestas and theatrical productions, and that her preference would have been to "banish" them from Spain altogether.[14] For Guzmán and for Queen Margarita, theatrical music unleashed "lascivious sounds that both in the poetry and in the music encourage dishonest behavior."[15] Most likely because of Margarita's distaste for theater and Philip III's preference for dancing, prior to Margarita's death in 1611 the royal court seems not to have organized important spectacle plays except for the series of *tableaux vivants* that were staged at Valladolid amidst the celebrations for the birth of prince Philip (the future King Philip IV) in 1605. Many years later, the official court historian Alonso Carillo remembered the dignified *saraos* and *máscaras* as more typical of Philip III's reign than the spectacle plays that were organized in later years. In his *Origen de la dignidad de Grande de Castilla* (Madrid, 1657) Carillo compared the sometimes "less than solemn" mythological spectacle plays of his own day with the decorous, non-dramatic entertainments of the reigns of Philip II and Philip III:

> In the epoch in which they attended and made more use of the court balls [*saraos*], the Grandees used to attend in their places with the ladies . . . After the *saraos* fell into disuse, they now attend the *comedias* more frequently,

[13] Document of 13 June 1585 (*E-SIM*, Estado, 1260, fol. 186^{r}), transcribed in Fernando Bouza (ed.), *Cartas de Felipe II a sus hijas* (Madrid, 1998), 122 n. 289: "En los saraos o festines donde la Infanta se hallare se ha de guardar la forma y orden que por acá se acostumbra, no consintiéndose otros bayles ni dançası que sean indecentes y no dignas de aquel lugar y ni en estas fiestas ni en las otras salidas públicas que hubiere deven hablar con las damas sino los que estuvieren en lugar con ellas."

[14] Diego de Guzmán, *Vida y muerte de doña Margarita de Austria* (Madrid, 1617), fols. 70^{r}, 148^{r}.

[15] Ibid., fol. 147^{r}: "Sonadas lascivas, que así en la letra como en la música mueven a deshonestidad."

and these entertainments, or other similar ones, are presented with less solemnity.[16]

The courtier-poet Antonio Hurtado de Mendoza also cited the royal decorum in his official published description of the first theatricals designed to entertain King Philip IV at Aranjuez in 1622. He took pains to describe the Aranjuez plays as special courtly entertainments whose decorum distinguished them from the everyday, plebian *comedia*:

> These performances do not admit the use of the vulgar name of *comedia*, but are instead called "an invention" to reflect the decorum of the palace....
>
> This [entertainment] which would surprise the common public if it were called a *comedia*, is called an invention at the palace, and cannot be evaluated by the precepts of the *farse* that it be a unified fable, because this one is put together from a disconnected variety.[17]

Many other writers shared this concern about the decorum of the palace plays, and between 1590 and 1648 the court began to cultivate its own, new kind of court play, in addition to the *saraos* and *máscaras* (which by no means disappeared). The new court plays were officially organized and designed by professionals, but played by court ladies, *meninos*, and members of the royal family. Musicians from the royal chapel provided music in some of these plays, and the choirs of the royal chapel also participated as an institution in at least one of them. Two theatrical inventions performed for the court of Philip III (*El premio de la hermosura*, a play by Lope de Vega, and *El caballero del sol*, by Luis Vélez de Guevara) were produced under the patronage of the king's *valido* or favorite, the duke of Lerma, at his country estate at Lerma near Valladolid in the years 1614 and 1617. None of the music for these plays survives, but we know from published descriptions that musicians in the royal service performed romances, ensemble songs, and courtly dances when called for by the texts of the plays.

In *El premio de la hermosura*, one of the most memorable musical scenes included a very moving performance of a sonnet sung as an elegy by a court lady, Doña Catalina de Acuña, in the role of Leuridemo.[18] Although there are very few extant sonnet settings by Spanish composers from this period, an earlier play per-

[16] Alonso Carillo, *Origen de la dignidad de Grande de Castilla: Preeminencia de que goza en los actos públicos, y palacio de los reyes de España* (Madrid, 1657), fol. 32^{v}: "En el tiempo que se frecuentaban y usaban más los saraos, solían asistir los Grandes en lugares con las Damas... Después que los saraos se han desusado, se frecuentan más las comedias, y estas fiestas, u otras semejantes se hacen con menos solemnidad."

[17] Antonio Hurtado de Mendoza, *Fiesta que se hizo en Aranjuez a los años del Rey Nuestro Señor D. Felipe IIII* (Madrid, 1623) [BNM, R-15515], fol. 4^{r}: "Estas representaciones que no admiten el nombre vulgar de comedia, y se le da 'invención' la decencia de palacio"; fol. 13^{r-v}: "esto que estrañara al pueblo por comedia, y se llama en Palacio invención, no se mide a los preceptos comunes de las farsas que es una fábula unida, [mientras] ésta se fabrica de variedad desatada."

[18] Concerning the documentary sources and music in *El premio de la hermosura*, see Stein, *Songs of Mortals*, 78–79. The most accessible edition of the text of the play is Lope de Vega, *Obras* (Biblioteca de autores españoles, 234), XXIX: 412.

formed in the 1590s for the court of Philip II, *La fábula de Dafne*, had also called for the decorous performance of a sonnet by a court lady in the role of the goddess Diana. She sang the well-known sonnet by Garcilaso de la Vega, "A Dafne ya los braços le crecían," to the accompanment of a guitar.[19] The second act of *La gloria de Niquea* (1622) began with a dedicatory sonnet sung first to a guitar accompaniment by a court lady in the role of a Nymph, and later repeated by an offstage choir of musicians.[20]

The centerpiece of the 1622 Aranjuez birthday celebrations, put on by queen Isabel for Philip IV, was *La gloria de Niquea*, with a text by the controversial count of Villamediana (who was said to be attempting to woo the queen). This was the first large-scale theatrical entertainment given during Philip IV's reign.[21] Ladies of the court played all of the principal roles and were assigned the solo songs, although their performances were reinforced by professionally designed scenery and visual effects. The expert musicians of the royal chapel (as anonymous choirs that sang from offstage, and as instrumentalists seated out of the audience's view) helped insure the "decorum" of this royal entertainment, the text of which was written by a highly-ranked courtier who did not earn a living as a professional dramatist. It is difficult to define the genre of *La gloria de Niquea*, and indeed of another later court play, *El nuevo Olimpo* by Gabriel Bocángel (1648), because they were such theatrical hybrids, much in the manner of the French *ballet de cour*. In performance they combined marvelously up-to-date visual effects, professionally designed choreography, spoken verse in Italianate poetic meters, and choral songs in concerted style, with solo songs in traditional Spanish meters. One song from *La gloria de Niquea*, a traditional romance sung by three nymphs (ladies in waiting), was reported to have left the audience in a state of magic "suspension" in spite of its technical simplicity. Another solo song from the same play also had an especially magical, persuasive effect when it was performed by a negro Portuguese maidservant famous for her voice. She arrived onstage as the allegorical figure of Night, costumed in a black dress encrusted with silver stars, and sang with sweetly "dark" tones to the accompaniment of a vihuela to soften the hero Amadis and weaken him through lyrical musical persuasion. This scene illustrates the way in which early-seventeenth-century Spanish court plays demonstrated the power of music and harnessed the effects of sensually persuasive song, although this "magic" song was nothing other than a romance performed in a traditional way as accompanied solo song. Another kind of music, sung by several mysterious unseen choirs, had the "magical" effect of soothing the spectators with its expansive sonority and concordant harmony, so that the discovery of an Inferno scene complete with leap-

19 See Garcilaso de la Vega, *Obras*, ed. Tomás Navarro Tomás (Madrid, 1924; repr. 1966), 215.

20 Concerning the indications for music in *La fábula de Dafne*, *El premio de la hermosura*, and *La gloria de Niquea*, and the extant repertory of Spanish sonnet settings, see Louise K. Stein, "Los músicos de la Capilla Real y la música de los festejos palaciegos, 1590–1648," in *La Capilla Real de los Austrias: Música y ritual de corte en la Europa moderna*, ed. Juan José Carreras and Bernardo J. García García (Madrid, 2001), 255–59, 267–68.

21 See the text in Conde de Villamediana, *Obras* (Madrid, 1643), and in Villamediana, *Poesía impresa completa*, ed. José Francisco Ruiz Casanova (Madrid, 1990), 1149–1227.

ing flames did not fill the audience with horror. In general in the early-seventeenth-century Spanish spectacle plays, solo songs were performed by amateur singers within their roles, but professional singers and instrumentalists from the royal chapel, divided into several anonymous choirs, provided the large, concerted, polyphonic pieces that accompanied scenes of supernatural effect and visual display.

Somewhat later in the reign of Philip IV, the first spectacle plays conceived by the professional dramatist Pedro Calderón de la Barca (1600–1681) were performed at court by professional actors and actresses with expertly designed italianate scenery and special visual effects. The extant texts for these plays, *El mayor encanto amor* (1635), *Los tres mayores prodigios* (1636), and *Auristela y Lisidante* (1637) call for special musical effects and audible cues to be provided by shawms, trumpets, and drums, just as did the *comedia* texts for the public theaters. The songs in them were performed in virtually the same traditional ways as they were in the *comedias* for the public theaters or in the earlier court plays, except that accompanied solo songs done by professional actress-singers in special roles (as divine messenger nymphs, for example) were a significant innovation.

While the professional musicians who had audibly enhanced the performances of earlier seventeenth-century court plays were royal musicians, they were not exposed to public view but sang or played in an anonymous choir hidden behind or above the scenery, clearly out of a concern for their royal decorum as the king's chapel musicians. This concern seems to have been greatly diminished by around 1650, when palace plays ceased to require the participation of singers from the royal chapel, although the core of the theatrical orchestra was a large continuo band of musicians on the royal payroll, most of whom also played in the royal chapel. The spectacle plays of Calderón from the 1630s were staged by companies of professional actors and actresses, and this meant that the persuasive, enchanting, or seductive songs embedded in them were performed not by amateur ladies of the court whose dignity was a central concern, but by professional actress-singers who were trained to appear on stage in public. This change seems to have had a significant effect on the kinds of solo song that could be performed in the palace plays. The extant music for a number of Calderón's later plays (the semi-operas, operas, and zarzuelas performed at court beginning in 1652) includes lyrical strophic airs or *tonadas* as well as through-composed declamatory airs and strikingly beautiful, difficult-to-sing recitative monologues and dialogues for the gods.

Although the early-seventeenth-century palace plays depended for their success on the work of Italian stage architects (Giulio Cesare Fontana from Naples, and then Cosimo Lotti from Florence), the early history of opera and related genres in the Hispanic dominions followed its own path, with only limited reference to operatic developments elsewhere in Europe. The first opera performed in Spain was *La selva sin amor* (1627), a tiny opera after the model of the Florentine pastorals that was only given twice, in December of 1627, for the royal family. It was designed above all to display the talents of Lotti, the stage designer brought to Philip IV from Florence, and the emphasis was on the visual, not the musical. Its libretto was written in Spanish especially for this court production by the prolific poet and dramatist Lope de Vega, although it is almost entirely in Italian poetic meters (only the brief *coros* are in Spanish octosyllabic lines). The music (apparently lost) was by Piccinini, the lute and theorbo player who was among Philip IV's favorite musicians, and who accepted the commission under pressure from the Florentine diplomats then serving in Madrid.[22] While Lope de Vega reported that he was "enraptured" to hear his entire text performed in song (recitative composed by the none-too-eager Piccinini with the help of a secretary at the Tuscan embassy), the production did not convince the Spaniards to cultivate opera. It seems to have inspired almost no critical reaction in Madrid in its time, and was all but forgotten by 1659–60 when the idea of performing a Spanish opera at court surfaced again and produced the two Hispanic operas designed to commemorate the marriage of María Teresa of Spain with Louis XIV of France—*La púrpura de la rosa* and *Celos aun del aire matan*, both with texts by Calderón and music by Juan Hidalgo (1614–1685).

It is safe to say that opera did not take root in Madrid in the early seventeenth century, even as a courtly entertainment, because the genre as first cultivated there was both impractical and difficult to accommodate within the well-established Spanish musical and theatrical conventions. The court composers at this early date were still unfamiliar with recitative, and for them the "art" of composition was demonstrated in the production of correctly contrapuntal polyphony, however ingenious in its setting of a text and its audible effects. "Composition" was likewise not understood to embrace the invention of simple, strophic solo songs that could be performed by any skilled amateur. At the same time, the traditions of performance that set professional musicians and actors apart from their non-professional counterparts did not include the expectation that actors would trade the freedom of exaggerated histrionic expression for the restriction of wholly sung roles, or that professional court singers (who were all male) would risk their dignity by appearing onstage in costume. Although professional acting companies seem to have included both male and female singers before 1650, it appears that male singers were not expected to sing solo songs onstage with any regularity. Ensemble songs (romances in polyphonic settings) sung simply by "músicos" in verisimilar situations were largely what male singers performed onstage in the public theaters (and offstage in the court productions) when they sang in plays. In the *zarzuelas*, semi-operas, and operas produced at the Madrid court after 1650, the principal sung roles were taken by professional actress-singers, even when the characters they played were gods such as Apollo and Cupid, or famous mythological males such as Cephalus and Adonis.

Music and Musicians in Church

While the actors who sang in the theaters may or may not have had any formal training in music, singers of church music were trained in the choir schools of churches and cathedrals all across the Hispanic world, well known for

22 See Stein, *Songs of Mortals*, 191–205; Whitaker, "Florentine Opera," 43–66.

their discipline and high standards. The Hispanic repertory of Latin-texted sacred music from the early seventeenth century includes masses and other liturgical compositions primarily in imitative counterpoint, for one or many choirs. Motets were composed to a very limited extent, to judge by the contents of the musical archives of cathedrals, convents, monasteries, and parish churches throughout the Iberian peninsula and in Mexico and Central and South America (in addition to numerous libraries in Europe and the Americas), which are instead replete with sacred villancicos. Although some of the villancicos from the later seventeenth century are accompanied solo songs with religious reworkings of formerly profane texts "a lo divino", the term *villancico* refers in this period to settings of vernacular sacred texts that honor all manner of religious festivities, especially Corpus Christi, Christmas, Epiphany, and Easter. Villancicos were performed in processions and in place of the responsories of Matins at Christmas, on many saints' days, and during the eight days of Corpus Christi. They incorporate a variety of musical textures—polychoral settings that call for a combination of vocal and instrumental choirs are the most typical—and normally include sections of strophic *coplas* and elaborate refrains known as *estribillos*, which may substitute for the standard *responsión*. Cultivated more prolifically even than large-scale psalm settings for multiple choirs, these vernacular and mostly festive pieces typify the brilliant sound of concerted music in the Hispanic Baroque. There are villancicos with or without instruments—harps and sometimes organ, violón, or guitars, usually *chirimias* and *bajoncillos*, but also later violins, oboes, and clarino trumpets—for many voices or for few, as well as a largely unstudied body of solo villancicos, some of them indistinguishable from sacred cantatas, and others like religious arias in eighteenth-century style. The most important repositories of Baroque sacred villancicos are the cathedral archives of Hispanic cities, although villancicos are also scattered through the music collections of libraries in Spain, Europe, the United States, and Latin America.

The importance of the vernacular and Counter-Reformation genre of the villancico in Hispanic culture cannot be overestimated. Pietro Cerone recognized the pervasive influence of the religious villancico early in the seventeenth century when he wrote: "I don't wish to say that the practice of the villancicos is bad, because it is accepted in all the churches of Spain, and to such an extent, that it seems as if no solemn occasion can be celebrated without them." Cerone had lived in Spain and served in the court chapel for nine years beginning in 1592. Admittedly a critic at some distance from his subject by the time he wrote his *El melopeo y maestro* (Naples, 1613), Cerone criticized the villancico especially for the characteristics that made it so popular and so effective as religious propaganda, namely its obvious *conceptismo*, its "diversity of languages" (with sections in languages other than Castilian and in dialect or pseudo-dialect for *Asturianos*, *Gallegos*, *Portugueses*, *Vizcaínos*, *Gitanos*, *Negros*, or *Indios*, for example), its quotation from theatrical songs and profane, popular *bailes*, and use of comic dialogue. For Cerone, these elements "turn God's church into a public theatre or recreation room." Sensitive to the power of the genre, which remained vigorous through the first half of the eighteenth century, the *cabildos* or chapters of many cathedrals agreed time and again to clean up the villancicos, given the sometimes scandalous conduct of the faithful upon hearing them. Villancicos were heard by people of all social classes at church and in both rural and urban settings, because all kinds of Spanish composers produced them, from the most distinguished of court musicians to the masters of cathedral music and those who composed or arranged music for parish churches.

As the voluminous correspondence among chapel-masters such as Miguel Gómez Camargo and Miguel de Irízar makes clear later in the century, the texts and the music of the villancicos circulated widely and rapidly in manuscript copies.[23] The publication of Pedro Rimonte (or Ruimonte), *Parnaso español de madrigales y villancicos a quatro, cinco et seys* (Antwerp, 1614) was exceptional. Rimonte was principal chamber musician to the archduchess Isabel Clara Eugenia and archduke Albert in Prague. His printed collection offers secular villancicos and madrigals with Spanish texts, whereas the typical seventeenth-century villancico has little in common with the madrigal and was almost exclusively preserved in manuscript. Villancico texts, on the other hand, were collected and published in small booklets, including those sung in many cathedrals and in the royal chapels in Madrid.

In their music, as in their texts, early-seventeenth-century Spanish villancicos demonstrate the persistence of native Spanish musical traits—especially the pervasive use of hemiola and syncopation—in an age in which musical style elsewhere in Europe was becoming increasingly homogenized. Although the idea of a recognizably Spanish style only became controversial in a later period (around 1700) when the genre eventually absorbed italianate "foreign" and "modern" styles, most seventeenth-century villancicos sound clearly designed to delight and instruct through musical gestures and conventions rooted in vernacular music and native musical practices. The villancicos are "composed" music, but they are designed to sound as spontaneous as "performer's" music; they are composed to exhibit precisely those traits that listeners might have associated with popular music or lowly *bailes*—extended hemiola and syncopation, an impulse toward improvisation, the inclusion of popular refrains, occasional guitar effects (and the real inclusion of guitars as continuo instruments), patterned bass lines, and dance rhythms.

While Spanish musical culture in the seventeenth century was not isolationist in any sense (many foreign musicians worked in Spain, and foreign music was played at court), it seems important to ask if Spanish musicians and composers of the mainstream were best served in their careers by cultivating conventional and traditional kinds of music. In the 1660s, when the Earl of Sandwich was posted in Madrid as a special ambassador, he found the people there full of "liberty and extravagance," and their manner of playing music, as "agreeable, soft and passionate" (perhaps referring to the sound of small ensembles based on plucked and strummed

[23] Miguel Querol Gavaldá, "Corresponsales de Miguel Gómez Camargo," *Anuario musical*, 14 (1959), 165–77; José López-Calo, "Corresponsales de Miguel de Irízar (1)," *Anuario musical*, 18 (1963), 197–222, 20 (1965), 209; Carmelo Caballero, "Miguel Gómez Camargo: Correspondencia," *Anuario musical*, 45 (1990), 67–102; Carmelo Caballero Fernández-Rufete, "Aportación documental al estudio de Miguel Gómez Camargo," *Revista portuguesa de musicologia*, 1 (1991), 109–27.

instruments with gut strings). Sandwich noted that generally the Spaniards had no taste for foreign music: "They love such tunes as the Trumpetts, but especially the ordinary tunes of Spayn as a mariona, Chicona [*sic*; chacona] or pasacalle."[24] Sandwich had first-hand experience because he was an amateur musician and sought opportunities to play chamber music at court.[25] The "ordinary tunes" or *bailes* of Spain, which Sandwich recognized because they were already famously popular far beyond her borders, retained their popularity and useful versatility well beyond the seventeenth century, though some of them had come into the musical vernacular as early as the late fifteenth century, or had been brought to the Iberian peninsula from the New World in the sixteenth century. These tunes, heard in dance music that served nobles and commoners alike, in romances and villancicos and in instrumental *glosas* and *diferencias*, are what early-seventeenth-century listeners in Spain and abroad recognized as essential in the Spanish idiom.

[24] Frank Reginald Harris, *The Life of Edward Montagu, K.G., First Earl of Sandwich (1625–1672)*, 2 vols. (London, 1912), II: 90.

[25] As quoted ibid., II: 112, Sandwich later described playing viols at the Buen Retiro palace with Don Juan José of Austria (Philip IV's illegitimate son), when suites from the "Royall" consort music of William Lawes and Flemish "light airs " were played through.

23

EARLY OPERA: THE INITIAL PHASE

Giuseppe Gerbino
Iain Fenlon

WHEN Nino Pirrotta wrote that "few other genres have their beginnings as precisely determined as opera," and that "its landmark is the first performance of *Euridice*, with music by Jacopo Peri" (6 October 1600), he was articulating the settlement of a dispute whose claims and interests remain difficult to untangle, both theoretically and descriptively.[1] The solution of the dispute largely depends on what we choose to isolate as the essence of the new musical theater. For Pirrotta it was the development of a declamatory style linking music to speech patterns, that is, of a recitative style. Peri's achievement in this area—the formulation of the linguistic principles underlying his theory of recitative as well as the demonstration of such principles in the "realistic eloquence"[2] of his style—is what ultimately made his *Euridice* the archetype of opera in the eyes of modern historians.[3]

[1] Nino Pirrotta and Elena Povoledo, *Music and Theatre from Poliziano to Monteverdi* (Cambridge, 1982; Italian orig., Turin, 1969, rev. 1975), 237.

[2] Ibid., 245. Besides Pirrotta, attempts at explaining the essence of Peri's *recitativo* may be found in Howard Mayer Brown, "How Opera Began: An Introduction to Jacopo Peri's *Euridice* (1600)," in *The Late Italian Renaissance, 1525–1630*, ed. Eric Cochrane (London, 1970), 401–43; Claude Palisca, "Peri and the Theory of Recitative," *Studi musicali*, 15 (1982), 51–61; repr. in idem, *Studies in the History of Italian Music and Music Theory* (New York, 1994), 452–66. John Walter Hill, "Beyond Isomorphism toward a Better Theory of Recitative," *Journal of Seventeenth-Century Music*, 9/1 (2003) (http://www.sscm-jscm.org/jscm/v9/no1/Hill.html), has recently proposed an approach to the study of early recitative based on intonational and metric phonology.

[3] The year 1600 was ratified as the "official" birth date of opera by a number of events organized in 2000 to celebrate the 400th anniversary of the performance of Peri's *Euridice*. They included three conferences (in Florence, Urbana-Champaign, and Paris), whose proceedings were published respectively in *Lo stupor dell'invenzione: Firenze e la nascita dell'opera*, ed. Piero Gargiulo (Florence, 2001); "In Armonia Favellare: Report of the International Conference on Early Opera and Monody to Commemorate the 400th Anniversary of the Italian Music Dramas of 1600, Held at the University of Illinois, Urbana-Champaign, October 5–8, 2000," *Journal of Seventeenth-Century Music*, 9/1 (2003) (http://sscm-jscm.press.uiuc.edu/jscm/v9no1.

The heated argument that witnessed the birth of court opera defines it both as a cultural phenomenon and as a historiographical concept. Peri and his two rivals, Giulio Caccini and Emilio de' Cavalieri, may seem to share with modern scholarship the desire, or perhaps the need, to explain the origins of this most unusual invention. In actuality, their "emplotted accounts" imposed the structure of a narrative on a series of events whose meaning derived from a conflict of authorship and the institutionalization of the early operatic experiments as court ceremonies. Concomitantly, and more importantly to us, they gave verbal expression to a wide compass of practices and ideas that shaped the humanistic concern with music, speech, and theater, the mechanisms of artistic patronage, and the relationship between the Florentine cultural aristocracy and the Medici court.

The starting point of the public declarations that prefaced the publication of Peri's, Caccini's, and Cavalieri's first demonstrations of the new theater was the unattainable model of Greek drama. "It has been the opinion of many," Ottavio Rinuccini wrote in the dedication to Maria de' Medici of his libretto of *Euridice*, "that the ancient Greeks and Romans, in representing their tragedies upon a stage, sang them throughout. But until now this noble manner of recitation has been neither revived nor (to my knowledge) even attempted by anyone, and I used to believe that this was due to the imperfection of modern music, by far inferior to the ancient."[4] The sharply focused tone of this opening statement defines the co-ordinates of Rinuccini's classicist horizon, but the rationale of his claim is anything but transparent. Leaving aside for a moment the issue of musical recitation, one could rightly object, for example, that the early opera libretti signed by Rinuccini in the 1590s did not even remotely look like any tragedy written in classical antiquity. They are in every respect pastoral or mythological fables of Ovidian inspiration. Indeed, many of those who were able to attend performances of *Dafne* and *Euridice* continued to refer to them as *pastorali* or *pastorelle* in their letters, accounts, or diaries.[5] Cultural habits were surely stronger than any theoretical argument. And yet Rinuccini, Peri, Caccini, and even Cavalieri chose to draw an ideal line that connected the modern musical theater with ancient tragedy.

There were two centers in Rinuccini's discourse, and it may be useful to keep them separate: the first, and perhaps more important, was the undemonstrable

html); and *La Naissance de l'opéra: "Euridice" 1600–2000*, ed. Françoise Decroisette, Françoise Graziani, and Joël Heuillon (Paris, 2002). Not everybody agreed on the historiographical significance of the anniversary; among the dissenting voices is Silke Leopold, "Die Anfänge von Oper und die Probleme der Gattung," *Journal of Seventeenth-Century Music*, 9/1 (2003) (http://www.sscm-jscm.org/jscm/v9/no1/Leopold.html).

[4] The full text with an English translation may be read in *Composing Opera: From "Dafne" to "Ulisse Errante"*, ed. Tim Carter (Cracow, 1994), 15–19. Jacopo Peri expressed the same point of view in the preface to the edition of the music: "in the opinion of many, [the Greeks and Romans] sang their tragedies throughout on the stage." See ibid., 25, and Oliver Strunk (ed.), *Source Readings in Music History*, rev. edn by Leo Treitler (New York and London, 1998), 659–62.

[5] An extensive survey of such accounts may be found in Warren Kirkendale, *The Court Musicians in Florence during the Principate of the Medici, with a Reconstruction of the Artistic Establishment* (Florence, 1993), 194–210.

but generally accepted idea of the superiority of ancient music *vis-à-vis* modern practice; the second stemmed from the humanistic debate on Greek and Roman tragedy. The investigation of classical drama and the relative merits of ancient and modern music reflected the intellectual interests of a segment of the cultural elite and minor nobility of Florence led first by Giovanni Bardi (in the 1570s and 1580s) and then, after his departure from Florence in 1592, by Jacopo Corsi (both, like Rinuccini, were members of the Accademia degli Alterati).[6] Among the most important documents of this activity is a seminal series of writings born of the collaboration between Vincenzo Galilei (whose musical studies were sponsored by Bardi) and the Florentine humanist Girolamo Mei (who at the time of his correspondence with Galilei resided in Rome).[7] Caccini, not Peri, seems to have been the musician most closely associated with Bardi and Galilei, even though unmistakable echoes of the ideas that were developed in those years found their way in the aesthetic claims of Peri as well. To judge from the extant letters and essays, Galilei's chief interest was the theory and practice of Greek music, and only secondarily ancient theater. In 1572 Galilei wrote to Mei, the recognized authority on Greek music theory, with a list of problems that he had not been able to solve. Mei's reply was uniquely momentous and novel in its impact. Simply put, it forced his fellow Florentines to rethink what music is and does.

The overarching question that drove the argument of Mei's long letter was not new: why does modern music no longer seem to be able to produce the extraordinary effects described by the ancients? But Mei's answer developed an oddly original and radical idea. The ancients did not know polyphony. His study of the sources had led him to the conclusion that their music must have been exclusively monophonic. And this was the "secret" of the marvelous power of ancient music to move listeners. Mei admitted that solo singing would seem to allow a rather limited expressive range, only to rebuke this false belief by arguing (or better, imagining) that the Greek poets and singers used melody as a natural projection of linguistic structures, in order to "express completely and with efficacy all that they sought to convey when speaking through the medium and with the aid of the highs and lows of the diastematic voice, as in their idiom a voice moving by intervals was called, to distinguish it from the continuous voice of common speech. This was accompanied by a methodical tempering of the rapidity and slowness of the voice in pronouncing its units of time, according to how each of those tempos by itself naturally fits some determinate affection."[8] In the last analysis, Mei continues, the true difference between modern and ancient music is one concerning the end of music itself. In principle, both musical systems are laudable, but we should

[6] On the Accademia degli Alterati, see Claude Palisca, "The Alterati of Florence, Pioneers in the Theory of Dramatic Music," in *Studies in the History of Italian Music and Music Theory*, 408–31.

[7] See *Girolamo Mei (1519–1594): Letters on Ancient and Modern Music to Vincenzo Galilei and Giovanni Bardi*, ed. Claude Palisca (American Institute of Musicology, 1960), and *The Florentine Camerata: Documentary Studies and Translations*, ed. idem (New Haven, 1989).

[8] Mei, in *The Florentine Camerata*, 74.

not expect our music to achieve a goal it does not set itself to achieve, for ancient (monophonic and language-oriented) music aimed to arouse the passions of the soul as an enhanced manifestation of the natural communicative functions and properties of language, whereas modern (polyphonic) music aims only at pleasing the ear:

> As to the marvelous effects of the music of the ancients in moving affections and not finding any trace of this in the modern, if we wish to look with a straight eye at the matters discussed above, it may happen that we shall marvel no more at the [effects], because our [music] does not have the same goal. This may be because ours does not have any means of accomplishing this as the ancient did, since it has as its object the delectation of the sense of hearing, whereas the ancient had the object of leading someone else to the same affections as one's own.[9]

The implications of this redefinition of the nature of music were manifold and to some extent attuned to various strands of the intellectual discourse of the last decades of the sixteenth century. Mei himself touched upon them in his essay: the relationship between language and music, language and reason, reason and senses, music and senses. Galilei, Bardi, Caccini, and Peri, in contrast with Mei, all came to believe that the limits of modern music were not only explicable but also expandable. A period of experimentation followed. Indirect evidence suggests that its coordinates were defined by the key concepts of monody (although the term itself is much later) and the affective essence of song. But in the 1590s it would seem that such experimentation entered a new phase: theater became the proving-ground of the capabilities of modern music. Speaking of *Dafne*, Peri wrote in the preface to the 1601 edition of *Euridice* that "it pleased the Signori Jacopo Corsi and Ottavio Rinuccini (as early as 1594) that I . . . should set to music the tale of Daphne, written by Signor Ottavio, to make a simple trial of what the song of our age could do."[10] The renewed emphasis on theater may have coincided with the ascent of Corsi as main sponsor of the Florentine musical avant-garde, redefined in the collaboration with Peri and Rinuccini after Bardi's departure from Florence (Galilei had died in 1591), and the related intensification of contacts with the Medici court. Bardi gradually lost favor with the Medici when Ferdinando I became grand duke in 1587. By contrast, in the 1590s Corsi's fortunes with the ducal family were on the rise.[11] The production of Rinuccini's *Dafne* in the Corsi palace with music by Peri and Corsi himself (Carnival 1597/98) was still a private endeavor, although at least one performance took place at the Palazzo Pitti the following year. *Euridice*,

[9] Ibid., 66.

[10] Peri, in Strunk, *Source Readings*, 659.

[11] On Giovanni de' Bardi, see *Neoplatonismo, musica, letteratura nel Rinascimento: I Bardi di Vernio e l'Accademia della Crusca* [Florence 1998], ed. Piero Gargiulo, Alessandro Magini, and Stéphane Toussaint (Prato, 2000), esp. the essays by Tim Carter and Stefano La Via. Corsi's career is detailed in Tim Carter, "Music and Patronage in Late Sixteenth-Century Florence: The Case of Jacopo Corsi (1561–1602)," *I Tatti Studies: Essays in the Renaissance*, 1 (1985), 57–104.

however, again the result of collaboration between Peri and Rinuccini with some (unwelcome) contributions by Caccini, was offered as a wedding gift for the entertainments celebrating the marriage of Maria de' Medici (Ferdinando's niece) with Henry IV of France. Seen against the backdrop of the complex patron–client relationship regulating the political power that the Medici exerted on the local nobility, often through the symbolic exchange of cultural capital, this was the event that in the last analysis turned the humanistic fantasies of the Florentines into court opera. The Mantuan court's direct sponsorship of opera in 1607 and 1608 (resulting in the productions of Claudio Monteverdi's *Orfeo* and *Arianna*) was already a sign of the definitive institutionalization of opera as a courtly ritual, one that Marco da Gagliano in the preface to his setting of *Dafne* (1608) defined as a "spectacle truly of princes."[12]

That the search for a modern music worthy of the teachings of the ancients should eventually lead to theater is not difficult to understand. The cultural icon of tragedy was always present in the background of the philological investigation on ancient music. But the claim that a work such as *Euridice* belonged, for its forms and contents, to the dramatic and psychological universe of tragedy deserves, as was already suggested, a closer look.

The debate on tragedy accompanied the humanistic reflection on genre theory throughout the sixteenth century. It was animated by the desire to recreate in Italian a form of theater that emerged from the past as an ambiguous object of admiration. The idea of tragedy (both as a literary genre and as a conceptual category) pursued by sixteenth-century humanists and playwrights belonged to a civilization that by the time of the publication of Gian Giorgio Trissino's pioneering *Sofonisba* (1524) was over two thousand years old. The cultural distance was enormous. Issues of form occupied a large portion of the critical and literary practice of the time: what type of verse should be adopted, how long the play should last, what function the chorus should fulfill, whether or not the play should be divided into acts and scenes, etc. This formalistic orientation is understandable if we bear in mind that what poets sought to extrapolate from the few available texts was not so much what ancient tragedy was as what modern Italian tragedy ought to be. The real problem for them, however, was the spirit of ancient tragedy, the vision of the human condition that it portrayed, the notions of destiny, pity, fear—in a word, the very essence of tragic plot. At this level, ancient and modern ways of thinking were not easily reconcilable.

Aristotle's *Poetics* entered mainstream critical theory in the 1540s (thanks in part to Alessandro de' Pazzi's bilingual Greek and Latin edition). Aristotle provided the key concepts of the philological and philosophical investigation, but not necessarily the answers to the most pressing questions. On the contrary, the theory of tragedy developed in tandem with the notoriously litigious exchange of competing commentaries on the Aristotelian text. The first author to attempt a systematic codification of modern tragedy on the basis of conceptual criteria defined in the

12 Marco da Gagliano, preface to *La Dafne* (Florence, 1608; facs. Bologna, 1970).

Poetics was Giovanni Battista Giraldi Cinzio (1504–1573), the author of an important series of *Discorsi* on tragedy, comedy, epic poetry, and pastoral theater.[13] The impulse towards a reinterpretation of the concept of tragedy that could fit modern sensitivity is already apparent in Giraldi's writings. Among his innovations were at least two that anticipated a critical perspective psychologically very close to early operatic experiments. Giraldi defended the so-called "tragedy with a happy ending" as the dramatic structure most appropriate to modern theatrical practice. He also touched upon a problem that Aristotle never fully explained, namely the nature of the pleasure that we derive from the experience of tragedy. Sidelining the idea that the proper pleasure of tragedy was linked to the pleasure of learning from *mimesis*, Giraldi emphasized the purely affective, oddly satisfying dimension of the human response to experience of painful emotions: "tragedy has a pleasure of its own, and in that weeping (*pianto*) one discovers a hidden pleasure, which makes it pleasing to the listener, attracts the attention of the soul, and fills it with marvel."[14] It was an intuition that would find application in the centrality of the topos of the lament within the ideal of drama embodied by early opera. One might argue that the psychological paradigm to which early opera gave voice coincided precisely with this aesthetic of the bittersweet pleasure of *pianto*, an aesthetic that, especially when compared with the ethical outlook of the Aristotelian notion of catharsis, indeed manifested itself as the sign of a cultural gap that the formalistic imitation of the ancients could no longer bridge.

In the quest for modern tragedy, opera proposed a somewhat radical solution, radical because it focused all its efforts on a decidedly marginal aspect of the humanistic debate, the hypothesis that ancient theater was sung throughout. Both Rinuccini and Peri smoothed over the historical uncertainties of such a claim by appealing to the "opinion of many" in this matter. But the many were most likely to be very few. One can mention with certainty only three names: Girolamo Mei, Francesco Patrizi, and Vincenzo Galilei.[15] However, when read within the context of the "modernist" orientation of the dramatic theory that sought to validate—with the help of the ancients—its own theatrical practice and taste, the point that the "inventors" of opera were trying to make reveals a cultural relevance much deeper than its philological weaknesses.

Well aware of the distance that separated his own contribution to the development of this genre from the ancient model, Rinuccini famously assigned the

[13] On Giraldi's dramatic theory, see Daniel Javitch, "The Emergence of Poetic Genre Theory in the Sixteenth Century," *Modern Language Quarterly*, 59/2 (1998), 139–169; Luigia Zilli, "Fonti italiane della teoria tragicomica," in *Dalla tragedia rinascimentale alla tragicommedia barocca*, ed. Elio Mosele (Fasano, 1993), 51–59.

[14] Giovanni Battista Giraldi Cinzio, *Discorsi intorno al comporre rivisti dall'autore nell'esemplare ferrarese Cl. I 90*, ed. Susanna Villari (Messina, 2002), 316.

[15] See Claude Palisca, *Humanism in Italian Renaissance Musical Thought* (New Haven, 1985), 408–26.

Prologue to *Euridice* to the personification of Tragedy itself, who was called on stage to declare that she was no longer what she used to be:

> No longer of blood shed by innocent veins,
> nor of eyes put out by the insane tyrant,
> unhappy spectacle to human sight,
> do I sing now on a gloomy and tear-filled stage.
>
> Away, away from this royal house
> maudlin images, shades of sorrow!
> Behold, I change my gloomy buskins and dark robes
> to awaken in the heart sweeter emotions.[16]

At first sight, this prologue may appear to have had the sole function of justifying the happy ending that Rinuccini had chosen for his version of the story of Orpheus and Euridice. But what are these "sweeter emotions" that Tragedy almost paradoxically invokes as her own? Rinuccini's words echo Giraldi's notion of "tragic pleasure" as an emblem of modern man's understanding of himself. One might even suggest that such sweeter emotions are to be found in the long-standing tradition of the Renaissance philosophy of love, which tended to conceptualize this most mysterious of human emotions precisely as a paradox, as the source of an indefinably pleasant suffering. Thus, the love-sorrow of modern tragedy came to represent for sixteenth-century society what the heroic sorrow of tragedy had represented for ancient Greek and Roman societies.

The theatrical dimension of the new music had also the advantage of translating the humanistic interests of the cultural elite into a spectacle consistent with the type of entertainments that were customarily organized for the prestige and leisure of the court, which included hybrid forms of dramatization (mixing dance, poetry, and music) inspired by the pastoral fashion of the time. By the end of the sixteenth century, pastoral entertainments had saturated the lifestyle of Italian courts. In a sense, the discourse on modern tragedy reconciled humanistically-shaped beliefs about music with the ordinary experience of the representational and self-fashioning practices of the court. Divided between the idealized distance of ancient tragedy and the semantic vitality of contemporary theater, opera solved an instinctual paradox by turning the theatrical taste of the moderns into the medium through which to relive the experience of the ancients. Early historiographers such as Giovanni Battista Doni sought to explain the mythological or pastoral content of opera by appealing to the principle of verisimilitude (gods, demigods, and shepherds were traditionally said to have had poetry and music as their natural language).[17] But it might be equally argued that what Doni really sought to ra-

[16] Trans. Howard Mayer Brown, 1967.

[17] Giovanni Battista Doni, "Trattato della musica scenica," ed. in Angelo Solerti, *Le origini del melodramma* (Turin, 1903), 203–5. The problem of musical-dramatic verisimilitude in early opera is discussed in Gary Tomlinson, "Pastoral and Musical Magic in the Birth of Opera," in *Opera and the Enlightenment*, ed. Thomas Bauman and Marita McClymonds (Cambridge, 1995), 7–20.

tionalize was the discontinuity between the tragic pretence of the theory and the pastoral subject matter of the libretti set to music. The popularity of pastoral fiction preceded and spilled over outside issues of verisimilitude, which never became a major concern for Rinuccini, Peri, or Caccini. Rather than a shrewd choice of dramaturgical nature, the prevailing and somewhat puzzling themes of early opera embodied the singular function that mythological and pastoral modes of representation came to fulfil in the courtly culture of late-sixteenth-century Italy.[18]

Corsi would seem to have played an instrumental role as mediator between the academic projects of the cultural elite of Florence and the rituals of the Medici court. To be sure, among the three claimants, Emilio de' Cavalieri, who under the new duke served as superintendent of the Medici musical establishment, was the nobleman-composer most closely associated with the court's official culture. In the 1590s he experimented extensively with musical theater. However, the three pastorals in music (now lost) staged for the Medici court during those years seem to have lacked the ideological apparatus that would characterize the dispute of 1600, and his *Rappresentatione di Anima et di Corpo*, produced in Rome for the Congregation of the Oratory, fell outside the social space and theoretical structures of court opera.[19] Nonetheless, Cavalieri's pastorals raise a broader issue that has gradually emerged in the course of this discussion, namely the relationship between opera and pre-existing forms of musical entertainments for the court.

Claims to innovation such as those put forth by Peri, Caccini, and Cavalieri inevitably stressed the novelty and originality of the new theater. But the tensions within their writings reveal an unresolved compromise between theoretical proclamations and long-established practices of solo singing and musical representation. Peri's and Caccini's competing accounts of how they created the new singing style bear the signs of this unresolved compromise. Peri's description emphasized the self-reflective nature of his investigation. Theory and observation preceded what he characterized as a newly discovered way of manipulating the musical properties of language, which, "rejecting every other type of song heard up to now," in turn aimed at recapturing the expressive power of ancient music.[20] Conversely, for Caccini the new style was not invented or artificially engineered but simply found in the musical vocabulary of his own time, in a style of singing that he had long practiced. Bardi, he says, had the sole merit of recognizing in the music of the moderns the lost voices of the ancients: "This is . . . the manner that Your Lordship, in the years when Your Lordship's *camerata* was flourishing in Florence, . . . declared to be that used by the ancient Greeks when introducing song into the presentations of

[18] The relationship between "modern" tragedy, early opera, and the pastoral ethos of the late sixteenth century is investigated in Giuseppe Gerbino, "Orpheus in Arcadia: The Creation of Pastoral Mode in the Sixteenth-Century Madrigal" (PhD dissertation, Duke University, 2001), 445–66.

[19] For a defense of Cavalieri's contribution to the creation of opera, see Warren Kirkendale, *Emilio de' Cavalieri, "Gentiluomo Romano": His Life and Letters, His Role as Superintendent of all the Arts at the Medici Court, and His Musical Compositions* (Florence, 2001), 185–212.

[20] See Jacopo Peri, preface to *Le musiche sopra l'Euridice* (Florence, 1600 [1601]); Eng. trans. in Strunk, *Source Readings*, 659–62.

their tragedies and other fables."[21] Despite the obvious bias of his autobiographical reportage, Caccini bore witness to unspoken assumptions typical of late Renaissance humanism, or at least of a generation of humanists who looked at classical antiquity to find a reflection of themselves.

G.G.

OTHER novelties alleged by modern historians imply discontinuity with previous musical practices, with a special position being reserved for a handful of "transitional" works (the Florentine *intermedi* of 1589, the lost pastorals of Emilio de' Cavalieri and Laura Guicciardini, etc.), works that are deemed to possess the essential characteristics of being sung throughout on the one hand and of containing elements of declamatory writing on the other. In this process, the primacy of Florence as the place where early opera was evolved is reasserted, thus mapping music history onto a well-established historiography of the Renaissance itself that ultimately derives from the enormous influence of the Vasarian model. To switch the focus, it is important to recognize that, in terms of its ideological means and purposes, methods of finance, and structures of production and performance, early-seventeenth-century court opera was virtually indistinguishable from the various types of court spectacle that had preceded it (and continued to surround it): the *intermedi*, jousts, and other set-piece genres performed in princely contexts throughout the peninsula, often in celebration of important dynastic occasions. Such entertainments were usually a product of the court itself, in the purely practical sense that the end results were a combined effort of poets, engineers, carpenters, musicians, singers, dancers, painters, and others who were permanently employed there, and were presented within the confines of the court.

Early-sixteenth-century court entertainments were usually given in the larger rooms within the palace complex, known to many in the audience from other contexts, transformed for the purpose through the construction of temporary structures made of painted wood and gesso painted to simulate marble. Such transformations were merely the first phase of a sequence of essentially theatrical experiences that constituted the spectacle itself. During the second half of the Cinquecento, as dramaturgical demands increased, stage machinery became more elaborate, and the attraction of the Vitruvian example became more intense, fixed court theatres became the norm. One of the earliest to survive, designed by Vincenzo Scamozzi for Sabbioneta, Vespasiano Gonzaga's model city near Mantua, quotes directly from classical antiquity;[22] it is obviously also heavily indebted to Andrea Palladio's slightly earlier Teatro Olimpico,[23] commissioned by an academy in Vicenza and inaugurated in 1585 with a performance of Orsatto Giustiniani's translation of *Oedipus rex*, whose choruses had been set to music by

21 Giulio Caccini, preface to *L'Euridice composta in musica in stile rappresentativo* (Florence, 1600); Eng. trans. in Strunk, *Source Readings*, 606.

22 Stefano Mazzoni and Ovidio Guaita, *Il teatro di Sabbioneta* (Florence, 1985).

23 Licisio Magagnato, *Il teatro Olimpico*, ed. Lionello Puppi (Milan, 1992).

Andrea Gabrieli in a spare and uncompromising style of unaccompanied choral recitative.[24] It is, in fact, the only surviving example of music written to the text of a tragedy, as well as a gentle reminder that the history of sixteenth-century theatrical music takes in cities other than Venice, social environments other than the court, and forms other than the *intermedio* and the pastoral. The ducal theatre at Parma, built for the Farnese and one of the most elaborate and well documented of the period, makes an accommodation with more recent practice through the incorporation of a proscenium arch, which had also been a feature of Bernardo Buontalenti's earlier Medici Theatre in the Uffizi, in effect a temporary transformation of an existing room into a typical hall theatre.[25] For the theatre constructed for the 1589 Florentine wedding, the same general plan was again followed.[26] Common to both were the steps joining stage to auditorium, a characteristic of court theatre that facilitated movement between the two areas, something that was technically useful (and sometimes symbolically significant) in productions of the *balletto di corte*, where the mingling of performers and audience often served an overtly ideological purpose.

Within these reserved and imposing spaces court spectacles were performed, often in the presence of the prince himself, before a carefully selected and socially exclusive audience hierarchically seated according to rank. Through words, music and, above all, astonishing scenic effects, these largely aristocratic elites, both local and "foreign," were presented with entertainments whose primary purpose was the delivery of thinly disguised political and ideological messages, usually involving elaborations of the theme of dynastic continuity as a guarantee of peace and prosperity. In these terms the Florentine *intermedi* of 1589, Claudio Monteverdi's *Arianna* to a text by Ottavio Rinuccini (Mantua, 1608), and the extravagantly scenic *Le nozze degli dei*, a "favola cantata in stile recitativo" with a libretto by Giovanni Carlo Coppola set to music by a team of five composers under the direction of Ferdinando Saracinelli (Florence, 1638), all rely on similar ideological imperatives, technological and spatial resources, and systems of production.

Such continuities are evident from the considerable amount of surviving documentation that surrounds the Florentine 1589 *intermedi*, the most famous and certainly the most elaborate set of the entire century, designed to be performed between the acts of Girolamo Bargagli's comedy *La pellegrina*.[27] Divided into separate units by Bardi, their common subject matter is music, or rather classical

[24] For the most recent edition, see the *Edizione nazionale delle opere di Andrea Gabrieli, [1533]–1585*, XII (Milan, 1995); for a discussion of the music, Nino Pirrotta, "I cori per l'*Edippo Tiranno*," in *Andrea Gabrieli e il suo tempo* [Venice 1985], ed. Francesco Degrada (Florence, 1987), 272–92, also in Nino Pirrotta, *Scelte poetiche de musicisti* (Venice, 1987), 43–61.

[25] Detlef Heikamp, "Il Teatro Mediceo degli Uffizi," *Bolletino del Centro Internazionale di architettura Andrea Palladio*, 16 (1974), 323–32.

[26] Cesare Molinari, *Le nozze degli dei* (Rome, 1968), 13–35; Pirrotta and Povoledo, *Music and Theatre*, 365–83; Mario Fabbri et al., *Il luogo teatrale a Firenze* (Milan, 1975), 105–8.

[27] Alois M. Nagler, *Theatre Festivals of the Medici* (New Haven, 1964), 58–69; James M. Saslow, *The Medici Wedding of 1589: Florentine Festival as "Theatrum Mundi"* (New Haven and London, 1996). In addition to Fabbri et al., *Il luogo teatrale*, much of the relevant documentation is also illustrated in a more recent exhibition catalogue; see Maria Adelaide Bartoli

myths about Neoplatonic concepts of music, illustrated in allegories and through symbolic figures. Three of them deal with the supreme harmony of the cosmos, while the remaining three represent the power of human harmony; the resulting thematic unity is unprecedented. In keeping with the political dimension of the genre, the 1589 *intermedi* take the idea of the power of music as the basic material for the celebration of a dynastic marriage. The sheer scale of these six *intermedi*, which completely overshadow the play itself, responds to a set of contemporary ideas derived from theories of princely decorum in which liberality, erudition, and above all *magnificenza* were all considered to be regal virtues, a belief that is here potently expressed in a spectacle of great elaboration, based on classical mythology. Equally important in this configuration is the evocation of "wonder" as an experience, a prerequisite clearly catered to by costumes, lighting, and particularly scenic effects; their deployment of elaborate stage action and machinery is just one way in which these *intermedi* anticipate seventeenth-century operatic practice. Indeed, a large part of the historical importance of the 1589 *intermedi* is that they are constructed out of the musical and theatrical elements from which the genre of opera itself grew within a decade in the same city. "Wonder" was also a necessary ingredient of the music, designed to stupify the listeners through the virtuosity of the performers, or the sheer size of the forces required.[28] Competition was great between the Italian courts to secure the most agile voices and the most able choreographers and to construct the most advanced theatrical machines, as expressions of princely virtue. An intense instance of this rivalry between dynasties (who were themselves genealogically connected), occurred in 1608 when the Gonzaga in Mantua and the Este in Ferrara competed for novelty in mounting extensive wedding celebrations at more or less the same moment.[29]

These various threads—political, mythological, technological, scenographical, choreographic, and musical—all come together in the final *ballo* of the 1589 *intermedi*. The scene itself is modeled on a passage in the second book of Plato's *Laws* that treats of the gods' gift of music and dance to mortals. In the size of its conception and the intricacy of its choreography, Cavalieri's dance is certainly full of "wonder:" the elaborate machines bring the gods from their clouds to the stage, and the brilliance of the costumes proclaims the magnificence of the provider of this particular feast for the eyes and the ears. In the final stanzas the allusions accumulate. The dance itself is already a symbol of authority and order. Now Plato's gods, descending, merge with the couple through whose union that authority and order will be extended and consolidated. It is difficult to find another passage in the *intermedio* repertory where the message is so bluntly stated, the language so unsubtle, the music so direct. Other aspects of the 1589 finale are also important

Bacherini, *"Per un regale evento": Spettacoli nuziali e opera in musica alla corte dei Medici* (Florence, 2000).

28 For an edition, see *Les Fêtes du mariage de Ferdinand de Médicis et de Christine de Lorraine (Florence, 1589)*, 1: *Musique des intermèdes de "La Pellegrina"*, ed. D. P. Walker (Paris, 1963).

29 Iain Fenlon, "The Origins of the Seventeenth-Century Staged Ballo," in *Con che soavità: Studies in Italian Opera, Song, and Dance, 1580–1740*, ed. Iain Fenlon and Tim Carter (Oxford, 1995), 13–40 at 34–39.

for the subsequent history of opera and dramatic music. In terms of size alone, the conception is unparalleled in the repertory of sixteenth-century theatrical dance, as is the ingenious sequence of rhythmic variations on the simple musical material announced in the opening and closing sections of the piece, variations that also exploit the contrast between full texture and three-voice material. The overall design is almost entirely symmetrical, with only the coda falling outside the scheme.[30] The result is the extension of the time dimension that the concertato method of organization made possible; by operating different permutations and variations, much larger structures could be created. All subsequent operatic finales followed the same strophic method of construction, sometimes employing merely two stanzas as in Monteverdi's *Orfeo*, sometimes as many as eight as in Peri's *Euridice*. In terms of operatic history, the finale of the 1589 *intermedi* probably exercised more influence on subsequent works than any other single number.

This brings us to a further point, namely the importance of the literary text of the 1589 *intermedi*, which anticipates many of the themes and conventions of the early opera libretto. The prominence of Apollo, for example, whose battle with the Python is staged in the third *intermedio* and who, in the sixth, descends with the spirits of Harmony and Rhythm to bring peace to earth and joy to the assembled nymphs and shepherds, anticipates the subject-matter of the first operas: Peri's *Dafne*, in which Apollo's victory over the Python forms the initial episode, Peri's *Euridice*, which concludes with a chorus of praise to Apollo, and Monteverdi's *Orfeo*, where Apollo similarly rescues Orpheus from the Bacchantes at the end of the work (which is probably an addition to the original Striggio–Monteverdi text). But the importance of Rinuccini as the poetic inspiration behind the composers and producers of the 1589 *intermedi* goes beyond any such details. In the *intermedi*, for which he wrote the lion's share of the texts, Rinuccini tested both his imagination and his awareness of what music could and should do in drama. This places him in a precise intellectual context, since the texts of the *intermedi* are less a characteristic expression of the Florentine tradition of court entertainments than of the concerns among the elite of the Accademia degli Alterati, of which Rinuccini was a member. It was as a result of these trials that Rinuccini proceeded to write a number of librettos, from Peri's *Dafne* to Monteverdi's *Arianna*, in each of which he expanded and solidified the technique of *poesia per musica*. It is true to say that it was on the territory staked out by Rinuccini and his composers that the subsequent development of opera was based, and that the 1589 *intermedi* are central to understanding it, since they represent not only a high point of the Florentine *intermedio* tradition itself but also the transition to the new genre that, in the guise of court opera, fulfilled similar cultural purposes.

It was in order to pursue the essentially political dimension of the form that detailed descriptions were published, their primary function being as a vehicle for propaganda, for disseminating beyond the immediate audience the sense of wonder that the performance, with its celebration of the familiar complex of princely virtues, had evoked. It is this, rather than facilitating further performances (which,

30 F. W. Sternfeld, *The Birth of Opera* (Oxford, 1993), 95.

stripped of their precise, local, dynastic meanings would make little sense anyway), that was also the principal function of engravings showing the sets; here too the 1589 *intermedi* established a practice that was widely followed in the seventeenth century. Undoubtedly the same is true for Malvezzi's edition of the 1589 music, which was modeled on Antonio Gardano's publication of the music for Cosimo de' Medici's marriage to Eleonora of Toledo, published exactly 50 years earlier.[31] The scores of the Peri–Rinuccini *Euridice*, Caccini's setting of the same text, Marco da Gagliano's *Dafne* (written for the 1608 Gonzaga wedding celebrations in Mantua), and Monteverdi's *Orfeo* were all published, the latter twice, Ricciardo Amadino's apparently puzzling decision to issue a second edition (without dedication) being presumably made to satisfy the collectors' market for music associated with exclusive environments and grand occasions. Certainly the volume itself, which appeared without dedication and which takes Amadino's first edition as its source and as the model for its typographical layout, shows scant sign of corrections, authorial or otherwise. In short, there is little to suggest that the earliest operas were anything more than rather recherché works of limited musical appeal but considerable political weight as the bearers of ideological meanings. Since all these memorial editions allowed much wider access to works that, in their original versions, had been devised for socially restricted use, they were also, in printed form, signifiers of social cachet. Early opera librettos are in a different class of material, since their prime function was to provide a text and describe the meaning of the action to the necessarily restricted and elite audience (who presumably had them to hand in performance), some of whom clearly only appreciated the immediately accessible elements of the spectacle rather than their often heavily allegorical meanings.[32]

Both *intermedi* and court opera were ideally suited as a vehicle for the demonstration of "conspicuous consumption," a concept that social historians have identified as central to their discussions of the behavior of sixteenth- and seventeenth-century European elites.[33] In these formulations, Italian aristocrats of the period do not fit into the conventional model of "economic man," in the sense that they were concerned not merely with profit and thrift but rather with generating a steady income to spend on luxury goods. This behavior, seen by both contemporaries and later moralizing historians as irrational and wasteful, was motivated by emulation, the need for socially rising groups to imitate the lifestyles of those of a higher social

[31] See Mary S. Lewis, *Antonio Gardano, Venetian Music Printer 1538–1569: A Descriptive Bibliography and Historical Study*, I (New York and London, 1988), 246–49, for a bibliographical description of the edition, and for an edition, Andrew C. Minor and Bonner Mitchell, *A Renaissance Entertainment: Festivities for the Marriage of Cosimo I, Duke of Florence, in 1539* (Columbia, MO, 1968).

[32] Werner Friedrich Kümmel, "Ein deutscher Bericht uber die florentinischen Intermedien des Jahres 1589," *Analecta musicologica*, 9 (1970), 1–19.

[33] Peter Burke, *The Historical Anthropology of Early Modern Italy: Essays on Perception and Communication* (Cambridge, 1987), chap. 10; idem, *History and Social Theory* (Ithaca, NY, 1992), 67–69.

standing.[34] In late-sixteenth- and early-seventeenth-century Italy the idea was related to that of *magnificenza*, which acted as a mechanism for converting wealth into status and power and which, in turn, was merely one word in a rich vocabulary that contemporaries used to describe elite lifestyles. For families who had already arrived at the summit, conspicuous consumption was regarded as a duty, necessary to avoid loss of face and to sustain the honor of the dynasty.[35] Its function was to distinguish between families who, as well as being dynastically linked, were also both rivals and equals at the same time. In this process, awareness of the power of symbolic forms of expression of precisely the kind with which contemporary courtly theatre is crowded is fundamental to the struggle for higher status,[36] and competition is the unavoidable result. In these terms, the distance between the operas promoted by the Medici and the "private" presentation of the Peri–Rinuccini *Euridice* is not as great as it first appears, while the close parallels between its music, text, and drama, and that of the Monteverdi–Striggio *Orfeo*, which have been so frequently noted,[37] are to be understood in relation to these issues as well as in terms of artistic emulation. The same is true of the Orpheus myth itself, the shared basis for a number of early court opera librettos.

While the earliest phase of court opera occupies a central position in the writings of those nineteenth- and twentieth-century music historians who have judged the phenomenon to be the *fons et origo* of the entire operatic tradition, the historical reality was different, as more recent writers have reminded us.[38] Furthermore, the critical reaction to the first operas was not overwhelmingly enthusiastic, and it is clear that the more familiar features of the *intermedio* tradition were thought to be preferable by many in court circles. For at least some of those accustomed to the imposing sonorities of the *intermedio* tradition, the new Florentine singing style could sound dry and sterile. A member of the audience for *Euridice* compared it to the "chanting of the Passion," while one of Cardinal Aldobrandini's entourage who was present at the performance of *Il rapimento di Cefalo* candidly remarked that "the style of singing easily led to boredom."[39] In this sense, too, early opera was

[34] Richard A. Goldthwaite, *Wealth and the Demand for Art in Italy 1330–1600* (Baltimore and London, 1993).

[35] Burke, *The Historical Anthropology of Early Modern Italy*, 134.

[36] Roy Strong, *Art and Power: Renaissance Festivals, 1450–1650*, 2nd edn (Woodbridge, 1984), esp. 98–125, 126–52.

[37] See, *inter alia*, Nino Pirrotta, "Monteverdi and the Problems of Opera", in *Music and Culture in Italy from the Middle Ages to the Baroque*, 235–53; Barbara Russano Hanning, *Of Poetry and Music's Power* (Ann Arbor, MI, 1980), chap. 3; Gary Tomlinson, "Madrigal, Monody, and Monteverdi's 'Via Naturale alla Immitatione,'" *Journal of the American Musicological Society*, 34 (1981), 60–108.

[38] See Lorenzo Bianconi, *Music in the Seventeenth Century*, trans. David Bryant (Cambridge, 1987), 161–70.

[39] Both quotes are taken from Claude Palisca, "Cavalieri, Emilio de'," in *The New Grove Dictionary of Music and Musicians*, 2nd edn, ed. Stanley Sadie and John Tyrrell (London, 2001), IV: 20–23. See also the remarks of Vincenzo Giustiniani (*c.*1628), in *Hercole Bottrigari: Il Desiderio . . . ; Vincenzo Giustiniani: Discorso sopra la musica*, trans. Carol MacClintock (American Institute of Musicology, 1962), 77: "This recitative style . . . proved to be so crude and without variety of consonances and ornaments that if the ennui that was felt had not been mitigated

probably a comparatively marginal entertainment in the eyes of contemporaries when judged alongside the comedies, jousts, tournaments, and *naumachiae* that made up most of the bill of fare in any extended sequence of dynastic celebrations. The one exception, of course, was the Monteverdi–Rinuccini *Arianna*, which enjoyed a good deal of popularity during the first half of the seventeenth century. Yet even in this case, the enthusiasm was not so much for the complete opera *per se*, but rather for its celebrated lament, as Severo Bonini's remarks and the surviving sources reveal.[40]

On the other hand, the unusual sense of self-consciousness that accompanied the creation of Florentine court opera well as the critical insights of the individuals involved in this project had an effect at once unexpected and long-lasting. They contributed to the formation of a "Platonic idea" of opera, of what opera ought to be *vis-à-vis* what opera was and later became, especially in the public market of the opera houses. It was the unique bond between the cultural institution of humanism and the political institution of the court that transformed the foundational myth of ancient drama into an object of nostalgic veneration as well as an archetype of artistic reform that over the centuries would yield multiple effects. As late as 1758, Francesco Algarotti still believed that under the aesthetic rule of princes endowed with fine judgment opera would again become the living image of Greek tragedy.[41]

I.F.

by the presence of such performers, the audience would have left the seats and the room quite empty."

[40] See Severo Bonini, *Prima parte de discorsi e regole sopra la musica*, trans. MaryAnn Bonino (Provo, UT, 1979), 151, where it is claimed that no musical household lacked a copy of the Lament.

[41] Francesco Algarotti, *Saggio sopra l'opera in musica* (Livorno, 1758), 84. On this point, see Bianconi, *Music in the Seventeenth Century*, 165–67.

24

ENGLAND, *i*: 1485–1600

Roger Bray

Before 1560

In order to understand the context of the period before 1560 we need to look at the early Tudor period from 1485.[1] The Englishness of the early years of the fifteenth century that had been noted abroad by Martin le Franc and Tinctoris[2] was strongly developed by the early Tudor composers. Continental influence is found growing as the sixteenth century proceeds—from France (the courtly love ethic's influence on secular music, the *pavane*, and the influence of the chanson on the early English anthem), Italy (the galliard, and the presence of Italian instrumentalists at Henry VIII's court), and Spain (in keyboard music)—and a small but relatively cosmopolitan group of continental composers lived and worked in England, some of them for fairly extended periods, notably Cabezón and de Monte, who were attached to Philip of Spain's retinue, Jacquet of Mantua, who seems to have worked at Magdalen College, Oxford, and Philip van Wilder, who worked at the royal court as one of Henry's household musicians.[3] There are nonetheless several native characteristics typical of English music of this period, some of them unique; fuller texture, larger choral compass (from the lowest bass note to the highest treble note), ornateness, massive sturdiness, exploration of contrasting scoring and sonorities, and esoteric construction; and most important, towards the middle of the sixteenth century we find English traits, especially

[1] The most recent detailed histories of English music of the 16th century are John Caldwell, *The Oxford History of English Music*, I: *From the Beginnings to c.1715* (Oxford, 1991), and Roger Bray (ed.), *The Blackwell History of Music in Britain*, II: *The Sixteenth Century* (Oxford, 1995). Their extensive bibliographies also include sources of editions of the music. There is much useful detail in Frank Ll. Harrison, *Music in Medieval Britain* (London, 1958; 4th edn, Buren, 1980), and David Wulstan, *Tudor Music* (London, 1985).

[2] Harrison, *Music in Medieval Britain*, 250, 257–58.

[3] See also Tim Carter, "Secular Vocal Music," *Blackwell History of Music in Britain*, II: 147–209 at 157–59, and Caldwell, *Oxford History of English Music*, I: 261–62.

rhythms, that are the result of a growing familiarity with setting the English language, especially its use in the earliest Anglican music.

Music for the liturgy

The fuller texture and fuller-sounding chords, with their sixths and thirds, are typical of Dunstaple in the mid-fifteenth century, whose work demonstrates well-judged and varied harmonic rhythm, and they are amply demonstrated in music from the Eton Choirbook (*GB-WRec* 178, *c.*1490–*c.*1515),[4] but the Tudors added two important qualities: the music was now leisurely and massive, and these qualities become important features throughout the sixteenth century. The music can be leisurely even when ornate, because the underlying harmonic rhythm moves slowly, as in the solo passages from the Eton Choirbook and Robert Fayrfax's masses, when the arrival at the final syllable of a melisma (and therefore usually the cadence) seems to be put off over and over again; or when a lengthy point of imitation gradually unfolds, as in works such as Christopher Tye's mass *Euge bone* or Thomas Tallis's mass *Puer natus est* (in each case in the Benedictus: both works date from the reign of Queen Mary, 1553–58). Indeed, it is sometimes the number of parts that have to have the point that causes this; *Puer natus* is for seven voices, while, slightly later in the century, the massiveness of Tallis's forty-voice motet *Spem in alium* is partly a result of the remorseless progress of the points of imitation through the parts. The leisureliness is also found in the works based on a lengthy cantus firmus, especially the instrumental *In nomine*, in which the cantus firmus always pursues its unhurried course in equal note-values. The massive quality arises partly from this leisureliness, also paradoxically from urgency, as when John Sheppard brings his contrapuntal entries in as quickly as possible (thus maintaining the fullest possible sound), also from the closeness of harmony possible in counterpoint for five equal voices (as in Sheppard's five-part *Spiritus sanctus procedens*), and also from the sheer size of the choirs being deployed (six parts used as a standard, rising to nine, thirteen, or forty parts on occasion and permitting striking antiphonal effects between the sub-groups of the ensemble). English composers thoroughly explore the various contrasts that are possible within the scoring they adopt, such as full choir versus reduced scoring (and therefore effectively loud versus soft), all singers of a part versus solo, high versus low, counterpoint versus homophony, plain figuration versus ornate, and fast harmonic movement versus slow. The exploration of the possibilities of contrast has sometimes been associated with the beginning of the so-called "Baroque" style around 1600, but all these techniques are found in the Eton Choirbook around 1500; indeed, they are all found in a single work such as Robert Wylkynson's nine-voice *Salve regina*.

The fact that English composers were excellent judges of the sound of their music was partly the result of the relatively standardized nature of the choirs for which they wrote.[5] It is no coincidence that the majority of composers who

[4] Caldwell, *Oxford History of English Music*, 1: 189–208.

[5] Wulstan, *Tudor Music*, 192–249.

contributed to the first great liturgical source of the Tudor period that survives, the Eton Choirbook, were associated with the educational institutions that had recently been founded with generous provision for a larger choir than was found in other establishments, such as the monastic or secular (non-monastic) cathedrals. Chief amongst these were colleges at Oxford and Cambridge, such as Magdalen College, Oxford, sometimes with their sister establishments, such as King's College, Cambridge, and Eton College, each of which had sixteen boy choristers and either eight or ten men, which was much larger than the polyphonic choirs in cathedral Lady chapels. With these forces available composers could explore the use of great masses of sound and the various types of contrast mentioned above.

In this they were helped by their establishments' liturgical requirements, which often specified occasions where music was to be sung in a situation that positively encouraged the display of technical skill. Polyphonic music had previously been largely confined to the Lady chapel of cathedrals and to a limited number of liturgical observances such as the Lady Mass. These new educational colleges did not have a Lady chapel but instead performed some of their most complex pieces within a peculiarly English liturgical occasion, the Evening Antiphon to the Virgin, after Compline, in which (to take Eton as an example) the choir processed into the antechapel and sang a Marian antiphon before an image of the Virgin Mary.[6] The need to provide music for this usage accounts for most of the repertory of the Eton Choirbook. The custom was adopted elsewhere, sometimes with local variations; at St Paul's Cathedral, London, a Guild of the Name of Jesus was refounded in 1507 to pay the choir to process into the crypt after Compline every day, where they sang a Jesus antiphon (and it was very probably for this occasion that Fayrfax wrote his *O bone Iesu* works).[7] Since the main content of this observance was the singing of an antiphon, it is not surprising that these antiphons became huge works that displayed the full capabilities of composer and choir. Polyphony was not always used in every establishment: one local usage, laid down by the founder's statutes at Magdalen College, Oxford, was the recitation of *Libera nos, salva nos* upon rising and before going to bed; plainsong must have been the norm for this, but the polyphonic settings by Sheppard stand as an excellent example of music for a special occasion.[8]

Another important feature of English sacred music, especially in the setting of the Ordinary of the Mass, is its extremely esoteric construction. This esotericism is not peculiar to English music but was developed in a unique way. Its origins lie in the orderly phrase structure of some fourteenth-century works (not only English works, though the motet *Thomas gemma Cantuariae* is a good example) and the organized layout of the isorhythmic motet, but the idea was developed in a more consistent way, showing an unbroken tradition via Leonel Power, Walter Frye, and the composers of the Eton Choirbook, whereas on the continent only isolated

[6] Harrison, *Music in Medieval Britain*, 162.

[7] Roger Bray (ed.), *Robert Fayrfax: Complete Works*, 1: *O bone Iesu*, Early English Church Music, 43 (London, 2002), p. ix.

[8] Wulstan, *Tudor Music*, 273.

examples are available in the latter part of the fifteenth century. The technique then became markedly more complex in England when applied to the Mass, even compared to, for example, Obrecht's mass *Maria zart*.

In one of Fayrfax's earlier masses, *Albanus*, a quasi-isorhythmic layout of the cantus firmus is used whereby the nine-note extract from a plainsong is laid out in prime, inversion, retrograde, and retrograde inversion, each version usually having its own rhythm; in this mass, too, Fayrfax makes the lengths of movements and of music on the cantus firmus and that not using it proportionally related.[9] In his later masses *Tecum principium* and *O quam glorifica*, the cantus firmus is laid out in such a way that the amount of music requiring coloration is proportionally related to the amount of music in plain notation, and then the whole structure, including the sections not written around the cantus firmus, exhibits proportional relationships in a huge scheme that takes in all four movements (English composers only set Gloria, Credo, Sanctus, and Agnus Dei, omitting a polyphonic Kyrie).[10]

If the development of the votive antiphon was the result of the patronage of the new educational foundations, the development of the esoteric mass seems to be a result of the patronage of Lady Margaret Beaufort, countess of Richmond and Derby and mother of Henry VII, and an extremely influential political figure and patron after the accession of her son in 1485. All the earliest group of composers who practiced this style were associated with institutions over which she had influence and patronage. George Newton, mentioned by Whythorne and Morley as a composer of "speculative" or extremely complex music (all of his music is lost), and Robert Cowper were both members of her chapel. Both were doctors of music at Cambridge (also in Lady Margaret's sphere of influence; she founded two colleges and the chair of divinity there), as was Fayrfax, whom she patronized in the commissioning of the mass *O bone Iesu*.[11] Lady Margaret's links with the Fayrfax family are closer and probably personal, for she spent her childhood in the 1440s at Maxey Castle, two miles from Fayrfax's father's home in Deeping Gate, Northamptonshire (he was one of her tenants), and some of Fayrfax's older siblings at this time had as godmother Lady Margaret's half-sisters and other members of her family. Her seat (which operated effectively as a subsidiary royal court) at Collyweston from 1499 to 1509 was only ten miles away, and it is therefore possible that Fayrfax, who by 1497 was at the Chapel Royal in London, came into contact with members of her chapel at this time, because there were very close links between the courts of mother and son. Thus George Newton may have been Fayrfax's teacher and the instigator of the carefully structured and proportioned layout. Among the composers of this generation the technique is even more complex in the surviving

[9] Roger Bray, "Sacred Music to Latin Texts," *Blackwell History of Music in Britain*, II: 46–93 at 46–73; idem, "Music and the Quadrivium in Early Tudor England," *Music & Letters*, 76 (1995), 1–18; idem, "Editing and Performing *Musica Speculativa*," in *English Choral Practice, 1400–1650*, ed. John Morehen (Cambridge, 1995), 48–73.

[10] Full information and analysis in Roger Bray (ed.), *Robert Fayrfax, Complete Works*, II: *Masses Tecum Principium and O quam glorifica*, Early English Church Music, 45 (forthcoming).

[11] Bray (ed.), *Fayrfax: O bone Iesu*, p. ix.

masses by Thomas Ashwell and almost as intricate in the music of the slightly later Hugh Aston and John Taverner. The influence of Lady Margaret's establishments continued even after her death in 1509, for Ashwell and Taverner were both associated at various times with Tattershall College, Lincolnshire, which fell under her sphere of influence (its warden from 1502 to 1513 was also dean of her Chapel), while Aston worked at Leicester, which was also within her influence.

English music is also a perfect bridge between the academic and the practical, for another unique feature in England of the time was the awarding of bachelor and doctor of music degrees at Oxford and Cambridge Universities with a composition exercise as the prerequisite, a practice that still exists today. In addition to doctors Newton and Fayrfax, Aston was an Oxford bachelor of music, while Fayrfax's doctoral incorporation exercise for the Oxford DMus in 1511 is the extraordinarily complex and esoteric mass *O quam glorifica*. However, it cannot be stressed strongly enough that this learned, intricately proportioned and structured music works excellently as sound. Indeed, according to the logic of the time, carefully structured music was certain to sound good, because it reflected back towards God the balance and order with which he had endowed the universe, thus embodying the concept (described by Plato, adopted by the Christian Church, and transmitted into medieval thinking by Boethius) that God had "ordered all things by measure, and number, and weight" (Wisdom 11: 17–20, AV).

In this respect music in England may be compared with other arts, especially architecture, where Nikolaus Pevsner makes the point that what may appear to be conservatism may simply be Englishness.[12] In his study on Englishness, Pevsner identified various characteristics with an incomer's dispassionate eye, showing how architecture from the twelfth century until the sixteenth and beyond emphasized various features, notably extreme height and emphasis on verticals (for which he gave Ely Cathedral and the Nine Altars Chapel at Durham Cathedral as examples), extreme length and elongation (exemplified by several cathedral naves, together with the English liking for the full-length portrait), love of surface decoration (exemplified by Lincoln and Wells Cathedrals), compartmentation (exemplified by the layout of almost every cathedral and large parish church in the country because of the way in which chapels are added to form what is effectively a series of rooms).[13] Since our composers worked in the very buildings that reflected this Englishness, it is tempting to translate these characteristics into music: the length and elongation become the prolongation of phrases and avoidance of cadence typical of Fayrfax, for example; the excessive height is mirrored in the peculiarly English treble voice; the love of surface decoration corresponds to the ornateness of the "Eton" style; and the compartmentation is mirrored by the division of works into passages for contrasting forces. However, it is not correct to say that composers mimicked architectural principles: quite the reverse, for at this time architects based their structural principles on the proportional and mathematical structure

[12] Nikolaus Pevsner, *The Englishness of English Art* (London, 1956), 83.
[13] Ibid., 81–111.

of music, as Leone Battista Alberti (1404–1472) says in his *De re aedificatoria* (1452):

> The numbers by means of which the agreement of sounds affects our ears with delight are the very same which please our eyes and minds. . . . We shall therefore borrow all our rules for harmonic relations from the musicians to whom this kind of numbers is extremely well known.[14]

These architectural techniques of careful proportion were not confined to Italy. In 1480 we find William Botoner alias Worcestre measuring the new Divinity School in Oxford (constructed 1430–55) prior to vaulting:

> The new school of divinity with the library above . . . contains in length 30 yards, each yard of three feet, and in breadth 32 feet, and in height from the bottom up to the upper "walplate" of "fretstone" 80 feet, and in height to the new vault or arch now worked in the year of Christ 1480, from the ground or floor level 32 feet.[15]

This gives 90 : 80 or 9 : 8 as the proportion of length to height of the complete building, 32 : 32 as the proportion of breadth to height of the lower floor, and 32 : 48 or 2 : 3 as the proportion of the height of the lower floor to that of the upper floor, 9 : 8 and 2 : 3 being ratios extremely well known to musicians as those of the tone and fifth respectively.

Early Tudor liturgical music, then, exactly matched the ritual needs of the Church, and its performance was strictly prescribed. Most of the music that one might hear in a pre-Reformation cathedral or collegiate chapel would be plainsong, but choirs also cultivated an improvisational technique known as *faburden*, whereby, reading only the plainsong, three parts could be achieved, one shadowing the plainsong a fourth above, the plainsong in the middle, and a third voice generally a third below it (giving what we today would call six–three chords), falling to a fifth below it at cadences (to a final root position with a bare fifth). The outbursts of composed polyphony in six or more parts in alternation with plainsong or faburden would therefore provide yet another type of contrast.

The utilitarian nature of the music also explains the fact that composers normally used plainsong as the basis of their music. In the antiphons of the Eton Choirbook, a plainsong tune (or, in Magnificat settings, a faburden) is selected for use in slow notes in the tenor in the full passages; in masses the choice of plainsong tune seems to be governed by personal factors, or perhaps the devotional preferences of a patron rather than a liturgical occasion, and it seems that composers deliberately avoided using a plainsong that had been used before; as we have seen, these cantus-firmus melodies are usually laid out in a highly complex and mathematical way. When the setting of responsories and hymns became popular in the 1530s and 1540s in the works of composers such as Taverner and Sheppard, the appropriate

[14] Quoted by Rudolf Wittkower, *Architectural Principles in the Age of Humanism* (London, 1949), 110.

[15] See John Harvey, *Gothic England* (London, 1947), 171.

plainsong usually moved in steady values in one of the voices (not necessarily the tenor). Though based on plainsong or faburden, however, English music is not in any sense restricted by it, and indeed, when listening, it is frequently impossible to tell it is present. Nor does the restriction of a cantus firmus unduly affect the harmonic or contrapuntal flow, such is the skill with which composers write around it, though the fact of its being relatively slow-moving does add to the typical English sturdiness. When it can be heard clearly, it is because the composer wishes it to be heard, as when it appears in the bass supporting the cascading counterpoint of Sheppard's *Libera nos, salva nos*, or when it appears in equal note-values towards the end of a Mass, earlier parts of which have seen it subjected to various treatments. Indeed, it is so frequently the case that the final (or near-final) passage of cantus-firmus writing in a mass is in equal values, from Fayrfax's *Albanus* through Taverner's *Gloria tibi trinitas* to Richard Alwood's *Praise him praiseworthy*, that there is a sense in which the composer is writing a set of variations in reverse, with the plainest statement last. The pertinent passage in *Gloria tibi trinitas*, at "in nomine" in the Benedictus, became the model for a whole new, peculiarly English instrumental and keyboard genre, the *In nomine*, itself providing a structure for the development of the art of variation for the next 150 years.

Whether or not there is a section written around the plainsong in equal values towards the end of a mass, composers increasingly demonstrate their sense of pace and balance by writing music of particularly great beauty and technical interest in their final Agnus Dei; they knew how to use harmonic and contrapuntal techniques to achieve moments that send a tingle down one's spine. Fayrfax introduces limpid unprepared fourths of great originality and very great beauty in the final passage of the Agnus Dei of *Tecum principium*, Tallis achieves an effect of great repose at the end of *Puer natus* (while actually giving birth to a new plainsong tune by a complex procedure of adapting the plainsong itself), Sheppard produces a memorable harmonic shift (of which he is a master) in the final passage of *Cantate*, while Tye produces a 4-in-2 canon of immense beauty for the upper voices in the Agnus Dei of *Euge bone*. Indeed, the careful way words are set leads to further speculations suggesting some kind of triangular relationship between Tallis's mass *Puer natus*, Tye's mass *Euge bone*, and Tallis's prayer for forgiveness, *Suscipe quaeso Domine*, scored for the same unusual seven-part choir as *Puer natus*. Both the masses have an unusually long and clear point of imitation at "Benedictus qui venit" in the Sanctus, which is allowed to run its course before succeeding voices (after the first two) come in, and the point in Tye's work is the same as the opening point of *Suscipe quaeso*, suggesting that special prominence is being given to this passage. If all three works were written for the occasion in winter 1554 when Cardinal Pole absolved England for its Protestant heresy, then maybe Cardinal Pole was the "good man" (of Tye's title) that came "in the name of the Lord," in which case perhaps the "child who is born" (Tallis's title) is England reborn to Catholicism.[16]

[16] Bray, "Sacred Music to Latin Texts," 80.

Instrumental music for keyboard or ensemble

Keyboard music, too, was largely governed by liturgical requirements before 1560; by far the major part of this repertory consists of organ masses and hymns, that is, polyphonic organ pieces either written around a cantus firmus or alluding to it tonally, for *alternatim* performance with the plainsong itself or possibly its faburden. The principal composers are John Redford, William Blitheman (also called John), and Tallis. Just as we have seen that one way of looking at the choral mass is to see it as a type of variation on a cantus firmus, so it is possible to see the succeeding verses of an organ hymn in a similar light, with each treating the cantus firmus in a different way (Blitheman's *Eterne rerum conditor* is a good example), and it is this characteristic, together with certain striking harmonic and figuration techniques, that led Apel to find "a clear relationship" between the keyboard music of England and Spain as a result of direct links between the two Chapels Royal (which included Antonio de Cabezón and Tallis) at the wedding of Mary Tudor to Philip of Spain in 1554.[17] More recent writers are divided on this: Doe is rather cool, and Ward downright hostile, but Caldwell notes some "bold" dissonances and furthermore finds links between Tudor ground-bass patterns and those of Spain and Italy.[18]

The very small number of early Tudor keyboard pieces that are not liturgical certainly explore the idea of variation in various ways; Aston's *Hornpipe*, the anonymous *My Lady Carey's dompe* (which may also be by Aston), and *Upon la mi re* are good examples, the *Hornpipe* being on a ground consisting of only two notes, as is, effectively, *My Lady Carey's dompe*, but the figuration and variety achieved upon these simple patterns is remarkable. The hornpipe is a dance, as is another piece from the same manuscript (*GB-Lbl* Royal App. 58), *The short Mesure off My Lady Wynkfyld's Rownde*. The "dompe" may simply be a dance (as in Nicholas Udall's *Ralph Roister Doister*, 1553) or it may be a dirge, genuine or affected (Shakespeare uses the term for an affected melancholic love-song in *Two Gentlemen of Verona*, III.ii.85). Lady Carey was Mary Boleyn, sister of Anne Boleyn and mistress of Henry VIII, married to one of his courtiers, Sir William Carey; if her "dompe" were a genuine dirge it would probably have been for her husband's death in 1528. The same manuscript illustrates a strong French influence on dance, in keeping with the courtly-love ethic of the court, but the early stage of a peculiarly English combination is also found, the pavan and the galliard, both dances of Italian origin which came via France; the two occur in close proximity and may have been paired

[17] Willi Apel, *The History of Keyboard Music to 1700* (Bloomington, IN, and London, 1972; orig. pubd as *Geschichte der Orgel- und Klaviermusik bis 1700*, Kassel, 1967), 157 and n. 87, which refers to M. S. Kastner, "Parallels and Discrepancies between English and Spanish Keyboard Music," *Anuario musical*, 7 (1952), 77ff.

[18] Paul Doe, *Tallis* (London, 1968), 60; idem, "Tallis", *The New Grove Dictionary of Music and Musicians*, 2nd edn, ed. Stanley Sadie and John Tyrrell (London, 2001); John M. Ward, "Spanish Musicians in Sixteenth-Century England," in *Essays in Musicology in Honor of Dragan Plamenac*, ed. Gustave Reese and Robert J. Snow (Pittsburgh, 1969; repr. New York, 1977), 353–64; Caldwell, *Oxford History of English Music*, I: 342.

already by this time. The use of the keyboard in dance, and the use of keyboard as a medium in which the idea of variation was explored, were both to become important in the latter half of the century; they can be seen to have early roots.

Just as there is very little secular keyboard music of the period before 1560, so there is very little surviving ensemble music, and even some of this is textless vocal music for vocalization, a fact confirmed by the appearance of three such pieces in *XX Songes* (printed 1530; see below). It is in the field of instrumental ensemble music that the clearest evidence of direct continental influence is seen, because many of the players employed at court were foreign, notably Jewish players from Italy. Henry VIII employed large numbers of instrumentalists, loud and soft, for a variety of occasions, 15 trumpeters and 20 other players at the beginning of his reign in 1509, and 18 trumpeters and 32 other players by the time of his death in 1547[19]—but very little indication survives of what they performed. It is possible that a small anthology of dances, copied at the end of the "Lumley" part-books (see below for fuller details) may preserve some court dances for use in a noble domestic setting. Otherwise, the music of "Henry VIII's Manuscript" (*Lbl* Add. 5465), which although it is usually thought of as a song-book actually contains more textless pieces than texted, includes several Franco-Netherlandish instrumental works, with the English contributions showing a style similar to that of the part-song, but with some use of esotericism in puzzle canons and solmization exercises.

Secular vocal music

In England before the Reformation "secular" must include everything that is not liturgical, and therefore may also include music to English words on a sacred theme, for domestic devotional use, as well as overtly non-religious music, whether political or amorous. During the early Tudor period secular musical activity was centred upon the court of Henry VIII. There are two main genres: the carol, inherited from the earlier fifteenth century, with its characteristic use of a refrain that begins, alternates with, and concludes the verses; and the part-song, a contrapuntal style adapted from liturgical music, though on a smaller scale, whereby phrases begin imitatively and there is a long melisma on the penultimate syllable of each line of text. A characteristic English trait is the juxtaposition of texts expressing courtly love with texts of a homely, earthy, hands-on approach to love, mirroring the attitude at Henry VIII's court, where, especially in the early years during Henry's marriage to Catherine of Aragon, the courtly-love ethic was embraced, apparently imported in emulation of the Burgundian court, while at the same time Henry sired at least two illegitimate children. There are examples of carols devotional (Sheryngham's *A gentyll Jesu*), political (Edmund Turges's *Enforce yourselfe as Goddis knyght*), courtly (William Cornysh's *Yow and I and Amyas*), and earthy (Cornysh's *Blow thi horne hunter*), and similarly part-songs devotional (Richard Davy's *A blessid Jesu*) and courtly (Cornysh's *Benedicite whate dremyd I this nyght*),

[19] John Harper, "Ensemble and Lute Music," *Blackwell History of Music in Britain*, II: 263–322 at 268.

both with refrain. The carol tends to give way to the part-song with refrain (where the refrain does not begin the song as well as alternating with the verses). There are no real political or amorous part-songs: the nearest are a political canon (Thomas Farthing's *Aboffe all thynge / Now lete us synge*, recalling the long-standing English love of canon, ever since the thirteenth-century *Sumer is icumen in*) and the anonymous lasciviously macaronic *Up Y arose in verno tempore*. Some songs adopt the AAB form of the *ballade*, and hence we find again an English naturalization of continental genres, such as the carol itself and the *lauda spirituale*, together with actual examples from the continent, such as the Netherlands piece *O waerde mont* (appearing in Henry VIII's MS as *Ough warder mount*).[20] This inaccurate title is a good example of the cavalier attitude of the English towards foreign languages, but it also reflects the fact that the English language itself developed rapidly during the sixteenth century and assimilated many foreign words. In court revels the homeliness is described in so many words in the case of the "homely mermaides, one of them a man mermaide, the other a woman; . . . and in every of the said mermaides a Childe of the Chapell singing right sweetly."[21]

Although an important feature of English music before the 1580s is the lack of a music-printing culture, there are isolated examples that show that attempts were made to establish one. The earliest such example is the *XX Songes* of 1530, most of the contents of which are courtly and devotional songs. No complete copies survive, whether because they were well-used and eventually fell to pieces or because they were little used and soon discarded, or even because few were purchased; it is difficult to tell how popular this book was, but it was an experiment not to be repeated for many years to come. However, the idea of printing music eventually became well-established in the area of devotional music, and the title page of the earliest metrical version of the scriptures makes its audience and performance context clear; Tye's *Actes of the Apostles* (1553), published during the reign of the Catholic Queen Mary, is clearly intended for private use: "The Actes of the Apostles, translated into Englyshe Metre . . . by Christofer Tye . . . wyth notes to eche Chapter, to synge and also to play upon the Lute, very necessarye for studentes after theyr studye, to fyle theyr wyttes, and also for all Christians that cannot synge, to reade the good and Godlye storyes of the lyves of Christ hys Appostles." This led, soon after the Elizabethan Reformation, to the appearance of metrical psalters whose title pages make it quite clear that they are mainly intended for performance in the home, but may also be used in church (see below).

If English secular song before the 1580s seems unfocused and difficult to define, it is because the music was pressed into service for a variety of functions (one of the chief advantages of the lack of a print culture is the fact that a manuscript compiler would collect only the works he wanted—for whatever reason—which is more revealing of the tastes of the time): keyboard and lute versions of songs and sacred works (frequently without words) are found, as is performance by instrumental ensemble, but it is perhaps something of a surprise to find secular music adapted

20 Carter, "Secular Vocal Music," 153.

21 Ibid., 156.

to make an anthem, as happens with Sheppard's *O happy dames* (*I will give thanks unto the Lord*) and even Cornysh's amorous song *Blow thi horne hunter* (*O Lord our Lord how marvellous*);[22] the Sheppard survives in an anthology made in Suffolk by Thomas Hamond (*Lbl* Add. 30480–84), a collection that may itself have been intended for domestic devotional and recreational use but presumably drew for this part of its repertory on liturgical Anglican sources, while the Cornysh is in a collection (the "Lumley" part-books, *Lbl* Royal App. 74–76) apparently copied about 1550 for use in the private household chapel of the Fitzalan family at Nonsuch. Tallis's *Purge me O Lord* is thought to show adaptation in the other direction, having been adapted to make a secular song (*Fond youth is a bubble*).[23]

The Reformation in England

The period of adaptation, uncertainty, and experimentation caused by the Reformation lasted longer in England than anywhere else in Europe because of the centralized power of the monarchy and the differing religious viewpoints of Henry VIII's three children, offspring of three different mothers; the consequent see-sawing between the Catholic and Anglican Protestant rites taxed composers' skills to the utmost. The gradual introduction of the English language began during the last ten years of Henry's reign, with the setting up of English Bibles in churches from 1537 and the introduction of English for the lesson at "Evensong," as Vespers was already called, from 1543. It was Archbishop Cranmer, reporting on his progress in translating the festal processions, who in a letter to Henry coined the memorable phrase, when he said that the music should be "as nere as may be, for every sillable, a note"; as Caldwell points out, this must have been in 1544.[24] This was, in any case, the direction that the Latin Mass had been taking in the shorter masses of Taverner (e.g., *Christe Iesu*), who died in 1545, and Ludford's Lady-masses. Edward VI, who succeeded Henry in 1547, was Protestant, but he died in his teens only six years later, to be succeeded by the Catholic Mary Tudor; she did not produce the Catholic heir that she and her party so wished for, and so on her death in 1558 her half-sister Elizabeth succeeded her. The account of the Elizabethan Reformation will be given below, but here we must note the substantial activity in setting sacred music to English texts, starting as early as the 1540s with texts for private devotions from books such as the *King's Primer* (1545), accelerating and moving into the church when Edward's and Cranmer's English Prayer Books appeared in 1549 and (slightly revised) in 1552.

Settings begin to appear of the components of the new English service, the translated Te Deum and Benedictus for morning service, and Magnificat and Nunc dimittis for evening service together with some examples of the anthem, the

22 Neither of these is identified in Ralph T. Daniel and Peter le Huray, *The Sources of English Church Music, 1549–1660*, Early English Church Music, Suppl. 1 (London, 1972); they are respectively anonymous pieces nos. 204 and 302.

23 John Morehen, "English Church Music," *Blackwell History of Music in Britain*, II: 94–146 at 104.

24 Caldwell, *Oxford History of English Music*, I: 269. See also Wulstan, *Tudor Music*, 278–92.

successor to the pre-Reformation evening antiphon ritual, which seems to have found its way into the service from an early date. It was made clear to musicians that a syllabic style was needed so that the words could be understood by the people, and thus a new homophonic style based on the French chanson was adopted; however, composers soon started to introduce contrapuntal entries in the second half of the piece, when the gist of the text had become clear and perhaps the need for clarity and hence a syllabic setting was not so important; examples such as Tallis's *If ye love me* and Sheppard's *I give you a new commandment* are typical; both were included in the only printed anthem source from this period, collected by the printer John Day (*Certaine Notes*, 1560). The influence of these early liturgical settings to English texts was profound and long-lasting, and it will be explored further below.

1560–1600

WHEREAS before about 1560 English composers put their most serious effort into church music, the growing interest in humanism after the Reformation led to a much wider range of genres available to composers. During the latter part of the century many aspects of the Englishness that we have identified above continued; the prolongation of phrases and avoidance of cadence is found particularly in Byrd's Latin motets, the extreme height is still mirrored in those few works using the peculiarly English treble voice (though this was now less common), the love of surface decoration is found in the keyboard variations, and the compartmentation is found in the verse anthem, fantasia, and variation. The love of contrasts (high versus low, etc.) of the pre-Reformation period is retained in the positioning of the choir in the Anglican context, divided into two halves (*decani* and *cantoris*, or the dean's side and the precentor's side), facing each other and therefore with an opportunity for antiphony, which is usually taken, especially in the settings of the canticles.

Musical careers

This growth of humanist thought is also reflected in the now much wider range of careers in music. Although the Church was still an important source of employment and patronage, a life in music outside the established Anglican church became possible for musicians, as seen in the careers of composers such as John Dowland, John Wilbye, George Kirbye, Thomas Greaves (who were employed as court or household musicians), Anthony Holborne (a lawyer), Giles Farnaby (a cabinet-maker and maker of musical instruments), Michael Cavendish and Ferdinando Richardson alias Heybourne (minor noblemen and courtiers). One source of employment open to Italian musicians, as a composer employed by an *accademia* or a confraternity, was not available to the English because no such organizations existed in England. At the end of the century Boethius's classification of three ranks of musician still informed professional musical life and the awarding of degrees at Oxford and Cambridge: firstly, performers, who "act as slaves . . . [because] they are totally lacking in thought"; secondly, "those who compose songs, . . . not so much by thought and reason as by a certain natural instinct"; and thirdly, the true musician (*musicus*) who "acquires an ability for judging . . . the composition as a whole . . . [and] forming judgments according to speculation or reason relative and appropriate to music."[25] Whereas court musicians during the early Tudor period generally confined themselves to performing and were therefore of the lowest rank, court and household musicians now began to aspire to Boethius's second rank of musician (and some, such as Dowland and Farnaby, took degrees, raising themselves to the third rank), so composition was no longer the exclusive preserve of church musicians.

To this list of musicians not employed by the Church we can add, certainly after 1584 and probably soon after 1581, William Byrd himself, who after 1584 was plainly not actively fulfilling his employment as one of the Gentlemen of the Chapel Royal. In this year he was the subject of an order defining where he was to be found and therefore where he was expected to attend church service on a Sunday, and the fact that this was his home village of Harlington confirms that he was not at the Chapel Royal; this opened the way for him to be charged with recusancy (a recusant being a Catholic who refused to attend Anglican services), a charge which obviously would have been impossible if he had been attending services in the Chapel. Furthermore, he was questioned by the authorities in connection with both the main Catholic plots of the 1580s (the Throckmorton plot of 1583 and the Babington plot of 1586).[26] The appointment as a Gentleman of the Chapel was for life, and Byrd never resigned, but he must have spent most of his stipend paying substitutes, and so we may say that the Chapel was no longer his principal source of disposable income after this date. This also means, incidentally, that all his Anglican church music must have been written before 1584; most of his anthems and services are accepted as early works, but his Great Service, a truly impressive work by any standards, must also come from before this date. In fact, there is no reason to think it any later: in its earliest surviving source (*Lbl* R.M. 24.d.2, "Baldwin's Commonplace Book," which contains scored extracts only) it appears in a section which dates from the 1590s, when it had evidently already fallen out of the Chapel Royal repertoire; the copyist John Baldwin, himself a member of the Chapel, copied only five of the six or seven voices of some of his chosen extracts, indicating that his archetype (presumably the original Chapel partbooks) was already incomplete by the 1590s.

In general, the new patrons were a mixture of the nobility (old and new), the

[25] Boethius, *De institutione musica*, trans. Calvin Bower as *Fundamentals of Music* (New Haven, 1989), 51; see also Roger Bray, "Music and the Quadrivium in Early Tudor England," *Music & Letters*, 76 (1995), 1–18; idem, "Music and Musicians in Tudor England: Sources, Composition Theory and Performance," *Blackwell History of Music in Britain*, II: 1–45 at 16–21.

[26] John Harley, *William Byrd, Gentleman of the Chapel Royal* (Aldershot, 1997), 74; David Mateer, "William Byrd's Middlesex Recusancy," *Music & Letters*, 78 (1997), 1–14. The closeness of the dates of the order defining Harlington as his home (17 Feb. 1583/84) and the meeting at which he helped the authorities with their enquiries (22 Feb. 1583/84) is no coincidence.

new administrative civil-servant classes, and those members of the middle class with education and refinement, and Byrd had patrons from most of these classes, ranging from the Earl of Worcester, the Howards (especially Henry Howard, later Earl of Northampton), Northumberlands, and Arundels, through Lord Paget, who was relatively new nobility, to Sir John (later Lord) Petre, one of Elizabeth's senior civil servants, and on to the middle classes both conforming and recusant, who bought his printed books. This contact with the Catholic gentry did him no harm socially, for his crowning social success was to marry his son and heir Christopher to Catherine More or Moore of Barnborough near Doncaster, Yorkshire, great-granddaughter of Sir Thomas More and descended on her mother's side from the Scrope and Clifford (Cumberland) families.[27] This firmly established Byrd's Catholic connections and distantly related his family to the Percys (Northumberlands), Cliffords (Cumberlands), Howards, Scropes, Dacres, Vauxes, Careys (Hunsdons), and Spencers of Althorp. Byrd's circumstances were unique, and no other composer could have achieved this free-lance status, partly because he enjoyed the protection of the queen and the nobility and partly because he still held (until 1596) the printing monopoly under which he and Tallis had published the *Cantiones . . . sacrae* of 1575. It is no coincidence that his publishing activity sprang to life again after a long hiatus in 1588, in his new financial context, soon after the deaths of both Tallis and his printer Thomas Vautrollier, who as a Huguenot refugee was not inclined to print Latin motets.

The concept of the customer is another important novelty of the Elizabethan period. There are few examples in the early Tudor period of personal patronage, because the final customer was generally the Church or the Court, which did not need wooing, and at least sacred compositions were not affected by the views of the customer. By the end of the century the dedication of a book of madrigals to a nobleman was simply a formal way of extracting an extra fee; the people for whom the music was intended were the performers (and in England primarily only the performers; there is not much evidence of an audience culture). Performers are in a good position to appreciate surface effects and the rather superficial illustration of the text at a simple level. This is true of church music too, for there are opportunities to use restrained word-painting in canticles and anthems, and hence there is little interest by composer, performer, or listener in structure for its own sake. The two groups of pieces for which we do not often find dedicatees—the fantasia and *In nomine* for keyboard or instrumental ensemble—are also the most introspective, and perhaps the genres most aimed at serious musical statements. The equivalent of these in vocal music is the substantial Latin motet as composed by Byrd, though there is a Catholic recusant subtext here.

[27] Joseph Hunter, *South Yorkshire* (London, 1828–31; repr. 1974), 1: 372–6. Sir Thomas's daughter and son-in-law were patrons of Tallis.

Anglican church music: language and rhythm

The most English feature of the Elizabethan period is of course the English language, which was itself rapidly developing, and towards which composers were showing a quickly developing confidence and spirit of experimentation. If we praise Italian madrigalists for the imaginative way in which they use, indeed exploit the Italian language, then we should likewise praise English composers in relation to the English language and assert that the best setters of Anglican church music and English madrigals are the English, an obvious but often overlooked truism. From the 1540s sacred music had been set in English, and so by the time composers came to set music in English for the Anglican church, and later for madrigals, their relationship with the language was well developed, and there were already many years of experience to draw on. Their style is quite restrained, because church texts are not written specifically to provoke illustrative music, but when the the proud need scattering and the mighty need putting down from their seat they are accorded appropriate treatment, more or less from the earliest settings and certainly from the settings of John Sheppard (before 1553) onwards.

The most important influence on the setting of the English language was Cranmer's penchant for starting verses and half-verses with conjunctions such as "for" and "and" in his Books of Common Prayer (1549 and 1552), and it is particularly noticeable in the English Magnificat ("My soul doth magnify the Lord"), compared to its Latin version with which composers were familiar before the Reformation; this text, of course, came to be set to music hundreds of times over the following centuries. True, his translation frequently echoes the familiar Latin version, where "et" becomes "and," or follows the requirements of the grammar by the transposition of "Ecce *enim*" to "*For* behold"—but note the difference of rhythm between the Latin and the English; however, he goes further by the simple fact of his translating "quia" as "for," rather than "because" (and so "Quia respexit," "Quia fecit magna," and "Quia viderunt" became "For he hath regarded," "For he that is mighty," and "For mine eyes have seen"). The two-syllable "quia" has its accent on the first syllable, the two-syllable "because" has its on the second syllable, but the one-syllable "for" is treated flexibly depending on what follows, and so the difference is substantial from the point of view of the person who is going to set the text, and the fact that in the Magnificat and the Nunc dimittis, which quickly became the most commonly set canticles of the reformed church, most of the verses and half-verses start "and" or "for" led composers almost immediately to the English sprung off-beat rhythm that has been used to secure the forward momentum of English music ever since. This rhythm (minim rest–semibreve–minim, etc.) is hardly found at all in the very earliest settings (in, for example, the Wanley partbooks, *GB-Ob* Mus. Sch. e.420–22), but it starts to be found in the settings by Sheppard, which must be Edwardian because Sheppard died in December 1558 or January 1559; indeed, to judge from his generally dynamic approach to rhythm, Sheppard may well have been its first main developer, because it is found only once in his setting of the Lord's Prayer, where there are several opportunities, whereas in his truly remarkable Second Service it is ubiquitous, and he also extends its use to "he."[28] The usefulness of this rhythm lies in its ability to provide continuity between the end of one phrase where the counterpoint has become very lively and the opening homophony of the next. This is very effective in the Magnificat, where there are many verses in which contrasts are set up, and the music must therefore move between moods in quick succession if it is to reflect them.[29]

Secular vocal music

After the Reformation, "secular" must include everything that is not exclusively to be performed in an Anglican liturgical setting, and therefore may comprise almost everything that was written (including Anglican church anthems but not canticles), owing to the great flexibility of performing context of the time. In secular music there is much more activity than in the first half of the century, and for a much wider range of performer and listener, including many types of secular vocal music (notably devotional music for both Anglicans and recusant Catholics, solo songs for accompaniment by the lute or instrumental ensemble, and part-songs and madrigals for purely vocal performance, most of which was for performance by a solo voice or one voice per part), and instrumental music (for keyboard, lute, or ensemble).

The provision of domestic devotional music may be explained by the religious situation in England. As we have seen above, it was with this market in mind that the first sign of the development of a speculative publishing culture had occurred, with Tye's *Actes of the Apostles* of 1553. The printer John Day continued to try to develop it with his metrical psalters, whose title pages make it quite clear that they are mainly intended for performance in the home but may also be used in church. In 1562 the first edition of what was to become the standard metrical psalter appeared. Its title-page sets out the intended performance circumstances: "The Whole Booke of Psalmes, collected into Englysh metre by T. Starnhold I. Hopkins & others: conferred with the Ebrue, with apt Notes to synge the*m* withal, Faithfully perused and alowed according to thordre appointed in the Quenes maiesties Iniunctions. Very mete to be used of all sortes of people privatelye for their solace & comfort: laying apart all ungodly Songes and Ballades, which tende only to the norishing of vyce, and corrupting of youth." Many later editions print hexachord syllables alongside the music notation, demonstrating even more strongly that they are intended for amateurs. There is a similar message in the note at the end of Archbishop Parker's Psalter (1560s), with tunes by "Talys:" "The Tenor of these partes be for the people when they will syng alone, the other parts, put for greater queers, or to suche as will syng or play them privatelye." Day also tried to establish the printing of liturgical music in his *Certaine Notes* (1560), the full title of which, in contrast to the examples just mentioned, does not mention domestic use: "Cer-

[28] Sheppard's Second Service is in David Wulstan (ed.), *An Anthology of English Church Music* (London, 1971), 59; the original version of the Lord's Prayer, to a pre-1552 translation, is ibid., 149.

[29] Wulstan, *Tudor Music*, 314–40.

taine notes set forth in foure and three parts to be song at the morning Communion, and evening praier, very necessarie for the Church of Christe to be frequented and used: & unto them added divers godly praiers & Psalmes in the like forme to the honor & praise of God."

A few years before Tallis and Byrd were granted the printing monopoly, both Day and Vautrollier published secular music: the former in 1571 with the *Songes* of Thomas Whythorne, avowedly Italian-inspired, and the latter in 1570 with the chansons and secular motets of Lassus's *Recueil du Mellange* (thereby showing French influence). Neither of these led immediately to any strong English secular music-printing tradition, however, and Whythorne recorded his disappointment in the sales of his book, which he attributed to Day's poor quality of printing and marketing. Tallis and Byrd addressed a different group of purchasers, the large number of Catholic recusants, in their joint *Cantiones... sacrae* (1575); these were also the target for Byrd's two books of printed Latin motets (the two books of *Cantiones sacrae*, 1589 and 1591), published after Tallis's death when Byrd operated the monopoly alone, although it is difficult to imagine that many such households had the forces to acquit themselves well with these works, which are demanding and complex. Byrd's psalms and devotional songs in his English printed collections such as *Psalms, Sonets and Songs* (1588) and *Songs of Sundrie Natures* (1589) would have been aimed at these Catholics as well as at Anglicans, thus showing great commercial shrewdness. The provision of large amounts of devotional (and eventually, with the publication of Byrd's *Gradualia* in 1605, Catholic liturgical) music for the domestic market is an important feature of English music.

The fine English disregard for foreign words that had been noticeable earlier continues when we hear of the "Lavoltos" danced by Marson's nymphs and shepherds in the *Triumphs of Oriana* (1601), *la volta* being one of the queen's favourite dances, but the English had always had a healthy interest in things continental (we have already mentioned above the anglicized Norman cathedral of the twelfth century and the tudorized French courtly-love ethic of Henry VIII's reign), and their interest increasingly turned to Italy as the sixteenth century progressed. As ever, they were prepared to take a long hard look before deciding how they would anglicize Italian music. Direct comparison between English music and that of the continent is generally inappropriate, but we have the musicians of the time to blame for the fact that we feel we should try. Byrd and Tallis, in the preface to their 1575 *Cantiones... sacrae*, set out to create a climate in which it is accepted that English music (in this case Latin-texted counterpoint) is as good as any on the continent, and Byrd, in one of the early collections of translated madrigals (Watson's *Italian Madrigalls Englished* of 1590, of which he was the publisher), seems intent on showing that he can write a perfectly good madrigal (*This sweet and merry month of May*) if he chooses to, but generally chooses not to do so; while Morley, in his marketing of the English madrigal unashamedly points his customers towards Italian models and translations, while taking the most promising features and anglicizing them. In their naturalization of foreign genres the English added local touches, notably homeliness and earthiness; the "homely mermaides" (of either sex) of Henry's reign have now, in Holmes's madrigal (also for the *Oriana* volume), become nymphs and shepherds feasting on "clowted cream," and the Englishness is apparent in the scenes from a rustic wedding in Morley's *Arise get up my dear* (1593) and from a morris dance in his *With bagpipes who comes?* (1594), while the jolly fosters and hunters of Henry's day continue their endless pursuit in works such as Morley's *Besides a fountain* (1594) and Campion's *It fell on a summer's day* (1601). But they all act in a very English way: fair Phyllis, of Farmer's eponymous madrigal, is the typical nymph-next-door, and all that the suitors need most of the time, with characteristic English sobriety, is to fall a-kissing.

If "The great achievement of the [Italian] madrigal is its success in making words sing,"[30] and if "[Italian] composers went on thinking that the way to capture the essence of a poem was to bring to musical life the *affetti* of individual words and phrases, and they continued to use a mixture of what we consider naïve and sophisticated methods to do so,"[31] then this applies equally to the English. However, one important way in which the two traditions differed lies in the way the pieces hold together, especially as the century progressed, for whereas in Italy "composers responded not so much with a new vocabulary of affective devices as with an increased ability to shift quickly from one device to another, and an increased willingness to interrupt the 'discursive' flow of the musical syntax with sudden changes of figure and texture,"[32] in England the lack of sudden shifts, the onward pace of the music, and the smooth transition between these short illustrative moments are more important. Weelkes's madrigal *Thule the period of cosmography* (1600), one of the best madrigals of the period, is an excellent example of English writing and demonstrates this well. Its chief English characteristic is its homogeneity and sense of pace; it is never episodic and never comes to a full stop and a restart. It takes full advantage of the English language (especially the alliterative qualities of "full of flying fishes" and "cochineal and china dishes," both set to fast music, the latter off-beat, the better to emphasize the "ch" sound), but it also manages to incorporate several exotic geographical names (Thule, Hecla, Fogo, Etna, Andalusia) to reflect the exploration exploits of a seafaring nation. It illustrates simple pictures such as the triangular shape of Sicily ("Trinacria") by moving very briefly into triple time, the sulphurious eruptions of Mt Hecla by furious fast notes (smoke and fire) within a held chord (rock), and individual words and phrases such as "flying fishes" and "higher" in the typical English restrained madrigalian style, never dwelling for more than a few beats on the picture but moving briskly on. The methods of moving on are the tried and trusted techniques of harmony, counterpoint, and the well-established English sprung rhythm (see above). The harmony at "doth *melt*" and "These things seem *wond'rous*" is mildly but not excessively chromatic and so provides a moment of emphasis without holding up the forward thrust, while there is a good example of double counterpoint at the beginning, where "Thule" is set to two semibreves to illustrate its island status, accompanied by an upward scale to illustrate distance. William Camden in 1586 took Thule to be Shetland,

30 James Haar, *Italian Poetry and Music in the Renaissance* (Berkeley, 1986), 50.

31 Ibid., 111.

32 Ibid., 134.

but according to legend it was supposed to be six days' journey north of Britain, so Tovey was probably right when he painted a pleasing picture of its being Iceland looming out of the top of the map in Mercator's new projection (1599), as its semibreves loom out of the highest voice, which shows how very modern poets and composers could be.[33] Weelkes combines chromaticism with counterpoint at "how strangely Fogo burns," while the off-beat sprung rhythm is found at "*Whose* sulphurious stream" to pick up a new phrase with urgency after the fragmented and jagged counterpoint associated with Hecla; the extension of this rhythm from the method of setting "and," "for," and "he," as discussed earlier, shows an excellent sense of development of its linking function, for "whose" is a prime example of a pronoun looking both forwards and backwards.

But it is to the picture of the Children of the Chapel Royal disguised as mermaids, from Henry's court revels, that we must return, because the use of boy choristers developed into companies of boy actors; the Children of St Paul's were available for free-lance engagements from at least as early as 1552, when Princess Elizabeth saw them, and they performed before her as the new queen in 1559 at Nonsuch Palace when she was entertained by Henry Fitzalan, Earl of Arundel, while the Children of the Chapel Royal performed at Court under Richard Edwards from 1561 (Edwards was a playwright as well as a composer), and these companies continued until about 1600, sometimes competing with the adult companies (in which, of course, the female roles were played by boys anyway). Obviously, any songs for such plays would have to have a treble line and some kind of instrumental accompaniment, since there were no lower voices available to provide a harmonic basis, and so in the theatre a group of viols, or if possible a plucked instrument, served this role. By the 1580s the boy-actor song had moved outside the theatre into three significant areas: into church as the verse anthem, and into the chamber as the consort song or the lute song. The development of the verse anthem is entirely logical in this context, for these were the same singers, though here with the support of the organ and men's voices, and it is equally natural that the work thought to be the first verse anthem, *When as we sat in Babylon*, should be by Richard Farrant, who is also noted for his play-songs, such as *Ah alas you salt sea gods*.[34] Since Farrant died in 1580, this also establishes the date by which the verse anthem had been developed. The term "verse anthem" is at first entirely appropriate, because the earliest examples set their text, usually from metrical versions of the psalms, verse by verse, with the soloist starting and the chorus echoing in full harmony the end of his phrase. The accompaniment is by the organ, which itself had peculiarly English qualities, because it is a transposing instrument that

33 As reported by Joseph Kerman, *The Elizabethan Madrigal: A Comparative Study*, (New York, 1962), 231–32. Camden's *Britannia* was published in Latin in 1586 (not in English until 1610), but Mercator's projection was even more up-to-the-minute: though originally published in 1569 it had only just been published in England, in Edward Wright's version of 1599, in *The Principall Navigations, Voiages, Traffiques and Discoveries of the English Nation* (London, 1598–1600), compiled by Richard Hakluyt.

34 Morehen, "English Church Music," 123–24; Carter, "Secular Vocal Music," 178.

developed in a particular way to cover specific needs.[35] The "verse" genre then spread quickly to the Service; Byrd's Second Service, which may be dated before 1584 (or even before 1581, for reasons stated above), is probably the earliest example and shows again how he mastered a genre before moving on and never using it again. It is Byrd, too, who bridges the gap between the verse anthem and the domestic consort song, in his English prints of 1588 and 1589; although he provides texts for all voices for all pieces, whether obviously secular, (e.g., *Though Amaryllis dance in green*) or devotional (*Lullaby my sweet little baby*) in an attempt to make them look like madrigals appropriate for purely sung performance, he annotates one voice "the first singing part" and indicates that they were originally conceived for, and should ideally be performed by, one voice and viols, thus giving rise to the "apt for voices and viols" tag applied to most of the later printed madrigal prints, even when the words of these were primarily conceived as all-sung. Again, many of Byrd's works in these printed collections are metrical psalms, though not necessarily set in standard verse-anthem format, indicating that they are for the domestic market.

Instrumental music

The English liking for a firmly-settled performing medium has been noted several times already. In pre-Reformation sacred music we have noted that the choirs for which the composers were writing were fairly uniform in size and entirely uniform in composition, and we have seen the development of the consort song, which relies on a known and established accompaniment (a group of viols) for accompaniment, and indeed the lute song, which relies on the sound of the lute. Nor is it surprising that in instrumental ensemble music the liking for a settled performance grouping led to the cultivation of the consort of viols and the mixed (or broken) consort (almost invariably violin, flute, lute, cittern, bandora, and bass viol), for which Morley wrote his *First Booke of Consort Lessons* (1599).[36] We have also noted the interest shown during the first half of the century in the concept of variation, from audible variation (in keyboard works based on grounds) to largely imperceptible cantus-firmus variation in masses (though with statements of the cantus firmus that in some cases become ever more perceptible as the mass proceeds). It is not surprising, then, that in instrumental music of the second half of the century the variation continued to be cultivated, in solo music (both for keyboard and for lute) and in instrumental ensemble music. However, no matter the medium for which a work was conceived, the English were flexible when it came to actual performance, as may be judged from the title and contents of a manuscript called "In nomines and other solfainge songes,"[37] indicating that instrumental pieces were sometimes sung (vocalized or to their "sol-fa-ing" syllables).

[35] Keith Elcombe, "Keyboard Music," *Blackwell History of Music in Britain*, II: 210–62 at 254–56; Wulstan, *Tudor Music*, 198–202.

[36] Harper, "Ensemble and Lute Music," 307.

[37] *GB-Lbl* Add. 31390.

In instrumental ensemble music it is possible even to advance a reason and context for the particular developments that occurred in the 1560s, which led to the later triumphs in this genre, for John Harper has perceptively pointed out that one major name is missing from his list of composers of such music during the 1560s: John Sheppard.[38] This strongly suggests that composers turned in this decade to their stock of Catholic liturgical music, with a view to giving it a new lease of life once it became clear that it was not going to be needed for liturgical use again. Sheppard, who died by early 1559, was therefore not in a position to promote his music in this way, but his surviving near-contemporaries (notably Tallis, Tye, and Parsons) were. The earliest apparently instrumental works were stylistically derived from sacred choral music, and some of them, such as Tye's *Rubum quem* (no further text) may have been actual Latin-texted works; the very earliest such work, Taverner's original *In nomine*, certainly is. Hence, the derivation of such pieces from motet to instrumental piece and then to vocalization shows typical English pragmatism. The English liking for cantus-firmus-based genres is seen not only in their development of the *In nomine* but also in their use of other cantus firmi, such as the hexachord (though this too had its roots in the pre-Reformation mass, since Avery Burton wrote one on this cantus firmus), and of ostinati (the difference being that ostinati are brief and incessantly repeated, though this too may have its roots in works such as Aston's mass *God save King Harry* and Alwood's mass *Praise him praiseworthy*, both based on the same five-note figure).

There is a virtually complete lack of interest in the use of secular melodies as the basis of Masses; the three *Western Wind* masses (by Taverner, Tye, and Sheppard) provide the only examples. There were no "armed men" in England. However, this is more than compensated for by the extensive exploration of secular and popular tunes in the variation, particularly but by no means exclusively the keyboard variation, whose works raise this genre to an early peak. The idea of variation is also found in keyboard settings of dances, with the pavan and galliard, now paired, providing a template. Byrd's variations on popular tunes or ostinati, such as "Walsingham" for keyboard, and "Browning" for viol consort, and his pavans and galliards, in which each section is repeated with variation, are of very high quality, as are the keyboard works of John Bull, one of which sets the hexachord progressively rising by a tone and therefore using notes that would sound painful on anything but some kind of well-tempered instrument.[39] It is difficult to imagine the dances actually being danced, though they are of course set in such a way that they could be, and this use of dance therefore provides the vehicle for complex compositional skill, leading in 1604 to one of the most extraordinary achievements of this period, Dowland's *Lachrimae* pavans, seven pavans for five viols and optional lute, presented as if they are to be performed in succession (and very well they work if performed thus, with their sustained passion), dance being used here as the medium for a substantial work showing progressive emotion in several "movements," except that all these use the same framework. Caldwell applauds their intensity of

38 Harper, "Ensemble and Lute Music," 279.
39 Elcombe, "Keyboard Music," 240.

expression while "missing . . . a sense of progression," and observes that "the pieces might be played in any order, or a selection made, without noticeable loss,"[40] which is true, but the tension would still build up, which is in itself a remarkable achievement, probably because they seem like variations without exactly being so, but more like variations on an idea. The full title, "Lachrimae, or Seaven Teares figured in Seaven Passionate Pavans, with divers other Pavans, Galiards, and Almands," sets the context of the first seven pavans, and the instrumentation combines the homogeneous consort of viols with the plucked lute, an effective combination of two well-established characteristic English sounds.

In one sense the fantasia, as developed by the English, whether for solo keyboard, solo lute, or consort, is in stark contrast to the *In nomine* and the variation, since it is free of the constraints of the pre-existing tune, but in another sense the cultivation of the fantasia runs parallel to that of the *In nomine*, since both set imitative points in such a way as to build the tension progressively; the particularly English view of the fantasia is well expressed by Morley, who defined it as "the chiefest kind of musicke which is made without a dittie . . . when a musician taketh a point at his pleasure, and wresteth and turneth it as he list, making either much or little of it as shalle seeme best in his own conceit."[41] Very few works are actually entitled "fantasia," but many agree well with this definition.

THE death of Elizabeth in 1603 is often taken as a cultural watershed, but many of the greatest achievements of the age were still to come: Byrd, though aged over 60, was to live for another 20 years, Dowland was about 40 but was to live for another 23 years, while the younger generation still had much of their composing career ahead of them: Tomkins (31) still had 53 more years, and Weelkes (27) still had 20. Gibbons (20) had hardly begun, and although he was to die at the early age of 42 his music is the apotheosis of the Elizabethan style while looking forward as far ahead as Purcell.

[40] Caldwell, *Oxford History of English Music*, I: 474.

[41] Thomas Morley, *A Plaine and Easie Introduction to Practicall Musicke*, (London, 1597), 181; see *New Grove*^{2} s.v. "Fantasia."

25

ENGLAND, *ii*: 1603–1642

Jonathan P. Wainwright

This chapter is concerned with English music during the reigns of the first two Stuart monarchs: James I (James VI of Scotland) who acceded to the throne in 1603 on the death of Queen Elizabeth I, and Charles I who succeeded James I in 1625. The date 1642 is a convenient one at which to conclude, for although Charles I was not to die on the scaffold until 1649, 1642 represents the beginning of the Civil War, the King's forced withdrawal from London, and the effective closing down of the country's leading musical institutions. The chapter will concentrate unashamedly on London—not because there was a lack of music in the provinces, but because it was to London, and to the court in particular, that the country looked for the latest musical fashions. The foremost musicians and composers were attracted to London; and the court system, which resulted in the constant movement of noblemen and their households to and from the city, undoubtedly aided the dissemination of music. We should not assume, however, that the high standard of music in London was necessarily replicated countrywide.

It is fortuitous that, in beginning with the accession of James I in 1603, we can avoid using the date 1600—in traditional music-historiography the beginning of the Baroque era—for that date has no real significance for English music, and the term "Baroque" is rarely used in relation to the latter until the Restoration (1660). English music in the first half of the seventeenth century, it is fair to say, was generally rather conservative in nature (certainly in comparison to some other parts of Europe), and its assimilation of Italianate "progressive" elements was relatively late and haphazard. This highlights one of the problems of the traditional Italian-centered historiographical construct. There is no doubt that, in terms of musical styles, many "Baroque" innovations began in Italy (even if, in reality, they evolved slowly in terms of performance practice rather than appearing suddenly in print)[1]

[1] For a critique of the pre- and post-1600 polarization in music historiography, see Jonathan P. Wainwright, "From 'Renaissance' to 'Baroque'?" in *From Renaissance to Baroque*, ed. Jonathan P. Wainwright and Peter Holman (Aldershot, 2005), 1–21.

and that other European countries were influenced, at different times and to different degrees, by musical ideas of Italian derivation. These influences were assimilated into the indigenous musical traditions in a complex manner related to social, political, and cultural factors, but a degree of reliance on Italian innovations does not, of course, make those European musical cultures "backward" or second-best. Such notions are no longer acceptable; and one of the advances in recent writings on music history has been the acceptance that so-called "peripheral" European cultures should be assessed as much in relation to their own historical context and in terms of their own indigenous traditions as from an Italianate perspective. This brief essay will attempt to do just that in relation to English music from 1603 to 1642.

Consort Music

Many noble households had chests of viols for domestic music-making; consort music was also an important pastime at court. In James I's reign the King's Musick, the secular branch of the royal musical establishment, employed about 40 musicians, divided into various groups of Renaissance-style consorts. The flutes, shawms and sackbuts, recorders, and violins were assigned to the public parts of Whitehall Palace, whereas the quieter instruments, such as the lutes and viols, performed in the Privy Chamber. The repertory of "public" court music was dance music, played by various ensembles including the orchestral violin band that performed in the traditional five-part layout of one violin part, three viola parts, and bass (usually without continuo). We should remember that in England early in the seventeenth century the violin was primarily associated with dancing and was not classed as an instrument for "serious" music.[2] The string repertoire performed in the Privy Chamber was far more esoteric. Of foremost importance is the music composed for consorts of viols (in combinations of treble, tenor, and bass instruments with or without organ). The musical style of the early-seventeenth-century fantasias and *In nomines* was definitely that of the "Renaissance" rather than the "Baroque" (if these terms must be used), for they utilize contrapuntal imitative structures rather than the new "Baroque" musico-rhetorical devices. It seems that the continental canzona and sonata styles did not have a real impact on English instrumental music until after 1660.

The conservative nature of the viol consort repertoire is highlighted by the fact that the early years of the seventeenth century saw a renewed interest in the *In nomine*—a type of contrapuntal consort piece written using the plainsong Sarum antiphon *Gloria tibi Trinitas* as a cantus firmus. The origin of this specifically English tradition can be traced back to the "In nomine Domini" section of the Benedictus of the six-part mass *Gloria tibi Trinitas* by John Taverner (*c.*1490–1545). But just why this particular section became detached from the mass as an independent

2 See Peter Holman, *Four and Twenty Fiddlers: The Violin at the English Court, 1540–1690* (Oxford, 1993), *passim.*

instrumental piece and then formed the basis of a long-running tradition of setting the plainsong (which ended 150 years later with Purcell) is something of a mystery. Perhaps it was in some sense a homage to English sixteenth-century music and to Taverner in particular. Most likely it relates to the concept of "imitatio" or emulation, and the "In nomine" is the English equivalent of the Franco-Flemish "L'homme armé" tradition. The *In nomine* no. 1 for six parts (Example 25.1, overleaf) by Alfonso Ferrabosco the younger (*c.*1575–1628) may be considered typical; we should note, in particular, the skillful contrapuntal invention surrounding the long notes of the cantus firmus.

This emphasis on the contrapuntal is also the primary feature of the most important instrumental form of the seventeenth century, the fantasia or fancy. As late as 1667, in his *Compendium of Practical Musick*, Christopher Simpson still considered the fantasia the "chief and most excellent" form of chamber music. He explained the fantasia as follows:

> In this sort of Musick the Composer (being not limited to the words) doth employ all his Art and Invention solely about the bringing in and carrying on of... Fuges [here meaning merely imitative points].... When he has tried all the several wayes which he thinks fit to be used therein; he takes some other point, and does the like with it; or else, for variety, introduces some *Chromatick* Notes, with Bindings and Intermixtures of Discords; or, falls into some lighter Humour like a Madrigal, or what else his own fancy shall lead him to: but still concluding with something which hath Art and excellency in it.

There are two particular points of interest here. Firstly the emphasis on variety; thematic unity was not a priority, in fact far from it, for it seems that contrast and balance were the important factors. The other important thing was the mention of the madrigal. We should remember that there was a long-standing tradition of copying Italian madrigals in England and that the copyists of manuscripts, or the publishers of printed music, would often give the performers the option of performing these imported madrigals vocally or on instruments, using the phrase "apt for voice or viol." Numerous late-sixteenth- and early-seventeenth-century consort-music manuscripts contain, amongst the fantasias and *In nomines*, textless Italian madrigals—by Luca Marenzio (1553/4–1599), Claudio Monteverdi (1567–1643), and their contemporaries—intended for performance by viol consort. It seems that English composers learnt much from Italian madrigals: in particular the manipulation of motifs in relation to texture, scoring, harmonic tension, pace, and changing metre.

At court, it was not only the King who employed musicians; his children also had musicians in their personal households. Prince Henry's household was formed in the winter of 1609–10, and until his untimely death in the autumn of 1612 it was the focus of many important artistic and scientific developments.[3] Prince Henry's musical activities were also noteworthy: his household musicians formed the

[3] See in particular Roy Strong, *Henry Prince of Wales and England's Lost Renaissance* (London, 1986).

Ex. 25.1 Alfonso Ferrabosco ii, *In nomine* no. 1 a 6, mm. 1–11
Alfonso Ferrabosco ii: The Six-Part Works, ed. David Pinto (Harpenden, 1990), II: 18

first new group to be added to the royal music since Henry VIII's reign (a group consisting mainly of singer-lutenists), and his musical patronage is notable for its Italianate interests, particularly in his employment of the musician Angelo Notari

(1566–1663).[4] After Charles was created Prince of Wales, on 3 November 1616, he appointed 17 musicians to his household; these included the six singer-lutenists he inherited from his brother's musicians, to whom he added six more of his own. [5]

However, it was in the field of string-consort music that Prince Charles's musicians really made their mark. Charles, while still Prince of Wales (1616–25), employed four of the most eminent composers of consort music: Alfonso Ferrabosco the younger, John Coprario (*c.*1570/80–1626), Orlando Gibbons (1583–1625), and Thomas Lupo (1571–1627), and together they were responsible for extending the range of scorings employed in the English fantasia idiom and for the introduction of the violin into contrapuntal music. Prince Charles was himself a skilled performer on the bass viol (having been taught by Alfonso Ferrabosco) and according to John Playford "could play his part exactly well on the Bass-Viol, especially of those Incomparable Fancies of Mr. Coperario to the Organ."[6] Although the violin

[4] Ian Spink, "Angelo Notari and his *Prime musiche nuove*," *The Monthly Musical Record*, 87 (1957), 168–77; Pamela Willetts, "A Neglected Source of Monody and Madrigal," *Music & Letters*, 43 (1962), 329–39; eadem, "Autographs of Angelo Notari," *Music & Letters*, 50 (1969), 124–26; Holman, *Four and Twenty Fiddlers*, 201–5; Jonathan P. Wainwright, *Musical Patronage in Seventeenth-Century England: Christopher, First Baron Hatton (1605–1670)* (Aldershot and Brookfield, VT, 1997), 162–65, 191–94.

[5] For details, see Andrew Ashbee, *Records of English Court Music*, IV (Snodland, 1991), 216–30.

[6] John Playford, *An Introduction to the Skill of Musick*, 10th edn (London, 1683). This is the first edition to make reference to the King's performing ability; previous editions that contain the section are concerned only with the King's musical preference: "And for Instrumental Musick none pleased him like those incomparable Fantazies for one Violin and Basses Viol, to

had first appeared at the English court in 1540, it was used almost exclusively for dance music until about 1620. Coprario was one of the first composers to use the violin in contrapuntal consort music. In 1622 Prince Charles formed a violin and viol ensemble[7]—"Coperario's Musique"—that consisted of Lupo, John Woodington, and Adam Vallet (violins), Ferrabosco II and Coprario (viols), and Gibbons (keyboard).[8] Once the violin had become established as an instrument for "serious" contrapuntal chamber music, court composers began experimenting with new forms and scorings using mixed groups of violins and viols with keyboard (usually organ) or theorbo continuo. Coprario, William White (1571–1634), and John Jenkins (1592–1678) composed works for two bass viols and organ; Lupo for two treble and two bass viols; and Lupo, White, Thomas Tomkins (1572–1656), and Jenkins for two treble and one bass viol; in all these scorings the treble viol could be replaced with the violin. From the point of view of later development, the combination of two trebles (or violins) and a bass is important, for we would appear to have here the nascent trio-sonata texture (although the organ part cannot yet be called a true basso continuo part). One of the new forms to emerge was the fantasia-suite, a fixed three-movement sequence of fantasia and two dances: an almain and a galliard that usually concluded with a short coda in duple time.[9] This form appears to have been invented by Coprario and seems to have remained a court genre until the Civil War, after which it was more widely disseminated. One example must suffice: the opening of the Fantasia from Coprario's fantasia-suite no. 4 for two violins, bass viol, and organ (Example 25.2, overleaf). The essential nature of the keyboard part is apparent, as is the contrapuntal mastery.

Another new fantasia scoring that appears to have had its origins in the experiments that were taking place in court circles in the 1620s was that of the "Great Dooble Base" fantasias, so called because they use (together with a violin or treble viol and a tenor or bass viol) an instrument a size larger, and tuned a fourth lower, than the normal bass viol. The best known examples are Orlando Gibbons's three- and four-part "Great Dooble Base" fantasias. The importance of these court consort pieces cannot be overestimated, for they stand at the head of a tradition that was to culminate in the trio sonatas of Henry Purcell and, as such, perhaps herald the beginnings of the English musical Baroque.

Charles's accession to the throne on 27 March 1625 created a problem. The new king already had a sizeable household of his own which he needed to somehow amalgamate with the personnel he inherited from his father. Charles's solution was to retain most of both households with their existing salaries; only seven of

the organ, Composed by Mr. Coprario" (4th–7th edns: 1664, 1666, 1667, 1670). All editions subsequent to 1683 repeat the version of the 10th edn.

7 Dated from John Woodington's petition to Charles I (12 May 1625), in which he states that he had been a member of "Coperario[']s musique 3 yeres" (*GB-Lbl* Add. 64883, fol. 57^{r}).

8 Ashbee, *Records*, IV: 217–30.

9 The term "Fantasia-suite" is modern; see Christopher D. S. Field, "Fantasia-suite," *The New Grove Dictionary of Music and Musicians*, 2nd edn, ed. S. Sadie and J. Tyrrell (London, 2001), VIII: 558–59.

his musicians from his time as Prince of Wales were not reappointed.[10] The extra numbers of musicians necessitated a reorganization of the royal music, and the various groups of musicians (such as the "Musicians for Lutes and Voices" and the "Musicians for the Violins") came under the overall control of the "Master of the Musicke," Nicholas Lanier (1588–1666), whose duty it was to oversee both the "public" and the "private" secular music-making at court. Lanier, the first holder of the post of Master of the King's Musicke, was appointed in 1626 at a salary of £200 per annum, [11] and his service to the king extended beyond musical matter, for he was sent to Italy a number of times between 1625 and 1628 to negotiate the purchase of paintings from the Gonzaga collection at Mantua.[12] The "King's Musicke" provided musical entertainment for court dinners, for dancing, for masques, "play nights," and intimate chamber music. However, it seems that the most progressive music was reserved for the more intimate surroundings of the Privy Chamber. The "Private Musick" performed chamber music and vocal pieces for the king's private delectation, and the musicians continued the innovative work pioneered when Charles was still Prince of Wales.

The confidence of the Caroline court's musical establishment must have taken a knock in the later 1620s with the deaths of a number of its foremost musicians: Orlando Gibbons died suddenly at Canterbury on 5 June 1625 while the court was awaiting the arrival of Queen Henrietta Maria from France, Coprario died in the summer of 1626, Lupo in the winter of 1627/28, and Ferrabosco in March 1628. But the court's musical identity was reaffirmed in 1635 with the appointment of William Lawes (1602–1645) as a "musician in ordinary for the lutes and voices,"[13] and the image of a progressive musical culture was secured. William Lawes's links with the court must predate his appointment in 1635. The earliest version of his Royal Consort (suites of dances) appears to date back to the early 1630s, and thus it is possible that he was composing for the "Lutes and Voices" several years before his official court appointment. His elder brother Henry (1596–1662) was appointed as "a musician for the voices" in 1631;[14] this would presumably have given William access to court musicians, if not to the court itself. William Lawes's consort music represents some of the most adventurous instrumental music of the time, and his fantasia-suites and his Harp Consorts, in particular, single him out as the heir to Coprario.[15] Towards the end of the 1630s Lawes returned to the composition of fantasias in more traditional scorings with his Consort Setts for five and six viols and organ.[16] This may at first seem surprising, but it appears that the more

[10] Holman, *Four and Twenty Fiddlers*, 226.

[11] Ashbee, *Records*, III: 19.

[12] See Ian Spink, "Lanier in Italy," *Music & Letters*, 40 (1959), 242–52; Michael I. Wilson, *Nicholas Lanier: Master of the King's Musick* (Aldershot and Brookfield, VT, 1994).

[13] Ashbee, *Records*, III: 82.

[14] Ibid., 57.

[15] See Murray Lefkowitz, *William Lawes* (London, 1960), 88–125; Holman, *Four and Twenty Fiddlers*, 262–65; David Pinto, *"For ye Violls": The Consort and Dance Music of William Lawes* (Richmond, 1995), *passim*.

[16] See ibid., 70–140.

Ex. 25.2 John Coprario, Fantasia-suite no. 4, Fantasia, mm. 1–11
John Coprario: Fantasia-Suites, ed. Richard Charteris (London, 1980), 127

old-fashioned viol fantasias remained in the court repertoire and were performed alongside the more progressive pieces until the outbreak of the Civil War in 1642.

Music for Solo Instruments

The first quarter of the seventeenth century was a great period for English keyboard music. The virginalist school of William Byrd (*c.*1540–1623), John Bull (?1562/63–1628), Giles Farnaby (*c.*1563–1640), Orlando Gibbons, and Thomas Tomkins composed fantasias, plainsong settings, dances, and variations on well-known tunes for virginals, spinet, harpsichord, regal, or chamber organ. The best-known sources of keyboard music of this period are the so-called Fitzwilliam Virginal Book, which is thought to have been copied by Francis Tregian between 1609 and 1619,[17] and a small engraved volume of 21 virginal pieces by Byrd, Bull, and Gibbons entitled *Parthenia or the Maydenhead of the first musicke that was ever printed for the virginalls* (London, [1612/13]). The wealth of forms used in the virginalists' music is notable, ranging from stylized dance settings (usually of the pavan and galliard, but later also of the almain and corant) to contrapuntal fantasias and variation settings. We also find settings based on plainsong cantus firmi (including the *In nomine,* already referred to); such pieces had, by the early seventeenth century, lost all connection with liturgical organ music. John Bull's music, in particular, is notable for its high degree of virtuosity and harmonic adventurousness. Bull, who left England for the Low Countries in 1613 (owing to a scandal of a sexual nature), helped transmit the English virginal style to continental composers such as Jan Pieterszoon Sweelinck (1562–1621). This is one of the few times in music history where English music can be shown to have influenced continental music rather than vice versa. The popularity of virginal music seems to have

[17] *GB-Cfm* Mus. 168 (32.g.29).

declined in the years after about 1625. This may have been to do with new trends at court associated with the change of monarch in 1625. The fantasia survived as the only form of solo organ music under the title "verse" or "voluntary."

The so-called Golden Age of English lute music was *c.*1590–1620. Surviving manuscripts of that period confirm the quality and quantity of the music written during the period: some 45 important sources contain more than 1,500 pieces.[18] This is a considerably larger repertoire than that for keyboard (although most lute pieces are shorter). Lute music was in composed in the same forms as keyboard music but with a greater emphasis on the homophonic dance forms. Some polyphonic fantasias exist, as do variations on popular melodies (particularly ballad tunes). John Dowland (1563–1626) was the most influential lutenist-composer of the period. He appears to have favoured the galliard as a form for his lute compositions, but he also composed pavans, almains, and fantasias. His most popular piece was the pavan *Lachrimae*, which can be found in about 100 manuscripts; he later turned it into the song *Flow my tears* in his *Second Book of Songs or Ayres* (London, 1600) and then into a five-part instrumental setting published in *Lachrimae or Seven Teares* (London, 1604).[19] Dowland's galliards, pavans, and almains for lute are abstract instrumental pieces and not intended for the dance floor. The prestige of the English school of lutenist-composers declined after the death of Dowland in 1626. The lyra viol (see below) superseded the lute as the popular instrument for the amateur player, and with the coming of Queen Henrietta Maria (Charles I's wife) there developed a fashion for all things French. This changing taste is documented in the contents of a lute manuscript compiled by Edward, Lord Herbert of Cherbury, between *c.*1619 and *c.*1640:[20] as well as music by Dowland and his contemporaries, it contains a large amount of music by the French composer Jacques Gautier (fl. 1617–49), who had been appointed at the English court in 1622.[21]

Lutes were not the only plucked solo instruments in use in England in the early seventeenth century. Wire-strung plucked instruments such as the cittern, bandora, and orpharion vied in popularity with the lute, and each has a small but characteristic repertoire. Mention must also be made of the lyra viol, a bowed instrument whose music was—like that of the plucked instruments mentioned above—notated in tablature. As an instrument it differs little from the bass viol used in consort music—basically it was smaller—but it has a large and important repertoire associated with it. Composers such as Coprario, Jenkins, William Lawes, Charles Coleman (d. 1664), and Christopher Simpson (*c.*1602/6–1669) produced music for the instrument characterized by chordal and pseudo-polyphonic textures, as it was capable of multiple stopping.

18 For full details, see Matthew Spring, *The Lute in Britain: A History of the Instrument and its Music* (Oxford, 2001).

19 For full details, see Peter Holman, *Dowland: Lachrimae (1604)* (Cambridge, 1999).

20 *Cfm* Mus. 689.

21 Ashbee, *Records*, III: 227–29.

Church Music

The foremost English religious establishment for music was the Chapel Royal, a body of persons within the Royal Household responsible for the ordering and performance of divine service in the sovereign's presence (whether it be at Whitehall, Hampton Court, Windsor, or elsewhere). In the seventeenth century the Chapel Royal comprised (with occasional fluctuations) a dean and 32 "Gentlemen," of whom seven or eight were chaplains and the rest "singing-men." A sub-dean, who was responsible for the daily running of the chapel, was elected from the chaplains, and the organists and a Master of the Children, responsible for the twelve choristers, came from the ranks of the singing-men.[22] The basic musical duties of the Chapel Royal were performance at morning and evening prayer, but they also performed at royal christenings, weddings, and funerals and at state occasions such as coronations. Gentlemen were paid £40 a year and, according to the "Orders for the Attendance" drawn up while William Laud was dean (1626–33), were required to attend daily, one month on and one month off (i.e. only half the Gentlemen were on duty), except for Sundays and major festivals when all were required to attend.[23] This system, together with the good holidays (three months in the summer and eight other weeks over the year), enabled some Gentlemen to also hold posts at nearby foundations such as St Paul's or Westminster Abbey. The prestige and attractive rates of pay meant that many of the country's best composers and singers were employed as Gentlemen, and, in both repertoire and performance standards, the Chapel Royal provided a model for cathedrals and collegiate establishments to follow.

From a twenty-first-century perspective, the foremost composer of sacred music living in the first twenty years of the seventeenth century was William Byrd. However, Byrd cannot be regarded as representative. He was, as is well known, a Catholic, and, even though he maintained his position at court, Byrd spent the last twenty or so years of his life in semi-exile at Stondon Massey in Essex. Here he was close to a Roman Catholic community centered around the household of Sir John Petre. This was the context for Byrd's last great collection of sacred music: the *Gradualia* (two books: London, 1605 and 1607), Latin settings for the Proper of the Mass (his three settings of the Ordinary had been separately published in the 1590s), no doubt designed for use in recusant worship. This, then, is "unofficial" sacred music. The English anthems and services performed in the Chapel Royal and the cathedrals, churches and collegiate establishments represent the "official" sacred music of the day. Some of Byrd's English music must date from the Jacobean period, such as the psalm settings published in his *Psalmes, Songs and Sonnets* (London, 1611), but these are mostly examples of "domestic" sacred music—devotional music rather than music for the liturgy. The compositions of Orlando Gibbons, Thomas Weelkes (1576–1623), and Thomas Tomkins are more representative. Two

22 See E. F. Rimbault, *The Old Cheque-Book . . . of the Chapel Royal* (London, 1872); and David Baldwin, *The Chapel Royal: Ancient & Modern* (London, 1990).

23 Rimbault, *Old Cheque-Book*, 71–3.

anthems by Gibbons, the "full anthem" *Almighty and everlasting God* and the verse anthem *This is the record of John*, may be considered as typical. A "full" anthem is an *a cappella* piece that does not utilize "verse" or solo sections (the survival of numerous organ parts to full anthems suggests that they were usually accompanied, the organist playing a type of *basso seguente* and doubling some or all of the voices). Gibbons's *Almighty and everlasting God* is an exquisite example: it is a simple four-voice setting, and the text, the collect for the third Sunday after Epiphany, is set polyphonically throughout with dovetailing imitative sections; the words are set almost entirely syllabically, and there is little text repetition. Although the anthem is thoroughly polyphonic in conception, the words match the music beautifully, and the meaning is delivered with absolute clarity. The same is true of Gibbons's *This is the record of John*, one of the best known examples of the "verse anthem." Here the use of "verses" for solo voices and instrumental accompaniment aids the declamation of the narrative text (John 1: 19–23). Many verse anthems, like *This is the record of John*, appear in manuscripts with viol consort accompaniments. These are the result of domestic or devotional performances, for, although there was a long-standing tradition in England of training choristers to play the viol, there is little evidence that consorts of viols were actually used in cathedrals and churches in a liturgical situation.

As the two Gibbons examples demonstrate, sacred and devotional music in England remained conservative in approach and showed little or no awareness of the so-called *stile nuovo*. The only publications to contain *stile nuovo* sacred compositions before the Commonwealth period were Walter Porter's *Madrigales and Ayres* (London, 1632)[24]—a single sacred work, "Praise the Lord"—and William Child's *The First Set of Psalmes of III. Voyces, Fitt for private Chappells or other private meetings with a continuall Base either for the Organ or Theorbo newly composed after the Italian way* (London, 1639).[25] It is noteworthy that as late as 1639 Child is describing his psalms as "after the Italian way" as if it was something unusual. The title of Child's publication also emphasizes the private nature of his music, as if "modern" Italianate music was considered best suited to private devotional meetings rather than public liturgy. However, Child's psalms, despite the title of the publication, are relatively conservative in approach, with little obviously of "the Italian Way." Latin motets composed by Richard Dering (*c.*1580–1630), composed in the 1620s, perhaps represent the earliest essays in the Italianate small-scale *concertato* style by an English composer; but the performance context was most likely Queen Henrietta Maria's Roman Catholic Chapel, and they cannot be seen as representative of mainstream English church music. With just a few exceptions, the Anglican liturgical repertoire, as performed in cathedrals and the Chapel Royal, was extremely conservative. This is reflected in the contents of John Barnard's *First Book*

[24] See Ian Spink, "Walter Porter and the Last Book of English Madrigals," *Acta musicologica*, 26 (1954), 18–36; idem, "An Early English Strophic Cantata (Porter's *Farewell*)," *Acta musicologica*, 27 (1955), 138–40. Spink stresses the progressive Italianate elements in Porter's *Madrigales and Ayres.*

[25] Robert Thompson, "George Jeffreys and the *Stile Nuove* in English Sacred Music: A New Date for his Autograph Score, British Library Add. MS 10338," *Music & Letters*, 70 (1989), 318.

of Selected Church Musick (London, 1641): of the 21 composers represented in the publication, nine were born before 1550 and none was born after 1600. Although Barnard purposely excluded works by living composers, even so, the conservative nature of the Anglican liturgical repertoire is revealed.

Music Printing and Publishing

Music printing and publishing came late to England. Although liturgical books with plainsong and metrical psalms had appeared in print, virtually no other music was printed in England until the 1570s. Even when music printing became established in England, the favoured method for the reproduction and dissemination of certain repertories (instrumental and church music in particular) remained manuscript. In this respect England lagged behind the Continent. The reason for the English reluctance to embrace a print culture is difficult to assess: it may have been partly due to the monopoly granted by Queen Elizabeth in 1575 to Thomas Tallis and William Byrd (Tallis died in 1585, and his patent was assigned to Thomas East in 1588) for the printing of "songe or songes in partes, either in English, Latin, Frenche, Italian, or other tongues that may serve for musicke either in Church or chamber, or otherwise to be either plaid or soonge"; the monopoly even extended to the printing of music paper.[26] It is possible Tallis and Byrd's lack of business acumen acted as a impediment to the development of English music printing and publishing. Things improved slightly when East took over the patent and published the first book of Nicholas Yonge's *Musica Transalpina* and Byrd's *Psalms, Sonets and Songs* (both 1588), but only in 1596, with the expiry of the Byrd–East monopoly, was there a real increase in music publication. Particularly noteworthy were Peter Short's publication of Thomas Morley's *Plaine and Easie Introduction to Practicall Musicke* and John Dowland's *First Book of Songes or Ayres* (both 1597). However, this success was short-lived, for in September 1598 Thomas Morley was granted the music monopoly and chose William Barley as his partner rather than East or Short. When James I came to the throne in 1603 he suspended all monopolies but in 1606 reintroduced the music patent under the assignee of William Barley. This was not good news for music printing and publishing: Barley was more interested in ballads than in music and produced, on average, only five titles a year between 1607 and 1612. Barley died in 1614, and between then and the first publications of John Playford in 1651 scarcely two dozen music books were printed. Whether by choice or not, the favoured method of music reproduction and dissemination in England remained manuscript. The chief repertoires to benefit from dissemination in print form were the madrigal and the lute ayre.

26 See Robert Steele, *The Earliest English Music Printing* (London, 1903; repr. 1965); D. W. Krummel, *English Music Printing, 1553–1700* (London, 1975); and Iain Fenlon and John Milsom, "'Ruled Paper Imprinted': Music Paper and Patents in Sixteenth-Century England," *Journal of the American Musicological Society*, 37 (1984), 139–63.

Secular Music: Madrigals, Songs and Ayres

At the beginning of the seventeenth century the English madrigal was at the height of its popularity. Following the success of Nicholas Yonge's *Musica Transalpina* (two parts: London, 1588 and 1597) and Thomas Watson's *Italian Madrigalls Englished* (London, 1590), and the promotion of the English madrigal by Thomas Morley (1557/8–1602), nearly all English composers (except Byrd) had become fascinated with the genre. In the first two decades of the seventeenth century composers such as Thomas Weelkes, John Wilbye (1574–1638), and Michael East (*c.*1580–1648) continued the Elizabethan tradition and produced pieces ranging from the charmingly light canzonetta-type to the serious madrigal.[27] A striking example of the latter is Wilbye's six-voice *Draw on sweet night*, published in *The Second Set of Madrigales* (London, 1609). This expressive and intensely melancholy madrigal represents the "English madrigal school" at its best. Ultimately, however, the "school" was short-lived (the last madrigal books were produced in the 1620s), and it has to be admitted that the early-twentieth-century nationalistic promotion of the genre was rather overenthusiastic. It is important to realize that, alongside the madrigal, England maintained its native tradition of song. Byrd and Gibbons, in particular, composed consort songs for solo voice or voices and viol consort accompaniment. The title of Gibbons's 1612 publication, *The First Set of Madrigals and Mottets of 5. Partes: Apt for Viols and Voyces*, reveals the typical performance possibilities of such music: *a cappella*, or performance by a consort of viols or by a mixture of voices and viols were all equally possible. The title also reveals the ambiguities of genre terminology: the "anthems" are actually devotional pieces, and the best-known "madrigal" in the collection, *The silver swanne*, is really a consort song that works at least as well performed by a solo singer accompanied by four viols as it does performed by five voices.

In the first decade of the seventeenth century the madrigal and the consort song gained a competitor in the form of the lute ayre, a vogue that began in 1597 when John Dowland published his *First Book of Songes or Ayres* (London, 1597). The collection proved so successful that it was reprinted at least four times between 1600 and 1613. Dowland went on to publish three more collections of lute ayres, and soon other composers followed suit, notably Thomas Campion (1567–1620). These songbooks were published in a large folio size and usually in "tablebook" format: as well as the parts for the solo voice and lute (the latter in tablature), optional parts for bass viol and other voice parts (alto, tenor, and bass) were printed each facing in different directions, so that performers seated around a table could use a single copy with ease. Again we see the flexibility in performance options that so characterize the time. If viols were to play the optional vocal parts, then the relationship with the consort song also becomes apparent; conversely, it should be noted that consort songs were also sometimes arranged for voice and lute. The words in these lute ayres were set simply and effectively while leaving any contra-

[27] See Joseph Kerman, *The Elizabethan Madrigal: A Comparative Study* (New York, 1962).

puntal ingenuity to the lute accompaniment. Gradually, however, the accompaniments show a tendency towards simplification with more chordal writing. Thus there is a gradual move towards the "continuo song," where only the melody and the bass were notated and the harmony was filled out by the lutenist or theorbo player.

The songs of Henry Lawes perhaps best represent this genre. Over 430 songs by Lawes survive; many were the product of court circles in the 1630s. He set over 40 poems by Carew and at least 14 by Herrick, as well as poems by Suckling, Waller, Milton, Lovelace, and Cartwright. The musical style that Lawes adopted in his songs—often freely declamatory, sometimes even approaching recitative—was ideally suited for an effective and direct projection of the text.[28] The close relationship between Lawes and the Caroline court poets is reflected in the title pages of the printed songbooks and poetry collections, and, in the words of David Greer, "in this courtly milieu . . . it is possible to discern something of that rapport between writer and musician that had earlier been a feature of French and Italian cultural life."[29]

The New Style

If we follow the traditional musico-historical method and look for Italianate "progressive" elements, then the "new style" was relatively late in being assimilated in England. Nicholas Lanier is generally credited with the introduction of true *stile recitativo* to England following visits to Italy between 1625 and 1628 (primarily to negotiate the purchase of paintings for Charles I from the Gonzaga collection at Mantua). Lanier's *Hero and Leander* includes true English recitative and—in traditional historiographical terms—must be considered as "progressive." *Hero and Leander* may or may not be the first example of English recitative,[30] but we should be aware that Italian monodies had been available in England from about 1610 onwards through publications such as Robert Dowland's *Musicall Banquet* (London, 1610) and Angelo Notari's *Prime musiche nuove* (London, *c.*1613).[31] Although the precise relationship between Italian monody and the English declamatory style is difficult to assess, owing to the different characteristics of the Italian and English languages, monody must have provided the underlying principles for the development of an English recitative.[32]

[28] For full details, see Ian Spink, *Henry Lawes: Cavalier Songwriter* (Oxford, 2000), 23–50.

[29] David Greer, "Vocal Music, I: Up to 1660," in *The Blackwell History of Music in Britain*, III: *The Seventeenth Century*, ed. Ian Spink (Oxford, 1992), 169.

[30] See McD. Emslie, "Nicholas Lanier's Innovations in English Song," *Music & Letters*, 41 (1960), 13–27; Vincent Duckles, "English Song and the Challenge of Italian Monody," in *Words to Music*, ed. Vincent Duckles and Franklin B. Zimmerman (Los Angeles, 1967), 3–42; Peter Walls, *Music in the English Courtly Masque, 1604–1640* (Oxford, 1996), 86–103.

[31] See Ian Spink, "Angelo Notari and his *Prime Musiche Nuove*;" Wainwright, *Musical Patronage*, 162–65.

[32] For a full examination of this issue, see Peter Walls, "The Origins of English Recitative," *Proceedings of the Royal Musical Association*, 110 (1983/84), 25–40; Ian Spink, *English Song:*

In certain court-related circles the interest in Italian music was extensive, particularly in the 1630s: the published catalogues of the London bookseller Robert Martin indicate that the most up-to-date Venetian music was easily obtainable in London.[33] One of Robert Martin's main customers was Sir Christopher Hatton III—later 1st Baron Hatton—who was to become Charles I's Comptroller of the Household during the Civil-War years when the Court was based in Oxford (1643–46). Hatton collected a large library of Italian music (the bulk of which survives today in Christ Church, Oxford), from which his musicians made manuscript copies, probably for performance at the Oxford Court.[34] The most important musician in Hatton's employ was the organist and composer George Jeffreys (*c.*1610–1685). It was undoubtedly Jeffreys's exposure to the Italian music in the Hatton collection—particularly the small-scale *concertato* motets written by contemporaries of Monteverdi such as Alessandro Grandi (1586–1630)—that led to Jeffreys's most successful compositions; his Latin motets (many written before 1646) show a complete assimilation of the Italian *seconda pratica* style.[35] The political situation (Civil War and Commonwealth) and the circumstances in which Jeffreys worked (as steward to the impecunious Hatton family) assured that his music was not widely disseminated and that he had little influence on either his contemporaries or on the succeeding generation of English composers.

Music for the Stage

The challenge to anyone making an assessment of English stage music in the first half of the seventeenth century is to avoid writing anachronistically and from an Italian opera-centered perspective. A traditional historiographical construction would note that the development of opera in Florence, Mantua, Rome, and Venice in the first half of the seventeenth century had far-reaching effects in the rest of Europe and suggest that it improved beyond measure any indigenous stage traditions. The fact that England did not fully embrace all-sung Italianate opera until the eighteenth century was something of an embarrassment to many music historians who judged English dramatic music purely by continental stand-

Dowland to Purcell (London, 1974; rev. 1984), chap. 2: "The New Men and the New Music," 38–71; Walls, *Music in the English Courtly Masque*, 86–103.

33 See Donald W. Krummel, "Venetian Baroque Music in a London Bookshop," in *Music and Bibliography: Essays in Honor of Alec Hyatt King*, ed. Oliver Neighbour (London, 1980), 1–27.

34 For full details, see Wainwright, *Musical Patronage*, *passim*. For the suggestion that Italian music from the Hatton collection was performed at the Roman Catholic services of Queen Henrietta Maria, see idem, "Images of Virtue and War: Music in Civil War Oxford," in *William Lawes (1602–1645): Essays on His Life, Times and Work*, ed. Andrew Ashbee (Aldershot and Brookfield, VT, 1998), 121–42.

35 For full details concerning Jeffreys, see Peter Aston, "George Jeffreys," *Musical Times*, 110 (1969), 772–76; idem, "Tradition and Experiment in the Devotional Music of George Jeffreys," *Proceedings of the Royal Musical Association*, 99 (1972/73), 105–15; Thompson, "George Jeffreys and the *Stile Nuove*," 317–41.

ards.[36] However, English stage music has to be considered on its own merits and without any sense of apology for the fact that England did not develop all-sung opera during the seventeenth century.

The English stage tradition was one of spoken drama in which music played a subsidiary role. Theaters employed musicians to provide interval music, dance music, sound effects, and accompaniments for songs. In Elizabethan times these songs had been popular tunes (as in Ophelia's mad scene in Shakespeare's *Hamlet*), but in the early years of the seventeenth century the King's Men, Shakespeare's company, started to commission songs specifically for their productions. Robert Johnson (*c.*1583–1633) was the most talented composer to provide songs for the Jacobean and Caroline theater. The musical heritage of his songs is that of the choirboy theatres of the Elizabethan period. Court composers had developed the consort song (for voice and four viols) for performance by choirboys in productions that ranged from morality plays to histories and imitations of classical dramas. A number of the choirboy consort songs survive in arrangements for lute accompaniment, and in the seventeenth century we find the accompaniment reduced to a bass line alone (for performance by lute with "realized" harmony or by bass viol alone). Johnson's songs for the "adult" theatres are notable for their use of a more declamatory style. They appear in manuscript sources with an unfigured bass for theorbo (rather than the tablature of the lute ayre) and, as such, may have been influenced by Italian monody (see above).

The other English "stage" tradition is the court masque, which gained a new lease of life at the beginning of James I's reign owing to his wife Anne of Denmark's enthusiasm for the genre and because of the talent of the architect Inigo Jones and the playwright Ben Jonson, who collaborated on a number of productions. Both James I and Charles I were prepared to spend considerable amounts of money on these large-scale entertainments in order to present a royal image of affluence and sophistication to court visitors such as foreign ambassadors. The productions were based on allegorical or mythological themes, and, although essentially vehicles for aristocratic dancing, the masques also contained speech, vocal music, and elaborate sets. The musical element of these masques has, until recently, been undervalued. This is partly because the surviving music for the Jacobean and Caroline masques is scattered amongst manuscripts that were often copied long after the original production, and the songs, choruses, and dances often survive in a fragmentary or rearranged state for domestic use.[37] The dance element of the Stuart masques was heavily influenced by French dance, and the style of the songs, by the likes of Lanier, Ferrabosco II, and Johnson, has been noted in the previous sections. Perhaps the most elaborate masque of the period was James Shirley's *Triumph of Peace*, which was performed at the Banqueting Hall at Whitehall under the auspices of the Inns of Court on 3 February 1634 at a cost of £21,000. Uniquely, papers relating to the production have survived intact. They reveal that three types of music—songs and dances and "loud music" mostly by William Lawes—were

[36] See, e.g., E. J. Dent, *Foundations of English Opera* (Cambridge, 1928), 1–42, 230–34.

[37] See in particular Walls, *Music in the English Courtly Masque.*

performed by three separate ensembles and that the musicians numbered over 40 in total.[38] It is ironic that it was from the Banqueting Hall in Whitehall—the place where the court masques were usually performed and where the royal image was fashioned—that Charles I emerged to mount the scaffold in January 1649.

THE word "conservative" has been used a number of times in the course of this essay. Although some court-related circles were absolutely up to date and received "new style" Italian music hot off the presses, English musical culture was not generally—in traditional historiographical terms—"progressive." The danger when using such expressions is that there is an allied implication that high quality can only be associated with the "progressive." This is not the case. The English viol consort repertoire, for example, may be "old-fashioned" in its systematic use of a contrapuntal idiom, but the quality of much of the music is undeniable. Indeed, if early-seventeenth-century English music is judged within its own historical context and in terms of its own indigenous traditions, then the achievement is truly remarkable. English composers may have been slow to respond to the new "Baroque" styles, but, as research has progressed on the music manuscripts associated with the Jacobean and Caroline courts, more and more we have come to realize that the courts' adventurous and sophisticated artistic tastes were of great significance. The monarch was surrounded by the best musicians of the age and was able to create an active and progressive musical culture at court, and it was to the court that the country looked for the latest musical fashions. There is little doubt that, had it not been for the breakdown of the court system in the lead up to the Civil War, new compositional styles would have been disseminated more widely, and English music would have "developed" apace. In the event, the fulfillment of the Stuart courts' musical promise had to wait until the Restoration, but this does not negate the achievements of English composers of the period 1603–42.

[38] For details, see Murray Lefkowitz, "The Longleat Papers of Bulstrode Whitelocke: New Light on Shirley's *Triumph of Peace*," *Journal of the American Musicological Society*, 18 (1965), 42–60; Andrew J. Sabol, "New Documents on Shirley's Masque *The Triumph of Peace*," *Music & Letters*, 47 (1966), 10–26; Kevin Sharpe, *Criticism and Compliment: The Politics of Literature in the England of Charles I* (Cambridge, 1987), chap. 5: "The Caroline Court Masque," 179–264.

26

INSTRUMENTAL MUSIC

Victor Coelho
Keith Polk

INSTRUMENTAL music from the beginning of the sixteenth century to roughly 1640 bristled with a new creative energy. In the previous century, many types of musicians—from lutenists and fiddlers to wind and percussion players—had found an increasingly enthusiastic market for their services, thus laying a secure foundation for the subsequent growth of instrumental styles. Yet, the outbursts shortly after 1500 in all branches of activity, and in all regions of Europe, remain astonishing in their scope. Almost all courtly ceremonies and private social rituals called for the participation of instrumentalists, from solo players in private settings to large mixed ensembles playing for state banquets, wedding ceremonies, theatrical productions, and even church services. The widespread circulation of instrumental music was facilitated by the advent of music printing, which created a new class of amateur players whose appetite for the latest musical tastes resulted in an entire repertory of instrumental transcriptions, arrangements, and imitations of the popular vocal music of the day. By the mid sixteenth century, instrumental styles were also often highly sophisticated artistic creations, with complex polyphonic repertories revealing a deep knowledge of both learned written styles and unwritten improvisatory practices.

It is not an overstatement to say that Renaissance European centers everywhere during this period teemed with instrumentalists, many of them highly skilled and thoroughly integrated into the mainstream of the musical culture. In fact, in many cities of even moderate size—Leuven in the Low Countries, Nördlingen in Germany, Lille in France—civic ensembles provided for citizens the primary medium for their hearing of sophisticated, up-to-date polyphony, both improvised and by leading composers. Similarly, widespread knowledge of the sacred vocal repertory of Josquin des Prez, Jean Mouton, and others, was spread largely through lutenists' and keyboardists' arrangements of these pieces, which allowed this music to surmount the walls of the chapel and enter into secular domestic settings and popular print culture. And popular chansons and madrigals by Crecquillon, Sermisy, Arcadelt, and Rore provided instrumentalists with an enormous repertory of "standards," which they arranged, varied, and marketed through a profitable publishing industry. In short, whether it is Siena, Florence, Augsburg, or Lyons, instrumental music was fully embedded in all of the most visible of Renaissance activities, social and political, and formed a vital element in the artistic landscape, fully contributing to all of the major developments and trends in Renaissance music.

An understanding of the contributions of instrumentalists is essential in any accurate assessment of the culture of the Renaissance. The following discussion, then, proposes an ordered discussion of a musical tradition of immense breadth, ranging from improvised to written styles, functional music (like signaling and dance music) to "art" styles (like the fantasia and toccata), and an itinerary that takes us from small German market towns to the major urban centers of royal patronage and the publishing trade.

Let us begin with some over-arching themes. A central concept (valid despite some overgeneralization), according to the late Howard Brown, is the gradual "emancipation of instrumental from vocal music" that took place at the beginning of the sixteenth century.[1] This can be seen not only with the emergence of new instrumental forms and idioms that had no basis in vocal music, as in the early ricercar, toccata, and dance variation, but also with the *types* of sources, which were increasingly written or published for exclusive use by instrumentalists. Another theme—this something of a paradox and not so well recognized in the scholarly literature—is the close relationship that existed between instrumental and vocal forces.[2] That is, in our attempts to establish the ways in which "emancipation" may have worked to separate instrumental from vocal, we should not lose sight of the fact that some of the finest "vocal" pieces of this era, like Giovanni Gabrieli's 14-voice *In ecclesiis* (1615), the final *ballo* of the famous 1589 Florentine *intermedi*, or even the first great "aria" in operatic history, Monteverdi's "Possente spirto" (*L'Orfeo*, 1607), are those that combined and contrasted vocal and instrumental forces.

In a somewhat different vein, a third development concerns the relationship between the composer and the player. In 1500, professional instrumentalists were known primarily as extempore musicians, their creations consisting usually of improvisations even in elaborately contrapuntal performances; very few players of this time, in fact, were ever known to engage in written instrumental composition. By 1600, on the other hand, the balance had shifted dramatically. The Gabrielis, Monteverdi, Schütz, Scheidt, Tallis, Dowland, Morley, Byrd, and Gibbons—all vocal composers of the first order— were all formally trained instrumentalists. This shift in the status of the player was a gradual process, and the improvisatory

1 Howard Mayer Brown, *Music in the Renaissance* (Englewood Cliffs, NJ, 1976), 257.

2 For a discussion of fundamental connections between instrumentalists and vocal music, see Howard Mayer Brown, "The Instrumentalist's Repertory in the Sixteenth Century," in *Le Concert des voix et des instruments à la Renaissance*, ed. Jean-Michel Vaccaro (Paris, 1995), 21–32. An excellent recent study that extends Brown's main thesis concerning the centrality of the lute in 16th-century music is John Griffiths, "The Lute and the Polyphonist," *Studi musicali*, 31 (2002), 89–102.

traditions continued as a kind of subsurface current throughout the sixteenth century. We will begin with a survey of the instruments of the era, which provides a crucial underpinning to understanding developments within the various repertories. This will be followed by a treatment of the musicians themselves, both professional and amateur, with a focus on the relationship between patronage and style, and the influence of printing. The final section will deal with the repertories of instrumental music, describing first the various genres, followed by a discussion of the contributions of the various regions of Europe.

Renaissance Instruments

Treatises and manuals

One measurement of the new status of instrumental music (and its players) after 1500 is the regular appearance of treatises ranging from eminently practical "how to" information about performance to comprehensive encyclopedic descriptions and illustrations of instrumental families. Between these two poles lies an indispensable corpus of books, prefaces, manuals, and treatises that are still consulted today by early-music practitioners for information about instruments and instrumental performance. Because of the newer techniques that were required for many instruments after the sixteenth century, printed books, especially those for plucked-string instruments, often contained prefaces explaining the rudiments of notation and technique.[3] All of the Petrucci lute books, for example (1507, 1508, 1520), contain rules "for those who do not know how to sing [i.e. read notation]," testifying to the new class of amateur musicians to whom instrumental prints were now marketed. More detailed information and instructions of greater breadth are found in vihuela books, which addressed such issues as tempo and style. Many of these rudimentary prefaces disappear from prints after around 1550, since reading tablature was taken for granted. By the beginning of the seventeenth century, it was necessary once again to explain recent developments in instrumental performance, which were equal in scope to the changes occurring in vocal music of the same period. The prefaces to publications by Frescobaldi (1611), Piccinini (1623), and Kapsberger (1626, 1640) all describe (but never prescribe) the use of more specific techniques—arpeggiation, ornamentation, slurring—within the context of a new stylistic aesthetic, illustrating the increasing disconnection between notational conventions and performance practice.[4]

[3] For an excellent survey of prefaces to Italian lute books, see Dinko Fabris, "Lute Tablature Instructions in Italy: A Survey of the *Regole* from 1507 to 1759," in *Performance on Lute, Guitar, and Vihuela: Historical Practice and Modern Interpretation*, ed. Victor Coelho (Cambridge, 1997), 16–46.

[4] A clear discussion of 17th-century Italian keyboard practice within the context of Frescobaldi's prefaces is in Frederick Hammond, *Girolamo Frescobaldi* (Cambridge, MA, 1983), 222–52; on the performance practice of Italian lute music of the same period, see Victor Coelho, "Authority, Autonomy, and Interpretation in Seventeenth-Century Italian Lute Music," in *Performance on Lute, Guitar, and Vihuela*, 108–41.

More encyclopedic knowledge of instruments, tunings, and even playing techniques are contained in several important treatises. Sebastian Virdung's copiously illustrated and influential *Musica getutscht* (1511) is the first printed treatise offering a general discussion of instruments and, significantly, is written in an accessible vernacular. Virdung covers the lute, clavichord, and recorder in particular detail, explaining tunings, stringing, and notation, as well as features of performance practice. Subsequently, Martin Agricola's *Musica instrumentalis deudsch* (1529/45) is one of many treatises that were indebted to Virdung. Michael Praetorius produced the most comprehensive and authoritative of these efforts with *De organographia* (vol. II of his *Syntagma musicum*, Wolfenbüttel, 1618). Praetorius, a fine organist and composer, brought exceptional range to his theoretical writings, and *De organographia* presents a revealing panorama of the instrumental colors available to late-Renaissance performers.[5]

After about 1520 a brisk market developed for more detailed instruction, and musicians, printers, and publishers rushed to satisfy these new demands. Among the more prominent volumes were those on the playing of *passaggi* on recorder (Ganassi, 1535) and on viol (Ganassi, 1542; Diego Ortiz, 1553), while Bermudo (1555), Sancta María (1565), and Cabezón (1578) provided information especially useful to vihuela and keyboard players.[6]

These are just a few among the outpouring of volumes representing Renaissance market forces at work. Note that the focus was on amateurs; no such wide demand (i.e. no wealthy clientele) existed for instruction books on, for example, cornetto, shawm, or trombone, all instruments exclusively for the professional. Praetorius, however, did cover all manner of instruments in his discussion, both those for amateurs and those for professionals; this had also been true of his predecessors.

[5] For these three treatises, see Sebastian Virdung, *Musica getutscht: A Treatise on Musical Instruments (1511)*, trans. and ed. Beth Bullard (Cambridge, 1993); Martin Agricola, *Musica instrumentalis deudsch: A Treatise on Musical Instruments (1529 and 1545)*, trans. and ed. William E. Hettrick (Cambridge, 1994); Michael Praetorius, *Syntagma musicum*, II: *De organographia*, parts I, II, trans. and ed. David Z. Crookes (Oxford and New York, 1986).

[6] For these treatises, see Agostino Agazzari, *Del sonare sopra il basso* (Siena, 1607; facs. Milan, 1969), trans. Oliver Strunk, *Source Readings in Music History*, 1st edn (New York, 1950), 424 ff.; Juan Bermudo, *Declaración de instrumentos musicales* (Ossuna, 1555; facs., ed. Macario S. Kastner, Kassel, 1957); and for a new translation of Bermudo's chapters on the vihuela, see Dawn Astrid Espinosa (trans.), "Juan Bermudo: 'On Playing the Vihuela'," *Journal of the Lute Society of America*, 28–29 (1995–96); Antonio de Cabezón, *Obras de musica para tecla arpa y vihuela*, compiled by Hernando de Cabezón (Madrid, 1578), ed. Felipe Pedrell and Higinio Anglés (Barcelona, 1966), ed. Claudio Astronio (Bologna, 2001); Girolamo Diruta, *Il Transilvano* (1593, 1604; facs., ed. Edward Soehnlen and Murray Bradshaw, Buren, 1983), also ed. as *The Transylvanian = Il Transilvano*, trans. and ed. Murray Bradshaw and Edward Soehlen (Henryville, PA, 1984); Sylvestro di Ganassi, *Opera intitulata Fontegara* (Venice, 1535), ed. Christine Vossart and Jean-Philippe Navarre (Spirmont, Belgium, 2002); idem, *Regola rubertina* (Venice, 1542), parts I, II, ed. Hildemarie Peter (Berlin, 1972); Diego Ortiz, *Trattado de glosas sobre clausulas y otros generos de puntos en la musica de violones* (Rome, 1553; facs. Florence, 1984); new edn in four languages of the original Spanish and Italian edns, ed. Annette Oterstedt, Eng. and Germ. trans. Hans Reiners (Kassel, 2003); Tomás de Sancta María, *Libro llamado Arte de tañer fantasia* (Valladolid, 1565), trans. and ed. Almonte Howell jr and Warren Hultberg (Pittsburgh, 1991).

Moreover, Agazzari in 1607 provided an extensive commentary on how instruments were to be combined in practice, and his views were directed particularly to the performances of professionals.

Keyboard

The organ remained the central instrument for the professional keyboard player throughout the sixteenth and early seventeenth centuries. The essential features of the "modern" instrument, including multiple manuals, pedals, and separable stops, had developed already by the early sixteenth century, replacing the portative organ (played with one hand while the other pumped the bellows), which had fallen out of regular use. The one-manual positive organ, a portable instrument, continued to be used in church and chamber performances. Various types of stringed keyboard instruments, such as harpsichords, virginals, and clavichords, increased in popularity, particularly in Italy and England, especially as instruments for accomplished amateurs. Around forty harpsichords, almost all Italian, survive from before 1600 (though none from before 1500), revealing brass- or iron-strung instruments with a $1 \times 8' + 1 \times 4'$ disposition and a range from *C* or *E* to f'''', as well as some instruments, after 1570, with $2 \times 8'$ stops. The specific call for such instruments after 1550, particularly in association with the doubling of bass parts, verifies the growing awareness of the importance of "foundation voices" in instrumental textures.[7] By 1600, the dominance of Venetian keyboard makers had been challenged by the important Ruckers dynasty of harpsichord and virginal makers from Antwerp, whose work featured a four-octave range (usually C–c''') and included two-manual models, often with elaborate case decorations. Their instruments were much in demand all over Europe, and some were even shipped to the New World.

Plucked strings

For most of the sixteenth century, the lute challenged the primacy of the organ at the professional level, with lutenists occupying prestigious positions at both the papal and princely courts. In addition, the lute was clearly the preferred instrument for amateurs, many of whom, as we can tell from personal manuscript sources, were very skilled players, if stylistically conservative. Virtually all of the extant sources of lute music from this period testify to the abilities and tastes of amateurs. Surviving instruments, treatises, and paintings have been helpful in showing the various sizes of lutes that were built and played before 1500. While an increasing standardization is clearly evident in the sixteenth century, the lute continued to vary in size in accordance with the demands of musical composition. In the fifteenth century, the instrument had five courses and was played with a plectrum, which did not preclude the playing of simple polyphonic textures. Shortly before 1500, a fundamental change in lute technique resulted from abandoning the plectrum in favor

[7] Howard Mayer Brown, *Sixteenth-Century Instrumentation: The Music of the Florentine Intermedii*, MSD 30 (American Institute of Musicology, 1973), 80.

of the fingers, which allowed lutenists to arrange more complex vocal works for their instrument, as well as stimulating a change in how lutes were built.[8]

The most common type of lute for both solo playing and accompaniment during the first half of the sixteenth century was a six-course instrument in which all but the highest string (the *chanterelle*) were doubled at the unison or octave. The most common tuning was *G–c–f–a–d′–g′* (or *A–d–g–b–e′–a′*), though larger bass lutes pitched a fourth lower as well as high-pitched soprano lutes were also used, particularly in works for lute ensemble. By the end of the century seventh and eighth courses were being called for in solo music (tuned to *F* and *D*), and by the beginning of the seventeenth century in France and the Low Countries ten-course instruments were common.[9] Aside from their extensive use as solo instruments, lutes were judged most felicitous for accompanying voices, and this led to the development of larger lutes with many extra bass strings, such as the 14-course archlute, tuned like a six-course lute but with eight diatonically-tuned bass strings attached to a long neck extension, and the theorbo (synonymous with *chitarrone*), a 14- to 18-course instrument with a somewhat different tuning whose extraordinary projection and increased lower range made it the ideal instrument for accompanying monody.[10]

Mention must be made of the vihuela, which for all practical purposes can be described as the lute of Spain. In what appears to be an expression of cultural sovereignty, the lute virtually disappears following the expulsion of the Arabs and Jews from Spain in 1492, to be replaced by the vihuela, a guitar-shaped instrument of six (occasionally seven) courses that was tuned exactly like a lute.[11] The vihuela can be documented in Spain from the last quarter of the fifteenth century into the seventeenth century, with its greatest period of use occurring between 1536 and 1576, when seven vihuela tablatures were published containing solo music and songs of extremely high quality. It was also used in early-sixteenth-century Italy, particularly in Spanish-dominated Naples, and some early lute publications specify lute or *viola* (Francesco da Milano, 1536). And in one of the most memorable passages about music in Castiglione's *Cortegiano* (*c.*1511), the practice of "singing poetry to the viola [vihuela]" is the response to the question of what is the "best music of all"?

The guitar also has a rich history during this period, especially in France, Italy, and Spain. The "Renaissance" guitar is a small four-course instrument (tuned like the highest four strings of the modern guitar, but pitched usually a fourth higher).

[8] For an accessible general history of the lute through the Renaissance, see Douglas Alton Smith, *A History of the Lute from Antiquity to the Renaissance* (Lexington, VA, 2002).

[9] For a clear discussion of lutes in the Renaissance, see Paul O'Dette, "Plucked Instruments," in *A Performer's Guide to Renaissance Music*, ed. Jeffery Kite-Powell (New York, 1994), 139–53.

[10] For a discussion of the theorbo as a continuo instrument, see Kevin Mason, *The Chitarrone and its Repertoire in Seventeenth-Century Italy* (Aberystwyth, 1989).

[11] Two excellent studies of vihuela performance and history are by John Griffiths, "The Vihuela: Performance Practice, Style, and Context," in *Performance on Lute, Guitar, and Vihuela*, 158–79; idem, "At Court and at Home with the *Vihuela da Mano*," *Journal of the Lute Society of America*, 22 (1989), 1–27.

The earliest printed works are the exquisite pieces included in Mudarra's vihuela tablature from 1546, and by the mid sixteenth century a thriving print culture of guitar music was sustained in France through the efforts of enterprising publishers who marketed this music to a large amateur clientele. As with the lute, the guitar underwent a significant "upgrade" in the late sixteenth century. By 1600, it had grown significantly in size and added another string, a development that went hand in hand with the introduction of new strumming techniques that were soon combined with the plucking techniques inherited from its Renaissance counterpart. Its ease of playing and the development of an immensely practical tablature system (*alfabeto*) that was unique to the guitar, led to a virtual frenzy for the instrument in seventeenth-century Italy, much to the chagrin of conservatively-minded purists who lamented the parallel decline of the lute at the hands of this loud, appealing, and accessible new instrument. Many early Florentine sources of monody are intended for guitar accompaniment, testifying to the instrument's visible presence in the newest styles of the day.[12]

Clearly, fascination with novelty and experimentation characterized the age, and other plucked stringed instruments emerged from time to time. Some made only an ephemeral appearance, others left a more lasting mark. The cittern, a melody instrument more flat-backed than the lute and played with a plectrum, was described by prominent theorists and attracted a sizeable repertory. The popularity of the cittern was such that the instrument in turn spawned several larger relatives, similar in basic shape and playing technique, such as the ceterone and the bandora. Retaining the pear-shaped body of the lute, but also played with a plectrum was the mandora. Because they were played with a plectrum, both the mandora and the cittern were well suited to broken consorts and for accompanying dancing when a more penetrating sound would have been appropriate.

Viols and violins

No changes in instrumental music were more marked than those affecting bowed-string instruments. Instruments popular in the fifteenth century, the rebec and the fiddle, were pushed aside by newcomers such as viols and violins. Viols were well established on the scene by 1520, having been introduced into Italy from Spain in the course of the late fifteenth century. This was a family of instruments from soprano through bass, all generally bowed in downward position (the larger sizes between the legs, *da gamba*), with sloping shoulders and a fretted fingerboard, and usually with six strings. The tuning pattern was similar to that of the lute; the bass, for example, could be tuned as *G–c–f–a–d′–g′* (though the absolute pitch was not fixed). The instruments were of delicate construction and produced a refined

[12] For a general history of the guitar during this period, see James Tyler and Paul Sparks, *The Guitar and its Music: From the Renaissance to the Classical Era* (Oxford, 2002); much information on primary sources of the 17th-century guitar has been compiled in Gary R. Boye, "The Baroque Guitar: Printed Music from 1606–1737" (http://www.library.appstate.edu/music/guitar/home.html; accessed 16 Feb 2006).

sound that was ideal for intimate chambers. They were highly favored by amateurs, but were also played by professionals.[13]

The violin was introduced, evidently as a family of instruments, early in the sixteenth century and was incorporated into ensembles sometime between about 1520 and 1550. It was a sturdier instrument, tuned in fifths, and produced a more penetrating timbre well suited to more open spaces, such as dance halls. From the initial stages the violin was an instrument for professionals (it was not considered suitable for those of "gentle birth") and was often taken up as an optional doubling by players in wind bands. During most of the second half of the sixteenth century it operated on more or less equal footing with other soprano instruments, particularly the cornetto and shawm, but gradually achieved prominence. By early in the seventeenth century the violin band was supreme, especially in Italy, and formed the basis for the new concept of a larger, relatively fixed ensemble, the orchestra.[14] This was not a rapid change, however, and wind instruments remained central to professional music making for much longer than has been recognized.

Wind instruments

By 1520 the wind band of shawms and trombone had for many years been the core ensemble for courtly and civic ceremonial occasions. The bands then were often five- or six-part, with two trombones and three or four shawms of varied sizes. During the first half of the sixteenth century the bands expanded both in size, but more particularly in the range of optional instruments that the players could pick up to achieve contrasts of timbre. The double-reed shawm itself had been built in two basic sizes earlier (discant and tenor, with the tenor usually called the bombard). This became a full family of instruments, covering all registers. The bass instrument, however, was too long and bulky for convenient use, and was soon replaced by an instrument with a doubled tube. Known by several names (*curtal* and *fagotto*, for example), instruments in this basic shape were the forerunners of the modern bassoon.[15] The trombone, too, was altered: the bell was made with less flare, which resulted in a more covered sound that matched agreeably with voices. The doubled slide became, finally, universal, and the trombone, too, was made in several sizes.[16]

The shawm-and-trombone framework provided the fundamental wind ensem-

[13] On the viol, see Ian Woodfield, *The Early History of the Viol* (Cambridge, 1984). Though popular with amateurs in England, Germany, and Italy, the French seem to have restricted the instrument to professionals; see Daniel Heartz, "Sources and Forms of the French Instrumental Dance in the Sixteenth Century" (PhD diss., Harvard University, 1957), 15–17.

[14] For a review of the history of the violin, see Peter Holman, *Four and Twenty Fiddlers: The Violin at the English Court, 1540–1690* (Oxford, 1993), 1–31.

[15] Characteristic of a developmental stage, several different approaches in terms of construction evolved in the early and mid 16th century. For a knowledgeable, coherent, and well illustrated discussion, see David Munrow, *Instruments of the Middle Ages and Renaissance* (London, 1976), 39–45.

[16] The smaller sizes were apparently very rare, and even the bass trombone was unusual. One use for the trombones was to double voices, with the soprano range usually covered by the cornetto.

ble throughout the sixteenth century, but a bewildering assortment of optional instruments was developed by the fertile imaginations of makers of that experimental age. Alas, with their reliance on improvisational practices, wind players seldom bothered to write down anything specific about what they were doing. One group of instruments was made with two or more tubes doubling on themselves, being very convenient to carry and play. Those played by taking the reed directly into the lips included the sordun, courtaut, and rackets; of these the bass racket seems to have found some consistent acceptance in practice.[17] In another group a double reed was "capped" inside a small cylinder, and the reed was activated by blowing through a small hole in the top of the instrument. The most common and effective of these were the crumhorns, cylindrical-bore instruments that produced a buzzing but engaging tone quality. These were made in complete families and apparently played most often as a consort. The capped instrument could also be made with an expanding bore, as in the *rauschpfeife* and the *schreierpfeife*, which could produce a much more penetrating sound. These instruments appear occasionally in sixteenth-century sources but seem to have found little general acceptance. Almost all of these optional instruments, even the crumhorns, appear to have gradually dropped out of use after the first decade or so of the seventeenth century.[18]

Of far greater viability was the cornetto, a hybrid instrument played with a small cup-shaped mouthpiece (as in brass instruments), but with finger holes (as with woodwind instruments). Few instruments suited the musical demands of the era from about 1500 to 1650 so aptly. The cornetto could match the dynamic range of the shawms and trombones in outdoor performances but also blend to lovely effect with the vocal choir. It was extremely agile in the hands of a skillful player, although it was difficult to master and was exclusively an instrument of the professional. The success of the instrument was so extraordinary that it replaced the shawm in some wind bands. Both Monteverdi and Schütz, for example, called for cornetts and trombones in their scoring, without any reference to shawms.[19]

Recorders and transverse flutes found a perhaps less spectacular but more long-term place. Both were played by amateurs and professionals. The recorder was well suited to sixteenth-century tastes, with its "deliciously mellow" sound (Munrow) and considerable agility. The recorder was most often played in consorts and was made in a great variety of sizes, which gave overlapping ensemble options. The very smallest instruments could be shrill and the largest cumbersome to play, but contemporary inventories consistently list twenty or more recorders, which suggests that players took advantage of all sizes. The transverse flute had an astonishing vogue, beginning around 1500, especially in France. Seldom mentioned or illustrated in the fifteenth century except as a kind of military-band instrument

[17] See Munrow, *Instruments*, 46; see also Jeffery Kite-Powell, "Crumhorn," in *A Performer's Guide to Renaissance Music*, 63–68.

[18] For the exceptional lingering of the crumhorn in French practice, see Munrow, *Instruments*, 49.

[19] Most such scorings, it should be added, were those that co-ordinated wind instruments with voices, contexts in which the cornetto would, of course, be more effective than the shawm.

(paired with the field drum), its popularity was such that an inventory of Henry VIII's instruments included 70 flutes, and a Stuttgart court inventory of 1589 listed 220 (compared with 48 recorders).[20] Flutes were made in only three principal sizes (alto, tenor, and bass), had a wider range than recorders, and were in certain respects more successful within ensembles.

Trumpet ensembles in the sixteenth century still maintained their primary role as symbols of stature. In northern Europe particularly the clangor of trumpets was equated with royalty, and everywhere the sound indicated high station.[21] Tradition continued to dictate that trumpeters formed a class of performers distinct from other instrumentalists, following a practice in place for more than a century. This convention was occasionally diluted, in that some courts and a few cities seem to have combined the functions of trumpeter with that of general instrumentalist, probably as a cost-saving measure (the court of Denmark was an example, as were the Dutch cities of Amsterdam and Haarlem). By the sixteenth century, as Peter Downey has shown, the specialized playing techniques of the various registers, most strikingly that of the highest *clarino* range, were well advanced. The repertories of trumpet bands were still rudimentary, however. The maturation of sophisticated musical structures in pieces for trumpet took place after the period under consideration here.[22]

The listings given here have been intended to highlight those instruments most central to musical practices between about 1520 and 1640. A considerable number of instruments have not been included. The harp, certainly an instrument of great beauty, was widely admired when it appeared in the hands of a gifted player, and it seems to have been more widely used than is easily appreciated. References to the harp are inconsistent in contemporary accounts, however, and it had no regular role, for example, in ensemble practices.[23] The bagpipe and pipe and tabor, too, claimed special audiences, but ones that fall outside the central concern here.[24]

[20] For a detailed discussion of the recorder and flute, see Herbert Myers, "Recorder," "Renaissance Flute," in *A Performer's Guide to Renaissance Music*, 41–62. Concerning the inventories, see Munrow, *Instruments*, 54.

[21] Some leading Italian cities such as Bologna, Florence, and Venice had long maintained trumpet ensembles. They were much rarer in the north (Ghent, which as with the Italian cities supported a trumpet ensemble distinct from its civic shawm ensemble, was one exception).

[22] Important steps had been taken by the early 17th century, and Fantini's treatise on trumpet playing was published in 1638. See Don Smithers, *The Music and History of the Baroque Trumpet before 1721* (Syracuse, NY, 1973), 75–86. When trumpeters picked up other instruments such as shawms and cornets, their repertories were of course not so restricted. See also Peter Downey, "The Trumpet and Its Role in Music of the Renaissance and Early Baroque" (PhD diss., Queen's University of Belfast, 1983).

[23] Anthony Newcomb, "Secular Polyphony in the 16th Century," *Performance Practice: Music before 1600*, ed. Howard Mayer Brown and Stanley Sadie (London and New York, 1989), 231, stresses the importance of the harp when it did appear, pointing out that some of the "most famous singers of the century . . . were harpists." The English court, it should also be noted, maintained a regular place for harpists; see Walter L. Woodfill, *Musicians in English Society from Elizabeth to Charles I* (Princeton, 1953), 296–306.

[24] For a more extensive discussion of instruments see the appropriate chapters in *A Per-*

Like and mixed ensembles

Finally, notions of ensemble practice responded with great elasticity to changing conditions. In one direction, fairly fixed concepts of like combinations had developed by about 1500, and consorts of flutes, recorders, and viols continued to be favored throughout the century. As a kind of culmination to this approach, the famous "twenty-four violins" of the seventeenth-century French court were an exclusively string band—as was the matching ensemble at the English court. In another direction, mixed consorts, too, including lutes, viols, recorders, harpsichords, and other such instruments, were commonly heard, also throughout the century. Moreover, although the medieval division of instruments into loud and soft categories had disintegrated to a great extent by 1520, players still tended for many decades to fall into the traditional patterns, but new options did evolve. The shawm band, still ubiquitous as the primary loud ensemble, broadened its performance doublings to include the cornetto and (especially for dance music) the violin.[25] Professional players of lute and keyboard instruments, too, seem to have followed career paths similar to the "soft" minstrels of the fifteenth century (they were more often soloists than was the case with wind players, for example).

By about 1570 newer concepts arrived, and as their vitality became increasingly irresistible older approaches began to fade. One of these new concepts, as observed once again by Howard Brown, lay with the stress placed on the division of labor between melodic voices and "foundation" voices. The soprano/bass duality, evidently as an improvisatory framework, was basic to dance music, clearly so by about 1570. In instrumental music, the arrival of the basso continuo practice about 1600 had been prepared by several decades of prior development in song accompaniments. Another was the emphasis on grand sonorities that combined vocal forces with wind, string, and keyboard instruments, as specified by Giovanni Gabrieli, Monteverdi, and Schütz. Yet another was the emergence after about 1610 of a new ensemble, centered on a string band with underpinning of continuo instruments, to which would be added *ad libitum* a variety of wind instruments.

Society, Patronage and Instrumental Musicians

Population throughout Europe increased substantially in the course of the sixteenth century, and the effect of this growth on music was clear and lasting; one specialist has estimated the rate as about a 25-percent growth from roughly 69 million to 89 million.[26] In leading cities such as Amsterdam, Antwerp, London,

former's Guide to Renaissance Music; Munrow, *Instruments*; Brown, *Sixteenth-Century Instrumentation.*

[25] In the 16th century players able to double on shawm and violin were rather common; by about 1600, however, the violin became increasingly a specialty. Players of shawms and violins were in any case almost invariably professionals. Note that with recorders, flutes, and viols, however, amateur and professional interest overlapped.

[26] Harry A. Miskimin, *The Economy of later Renaissance Europe, 1400-1600* (Cambridge,

and Paris, the effects were particularly dramatic, and increases were considerably higher. Population growth was tied to an increase in economic activity, which in turn was accompanied by striking examples of an increase in personal wealth. In critical regions, especially England, France, and Spain, growth was accompanied by centralization of political power with vastly increased resources available to monarchs. Such growth had an impact on music in two important ways. The first was that greater resources were available for the support of professional musicians. The second was, as we have already noted above, that many more wealthy amateurs actively participated in music-making.

Royal taste exercised a determining influence on the patronage of professional musicians, and the fact that heads of state controlled higher levels of discretionary income was quickly reflected in a larger personnel of resident instrumentalists. The growth pattern was already clear early in the sixteenth century, as the number of musicians supported by Maximilian I of Habsburg about 1515 was almost double that of those of the imperial court of some fifty years earlier. Similarly, Pope Leo X, François I, and Henry VIII engaged significantly larger instrumental forces than had been the case in the late fifteenth century, snaring in the process the services of the most prized virtuosos, including the lutenists Gian Maria Giudeo, Francesco da Milano, and Albert de Rippe and the keyboardist Marc'Antonio Cavazzoni.[27] The internal organizations of these new establishments were quite similar, which reflects the intense competition (and imitation) that characterized court life of the era. The wind bands remained the core units, but expanded to between six and eight. The players' basic assignments centered on shawms and trombones (still a successful medium for dance music), but performances on cornetts, crumhorns, recorders, and even string instruments were also routine. One or two keyboard specialists were available, along with two or three lutenists. A new group comprised the string players. Early in the century these were violists, but gradually violinists were added as well. Again, because the violinists were so often involved in improvised performances, the evolution around 1550 remains murky, but by 1600 the pattern is unmistakable as more musicians are labeled specifically as violinists. The establishment of the "twenty-four violins of the King," early in the reign of Louis XIII (who assumed the crown in 1610) capped this development, and when it had run its course the total number of court players was almost doubled.[27]

1977), 20–28. See also Jan A. van Houtte, *An Economic History of the Low Countries, 800–1800* (London, 1977), 123–35.

[27] Very few documents survive concerning the French court, especially under François I, as has been shown by Christelle Cazaux, *La Musique à la cour de François Ier* (Paris, 2002), and while the general outlines of support are reasonably clear, details are scanty. For the English court, however, documentation is extensive, and developments can be followed step by step. By 1612 there were twelve players engaged there as regular members of the string band (with at least five others who could also join forces). By 1631 the fixed membership was at least 14, with a clear distribution into five sections (Holman, *Four and Twenty Fiddlers*, 178–79, 234–35; see also Woodfill, *Musicians in English Society*, 303–4). In spite of poor documentation, it would appear that leadership emanated from the French court, especially given the enthusiastic participation by Louis XIII in dance performances, which were central to the performances of the court violinists. See Robert M. Isherwood, *Music in the Service of the King: France in the*

The smaller courts, while they could not command the resources of the monarchies, still managed to provide significant backing for instrumental music. The courts of Italy, especially Ferrara (Este), Florence (Medici), and Mantua (Gonzaga), were especially important in the development of a brilliant circle of lutenists and string players. Those in Germany (especially Munich and Dresden) made possible the kind of environment that produced the massed sonorities called for by Praetorius and Schütz. By the early seventeenth century the center of courtly patronage in Italy had moved to Rome, in the hands of wealthy families such as the Aldobrandini, Bentivoglio, and, in particular, the papal circle of Pope Urban VIII (r. 1624–44) and his nephews Francesco and Antonio Barberini, who were crucial in the patronage of the most influential keyboard composer of the early seventeenth century, Girolamo Frescobaldi, as well as the lutenists Piccinini and Kapsberger.

Of course, some of the most important patrons of instrumentalists were the city governments themselves, which subsidized stables of professional instrumentalists. Already strong in the fifteenth century, these groups tended to increase in size after 1500. In cities of modest population that had engaged three players around 1480, four became the norm by 1550. Larger cities, such as Antwerp, Augsburg, and Bologna enlarged to between six and eight players. Civic ensembles, like their counterparts at chapel and court, widened the range of instrumental doubling, which was reflected in the very names. The "city pipers" (*stadspijpers*) of Antwerp became the "city players" (*stadsspeellieden*), just as the "shawms and trombones" (*piffari* and *tromboni*) of Bologna assumed the more prestigious nomenclature of "musicians" (*musici*) of the city, in both cases by about 1550.[28]

The relationship between patronage and decisive changes in both vocal music and music for lutenists and organists has been recognized for some time. But the names of outstanding musicians associated with professional wind ensembles remind us that these groups, too, should not be overlooked even though their specific contributions are veiled and difficult to assess. Susato, an editor, composer, and the leading music publisher of his era in the Low Countries, began his career as a trombonist in the civic ensemble of Antwerp. Jean d'Estrée (who published several volumes of instrumental music in Paris at mid-century) was a shawmist in the court band of the French crown. The Hessen brothers (who also published dance music) were city musicians in Breslau, and even Hans Leo Hassler served as the leader of the city music of Augsburg. Members of courtly and civic wind ensembles (some of whom shifted their focus to cornetts and stringed instruments, but many of whom remained loyal to shawms and, especially, trombones) continued to interact in music making at the highest artistic level. Their improvisatory skills have blurred our historical perspective, but the contributions of professional ensemble

Seventeenth Century (Ithaca, NY, 1973), 88–113. Note that while the violin has been considered an Italian fashion, most of the players at both the French and English courts were locals.

[28] For Antwerp, see Godelieve Spiessens, "De Antwerpse stadsspeellieden, Deel I: 15e en 16e eeuw," *Noordgouw: Cultureel tijdschrift van de provincie Antwerpen*, 9 (1969), 25; for Bologna, see Osvaldo Gambassi, *Il Concerto Palatino della Signoria di Bologna* (Florence, 1989), 618–21.

players were key elements in the rapidly changing musical scene of the sixteenth and early seventeenth centuries.[29]

Enthusiastic amateurs with means, both at court and in cities, formed another crucial layer in the culture of instrumental music. They played music constantly in the sixteenth century, creating markets for teachers, for instruction books, and for manuscript and published collections of music. Amateurs undoubtedly followed the lead of professionals concerning the technical details of music making, but they played a forceful and often definitive role in matters relating to musical taste and repertory. In many ways it is due to them that a certain canon of "classics" was formed during the sixteenth and early seventeenth centuries. The many arrangements of vocal pieces for lute and vihuela (called intabulations) that were published after 1500 are good examples that reveal the public's taste for French chansons, especially those by Crecquillon, Sermisy, and Lassus, madrigals by Arcadelt (the closest phenomenon to "The Beatles" of the Renaissance, with a popularity spanning over a hundred years) and Rore, and masses and motets by Josquin, Morales, Gombert, and Palestrina. The latter represent a particularly interesting recontextualization of genres and purpose, in which sacred music, originally intended for liturgical service, is *secularized* by stripping it of its Latin text and liturgical function, and further both *domesticized*, through performing the work at home and truncating its form (lutenists and vihuelists, for example, intabulated only parts of a Credo or a Gloria), and *vernacularized*, through the addition of scales, ornaments, and other textures borrowed from instrumental idioms.

Growth and development have been emphasized, but darker forces were afoot as well. Plagues and famine had lurked throughout late medieval and early modern times, but their devastations tended to be relatively short-term. The religious wars of the late sixteenth and early seventeenth centuries were quite a different matter. The ravages of the Thirty Years' War, which began in Germany in 1618, so decimated the staff of court musicians that Schütz could no longer count on an ample number of players—in his *Sacrae symphoniae* he drastically reduced his scoring as a result, as Stravinsky would do three centuries later in the face of a drastic shortage of musicians during the First World War. The longer conflict waged by the Spanish crown in Flanders was even more cataclysmic. Some cities reduced their expenditures for music, and cities such as Leuven, Mechlin, and Dendermonde eliminated musical subsidies entirely. "It is inappropriate at the present time to support the civic ensemble," reads the 1578 account book from Mons, "given that the money is needed for the fortifications of the city."[30] Such defenses proved crucial as this war ground on for decades. The loss of life was appalling, and musicians, too, were recorded among those cut down. For a generation, musical life was blotted out, with even more long-term effect in vocal music than in instrumental. The conclusions may be obvious, but deserve restatement none the less. Musical culture is elastic, and it can survive disasters of short duration. Long-term conflict, with incessant

[29] With the ascendance of the violin in the early 17th century, the wind bands finally went into decline as they lost their vital link to main-stream musical activity.

[30] Léopold Devillers, *Essai sur l'histoire de la musique à Mons* (Mons, 1868), 16.

diversion of resources for defense and for the pursuit of war, is another matter. The economies of both Flanders and Spain were dismembered, many of their institutions shattered, and their brilliant musical cultures destroyed. Other regions, it must be added, fared much better during this era. The patronage frameworks of England and Italy, for example remained quite secure. The same was true for Germany to the extent that, though damage ran deep in some regions, most recovered, and German instrumental music remained a vigorous force.

The Repertories

Instrumental performance of vocal music

Through the greater part of the sixteenth century singers and players shared much in terms of styles and repertories. Excluding collections for solo instruments, title pages of the published repertory routinely stated that the contents of volumes could be performed by "voices or instruments."[31] Instrumentalists, though, especially professionals, would have adapted the musical texts to suit their own needs, often dividing long notes, embellishing cadences, filling in rests, specifying precise chromatic alterations, rendering other passages more idiomatic, transposing, and sometimes altering the form.

Ornamentation of pre-existing texts, that is, the extensive elaboration of given melodic lines, was the primary means of adaptation through much of the sixteenth century. This is one aspect of instrumental practice that is reasonably clear. Even though this was a spontaneous technique to be applied in the course of a performance, the procedures of decoration are well described in several manuals.[32] These instruction books, many written by practicing professionals such as Silvestro di Ganassi, Diego Ortiz, and Girolamo dalla Casa, reveal that divisions (as such decorations could be called) were applicable to all instruments, including flutes, viols, keyboard instruments, lutes, and vihuelas.[33] Furthermore these sources also show that while details varied from one writer (and one instrument) to another, the essential principles that underlay decorative techniques were shared through various mediums. The examples in musical sources show that, at their best, elaborations could lend graceful elegance. At their most perfunctory, they can appear, at least to our tastes, mechanical and tedious, as in Italian lute music of the first decades of the sixteenth century and much of the German organ repertory between about 1530 and 1590.

[31] Susato characteristically described his chanson prints as "convenable tant à la voix comme aussi propices à jouer de divers instruments;" and note that while he did issue one volume of dance music, he published not a single volume of imitative fantasias or ricercars for ensemble instruments.

[32] For a discussion of the manuals, see Howard M. Brown, *Embellishing 16th-Century Music* (Oxford, 1976), pp. vii–xiv.

[33] For a listing of the treatises, see the "Bibliography of Sources to 1600; Sixteenth-Century Treatises that Include Information about Performance Practice," in *Performance Practice: Music before 1600*, 269–71.

Another genre in which the same music served both instrumental and vocal purposes was the intabulation. At its simplest, an intabulation was an arrangement of a vocal model notated in tablature for lute, vihuela, or guitar, or occasionally keyboard, though the term has been applied to any instrumental arrangement for plucked string or keyboard whether or not it is in tablature. The making of intabulations was a central concern (perhaps *the* central concern) of lutenists, and in fact the majority of the surviving lute repertory consists not of fantasies or dances but intabulations, which both testifies to instrumentalists' close knowledge of the latest trends in vocal music and provides a barometer for gauging the popularity of these pieces. Often, intabulations were faithful renderings of the vocal model in all respects, resembling little more than transcription, albeit occasionally transposed and modified for the size of instrument at hand. At the other extreme are highly embellished examples in which the original vocal contours are barely visible (or indeed, audible) beneath a swirl of ornamentation and cadential embellishment. The fact that intabulations are not entirely "original" works but arrangements of vocal models should underscore their importance, not only in the context of the popularity they clearly enjoyed in the sixteenth century but also about what they can tell us about Renaissance musical composition. First of all, intabulations were made for a variety of reasons: as a pedagogical process through which a player can understand the contrapuntal workings of a vocal model; as a practical means of reducing vocal parts for the sake of accompanying; as self-standing solo pieces; and as an aid in composition, in which the intabulation may have acted as a kind of "pseudo-score" that composers used to mediate the eventual scoring of vocal parts. Contemporary descriptions of intabulation methods contained in treatises by Le Roy, Bermudo, and especially Vincenzo Galilei show further how intabulations can teach players how to compose works in this vein, such as fantasias.

The lute song was another genre with a massive debt to the vocal repertory. Many settings for lute and voice were published in the early sixteenth century, including works originally written in parts derived from the frottola and early madrigal repertories. These pieces were in almost all cases adaptations of pieces originally written in parts. In the lute settings one line (usually the discant) would be left for voice, and the others, often just the tenor and bass, played by the lute (other plucked instruments would also have been acceptable), maintaining as close as was feasible the original voice-leading. This approach of reducing polyphonic repertories for lute and voice dominated for decades and forms the background for the emergence of accompanied monody at the end of the century.[34] The appearance of the French *air de cour* and the English ayre of around 1600 signaled yet another development that was evidently conceived specifically to take advantage of the special capabilities of the lute. The lute songs of Dowland and the other Elizabethan songwriters—Pilkington, Campion, Rosseter, Ferrabosco, and Danyel—contained newly composed accompaniments (that is, they were not derived

[34] The evolution of the lute song repertory towards accompanied monody is treated in Kevin Mason, "*Per cantare e sonare:* Accompanying Italian Lute Song of the Late Sixteenth Century," in *Performance on Lute, Guitar, and Vihuela*, 72–107.

from previously existing vocal parts) and represent magnificent examples of the type.[35]

The transformation of the canzona furnishes a striking example of successful adaptation of vocal music to instrumental ends. During the earliest phases, Italian musicians simply took over French chansons, as in Gardano's 1539 print *Canzoni francese a due voci . . . buone da cantare et sonare.* Instrumentalists were certainly drawn to these pieces by their straightforward rhythmic and attractive melodic qualities, by the popularity these works enjoyed among the general public, and by their clearly audible formal structures (ABA, ABCA, and ABB, for example). The next steps are unclear, as there seem to be mid-century prints of *canzoni francese* for which no vocal models have been found, but certainly by about 1570 the canzona had become an instrumental piece (a Vincentino publication of 1572 included one *canzon da sonar*).[36] The late-sixteenth- and early-seventeenth-century canzonas maintained an appealing melodic style and sprightly rhythms but exploited unmistakably instrumental effects, both in the ensemble versions (those, for example, by Claudio Merulo, Giovanni Gabrieli, and later Samuel Scheidt) and in those for keyboard (Andrea Gabrieli, Merulo, and the seventeenth-century master of the form, Frescobaldi). In this late stage the canzona became so close in basic vocabulary to the mid-century ricercar and fantasia that it can be more appropriately discussed together with them (see below).

One final instrumental category may be included under the rubric of "vocal music." Toward the end of the sixteenth century composers increasingly exploited the potential of contrasting specific instrumental colors with voices. Indeed, the largest body of pieces in which composers precisely demanded such instruments as violins, cornetts, and trombones were vocal works. The Italians provided leadership in this area in two distinct directions. Giovanni Gabrieli explored contrasts of large masses of sound, with twelve and more individual parts split into two, three, or more choirs, differentiated by various vocal, wind, and string timbres. His lead was followed by several distinguished Germans, including Hassler, Praetorius, and Schütz. Monteverdi, moving in another direction (also followed by Schütz), preferred to exploit the tone quality of a few voices (often just one or two, supported by continuo) contrasted with blocks of sound provided by an instrumental ensemble. The instrumental group often provided formal cohesion by restating initial material, as with the ritornello, creating a rondo-like affect.

Dance music

Massive quantities of dance music poured from presses all over Europe throughout the era, including music for lutes (both solo and duos), various keyboard instruments, and ensembles. Despite the abundance of source material, however,

[35] On this repertory, see Brown, *Music in the Renaissance*, 270–71; see also David Tunley, "Tunings and Transpositions in the Early 17th-Century French Lute Air," *Early Music*, 21 (1993), 203–9.

[36] Ernst Meyer, "Concerted Instrumental Music," in *The Age of Humanism 1540–1630*, ed. Gerald Abraham, The New Oxford History of Music, IV (London, 1968), 565.

uncertainties remain concerning quite basic issues. It is clear that this music was designed to be played, but by whom? Also, this was dance music, but was it ever used as raw material for use on the actual dance-floors of the time, or was published dance music an idealized repertory intended for solo instrumental performance, like a Bach gigue or a Chopin waltz?

It now seems clear, after the work of such scholars as Daniel Heartz and Howard Brown, that the publications, at least those for ensemble, were apparently designed for amateurs.[37] Much of this repertory is uncomplicated, comprising either simple harmonized tunes or strings of various kinds of variations. Furthermore, when instruments are indicated, such as flutes and recorders, they are those most likely to be played by amateurs. It follows, then, that the music would not have been heard on the dance floor, for sixteenth-century amateurs were usually either members of the aristocracy or from wealthy urban circles. These men and women would never have played for dancing, which was a task for hired professionals and one that was beneath those of higher station. Lute publications, too, almost always contained dance music (though it is interesting to note that the published output of papal lutenists like Francesco da Milano and Perino Fiorentino and royal lutenists like Albert de Rippe almost completely exclude dance or variation settings).

Still, this music probably does at least mirror contemporary developments in dancing, which, is itself a gauge of social customs and class function. The Attaingnant repertory of about 1530, for example, shows that the fifteenth-century *basse dance*, a refined, ceremonial, and almost ritualistic dance, had been replaced by the modern, and more simple, *basse dance commune*, as well as by the pavan, gagliarda, saltarello, and branle, dances whose origins run the gamut of domestic, international, urban, and rural.[38] Moreover, the medieval technique of basing a structure on a dance tune stretched out in the tenor with improvised counterpoint above and below, had been replaced by a very different approach. The new *basse dance*, for example, was for four parts, with the melody usually in the superius and with a bass part that is noticeably more harmonic in its voice leading. In addition, this new dance was made up of short, clearly articulated phrases that were repeated, resulting in a much more transparent formal structure. Finally, the *basse dance commune* was frequently paired with a concluding faster dance, often in a contrasting meter, similar to the pavan/galliard, passamezzo/saltarello, and the German *Hoftanz/Nachtanz* pairs that are ubiquitous in lute books. While certainly normative, such pairings were not fixed, however, as other combinations were possible, and many dances could be done singly (these included the branle, tordion, and piva).[39] In the later sixteenth century new dances were arriving yet again, especially the allemande and courante.

[37] Heartz, "Sources and Forms," 13–14; Brown, *Music in the Renaissance*, 269. See also Dietrich Kämper, "Studien zur instrumentalen Ensemblemusik des 16. Jahrhunderts in Italien," *Analecta musicologica*, 10 (1970), 156–59.

[38] Daniel Heartz, "The Basse Dance; Its Evolution circa 1450 to 1550," *Annales musicologiques*, 6 (1958–63), 321–7.

[39] On the various dance types, see Daniel Heartz, *Preludes, Chansons and Dances for Lute* (Neuilly-sur-Seine, 1964), pp. xxxi–liv.

It appears certain that when professionals performed for dancing they followed the main developments outlined by the published repertory as they improvised. They would have certainly played the same kinds of dances, though clearly without the fast diminutions as found, for example, in the lute branles by Le Roy or the long (and sometimes rambling) divisions one encounters in the dance settings by the prolific blind lutenist from Trieste, Giacomo Gorzanis. A more plausible example of the musical style that was used for dancing is given by three Italian dance treatises, *Il ballerino* (1581) and *Nobiltà di dame* (1600),[40] both by Fabritio Caroso, and *Le gratie d'amore* (1602) by Cesare Negri. All three treatises provide musical examples in lute tablature following the description of the steps of the dance. The settings are simple and set in regular phrases, and generally homophonic with only slight extensions of scales. Furthermore, a handful of French and English manuscript versions of sixteenth- and early-seventeenth-century dance pieces have survived, evidently reflecting the practices of professionals. In these pieces only two parts are given (soprano and bass); therefore the older tenor-based cantus-firmus tradition had been abandoned, and the task of the performers in this era was centered on the spontaneous creation of inner parts to fill out the texture. In terms of internal forms, evidently the clearly articulated phrases and the repeated sections were also retained. Finally, the manuscript versions, and published pieces by expert instrumentalists such as Susato, show that in the dance pairs the faster concluding dance was frequently treated as a variation of the first.

The published dance repertory also reveals that composers utilized dance pieces in various ways to build larger musical structures. One way to accomplish this was to add further dances to the dance pairs. By the later sixteenth century sets of three dances were fairly common, and by shortly after 1600 four and more could be strung together. The content was not yet fixed, but the allemande and courant were usually the common building blocks around which other dances could be grouped (cf. the "Royall Consorts" of William Lawes).

Yet another approach to extending dance structure was variation. One way to do this was to vary a bass pattern. Spanish composers were among the first to work with this idea, but it was the Italians who developed such standard patterns as the *passamezzo moderno* (I–IV–I–V...) and *passamezzo antico* (I–VII–I–V...), the Romanesca, or *Guardame las vacas* as it was known in Spain (III–VII–i–V...), and the Folia (I–V–I–VII ...). Another approach, one favored especially around 1600, was to state an entire dance melody, then to follow this with a set of variations in which the framework of the original melody provided the basis for elaboration. Byrd and Gibbons provided splendid examples.

English musicians enriched the dance literature in other ways. In their hands the pavan became a highly expressive and serious work. The efforts of Dowland, Phillips, and Brade were of such stature that they became the "main vehicle for the dissemination of the English consort style in northern Europe"(Holman). Indeed, the great impact of English composers abroad deserves much more emphasis that

[40] Fabritio Caroso, *Nobilità di Dame: A Treatise on Courtly Dance, Together with the Choreography and Music of 49 Dances*, ed. and trans. Julia Sutton (Oxford, 1986).

it has received, and this impact was largely through dance settings, many of which, like Dowland's *Lachrimae* pavan, were disseminated widely throughout England and the Low Countries in both solo and ensemble versions.[41] The English (and some German composers who followed their lead) set pairs of dances, particularly pavans and galliards, but they also assembled collections in which several dances of one type would be given in series, which again underlines the point that little uniformity can be expected from instrumental practices during this period. Another English contribution has been termed the "fantasia-suite," a form favored by Coprario, which would begin with a fantasia followed by an almain and a galliard.[42]

Finally, it should be noted that though dance settings in this era were often modest pieces, it was in this repertory that composers and performers explored elements that were key to later developments. These included a focus on the bass (especially in dance variations), concern with relationships between movements (as in Susato's dance pairs), and textures with polarized soprano and bass.

Improvisatory types, intonations, preludes, and toccatas

In the early sixteenth century there was not yet an established set of rules for audience behavior as exists now (such as it is) for modern concerts. We can assume that one of the conditions commonly facing the musician was the distracting chatter of conversation. We know from a contemporary description of a performance by Francesco da Milano that the way he quieted his listeners was to strum a few chords and play a few running lines—in short, to play a kind of prelude.[43]

Such pieces were useful to musicians in both secular and sacred contexts. They went by a variety of names, the most common being toccata, prelude, preamble, and intonation. Some of the earliest were called "tastar de corde" (literally, "a touching of the strings") or more commonly "ricercar" (between about 1508 and 1536), but by mid-century "tastar" was replaced by its cognate "toccata," while "ricercar" was now applied to pieces consistently imitative in texture, making the term synonymous with the fantasia. Preludial-type pieces were always idiomatic, reflecting the capabilities of the instrument for which they were conceived. They also seem very close to improvisations, with great flexibility in terms of form, and could combine chordal passages, running scale patterns, and even imitative segments.[44] Many are of slight musical value, but Italian composers in the late sixteenth century, Andrea

[41] Holman, *Four and Twenty Fiddlers*, 163.

[42] John Caldwell, *The Oxford History of English Music*, I: *From the Beginnings to c.1715* (Oxford, 1991), 479. See also Christopher D. S. Field, "Consort Music I: Up to 1660," in *The Blackwell History of Music in Britain*, III: *The Seventeenth Century*, ed. Ian Spink (Oxford, 1992), 235.

[43] The passage, written by the jurist Jacques de Vintimille and cited by Pontus de Tyard in 1555, contains the following: "The tables being cleared, he chose [a fantasia] and, as if tuning his strings, sat on the end of a table seeking out a fantasia." Quoted in H. Colin Slim, "Some Possible Likenesses of Francesco Canova da Milano (1497–1543)," in idem, *Painting Music in the Sixteenth Century: Essays in Iconography* (Aldershot, 2002), 5.

[44] On the background of the toccata, see Murray Bradshaw, *The Origin of the Toccata*, MSD 28 (American Institute of Musicology, 1972).

and Giovanni Gabrieli and Claudio Merulo, for example, succeeded in producing pieces of lasting interest.

Variations and cantus-firmus settings

The earliest and most consistent uses of variation techniques were those found in dance music, as discussed above. Two later types may be mentioned briefly. In the first, the concept of repeated bass patterns, as in the Spanish and Italian dance types, or the repertory of sixteenth-century "grounds," led by the early seventeenth century to more ambitious structures built on bass ostinatos. Monteverdi made particularly effective use of this approach. In the second, which appears to have begun in mid-sixteenth-century Spain, composers took over the devices of those dance variations in which a melodic structure was stated, then followed by a set of varied alterations in which each successive statement was clearly set apart (as in the English sets found in such sources as the Fitzwilliam Virginal Book). These variation sets were based on either popular songs or sacred melodies (examples of both are also found in the English repertory). This approach spread to the Low Countries (especially in the works of Sweelinck) and appears to have reached from there into Germany. Scheidt and Schein emphasized sacred settings within their output of variation types and developed an array of variation techniques, especially in music for organ.

No change in performance practice was more fundamental than that concerning the use of a cantus firmus. Improvisation around a borrowed melody (with the tune in longer notes, most often in the tenor, surrounded by more sprightly counterpoint) was central to music-making until the late fifteenth century. This practice, in its most strict manner, rapidly lost its principal role after 1500. In dance music, as seen above, the tenor-based structure yielded to one based on a soprano melody with supporting lower parts (in sacred music and in such pieces as the ricercar it yielded to a structure based on imitation). Still, the cantus-firmus principle was by no means abandoned, and borrowed melodies certainly continued to be a staple item in the practices of church organists everywhere. The approaches of Germans, from Hofhaimer through Scheidt, were varied and imaginative. The French, to judge from the publications of Attaingnant and the later ones by Titelouze, were less adventurous in this regard. The early generation of Italian and Spanish organists led by Girolamo Cavazzoni and Antonio Cabezón, on the other hand, produced brilliantly original works. This artistic level was maintained by later Italians, particularly Andrea and Giovanni Gabrieli and Frescobaldi.

Imitative types: ricercar, fantasia, canzona per sonare

As instrumental music continued to develop in the sixteenth century, composers increasingly dispensed with such traditions as relying on borrowed melodies, fixed dance patterns, or repeated basses. The most ambitious efforts were in imitative pieces such as the ricercar and fantasia. What remains striking is how sophisticated were some of what were apparently the earliest examples.

In many of the lute ricercars (or fantasias) by Francesco da Milano, most written in the late 1520s and early 1530s while the lutenist worked at the papal court, two or three interrelated ideas, each one usually developed in imitation, serve to unify the piece, with astonishingly subtle alterations.[45] The variety of influences demonstrated in these works show how thoroughly Francesco, like other instrumentalists, adopted the sectional contrast used in the motet or the French chanson—duets vs tutti, homophony vs imitation—which was combined with a thoroughly idiomatic style. Other ricercars of Francesco are monothematic, and a few embed quotes from vocal music, which demonstrate aspects of the same parody and paraphrase technique used in sacred vocal polyphony. Much the same can be said of the counterparts for organ by Francesco's contemporary Girolamo Cavazzoni. In Spain, Antonio de Cabezón, too, produced masterful contrapuntal pieces, which he termed *tientos*. Modern scholars have often pointed out the similarities in the ricercars of around 1540 with imitative structures in contemporary motets. Drawing attention to the common element, however, should only serve to heighten our awareness of the fact that the best of the instrumental versions are not at all interchangeable in technique with their vocal counterparts. Evidently this approach was uniquely instrumental from very early in its development.

While the ricercar (or fantasia) of the first half of the century showed a plurality of approaches—clearly commensurate with the vihuelist Luis Milán's definition in 1536 that a fantasia derives "from the fantasy and skill of the author who created it"—the works in this genre after 1550 conform more to a norm; a fantasia was a piece built up of successive contrapuntal sections, or points of imitation. By the end of the century the internal sections tended to be longer, fewer in number, and more clearly articulated. Some were monothematic, although this was by no means a standard feature. An example of the multisectional ricercar, with clearly contrasting sections, and a return to initial material, is the well-known *Ricercar del duodecimo tono* of Andrea Gabrieli.[46] Ricercars all but disappear from the Italian and French lute repertory after 1600, but they continue in Italian keyboard music, whose master in this period was Frescobaldi. The formal procedures also attracted the finest composers in the north. Byrd, Dowland, Gibbons, Sweelinck, Scheidt, and Schein, for example, all produced fine pieces in this genre.

After about 1590 many pieces called canzonas should be included within the general type. More refined distinctions may be made with some composers. For some, ricercars tended to be keyboard works, while canzonas were ensemble pieces. For those who observed this distinction, historical hindsight permits the suggestion that the later ensemble sonata evolved from the canzona and fugue from

[45] On the ricercars of Francesco da Milano, see Arthur J. Ness, *The Lute Music of Francesco Canova da Milano (1497–1543)* (Cambridge, MA, 1970), 4–7; see also Heartz, *Preludes, Chansons and Dances*, pp. xv–xvii; Victor Coelho, "Papal Tastes and Musical Genres: Francesco da Milano 'il divino' (1497–1543) and the Clementine Aesthetic," in *The Pontificate of Clement VII: History, Politics, Culture*, ed. Kenneth Gouwens and Sheryl E. Reiss (Aldershot, 2005), 277–92.

[46] Available in Archibald T. Davison and Willi Apel, *Historical Anthology of Music* (Cambridge, Massachusetts, Harvard University Press, 1946), 1: 147–48.

the ricercar. Still, the titles applied by composers about 1600 were by no means fixed. Frescobaldi, for example, composed pieces he called variously canzonas, fantasias, and ricercars. His fantasias and ricercars were the most similar in that both involved extensive imitative reworking of the ideas stated at the outset. His canzonas tended to be more varied melodically and rhythmically and to have more clearly defined sectional structure, but they fall nonetheless into a style that other composers might have called ricercars. The flexibility of terminology is vividly illustrated in the ricercar by Andrea Gabrieli mentioned above, a piece that fits many of the stylistic criteria of the canzonas by his nephew Giovanni.

New arrivals around 1600: concerto, ritornello, sinfonia, sonata

By late in the sixteenth century, roughly 1590, new terms began appearing on title pages and scores. Their meanings varied from place to place and from time to time, but they were unified in one sense: they indicated the presence or the participation of instruments. This presence was almost always allied to the newer trends of the era. Among these certainly one of the most important was that the participation of professional musicians finally emerges clearly. Attaingnant had published his dances almost certainly for use by amateurs, but when Giovanni Gabrieli called for cornettists, trombonists, and violinists in his scores, he was specifically requiring the presence of professionals.

The term *concerto* appeared in several title pages around the turn of the century, but it was not itself attached to individual pieces contained within the prints. What the term was evidently intending to communicate was that, among the works in the volume, one could anticipate the general co-operation of instruments with voices. The term that would more often be found in the scores themselves (as opposed to the title pages) was *concertato*, which indicated contrasting elements within the piece in question. It could be inserted, for example, to identify a grouping that included vocal and instrumental forces, when these forces were inserted in contrast to more purely vocal units.

The designation *ritornello* was most often used in the early seventeenth century to identify an instrumental segment within a larger vocal work. This instrumental segment could reappear, and would often then result in a kind of rondo form. Monteverdi used this device with telling affect, as in *Chiome d'oro* from his Seventh Book of Madrigals (1619). In the ritornello of this piece, the upper two instrumental voices imitate and interact with each other above an ostinato bass. The bass then continues in the vocal sections, providing a tautly unified overall structure.

The term *sinfonia*, too, is most often found in music about 1600 (as with Gabrieli, and later with Schütz) as a label for instrumental segments within larger works that incorporate voices. In this context, however, the sinfonia was not usually repeated, as was the case with the ritornello. Rather less often, the term could indicate independent works; such pieces were written by Banchieri, Rossi, and Viadana. These independent works were multisectional in structure and similar in style to canzonas. Otherwise, sinfonias during this era were not standardized in terms of textures, forms, or instrumentation.

The term *sonata*, from about 1550 through the early seventeenth century, designated not a particular form or even procedure, but simply that the pieces were played rather than sung. Beyond this very general definition it is probably fruitless to try to establish any more specific definition. Individual composers, of course, did have some reasonably definite ideas about what kind of composition might be designated a sonata, but these tended to be quite idiosyncratic. Cima published a set of sonatas in 1610 that included textures calling for two violins above a bass, while others, such as Merula, produced pieces that are very much like canzonas. Giovanni Gabrieli evidently included several related but different kinds of pieces within the general rubric. With his well-known *Sonata pian'e forte*, he apparently intended to indicate a piece for antiphonal choirs that fell somewhere between the more grave style of his ricercars and the more spirited character of his canzonas. His *Sonatta per tre violini* (published in 1615), however, calls for only three parts, often in imitation, above a figured bass. For the period considered here, the prudent attitude would be to consider each piece called a "sonata" very much on its own merits. Only after about 1640 did more specific understandings about the sonata as a genre develop.

Regional Developments

Italy clearly produced the most instrumental music, of the greatest variety, over the longest span. Italian organists reached the front rank of their profession early in the sixteenth century, with a roster of talent that ran in an unbroken line from Cavazzoni to Frescobaldi. Italians produced all types of music for organ, but they were especially important in the evolution of the *canzona francese* from simple transcriptions of vocal models to a significant kind of instrumental music, and similarly in the evolution of the ricercar from a piece which followed principles of vocal music to an independent instrumental form of the highest artistic merit. It was Italians, too, who first employed the organ as a *concertato* instrument supporting the basso continuo. Significant in these developments were Andrea Gabrieli and Banchieri in the second half of the sixteenth century, Merulo and Giovanni Gabrieli about 1600, and Frescobaldi.

Italy was graced with masterful lutenist composers from the beginning of the era, with Marco dall' Aquila, Francesco da Milano, Giovanni da Crema, and the Mantuan Alberto da Ripa (Albert de Rippe), while later figures included Vincenzo Galilei and Simon Molinaro, the last two being skilled composers of vocal music as well—a trait that shines through in their fastidious concern with voice-leading in their lute compositions. Among the early lute pieces, especially important were the ricercars, but Italians skillfully produced music for all genres: intabulations of vocal music, pieces for voice and solo lute, and dance movements.

In ensemble music Italians also seized leading roles in all fields. In wind music, the prestige of Italians is demonstrated by Ganassi and Dalla Casa (both members of the civic wind ensemble of Venice), who produced authoritative treatises on the art of ornamentation. By about mid-century, the reputation of Italian cornettists was exceptionally high. Orologio, for example, not only traveled throughout Europe as a virtuoso on his instrument but was a composer of considerable merit. Ensemble string music through most of the sixteenth century was considered an Italian creation, and players imported in this era into the courts of France and England were largely Italian. Both the viol and the violin reached their definitive forms in Italy. Many early viols were produced by German makers, but by the turn of the seventeenth century the dynasties of brilliant Italian makers were well established. Moreover, it was Italy that began to pour out violin virtuosi who soon captivated most of Europe. By about 1610 came the production of idiomatic pieces by such composers as Marini and Cima, which exploited the particular virtues of the instrument. Forms were by no means standard, but early examples of solo and trio sonatas and of sonatas in essence on the *da chiesa* and *da camera* model were being produced by Italian composers around 1630 and were soon to be emulated through much of Europe.

Germany came the closest of the European regions to matching the outpouring that characterized Italy. Early in the sixteenth century, such German organists as Hofhaimer and Schlick had established Germans as the leading players and composers of the era. In the middle years of the century the organ was no less extensively cultivated, but the emphasis of organ composers on elaborate ornamentation resulted in a music that has not worn well for later generations. By the end of the century, though, younger organists of brilliant talent arrived on the scene. These included Praetorius, Scheidt, and Schein in the north and Hans Leo Hassler in southern Germany. The emphasis in the earlier period was on intabulations and dance music, but by about 1600 the German masters were particularly successful with imitative ricercars and canzonas and with various kinds of variations.

Germany could claim very competent lutenists, including Hans Judenkünig, Hans Gerle, and Hans Newsidler, during the first half of the sixteenth century. The emphasis in their written works, as with their keyboard colleagues, was on intabulations and dance pieces, of which many settings were cognates with Italian works. The next generation, including Melchior Newsidler and Sebastian Ochsenkun, were as gifted as players, and much of the music of the younger Newsidler is both distinguished and challenging. The works of the Transylvanian lutenist Valentin Bakfark must be included here; his long and complex fantasias were of the highest caliber.

German courts and cities supported first-class professional ensembles through most of the era (until financial setbacks resulting from the wars beginning in 1618), and it is also clear that enthusiastic circles of amateur performers had sprung up, especially in the larger cities. Little music was composed for ensembles, however, as most German publications through the sixteenth century continued the pattern of offering vocal music for *ad libitum* instrumental use. By about 1590, and especially after the turn of the century, came an outpouring of compositions for ensembles. These were dominated by dances, written by such composers as Hassler, Melchior Franck, Scheidt, and Schein (as well as an influential group of English composers resident in Germany).[47] Of greater artistic interest were the works of Praetorius, Schütz, Scheidt, and Schein, that combined ensemble instruments with voices.

French instrumental music, as reflected by published collections, was curiously erratic. Attaingnant published several volumes of keyboard music early in his career; this was followed by nothing of lasting interest until the publication of Jean Titelouze in 1623. The Low Countries were similar in that one figure, Sweelinck, towers above all others. A good deal of lute music was published in France (by Attaingnant, Moderne, Gorlier and others), containing exceptional compositions by two transplanted Italians, da Ripa (de Rippe) and Paladino (Paladin), and in the Low Countries (by Phalèse in Leuven), but most of the music was more competent than distinguished.

The same presses in Paris, Lyons, Antwerp, and Leuven churned out quantities of ensemble music, mostly devoted to dance sets. Much of this music is charming and effective for casual amateur performance and is beautifully adapted to its purpose. It should also be noted that, as reflected in the publication of instrumental music, activity slowed in France during the worst of the religious conflicts in the last two decades of the sixteenth century, and it stopped almost completely in the southern Netherlands—Susato himself fled Antwerp, evidently owing to the threat of religious persecution.[48] By early in the seventeenth century, however, conditions in France stabilized, and the establishment of the "twenty-four violins of the King" was a key development in the history of French instrumental music.

The musical taste of professional ensemble instrumentalists was dominated by that of the French court, and this appears to have centered almost exclusively on dance music, although an important volume of *fantasies* by Eustache Du Caurroy was posthumously published in 1610. French professionals, at any rate, showed little inclination to indulge in the newer Italian genres such as sonatas and sinfonias. Very little has survived in contemporary manuscripts of court dances, but the collection assembled slightly later by Philidor apparently gives a good idea of the nature of the repertory. French court dances were written down in two parts only, soprano and bass. The dance ensemble performed in five parts, and the inner three parts were apparently improvised.[49] A further verification of this practice is provided by a series of contemporary English manuscripts reflecting the same approach.[50] Taken with iconographic evidence of numerous illustrations of instruments playing for dancing, in none of which are the players shown playing from written music, these manuscript collections underline the point that improvisational practice continued to be a central feature of performance throughout the period under consideration here.

47 On English composers in Germany, see Holman, *Four and Twenty Fiddlers*, 156–72.

48 Kristine Forney, "New Documents on the Life of Tielman Susato, Sixteenth-Century Music Printer and Musician," *Belgisch tijdschrift voor muziekwetenschap*, 36–38 (1982–84), 18–52.

49 On the repertory, see Isherwood, *Music in the Service of the King*, 94–102; see also 367 n. 75.

50 See Holman, *Four and Twenty Fiddlers*, 189–94, 238–41; on the influence of French musicians in England, see ibid., 108, 230–33.

Spanish instrumental music appears to have been characterized by very uneven production. Relatively little keyboard music was published there, but the surviving works of Antonio de Cabezón reveal him to have been a master whose works can stand next to any of his contemporaries. Liturgical music for organ formed a significant portion of his output, but his intabulations and pieces based on variation technique offer splendid examples of the genres. Of special interest are pieces he titled *tientos*, similar in style to the Italian ricercars, but with a fascinating subtlety of counterpoint. None of the Spanish keyboard composers of the later sixteenth century were of the same caliber.

Several fine vihuela composers appeared in quick succession in the two or three decades after Luis Milán's *Libro de vihuela de mano intitulado El maestro* (1535/36), the most significant of whom were Luis de Narváez, Alonso Mudarra, and Miguel de Fuenllana. These composers produced idiomatic pieces, fantasias, intabulations, and variations sets of consistently high distinction, and the collections of Mudarra and Fuenllana also contain some of the earliest works for the Spanish guitar.

Ensemble music in Spain has attracted little scholarly interest until quite recently. One significant development was that the more important churches in Spain began remarkably early to engage staffs of wind players on permanent contracts.[51] By about 1530 this appears to have been a general trend. Some Spanish wind players were evidently quite capable, but a decline in ensemble music appears to have set in by late in the century, at least in the respect that players in Spain appear to have been slow to adapt to newer trends around 1600. Certainly little original written music of artistic merit seems to have been produced.[52]

Music in England, in contrast to that of Spain and the southern Low Countries, reached a peak in the late sixteenth and early seventeenth centuries. A few sources of keyboard music survive from the earlier sixteenth century, but scores of fine composers seem to have burst on the scene around 1590. The breathtaking quality of so many pieces by such a variety composers testifies yet again to the richness of instrumental music of the era. Byrd, Bull, and Gibbons may be selected as those most consistently of top rank, but such composers as Giles Farnaby, Morley, Peter Philips, and Thomas Weelkes also produced works of great beauty. The range of music spans all types, but outstanding are the fantasias (again the equivalent of the Italian ricercars) and variation forms. A particular English trait was the preference for the virginal, although the organ was not neglected. Our knowledge of English keyboard music is established not only by fine prints but also by extensive manuscript anthologies such as the Fitzwilliam Virginal Book.

Relatively little lute music was published in England until fairly late in the sixteenth century, although fine lutenists were performing there throughout the era. The great master was John Dowland, whose music is simply exquisite (his output includes fantasias, dances, and variations, and of course lute songs). Outstanding

[51] Kenneth Kreitner, "Minstrels in Spanish Churches, 1400–1600," *Early Music*, 20 (1992), 533–46.

[52] On the situation in Spain, see Douglas K. Kirk, "Churching the Shawms in Renaissance Spain: Lerma, Archivo de San Pedro Ms. Mus. 1" (PhD diss., McGill University, 1993).

among his colleagues were John Johnson, Daniel Bachelar, and Francis Cutting, whose works are mostly contained in manuscript.[53] One odd feature is that some of the finest English composers so little exploited the instrument. We have only a single lute work by Morley, only a handful of lute pieces can be attributed to William Byrd (and some of them are simply transcriptions of his keyboard works), and Gibbons and Weelkes wrote none at all.

Ensemble music found a ready audience in England. The viol had an extraordinary vogue among English amateur musicians, which seems to have engendered a matching repertory of dances, imitative pieces, and variations. The tradition of cantus-firmus settings (which continued to appear for decades) based on the *In nomine* theme was a peculiarly English phenomenon. The contrapuntal pieces of Byrd and Dowland represent an artistic high point (including Byrd's settings for solo voice and viols). Music for broken consorts was not neglected, with Morley's *First Booke of Consort Lessons* (1599) being a landmark set. Excellent wind ensembles were available both at court and in the larger cities, and fine professional string players were available as well (many of them at first Italian players of both viol and violin; later on French influence was more prominent). Peter Holman has recently described the development of the string ensembles at the English court, showing that the tradition there was quite vigorous and similar to that of the French court. Indeed, the demand for instrumental music at court in the first two or three decades stimulated a first-rate repertory by such composers as Orlando Gibbons and Coprario. The distinguished tradition was continued in the next generation with the works of William Lawes.

An underground style?

Ample evidence suggests that a significant body of musicians functioned beyond the range of written music throughout the sixteenth century. We have seen, for example, the startling maturity of some of the earliest examples of written pieces in such genres as the imitative ricercar, which hints that such pieces may have existed earlier in unwritten form. The evidence of French and English dance music is more explicit, as we have preserved examples of pieces written for two parts, soprano and bass, which were evidently intended as a shell inside which further parts would be improvised. We also know from the comments of outstanding players such as Ganassi that it was simply assumed that instrumentalists would not only perform written music, but also that they could on the spot create polyphonic music to match the needs of any particular occasion. The question remains, however, as to what, if anything, may be established concerning this "underground" music.

We can be reasonably sure that the repertories followed along the lines of written sources. Dance music, of course, and variation forms would have been

[53] For an exemplary study of English lute music of the period, see Matthew Spring, *The Lute in Britain* (Oxford, 2001).

standard fare. The application of divisions, as mentioned above, was by its very nature a spontaneous practice. One useful approach might be to determine areas in which improvisation might have been improbable. Textures that involved six or more voices, especially when one choir might be contrasted with another, would be highly unlikely contexts for improvisation (and it should be noted that it was in precisely this kind of piece where specific instruments were indicated). The extensive exploration of chromatic progressions, too, would have been very difficult if not written down. Imitation, however, though difficult, would of itself not have posed insuperable difficulties for skilled players. Contemporary treatises, at any rate, indicate that improvised imitative counterpoint was expected from competent musicians. It may not be possible to reconstruct the practices of the sixteenth century (or even desirable, given our lack of any verification as to the accuracy of our efforts). We should at least be aware, however, that in considering what remains of instrumental music of the era, it is just that, a remnant. Much is gone, almost without a trace. There may have been brilliant ensemble music heard in France in the late sixteenth century, for example, or fine imitative keyboard pieces in Germany, or worthy lute ayres heard in England around 1540. We have only the faintest of traces that signaled their presence, and as improvisations they vanished completely with the passing of their age.

SUPPLEMENTARY BIBLIOGRAPHY TO THE PAPERBACK EDITION

This selective bibliography contains additions to critical work since the volume was first published in 2006. Entries relevant to more than one chapter are given in both places.

1. Renaissance Humanism and Music – Gary Tomlinson

Gerbino, Giuseppe. *Music and the Myth of Arcadia in Renaissance Italy*. Cambridge: Cambridge University Press, 2009.

Palisca, Claude V. *Music and Ideas in the Sixteenth and Seventeenth Centuries*. Urbana and Chicago: University of Illinois Press, 2006.

Welch, Anthony. *The Renaissance Epic and the Oral Past*. New Haven: Yale University Press, 2012.

2. The Concept of the Renaissance – James Haar

Strohm, Reinhard. "The Difference of Early European Music", in *Essays on Renaissance Music in Honour of David Fallows: Bon jour, bon mois et bonne estrenne*, ed. by Fabrice Fitch, and Jacobijn Kiel. Woodbridge: Boydell Press, 2011, pp. 380–388.

Tomlinson, Gary. "Self, Other, and the Emergence of Musical Modernity", in Gary Tomlinson, *Music and Historical Critique. Selected Essays*. Aldershot: Ashgate, 2007.

3. The Concept of the Baroque – Tim Carter

Davidson, Peter. *The Universal Baroque*. Manchester: Manchester University Press, 2008.

Dejans, Peter, ed. *Towards Tonality: Aspects of Baroque Music Theory*. Leuven: Leuven University Press, 2007.

Heller, Wendy. *Music in the Baroque*. New York: W.W. Norton & Company, 2013.

Stauffer, George B., ed. *The World of Baroque Music: New Perspectives*. Bloomington: Indiana University Press, 2006.

4. Italy, *i*: 1520–1560 – Giulio Ongaro

Cardamone, Donna G., and Cesare Corsi. "The Canzone Villanesca and Comic Culture: The Genesis and Evolution of a Mixed Genre (1537–1557)". *Early Music History*, 25 (2006), pp. 59–104.

Cummings, Anthony M. "Music and Theatre in Leo X's Rome", in *"Uno gentile et subtile ingenio": Studies in Renaissance Music in Honour of Bonnie Blackburn*, ed. by Gioia Filocamo, and M. Jennifer Bloxam. Turnhout: Brepols, 2008, pp. 683–693.

McKinney, Timothy R. *Adrian Willaert and the Theory of Interval Affect: The "Musica nova" Madrigals and the Novel Theories of Zarlino and Vicentino*. Farnham and Burlington: Ashgate, 2010.

Van Damme, Simon, ed. and intro. *Adrian Willaert*, special issue of the *Journal of the Alamire Foundation*, IV/1 (2012).

5. Italy, *ii*: 1560–1600 – Noel O'Regan

Charteris, Richard. *Giovanni Gabrieli and his Contemporaries: Music, Sources and Collections*. Farnham and Burlington: Ashgate, 2011.

Moroney, Davitt. "Alessandro Striggio's Mass in Forty and Sixty Parts", *Journal of the American Musicological Society*, 60 (2007), pp. 1–70.

Newcomb, Anthony. "Luzzaschi's Setting of Dante: 'Quivi sospiri, pianti, ed alti guai'". *Early Music History*, 28 (2009), pp. 97–138.

——. "Giovanni Maria Nanino's Early Patrons in Rome". *The Journal of Musicology*, 20/1 (2013), pp. 103–127.

O'Regan, Noel. "Church Reform and Devotional Music in Sixteenth-century Rome: the Influence of Lay Confraternities", in *Forms of Faith in Sixteenth-Century Italy*, ed. by Abigail Brundon, and Matthew Treherne. Aldershot: Ashgate, 2009, pp. 215–232.

Wistreich, Richard. *Warrior, Courtier, Singer: Giulio Cesare Brancaccio and the Performance of Identity in the Late Renaissance*. Aldershot: Ashgate, 2007.

6. Italy, *iii*: 1600–1640 – Tim Carter

Bowers, Roger. "Claudio Monteverdi and Sacred Music in the Household of the Gonzaga Dukes of Mantua, 1590–1612". *Music & Letters*, 90/3 (2009), pp. 331–371.

Carter, Tim, and Richard A. Goldthwaite. *Orpheus in the Marketplace: Jacopo Peri and the Economy of Late Renaissance Florence*. Cambridge, MA: Harvard University Press, 2013.

Cusick, Suzanne G. *Francesca Caccini at the Medici Court: Music and the Circulation of Power*. Chicago: University of Chicago Press, 2009.

Dell'Antonio, Andrew. *Listening as Spiritual Practice in Early Modern Italy*. Berkeley: University of California Press, 2011.

Fabris, Dinko, and Margaret K. Murata, eds. *Passagio in Italia: Music on the Grand Tour in the Seventeenth Century*. Turnhout: Brepols, 2013.

Monson, Craig A. *Nuns Behaving Badly. Tales of Music, Magic, Art, and Arson in the Convents of Italy*. Chicago: The University of Chicago Press, 2010.

7. Music for the Mass – Allan W. Atlas

Burn, D., and S. Gasch, eds. *Heinrich Isaac and Polyphony for the Proper of the Mass in the Late Middle Ages and the Renaissance*. Turnhout: Brepols, 2011.

Fallows, David. *Josquin*. Turnhout: Brepols, 2009.

Filocamo, Gioia, and M. Jennifer Bloxam, eds. *"Uno gentile et subtile ingenio": Studies in Renaissance Music in Honour of Bonnie Blackburn*. Turnhout: Brepols, 2008, esp. pp. 351–402, 403–490.

Kirkman, Andrew. *The Cultural Life of the Early Polyphonic Mass: Medieval Context to Modern Revival*. Cambridge: Cambridge University Press, 2010.

8. The Motet – Anthony Cummings

Rastall, Richard, ed. *The Secular Latin Motet in the Renaissance*, with a foreword by Leofranc Holford-Strevens. Lewiston, NY: Edwin Mellen Press, 2010.

Schmidt-Beste, Thomas, ed. *The Motet Around 1500: On the Relationship Between Imitation and Text Treatment?* Turnhout: Brepols, 2012.

Schubert, Peter N. "Hidden Forms in Palestrina's *First Book of Four-Voice Motets*". *Journal of the American Musicological Society*, 60/3 (2007), pp. 483–556.

Verbeke, Demmy. *Latin Letters and Poems in Motet Collections by Franco-Flemish Composers (c.1550-c.1600)*. Turnhout: Brepols, 2010.

9. France, *i*: 1520–1560 – Richard Freedman

Canguilhem, Philippe. "Deux recueils inconnus de Pierre Attaingnant retrouvés à Montauban". *Revue de musicologie*, 93/2 (2007), pp. 469–481.

Cavicchi, Camilla, Marie-Alexis Colin, and Philippe Vendrix, eds. *La musique en Picardie du XIVe au XVIIe siècle*. Turnhout: Brepols, 2012.

Coeurdevey, Annie, and Philippe Vendrix. *Musique, théologie et sacré, d'Oresme à Érasme*. Ambronay: Centre culturel de rencontre d'Ambronay, 2008.

Dumitrescu, Theodor. "Who Was 'Prioris'? A Royal Composer Recovered". *Journal of the American Musicological Society*, 65/1 (2012), pp. 5–65, 298–299.

Halévy, Olivier, Isabelle His, and Jean Vignes, eds. *Clément Janequin, un musicien parmi les poètes: Musique, voix et réalisme sonore à la Renaissance*. Paris: Société Française de Musicologie, 2013.

10. France, *ii*: 1560–1600 – Jeanice Brooks

Handy, Isabelle. *Musiciens au temps des derniers Valois (1547–1589)*. Paris: Champion, 2008.

McGowan, Margaret M. *Dance in the Renaissance: European Fashion, French Obsession*. New Haven: Yale University Press, 2008.

Orden, Kate van. "Children's Voices: Singing and Literacy in Sixteenth-Century France". *Early Music History*, 25 (2006), pp. 209–256.

Zecher, Carla. *Sounding Objects: Musical Instruments, Poetry and Art in the French Renaissance*. Toronto: University of Toronto Press, 2007.

11. France, *iii*: 1600–1640 – David Tunley

"Aspects of the French Baroque", *Early Music*, 38/1 (2010), pp. 59–118.

Cypess, Rebecca. "Chambonnières, Jollain and the First Engraving of Harpsichord Music in France". *Early Music*, 35/4 (2007), pp. 539–554.

Davy-Rigaux, Cécile, Bernard Dompnier, and Daniel Odon Hurel, eds. *Les cérémoniaux catholiques en France à l'époque moderne: Une littérature de codification des rites liturgiques*. Turnhout: Brepols, 2009.

Duron, Jean, ed. *Le prince et la musique: les passions musicales de Louis XIV*. Wavre: Mardaga, 2009.

12. Chanson and Air – Kate van Orden

Dobbins, Frank. "Strophic and Epigrammatic Forms in the French Chanson and Air of the Sixteenth Century". *Acta Musicologica*, 78/2 (2006), pp. 197–234.

Freedman, Richard, and Philippe Vendrix, eds. *Les livres de chansons nouvelles de Nicolas Duchemin, 1549–1568* <http://ricercar.cesr.univ-tours.fr/3-programmes/EMN/Duchemin/>.

Halévy, Olivier, Isabelle His, and Jean Vignes, eds. *Clément Janequin, un musicien parmi les poètes: Musique, voix et réalisme sonore à la Renaissance*. Paris: Société Française de Musicologie, 2013.

13. Madrigal – James Haar

Deutsch, Catherine. "*Antico* or *Moderno*? Reception of Gesualdo's Madrigals in the Early Seventeenth Century". *The Journal of Musicology*, 30/1 (2013), pp. 28–48.

Lewis Hammond, Susan. *The Madrigal: A Research and Information Guide*. New York: Routledge, 2011.

Meine, Sabine. *Die Frottola: Musik, Diskurs und Spiel, an italienischen Höfen, 1500–1530*. Turnhout: Brepols, 2013.

Newcomb, Antony. "The Ballata and the 'Free' Madrigal in the Second Half of the Sixteenth Century". *Journal of the American Musicological Society*, 63/3 (2010), pp. 427–497.

Newcomb, Antony, and Kate van Orden, eds. *The Italian Madrigal, 1550–1610, no. 1* and *The Italian Madrigal, 1550–1610, no. 2*, special issues of *The Journal of Musicology*, 29/4 (2012); 30/1 (2013).

14. The Netherlands, 1520–1640 – Kristine K. Forney

Deutsch, Catherine. "Pétrarque transalpin, de Cyprien de Rore à Claude Le Jeune. réception, imitation et jeux de miroirs intertextuels". *Revue de musicologie*, 97/1 (2011), pp. 3–34.

Forney, Kristine K. "Renaissance Piety and Ceremony: Antwerp's *Speellieden* at Work", in *Instruments, Ensembles, and Repertory, 1300–1600: Essays in Honor of Keith Polk*, ed. by Timothy McGee, and Stewart Carter. Turnhout: Brepols, 2013.

——. "A Proper Musical Education for Antwerp Women", in *Music Education in the Middle Ages and the Renaissance: Reading and Writing the Pedagogy of the Past*, ed. by Susan Forscher Weiss, Russell E. Murray, and Cynthia J. Cyrus. Bloomington: Indiana University Press, 2010, pp. 84–125.

Gordon, Bonnie. "The Secret of the *Secret Chromatic Art*". *The Journal of Musicology*, 28/3 (2011), pp. 325–367.

15. Music, Print, and Society in Sixteenth-Century Europe – Iain Fenlon

Fenlon, Iain, and Tess Knighton. *Early Music Printing and Publishing in the Iberian World*. Kassel: Reichenberger, 2006.

Lewis, Mary S. *Sources and the Circulation of Renaissance Music*. Farnham and Burlington: Ashgate, 2012.

Monson, Craig A., and Roberta Montemorra Marvin, eds. *Music in Print and Beyond: Hildegard von Bingen to The Beatles*. Rochester, NY: University of Rochester Press, 2013.

Orden, Kate van. *Music, Authorship, and the Book in the First Century of Print*. Berkeley: University of California Press, 2013.

——. "Josquin, Renaissance Historiography, and the Cultures of Print", in *The Oxford Handbook to the New Cultural History of Music*, ed. by Jane Fair Fulcher. Oxford: Oxford University Press, 2011, pp. 354–80.

16. Concepts and Developments in Music Theory – Karol Berger

Fenlon, Iain, and Inga Mai Groote, eds. *Heinrich Glarean's Books: The Intellectual World of a Sixteenth-Century Musical Humanist.* Cambridge: Cambridge University Press, 2013.

Judd, Cristle Collins. "Music in Dialogue: Conversational, Literary, and Didactic Discourse about Music in the Renaissance". *Journal of Music Theory*, 52/1, (2008), *Essays in Honor of Sarah Fuller*, pp. 41–74.

——, ed. *Musical Theory in the Renaissance.* Farnham and Burlington: Ashgate, 2013.

Mengozzi, Stefano. *The Renaissance Reform of Medieval Music Theory: Guido of Arezzo between Myth and History.* Cambridge: Cambridge University Press, 2010.

Schiltz, Katelijne, and Bonnie J. Blackburn, eds. *Canons and Canonic Techniques, 14th-16th Centuries: Theory, Practice, and Reception History. Proceedings of the International Conference, Leuven, 4–6 October 2005.* Leuven and Dudley: Peeters, 2007.

Smith, Ann. *The Performance of Sixteenth-Century Music: Learning from the Theorists.* Oxford: Oxford University Press, 2011.

17. Germany and Central Europe, *i*: 1520–1600 – Peter Bergquist

Bergquist, Peter. "'Omnia denuò multò quàm antehac correctius edita': Zu Leonhard Lechners Redaktion der *Selectissimae cantiones* am Beispiel seiner Lesart der Vertonung des Wortes 'patibulo' in Lassos Motette *Vexilla regis* LV 225". *Journal of the Alamire Foundation*, 5/1 (2013), pp. 93–104.

Eichner, Barbara. "Sweet Singing in Three Voices: A Musical Source from a South German Convent?" *Early Music*, 39/3 (2011), pp. 335–348.

Gasch, Stefan, Birgit Lodes, and Sonja Tröster. *Senfl-Studien.* Tutzing: Hans Schneider, 2012.

Lodes, Birgit, ed. *NiveauNischeNimbus: die Anfänge des Musikdrucks nördlich der Alpen.* Tutzing: Verlegt Bei Hans Schneider, 2010.

18. Germany and Central Europe, *ii*: 1600–1640 – David Crook

Fisher, Alexander J. *Music and Religious Identity in Counter-Reformation Augsburg, 1580–1630.* Aldershot: Ashgate, 2004.

——. *Music, Piety, and Propaganda: The Soundscape of Counter-Reformation Bavaria.* Oxford: Oxford University Press, 2014.

Frandsen, Mary E. *Crossing Confessional Boundaries: The Patronage of Italian Sacred Music in 17th-Century Dresden.* Oxford: Oxford University Press, 2006.

Johnston, Gregory S., ed. *A Heinrich Schütz Reader: Letters and Documents in Translation.* Oxford: Oxford University Press, 2013.

Lewis Hammond, Susan. *Editing Music in Early Modern Germany.* Aldershot: Ashgate, 2007.

Rose, Stephen. "Trumpeters and Diplomacy on the Eve of the Thirty Years War: The Album Amicorum of Jonas Kröschel". *Early Music*, 40/3 (2012), pp. 379–392.

Spohr, Arne. *"How chances it they travel?" Englische Musiker in Dänemark und Norddeutschland 1579–1630* [Wolfenbütteler Arbeiten zur Barockforschung, XLV]. Wiesbaden: Harrassowitz, 2009.

Varwig, Bettina. *Histories of Heinrich Schütz.* Cambridge: Cambridge University Press, 2011.

19. The Reformation and Music – Robin A. Leaver

Kim, Hyun-Ah. *Humanism and the Reform of Sacred Music in Early Modern England: John Merbecke the Orator and The Booke of Common Praier Noted (1550).* Aldershot: Ashgate, 2008.

Leaver, Robin A. *Luther's Liturgical Music: Principles and Implications.* [Lutheran Quarterly Books] Grand Rapids: Eerdmans, 2007.

Quitslund, Beth. *The Reformation in Rhyme: Sternhold, Hopkins and the English Metrical Psalter, 1547–1603.* Aldershot: Ashgate, 2008.

Willis, Jonathan. *Church Music and Protestantism in Post-Reformation England: Discourses, Sites and Identities.* Farnham and Burlington: Ashgate, 2010.

20. Renewal, Reform, and Reaction in Catholic Music – Craig Monson

Baker, Geoffrey. *Imposing Harmony: Music and Society in Colonial Cuzco.* Durham, NC: Duke University Press, 2008.

Crook, David. "A Sixteenth-Century Catalog of Prohibited Music". *Journal of the American Musicological Society*, 62/1 (2009), pp. 1–78.

Getz, Christine Suzanne. *Mary, Music, and Meditation: Sacred Conversations in Post-Tridentine Milan.* Bloomington: Indiana University Press, 2013.

Macy, Laura. "Geronimo Cavaglieri, the *Song of Songs* and Female Spirituality in Federigo Borromeo's Milan". *Early Music*, 39/3 (2011), pp. 349–358.

Morucci, Valerio. "Cardinals' Patronage and the Era of Tridentine Reforms: Giulio Feltro della Rovere as Protector of Sacred Music". *The Journal of Musicology*, 29/3 (2012), pp. 262–291.

Weaver, Andrew H. *Sacred Music as Public Image for Holy Roman Emperor Ferdinand III: Representing the Counter-Reformation Monarch at the End of the Thirty Years' War.* Farnham and Burlington: Ashgate, 2012.

Wuidar, Laurence. *Musique et astrologie après le Concile de Trente.* Turnhout: Brepols, 2008.

21. Spain, *i*: 1530–1600 – Todd M. Borgerding and Louise K. Stein

Fenlon, Iain, and Tess Knighton, eds. *Early Music Printing and Publishing in the Iberian World.* Kassel: Reichenberger, 2006.

Knighton, Tess, and Emilio Ros-Fábregas, eds. *Recent Research on Early Iberian Music in an International Context.* Kassel: Reichenberger, 2013.

Kreitner, Kenneth. "The Repertory of the Spanish Cathedral Bands". *Early Music*, 37/2 (2009), pp. 267–286.

Noone, Michael. "Processions to the 'City of the Dead': the Spanish Royal Chapel and an Anonymous Requiem from El Escorial", in *The Royal Chapel in the Time of the Habsburgs: Music and Ceremony in the Early Modern European Court*, ed. by Juan José Carreras, and Bernardo García García. English version edited by Tess Knighton. Translated by Yolanda Acker. Woodbridge: Boydell Press, 2005, pp. 144–161.

Ramos, Pilar. "Musical Practice and Idleness: A Moral Controversy in Renaissance Spain". *Acta Musicologica*, 81 (2009), pp. 255–274.

Rees, Owen. "Case Study: Seville Cathedral's Music in Performance, 1549–1599", in *The Cambridge History of Musical Performance*, ed. by Colin Lawson, and Robin Stowell. Cambridge: Cambridge University Press, 2012, pp. 353–374.

Rees, Owen, and Bernadette Nelson, eds. *Cristóbal de Morales: Sources, Influences, Reception*. Woodbridge: Boydell Press, 2007.

Robledo Estaire, Luis. "The Form and Function of the Music Chapel at the Court of Philip II", in *The Royal Chapel in the Time of the Habsburgs: Music and Ceremony in the Early Modern European Court*, ed. by Juan José Carreras, and Bernardo García García. English version edited by Tess Knighton. Translated by Yolanda Acker. Woodbridge: Boydell Press, 2005, pp. 135–143.

Ros-Fábregas, Emilio. "'Foreign' Music and Musicians in Sixteenth-Century Spain", in *The Royal Chapel in the Time of the Habsburgs: Music and Ceremony in the Early Modern European Court*, ed. by Juan José Carreras, and Bernardo García García. English version edited by Tess Knighton. Translated by Yolanda Acker. Woodbridge: Boydell Press, 2005, pp. 65–84.

"Urban Music in Renaissance Spain", *Early Music*, 37/3 (2009), pp. 355–416.

Walkley, Clive. *Juan Esquivel: A Master of Sacred Music During the Spanish Golden Age*. Woodbridge: Boydell Press, 2010.

22. Spain, *ii*: 1600–1640 – Louise K. Stein

Cramer, Eugene Casjen. *Studies in the Music of Tomás Luis de Victoria*. Aldershot: Ashgate, 2001.

Negredo del Cerro, Fernando. "The Royal Chapel as the Setting for Political Struggle: Praise for and Attacks on the Royal Favourite during the time of Philip IV", in *The Royal Chapel in the Time of the Habsburgs: Music and Ceremony in the Early Modern European Court*, ed. by Juan José Carreras, and Bernardo García García. English version edited by Tess Knighton. Translated by Yolanda Acker. Woodbridge: Boydell Press, 2005, pp. 229–245.

Robledo Estaire, Luis. "Questions of Performance Practice in Philip III's Chapel". *Early Music*, 22/2 (1994), pp. 199–216.

——. "El sermón como representación: teatralidad y musicalidad en la oratoria sagrada española de la Contrarreforma". *Revista de musicología*, 26/1 (2003), pp. 127–186.

Stein, Louise K. "The Musicians of the Spanish Royal Chapel and Court Entertainments, 1590–1648", in *The Royal Chapel in the Time of the Habsburgs: Music and Ceremony in the Early Modern European Court*, ed. by Juan José Carreras, and Bernardo García García. English version edited by Tess Knighton. Translated by Yolanda Acker. Woodbridge: Boydell Press, 2005. pp. 173–194.

Vicente Delgado, Alfonso de, and Pilar Tomás. *Tomás Luis de Victoria y la cultura musical en la España de Felipe III*. Madrid: Centro de Estudios Europa Hispánica, 2012.

23. Early Opera: The Initial Phase – Giuseppe Gerbino and Iain Fenlon

Brown, Peter, and Suzana Ograjenšek. *Ancient Drama in Music for the Modern Stage*. Oxford: Oxford University Press, 2010.

Calcagno, Mauro P. *From Madrigal to Opera: Monteverdi's Staging of the Self.* Berkeley: University of California Press, 2012.

Carter, Tim. "Monteverdi, Early Opera and a Question of Genre: The Case of Andromeda (1620)". *Journal of the Royal Musical Association*, 137/1 (2012), pp. 1–34.

Carter, Tim, and Richard A. Goldthwaite. *Orpheus in the Marketplace: Jacopo Peri and the Economy of Late Renaissance Florence.* Cambridge, MA: Harvard University Press, 2013

"Monteverdi", *Early Music*, 39/4 (2011), pp. 489–596.

Selfridge-Field, Eleanor. *Song and Season: Science, Culture and Theatrical Time in Early Modern Venice.* Stanford: Stanford University Press, 2007.

Whenham, John, and Richard Wistreich, eds. *The Cambridge Companion to Monteverdi.* Cambridge: Cambridge University Press, 2007.

24. England, *i*: 1485–1600 – Roger Bray

Brett, Philip. *William Byrd and His Contemporaries: Essays and a Monograph*, ed. by Joseph Kerman, and Davitt Moroney. Berkeley: University of California Press, 2007.

Dumitrescu, Theodor. *The Early Tudor Court and International Musical Relations.* Aldershot: Ashgate, 2007.

Marsh, Christopher W. *Music and Society in Early Modern England.* Cambridge: Cambridge University Press, 2010.

Ortiz, Joseph M. *Broken Harmony: Shakespeare and the Politics of Music.* Ithaca, NY: Cornell University Press, 2011.

25. England, *ii*: 1603–1642 – Jonathan P. Wainwright

Cunningham, John. *The Consort Music of William Lawes, 1602–1645.* Woodbridge: Boydell Press, 2010.

"Dowland anniversary" and "Performing Dowland", *Early Music*, 41/2 (2013), pp. 189–280, 295–329.

Holman, Peter. *Four and Twenty Fiddlers: the Violin at the English Court 1540–1690.* Oxford: Clarendon Press, 1995 [1993].

McCarthy, Kerry. *Liturgy and Contemplation in Byrd's* Gradualia. New York: Routledge, 2007.

Winkler, Amanda Eubanks. *O Let Us Howle Some Heavy Note: Music for Witches, the Melancholic, and the Mad on the 17th-Century English Stage.* Bloomington: Indiana University Press, 2006.

26. Instrumental Music – Victor Coelho and Keith Polk

Berney, Boaz. "The Renaissance Flute in Mixed Ensembles: Surviving Instruments, Pitches and Performance Practice". *Early Music*, 34/2 (2006), pp. 205–224.

Blackburn, Bonnie J. "'Il Magnifico Sigismondo Maler Thedescho' and His Family: the Venetian Connection". *The Lute: The Journal of the Lute Society*, 50 (2010), pp. 60–85.

Brinzing, Armin. *Studien zur instrumentalen Ensemblemusik im deutschsprachigen Raum des 16. Jahrhunderts*, Abhandlungen zur Musikgeschichte, ed. by Martin Staehelin. Göttingen: Vandenhoeck & Ruprecht, 1998, 2 vols.

Carter, Stewart. *The Trombone in the Renaissance: A History in Pictures and Documents.* Hillsdale, NY: Pendragon, 2012.

Ceulemans, Anne-Emmanuelle. *De la vièle médiévale au violon du xviie siècle: Étude terminologique, iconographique et théorique.* [Épitome musicale], ed. by Phillipe Vendrix, Marie-Alexis Colin, and David Fiala. Turnhout: Brepols, 2011.

Cypess, Rebecca. "Instrumental Music and 'Conversazione' in Early Seicento Venice: Biagio Marini's 'Affetti Musicali' (1617)". *Music & Letters*, 93/4 (2012), pp. 453–478.

Cyr, Mary. *Style and Performance for Bowed String Instruments in French Baroque Music.* Farnham and Burlington: Ashgate, 2012.

Göllner, Theodor, and Bernhold Schmid, eds. *Die Münchner Hofkapelle des 16. Jahrhunderts im europäischen Kontext.* [Bayerische Akademie der Wissenschaftern, Philosophisch-Historisch Klasse, Abhandlungen, Neue Folge, Heft 128] Munich: Verlag der Bayerischen Akademie der Wissenschaften, 2006.

Hoffman, Bettina. "The Nomenclature of the Viol in Italy", trans. by Richard Carter, and John Steedman. *The Viol da Gamba Society Journal*, 2 (2008), pp. 1–16.

Howard, Deborah and Laura Moretti, eds. *The Music Room in Early Modern France and Italy: Sound, Space and Object.* Oxford: Oxford University Press, 2012.

Kite-Powell, Jeffery T., ed. *A Performer's Guide to Renaissance Music.* New York: Schirmer Books, 2007 [1994].

Kreitner, Kenneth. "The Repertory of the Spanish Cathedral Bands". *Early Music*, 37 (2009), pp. 267–286.

Lasocki, David, ed. *Musicque de Joye: Proceedings of the International Symposium on the Renaissance Flute and Recorder Consort, Utrecht 2003.* Utrecht: STIMU, 2005.

McGee, Timothy. *Instruments, Ensembles, and Repertory, 1300–1600. Essays in Honour of Keith Polk.* Turnhout: Brepols, 2013.

McGowan, Margaret M. *Dance in the Renaissance: European Fashion, French Obsession.* New Haven: Yale University Press, 2008.

Myers, Herbert W. "The Musical Miniatures of the *Triumphzug* of Maximilian I". *The Galpin Society Journal*, 60 (2007), pp. 3–28, 98–108.

Nevile, Jennifer, ed. *Dance, Spectacle, and the Body Politick, 1250–1750.* Bloomington and Indianapolis: Indiana University Press, 2008.

Pio, Stefano. *Viol and Lute Makers of Venice 1490–1630 (Liuteria veneziana 1490–1630).* Venice: Venice Research, 2011.

Smith, Anne. *The Performance of Sixteenth-Century Music: Learning from the Theorists.* Oxford: Oxford University Press, 2011.

INDEX

Page numbers in **boldface** indicate important discussions of the topic.

Volumes already published

Machaut's Music: New Interpretations
edited by Elizabeth Eva Leach

The Church Music of Fifteenth-Century Spain
Kenneth Kreitner

The Royal Chapel in the time of the Habsburgs
Music and Court Ceremony in Early Modern Europe
edited by Juan José Carreras and Bernardo García García

Citation and Authority in Medieval and Renaissance Musical Culture
Learning from the Learned. Essays in Honour of Margaret Bent
edited by Suzannah Clark and Elizabeth Eva Leach

European Music, 1520–1640
edited by James Haar

Cristóbal de Morales
Sources, Influences, Reception
edited by Owen Rees and Bernadette Nelson

Young Choristers, 650–1700
edited by Susan Boynton and Eric Rice

Hermann Pötzlinger's Music Book
The St Emmeram Codex and its Contexts
Ian Rumbold with Peter Wright

Medieval Liturgical Chant and Patristic Exegesis
Words and Music in the Second-Mode Tracts
Emma Hornby

Juan Esquivel: A Master of Sacred Music during the Spanish Golden Age
Clive Walkley

Essays on Renaissance Music in Honour of David Fallows
Bon jour, bon mois et bonne estrenne
edited by Fabrice Fitch and Jacobijn Kiel

Music and Ceremony at the Court of Charles V
The *Capilla Flamenca* and the Art of Political Promotion
Mary Tiffany Ferer

Music and Meaning in Old Hispanic Lenten Chants
Psalmi, threni and the Easter Vigil Canticles
Emma Hornby and Rebecca Maloy

Lightning Source UK Ltd.
Milton Keynes UK
UKOW06f1308280716

279425UK00005B/143/P

9 781843 838944